Opera and Drama in Russia
As Preached and Practiced
in the 1860s

Russian Music Studies, No. 2

Malcolm Hamrick Brown, Series Editor

Professor of Music
Indiana University

Other Titles in This Series

No. 1   *Nationalism, Modernism, and Personal Rivalry
in Nineteenth-Century Russian Music*

Robert C. Ridenour

No. 3   *Musorgsky: In Memoriam,
1881-1981*

Malcolm Hamrick Brown, ed.

Opera and Drama in Russia
As Preached and Practiced
in the 1860s

by
Richard Taruskin

UMI RESEARCH PRESS
Ann Arbor, Michigan

Produced and distributed by
UMI Research Press
an imprint of
University Microfilms International
Ann Arbor, Michigan 48106

Library of Congress Cataloging in Publication Data

Taruskin, Richard.
Opera and drama in Russia as preached and
practiced in the 1860's.

(Russian music studies ; no. 2)
A revision of the author's thesis, Columbia University,
1975.
1. Opera–Russian S.F.S.R.–History and criticism.
I. Title. II. Series.

ML1737.T37 1981   782.1'0947   81-14780
ISBN 0-8357-1245-1   AACR2

Contents

List of Figures   *vii*

Preface   *ix*

Note on Transliteration   *xvii*

1   Glinka's Ambiguous Legacy and the
     Birth Pangs of Russian Opera   *1*

2   "This Way to the Future":
     The Case of Serov's *Judith*   *33*

3   *Pochvennichestvo* on the Russian Operatic Stage:
     Serov and His *Rogneda*   *79*

4   Drama Revealed Through Song:
     An Opera After Ostrovsky   *141*

5   *The Stone Guest* and Its Progeny   *249*

6   *"Kuchkism"* in Practice:
     Two Operas by César Cui   *341*

7   Epilogue   *427*

Appendix A: Synopses of the Serov Operas   *433*

Appendix B: Three Numbers from *Bogatyri*   *449*

Appendix C: *The Power of the Fiend*, Act I #7   *491*

Appendix D: Love Duets from *Angelo*   *519*

Bibliography   *543*

Index   *553*

List of Figures

1.1 Prince Odoevsky *xviii*

1.2 V.V. Stasov in 1852 *8*

1.3 Alexander Serov in 1845 *9*

1.4 Herman Laroche at the outset of his critical career *22*

2.1 "Wagner Leaps into the Future" *43*

3.1 Serov in the 1860s *78*

3.2 Apollon Grigoriev at the time of *Iakor'*. *80*

3.3 Alexei Verstovsky *103*

3.4 Stasov in the 1860s *127*

4.1 Alexander Ostrovsky at the end of the *Moskvitianin* period *142*

4.2 Vladimir Kashperov, Ostrovsky's collaborator on *The Storm* *155*

4.3 Konstantin Villebois *173*

4.4 The original set for the Shrovetide scene in Act IV of *The Power of the Fiend* *230*

4.5 Sariotti as Eryomka and Leonova as Spiridonovna in the première production of *The Power of the Fiend* *236*

4.6   Caricature by Fyodor Stravinsky of himself in role of
Eryomka   *236*

5.1   Alexander Dargomyzhsky, engraving after a photograph of the late
1850s   *250*

5.2   Serov and Dargomyzhsky (anonymous caricature from around the
time of *Rusalka*)   *259*

5.3   Nikolai Chernyshevsky around 1860   *259*

5.4   Montage of scenes from the première production
of *The Stone Guest*   *295*

6.1   César Cui around the time of *Ratcliff*'s première   *342*

Preface

Perhaps the fairest measure of Wagner's success as publicist in his own behalf is that anyone who links the words "opera and drama" still owes him an acknowledgment. Joseph Kerman discharged this obligation in his well-known book of 1956 by making "no apology for the Wagnerian title" of a work which, he maintained, was "far from Wagnerian."[1] I would like to make the acknowledgment if anything even more backhanded, with a plea that "the old tautology," as Kerman called it, need not necessarily have Wagnerian connotations at all. Kerman's claim, that "Wagner's operas and his writings forced the nineteenth century...to approach opera with a new high-mindedness," seems, on the face of it, self-evident. But an exception must be made for Russia. That high-mindedness existed independently there. Its sources were not to be found in Wagner's example, and its manifestations in operatic practice were essentially un- and even anti-Wagnerian.

High-mindedness, in any event, has always been a Russian specialty. The endemic strain of puritanical integrity that characterized the Russian thinker and set him apart has been dramatically described by Isaiah Berlin, and should be held cantus firmus-like in view by the reader of this or any study of Russian aesthetic attitudes.

> Nothing like it existed in the West; the total and unquestioning, at times fanatical, intellectual and moral dedication of the intelligentsia, its purity of character and unswerving pursuit of the truth, and the horror with which any lapse from integrity—collaboration with the enemy, whether state or Church or other obscurantist powers—was regarded by it, are probably unique in human history.[2]

Although Berlin wrote primarily about political and social thinkers, the attitude of stern rectitude he depicts no less aptly characterizes Russian aesthetics. Art was and is a moral issue to the Russian mind; nowhere else on earth has ars gratia artis been held in such contempt. An artist whose art was for the sake of art and not for the sake of truth was just as much a "collaborator with the enemy" as an artist whose art consciously served falsehood—and this is a view shared equally by the Lunacharskys and the

Solzhenitsyns. It is a Russian attitude that overrides and crosscuts all political or doctrinal differences, and the only Russians who opposed it—Nabokov, Stravinsky—were those cut off from Russia.

Only by keeping this essential moralism in mind can one hope to understand the bitterness with which Serov pursued *Ruslan and Liudmila* by the otherwise sacrosanct Glinka, or the venom with which his own *Rogneda* was excoriated by its critics. As Serov put it to Ostrovsky, "Honorable devotion to ideas" was all, was worth any sacrifice in friendship, in success, in personal satisfaction. Only the fanatical pursuit of truth as a moral good can explain the early Russian rejection of Romanticism (and with it, of Wagner), which conditioned so much of the operatic preachment and practice we shall be examining in the pages that follow. Russian art has always been a didactic art, and it is in this spirit that realism took hold and informed the Russian opera of the 1860s.[3]

Even Romanticism had to be called realism in Russia. When Apollon Grigoriev, one of the few Russian Wagnerites, hailed the works of that latest and most extreme exponent of German idealism in music, he called Wagner the apostle of "true realism," a supererogatory term that got Grigoriev into no end of semantic difficulties. But it would be an enormous mistake merely to note these difficulties and dismiss the term as an aberration, for to do so would be to dismiss the Russian mentality that invented it. Tchaikovsky, almost alone among important Russian musicians, admitted (to himself) that opera was "based on falsehood *(lozh')*," that is, on stylized illusion.[4] But even he was quick to turn around and assure us that this very falsehood served truth, understanding the latter word in the moralistically charged meaning it had for Herzen, Dobrolyubov or any other "progressive" thinker. "It seems to me," he wrote, "that I am truly gifted with the ability to express truthfully, sincerely and simply, in music, those feelings toward which the text aims. In this sense *I am a realist and fundamentally a Russian.*"[5] This is hardly a workable definition of "realist," and yet to the extent that it is one at all, it also, for Tchaikovsky, defined his Russianness.

"Music drama must be . . . above all, *drama*," wrote Serov, seemingly paraphrasing the title of Wagner's famous tract. Clearly then, any study in which Serov is given as much importance as he is here would have to acknowledge Wagnerian influence on Russian operatic "reforms." But Serov's patently Wagnerian sentence was penned before he so much as knew Wagner's name. Conversion to Wagnerianism brought no change of mind, merely confirmation of a viewpoint already held. And when this is grasped, Serov takes on new importance as representative of an essentially indigenous Russian tendency, rather than as an importer of "Western trends," as the *Harvard Dictionary* describes him.[6] A just assessment of Serov's contribution to the history of Russian opera is perhaps the most important "mission" of the present study, and this accounts for the seemingly disproportionate space accorded him.

The history of Russian music in the nineteenth century, and of Russian opera in particular, is in drastic need of rewriting. The language barrier has long prevented serious English-language work in the field, and the scholarly studies that have recently begun to emerge have concerned themselves mostly with the Soviet period.[7] The "golden age" of Russian music, the period from Glinka to Rimsky-Korsakov, has largely been left to dilettantes and popularizers. Basing their work on secondary sources and lacking access to the scores, these writers have been responsible for a perhaps unparalleled perpetuation of error and misevaluation.[8] Only in the realm of biography have there been any really reliable works, but even these have been belletristic in the main and have not contributed knowledge beyond what is available in Russian-language secondary sources.[9]

There has been no English-language work on the subject of Russian opera since Rosa Newmarch's volume of 1914, which was in any case little more than a mirror of the prejudices of Newmarch's acknowledged mentor, Vladimir Stasov, surely one of the most partisan and biased "historians" of art that ever lived. Readers of French are faced with a similar problem, for no less slanted is César Cui's *La musique en Russie* (Paris, 1880), a work approachable today only as a primary source. The 1860s, focus of the present study, are particularly inaccessible. The major figures of that decade are precisely those about whom Stasov (and consequently Newmarch) was least objective and most polemical. And the inaccessibility of their scores has made the decade a notably shadowy one in all the Western-language histories. Its coverage in Hofmann's *Un siècle d'opéra russe* (Paris, 1946) is symptomatic. Cui and Serov, together with Rubinstein, make up a little troika of also-rans, to whom are allotted a paltry twelve pages out of the twenty-four assigned to "L'Opéra russe après Glinka et Dargomijsky."[10] Gerald Abraham's brief article, "The Operas of Serov," in *Essays Presented to Egon Wellesz* (Oxford, 1966) is to date the only Western-language source that gives the reader any chance at all to acquaint himself with the actual music of Russian opera in the 1860s.

Even in Russian, the literature on the 1860s was until recently almost equally unsatisfactory. Vsevolod Cheshikhin's encyclopedic survey, *Istoriia russkoi opery* (Moscow, 1905), contains a wealth of factual information, but also a preponderance of snap judgments. And as is well known, the treatment of the Russian "classics" in the Soviet period has generally been characterized by an immoderate reverence that has precluded dispassionate evaluation. The 1860s have been slighted in the Russian literature hardly less than in the Western. There has yet to appear a biography of César Cui or a comprehensive study of his operas in any language. None of the three Russian biographies of Serov[11] deals to any useful extent with his music. The literature on Dargomyzhsky has been more extensive, but largely confined to the early period, up to *Rusalka*. The long-awaited third volume of Mikhail Pekelis's biography[12] would have rectified this imbalance, but the author's death has deprived us of it. As a result, the present study contains the most extensive treatment of *The Stone Guest* to be found in any language. Russian musicology's most fruitful accomplishment to date, with respect to opera in the 1860s, has been the abundant publication of well-edited primary sources—documents, letters, memoirs, contemporary reviews.

The bleak picture painted here was notably relieved, however, with the publication in 1971 of the second volume of Abram Gozenpud's monumental *Russkii opernyi teatr XIX veka*. At last there was a copious secondary source devoted precisely to the "missing" decade, and one in which questions of aesthetics were given adequate and fairly impartial coverage. While my debt to Gozenpud's work will be evident to the reader from the number of citations made from it in my own, I should like to point out the differences in emphasis between his study and mine. Gozenpud's is, as its title suggests, primarily a study of the operatic theater in Russia as an institution. Therefore, much attention is paid to matters that fall outside the scope of the present study—artists, productions, management—and hardly any to questions of literary and intellectual backgrounds or musical style. Moreover, Gozenpud's work is in the nature of a chronicle, in which works are taken up in the order of their premieres. This weakens the evaluation of aesthetic trends considerably. I have preferred to proceed composer by composer, and have placed my discussion of *William Ratcliff*, for example, after the chapter devoted to *The Stone Guest*, although the première of Cui's opera preceded the posthumous production of Dargomyzhsky's work by a good three years. Dargomyzhsky's example was an indispensable influence on Cui, and this relationship could not adequately have been explored had chronology been rigidly respected. All objections notwithstanding, though, Gozenpud's study is one of inestimable value. The third volume, which appeared in 1973, is perhaps the most valuable of all. It maintains the same high scholarly and critical standards as the first two, which means that for the first time such famous works of the seventies and early eighties as *Boris Godunov* and *Eugene Onegin* have been placed in a fully adequate historical perspective.

A few words about the history and scope of this study may be in order. It is a completely new work, based on my doctoral dissertation (Columbia University, 1975), which it supersedes and, I believe, invalidates. I have changed my mind on many points, incorporated a great deal of material that has come to light (or to my attention) over the last five years, tightened the arguments and polished the style. But most importantly, I now feel I have succeeded in accomplishing what the dissertation only dimly attempted: the fixing of the emergent Russian operatic school and its aesthetic moorings within the broader context of Russian intellectual history. I have not written a comprehensive survey of Russian opera in the 1860s. To do that, I would have had to cover many works—by Fitingof, Afanasiev, Artemovsky, Dütsch, Villebois and others—whose historical insignificance is matched only by their lack of musical interest. I have limited myself to those composers who dealt seriously and originally with problems of aesthetics. Serov and Cui did so both as composers and as professional critics, which makes the study of their work all the more interesting and revealing. And Dargomyzhsky was in word and deed the very model of the operatic "reformer." Because he did not interest himself in "theoretical" questions per se, Anton Rubinstein—perhaps the most prolific composer of the period—has been omitted from consideration here, except in passing. Although his works are competently written and not completely lacking in historical influence, I felt that to include them would have made it necessary to include the works of the insipid gentry listed above. This would have seriously deflected the study from its real theme. Rubinstein's "sacred opera" was essentially a false issue, for his new genre was merely the Mendelssohnian oratorio staged. Stage *Elijah* and you have a Rubinsteinian opera; take the staging away from *The Tower of Babel* or *The Macabees* and you have a Mendelssohnian oratorio. The subject is interesting, but the present study was not the place for its elucidation. For whatever the sacred opera was, it was not "opera as drama."

The idea of this book came to me in the course of writing my masters essay, *Vladimir Vasilievich Stasov: Functionary in Art* (Columbia University, 1968). The more I read of Stasov's vilification of Serov, the more interesting the latter became. Clearly, if so important a critic as Stasov regarded Serov—about whom I knew next to nothing and could find out little more in the literature available to me—as the archfiend of Russian music, he must have been a figure of considerable importance himself. And so I at first decided to give Serov the standard life-and-works treatment. Once I embarked on my research, however, it became clear that Serov's significance was revealed only in conjunction with the other composers and critics of his time, who pursued ends similar to his with means often diametrically opposed. The project was now an ambitious one indeed: to trace the emergence of the Russian operatic aesthetic from its seeds in the Stasov-Serov controversies over Glinka's legacy to its flowering in the "classical" repertoire, the works of Musorgsky, Tchaikovsky and Rimsky-Korsakov. I actually wrote the first draft of the dissertation in this form, with two immense chapters not included here, which took the study through the 1870s. The first of these concerned "Three Historical Operas"—*Boris Godunov, Pskovitianka* and *The Oprichnik;* the second, "Three Comic Operas after Gogol"—*The Fair at Sorochintsy, May Night* and *Vakula the Smith.* I am still convinced that the generic approach is the one best suited to the "classical" repertoire of Russian opera, rather than proceeding by individual composers. But the dissertation was breaking all reasonable bounds of length, and the valuable emphasis on origins and on

Serov's contribution was being swamped by the musically much more attractive and intrinsically more interesting operas of the seventies. For both of these reasons, I decided to amputate the final pair of chapters and save them for future use. The present study, then, is the result of an initial swelling and a subsequent shrinkage of scope.

One methodological note: I decided at the very outset to confine myself to vocal scores in my investigation of the music. Those aspects of the operas under discussion most germane to the theme—scenario, operatic "forms," declamation and prosody, treatment of the chorus—are all fully revealed in the more compact medium. Indeed, such works as *The Stone Guest* and *Marriage* existed only as vocal scores within their composers' lifetimes. But I am aware that a loss is involved, and that some of my remarks about Serov's Wagnerianism or lack of it, for example, may stand in need of revision in light of his orchestration. The instrumentation of *Judith,* at any rate, was the one feature of the opera that appealed to Wagner when Serov submitted the score for his judgment.

All dates throughout are according to the Julian (Old Style) calendar which in the nineteenth century was twelve days behind the Gregorian. I have never seen the point of adjusting dates unless Russian and Western events needed to be synchronized, which has not been the case here. (Otherwise the anomaly typified by Soviet commemoration of the "October Revolution" in November is confronted in a small way on almost every page.) The only exceptions are a few letters which were written abroad and double dated by their authors. Where this is the case, the double dating is maintained in the present context.

This study would have been impossible without access to documentary material and most particularly to scores which are unavailable outside Russia. I would like therefore to express my gratitude to the International Research and Exchanges Board for selecting me as a participant in their Graduate Student/Young Faculty Exchange with the Soviet Union for the academic year 1971-72. The opportunity to live and work for a year in Moscow enriched me far beyond the fulfillment of my academic project and far beyond my ability to express or repay. My stay in the USSR was further facilitated by the award of a Fulbright-Hays Traveling Fellowship, for which I am likewise grateful. I would also like to acknowledge my debt to Alexei Ivanovich Kandinsky, head of the Music History Department of the Moscow Conservatory, for his consultations and letters of introduction, and to the staffs of the Conservatory Library, the Lenin Library in Moscow, the library of the Kirov State Theater in Leningrad and the Saltykov-Shchedrin Public Library, also in Leningrad. I was given access to many nineteenth-century journals and newspapers which contained far more than music criticism, and to which access is often restricted. I encountered no difficulties whatever. My Moscow friend and fellow viola da gamba player Mark Vainrot performed prodigies on my behalf in securing beautiful, bound photocopies of rare scores, and a kind woman—whose name I never did get to know—behind the *"bukinis-ticheskii"* (second hand) counter of the music store on Neglinnaia Street was similarly helpful. She put aside for me any scores on my list that passed through her hands, so that I was able to buy for a pittance first editions of Serov's *Judith* and Cui's *Prisoner of the Caucasus.* Thanks to these individuals and others, I was able to assemble a personal library of vocal scores that surpassed my wildest dreams. Nor must I forget another friend, Hillar Taamal, who on my last day in the USSR—when I was naturally busy with personal affairs—devoted his entire day to securing for me the very last remaining item on my list, the libretto of the Kashperov-Ostrovsky *Storm,* on which I had given up, and which he presented to me in the course of our tearful farewells at the airport.

To Prof. Vladimir Ussachevsky of Columbia University go my warm thanks for the enthusiastic interest with which he approached my project, and his useful suggestions. Professors Edward Lippman, Joel Newman, Robert Maguire and Boris Schwarz were most kind and constructive in their comments, many of which have been incorporated into the text. Ms. Barbara Mueser, Index Editor of RILM Abstracts, was most helpful in matters of style and transliteration. My friend and neighbor, A.G. Murphy, has given generously of his professional editing skills whenever called upon.

Among those who helped me render this a readable book, Prof. Newman (once again) and my good friend Piero Weiss were indispensable, as were Joseph Kerman and Nicholas Temperley, who edited the first and second chapters for publication in *19th Century Music* and *JAMS,* respectively. I have tried to follow their example in the rest of the book. Finally to George Buelow and to Malcolm Brown, the editor of Studies in Russian Music, my thanks for their encouragement, their occasional prodding, and for the opportunity and incentive to write the book I wanted to write.

Richard Taruskin
October, 1980

Notes

1. Joseph Kerman, *Opera as Drama*, p. 3.

2. Marc Raeff, ed., *Russian Intellectual History* (New York, 1966), pp. 9-10.

3. This is not to suggest that artistic values were altogether neglected in Russia. Belinsky himself wrote that:

    When a work that claims to belong to the realm of art fails to meet [art's] requirements, it will be false, lifeless and dull, and no tendency can save it. Art can be the organ for certain ideas and tendencies, but only when it is art above all. Otherwise its works will be lifeless allegories, cold dissertations, but not living representations of reality (Vissarion Belinsky, *Sobranie sochinenii II* [Moscow, 1948], p. 752).

But this is really no qualification, since even here art is valued for its truth and its fidelity to reality.

4. P.I. Chaikovskii, *Dnevniki 1873-1891* (Moscow-Petrograd, 1923), p. 215.

5. V.N. Pogozhev, "Vospominaniia o P.I. Chaikovskom," in Igor Glebov, ed., *P.I. Chaikovskii: Vospominaniia i pis'ma* (Leningrad, 1924), p. 77. Emphasis added.

6. *Harvard Dictionary,* 2nd ed. (Cambridge, 1969), p. 745.

7. Worthy of special mention are *Soviet Composers and the Development of Soviet Music* by Stanley Dale Krebs (New York, 1970) and Boris Schwarz's monumental study, *Music and Musical Life in Soviet Russia, 1917-1971* (New York, 1972).

8. Particular offenders have been Richard Anthony Leonard's *History of Russian Music* (London, 1957) and James Bakst's *History of Russian-Soviet Music* (New York, 1966). The *History of Russian Music* by Gerald Seaman, the first volume of which was published by Praeger in 1967, was a disappointment—see reviews by Miloš Velimirovič [*The Musical Quarterly,* 55 (1969), pp. 408-17] and Malcolm Brown [*Notes* 26 (1969), pp. 24-26]—and the project has apparently been dropped by the publisher. Alfred Swan's *Russian Music and Its Sources in Chant and Folk-song* (New York, 1973) was a disappointment of another kind. A posthumous work by a great scholar, its sketchy and chaotic nature represents its state at the time of the author's death, not the book he intended to give us.

9. Typical of these have been two by David Brown: *Glinka* (London, 1974; reviewed by Richard Taruskin in *The Musical Quarterly* 61 [1975], pp. 141-51) and *Tchaikovsky: The Early Years, 1840-1874* (New York, 1978; reviewed by Malcolm Brown in *JAMS* 33 [1980], pp. 402-7).

10. The title itself is inappropriate, since Dargomyzhsky's last opera was written concurrently with Cui's *Ratcliff,* and not even begun until two of Serov's three had already been produced.

11. V.S. Baskin, *A.N. Serov (Biograficheskii ocherk)* (Moscow, 1890); Nikolai Findeisen, *Aleksandr Nikolaevich Serov: Ego zhizn' i muzykal'naia deiatel'nost',* 2nd ed. (Moscow, 1904); Georgii Khubov, *Zhizn' A.N. Serova* (Moscow, 1950).

12. Mikhail Pekelis, *A.S. Dargomyzhskii i ego okruzhenie I* (Moscow, 1966); *II* (Moscow, 1973).

Note on Transliteration

The transliterations that appear in the music examples and in Appendices B and C directly underlaid to the music follow not the Library of Congress system as in the text, but the so-called "international scholarly system" [cf. J. Thomas Shaw, *The Transliteration of Modern Russian for English-Language Publications* (Madison, Wisconsin, 1967)], which takes less space. The differences between it and the LC system are as follows:

LC	Int. Schol.
ch	č
sh	š
zh	ž
kh	x
ts	c
ia	ja
iu	ju
-yi	-yj
-ii*	-ij

*Where the second i represents the Russian *i kratkoe*.

Fig. 1.1   Prince Odoevsky

1

Glinka's Ambiguous Legacy and the Birth Pangs of Russian Opera

Everyone knows that the history of Russian opera as a living tradition begins with Glinka, mounting interest in his predecessors and contemporaries notwithstanding.[1] But Glinka's legacy posed serious problems to those who sought to build upon it. His two operas seemed to point in opposite directions, between which Glinka's heirs found themselves forced to take sides almost from the first. Precisely because everyone agreed that Glinka "placed the decisive boundary between the past and the future of Russian music,"[2] it became impossible to accept the contradictions in his achievement. The future of Russian music demanded the cultivation of the best seeds sown by the great composer and the exclusion of the rest; only when the Russian musical "school" was firmly on its feet could canonization and, with it, unquestioning acceptance take place. The question of what was wheat and what was chaff in Glinka was never fully resolved by his critics, and indeed, the achievements of succeeding generations of composers finally rendered the question superfluous. Composers made their own selections, performed their own grafts, and created their own hybrids, and Glinka could at last be retired from the polemicists' arena to a place among the unassailable "classics." But the early controversies played a decisive role in forming the characteristically high-minded Russian view of opera, and any understanding of Russian operatic aesthetics and criticism, "realist" or otherwise, must rest upon an examination of them. It was largely thanks to these sometimes acrimonious debates that César Cui was able to boast in 1889 that "operatic matters now stand with us on a higher plane than in Western Europe."[3]

The controversies we have in mind are not those which surrounded *A Life for the Tsar* at its premiere in 1836. The well-publicized comment that the new opera was *musique des cochers* never represented enlightened opinion; the progressive intelligentsia and the literary community (including both Pushkin and Gogol) all welcomed it. Significantly, it was seen by them from the very first as the beginning of that long-awaited new Russian school whose future development was nothing but a prophecy. The real question is why Glinka's first opera should immediately have been viewed in this way, when in fact there did exist other Russian operas that enjoyed considerable esteem.[4] Only a year before, Verstovsky's *Askold's Grave* had been very warmly received, but nobody had made any comparable claims for it. Nor had anyone seen great beginnings in the works of Cavos, Davydov, or the various Titovs.

The answer to this question is perhaps best suggested by the critiques of Prince Vladimir Fyodorovich Odoevsky (1804-69). Best known as a lyric poet and writer of Hoffmannesque short stories, Odoevsky was also a dilettante composer and Russia's leading musical feuilletoniste at the time of Glinka's operatic debut. Writing in the newspaper *The Northern Bee (Severnaia Pchela)*, Odoevsky hailed *A Life for the Tsar* as the harbinger of a "new element in art," for Glinka had "proved with his brilliant essay that Russian melody...may be elevated to the level of tragedy."[5] Not only did Glinka further, by means of superior talent and craft, the idealization of the Russian national musical heritage—"Russian melodies which however are not copies of any specific folk song," as Odoevsky put it—but he used this material in an unprecedented way, as the stuff of drama, the carrier and supporter of plot and characterization, whereas formerly "volkstümlich" melodies had played the same kind of decorative role in the Russian musical theater as everywhere else in Europe.[6] Odoevsky singles out for special mention Susanin's fourth-act monologue, where the "melody achieves the highest tragic style, while—something unheard of up to now—preserving in all its purity its Russian character. One must hear this scene to become convinced of the feasibility of such a union, which until now has been considered an unrealizable dream."[7]

Of course, one of the reasons why this union had been so considered is that prior to Glinka, Russian operas had never aspired to the tragic style at all. Previous Russian operas and quasi-operas with potentially tragic situations (e.g. *Askold's Grave*) had characteristically avoided tragic denouements by such standard devices as the last-minute rescue or the intervention of a deus ex machina. Thus in the previous operatic version of the Ivan Susanin story, by the Russified Italian Catterino Cavos (1815), Susanin's life is saved at the last moment by the sudden arrival of a detachment of Russian soldiers. Glinka's Susanin is allowed to die his historical (?) death, and his personal tragedy is then juxtaposed in the Epilogue with popular rejoicing at the Tsar's salvation. Here the *lieto fine*, if such it be, in no way detracts from, but rather enhances and apotheosizes by contrast, the loftiness of Glinka's tragic and patriotic theme.

Such contrasts are indeed fundamental; we have Glinka's own testimony that the possibility of drama through "the opposition of Polish music to Russian"[8] was one of the main attractions of his subject. He consciously set out to unite the principles of dramatic music with those of national music in an unprecedented "organic" fashion. Nor should we forget that *A Life for the Tsar* was the very first Russian work for the musical stage to dispense with spoken dialogue, which still survived from Russian opera's Singspiel days. Glinka's opera is almost self-consciously "advanced," right down to a kind of foreshadowing of leitmotiv technique.[9] What commended *A Life for the Tsar* to the intelligentsia, then, was its fusion of two progressive tendencies: it was the first serious musical drama by a Russian, and it brought the musical idealization of the Russian folk melos to a new height of accomplishment. These two tendencies fed one another and seemed to reveal, in their symbiosis, the path along which the organic development of Russian opera would proceed.

But when Glinka's second opera was heard, six years to the day after the first, those who had awaited a bold continuation down that path were sorely disappointed. For *Ruslan and Liudmila* apparently turned its back upon all that *A Life for the Tsar* had stood for. In place of the lofty theme of his first opera, Glinka now offered a musical treatment of Pushkin's mock-epic of 1820, a work decidedly out of joint with the times. A great favorite with today's formalist critics for its absence of "significance or symbolism," for its "perfect freedom from all emotional and intellectual dross,"[10] it had become by the 1840s a work much despised by progressive literati—so important was such "dross" becoming at this moment in Russian intellectual history. The leader of the new criticism was Vissarion Belinsky (1811-48), the quintessential "man of the forties," who wrote that Pushkin's poem was "nothing more than a fairy-tale, devoid of any sense of time and place or national character and hence of verisimilitude," and "in our time not even every schoolboy can find the will and patience to read it."[11] Glinka himself, by the time he came to write his autobiographical *Notes*, was a bit embarrassed by the subject and implied that Pushkin and he might have collaborated on a revision of the poem that would have brought it into conformity with more responsible views of art, had the poet's death not intervened.[12] But there is little reason to credit this tantalizing fantasy of a joint effort by Russia's greatest poet and her greatest composer, especially in view of the actual history of *Ruslan*'s libretto, a long, sorry tale that foredoomed the opera to dramaturgical failure.[13]

In both conception and execution, then, *Ruslan and Liudmila* was an about-face from the noble and dramaturgically successful opera seria that had preceded it. It belonged to another tradition, that of the "magic opera," the tradition of *Die Zauberflöte* and *Oberon*. And it could hardly serve the cause of the "organic" fusion of the dramatic and the national, since its literary source was an imaginary fancy with no real ties to the Russian epic tradition, and no aim or purpose beyond entertainment. Pushkin had jestingly clothed a thoroughly Westernized "Enlightenment" sensibility in the forms and rhetoric of the ancient *byliny*. Since, as Belinsky suggested, no nineteenth-century artist could really follow Pushkin in this, Glinka compounded his opera's difficulties by attempting to place the emphasis as far as possible on the epic gestures and romantic situations, with the aim of making substance out of what had been mere trapping in Pushkin. This led to incongruity of content and manner in the opera, to inconsistency of tone, and above all to paralysis of action. Moreover, the musical language of *Ruslan* was—inevitably—highly eclectic. Where in his first opera Glinka had striven for dramatically appropriate national character, the sources of *Ruslan*'s melodic material are rather self-indulgently promiscuous: Russian, Tatar, Caucasian, Persian, Turkish, Finnish (not to mention Farlaf's patently Italianate *buffa* music or the "artificial" Chernomor music with its whole-tone scale). Moreover, these tunes are in the main actual citations rather than imitations, and they are used as themes for set pieces, while dramatic scenes and situations are mostly carried by stylistically neutral music. The result was that local color was once again relegated to a decorative role, and lost the organic relationship to the drama that was the hallmark of *A Life for the Tsar.*

Paradoxically, one of the severest problems *Ruslan* posed for its critics was the quality of its music. The score abounds in dazzling displays of compositional virtuosity which placed Glinka among the most advanced and accomplished technicians in all of Europe, not only in Russia. While no one could claim that the new opera stood comparison with *A Life for the Tsar* as a musical drama, no one could fail to recognize that as a musical composition *Ruslan* represented an extraordinary advance. *Ruslan* thus became an opera impossible to accept and impossible to dismiss. Here was the classic dilemma of operatic theory crystallized in practice: the best possible music seemingly wedded to the worst possible libretto.

The case of *Ruslan* thus became a test of opera in general. Evaluation of this work was bound to set precedents. One could not praise or damn Glinka's second opera without facing up to problems as to the relationship of music and drama, of word and tone, of proper operatic subjects and their proper treatment—questions rarely dealt with explicitly in the rest of Europe before Wagner's tracts appeared.[14] The Russian school, then, was confronted with a philosophical crisis at the very beginning of its existence. There was the additional element of artistic patriotism, too, which did not help to clarify the issues. "He who would remain indifferent to an event of this kind," wrote Odoevsky in 1858, when *Ruslan* was revived after fifteen years' banishment from the stage, "is . . . not only no artist, but no Russian to boot." In the same letter, though, even Odoevsky is forced to admit that *"Ruslan's libretto must be redone,*—preserving all of Glinka's music, of course."[15]

At the time of *Ruslan's* premiere, Odoevsky, one of Glinka's intimates, had been one of the opera's few defenders in print. But his defense raised more problems than it solved. He dealt mainly in generalities, never even mentioned Glinka's opera by name, and excused the problems of the libretto by invoking its fantastic genre.

To seek drama in a fantastic work would be in vain. Drama in the fantastic fairy-tale world has its own peculiar conditions which belong to that world exclusively. Conflict among men, which constitutes one of the essential ingredients of earthly drama, is here brought to nought and there only remains struggle within the self and with non-human forces.[16]

For Odoevsky, then, as for any romantic, the fantastic is understood as a metaphor for the human condition. The differences, already noted, between Glinka's handling of *Ruslan* and Pushkin's indicate that the composer attempted to impose this view upon the poet's work as well. Ruslan's biggest moment in the opera is his apostrophe to the battlefield in Act II, just before his confrontation with the giant head. It represents a romantic *crise de coeur*, a "struggle within the self," after which Ruslan is rewarded with the sword he needs to do battle with the "non-human force," Chernomor. This scene may well have been foremost in Odoevsky's mind when he wrote of *Ruslan*. When Odoevsky proceeds to describe the place of music in fantastic drama, however, he gives expression to an idealist aesthetic which, even as it professes to justify the genre *Ruslan* represents, actually only underscores the problematic nature of all opera.

I admit it, I am the enemy of fantastic presentations on the stage. Theatrical forms are too crude to express the passions, vices, virtues, sufferings, and joys of the fantastic world. Scenic presentations require finished form, definiteness, while the character of a fantastic work is one of indefiniteness or infinitude.... But this does not apply to music. Music, by virtue of its limitless, indefinite form, can give a scenic presentation precisely what it lacks before it can be called fantastic. But for this yet another condition must be met: it is necessary that the spectator be able to immerse himself in his own inner, secret world and forget for a time all surrounding reality. This condition is the hardest of all, since everything distracts the spectator, even the beauty of the sets.[17]

One cannot escape the impression that Odoevsky's view of *Ruslan*, if taken to its logical conclusion, would take the opera out of the theater altogether and put it on the concert stage as an oratorio.[18] In any case, if music's major virtue is its indefiniteness of "content" and its stimulation of subjective reverie, this would seem to presage at best an uneasy relationship between music and any words or any stage situation whatsoever.

Ruslan had a few other defenders at the time of its premiere, notably the orientalist Osip Senkovsky (1800-1858), who was naturally much taken with the wealth of exotic material in the opera and its colorful, virtuosic handling.[19] But the conventional wisdom was summed up in one of the typically patronizing reviews that greeted the first production:

With respect to harmony the opera possesses high distinction but in melody it stands lower than *A Life for the Tsar;* as a technical accomplishment it has brought its author much glory and many adherents, but as an opera...*c'est une chose manquée.*[20]

This opinion long went unchallenged while *Ruslan* languished unperformed and *A Life for the Tsar* became the very staple of the repertoire. The mid-1850s, however, saw the rise of two musical writers of great talent and promise, in fact arguably the two most important critics in the history of Russian music. And with their appearance controversy about *Ruslan* was reborn on a new plane both of substance and of vehemence.

Alexander Nikolaevich Serov (1820-71) and Vladimir Vasilievich Stasov (1824-1906) had been close friends when they were both attending the St. Petersburg School of Jurisprudence in the late 1830s and early 40s. Serov made Glinka's acquaintance in 1842, the year of *Ruslan's* premiere. Stasov met Glinka through Serov, seven years later.[21] Boundlessly devoted to the great man, they collaborated on a number of memorial projects following his death in 1857, Serov, for example, making use of much unpublished documentary material in his friend's possession for his obituary of the composer.[22]

Stasov's memorial effort in 1857 went much further than any obituary. He undertook an ambitious monograph on Glinka, which was published toward the end of the year in three issues of the journal *The Russian Courier (Russkii vestnik).*[23] In addition to a biography, Stasov provided a worshipful critical evaluation and, what is most important for us, reopened the question of the relative merits of Glinka's two operas. Not surprisingly, in view of his crusader's zeal and his closeness to the late composer, the young critic came out on the side of *Ruslan.* But if this does not surprise us, it must certainly have shocked many of Stasov's readers, who were accustomed to the received notion that *A Life for the Tsar* was a masterwork and *Ruslan* a misfire. Not content merely to rehabilitate *Ruslan,* Stasov actually attempted to reverse the commonly held opinion. His treatment of *A Life for the Tsar* comes as no less of a shock to the modern reader who knows only the later Stasov, spokesman of the *kuchka,* jealous defender of realism and of the Russianness of Russian music: he attacks the self-conscious nationalism of *A Life for the Tsar* as naive and limiting, and denounces the whole tendency that the opera represents as a blind alley.

In the thirties there was a lot of talk among us about national character *(narodnost')* in art, and for this reason Glinka's opera naturally seemed the most apposite possible support for general theories and claims, and was the rallying point for subsequent argument and polemic. Nationalism *(natsional'nost')* was taken then in its most limited meaning, and so it was then thought that in order to impart national character to his work an artist had to put into it, as if into a new setting, that which already existed among the people, created by their spontaneous creative instinct. People sought and demanded the impossible: the amalgamation of old materials with new art. They forgot that the old materials belonged to their own time and that a new art, which had already succeeded in working out its own forms, needed new materials as well. . . . This purely material, eclectic, decorative method was accepted as the highest manifestation of national art, and no one cared even to try to understand what makes for true national character. . . . Thus it is not surprising that Glinka . . . was strongly taken with the idea of filling his opera with as many melodies as possible that were close to those of the simple Russian folk. But this is in no way essential: it is merely a detail, and *harmful* to art works in our time at that, for it only places superfluous, needless chains on the composer without adding anything of essence to his work. National character is contained not in melodies, but in the general nature of a work, in the *aggregate of the most diverse and extensive conditions.* Where these are not all met, the significance of individual melodies disappears, unquestionable though their popular derivation may be.[24]

But one looks in vain for any definition of those "conditions" which Stasov saw fit to italicize. The "material" expression of national character was indeed widely opposed by idealistic critics, among whom Stasov must be counted at this stage of his career, on the grounds that it violated the radical distinction they drew between the "essence" of an art work and its "external form." But it was clearly a difficult matter to define the "national" in more spiritual, less mundanely concrete terms. Stasov quotes with approval from a then unpublished critique of *A Life for the Tsar* by Nikolai Melgunov (1804-67), who saw national character as stemming miraculously and inexorably from the "Russian spirit" of a hypothetical great Russian composer (alas, not Glinka) who, without thought of imitating the music of the people, would steep himself in "musical science and experience," and would "include in his works all that is outstanding in prior schools." The mere fact of his being Russian would insure his creating "*his own* original *Russian music.*" National character, in this view, is a mystical thing, achievable not by act of will but only, as it were, by grace of "fresh, genuine talent."[25] Glinka had approached the question of national character materialistically and willfully, and as a result saddled his opera with a limited and stereotyped emotional range, especially as in Stasov's opinion he grasped the essence of folk music crudely and one-sidedly. "It would appear," he charged, "that right up to the end Glinka believed the chief trait of Russian national musical style to consist of the predominance of the minor mode, of ceaseless sorrow and melancholy." The result was monotony: "the whole opera took on the coloration of the minor mode, with its attendant sorrowfulness, its constant depression."[26]

Proceeding from Melgunov's assumptions, Stasov locates the best and most "original" elements in *A Life for the Tsar* in "the recitatives, the choruses and large ensembles and above all, the epilogue." He claims that here Glinka was inspired not by folk music, but took his cue from the "revolutionary" operas of Cherubini and Beethoven. Glinka's opera was no mere imitation of the heroic operas inspired by the French revolution, however—it was a continuation along the path. Beethoven and Cherubini's contribution had been a kind of "subject more suitable to oratorio than opera, where the main interest is neither love nor passion, nor any plot arising from these, but the rise and triumph of a great moral sentiment."[27] This had been Glinka's starting point, says Stasov, and from this the critic draws a conclusion that sets him radically apart from any other writer on Glinka. Far from raising folk song to the level of tragedy, as Odoevsky would have it, Glinka actually succeeded in

Fig. 1.2   V.V. Stasov in 1852

Fig. 1.3   Alexander Serov in 1845. The drawing
is by Stasov's sister Sophie.

negating tragedy and conflict-driven dramaturgy altogether, and *herein lay his highest achievement.* "This oratorio-like character introduced into opera constitutes a direct opposition to the present *dramatic* tendency," and Stasov leaves no doubt that he sees this as a good thing, for realistic drama lacks the "power to serve in the unfolding of a high moral climax."

Stasov's objections to the kind of "nationalism" Glinka practiced in his first opera, then, go much deeper than mere considerations of musical style. This "nationalism" makes for the intrusion of "verisimilitude" into the domain of art, which is properly one of idea and symbol. Even on the level of dramaturgy, verisimilitude, whether of character portrayal or of the setting of time and place, is seen to be an irrelevant and even backward criterion. Stasov leaves no room for doubt that he considers the conventional theater (of which he takes Mozart to be the operatic paradigm) to be moribund. The nineteenth century, he confidently asserts, was to witness the complete triumph of the kind of "antidrama" Glinka's opera represented. "Individual characters" would give way to "*types* embracing whole classes of individuals," and the inevitable loss in "vital representational power" would be more than compensated for by the gain in "high moral and idealistic feeling."

In view of the future development of Russian opera, to say nothing of Stasov's own future role in that development, this pronouncement is comical. It is difficult, moreover, to be sure whether Stasov really meant what he said or if he was merely trying to turn *A Life for the Tsar* into a foil for *Ruslan.* Certainly Stasov was never a stranger to tendentious argument, nor can it be a coincidence that his evaluation of *A Life for the Tsar* reads like everyone else's critique of *Ruslan.* By turning Glinka's first opera into a kind of trial balloon for the second, Stasov is able to reconcile their tendencies—a necessary feat if he is to prove that *Ruslan,* far from being "*une chose manquée,*" actually represents the consistent and deliberate continuation of the line begun with *A Life for the Tsar.* Thus, where Odoevsky had singled out for highest approbation the interpenetration of the national and the dramatic in *A Life for the Tsar,* Stasov contends that both these factors belong to an outmoded aesthetic; Glinka's truly new and valid contributions lie in the opera's "oratorio character" and its eschewal of traditional conflict dramaturgy— conveniently, the very "flaws" for which *Ruslan* was denigrated. Again conveniently, Stasov ignores in his argument Susanin's Act IV "scene in the woods" which was central to Odoevsky's evaluation. Stasov focuses rather upon the Epilogue—a static and stylized portrait of a nation rejoicing, the musical highpoint of the opera, but a type of scene that has no parallel in spoken drama (save perhaps the tableau vivant with which many nineteenth-century dramas concluded). The Epilogue lives through its music alone, and for this reason it may be directly linked with *Ruslan*—if and only if it can be shown that the antidramatic quality of Glinka's second opera was the result of design rather than of faulty or careless execution. The entire discussion of

Glinka's operatic legacy in Stasov's monograph seems to have been planned in order to make such a proof possible.

Stasov begins his exegesis of *Ruslan* with an array of quotations from the opera's early critics, to show that their hostility was founded upon a misunderstanding not only of Glinka's second opera, but of his first as well. Nor does Stasov spare *Ruslan*'s defenders, for they too failed to grasp the true significance of the work. The one name Stasov never mentions is Odoevsky's— for the very reason, perhaps, that Odoevsky's remarks on *Ruslan* quoted above seem to have furnished Stasov with his point of departure. Stasov, too, professes to find in the supernatural "the most grateful and the most auspicious theme for [musical] art," because "fairy tales and medieval or oriental legends make it possible to embody in the mysterious depths of sound those poetic images which could find place in no drama or tragedy, within no strictly historical or realistic framework, but whose charms are plain to any poetic temperament."[28]

But if a fantastic or supernatural subject is good because it severs the last fetters binding the composer's imagination to a given time and place, one can only wonder why Stasov stops there and does not view *any* external, specific subject matter—fantastic or not—as an unnecessary limitation for music. Again we are made aware of the tendentious nature of Stasov's argument: he is a romantic idealist to the extent that it serves the cause of *Ruslan* and not a step further. Serve the cause he does, though, and with a vengeance. Unconstrained fantasy had been at the root of what most critics had viewed as *Ruslan*'s weaknesses: the incoherence of the libretto, the almost total lack of action, the motley succession of unconnected tableaux, the composer's seeming self-indulgence in seeking outlandish pretexts for musical extravagances. Stasov sweeps all such objections away with Olympian disdain.

> In view of the significance of magical subjects for art works, nothing could be more senseless or absurd, nor could anything prove more decisively the absence of poetical instinct and sensitivity, than to demand of a magical opera those qualities that pertain to other operatic forms. Here what matters is not the subject itself, neither plot nor denouement; the task is not the development of psychologically true characters, but rather the embodiment of the composer's own poetical urges. The whole matter is one of detail, general atmosphere and breath of poetry.... One must set aside all ordinary operatic criteria from this opera's very first bars and not ask of *Ruslan and Liudmila* anything other than the solution of those poetical problems which were congenial to Glinka's spirit and which he therefore assigned himself.... *Ruslan*'s libretto is precisely the kind Glinka needed: as a result of the most varied circumstances it inadvertently came out in separate, almost unconnected pieces, simply strung like pearls on a golden thread. But Glinka's whole talent and skill was suited precisely to the production of *separate pieces*, not large coherent masses.[29]

The idea of a composer assembling the huge apparatus of opera for the sole purpose of expressing his subjective feelings and inchoate romantic yearnings strikes one as uneconomical at the very least. Most would be content, one would guess, with a mere *Charakterstück* for this purpose. Yet Stasov persists in measuring *Ruslan* exclusively by the standard of its fidelity to Glinka's soul, about which he presumes to speak with absolute authority. No paradox seems to be too blatant for him. We have already observed how Glinka, by giving such prominence to Ruslan's Act II monologue on the battlefield, had strayed far from the world of Pushkin even as he quoted from him. Stasov sees this monologue frankly as inconsistent with Ruslan's character in the opera—and for that very reason approves of it!

> Its first part, one of Glinka's best things, is an embodiment of a lyrical, contemplative idea belonging to our time and hardly appropriate to Ruslan. Glinka empathized with this thought, carried it within his own nature and therefore expressed it with all the lyric force of his genius. But the second part of the aria functions in the libretto as a representation of the true Ruslan, the hero, who was foreign to Glinka's nature, and therefore this part of the aria came out weak and colorless, a mere composition rather than a creation.[30]

The fact that the hero, Ruslan, holds the stage alone for this number only, whereas the subordinate character Ratmir, for example, has two large and dramatically pointless arias, was another long-standing cause for consternation regarding Glinka's handling of his subject. Not so, says Stasov, again for the reason that the true subject of the opera is not Ruslan, not Liudmila, but Mikhail Ivanovich Glinka.

> There was not a single character in *A Life for the Tsar* that could have united within itself so completely the themes closest to Glinka, and indeed in the present opera no other character than Ratmir presented such a rich prospect and such a fertile subject. As a result Ratmir emerged as the most sharply profiled image: he is the most heartfelt expression of Glinka himself, and the oriental melodies served the composer simply as a new and powerful means of portraying the movements of his own spirit.[31]

One of the most offensive of Glinka's transgressions, most critics felt, was the needless invention of Gorislava, Ratmir's inamorata, who plays no part in Pushkin's poem, nor in the opera's plot as such, but merely materializes in Act III to sing a cavatina. Stasov values her above Liudmila herself (who is "just as colorless and ill-defined as Antonida in *A Life for the Tsar*"[32]), for Gorislava, too, is Glinka's soul-surrogate on stage, whereas Liudmila is but a character in the silly story which supplies that despised but necessary evil, the plot. Both Gorislava's and Ratmir's arias (as well as Finn's ballad in Act II—another fatal case of plot paralysis) are praised by comparison with Glinka's finest songs and romances—as though what makes a good song, multiplied by a given number of pieces, will make a good opera.

    Given Stasov's postulate that Glinka's true subject in *Ruslan* was Glinka, and that this hidden subject is best brought out in precisely those parts of the opera that digress from the main line of the action, the upshot of his argument appears to be that the only truly inessential elements of the opera are the plot and the major characters. Where *Ruslan's* critics would have us excise Ratmir and Gorislava, Stasov would sooner see us dispense with Ruslan and Liudmila. Where the critics would have us tighten the plot and its development, Stasov would sooner see all pretense of plot abandoned. But even if we accept Stasov's criteria as valid, we are left unconvinced after all that Glinka's choice of subject was an expedient one. Could the composer not have found a story which could have served, without recourse to subplot and insertion, as metaphor for "the composer's poetical urges," had he truly wanted this? In the end it is this first condition, the choice of subject, that pulls the rug out from under Stasov's arguments.

So extreme are the opinions expressed by Stasov in his Glinka monograph, so determined does he seem to turn all previous evaluations of Glinka and his operas topsy-turvy, that one must suspect that the critic wrote more out of a desire to confound than to enlighten. When he returned two years later to the question of Glinka's operatic legacy, Stasov modified his argument almost beyond recognition, which only strengthens the feeling that the first time around he had not been entirely ingenuous. Undoubtedly, much of the change was due to the fact that in the meantime Stasov's evaluation of Glinka had been hotly disputed by his former friend, Serov.

We can trace Serov's attitude toward the Glinka operas much further back than Stasov's, and in doing so perhaps discover some of the sources of the latter's position in 1857. The two had engaged in a voluminous correspondence, which lasted from Serov's graduation in 1840 from the School of Jurisprudence, where the "romantic friendship" with Stasov had flowered, until the cooling of that friendship more than a decade later.[33] Only Serov's side of the correspondence has been preserved, thanks to Stasov's lifelong habit of saving every letter he received (a habit which has vouchsafed to us a wealth of documentary material concerning almost every important Russian artist of the nineteenth century). But one-sided though it be, the Stasov-Serov correspondence is of primary importance not only as a source of information about Serov, but as a faithful mirror of the aesthetic milieu in which both critics were formed. Romanticism was in full swing and Serov accepted its tenets absolutely. We are not surprised, therefore, to find in his letters many foreshadowings of the views Stasov was to express in the late 1850s. Serov, like Stasov, scoffs at the use of folk music as a material basis for art music, finding in it, just as Stasov would, too narrow a range of expression ("Melancholy and exuberance [*grust' i udal'stvo*]—that's all, that's the whole world"), and goes so far as to assert that "genius *must* be cosmopolitan." *A Life for the Tsar* is berated for its "kvass-patriotic, completely unoperatic, even altogether unstageworthy subject ... An entire half of the subject matter, the *Polish* element, is not even given a worthy representative! A dozen choristers cannot replace a single character."[34]

Again not surprisingly, Serov originally viewed *Ruslan* as something of an antidote to *A Life for the Tsar*. News of Glinka's new opera aroused the fond anticipation that it would rectify all the errors of the first and actually accomplish what the first had only promised to do: lay the foundations for what Serov called a Russian "dramatic national music."[35] But for Serov, as for so many, direct knowledge of the new work brought disappointment. He and Stasov had devised four criteria for evaluating operatic excellence: 1) the general poetic conception, 2) the choice of characters, 3) the plan and scenario, 4) the quality of the music and the orchestration.[36] From the first Serov acknowledged that *Ruslan* was seriously flawed in the first and third of these respects, but that he could not "help loving it for the second and fourth, which are really beautiful and seductive." The "dazzlingly beautiful fourth point," in particular, became a real moral dilemma for Serov, since it "did not allow strict criticism to penetrate to the depths of the *conception*,"[37] while it was this conception, the "first point," upon which he had based his own prescription for Russian opera, and his greatest expectations for *Ruslan*. The Russian magical subject had not served, as hoped, to strengthen the dramatic unity of *Ruslan*, but on the contrary had seduced Glinka into composing the kind of concert-in-costume that Serov would rather see the world outgrow. *Ruslan*, then, could serve the future of Russian opera only as a negative example. It was this object lesson, more than any other single influence, that brought Serov to his lifelong conviction that opera must never sacrifice those criteria which it shares with the spoken drama.

When in 1851 Serov became a professional music critic, he devoted his most important articles to the formulation of a coherent theory of opera as musical drama. In reviews of works by Mozart, Donizetti, Verdi, Meyerbeer, his beloved Weber, and particularly in an imposing, withering essay entitled "Spontini and His Music" written in 1852, Serov confirmed the fact that *Ruslan*'s failure had been the decisive trauma that entirely reformed his critical outlook. He now viewed dramatic viability as the sine qua non for opera. Even before his famous "conversion" to Wagner's theories, Serov was writing that opera's "main conditions are the same as those of *spoken* drama, that musical drama must be first of all—*drama*."[38] He inclined away from the magical toward the historical and from the national to the cosmopolitan— that is, he fled from Glinka into the arms of Meyerbeer, and, once he discovered *Oper und Drama* and *Das Kunstwerk der Zukunft*, from Meyerbeer to Wagner in his search for a model musical realization of his ideals. But since he never lost his belief in Glinka as the cornerstone of the Russian school, perhaps it would be fairer to say that in rejecting *Ruslan* he returned to *A Life for the Tsar*, whose merits he now felt he had formerly underestimated.

But Serov was far from eager to introduce the question of the relative merits of Glinka's operas into his public critical activity. His hesitation was no doubt conditioned first and foremost by his personal devotion to Glinka, who believed *Ruslan* to be his chef d'oeuvre. Moreover, Serov was no less ardent than Stasov in protesting *Ruslan*'s lapse from the active repertoire despite the opera's faults. *Ruslan* had become the focal point of a cause: the securing of "equal rights" for Russian opera in Russia.[39] Serov could hardly help this cause by venting his criticism of *Ruslan* in print, though, according to his "Memoirs of M.I. Glinka" (1860), he was not timid about expressing his opinions on the subject to Glinka's face.[40]

In any case, from 1851 to 1856 Serov went to great lengths to avoid controversial public statements about Glinka, even where the occasion seemed to call for them. How curious, for example, to read his review of *Ruslan* in piano-vocal score[41] and find not a word about the opera, only a detailed description of the arrangement. Serov made his first published comparison of Glinka's operas in the course of his enormous ten-installment critique of Dargomyzhsky's *Rusalka,* which appeared in 1856. The critic viewed Dargomyzhsky's opera approvingly as a continuation along the path indicated by *A Life for the Tsar,* despite its romantic, supernatural subject derived, like that of *Ruslan,* from Pushkin. Having said this much, Serov felt called upon to show why *Ruslan* was a blind alley for Russian opera, but he does so in the gentlest, most cautious terms. Taking for granted the botched libretto, he notes further that:

> One might make many reproaches against the music of this opera as well, particularly from the point of view of local color, to which the composer has allotted excessive importance. Alongside ancient Slavic elements, the composer has introduced many oriental episodes for the sake of variety, and has dwelt too long upon them at the expense of unity.... In later, maturer operas, a composer of M.I. Glinka's quality would have found a way to preserve all the peculiarities of his style without tying himself down in this way.[42]

All this is not so far from what Stasov had said in his Glinka monograph—except that Stasov had said it about *A Life for the Tsar,* and interpreted all the oriental numbers in *Ruslan* metaphorically. Such a view Serov could not adopt; far more a "realist" at this point than Stasov, he regarded "objects" strictly as objects, and hence the stylistic variety of *Ruslan* was only so much clutter for him. Serov's painfully-arrived-at conclusion was that self-conscious national coloration and dramatic strength were essentially at odds, the success of *A Life for the Tsar* notwithstanding.

In 1857, the year for eulogy where Glinka was concerned, Serov wrote the short "obituary essay" to which we have referred above. Speaking of the recently deceased, Serov felt himself under an obligation to say nothing but good and confined himself in his treatment of *Ruslan* to conventional praise of the "fourth point"[43]—the typical "liberal" attitude toward the opera, and a clear violation of the "organic" view of the genre which Serov consistently applied to everyone else's work. But Stasov's belligerently radical, untenable defense of the opera in the same year fired Serov's inclination to give expression to his true opinion without restraint.

An opportunity soon presented itself: the long-awaited revival of *Ruslan* in 1858, for which Serov himself had been loudly calling for years. The battle of *Ruslan's* reinstatement on the stage having finally been won, Serov now saw no danger in frankness and totally reversed his forgiving pose. Like Stasov, he could not resist sacrificing one Glinka opera at the other's altar, so he systematically overpraised *A Life for the Tsar*, while his criticism of *Ruslan* now probably exceeded anything he had previously expressed even in private. His review took on a stern moralistic tone that was all too easily misinterpreted as malicious and disrespectful to the great composer's memory:

> Glinka wrote two operas in all. One is a miracle of inspiration, a magnificent creation, a model of organic wholeness from its general conception down to its minutest details. The other is a conglomeration of individual strokes of genius and brilliant, profound musical beauties, somehow strung upon one of the most pitiful libretti in the world.... Having created his great first opera, which flows in its entirety from a unified dramatic conception, Glinka wished to show off in his second, to play the virtuoso *(virtuoznichat')* with his newly strengthened compositional gifts.... He imagined it possible to separate musical interest from scenic, he ignored the integrity of opera as play, and for all these transgressions against art he paid dearly with the failure of his heroic labors.... Let there be no objection to the effect that "the play is not the thing," that opera "is in no sense a drama but a musical work," that, in fine, "if the music is good, then all is well."... All that is given on a stage is drama, a living dramaturgical organism, or else it would be better never to raise the curtain.... What kind of opera is this, if its music produces a greater effect in the concert hall than on the stage? What kind of artistic creation is this, which gains when performed piecemeal rather than in its entirety?[44]

This preacher's and prosecutor's rhetoric is maintained through the entire article. Nor does Serov limit himself to the libretto in his castigation: now he attacks the very conception of the opera—his "first point," which we know to have distressed him as early as 1843:

> Pushkin's fairy tale in the jesting manner of Ariosto could never be called an altogether sorry subject for opera... but the opera's authors have addressed themselves to it incredibly badly, beginning with the fact that they have given the opera a "serious" turn... and thereby laundered all the gracious charm out of the text. The heroic strength of the Kievan knight and the oriental languor of Ratmir—these are the elements that reign in the music; everything else is pushed far into the background.[45]

Deliberately and mercilessly Serov singles out all the opera's musical highpoints for attack. The ingenious canon *(Kakoe chudnoe mgnoven'e)* following Liudmila's abduction, for example, "cools anew the dramatic action which has scarcely begun,"[46] since by its very musical structure it is slow in unfolding, at a moment where quickness of pace is of the essence. Glinka is guilty of mere decorativeness here, as in the great finale with its radiant reprise in the orchestra of the fourth-act Caucasian *lezginka*—"in Kiev, in Svetozar's palace, just as if the orchestra has mistakenly opened its music to the wrong act!" And Serov's objections to Glinka's treatment of Liudmila as a "pouting prima donna" explode into an orgy of sarcasm that spares no one: "The music is harmed by its reliance on virtuosity (imagine—'virtuosity' in a Russian prima donna!)."[47]

With this dour diatribe Serov had thrown down the gauntlet and it was now for Stasov to pick it up. Protocol demanded that he, too, await a pretext, and one was soon forthcoming.

On January 26, 1859, the Circus Theatre in St. Petersburg, the newly reestablished home of the Russian Opera, burned to the ground. Scores, sets, and costumes of seventeen operas were destroyed, among them *Ruslan,* which, as we have seen, had only the year before returned to the repertory after a fifteen-year hiatus. Stasov wrote an anguished article entitled "A Martyr of Our Time"[48] in the form of a letter to the editor of *The Russian Courier,* the same journal that had published his 1857 monograph. This time around, Stasov attempted to show that *Ruslan's* fate had been ill-starred from the very beginning, introducing a note of special pleading he had proudly avoided before. What is significant is that the history of *Ruslan's* misfortunes as Stasov now tells it begins with the libretto, whose immunity from all cavil was the mainstay of his prior argument. Where in 1857 *Ruslan's* libretto was "precisely the kind Glinka needed," in 1859 it is his chief stumbling block: "a kind of unprecedented drawing done by a dozen different artists, one drawing a hand, another a leg, one an ear, another an eye."[49] Glinka's achievement is viewed as a triumph over crippling handicaps, whereas previously everything was seen as proceeding smoothly from a consistent and congenial, if hardly "organic," conception. Stasov under fire is in full retreat.

Much space is again given to the ruthless sacrifice of Glinka's first opera to the advantage of the second. But this time Stasov takes a new tack in condemning *A Life for the Tsar:* once again the opera's monotony of tone is decried, but whereas formerly Stasov had cited the use of folklike materials as the reason for this, now he cites the subject and the libretto. What had been formerly hailed as high moral purpose is now held up to ridicule. The opera's purview is narrowed from the national to the merely patriotic, and even as such it is

such a one-sided and ungrateful subject that it inevitably forced the opera to take on a plaintive and melancholy coloration. Strictly speaking, the whole opera is designed as a celebration of passive self-sacrifice, but this provides material for only one scene and a few scattered phrases elsewhere.... There are properly only two characters: Susanin and the Polish troop division.... The magnificent Polish ball scene is an interpolated divertissement, unnecessary to the opera and false in its conception because it contains no individual personalities. Even more of an interpolation is the magnificent Epilogue to the opera, which is utterly undramatic.[50]

It would exceed the limits of patience to sort out all the reversals in this passage. Stasov is clearly enjoying a new tactical game—the ascription to *A Life for the Tsar* of all the faults generally laid at *Ruslan*'s door. But the trick backfired on the critic, since to complain of the absence of the conventionally dramatic is to abandon the "pure" romantic subjectivism of the 1857 monograph and to accept the dramatic as valid operatic criterion. Stasov can no longer pretend that *Ruslan* is simply a "portrait of the artist"; he now calls it an "epic" work, whose major assets are its "richness of coloring, strength, variety, beauty, vitality."[51] This is hardly "objective" terminology, but at least it does suggest that the critic now gives weight to those purely exterior aspects of the opera he had formerly affected to despise.

Stasov is now faced with a problem. While in 1857 he had disdained to defend *Ruslan* in the strict sense of the word, arguing rather that the opera's critics proceeded from false premises, he is now forced to prove that the opera is what they said it was not: a dramatically viable work. Stasov weasels out of this quandary by a rather sorry recourse to semantic pettifoggery: he asserts a radical distinction between the "scenic" and the "dramatic,"[52] claims that Glinka was deficient only in the first of these (in company with Gluck and Mozart, "except in the latter's comic operas"[!]), pontificates to the effect that the two qualities "are often confused, while they are in fact essentially different and do not often coexist within the same author," and yet—need we add—again fails to define his terms. For all its pugnacity, then, "A Martyr of Our Time" must be regarded as a capitulation. Never again was Stasov to deny that *Ruslan* was a dramaturgically flawed work, and he did not attempt another general characterization of the opera until 1901, when, in his synoptic *Art in the Nineteenth Century* he confessed that Glinka's talent was "completely devoid of the dramatic element." Only this, Stasov wistfully noted, "prevents *Ruslan* from being considered the greatest opera in the world."[53]

His arguments vitiated, Stasov began to indulge in captious attacks on Serov's credibility and competence as a critic. His main ploy was to portray his rival as the agent of a foreign power—Wagner and the *"Zukunftists"*[54]—a ploy which unfortunately has left its mark on Serov's place in history, since Stasov outlived his antagonist by thirty years and had plenty of time to malign him without contradiction. Ironically, he harped most of all upon Serov's alleged inconsistency of viewpoint, while in the *Ruslan* controversy it was Serov whose position remained consistent and he himself who vacillated and equivocated. Stasov's growing hostility towards *A Life for the Tsar,* for example, seems clearly to have been impelled by Serov's unswerving defense of the opera.[55]

But if Stasov was guilty of unfair tactics, Serov was no less guilty of faulty strategy, for he persisted in passing out ammunition to his chauvinistic detractors. Instead of leaving well enough alone, he kept introducing into the *Ruslan* controversy Wagnerian side issues which embroiled discussion in a host of obfuscatory irrelevancies. His article of 1860, "*A Life for the Tsar and Ruslan and Liudmila,*" contains the best dramatic analysis of Glinka's operatic legacy by any nineteenth-century critic, and might have put all polemics to rest once and for all, so masterly and convincing is Serov's summation of his position. But in the course of rehearsing his objections to Glinka's reinterpretation of his source, Serov observes that a "serious" magic opera must furnish a "*mythic* and *mystical* foundation for profound spiritual drama." It is not hard to guess that he had *Tannhäuser* and *Lohengrin* in mind, especially when he asserts explicitly with reference to the first of these that "it is time for all who are concerned with operatic music to know that there already exist in the world musico-scenic works in which the highest ideals of musical drama are *realized.*" Nor does Russia's leading *Zukunftist* stop there. After dismissing *Ruslan* by comparison to Wagner, he goes on to use the very same yardstick to praise Glinka's other opera, and this was very nearly his undoing. Serov wrote, in all sincerity and innocence, that

it would be the highest panegyric for our Glinka to say with pride that in Russia, ten full years before the Wagnerian revolution, there was an artist of genius who managed to create an opera on Russian national soil which approached the Wagnerian ideal *very closely.*[56]

This gratuitous comparison could not have been timed more poorly. It invited the misconstruction that Serov saw the Russian composer as a mere forerunner of the German, and the furies were not long in descending. Russia in the 1860s was a hotbed of Pan-Slavism, and Serov's antagonists had lost no time in surrounding Glinka's operas with a patriotic cult. As a result, Serov's name was linked with a subversive though nebulous "German party" associated with Anton Rubinstein and the new St. Petersburg Conservatory. Narrow nationalism and obscurantist Slavophilia were brought into play by opponents of the Conservatory in defense of "Pure Russian" manifestations in art, and at the forefront of this new and quite spurious Russian musical messianism we find V.V. Stasov in temporary alliance with all manner of reaction.[57] Exploitation of Glinka's operas as a rallying point for Pan-Slavism reached its height in 1867, when both of them were produced in Prague under Mily Balakirev's direction, as part of a festival of Slavic music. There can be no doubt that the festival was laden with political overtones in the setting of Austro-Hungarian Bohemia, and back in Russia Stasov greeted it with a strident series of articles in which the critic-turned-pamphleteer decried the neglect and hostility Glinka had consistently met with at home from the likes of Serov. The Czechs had shown how Slavs should treat the treasures of Slavic art, according to Stasov—with acceptance, with acclaim, with none of Serov's questioning and cavil. Glinka's bust was placed in the Czech Museum as part of the festival activities; Stasov describes the ceremony in a delirium of Pan-Slavist enthusiasm. The bust, he writes, was placed "precisely where it belongs—next to Shakespeare: the bust of the greatest operatic composer up to now should not be put anywhere else than next to the greatest dramatic writer."[58]

And if Glinka, who Stasov himself had admitted before—and would admit again—was "devoid of the dramatic," was now to be ranked as a dramatist only beside Shakespeare, this shows how complete, if tacit, was Stasov's capitulation before the force of Serov's arguments. As so often happens in such cases, the less ground Stasov had to stand on the shriller his tone became, and it is probably no coincidence that his most desperate plea on behalf of *Ruslan* comes from the article in which ad hominem attacks against Serov (and captious sniping at Serov's own operas, of which there were by that time two) reached a disagreeable height.

> In these accusations [against *Ruslan's* libretto] there is a measure of justice....I do not mean to deny them. There is, however, much to be said in the opera's defense. Let us admit that in certain scenes that follow one another the connection is in fact missing; one senses gaps. Well, they are just that—gaps—and nothing more. The score of *Ruslan* has always[!] seemed to me the kind of work in which certain parts have been left incomplete by the author or else lost. Imagine a Shakespearean drama, from which several important scenes have disappeared, scenes whose necessity no one can doubt. Imagine a poem by Byron, from which several crowning lines urgently demanded by the thrust of the poem have been torn out or unfinished. Imagine, finally, a precious statue, from which a hand, a leg, perhaps even the head, has been knocked off or left incomplete. All this would be a misfortune, an irremediable, irreversible misfortune. But merely because these sorrowful facts exist, are we any the less to value that which is, any the less to perceive the merits of that which is in fact before us, or, in keeping with Mr. Serov's fine logic, are we to reject such a work?[59]

Serov's response to this—in an immense essay entitled "Ruslan and the Ruslanists," published serially in his own short-lived "specialist-critical gazette," *Music and Theatre (Muzyka i Teatr),* in 1867—was merely the dry observation that "the comparison of this opera, on account of its deficiencies, with the most renowned torsos in the world of art, like the headless Vatican Hercules, only proves that such a panegyrist is himself headless, or at least—as the Russian saying goes—'without a Tsar in his head.' " In his treatment of *Ruslan,* Serov shows himself to be no slavish Zukunftist. While he approves in principle of the leitmotiv, he nonetheless opposes—along with the vast majority of Russian composers and critics—what he takes to be the "symphonization" of opera. He deplores the excessive dramaturgical importance of the orchestra in certain crucial parts of *Ruslan* just as vociferously in

1867, when he has had the opportunity to acquaint himself with at least parts of the *Ring,* as he had in 1860, when he thought of *Lohengrin* as the epitome of the "Wagnerian revolution." He continues to object to Glinka's treatment of the "bad" supernatural characters, Naina and Chernomor. Although Serov has some praise for the scene between Naina and Farlaf in Act II—"the *only one* in the whole opera with true theatrical effectiveness"—the conception is marred by the fact that Naina as a musical character "exists only in the orchestra; on the stage she merely feeds lines to Farlaf." And this tendency is carried to extremes with Chernomor, who is reduced to a mime role on the stage, but even so lacks support from the orchestral music, since

> the composer, carried away with the brusque savagery of the whole-tone scale he had invented for Chernomor, neglects to depict in the orchestra the gestures the character is to perform, even if we concede that it was right to limit his role to mime. In the orchestra we often hear a general description of a monstrous sorcerer with all his wickedness and power. On stage he is nowhere to be found, nor could it have been otherwise, since *the stage is not a symphony,* but demands detail work and particularities, a thing no composer can forget with impunity.[60]

One measure of the importance of the *Ruslan* controversy is the fact that almost the entire dramatis personae of nineteenth-century Russian music criticism cut its teeth on it. To the names of Odoevsky, Stasov and Serov we may now add those of César Antonovich Cui (1835-1918) and Herman Augustovich Laroche (1845-1904), representatives of the next generation— and the list of nineteenth-century Russian critics of real consequence is virtually complete.

Cui's anomalous position in the history of Russian music has been remarked often enough. Its beginnings can be observed in his tenacious espousal of a type of *Ruslan*-defense that even Stasov, beginning in 1859, found untenable. Where in 1857 Stasov had justified his preference for *Ruslan* with a high-flown if shaky theoretical construct, Cui defends the opera in grossly "hedonistic" terms. Flatly asserting that Glinka's second stage piece is "the world's greatest opera in terms of musical beauty, . . . a work from whose leavings one could make five or six excellent operas," Cui goes on to complain, in an article dating from 1864, his first year of critical activity, that

> *Ruslan's* libretto has been and is still being subjected to strong attack for its lack of unity, for its motley character, for its insufficiency of dramatic interest—*as if no operas have the right to exist except dramatic ones.* But besides its power to express the movements of the affections, music possesses another amazing faculty (and this more than any other of the fine arts, since the language of music is the least definite)—it can act upon the imagination, loose it from reality and transport it to the world of the supernatural. *Ruslan* is frankly a fantastic opera, a fairy-tale opera. There is no drama in it, but, on the other hand, what a wealth of scenic possibilities of the most variegated nature, what an enticing task for the

Fig. 1.4   Herman Laroche at the outset of his critical career.

composer such an opera is! He can give full rein to his fevered imagination! In this respect *Ruslan*'s libretto, aside from the discontinuities in the details, was no small help to Glinka in creating the musical miracles with which he has so liberally strewn his work. . . . Why is it so hard to understand why Glinka, carried away by his subject, should have written a series of brilliant scenes which only afterwards had somehow to be made to follow one upon the other? Is the incoherence of the subject not redeemed a hundred times over by the immortal beauties this same subject inspired?[61]

As for the concluding rhetorical questions, Serov had answered them four years earlier with a thundering negative:

The difference between the beauties of an organic artistic whole, a self-sufficient world whose beauty in no way detracts from that of its component parts, and a conglomeration of beautiful details, is unquestionably beyond those gentry for whom the music of an opera is candy and the libretto the candy dish.[62]

Laroche entered the fray in 1867, with an imposing essay that marked his critical debut at the age of twenty-two. In "Glinka and His Significance in the History of Music," the young critic defended Glinka against Serov's attacks from an entirely fresh point of view—for Laroche was a musical thinker like no other in Russia. An alumnus of the first graduating class of Rubinstein's Conservatory, the newcomer was committed to a "pure music" aesthetic that found little response among the more "progressive" musicians of the day, whether their allegiance was more to Wagner (Serov) or to Schumann-Berlioz-Liszt (the *kuchka*). If Laroche had a mentor it was Hanslick, whose *Vom musikalisch-Schönen* he was to translate into Russian some years later, and whose theories and formulations are already quite conspicuous in the early Glinka article. Where else but in Hanslick among nineteenth-century thinkers could Laroche have encountered ideas skeptical of the very viability of opera as an art form? "Having stepped out of the sphere of lyricism into that of drama," he writes, "music has come face to face with tasks that might seem incompatible with her true nature as an art of the indefinable."[63] Like Hanslick, Laroche recognizes certain resources of orchestration, rhythm, melody and harmony (ranked in order of increasing subtlety) through which music can attempt "representation." But the mistaken view of opera as music's highest calling, and the Wagnerian and Serovian doctrine that unity of tone and word is the highest goal of opera, had led to a preoccupation with these essentially peripheral properties far out of proportion to their true value, much to the detriment of music's intrinsic development.

It is in his very refusal to follow the trends Laroche deplores, in his insistence—as Laroche sees it—upon giving music its due, that Glinka shows the way out of the contemporary cul-de-sac. And it is particulary in *Ruslan* that he presents the very soundest solution to the problem of musical drama. Laroche's formulation is a deliberate paradox, however, for the critic knowingly calls dramatic the very characteristics of *Ruslan* that all other critics cited in denying the dramatic gift to Glinka altogether. In order to portray Glinka as a model operatic composer, Laroche is forced into some rather tricky reasoning.

First of all, Laroche postulates—as did Stasov in 1859—a fundamental distinction between the merely "scenic" and the dramatic. Unlike Stasov, however, Laroche actually attempts to define his terms. For him the dramatic is "the ability to create characters and to understand a stage situation in musical terms." This definition neatly evades the issue of music's relationship to words. Indeed, Laroche warns that to base musical drama upon moment-to-moment fidelity to the text is to invite the degeneration of vocal melody into recitative and to fail to distinguish adequately between characters. On the other hand, to base musical drama not on situation but solely on individualization of character is to permit full-blown lyric forms, and Laroche notes with approval that Glinka's recitative "always approaches arioso and cantilena, as opposed to the reigning *talkiness* of the run-of-the-mill variety." But avoidance of "talky" recitative will not alone guarantee that character will be portrayed with sufficiently "dramatic" profile. The composer must guard against excessive "subjectivity" of style (*pace* Stasov!), the trap into which Schumann fell in *Genoveva,* for example, an opera whose musical style is at once too personal and too consistent. For Laroche the seemingly indiscriminate conglomeration of styles that had been so often noted with disapproval in *Ruslan* was the opera's highest virtue, and set its composer apart from the unhealthy trends that dominated the times.

> [Glinka] alone, of all the musicians of this century, has written an opera that is almost entirely *objective,* depicting in its music not general indefinite feelings, not the sensibilities of the composer himself, but the passions and profiles of the characters; an opera in which some characters are embodied in sounds with such astounding accuracy, that were the words of the opera to disappear and the music alone remain, musical analysis could reconstruct the characters in all their plenitude, so precisely are they drawn in melody, rhythm, harmony, and instrumentation; an opera in which musical style follows with amazing plasticity the inexhaustible variety of the subject, depicting remote areas, capturing the spirit of the most diverse nationalities, drawing entire landscapes, sculpting figures and groups before us as if from marble; finally, an opera in which there is no room for patches and ballast, in which not a single note is written merely to fill up time, an opera where there are no secondary characters and superfluous scenes, but where every detail no matter how small is brought to its fullest fruition. . . . And what is most important, drama occupies far from last place among these elements—a specifically Glinkaesque dramaturgy that unites the austerity and profundity of Gluck with Mozartean plasticity and invention.[64]

Carried away, Laroche seems not to have noticed how his exaggerated praise of the opera's particulars contradicts almost point for point the theoretical argument that had led up to it. Some of his claims, indeed, are merely absurd (no dispensable characters or scenes!), and he is quick to contradict them when he gets down to cases. But in his talk of objectivity of style Laroche hints at what in the late sixties was becoming *the* issue of Russian art criticism in all media. Laroche could not foresee the direction the realist experiments of the ensuing decade would take, nor had he any knowledge of the rather extreme projects—*The Stone Guest, The Power of the Fiend*—that were in progress even as he wrote. When he learned of all this the critic was to recoil in horror and become Russia's leading musical antirealist. But at this point it was precisely in the "objectivity" of Glinka's operatic style—the root of his power of characterization and hence of his dramaturgy, deriving in large part from the composer's accurate observation and assimilation of various folk musics—that Laroche saw a way out of the post-Classical impasse of Western music, and not only for Russia. He cites a well-known passage from Ambros's *Kulturhistorische Bilder aus dem Musik-leben der Gegenwart* of 1860 to the effect that the torch must be passed from an exhausted *Mitteleuropa* to the peripheries, to America or to Russia. Laroche sneers at the first alternative, of course, but heartily seconds the latter and sees Glinka as the savior of European music much as contemporary Slavophiles saw Russia as savior of Europe generally.

> Ambros never guessed that long ago a Russian musical genius finished his career, one whose works, so fresh and healthy, contain within themselves the elements of renewal, capable of fertilizing new musical developments and laying the foundations of a new musical school. Diatonicism of melody, predominance of simple triads and modal cadences in harmony, absolute freedom of rhythm, all of these are elements fundamentally opposed to the musical current of our time: chromaticism, dissonant harmony, worn-out major and minor cadences, monotonous rhythm.[65]

Here we have a prescription for musical progress reminiscent of Verdi's, except that Laroche is perfectly in earnest. Significantly, what Laroche *really* values in Glinka has nothing to do with opera per se, but with questions of "pure" musical style. And that is natural, since the tacit assumption behind Laroche's critique of Glinka is that in music drama what matters most is music. All the musical trends the critic deplores, after all, stem directly or indirectly from poetry's rape of the art of tones in the nineteenth century. Glinka, "the Russian Mozart," remained for Laroche the last composer in or out of Russia who was entirely free of the Wagnerian delusion, and for that reason the last to be a force for artistic sense and reason.

No less than Stasov, Laroche was guilty of exploiting Glinka as a propagandist's dike against the Wagnerian tide, as if Glinka had somehow foreseen the wave of the future and sought with Laroche to quell it.

> If one wanted to write deliberately, as if to order, an opera in opposition to the Wagnerian system, then one could hardly create anything better suited to overturn that system than Glinka's score. Not only does the entire opera soar in realms of dream and fantasy, without

a single jot of everyday realism (that could be said as well, perhaps, of *Lohengrin* or the *Nibelungs*), but in the development of this fantastic plot there is nowhere to be found any pretense to what the French call *"une pièce bien faite,"* that is, external scenic coherence and logic. Nowhere does music waive a single right in the interests of strengthening the dramatic illusion. Swimming in a wide-open sea of harmonic and contrapuntal inspiration, the composer does not deny himself a single detail, does not cut short the development of a single motive where this might in fact have aided the quickness of action or eased the singers' roles. The results showed him to have been completely in the right.[66]

But this is mere "magic wand" criticism, in which all faults attributed to a work of art are miraculously transformed into virtues by sheer critical fiat. As so often happens in polemics, the object of debate has become a hobby horse, and the controversy has ceased to be informative about anything other than the antagonists themselves.

The fact, however, that eventually all the "Ruslanists" felt constrained somehow or other to find a dramatist in Glinka, only shows to what extent Serov was the most influential of the Russian critics—a position much bolstered, obviously, by his being simultaneously the dominant dramatic composer in Russia during the 1860s. Serov had succeeded in persuading even his antagonists that opera must be dramatically viable and must be judged ultimately by the same standards that apply to the spoken drama (not that his own operas necessarily measured up to this ideal!). Stasov, although he remained to the end Serov's bitter opponent on the subject of *Ruslan,* nonetheless had to concede Serov's fundamental premise, and nowhere is this more evident than in his rather pathetic little article, "The Original Plan of the Opera *Ruslan and Liudmila,*" which either by coincidence or design he published only after Serov's sudden death in 1871. Among Glinka's post-humous papers there had turned up a little notebook from the year 1838, in which Glinka had jotted down an outline scenario for his new opera and which he then seems to have forgotten about at once. The composer made no mention of such an outline in his autobiographical notes of 1854–55, where in fact the impression of harum-scarum working habits is more than confirmed. Thus, writes Stasov, having found this bit of paper,

> it is now necessary to defend Glinka even against himself. . . . had Glinka preserved his original intentions, the opera would have gained all that it now lacks: the main motives and events would have been preserved as they are in Pushkin's poem, and if they had been included in the final libretto, Glinka's wonderful opera would doubtless have gained much in dramatic action. It would have been irreproachable even from the scenic point of view.[67]

But not only is second-guessing of this sort inevitably futile, the document does not support Stasov's thesis. When we read that among these saving differences is a new character, unknown to Pushkin, Ivan-Tsarevich (Liudmila's brother), who was—by Stasov's too-candid assertion—envisioned only so as to gain a tenor for use in ensembles, we see that Glinka's first plan was hardly more dramatically responsible than the final one. Even were the opposite the case, it is hard to see how *Ruslan*'s reputation as a work of stagecraft could be saved by showing it to be the botched effort of a dramatic genius.

How far Stasov has come since 1857! Where his first work on the opera was a proud and belligerent promulgation of a new operatic ideal, he is now reduced to grasping at any straw that might salvage *Ruslan*'s reputation. Even within the *kuchka*, Stasov's own camp, *Ruslan* had long ceased to be a model. When Balakirev was toying with the idea of writing an opera in 1863, he wrote to Stasov that "the thought is continually weighing upon me, what is opera and what should it be," but he is quick to add, as if anticipating Stasov's reply, "*Ruslan* is not the answer—there one finds only beautiful music"[68]

Beautiful music, however, was all the public asked, apparently, and it is superbly ironical that all during the time these impassioned debates raged around *Ruslan,* the opera was steadily gaining ground with St. Petersburg audiences. Laroche and the "Ruslanists" naturally claimed this as a vindication of their various and mutually exclusive theories, but the most balanced summation was written—again naturally—by an outsider to these battles. In one of Tchaikovsky's rare critical articles, a review of the 1872 revival of Glinka's opera for the Moscow newspaper *The Russian News (Russkie vedomosti),* the young composer surveys with refreshing detachment the war that had recently come to an end with Serov's death, and in conclusion, gives the palm to the deceased.

Serov's judgment proceeded from that premise which was the motto of all his critical activity, namely, from the Wagnerian principle that "opera is musical drama."...[The "Ruslanists"], not relying on philosophical principles, not given to abstract aesthetic theorizing, decided that *Ruslan* was not only Glinka's best opera, but simply *the* best opera, an opera of operas, so to speak, the Tsar of operas. In *Ruslan*—so say these fiery but notably paradoxical feuilletonists—Glinka demonstrated greater creative strength in comparison with his first opera; he appeared fully armed with ripe mastery and went along paths entirely new to art, which he was the first to indicate. In *Ruslan,* according to them, Glinka declared himself a bold innovator and shook off the shackles of routine and convention, while in *A Life for the Tsar* he still submitted to old forms.... In comparing these two sharply conflicting viewpoints, one cannot help coming to the conclusion that Serov's criticism goes deeper and is the more rational.... It is a fact that large-scale works of art are to be valued not so much for pure strength of invention, as for perfection of form in which inventive force is to be channeled, for the balance of its parts, for the successful meshing of the idea with its external expression. *Ruslan* cannot be included among the model operas; it is simply a magical spectacle accompanied by outstandingly fine music. There can be no doubt that if our operatic repertoire were rich in remarkable works, or if Glinka had lived to write two or three more operas which came closer than *Ruslan* to satisfying the requirements of the stage and of dramatic interest, then *Ruslan* would be given more rarely and would be relegated mainly to the concert stage.[69]

The great value of the *Ruslan* controversy, as Tchaikovsky's review demonstrates, was that it made the question of music *versus* drama an open, hotly discussed, and almost obsessive one for practically all Russian musicians, whether or not they were parties to the original debate. There is not a Russian opera of the later nineteenth century that does not have a clearly defined "relationship" to *Ruslan*, whether pro *(Sadko, Prince Igor)* or con *(Boris Godunov, The Power of the Fiend.)*. And as a result it would be no exaggeration to say that of all operatic "schools" in the nineteenth century it was the Russian that most consistently, conscientiously, and explicitly wrestled with the problems of music's relationship to words, to libretto, and to stage situation. This is not to say that many nineteenth-century Russian operas after Glinka are models of prosody, fluidity of form, or dramatic truth. But even the least satisfactory from these points of view were written not in ignorance or neglect but in open awareness of what was universally acknowledged to be a crucial issue. And it should not be supposed that the primary impetus for this ferment in Russia was Wagner's impact, for all that Wagner's leading Russian adherent had played a leading, perhaps *the* leading role in bringing it about. Serov remained a lonely Russian Wagnerite, and by no means a perfect one. The history of the *Ruslan* controversy shows that Russia found her own way to music drama, and that the major impetus came from Glinka. But it was not the success of the master's first opera that pointed the way, it was the failure of the second.[70]

Notes

1. For a listing of secondary sources of information about Russian opera before Glinka, see Donald Jay Grout, *A Short History of Opera*, 2nd ed. (New York, 1965), p. 454 fn. To this should be added the most extensive treatment in a single English-language source of the "prehistory" of Russian music: Gerald Seaman, *History of Russian Music I* (New York, 1967). See also Seaman's briefer contribution to NOH VII, pp. 270-81.

2. Iurii Keldysh, *Istoriia russkoi muzyki*, (Moscow-Leningrad, 1948), I, 369.

3. Tsezar' Kiui, *Izbrannye stat'i* (Leningrad, 1952), p. 408.

4. As recently as 1939, in fact, Gerald Abraham attempted to topple *A Life for the Tsar* from its throne and show it to be the culmination of the "pre-Glinka" tradition, rather than the beginning of its own *(On Russian Music* [New York, 1939], pp. 2-19).

5. V.F. Odoevskii, *Muzykal'no-literaturnoe nasledie* (Moscow, 1956), p. 119.

6. See, inter alia, Catterino Cavos's *Ivan Susanin,* on the same subject as *A Life for the Tsar* (examples in *Istoriia russkoi muzyki v notnykh obraztsakh II,* ed. S.L. Ginzburg [Moscow, 1969], pp. 133-42).

7. Odoevskii, p. 124.

8. M.I. Glinka, *Zapiski* (Leningrad, 1953), p. 105.

9. For an early "leitmotivic" analysis of Glinka's opera, see A.N. Serov, "Opyty tekhnicheskoi kritiki nad muzykoiu M.I. Glinki: Rol' odnogo motiva v tseloi opere 'Ivan Susanin'," as published in Serov, *Izbrannye stat'i II* (Moscow, 1957), pp. 35-43.
    The formal and technical advances of Glinka's work were not greeted unanimously. Conservatives, especially political conservatives like Thaddei Bulgarin (Tadeusz Bulharyn, 1789-1859), publisher of the influential paper *Northern Bee (Severnaia pchela)*, saw in the elaborate and continuous music only a distraction from the patriotic theme, and called for a reinstatement of spoken dialogue, "so that [the opera's] content be made understandable to the public in all its magnitude.... The content is swamped by the uninterrupted singing" (quoted in A.A. Gozenpud, *Russkii opernyi teatr XIX veka I* [Leningrad, 1959], p. 71).

10. D.S. Mirsky, *Pushkin* (New York: Dutton, 1963), p. 40.

11. Vissarion Belinskii, *Sochineniia III* (St. Petersburg, 1857), 96.

12. Glinka, *Literaturnye proizvedeniia i perepiska I* (Moscow, 1973), p. 282.

13. See David Brown, *Glinka* (Oxford, 1974), chapter 9 for a detailed account of the history of *Ruslan*'s creation.

14. In the nineteenth century, anyway. Obvious parallels could be drawn between the critical attitudes to *Ruslan* which we shall be tracing and the many philosophical and aesthetic controversies which attended opera's infancy and enlivened the first two centuries of its history. But this would contribute little to the understanding of the positions of critics who for all we know never heard of Caccini, Algarotti, or Le Cerf de la Viéville. It would be best to say that in operatic criticism, as in so many other areas, ontogeny recapitulates phylogeny.

15. Letter to V.V. Stasov. Odoevskii, pp. 233, 237.

16. "Zapiski dlia moego pravnuka o literature nashego vremeni i o prochem," in Odoevskii, pp. 210-11.

17. Ibid., p. 211.

18. This proposal has in fact been made frequently, and still has its adherents. It was expressed to me in conversation by the Soviet musicologist A.I. Kandinsky, who added that the public and the press would never accept the idea, and to advance it openly in Russia today would be considered a sacrilege.

19. See Stasov, *Izbrannye sochineniia I* (Moscow, 1952), p. 470. Also Gozenpud, p. 168.

20. R. Zotov in *Severnaia pchela* (1842), no. 277. Quoted by Stasov, *Izbrannye sochineniia*, p. 467. The French phrase was to follow the opera around for many years (see Glinka, *Zapiski*, pp. 170, 172).

21. Glinka warmly recorded these meetings in his *Zapiski*, pp. 162 and 207.

22. The obituary was published in *Syn otechestva* 12 (1857), reprinted in Serov, *Izbrannye stat'i II* (Moscow, 1957), pp. 7-15. On Serov's collaborations with Stasov, see Tamara Livanova, *Stasov i russkaia klassicheskaia opera* (Moscow, 1956), p. 72; see also Serov's letter to Stasov, 27 February 1847, in *Muzykal'noe nasledstvo III* (Moscow, 1970), p. 181.

23. *Russkii vestnik*, October-December 1857. Reprinted separately (Moscow, 1955) and in Stasov, *Izbrannye sochineniia I*, pp. 379-524.

24. Stasov, *Izbrannye sochineniia I*, p. 425-26. Italics original.

25. Ibid., p. 248.

26. Ibid., p. 442. While Stasov's description is one-sided, it contains an element of truth. Counting the main set pieces of the opera (and excluding the Polish act and the Epilogue, as did Stasov himself), major and minor run neck and neck (eleven numbers apiece). But the major-mode pieces display the typical *peremennost'* (oscillation with the relative minor) of the Russian folk style, and the minor-mode list contains many more of the opera's most popular numbers than the major (both of Antonida's arias, the Act I trio which became the core of Balakirev's piano fantasy, Susanin's Act IV *scena* and aria, the overture, etc.). Curiously, the role of Vanya, so often criticized for its unrelieved melancholy and plaintiveness, is cast almost entirely in the major.

27. This and the next two quotations—ibid., p. 429.

28. Ibid., p. 472.

29. Ibid., pp. 472-73.

30. Ibid., p. 474.

31. Ibid., p. 475.

32. Ibid., p. 476.

33. The story of this friendship has been the subject of much speculation. Perhaps the most balanced treatment of its transformation into enmity can be found in the introductory article to the publication of the Stasov-Serov correspondence by A.A. Gozenpud and V.A. Obram (*Muzykal'noe nasledstvo I* [Moscow, 1961], 77-80). In this account both personal and "ideological" factors are given due weight, with the balance perhaps favoring the former.

34. Letters of March 15, April 18, and March 15, 1842. *Muzykal'noe nasledstvo I*, pp. 160, 171, 161.

35. August 14, 1841: "Russian opera needs a *magical* subject—so as to uncover all the riches of our mythology and express the true *Russian* view of *nature.* If such a subject were to be developed with a true knowledge of the Russian spirit, with burning enthusiasm and if it were to meet today's criteria for theatrical music—then a real path would be laid and the fate of Russian music would be decided! Perhaps we won't have to wait long for this—Glinka has nearly finished his second opera, *Ruslan and Liudmila.* I don't know this creation, but judging by the subject and the composer I rejoice in advance. Oh, since I chanced to make the personal acquaintance of M.I. Glinka, I believe in him as in a deity" (*Muzykal'noe nasledstvo I,* p. 130).

36. See Stasov's commentary to the Serov letters printed in *Russkaia starina* (1876), no. 12. This is partially reprinted in *Muzykal'noe nasledstvo I,* p. 297.

37. January 10, 1843. *Muzykal'noe nasledstvo I,* pp. 200, 209.

38. "Spontini i ego muzyka," in Serov, *Izbrannye stat'i I,* p. 371.

39. A permanent Italian troupe was set up in St. Petersburg in 1843. This was soon followed by the "banishment" of the Russian opera company to Moscow.

40. Serov, *Izbrannye stat'i I,* pp. 156-57. This article also furnishes us with some evidence that Stasov's strained defense of the opera originated with Glinka's own self-justifications or at least seemed motivated by the desire to lend support to them:

     One day [Glinka] told me straight out: "Well, there's no need for lengthy debate: *comme pièce de théâtre, comme opera enfin, c'est une oeuvre totalement manquée.*" But . . . if someone, relying on this frankness, were to start enlarging on the whole array of *shortcomings* in *Ruslan,* he would immediately meet with Glinka's most strenuous opposition. Resting on the most paradoxical ideas, Glinka would resort to any sophistry in order to prove that the opera could only have been *just* as it was, and that the whole fault was with the public, which had not matured to such a level of understanding and didn't know its own mind (p. 156).

41. *Izbrannye stat'i II,* pp. 23-27; originally published in *Muzykal'nyi i teatral'nyi vestnik* (1856), no. 16.

42. Ibid., I, p. 280.

43. Ibid., II, p. 13. "The weakness of the libretto will always be compensated by the striking beauties of the wondrous music."

44. A.N. Serov, *Kriticheskie stat'i II* (St. Petersburg, 1892), pp. 1019-21 passim.

45. Ibid., p. 1021.

46. Ibid., p. 1022. Serov apparently recognizes no "action" in the lengthy scene of the wedding feast.

47. Ibid., pp. 1026, 1022.

48. Stasov's original title ("Muchenitsa nashego vremeni"); the editors of the *Russkii vestnik* apparently did not appreciate the play upon the title of Lermontov's famous novel *A Hero of Our Time,* and changed the heading of the article to "Mnogostradal'naia opera" ("A Long-suffering Opera"). It is reprinted under its original title in Stasov, *Izbrannye stat'i o M.I. Glinke* (Moscow, 1955), pp. 50-65.

49. Stasov, *Izbrannye stat'i o Glinke,* p. 51.

50. Ibid., p. 60.

51. Ibid., p. 61.

52. Ibid., p. 62.

53. Stasov, *Izbrannye sochineniia III* (Moscow, 1952), p. 721.

54. Typical is the blistering attack on Serov which Stasov published under the title "The Answer of a Contemporary to Two Pronouncements of the Zukunftists," in the *Niederrheinische Musik-Zeitung* (reprinted in Stasov, *Izbrannye sochineniia I,* pp. 40-43). See fn. 39, Chapter 2.

55. The patriotic subject, formerly a "great moral sentiment," became downright offensive to the critic. To Balakirev he wrote.

     Perhaps no one has ever done a greater *dishonor* to our people than Glinka, who by means of his great music displayed as a Russian hero *for all time* that base groveller Susanin, with his canine loyalty, his henlike stupidity ["owllike," in the original Russian] and his readiness to sacrifice his life for a little boy whom, it seems, he has never even seen. This is the apotheosis of the Russian brute of the Muscovite strain and of the Muscovite era. ... But there will come a time when all of Russia will become that which was formerly desired only by its best citizens. At that time musical understanding, too, will be raised: Russia will cling ardently to Glinka but will recoil from this work, at the time of whose creation [Glinka's] friends and advisers, good-for-nothings of Nicholas I's time, insinuated their base poison into his talent. *A Life for the Tsar* seems an opera with a chancre that gnaws at it and ... threatens its life (Stasov and Balakirev, *Perepiska I* [Moscow, 1970], p. 130).

This remarkable passage has been given the widest possible play in Soviet criticism both as demonstration of Stasov's alleged proto-Bolshevism and as justification for today's performances of the opera to Gorodetzky's libretto, from which all mention of the Tsar has been removed.

56. Citations in this paragraph from Serov, *Kriticheskie stat'i III* (St. Petersburg, 1894), pp. 1301, 1309, 1310.

57. It was Stasov who penned the most vociferous attack upon the Conservatory, published in the *Northern Bee*, with whose reactionary policies he otherwise had little in common. See Stasov, *Izbrannye sochineniia II*, pp. 536-38.

58. Ibid., I, p. 169.

59. Ibid., p. 147.

60. Citations in this paragraph from Serov, *Izbrannye stat'i I*, pp. 252, 235, 231.

61. Tsezar' Kiui, *Muzykal'no-kriticheskie stat'i I* (Petrograd, 1918), p. 111.

62. Serov, *Izbrannye stat'i I*, p. 1298.

63. German Larosh, *Sobranie muzykal'no kriticheskikh statei I* (Moscow, 1913), p. 84.

64. Citations in this paragraph from ibid., pp. 140, 120, 109-10.

65. Ibid., pp. 49-50.

66. Larosh, *Izbrannye stat'i o Glinke* (Moscow, 1953), pp. 152-53.

67. Stasov, *Izbrannye stat'i o Glinke* (Moscow, 1955), pp. 124-25.

68. Letter of April 27, 1863. Stasov and Balakirev, *Perepiska I* (Moscow, 1970), p. 198.

69. P.I. Chaikovskii, *Muzykal'no-kriticheskie stat'i* (Moscow, 1953), pp. 52-54 passim.

70. A fairly recent study by Tamara Livanova ("Polemika A.N. Serova i V.V. Stasova ob operakh Glinki," *Opernaia kritika v Rossii, 2*, no. 3 [Moscow, 1969], pp. 333-61) deals with the same questions we have dealt with here, surveys the same materials—and reaches diametrically opposite conclusions. At the very least Livanova seems hampered by Stasov's present-day status in Russia (along with Glinka himself) as a national monument. His views have, since the 1930s and until very recently, been regarded as doctrine in Soviet cultural historiography, and the only critique to which his frequently contradictory and untenable youthful judgments are subjected consists of noting where they diverge from that perfect suspension of the critical faculties which characterizes his "mature" position. In the present instance this applies particularly to his "underestimation" of *A Life for the Tsar* and his failure to appreciate Glinka's "realism" not only in his first opera, but in *Ruslan* as well. As for Serov, his arguments are dismissed out of hand for failure to comprehend Glinka's "epic dramaturgy."

2

"This Way to the Future": The Case of Serov's *Judith*

Alexander Nikolaevich Serov occupies an unenviable position in the history of Russian music. As composer he is generally bracketed with Anton Rubinstein as one of the *manqués* at the peripheries of Russian opera, though even Rubinstein maintains a toehold in the living repertoire (in Russia, at least) with *Demon,* while Serov's operas have vanished from the stage.[1] As critic, the once-mighty Serov has been reduced to a blind worshipper of Wagner and equally blind persecutor of all that was new and healthy in Russian music.[2] We owe this grossly unfair assessment of his artistic and historical worth primarily to V.V. Stasov, indefatigable publicist that he was. Fortunate enough to outlive his rival by more than thirty years, Stasov had ample time to besmirch Serov's memory in a torrent of articles and essays.[3] As a rule, Stasov's views have been accepted uncritically by Western writers on Russian music, particularly the "pioneers" in the field—Newmarch, Montagu-Nathan, Calvocoressi—who based their early work directly on his synoptical essays, as Newmarch, at least, has frankly admitted.[4] That Serov has become a forgotten man even in his homeland was sadly illustrated in 1971, his centennial year, when no commemoration or reassessment occurred save one modest article in *Sovetskaia muzyka.*[5]

But many of the harshest critical evaluations of Serov have been made in ignorance of his work, and acquaintance has usually bred respect. Consider Gerald Abraham's two essays devoted to the composer. The first, included in a 1936 volume entitled *Masters of Russian Music,* rehearses the well-worn charges of Wagnermania, artistic opportunism and un-Russianness—the Stasovian legacy—while imparting little information about the music of Serov's operas beyond the clichéd judgment that in *Judith,* "the not shockingly original music [was] effective in a crude, secondhand Meyerbeerian way."[6] Thirty years later, taking a closer look, the English writer found much to admire.

It is something to have fashioned two such totally different works as *Judith* and *Hostile Power* [*Vrazh 'ia sila,* literally *The Power of the Fiend*], as well as the best pages of *Rogneda,* and to have breathed some real musical life into such puppets as the Jewish heroine and the evil Russian smith. These are surprising achievements. . . . [7]

Indeed, the quality of Serov's work always comes as a surprise to those who have known him only through the Stasovian propaganda mill. The fact is, though, that Serov was the foremost Russian composer of opera during the years when all the composers whose works form the "classical" post-Glinka repertoire were coming to maturity. None of them escaped his impact, whether their personal reactions to him were predominantly positive (Tchaikovsky) or negative (the Five). As a historical figure, then, Serov was anything but the cipher he now appears; he was an essential link between the Russian opera of the first half of the nineteenth century and that of the second.

Moreover, as composer and critic in one, Serov would seem a particularly fruitful object of study, since his dual career permits the direct comparison of theory and practice. Here, however, is precisely where the biggest problems have always arisen, since Serov the composer so often appears to be engaged in dubious battle with the precepts of Serov the critic. Paradox and apparent contradiction confront the investigator at every turn, and—again thanks to Stasov—Serov is rarely given the benefit of the doubt. His writings are assumed to mirror Wagner's—did Serov not write that "opera must always be drama?"—and so the writings are denied intrinsic importance. But since his operas are reputed to embody "not an atom of Wagnerian influence,"[8] not only is the importance of the operas denied in turn, but Serov is taken to task for somehow not living up to his critical ideals. Abraham ended the 1936 essay to which we have referred by quoting the typically upright Serovian pronouncement that "to write against one's own convictions [is] the worst of all intellectual crimes," then adding the typical Stasovian sally that "as long as he kept off staved paper, [Serov] never committed it."[9] But the "convictions" which Serov is so often accused of transgressing are frequently those merely attributed to him on the basis of the accuser's knowledge of Wagner. Unprejudiced study of his work reveals far more originality and consistency than he is usually credited with (along with perhaps an atom or two of genuine Wagnerianism in the music).

We shall focus first on *Judith,* Serov's first opera (or rather, his first finished and performed opera, since there were many earlier attempts in the course of the composer's protracted and frustrating "pre-career"). A treatment of the familiar Apocryphal story, long a favorite with composers of opera and oratorio, it was written at the very height of Serov's critical influence and at the time of his greatest involvement, both professional and personal, with Wagner. It was an avowed and "programmatic" attempt to realize the critic's ideals in sound. And, alone among Serov's operas, it was universally respected for its intentions, even by his antagonists. César Cui wrote of *Judith* that it was "the first conscious attempt in Russian opera to embody a truly contemporary view of art."[10] As such it has a unique and eminent claim on our attention.

When *Judith* had its premiere on May 16, 1863, its forty-three-year-old composer had already been Russia's foremost music critic for a dozen years, but as a composer he had never been taken seriously. The little he had written up to his fifth decade could all be described as juvenilia, and of that little, practically nothing had been performed or published. Such a retarded development may be unique in the history of music, and it could only have happened in Russia.

Though a man of exceptional intellectual gifts and an extraordinarily wide-ranging education, Serov was utterly deprived by force of circumstance of the opportunity for professional training in music. Thus, he joined the long and illustrious line of Russian musical autodidacts. But unlike Glinka or Dargomyzhsky, he was not a gentleman of leisure, free to devote his full time to the cultivation of his musical avocation, or to go abroad for instruction, as Glinka had done so profitably. And unlike Balakirev, Serov had no Ulybyshev to support him while he undertook his musical self-education. Formal training in composition in the Russia of Serov's youth was nonexistent. The first Russian conservatory was still decades in the future; musical opportunities were limited to the piano lessons all bourgeois households imposed on their children, and in these Serov's progress had not been such as to give his parents any cause for alarm. When, in December, 1835, Prince Pyotr Giorgievich Oldenburgsky founded the Imperial Jurisprudence School "for the education of young gentry for the judicial branch of the civil service," Serov's father saw a golden opportunity to prepare his gifted son for a career in his own footsteps, and Alexander was accepted and enrolled with advanced standing. Ironically, it was here at the school of law, where piano instruction was provided by no less a figure than Adolf Henselt, and where student concerts were an important part of the curriculum (Serov usually appeared as cellist), that he was inadvertently guided into a musical career.[11]

It was at the Jurisprudence School that Serov and Stasov met, and Stasov played an important role in nurturing his somewhat older friend's artistic dreams. It was Stasov who impelled him in 1840 to make his very first attempts at original composition, and the first of his operatic projects was likewise undertaken at Vladimir Stasov's suggestion (*Basurman* [*The Pagan*], after a romantic historical novel by Ivan Lazhechnikov which had come out in 1838). The only fruit the *Basurman* project seems to have borne, however, is that it gave Serov the pretext for discoursing at length, in letters to Stasov, on his operatic ideals. The habit of putting his thoughts about music down on paper was later to provide him with a career, but for the next dozen years he tried to make a go of the civil service while flitting from operatic project to project. He tried his hand during this period at *The Merry Wives of Windsor, La Meunière de Marly,* Gogol's *May Night* and other subjects, but practically none of this music has come down to us. In some instances, none seems to have been written; in others, Serov seems to have destroyed his work. All projects, however, were very thoroughly described in his correspondence with a characteristic mixture of winning enthusiasm and risible bumptiousness. To Vladimir Zotov, his prospective librettist for *The Merry Wives,* the untried but supremely self-confident young amateur wrote sententiously that "Shakespeare can be expressed only by music in which beauty of form is matched by truth of expression, and precisely such music (until now realized only in the operas of Mozart) is my ideal."[12] In later letters to Stasov, he amplifies a bit, expresses his conviction that a comic opera must proceed chiefly through ensembles, but warns that not even the tiniest character should be allowed to lose his individuality by being absorbed into the group. Here he would surpass Mozart, or at least circumvent some of the pitfalls his Viennese forerunner had fallen into.[13]

But all of Serov's operatic projects up to *May Night* inevitably foundered on the same reef—his utter lack of practical skill. From Simferopol' in the Crimea, where he was stationed as secretary to the presiding officer of the criminal court, he sought some help in matters of technique by correspondence with Osip Hunke (1803-83), a Czech-born music teacher and textbook author who was in the late 1840s in charge of the music division of the Imperial theatres in St. Petersburg. These correspondence lessons hardly amounted to more than desultory advice on "manier le contrepoint," as Serov put it in a letter to Stasov.[14] But they constituted the sum total of his formal training. In his later years, he took a certain understandable if perverse pride in his lack of schooling in music.[15] But Serov's was the pride of the self-made man, not the defiance of an iconoclast à la *kuchka.* His attitude toward technique and professionalism was always respectful, in contrast to the outspoken derision of the later Stasov.

All the abortive early projects became an embarrassment to Serov; as early as 1847, he dismissed nearly all that he had created up to then as "weak, thin, poor, childish, fit for burning."[16] The first work for which Serov later acknowledged paternity was *May Night,* on which he labored from 1849 to 1854, recasting it thoroughly in the process no less than three times; but in the end he apparently consigned it, too, to the flames.[17] In his autobiographical sketch of 1870, he gave as his reason his "dissatisfaction with his work from the point of view of its style, in which the influence of Glinka and that of the German classical models...were too evident," along with the impossibility for a "beginning composer" to achieve the "originality of form" the subject demanded.[18]

But besides the perpetual and frustrating battle he had to face with his own technical limitations, Serov had to contend with another handicap which was to plague him throughout his life. From the very first he could not get along with literary collaborators. Relations broke off with every one of his librettists, from Zotov, whom we mentioned before, through the motley parade of hacks with whom he temporarily allied himself in the course of work on *La Meunière de Marly*, to Praskovia Mikhailovna Bakunina,[19] who withdrew suddenly from the *May Night* project in 1853 and left the composer high and dry. The reasons given in Serov's letters are various, but such a recurrent pattern suggests a single underlying cause, and this is not difficult to locate in his personality, one of the most cantankerous imaginable. The story of his life is one of continual run-ins with all and sundry, including most assuredly the collaborators on his mature projects as well, and culminating in a veritable scandal with Alexander Ostrovsky over Serov's demands for alterations in the play that became his last opera, *The Power of the Fiend*. The difficulties he always experienced when it came to getting along with collaborators must have made Serov doubly receptive to the Wagnerian dogma that poet and composer be one and the same.

But he could never manage that, either. He had tried to go it alone as early as *Basurman*, but he simply lacked the literary gift. After Bakunina pulled out of the *May Night* project Serov wrote an agonized and uncharacteristically self-revealing letter to Vladimir Stasov's brother Dmitri:

> Wagner is a fine fellow to be able to write the *whole text* of his operas himself. With me, on the other hand, *verses* can be a major obstacle (in a few places I have occasionally rewritten the text, *tant bien que mal*). Besides the *making* of the text itself, I need someone from the *outside* to check the details of my libretto closely from the *theatrical* point of view. Here in the Crimea I have *no one at all* this time around ... From the purely esthetic angle I don't think I need another's eye or another's intellect. All this could be resolved in one or two months (if only the *right person* could be found). But there are also lacunae in the music itself, which without any trouble I could indeed fill right here in the Crimea, *once and for all,—if I were not I!* Sometimes I could absolutely cry—but the ideas I need in accordance with the ideals I have conceived—*simply won't come!*[20]

Then, too, there was the obstacle of material need. In the 1870 autobiographical sketch, Serov complained of "external circumstances which prevented him from devoting himself completely to work on [his operas]."[21] He was referring, of course, to the need to make a living, which had taken him against his will away from the musical centers and had thus robbed him not only of time but of stimulating contacts. In 1851 he finally decided that he could bear no more of the civil service and, resigning his commission, returned to St. Petersburg in defiance of his father. The elder Serov, though he had taken a sympathetic interest in his son's composing while it was merely a hobby, would not now countenance what he viewed as his renunciation of a responsible way of life, and cut him off. Plunged into a state of near-starvation, Serov began writing the articles that were to make his reputation. He could not support himself this way, however, and a year later he was forced to reapply for admission to the service and was reassigned to Simferopol', where he stayed until 1855. From that year until 1860 he once again tried his hand at professional music journalism and was able this time to remain alive on the proceeds of his pen. But financial pressures and the increasing demand for his work made him in those years a music critic and only that. From the period of *May Night* to that of *Judith,* Serov wrote practically no music at all, and all but gave up his fond dreams of a composer's career.

It has often been said that the history of Russian musical criticism begins with Serov, and this is true in the sense that the history of Russian music itself "begins" with Glinka. There were critics before Serov in Russia, but hardly a one was more than a dilettantish feuilletonist. The most gifted of them, Prince Odoevsky, is interesting as a musical writer largely because of the position he occupies in the broader realm of letters. The wealthy amateurs Ulybyshev and von Lenz had acquired a certain reputation for their books on Mozart and Beethoven respectively, but their eminence testifies above all to the weakness of the field. And then there were the hacks: the Rostislavs, the Arnolds, the Damckes. From his very first article,[22] Serov burst upon this world like a bombshell, and quite deliberately. He lost no time in taking on all his rivals and elders in acid polemic, attacking both Ulybyshev and von Lenz during his first years,[23] and continuing with a blistering exposé of Rostislav (1854) occasioned by the latter's publication of an "analysis" of *A Life for the Tsar.* These articles, though of course ephemeral, were the ones most noticed at the time. What makes Serov a critic of enduring importance, however, is the many essays he devoted to questions of opera and dramatic music. Here, too, he took on all existing schools, surveying the whole field in an extensive series of articles and finding everywhere a sad perversion of the Gluckian ideal of music drama, which consisted neither in gaudy virtuoso display, nor in "noisy choruses and Bacchanales, but in profound psychology, in communion between the souls of the characters and the soul of the spectator, in spiritual transports now passionate, now tender; in a word—in all that makes up the life of the spirit."[24]

"Spontini and his Music" was the article in which Serov gave first Russian voice to the well-worn reformist slogan that "the major criteria [of musical drama] are the same as those of spoken drama, that music drama must be, in fact, and above all, *drama,*" a position of which, he says, Gluck was the "discoverer."[25] For this blessed union to come about, however, it would be necessary to reconcile the demands of musical beauty with those of "truth of expression." Serov puts this in national terms: the reconciliation of the Italian and German schools. Although generally optimistic about the prospects, he is unwilling to make predictions, for

The question of the ideal for heroic opera, or, more simply, what heroic opera should be like in our time, is one which cannot be resolved by a critic, but by a new operatic genius, inclined toward the tragic genre. Almost nothing can be said for certain a priori: only the artist's genius can loose the Gordian knot.[26]

As fate would have it, though, the hero was not long in coming. A few months after the appearance of "Spontini," on August 16, 1852, Serov wrote to Stasov:

We must get together and talk about a certain Richard *Wagner*, whose work in three little volumes, *Oper und Drama* has been *very much* on my mind lately. This is a *terribly intelligent* man—he understands many things completely contrariwise to the *popular* view. Just the fact that he hates Meyerbeer and considers the Ninth Symphony the *crowning glory of all music* was enough for me to love his outlook and his whole nature. But despite all these *good things*, one must *renounce* the joy of considering him "one of us." . . . He does not pay respect where it is due and either goes too far a priori . . . or is simply talking through his hat, seeking theoretically to "justify" his unsuccessful practical ambitions in composition. (He himself writes operas—without the least aptitude for musical beauty.)[27]

Speaking of a priori assumptions, one wonders where Serov got his ideas about Wagner's music.[28] Ironically, he who was to be Russia's Perfect Wagnerite was initially rather coolheaded even about the theories. He goes on in his letter to Stasov to promise an article (which, alas, he never wrote) in which he would refute those points in *Oper und Drama* with which he disagreed. It is easy enough to guess what some of these differences were, and they were crucial, indeed. In the Spontini article he had come out against the view, ascribed there to Rousseau, that opera was an equal union of three arts. "To our way of thinking," Serov had written, "poetry's role . . . is far from being on a par with music's, and that of painting is yet further in the background."[29] And he agreed with Rousseau's rationalist viewpoint that the supernatural has no place in serious opera if musical drama is to move the emotions.[30] These views must be borne in mind if we are to understand Serov's own musico-dramatic works.

By the time he read *Das Kunstwerk der Zukunft,* Serov had sufficiently resolved his quibbles with Wagner's theories to be able to exclaim in a letter to Dmitri Stasov that "as a critic I am simply in love with him."[31] But still he remained cool, even hostile to Wagner's music. Serov's view of the German composer as late as 1856 is astonishingly patronizing and, what is more, virtually indistinguishable from the attitude that was soon to be characteristic of almost all Russian musicians *except* Serov.

As far as his operas are concerned, one can see in them an unquestionable gift, but everywhere an enormity of intention and pretension does battle with the author's feebleness as an artist, with his failure to cope with the technical side of things. That is why these operas, far from the model creations they appear to be to Liszt and the other Wagnerians, so often come across as the forced, tortured works of a very gifted but unfinished dilettante. The general impression of his music is one of unbearable boredom and a certain agonizing feeling of dissatisfaction.[32]

Skepticism gave way to discipleship in 1858. In that year Serov made his first journey abroad and heard *Tannhäuser* in Dresden. (The next year he heard *Lohengrin* in Weimar.) Now, for the first time hearing a Wagner opera in context and in its entirety, Serov was overwhelmed.

In the face of Wagner's creation, I was seized with the most *naive* astonishment, as if I had never before had any inkling of what theatre is, or drama, or opera! So stunningly new was this inspired solution of the great problem of fusing three separate arts.... Of all other operas which I know in actuality, that is, on the stage, not one can compare with *Tannhäuser* in "wholeness" of impression.[33]

Music that had been for Serov "merely curious" and "incapable of giving enjoyment from the 'musical standpoint'"[34] was revealed to be magnificent in conjunction with text and spectacle. The "Gordian knot" had been untied, and Serov could proclaim to the world, or at least to Russia, that "fifteen years after the creation of *Tannhäuser* it is time for all who are concerned with operatic music to know that there now exist in the world musico-theatrical works in which the highest ideals of musical drama are *realized*."[35]

Serov became convinced of the feasibility, indeed the necessity, of the Gesamtkunstwerk, and rejected music's right to an independent, self-sufficient existence. Particularly he scorned evaluations of Wagner based on the "pure musical" criteria he himself had applied previously.

Musical confections for the purpose of sonic foppery, whose goal is the mere amusement of the ear are—in the eyes of a true musician-artist—a degrading occupation for a thinking man, mere craft and industry. A piano concerto, let us say, without the slightest inner idea calling forth its whole stream of sounds, stands in our time decidedly in precisely the same relationship to *true* music, as a calico pattern stands in relationship to painting... Thus, without a program, without a definite dramaturgical plot (taking the word drama in its broadest sense), composing is unthinkable for Wagner. But from this it follows logically that *his* music demands, for full effect, the listener's close acquaintance with the music's *subject,* with its dramatic meaning and significance.... How great, then, is the impertinence of those obtuse souls who, not having troubled themselves to find out what is going on in the prelude to *Tristan,* the prelude to *Lohengrin* or the overture to *Der fliegende Holländer,* are beginning to *criticize* (!) these creations as more or less successful selections of tones![36]

In precisely the same terms he was later to defend his own works, and in this sense was consciously a "Wagnerian." But we should lose perspective on the relationship between Serov and Wagner if we forgot that it was the experience of Wagner's music drama, not his theories, that made Serov his admirer. If anything, Wagner's works only confirmed his feeling that union or no union, the most important of the arts in opera was music, and this fundamentally determined not only the nature of his appreciation of Wagner, but also his own creative methods, as we shall see. And in general, there is scarcely an idea Serov putatively got from Wagner that is not present at least embryonically in his articles and correspondence before he made contact with the German's theories or his music.[37] Therefore, while Serov may have invited the metaphor with his quasi-religious language—"I take pride that I can be [Wagner's] apostle in Russia"[38]—to speak of a "conversion" would be beside the point. What Wagner really did for Serov was to indicate—and this by his musical, not philosophical works—the path toward realization of the ideals Serov had possessed and professed independently.

Serov's greatest period of involvement with Wagner extended from the time of his exposure to *Tannhäuser* until his own debut as composer with *Judith*: altogether five years. His was a lonely voice in Russia where Wagner was concerned. His apostlehood brought him isolation from the young "Ruslanists" and Stasov, who suspected the motives of the Russian "Zukunftist,"[39] and from the Rubinstein-Conservatory-Russian Musical Society camp as well, whose conservatism, if not patriotism, was offended by the "music of the future." A series of lectures Serov undertook to acquaint St. Petersburg with his idol met with dismal failure.[40] Serov began to feel that there was no place for a Wagnerian in Russia, and even contemplated emigration to Germany, where he thought to "busy myself with fugues and things so that I can get a Doctor of Music degree from the University of Berlin."[41] This he did not do, but he was forced once again to reenter the civil service (this time as censor of foreign-language literature for the postal authorities), which was for him the greatest humiliation of all.

The misery of these years was somewhat assuaged by Serov's personal relations with the object of his adoration and cause of his distress.[42] He introduced himself to Wagner in Weimar in 1858. Five years later, in characteristic fashion, Wagner rather abused Serov's devotion during his Russian tour, but Serov's articles from this time show him proud to share the spotlight with the man of the hour. A contemporary caricature[43] shows "Wagner leaping into the future, while his Russian follower, A.N. Serov, acts as his courier and prepares horses at the way stations." Serov, posthorn to his lips, flies ahead on a snorting stallion, leading a train of miniature Valkyries and Nibelungs who are emanating from oversized, nondescript brass instruments (Fig. 2.1).

But if Serov's activities on behalf of Wagner seem in some way to have done him more harm than good, let us remember that it may well have been Wagner's example—the "proof" that the ideal was attainable—that reawakened his appetite for musico-dramatic creation. His Wagnerian "delirium" gradually gave way to renewed faith in his own powers and rededication to what he saw as his real calling. By late 1860 he wrote to Mariya Pavlovna Anastasieva (née Mavromikhali, a close friend from Simferopol' who had replaced the estranged Stasov as his number one confidante):

> Less than ever before have I a right to hesitate or doubt my artistic calling. I have won myself a certain notoriety; I have made a name for myself with my musical critiques and journalistic activities. But the main task of my life lies not in that, but in musical creation.[44]

Accordingly, he sought out Konstantin Ivanovich Zvantsev, whom he had known since 1857 and who was one of the very few other ardent Wagnerians in Russia, with the proposal that together they turn Pushkin's *Poltava* into an opera.[45] Zvantsev, for his part, had other ideas: he immediately began persuading Serov that La Motte Fouqué's *Undine* (in Zhukovsky's Russian translation) stood in urgent need of a new musical treatment, considering the poor quality of Count Lvov's opera on the subject (1846). The projected opera was to be a chip off *Lohengrin* in every way, with a libretto constructed almost entirely from Zhukovsky's verses so as to ensure proper weight and significance to the poetic element. One detail of their plan which Zvantsev later recalled is worth recording here:

> For some reason I especially put my faith in Serov's ability to orchestrate; I dreamed of a fantastic Berliozian orchestra and ... advised Serov not to assign Kühlebach to a bass voice, but to leave him mute and characterize him only symphonically, elementally. Serov agreed to this, the more readily since even without Kühlebach the opera would be amply supplied with basses.[46]

But those who know Serov's articles on Glinka's *Ruslan* will recall that this sort of thing was one of his primary objections to the dramaturgy of that opera, where Chernomor literally, and Naina virtually, "exist only in the orchestra." On the other hand, "symphonic characterization" was a cardinal tenet of Wagnerian procedure. With much benefit of hindsight, Zvantsev attributes the reason for *Undine*'s ultimate abandonment precisely to this point, suggesting obliquely that the mature Serov's theoretical outlook was conditioned to a large extent by the limitations of his own musical fantasy and his insecure autodidact's technique. Sorely and permanently disappointed in Serov for cooling to this, his pet project, Zvantsev wrote of the composer with all-but-Stasovian vitriol, reproaching him as a renegade Wagnerian who would willingly sacrifice principle to ambition.

> At that time I did not doubt in the slightest Serov's ability to draw inspiration from *Undine* and create something truly beautiful. But knowing his unstable character, immoderate vanity and impatience to gain fame as a composer with all possible speed, I trusted neither his constancy in this endeavor, nor his general ability to enter into a true collaboration.... If there can exist in art such visionaries as Hamlet and Macbeth, or sentimental dreamers

Fig. 2.1   "Wagner Leaps into the Future."

The massive scores that are weighing Wagner down
include *Tannhäuser* and *Siegfried.* The sign at the upper
left reads: "This way to the future." In the lower right
the public looks on nonplussed, musing (according to
the original caption): "Here's a how-de-do! Which way
to go, forward or backward?" The figures tugging at the
public's coat-tails are personifications of the conservative press. Says the one on the left, "To go forward, one
must go backward—to pre-Petrine times, if you please,"
while the figure on the right objects, "What are you
talking about? If you want to go forward, you must
stand still."

like Ophelia, Elsa, Agatha, Senta, Gretchen, then our Undine might also have had a perfect right to exist, had Serov only possessed sufficient moral strength, talent and truth of expression for the musico-dramatic embodiment of this wonderful figment of German poesy. But Serov was drawn in another direction, and the Realist party, when the time came, was the first to scoff at him—which served him right![47]

As it happened, it was Zvantsev himself who unwittingly gave Serov the nudge in the "other direction." On the evening of December 20, 1860, the two of them were sitting together in a box at the Mariinsky Theatre rented by the management of the journal *Iskusstvo (Art),* of which Serov was musical editor and for which Zvantsev, at Serov's invitation, was writing theatrical reviews. The Italian tragedienne Adelaide Ristori was appearing for a season of spoken drama. Her vehicle that evening was Paolo Giacometti's *Giuditta.* According to Zvantsev's oft-quoted account:

> During the interval after Holofernes' orgy . . . I said to Serov, "Well, what about that for an operatic finale?" Enraptured by this orgy, he cried out, "Of course! And I will certainly write an opera *Judith,* the more gladly because I've always been attracted by the stories and characters of the Old Testament!"[48]

At the time neither Zvantsev nor anyone else could have attached any particular importance to Serov's promise, considering his long history of unfinished work and the ease with which he had been carried away one moment and sidetracked the next on so many occasions in the past. But when, slightly less than a month later, Serov wrote to Zvantsev that he was putting the finishing touches to his musical version of the last scene of *Judith,*[49] it was apparent that Serov had been inspired "not in passing but in earnest."[50] His "pre-career" was, at long last, at an end.

> At last God has vouchsafed to me the time when I might say with Correggio, and not without a touch of pride, "Anch'io sono pittore!" I am not merely writing about music, I am writing music itself, acting the artist in the true sense of the word. My sails are spread, I am creating score after score, and on this account I am boundlessly happy and pleased with my fate.[51]

With these touching words, an ecstatic Serov informed Victor and Maria Anastasiev of his new project. In the same letter (February 5, 1861) he gave them this characteristically sanguine progress report:

> *Judith* so affected me that I have undertaken to write an Italian opera on this subject. I have begun with the last act, and the finale of the opera with its great triumphal hymn is already done, even down to the orchestration. I will offer it to the prima donna La Grua, who might agree to perform this scene in her benefit . . . and if this comes true, they will accept the whole opera for the next season, and I will write it straight through, without any corrections, in a couple of months.[52]

Here already is one of those typically Serovian paradoxes: Russia's most stiffly anti-Italian music-critic writing an Italian opera. Many heads have been scratched and shaken over this development, particularly by those for whom Russian music is under an obligation to be "national." But Serov was in all artistic respects an internationalist at this point in his career. And as the letter itself reveals, Serov the practical musician could not afford the luxury of Serov the critic's idealism.

Beginning in 1843, and well into the sixties, the Italian Opera at St. Petersburg was by far the most prestigious musical organization in the Russian capital. It boasted stars of international standing (Rubini, Viardot, Artôt), its productions were lavish, and its repertoire was actually more varied than its name would suggest (works by Meyerbeer, Auber and others were regularly included). By comparison, the Russian Opera was a mere provincial house which, aside from a few exceptional artists like Osip Petrov and Darya Leonova, could not compete artistically with the Italian troupe.[53] The theater lacked a really viable repertoire as well, at least in eyes as discriminating as Serov's. After Glinka only Dargomyzhsky had added significantly to it, with his *Rusalka* (1856). The rest of the Russian repertoire was decidedly lightweight, consisting of works by Verstovsky, Artemovsky, Dütsch, Villebois and others with whom Serov, perhaps, did not wish to be linked. The Italian opera was certainly the place to have one's operas performed, especially if one desired a reputation beyond the borders of Russia, and there is every reason to suppose that Serov—who had hobnobbed in Western Europe with Berlioz, Liszt and Wagner, and considered himself their colleague if not yet their rival—contemplated something more than local celebrity. Then, too, the play that had fired Serov's imagination had been an Italian one, and its leading lady an Italian actress who spoke her lines in her native language. From this he may have retained an impression of the drama strongly bound to the language in which he had made its acquaintance. Nor should we discount the ambiguities of his attitude toward Italian opera. Late in life he came to admire Verdi highly, and his rapture with Adelina Patti, who sang in St. Petersburg beginning in 1869, is well known, thanks to the capital his enemies made of it.[54] And in view of his ideas on the nature and purpose of operatic texts, which we shall examine presently, it would be perhaps unwise to draw too many conclusions about the nature of his operatic conception from the language in which he thought to cast it.

But the course of events completely overturned his plans. He presented his completed act to La Grua—a performer who enjoyed acclaim, be it noted, not only as virtuosa but as singing actress[55]—in April, 1861.[56] He received from her a rude shock: "The famous European prima donna, it goes without saying, disdainfully shattered the unknown Russian 'amateur's' dreams, reproaching him, while she was at it, for not having chosen a more effective text."[57] According to Zvantsev,[58] she also muttered something about not wishing to compete with her dear friend Ristori. And that is how *Judith* became a Russian opera.

Serov had to scrap the Italian libretto he had commissioned from Ivan Antonovich Giustiniani, "professor, bibliographer, *improvisatore* and ingenious master of rhyme," in the generous estimation of Zvantsev, who had secured his services for Serov.[59] Having yet again come to grief in his dealings with a librettist, he decided once more to try what he took to be the Wagnerian method. Quickly regaining his optimism, he wrote to Anastasieva at the end of the summer: "[I am] highly pleased with my work, and am writing my music swiftly and with a steady hand." He referred to the opera as "half finished," and looked forward to finishing the whole work by the end of November "when, God willing,... I will have only to concern myself with getting my opera into its rightful [!] place—the stage of my beloved Mariinsky."[60] By the end of November, however, he had only completed one more act in text and music, the first. This he sent, through a party referred to in his correspondence as "M.P.M.,"[61] to Balakirev for inspection, as an act of good will. Balakirev's patronizing response and Serov's infuriated reaction drove the first wedge into the rift that was ever to widen between Serov and the composers of the "New Russian School" from the moment he became their competitor.[62] The blow set him back considerably; not until another year had passed would he write "The End" on his score.[63] But there were other things the matter; work dragged on and on and no one knew why. Finally, in May, 1862, Serov called in a young "melomane," D.I. Lobanov, to assist him as versifier. At their first meeting Lobanov remarked:

> "Most likely you already have a libretto."
> "Not yet, but of course you know, my friend, that I would never entrust my imagination to strange hands... "
> "By this you mean...?"
> "I mean that no one will write a libretto for my opera but I: I am the composer, and at the same time I am the librettist.[64]

Lobanov wondered, naturally enough, what Serov had called him in for. The composer gave him a copy of the scenario,

> ... and asked me to furnish verses from it. "Only don't forget, old man, my firm request not to depart from my ideas or even from the expressions which you will find in my manuscript." [As work progressed] I received sheets from him, on which were sketched drafts of the text for the opera, partly in verse, partly in prose, and from these half-finished sketches I was to make verses throughout, according to the indicated musical rhythms and the sequence of action. Sometimes my work went for nought since I was inclined to depart from the dry Biblical locutions and Serov would revise my settings.[65]

In other words, from late 1861 until May 1862, Serov, far from writing his own "poem" in the Wagnerian fashion, had worked without a text, using only a rough scenario of his own devising, to which inserts and additions were continually made as the composer improvised the music.[66] Here is a second Serovian paradox: where Serov the critic was the most demanding advocate in the Russia of his time of the "organic" wedding of music and drama, Serov the composer could allow the inner acts of his opera to take shape in haphazard fashion with only the most vaguely defined "subject" as guide. As music accumulated, so did "dramatic situations," causing the opera to swell from a modest three acts to a "grand" five, and inevitably affecting deleteriously the structure of the drama. And this is yet another paradox. No less than Glinka, whose *Ruslan* he so severely chastised in print, he allowed himself to be carried away by his musical fantasy, especially in the portrayal of "oriental" pomp and hedonism. What had been a single climactic and spectacular Assyrian act in the original conception had to be split up into two. And this was a serious deflection from the dramaturgical principles Serov espoused in theory. Where all the other acts in *Judith* make stark contrasts with their neighbors—a Serovian sine qua non—Acts III and IV are absolutely parallel both in setting and in structure, and hence redundant. Both begin with picturesque scene-painting: in Act III this takes the form of Holofernes' march and the songs and dances of the odalisques; in Act IV an orchestral showpiece of an entr'acte and the ensuing chorus introduce Holofernes' orgy, in which we are treated to more dancing and to a kind of song contest between the commander and his eunuch Vagao. Then, in both acts, decorative entertainment (in the second instance amounting to far more than half the act's running time) gives way to highly charged confrontation of the principals, Act IV culminating in the murder.

Much of the divertissement, to be sure, is given some excuse by the scenario: the orgy is an integral part of the story, and even the reprise of the march (with orchestre d'harmonie onstage) is "justified" as depicting the Assyrians' preparations for war. But just as surely, to claim that all of it forms "an organic part of the action"[67] is at once to exaggerate and to miss the point. The sheer quantity of Meyerbeerian spectacle he provides, particularly in Act IV, reminds us inevitably of Serov's own cavils against the excesses of the grand opéra. "The picturesque is very important on the operatic stage," he had written in his critique of Spontini in 1852, "only let it not be the chief thing."[68] *Judith*'s fourth act notably violates this spirit of restraint. And the inclusion of dances in two consecutive acts is no less glaring an inconsistency in the work of a man who had written that dances are "out of place in lyric drama; they interrupt the action and distract the attention."[69]

Such a hypertrophy of divertissement was the inevitable result of exercising the musical imagination without the fetters and limitations that a more concretely specified set of situations would have imposed—the very "crime against art" Serov so loudly decried in the composer of *Ruslan*.[70] Even orchestration preceded the fixing of much of *Judith*'s text. Some parts of the opera were actually performed during the period in which Serov lacked a libretto. On February 26, 1862, the "Orgy and Bacchanalian Dances" at the beginning of Act IV were given minus the choral parts by Serov's friend Victor Kazhinsky at a concert in the Alexandrinsky Theatre. And the odalisques' songs and dances, along with Holofernes' march (Act III) were similarly performed in purely instrumental form in the summer of 1862 by Johann Strauss's orchestra at Pavlovsk.[71]

This brings us to paradox number four: Serov had long since taken up Wagner's cry that the composer of a musical drama must be his own librettist, and always was to claim as much for *Judith*. But in point of fact, *Judith*'s words, excepting those of the first act, were the work of a "committee," in which the composer seemed not even to occupy first place. Early in their collaboration Lobanov began to smell a rat. When Serov would modify Lobanov's work, the younger man noticed that "his verses were sometimes so artful, that I even began to wonder whether he had another collaborator besides me."[72] And although Serov hotly denied it to Lobanov, there were not one but two others. When he finally got around to thinking about a Russian text to replace Giustiniani's for the finale, Serov turned not to Lobanov but to Zvantsev, who had experience as an operatic translator and was then working on *Tannhäuser*. He sent him the Italian text for the fifth act, with the request that Zvantsev "transplant it to Russian soil, which for you should only be too easy." And he gave Zvantsev directions no less explicit and detailed than those he had given Lobanov, necessary because of the already-composed music: "I have marked all the rhythms for you in detail. I have also noted those places where it would be desirable to hew closer to the Bible than what came out in the rhymes of Signor Improvisatore."[73] And, as if two librettists working for him were not enough, he enlisted a third, this time a poet of real credentials, over whom he was in no position to exercise dictatorial control:

> Several gaps in the text, at those spots which demanded rhymed verse of greater finish than elsewhere (and which were difficult for me due to inexperience), forced me to seek the assistance of one of the foremost artists of Russian verse, Apollon Nikolaevich *Maikov* [1821-97], who had been interested in my work from its very inception.
> In the experienced view of A.N.M., the words of my opera, with their occasionally awkward treatment, lagged considerably behind the music in quality. In his good will toward me, A.N. overcame the scorn with which the literary man generally views the "opera libretto," and he devoted several evenings to a most attentive revision of my [!] text.
> Without touching the action of the play, or the makeup of any individual scene, my "collaborator" corrected many "deformities," as he called them, in the *facture* of my verses (which were very understandable and excusable, after all, in a man who had never written verses in his life) and in certain places... interpolated a few poetical images into the text itself, giving everywhere a greater profile and character to the speeches of the main personages.[74]

Maikov's contributions are a bit more extensive than Serov here implies. In the separately printed libretto, the composer scrupulously marked with asterisks those lines which were Maikov's rather than "his," and it is apparent that, for example, almost all of *Judith*'s lengthy Act II monologue is Maikov's work, as are the great majority of the opera's set pieces, obviously the places Serov mentioned where greater elegance of poetic style was needed. Maikov touched Act I (Serov's own) little, however, and Act V (Zvantsev's) not at all. It is characteristic that Serov denied the existence of each of his collaborators to the others, and it is obvious that only Maikov's eminence vouchsafed his contribution its due acknowledgement. To the end, though, Serov maintained that he, like Wagner, was his own sole librettist in *Judith*. Preposterous though this contention appears, his peculiar aesthetic outlook on opera permitted him to believe it quite sincerely.

Serov never wrote a tract comparable to *Oper und Drama,* but he did come close to giving systematic exposition to his operatic ideals in the course of his encyclopedic critique of Dargomyzhsky's *Rusalka,* published in ten install-ments in the influential *Muzykal'nyi i teatral'nyi vestnik (Musical and Theatrical Herald)* following the premiere in 1856. The theories and arguments set forth there are obviously colored by his knowledge of Wagner's tracts (though the height of his involvement with Wagner was to come later). Curiously, though, the result of Wagner's influence seems to have been mainly to lead Serov back to Rousseau's view of opera as an equal union of three arts, a view he had questioned, as we have seen, four years earlier.

"In my opinion," he wrote in 1856, "the components of 'opera' may be most conveniently viewed as three." And he proceeds to list and comment upon them thus:

1. The element of the poetical framework (the content and idea of the opera as a play)
2. The musical element (the expression of this idea through music)
3. The scenic, or theatrical, element (the realization of the idea of the text and the music by means of visible plastic images on the theatrical stage).

   Each of these three elements (text, music and staging) might dominate a given opera or certain of its parts to a greater or lesser extent, but in the complete absence of any of them the idea of "opera" is vitiated. From such a division of elements it is clear that, for example, the blatant incongruity of music and text (as in certain Italian operas of the "bravura" school) destroys the ideal of opera; but no less (even more, perhaps) is it destroyed by contradiction between that which is demanded by the nature of the play and the music, and that which we actually see on the stage (in the production and in the acting).[75]

Having made this division and ordering of operatic components, Serov goes on to break the first category down further. Here divergences both from Rousseau and from Wagner become apparent. But so closely does this personal operatic credo conform to Serov's practice in *Judith* that one must again conclude that composer and critic were not nearly so far apart as is commonly supposed, and that in both guises Serov was his own man.

One must definitely distinguish three stages in the text of an opera—stages of extremely unequal importance—which are often not distinguished but confused, and this confusion is inimical to true judgment of opera. These stages are:

1. The *plot,* as a poetical invention (la fable de la pièce, die Fabel des Stückes).
2. The musico-poetical disposition of the operatic ground plan—the "scenario" of the opera.
3. The words—the rhymed or unrhymed verses of the text.

The *first* of these stages is the most important one, both in relation to the opera as a dramatic composition and in relation to the opera as a theatrical presentation or spectacle, and even with regard to music. On the first stage depends the ability of the text to "inspire" the musician; on this same factor, together with the music and production, depends the interest and attraction of the opera and its whole fate.

The *second* stage . . . must be strictly and equally balanced between the requirements of the poet and those of the musician. This is often a very difficult task, and because of this there are so few operatic libretti with completely successful scenarios.

The *third* stage is altogether subordinate to the music. The music is written to a given set of "words," to be sure, but the musician writing the opera is inspired, of course, not by words, but by the situation of the given character or characters. This situation is in turn dependent upon the "plot" and "plan." Consequently, even for the composer himself, the "words" are not of primary importance. In them one need only observe a few conditions demanded by the music, that is, that the words be so adjusted as to assist, and never impede, the "musico-scenic impression."

For the listener, the words in most cases disappear behind the music, drown in an ocean of vocal and instrumental sounds. In keeping with this virtually inescapable evil, the libretto of an opera must be so made that the plot in its broad outlines be consistently clear and understandable almost without the assistance of words; that it be almost as simple and graphic as that of a ballet.[76]

Serov's ideal operatic scenario, then, is one that relies as little as possible on the intelligibility of the text, which means that the musical setting should rely as little as possible on recitative, let alone spoken dialogue (the *Singspiel* is for him an "anti-artistic" genre even in the hands of Beethoven). For this reason, plots must be chosen which make their appeal not by virtue of reason or logic, but which directly involve the senses and emotions. The hallmark of a good operatic scenario is vividly portrayed feelings: that of a good play, well developed ideas. That is why "dramas based on characters in whom rational thought predominates [are] essentially unmusical,"[77] (hence he specifically excludes Pushkin's *Boris Godunov*!) and at the same time why the subject of *Judith,* whose characters are at all times motivated by the strongest and most elemental passions, is ideal for opera, and *not* for the spoken drama.

By the same token, an operatic text that calls for much recitative is one that ought to be spoken and not sung; it depends for its effect upon its words, not upon the vivid portrayal of character and affect for which music is uniquely suited, and for which it must be given freedom. Serov's main quarrel with other critics of opera, notably Fétis, turns upon precisely this point—that they ascribe far too much importance to the text at the most local of its "stages," and hence assign far too much responsibility to the librettist as partner in the creation of the scenario. "The plan of an opera," Serov emphasizes, "in all that relates to the sequence of scenes (that is, here a duet, there a chorus, here an aria, there a finale with so many characters), is arrived at by *mutual agreement* of composer and librettist and sometimes," he insists, "belongs *more to the composer* than to the author of the words."[78]

Serov never perceived the gulf that separated this weighting of operatic elements from Wagner's. The whole thrust of *Oper und Drama* had been in favor of the "poem," the essential Wagnerian shaping force. Serov denies all shaping power to the text; as long as he controlled the first and second "stages" of *Judith*'s book, and made some small contribution even to the third, he felt himself entirely justified in claiming that he was his own librettist.

This short exposition of Serov's operatic theory is essential to an understanding of the curious preface to *Judith*'s libretto, wherein he is at pains to compare his opera to "prior dramas" on the subject, by which he means, besides the Giacometti vehicle he had seen three years before, the famous tragedy by Friedrich Hebbel, generally regarded as the finest dramatization of the Judith legend. Serov disagrees: his opera has every advantage over his predecessors' dramas, and for reasons obviously related to the theories we have examined.

> The main defect of these dramas consists first of all in the fact that they are *spoken dramas*, while this subject calls for a *musical* drama; secondly, in the fact that in the general and in the particular both of them depart from the legend and its inner content.[79]

On the necessity for the composer to be his own librettist, he asserts:

> Even the very best writer, precisely because he *is* a writer and not a musician, is incapable of creating a text for musical drama.

And on his own performance:

> Above all I strove, in writing the scenario of this play, to keep *as closely as possible to the text of the book of "Judith,"* drawing my scenic effects directly from the organism of the project as a whole, and bypassing the various extra characters and situations, with which neither the author of the Italian nor of the German drama were niggardly.[80]

The "extras" in Giacometti's *Giuditta* are easy enough to identify. They include such standard melodramatic fare as Judith's lover (an "Italian *primo tenore*," as Serov sneeringly recalls him), an odalisque in love with Holofernes and jealous of Judith, an episode in which the Hebrew high priest is captured and taken prisoner to Holofernes—and much else besides.[81] Serov's objections to Hebbel's tragedy are at once more difficult to isolate and more revealing. Serov admired the play; in his preface he admitted having been influenced by Hebbel's general plan.[82] But of the complex of psychological and metaphysical themes which so distinguish Hebbel's treatment of the legend there is little trace in Serov, for in his view such baggage is hardly less superfluous to the operatic composer than Giacometti's lovers and odalisques.[83] The "Biblical simplicity" Serov sought (and which Hebbel, be it said, despised) was beyond the reach of an author of spoken drama. Lacking the intensifying resources of music, the dramatic author has no choice but the deepening and rounding of character, the introduction of "conflicts," and—above all—the complication of action and motive. And so Hebbel's heroine is deeply ambivalent in her motives, while his Holofernes becomes a magnetic, Napoleonic figure, as capable of seducing Judith as she him. In the words of Hebbel's biographer, "the more or less symbolic opposition of Jewish woman and heathen warrior is a superficial one, compared with this tragic opposition of a man and woman with a fundamental affinity."[84] Judith's inner conflicts, set in motion by her unconsummated marriage, make her a true tragic heroine, whose personal anguish reaches its climax with wrenching irony precisely at her moment of triumph. She returns with Holofernes' head to a scene of celebration which, inwardly devastated, she finds unendurable. After the Jews rush off in pursuit of the leaderless Assyrians (Judith [thinking of the noble Holofernes]: "Das ist Schlächtermuth!"), she begs the remaining priests and elders that, should she request it, she be put to death. They are astonished, but only to her handmaiden does Judith confess her reason, in the play's chilling closing lines:

> Ich will dem Holofernes keinen Sohn gebaren! Bete zu Gott, dass mein Schoss unfruchtbar sei. Vielleicht ist er mir gnädig![85]

That Serov never for a moment thought to burden Judith (to say nothing of his audience) with such ideas is a perfect measure of the difference he perceived between the spoken and the lyric theater, and it was precisely because of this need on the part of the modern dramatist to saddle the action with such a weight of "meaning" that—as he avers in his preface—the Judith story was unthinkable in any but musical terms, and that only an operatic treatment could do it justice. So Serov systematically omitted everything in Hebbel's handling of the Judith story which might have compromised the unidimensional portrayal of the heroine. Her emotions are as blatantly "civic" and impersonal as Susanin's![86] If Judith's fatal ambivalence is present at all in Serov's drama, it is present only in an almost absurdly trivialized form, when Holofernes places a temptation in Judith's heart by offering to share Nebuchadnezzar's throne with her (Act IV).

On the other hand, a good deal of Hebbel's action did find its way into Serov's scenario.[87] Both dramatists center their first acts around Achior's admiring summary of the fate of the Jews. But Hebbel sets the act in the Assyrian camp, basing its action on chapters 3-6 of the Apocryphal book, while Serov opens his drama upon the scene of the siege of Bethulia (chapter 7), and summarizes the rest in Achior's recitative and aria. Holofernes' musings on the boredom of omnipotence and his angry yet fascinated response to the hardy defiance of the Hebrews are transferred (minus intellectual nuances) to Serov's Act III, his first "Assyrian" act.

Serov's Act II strikingly demonstrates both the extent of his indebtedness to Hebbel and their crucial differences of emphasis. The first part of this act has no true analogue in the Apocrypha at all, so his model can only have been Hebbel. In the Apocryphal account, Judith's resolution and decision are wholly implicit in her actions. Hebbel gives us an entire scene devoted to Judith's inner struggle and mastery of doubt. The unnamed "handmaiden" given passing mention in the Apocrypha becomes a major character: Mirza in Hebbel, Avra[88] (Judith's former wet-nurse and no maiden) in Serov. To Avra Serov transferred the arguments against opposing the Assyrians voiced in Hebbel's drama by Ephraim, Judith's suitor, a character he saw fit to eliminate. But where Hebbel used this act for his critical exposition of Judith's inner split, Serov is interested only in the broadest "contrast"—Judith's resolution (Act II) versus the despair of the rest of the Hebrews (Act I). When Hebbel's heroine recalls her dead husband it is with tortured memories of their failure to consummate their union. Serov's Judith bewails only the loss of a potential leader for her people. The narration of her husband's bizarre wedding-night visions is replaced in the opera by the "War Song of the Jews," a conventional "interpolated" number recounting the exploits of Yail, which Judith has Avra sing to boost her courage.

Hebbel's Act III, in which Judith rebukes the elders (Apocrypha: chapter 8) becomes the second part of Serov's Act II. Serov has the elders come to Judith, as it is in the original narrative, while Hebbel shifts the scene to the center of Bethulia for the crowd scene which corresponds to Serov's Act I. But where Hebbel's crowd scene is an anecdotal, colorful affair, Serov's is all ascetic "exposition."

The outward course of events for the rest of the drama, except for Ephraim's attempt on Holofernes (in Hebbel but not in Serov) and Holofernes' Boris-like hallucination (in Serov but not in Hebbel), is, in its broad outlines, identical in the two versions. Among the inventions of Hebbel adopted by Serov is Mirza/Avra's continued distrust of Judith's motives. But where Mirza had seen through to the underlying conflict that made Judith's fate truly tragic, Avra seems merely obtuse. The deed done, Serov's Judith returns triumphant to Bethulia bearing Holofernes' severed head, but not the burden of guilt her counterpart in Hebbel had to endure. She leads the inhabitants of the city in a closing canticle drawn directly from the Apocrypha, the scene with which Serov had begun under the direct impression of Giacometti's vehicle for Ristori.

But Serov's handling of the subject should not be regarded as a mere "operatic" impoverishment. By beginning his drama in Bethulia rather than the Assyrian camp (like Giacometti), but withholding Judith's appearance until the second act (like Hebbel), he actually effects a sturdier dramatic structure than either of his predecessors. In Serov's scenario the first two acts (Hebrew) are balanced against the third and fourth (Assyrian), while at the same time representing an internal contrast, as we have seen, of despair and resolution. The absence of women's voices (except for choristers) in Act I, and the virtually complete domination of Act II by Judith (dramatic soprano) and Avra (mezzo), make for another deliberate and theatrically effective contrast. The first and final acts—monumental "frescoes" framing the action, in which "the interest . . . is virtually entirely in the choruses,"[89] are also balanced by contrast: lamentation versus rejoicing. This reliance on contrast admittedly makes for a rather static conception of drama. But if Musorgsky was right to complain that "there is no action" in the first two acts,[90] the charge could be made with equal justice against Hebbel's drama, and often was.[91]

Penetrating beneath the level of scenario to what Serov called the "third stage" of operatic dramaturgy (the words of the libretto and their relationship to the music) we find Serov's performance entirely consistent with his theories and with his working habits—and diametrically opposed to the thinking of practically all the other leading Russian musicians of the day, especially those of the younger generation. Dargomyzhsky's famous rallying cry of the sixties ("I want music strictly to express the word; I want truth.") already suggests the difference: by placing the locus of "truth" at the level of the individual word of text, the composers who followed Dargomyzhsky's precept sought to banish rounded "forms" from their work and turn opera into an infinitely flexible, madrigalistic, "melodic recitative," in César Cui's formulation.

Though Serov could be sympathetic to such an approach as critic, as his review of Rusalka amply demonstrates,[92] the same essay contains the classic formulation of Serov's own operatic principles, where a far broader and more generalized view of the text-music relationship is advocated. Not only did Serov the critic promulgate such a relationship between text and music, but Serov the composer's working methods made it the only one possible. Devaluation of the verbal element per se may be plainly observed both in the treatment accorded the "third phase" in much of Judith, and in its sheer quality.

The relationship between text and music in Judith is often a rather casual one, and Serov took an occasionally offhand approach to that most sacred of Russian sacred cows, declamation. For this he was angrily attacked by those who, like the young kuchkists and Stasov, equated correct prosody with dramatic truth, and he became embroiled in pointless debate with even his friendliest critics over niceties of accentuation. When Rostislav (Theophil Tolstoy) suggested that the subject of the choral fugue in Act I (Ex. 2.1) betrays by its declamation (e.g., the placement of the unaccented syllable "za-") the fact that the music preceded the words in the process of composition— an observation not only astute but accurate—Serov denied it in the most arrogant, tautological terms.

I am outraged to the depths of my being, I actually have fits whenever it is suggested to me that I do not know the "prosody" of my own native language! Russian prosody might perhaps be unknown to the esteemed Director of the Russian Conservatory, who jabbers and scribbles in three or four languages equally illiterately (since all these languages are foreign to him), but a Russian composer who has written his own text for his opera must at least know prosody. I am ready to argue not only with you, but with a whole legion of critics and connoisseurs (if such a legion could be found in Russia) that mistakes or slips in Russian prosody do not and cannot exist in my score, just as there cannot be mistakes in harmony, though my harmony be in a thousand places condemned by thousands of Zarembas [Nikolai Ivanovich Zaremba (1821-79), Professor of Harmony at Rubinstein's Conservatory] and Fétises. If I felt I did not know my business, I would never have decided to make my debut as a composer in the public arena ... You have every right to discuss and criticize my views on art, my principles, or my style—*c'est toujours discûtable.* But in matters of knowledge and technique I cannot accept lessons from anyone.... I have never had professors and I do not recognize them.[93]

Ex. 2.1.   Serov, *Judith,* choral fugue in Act I (vocal score, Moscow: Gutheil, ca. 1885)

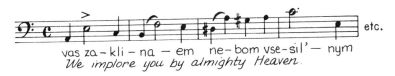

Serov's loud protestations notwithstanding, many of *Judith*'s most effective pages, if approached from the prosodic or declamational point of view, will look ineffective or even downright silly. Obviously, it follows that this is not the best critical yardstick to apply, even though such an approach was favored above all others by Serov's hostile critics like Cui. But taking a close look at one number from this standpoint will repay us with a glimpse of his working relationship with his phantom collaborators. One of the most extended and "symphonic" musical numbers in *Judith,* the chorus of Assyrians that heralds the heroine's appearance in Act III,[94] is based on the following text:

Prishlá k nam evréika krasý nebyváloi,	A Jewess of unheard beauty has come to us;
V shatër k Oloférnu stremítsia oná;	she is headed for Holofernes' tent.
K vozhdú Assiríian zheláet predstát',	She wishes to stand before the Assyrians' leader.
Chegó ona khóchet ne znáet niktó!	Nobody knows what she wants.

Vót uzh druz'iá krasotá!	Now there's a beauty, friends!
Ákh chto za grúd', chto za óchi!	What a breast, what eyes!
Négoiu, strást'iu polná;	She is full of tenderness and passion.
Vsékh nas pleníla sobói!	She has captivated us all!
Evréev nam nádo mechëm istrebít',	We must destroy the Jews by the sword;
Oní nam ne stráshny,	They hold no terrors for us.
No zhénshchiny ikh krasói svoéi	But their women, with their beauty,
Mógut ves' mir pokorít'!	Could conquer the whole world!

On these twelve lines (presumably Lobanov's), Serov turned out 283 measures of music (not counting the orchestral introduction and postlude). Or rather, these twelve lines of text were obviously stretched over 283 bars that were ready and waiting for them. The lines of text, and fragments of them, are all repeated interminably and juxtaposed with one another in all kinds of combinations. Peculiarities of prosody strengthen the impression of a marriage of convenience between word and tone. In the first setting of the first quatrain, the music follows its own quite natural scheme of symmetrical phrase repetitions, but repetition of words seems to follow no plan whatever, save the supplying of the needed number of syllables. Nor does the opposition of syllabic and melismatic prosody seem to arise from any consideration of textual meaning, but is apparently the result of an occasional insufficiency of syllables to cover the preexistent notes. The setting of the last two lines of the first stanza seems particularly ineffective: they are set to identical music but do not rhyme; a repetition of text as well as music might here have been an improvement, but Serov needed to get through the first stanza, so as to make the beginning of the second stanza coincide with his "second theme" (Ex. 2.2).

Here the melismas on "zhelaet" and "znaet" are not such as might have been suggested to the composer's imagination by the text. Such melodic flourishes, which seem to have no relation to the words on which they are sung, are common enough in *Judith,* and continually remind us that their composer believed music to be the medium only of the most generalized expression, and rarely attempted to follow with his music the transient, fugitive images and associations of the text at the more local range favored by the next generation of Russian composers. The rhythmic dickering to which he subjects the melody in the second line, moreover, again suggests "contrafactum."

The nature and structure of the chorus's "poem" is itself revealing. The first quatrain is in strict dactylic tetrameters, the second in a catalectic dactylic trimeter. But in the third quatrain Lobanov was evidently hard pressed to find words to fit Serov's music, for here the four lines contain respectively four, two, four and three feet. And even then Lobanov was not entirely successful, since the word "svoéi" in the third line consistently appears with the accent displaced to the first syllable. The setting of this line is otherwise notable as an

Ex. 2.2.   *Judith,* chorus of Assyrians in Act III (excerpt, vocal
parts only)

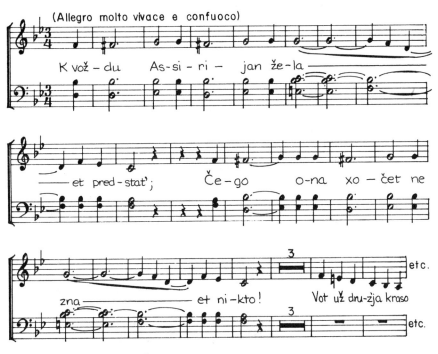

Ex. 2.3.   *Judith,* chorus of Assyrians in Act III (excerpt, three
choruses in unison)

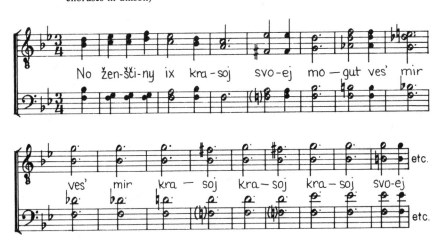

exceptionally, almost comically telling example of fragmentary text repetition: "No zhenshchiny ikh krasoi svoei mogut ves' mir, ves' mir krasoi krasoi krasoi svoei mogut krasoi svoei mogut ves' mir pokorit' ves' ves' mir pokorit'" (Ex. 2.3).

These "weaknesses" of prosody in the Assyrians' Chorus are easily enough explained, even justified, by Serov's wish to herald Judith's entrance with an enormous choral-orchestral fanfare. The intent is not so much dramatic as decorative—one of his characteristic "frescoes." But the same habits of prosody, evidence of the same working routine, can be observed in "dramatic" scenes as well. In his Act III arioso, Holofernes gives vent to his impatience (!) by endlessly repeating the lines of his short text (especially the line, "A tut stoím i smótrim na zhálkoe gnezdó [But we just stand and gape at that pitiful tribe]"), stretched as if by Procrustes himself across seven full pages of vocal score.[95]

Serov's contemporaries tended to exaggerate his Wagnerianism as much as later commentators have discounted it. Theophil Tolstoy, writing as Rostislav, summed up the Russian composer's debt to the German by noting in his "Analysis" of *Judith* that both of them "reject virtuosity" and "avoid melody."[96] And as late as 1890, Vladimir Sergeevich Baskin found "endless melody" and no end of "orchestral development" in *Judith*.[97] Serov himself was among those who saw *Judith* as patently a "Wagnerian" opera. In the interview with Tolstoy (quoted in footnote 86 of this chapter) after explaining why he had sought to avoid "Glinka's footsteps," he addressed himself quite seriously to his interlocutor's remark, made "not without a certain malice," that instead he had followed the footsteps of the German master. "That's another story," he retorted. "Wagner is as yet completely unknown here; let our public acquaint itself with his style and procedures in *Judith*."[98]

But wherein does this "Wagnerianism" reside? It is surely not to be sought in Serov's musical style as such, for there one can observe only the faintest traces of Wagner in Serov's eclectic mix,[99] and, at that, only because one is naturally on the lookout for them. So, in one sense one can agree with Gerald Abraham's conclusion that "whatever Serov has in common with Wagner is due to common factors in their musical ancestry: Spontini, Halévy and, above all, Meyerbeer."[100] But Serov's Wagnerianism was no simple matter of musical mimicry. Rather, it was a matter, as Serov himself averred, of operatic "procedure," the interrelating of music and dramatic situation. From the standpoint of operatic dramaturgy and form, none of the figures Abraham mentions could have provided Serov with a model. Nor will it do to point to *Rusalka* as a point of departure, however the composer of *Judith* may have admired that work. For the famed and much-touted dramatic scenes of Dargomyzhsky's opera are essentially extended *stromentato* recitatives, a form which Serov almost totally excluded from *Judith,* and which, indeed, his working methods rendered unfeasible.

No, Wagner and only Wagner was for Serov the paradigm of sensible and resourceful application of music to dramatic situations. But before we can find Wagner in Serov we must remember first that it is *his* Wagner, not necessarily ours, that we will find; and second, that there were fundamental disparities between the Russian composer and the German (perhaps unrecognized by Serov himself) which necessarily hindered any similarity of result, however close the intentions may have been.

To deal with the latter first: it is obvious that one cannot write a truly "Wagnerian" opera unless one writes it according to Wagner's method. That is, not only must the author of the music and of the play be the same (and here, for the sake of argument, let us grant Serov his conceit), but the words must necessarily precede the music. Most of Serov's music, imagined in response not to a "poem," but to an "image" or "situation," was shaped "abstractly." And since Serov's musical imagination—or his technique, which for our purposes amounts to the same thing—admitted little in the way of ongoing, developmental form, it was inevitable that his music lacked anything resembling the plasticity of Wagner's.[101] Nor can one be sure that he even considered such "symphonic" form desirable.[102]

What, then, did Serov consider the essence of "Wagnerianism" to be? The closest to an explicit formulation can be found in a heated defense of Wagner which Serov penned in answer to a certain Paul Smith, a follower of Fétis, who had published an attack on Wagner's reforms in the *Revue et Gazette Musicale* at the time of Wagner's Parisian concerts of 1860—or just before Serov embarked on the composition of *Judith*. He attempts here to strip away the smokescreen of verbiage surrounding Wagner's notorious theories[103] and to view Wagner's dramas as the culmination of a steady historical process rooted in Gluck and Mozart.

The greater part of the first act of *Don Giovanni* is taken up by the *introduzione* and the enormous *finale,* created according to the demands of the scenic action, and not by cutting it up into arias, duets, and the like. In *Figaro* practically the whole second act and practically all of the fourth act consist of through-composed *finales.* At the same time, all Figaro's arias seem rhetorical patches, as does, for example, the aria "Il mio tesoro" in *Don Giovanni.* In *Die Zauberflöte,* each act is half taken up with finales. The arias in this opera are its weaker side.

Now, if we understand and sense that the form of a *finale* or an *introduzione,* a linked sequence of monologues, duets, trios, recitatives, melodramas, choruses and ensembles [*penie mnogogolosnoe*] and so on, according to the demands of the dramatic plan—that is, the form of *free* development of musico-dramatic scenes, *without the slightest concession to the rhetorical* for the benefit of the singers—is precisely that form which answers completely to the ideal of combining dramatic poetry and music as Gluck had already conceived it— then it will become the most natural matter for a composer-poet, for whom the most important thing is not the creation of separate items of musico-scenic representation (as it is for Meyerbeer, for example), but for whom on the contrary (as it was for Beethoven), the most important thing is the poetic *idea* of the artistic creation in its entirety, that such a composer, I say, living in our time—after the operas of Mozart, Beethoven, Cherubini, Méhul, Spontini, Rossini, Weber, Marschner, Meyerbeer—had to arrive at this system: *to turn every act of his opera* into one uninterrupted *finale* (or *introduzione* and *finale* connected). There is the whole layout of the Wagnerian operas in its broad features.

Where the subject, according to the meaning of the drama, demands a monologue, there is a *monologue* in Wagner's music (not an "aria," because this word brings with it the idea of Italianate, conventional, rhetorical stereotype, inhibiting dramatic truth). Thus, in *Tannhäuser*, Elisabeth's monologue at the beginning of the second act, and her prayer at the beginning of the third; Tannhäuser's big third-act narrative of his pilgrimage; and in the same act Wolfram's lyrical song to the evening star. The whole scene of the song contest is a series of monologues for each of the Minnesingers (these monologues are of a lyrical character, in very much the same form as many of Schubert's songs or the romances of our own Glinka).

In *Lohengrin*, Elsa has two monologues, in the first and in the second act; there is a monologue for the king and there is Lohengrin's long narrative about the secrets of the Holy Grail at the drama's climax.

Where the meaning of the dramatic plan demands the interaction of two characters—even Wagner promptly provides a duo. The scene of Tannhäuser and Elisabeth, for example, at the beginning of the second act—a formal duet, in its structure even highly reminiscent of the duet of Florestan and Leonora in the first act of *Fidelio*. The beginning of *Tannhäuser*, in fact, is a duet for Tannhäuser and Venus.

In *Lohengrin* there are three huge scenes (Ortrud and Telramund, Ortrud and Elsa, Elsa and Lohengrin) which proceed as duets (but not, of course, in thirds and sixths!). The last part of the first act of *Tannhäuser* is a delightful septet for male voices.

In the first act of *Lohengrin* the prayer before the knightly combat is the most transparent crystalline quintet with chorus.

What's all the fuss about?[104]

For Serov, then, Wagner represented nothing more revolutionary than the most successful response to date to the "continuous finale" for which German idealist critics like Lessing and Herder had been calling for years. To the extent that Serov's technique and working methods allowed him to achieve it, we will find his Wagnerianism in the continuity and flexibility of his "forms." And conversely, one might add, the extent to which Serov fell short of this goal as a result of composing without a text will be the extent to which his music will consist—to borrow his own clumsy locution—of "separate items of musico-scenic representation," notably in the Assyrian acts. And this, along with his rather impersonal, eclectic style, accounts, more than anything else, for the resemblance to Meyerbeer, which has escaped no one.

Act V of *Judith,* which contains the music Serov wrote in his first flush of enthusiasm, is an excellent example of the "continuous finale" he aspired to. It is executed on a vast scale; some of the members of the "chain" are in themselves quite extended compositions. But no "link" is allowed to come to a full stop. The very elaborate chorus of starving Judeans, for example, is cut off on a deceptive cadence by the offstage music of Judith's approach. Previously it had been interrupted twice, for speeches by Achior and the high priest Eliachim. The latter is introduced by a climactic diminished-seventh chord which finishes off another major section of the chorus on a note of similar unfinality. The only "perfect cadence" in the entire act is the concluding one, at the culmination of Judith's canticle with chorus, a splendiferous and decidedly "operatic" number which nonetheless has its origins and counterpart directly within the Biblical story (chapter 16).[105] It is, as Serov would have said, motivated from within the "dramatic plan."

Act I, the second to be composed, exhibits even more manifestly "Wagnerian" formal—and now let us add, tonal—characteristics (alongside its prima facie Wagnerian-ness as the one act whose words are really the composer's). Nominally in E minor, the first scene opens with a kind of extended dominant pedal,[106] but the primary functions of the key are never asserted. The opening recitative scene reaches its climax in Eliachim's arioso, which makes its cadence on G, following which the first chorus wrenches the tonal center back to E minor. But once more cadences are suppressed, and when a concluding E major chord is sounded right before the fugue (quoted in Example 2.1 above), it clearly plays the role of dominant to A minor. The fugue is cut off on a diminished-seventh chord, and is linked by a line of arioso for the priest Ozias to a reprise in the opening key. And only here is an authentic cadence on E minor allowed to occur, coinciding with the people's desperate decision to surrender to Holofernes. The decisive moment on stage is confirmed by the music. Ironically, it was Stasov who saw Serov's "Wagnerianism" most clearly as residing in the "general aspiration to formlessness which of course is the best aspect of the whole opera."[107]

Indeed, Serov seems to have possessed a considerable awareness of the potential relationship between musical and dramatic tensions, and the possibility of articulating the "movements" of both in conjunction. And despite the freedom of his handling of "key," he was also sensitive to the tonal unity of his opera, and, like Wagner, saw tonal relationships as analogues to dramatic ones. The outer acts are both centered on the key of E major-minor, however rare their cadences. The first act ends quietly and with a characteristically Serovian "fade-out,"[108] which lends all the more musico-dramaturgical significance to the huge final cadence of the last act. The key of the outer acts is consistently associated with the Hebrews. The Assyrian acts are predominantly in D major-minor while the key of C minor is reserved for Judith herself, with Avra's utterances mostly in F minor. The deliberateness of this set of key associations is confirmed by Serov's use of these keys outside the acts to which they are "indigenous." Thus the "War Song of the Jews" in Act II is in the "Hebrew" tonality of E major, while the rest of the act is in the Judith and Avra keys except for the duet of Ozias and Charmi, elders of the people, which again reverts to a tonality associated with Act I. Similarly, when Judith appears for the first time in Holofernes' camp, she brings "her" key with her.

Serov strove for musico-dramatic unity in melodic, as well as tonal, details. Unsubtle though Holofernes' musical characterization may be, it is executed with remarkable and imaginative consistency. All his numbers, and all numbers associated with him, share important musical aspects far beyond the brassy orchestration which they have most obviously in common. A three-note "headmotive," *D-E-F*(♯), unifies all the Holofernian numbers (Ex. 2.4): the march (a),[109] the Act III arioso (b), the triumphant chorus at the end of the third act (c), and Holofernes' martial air in Act IV (d).

Ex. 2.4.   *Judith,* "headmotive" uniting Holofernian numbers

a. the march in Act III (vocal score, p. 169)

b. the arioso in Act III (pp. 161-2)

c. the chorus at the end of Act III (p. 216)

d. Holofernes' martial air in Act IV (pp. 264-5)

The motive also figures conspicuously in Holofernes' dramatic repliques, though often transposed to other keys (Ex. 2.5).

Ex. 2.5.   *Judith*, further use of headmotive in Holofernes' part, Acts III and IV

a.

b.

c.

d.

e.

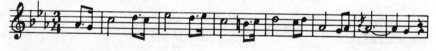

Net!   na pre-stol   ja sjadu sam ca-rěm!
No! I'll sit myself upon the throne as King!

f.

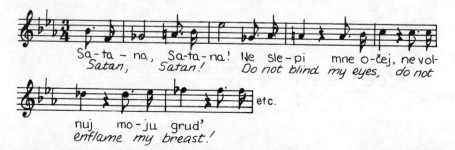
etc.

Pust' bog pri-dět tvoj   sam!
Let your god himself appear!

Judith is also provided with characteristic themes, mostly drawn from her Act II monologue. And when she quotes Achior's words to Holofernes[110] she also quotes his music.

Though these devices of thematic association undoubtedly have their source in Serov's affinity for Wagner, it is far too much to call such headmotives and reminiscences "leitmotives," as Baskin, among others, has done. The term, properly used, implies an "autonomous" symphonic treatment essentially alien to Serov's musical mentality. Serov's are static identifying motives which rarely change character in response to dramatic vicissitudes. The one significant exception is worth quoting, however. Judith's momentary anguish of temptation in Act IV is based on a striking chromatic transformation of the opening oboe theme of her Act II monologue. It seems significant that the two passages come from the last two scenes of the opera to have been composed (Ex. 2.6).[111]

Ex. 2.6.   *Judith,* chromatic transformation of a theme

a. Judith's monologue in Act II, opening oboe theme

b. Her moment of temptation in Act IV

Sa-ta – na,   Sa-ta-na!   Ne sle-pi   mne o-čej, ne vol-
Satan,   Satan!   Do not blind my eyes, do not

etc.

nuj   mo-ju grud'
enflame my breast!

But Serov's efforts to construct a continuous musico-dramatic discourse are everywhere hampered, it must be admitted, by the short-windedness of his musical ideas. Stasov, for all his malice and hyperbole, was once again not far from the mark when he shrieked to Balakirev after the premiere that Serov "cannot write two coherent pages of music; he has to interrupt the flow every five measures, or else it comes out academic, somehow fugal."[112] Serov's imagination generally came up with two- or four-bar phrases, which he usually developed through repetitive and symmetrical rhythmic sequences. Therefore even the shortest links in Serov's structural chain—say, a bridging line of recitative—is likely to be rhythmically square and disconcertingly "singsong." Extended scenes and monologues—Judith's in Act II, Holofernes' in Act III—are best understood as discrete little chains within chains. Judith's monologue, the longest such scene in the opera by far, contains what could easily pass for four short, rhythmically obvious "arias" linked by modulatory bridges which are themselves rhythmically "rounded" and stable. The result of all this, as Musorgsky was quick to point out, was that "*Wagner's Kindchen* doesn't look like his daddy; *he couldn't measure up to him.*"[113] Wagner himself evidently agreed, for upon being presented with the score during his St. Petersburg tour just before *Judith*'s premiere, all he found to say was, "Well, it's clear that you know how to orchestrate."[114]

Before closing the case of *Judith*, a few words should be said about its performance, for this was in some ways the most remarkable and influential aspect of the opera. In keeping with his view of himself as sole creator of his opera, Serov attempted as far as possible to supervise and control all aspects of its production. In this he was not entirely successful; the Imperial Theaters Directorate was not prepared to allot sufficient funds to cover an entirely new staging. The sets, like much of Serov's Assyrian music, were of the all-purpose "oriental" variety, and had actually served for recent perfomances of *Nabucco* and *Semiramide*.[115] The choreography, by Alexei Bogdanov, was likewise of the most conventional sort, and so offended Serov that he insisted upon its being replaced in Act IV by a tableau vivant.[116] The costumes, on the other hand, were the result of a collaboration between the author and the well-known archaeologist Nikolai Veniaminovich Nabokov, who drew upon historical data for an accurate representation of ancient Judean and Assyrian attire.

But the production's most impressive feature, and one which may have had a greater impact upon the future of Russian opera than Serov's music itself, was the composer's casting and coaching of the two principals. Serov rejected the established singers of the Russian Opera, preferring to seek out two unknowns whom he could more easily mold to his desired conception. Judith was played by Valentina Bianchi (1839-84), Swiss by birth and a graduate of the Paris Conservatoire. Serov called her "a singer of enormous voice and German musicality."[117] She had a remarkable range and was able to sail over Serov's noisy orchestration with ease. One critic, pointing out her defects, noted that the "constant sobbing in her singing, her forced high notes of piercing timbre, her howling phrasing," as well as her "passion [and] inner fire," rendered her unsuited to Russian opera, thinking evidently of Glinka and the earlier Dargomyzhsky, whose music demands a refined, bel canto style of execution.[118] But the role of Judith was made for a voice like Bianchi's. It broke new ground in Russian opera, and was viewed with alarm by Glinka's admirers. Cui, for example, wrote that the opera's greatest fault was "the ungrateful part of Judith herself: it is written extremely high in tessitura, shrilly and clumsily for the voice; the performance of such a role is tiring for the singer and injurious to her voice. Even the recitatives are written excessively high."[119] But of course this extremity of range was part of the characterization, and Serov carefully coached Bianchi at her home for months before the premiere, so that her performance, which critics tended to find overly melodramatic,[120] was beyond question a faithful realization of the composer's intentions.

Even more novel and startling was the performance of Mikhail Ivanovich Sariotti (1839-78), a debutant who created a sensation in the role of Holofernes. "A singer of limited vocal means but outstanding gifts as *singing actor,* performing with sense and meaning," according to Serov,[121] Sariotti, under the composer's strict tutelage, managed to create a wholly new and specifically Russian type of singer, and was the most important single contributor to the opera's astounding and unexpected success. He was also the focal point of heated critical controversy. Cui was horrified at Sariotti's performance, but correctly perceived that his quarrel lay not with the singer but with the composer.

> It is hard to say anything against Mr. Sariotti while the author is on hand and while Sariotti is in all probability singing and acting on Mr. Serov's instructions. Consequently, to take issue with the merits of Sariotti's performance means questioning the author's understanding of Holofernes as a personality. But what else can one do? Finding Sariotti's performance talented, I find it at the same time monstrous. In the third act it is only a question of *extreme* exaggeration and tastelessness, but in the entire fourth act what we hear from Mr. Sariotti is not singing at all, but raucous bellowing. If Mr. Serov were really aspiring to precisely this, then he probably would not have written a vocal part, but merely indicated "Holofernes declaims hoarsely."[122]

What Serov and Sariotti had accomplished was a decisive break with the traditions of the *basso cantante* (upheld in Russia by Osip Petrov and the role he created, Ivan Susanin),[123] and its replacement by the parlando manner that became the very trademark of the Russian basso. The line of dramatic bass and baritone roles that so conspicuously stud the Russian operatic firmament—Khovansky, Galitzky, Ivan the Terrible (not to mention Boris Godunov)—can be traced back to Holofernes, and the noble dynasty of singing actors culminating in Fyodor Stravinsky and Chaliapin—to Sariotti. Even Cui was forced to admit, with regard to *Judith*'s fourth act, where Holofernes/Sariotti's raving and howling had been most objectionable, that "it is guided by intentions of dramatic truth, such as had never existed among us before *Judith*."[124] Coming from a *kuchkist* that is high praise indeed, topped only by Tchaikovsky's avowal—as late as 1892!—that "after *Don Giovanni* I love most *A Life for the Tsar*... and Serov's *Judith*."[125] Tchaikovsky's linking of these names was far from fortuitous. If not the epoch-making work some thought it to be at the time of its premiere, *Judith* nonetheless deserves to be remembered as the first musical drama in Russia which was self-avowedly a "music drama," which sought to do consciously and in a principled way what Glinka had done instinctively. Though hardly commensurate with Glinka's, Serov's claim as a founding father of the Russian school is nonetheless genuine, and without knowing him we cannot really know those who followed.[126]

Notes

1. The most recent production of a Serov opera (unless one wants to count a recent *Judith* in Buryat Mongolia!) was the Bolshoi's staging of *Vrazh'ia sila* in a revision of Asafiev (1947)—a failure. *Judith* was given only as long as Chaliapin was around to sing Holofernes, while *Rogneda* did not survive the Revolution. Diaghilev's Paris production of *Judith*'s Assyrian acts in 1909 (a Chaliapin vehicle) remains the only non-Russian staging Serov's work has ever been accorded.

2. He was rehabilitated somewhat (as critic only) after the "Zhdanovshchina" of 1948. As one whose writings could be used to uphold the Party resolution on preserving the traditional values of Russian music, Serov was treated to an edition of his *Selected Articles* (vol. I: Leningrad, 1950; vol. II: Moscow, 1957), edited by Giorgii Khubov, who wrote a lengthy introduction entitled "Alexander Serov: Militant Realist." Khubov is also the author of a biography which appeared at the same time, and which displays the same slant (*Zhizn' A.N. Serova,* Moscow, 1950).

3. The most influential of these were the synoptic essays "Twenty-five Years of Russian Art" (1882), and "Art in the Nineteenth Century" (1901). "The Brakes on New Russian Art" (1885), a sort of companion piece to the former, records twenty-five years of Russian criticism with which Stasov disagreed, and singles Serov out for a special excoriation. All of these may be found in the three-volume edition of Stasov's writings: V.V. Stasov, *Izbrannye Sochineniia* (Moscow, 1952). An idea of the viciousness of Stasov's diatribes against Serov may be gained from the recent translation of the musical section of "Twenty-five Years," in Vladimir Stasov, *Selected Essays on Music,* trans. Florence Jonas (New York, 1968), pp. 84-90.

4. *The Russian Opera* (New York, 1914), p. 148.

5. A.A. Gozenpud, "Opernoe tvorchestvo A.N. Serova," *Sovetskaia muzyka* (1971), no. 7, pp. 91-105. Gozenpud, a long-established expert in the field of "classical" Russian opera, has been leading a determined effort on the part of a number of senior Soviet scholars to put

Serov back into proper perspective. The most extensive and objective treatment of the composer to be found in Soviet musicological publications is in the second volume of Gozenpud's *Russkii opernyi teatr XIX veka* (Leningrad, 1971). A more recent publication is G. Abramovsky's article on *Rogneda,* published together with some letters and memoirs of Serov in *Sovetskaia muzyka* (1976), no. 12, pp. 92-101. In the latter piece, Serov's close ties to literary figures not particulary honored in the Soviet Union (Grigoriev, Averkiev, the *"pochvenniki"*) is given some long-overdue emphasis.

6.   "Serof," in M.D. Calvocoressi and Gerald Abraham, *Masters of Russian Music* (London, 1936), p. 88.

7.   "The Operas of Serov," in Jack Westrup, ed., *Essays Presented to Egon Wellesz* (Oxford, 1966), p. 183.

8.   Paul Henry Lang, *Music in Western Civilization* (New York, 1941), p. 948.

9.   *Masters of Russian Music,* p. 96.

10.   Tsezar' Kiui, *Muzykal'no-kriticheskie stat'i* (Petrograd, 1918), p. 184.

11.   On the musical life of the school, and Serov's role in it, see the fifth section of Stasov's memoir of 1881, "The School of Jurisprudence Forty Years Ago" ("Uchilishche pravovedeniia sorok let tomu nazad," *Izbrannye sochineniia II,* pp. 345-63). Details of Serov's civil service career, his early attempts at composition and his musical self-education are given in English in Abraham's article in *Masters of Russian Music,* which gives as much biographical information as the Western reader is likely to want. In Russian, Nikolai Findeisen's monograph, *A.N. Serov, Ego zhizn' i muzykal'naia deiatel'nost',* 2nd ed. (Moscow, 1904)—Abraham's main source—gives a great deal more than that.

12.   September 14, 1844. Cited in V.S. Baskin, *A.N. Serov* (Moscow, 1890), p. 30.

13.   "[In the *Figaro* sextet,] Don Curzio transgresses seriously . . . since he is stuck in simply for the sake of a tenor and repeats (in words and *music*) what the Count sings. I cannot forgive Mozart for this" (October 20, 1844. *Muzykal'noe nasledstvo I* [Moscow, 1962], p. 263).

14.   June 12, 1847. *Muzykal'noe nasledstvo II* (Moscow, 1966), p. 196.

15.   In his autobiographical sketch of 1870, Serov affirmed with his usual immodesty (and, also characteristically, in the third person): "In all technical matters of the composer's trade, Serov had no guide—we repeat—*no one,* except the classic scores and his own imagination" (*Izbrannye stat'i I,* p. 69).

16.   To Stasov, April 17, 1847. *Muzykal'noe nasledstvo II,* p. 179.

17.   The usual reason given is Stasov's sudden and curt rejection of the opera, for which we have no direct evidence, only surmises based on Stasov's sarcastic markings on one of his letters from Serov (December 1, 1851) in which the latter had waxed particularly enthusiastic about his work—markings undoubtedly entered long after the fact (cf. *Muzykal'noe nasledstvo III* [Moscow, 1970], pp. 108-9). More likely, the opera was never finished. Mention of it in Serov's correspondence suddenly breaks off in 1854, and up to that point he had always referred to it as a work in progress. If he destroyed the work it could hardly have been before May 8, 1855, for on that date he inscribed the opening bars of Levko's serenade—the opening number of the opera in its final form—in Liudmila Shestakova's album, which he scarcely would have felt like doing if by that time the opera had come to its reputed unhappy end. Thus, a considerable period is unaccounted for in the history of *May Night,* and the question remains why not one note (save the album inscription) has survived. All questions of burning aside, various numbers from the opera's various versions had been

circulating widely among Serov's friends and acquaintances both in St. Petersburg and in the Crimea. Not even Hanna's prayer, which was publicly performed with orchestra as early as 1851 (on the initiative of Stasov, who was still so devoted to Serov as to make the fair copy of the score himself [cf. Findeisen, p. 62]) seems to have been preserved, although it had been deleted from the final scenario of the opera (see Serov to Stasov, January 7, 1853, *Muzykal'noe nasledstvo III*, p. 150) and hence presumably would not have been affected by the alleged conflagration. Findeisen assumed that it existed somewhere, as of 1904. Perhaps it still does.

18. *Izbrannye stat'i I*, p. 69.

19. A cousin of the famous anarchist. Serov became acquainted with the Bakunin family during his years in Simferopol', and became rather close to the anarchist's brother Alexei. But when Rosa Newmarch asserts confidently that in the Crimean city Serov "made the acquaintance of the revolutionary Bakunin, who had not yet been exiled to Siberia," and adds even more confidently that "the personality of Bakunin made a deep impression upon Serov, as it did later on Wagner" (*The Russian Opera*, p. 46), this is pure fantasy. Mikhail Bakunin was abroad from 1840 to 1851, when he was extradited to Russia and sent immediately into exile. Serov never met him.

20. August 13, 1853. *Muzykal'noe nasledstvo III*, p. 167.

21. *Izbrannye stat'i I*, p. 69.

22. *Muzyka i virtuozy* ("Music and the Virtuosi"), published in *Biblioteka dlia chteniia* in April, 1851 (Serov, *Izbrannye stat'i II*, pp. 525-38).

23. Serov's dispute with Ulybyshev attracted the attention of Liszt, who summarized the young Russian critic's article "Mozart's *Don Giovanni* and its Panegyrists" with approval in "Ulibischeff gegen Seroff, Kritik der Kritik" (*Neue Zeitschrift für Musik*, January, 1858), which was Serov's first notice abroad. Liszt and Serov had been acquainted since 1842, when the virtuoso had toured St. Petersburg (for a charming memoir see Stasov, "Uchilishche pravovediniia sorok let tomu nazad," part VII [*Izbrannye sochineniia II*, pp. 377-88]).

24. *Izbrannye stat'i I*, p. 373. Serov's many strictures against the grand opéra are not without their irony, coming as they do from the man who in a few years was to become notorious as the "Russian Meyerbeer." Actually, his correspondence reveals an ambivalent attitude toward the composer of *Robert le Diable* and *Le Prophète*. He who in 1841 was for Serov "le favori de mon âme" (*Muzykal'noe nasledstvo I*, p. 107) had become five years later a mere "Jew charlatan" *(zhid-sharlatan)* (October 28, 1846. Cited from Baskin, p. 28. In *Muzykal'noe nasledstvo II*, p. 141, the coarse expression is suppressed).

25. *Izbrannye stat'i I*, p. 371.

26. Ibid., p. 386.

27. *Muzykal'noe nasledstvo III*, p. 127.

28. Serov did not hear any in orchestral performance until 1856. His reaction then was still far from adoring. See his *Otchët o kontserte filarmonicheskogo obshchestva*, quoted in Findeisen, p. 69, and partially in English in *Essays Presented to Egon Wellesz*, p. 172.

29. *Izbrannye stat'i I*, p. 373. In 1857 Serov still considered that "the union of all the arts on the stage, of which Wagner dreams, is an almost unrealizable Utopia" (*Muzykal'nyi i teatral'nyi vestnik* [1857], no 36. Cited in Findeisen, p. 69).

30. *Izbrannye stat'i I*, p. 371.

31. August 13, 1853. *Muzykal'noe nasledstvo III*, p. 168.

32. Quoted from F.M. Tolstoi, "Vospominaniia o Serove," *Russkaia starina* (1874), p. 345.

33. "Pis'ma iz-za granitsy," July 30/August 11, 1858. *Izbrannye stat'i I*, pp. 515-6.

34. Findeisen, p. 69.

35. Serov, *Kriticheskie stat'i III* (St. Petersburg, 1894), p. 1309.

36. *Izbrannye stat'i I*, p. 556. The reference to a piano concerto is a typical dig at Anton Rubinstein, a target Serov always found irresistible.

37. A good example and a very early one is the huge letter, already alluded to in passing, wherein Serov describes to Stasov his very first operatic project, *Basurman* (August 18, 1843. *Muzykal'noe nasladstvo I*, pp. 231-37.). A couple of relevant excerpts—the first, on the opening of the third act of *Der Freischütz:*

> I can never rejoice enough or *without tears* [at this scene]—we are still filled with the horror and gloom of the somber Wolf's Glen—and all of a sudden the curtain rises—a calm, tranquil room, in which, through the green window drapes, a ray of sunshine brightly gleams, and *about the sun*, in which is so palpable the presence of God, and *about the clouds*, Agatha and the cello sing together! There is poetry, there is scene-painting, there is music— *all together!* (Such, in my estimation, must opera always be, and not in one or two scenes, but throughout . . .).

On freedom of operatic form:

> It seems to me, that in this incessant *excitement*—happiness versus misfortune—good versus evil— is precisely the definition of true drama. . . . You will grant that in my opera there will be *lots* of dramatic life, so much, that for the usual division into arias, duets and trios there will hardly be room—or rather, there *will* be, but extremely little in comparison with *through-composed* scenes, where the action will be carried now by one character, now several, now almost all, now *all* and even by the *chorus!* And this, as you see, is not *par principe*, but only because it is necessary. . . . My opera, whose material in its richness would suffice for three operas, will positively *boil* with scenic vitality; one scene of true drama followed by another, even *hotter*, and the spectator's relief (which is necessary in any dramatic creation, all the more in an *intensified*, that is, musical one) will be provided only by those scenes in which a quiet, peaceful, spiritual charm will enter into rivalry with the fiery dramatics of the other parts of the opera.

In one neatly turned passage, Serov speaks of dissonance in metaphorical terms: both as a musical phenomenon and as a psychological, dramaturgical one ("Anton's arrival in Muscovy sets off a chain of dissonances."). In his operatic world, the one reflects the other. This rather sophisticated view of music as the expressive analogue of drama leads him to the surprising (yet "logical") conclusion that the *lieto fine* is necessary, since dissonances, whether musical or dramaturgical, must be resolved.

38. To M.P. Anastasieva, March 19, 1860. Cited in Baskin, p. 44.

39. The term was actually Rostislav's but Stasov lost no time in taking it up. Typical is the attack on Serov which Stasov published under the title "The Answer of a Contemporary to Two Pronouncements of the Zukunftists," in the *Niederrheinische Musik-Zeitung* (reprinted in Russian in Stasov, *Izbrannye sochineniia I*, pp. 40-43). The two pronouncements of Serov which gave Stasov his pretext were actually made, not in defense of Wagner, but in defense of Beethoven against Ulybyshev: (1) *Das Criterium des musikalischen Gesetzes liegt nicht in den Ohren des Consumenten, es liegt in der Kunstidee des Producenten;* (2) *Wenn eine*

Theorie nicht mit der Praxis eines Weltgenies stimmt, da wird sie nie bestehen, denn die Kunst lebt ihr Leben nicht in Büchern, sondern im Kunstwerk. Irritated by the "Caesaristic" emphasis on the freedom of the transcendent individual, Stasov moved in quickly to expose the promulgator of these "pronouncements" and the "guild of Zukunftists" he is said to represent: "The *Zukunftist* guild is primarily a guild of dilettantes, immature artists and hence mainly of rationalizers. ... It is enough for a Zukunftist to write five measures of his zukunftist music, so as then to write five reams 'on the meaning and content of those five measures.'... A true artist does much and says little [while] he who has not a jot of talent but lots of ambition will gladly join the new guild, which opens up such a wide field for dilettantism and casuistry. What a true and reliable asylum for all manner of absurd music and absurd discoursing on art! Mr. Serov has served up a tasty dessert for them all with his pretty aphorisms."

40. "... only forty in the audience! I didn't make a penny!!! I am paying for the lights at my lectures with my articles! There's Petersburg for you." (To Anastasieva, April 7, 1859. Quoted in Baskin, p. 43.)

41. Baskin, p.44.

42. For a full account of these, see Oscar von Riesemann, "Alexander Seroff and His Relations to Wagner and Liszt," *Musical Quarterly* 9 (1923), pp. 450-64.

43. N. Stepanov in *Iskra* (1863), no. 13. Reproduced in Findeisen, p. 105.

44. November 9, 1860. Quoted in Baskin, pp. 41-42.

45. This poem later served Tchaikovsky as the basis for his opera *Mazepa* (1884).

46. K.I. Zvantsev, "Vospominaniia ob A.N. Serove i pis'ma ego," *Russkaia starina* 59 (1888), p. 378.

47. Ibid.

48. Ibid. See also *Essays Presented to Egon Wellesz*, p. 172.

49. January 17, 1861. Zvantsev, p. 382.

50. Findeisen, p. 88.

51. *Russkaia starina* 21 (1878), p. 159.

52. Ibid.

53. Serov himself had remarked on this state of affairs in one of his critiques of *Ruslan and Liudmila* when he jeered at the very possibility of "virtuosity in a Russian prima donna!" (*Kriticheskie stat'i II* [St. Petersburg, 1894], p. 1022). The quality of the Russian Opera's productions was to improve dramatically in the 1860s (see A.A. Gozenpud, *Russkii opernyi teatr XIX veka II* [Moscow, 1971], pp. 5-42).

54. Not that Serov himself made any secret of it. He even composed for Patti a coloratura vehicle in Italian entitled "Ave Maria d'una penitente," which the diva actually sang in his memory in 1871.

55. See Gozenpud, *Russkii opernyi teatr I* (Moscow-Leningrad, 1969), p. 179.

56. In his autobiographical sketch Serov gives the month as February, but his letters contradict him (cf. Findeisen, p. 95).

57. A.N. Serov, "Autobiographical Sketch," *Izbrannye stat'i I*, p. 73.

58. *Russkaia starina* 31 (1888), p. 652.

59. See Findeisen, p. 94.

60. September 10, 1861. *Russkaia starina* 21 (1878), p. 161.

61. Abraham (*Essays Presented to Egon Wellesz,* p. 173) assumes that this was Modest Petrovich Musorgsky, but a far more plausible candidate, because a far more interested party—and one, moreover, on whom the composer often relied—was his confidante Anastasieva, who in St. Petersburg liked to use her exotically Caucasian maiden name, Maria Pavlovna Mavromikhali.

62. For the exchange of letters (all addressed to "M.P.M."), see *Russkaia starina* 9 (1874), pp. 351-52; partial English translation (of Balakirev's side only) in Abraham, *Essays.* Serov's relations with the young Balakirev circle from 1856 to about 1860, when he was still identified as critic only, had always been extremely cordial; indeed the most encouraging notices the future *"kuchkists"* received for their early works were from Serov (see, for example, *Izbrannye stat'i I,* pp. 339-42; "Tri poslednie vechera Russkogo Muzykal'nogo Obshchestvo," I, pp. 565-67 [Review of choruses from Cui's *Prisoner of the Caucasus*]; scattered reviews collected under the heading *"Muzykal'naia khronika,"* in *Izbrannye stat'i II:* pp. 612-13 [Cui, Scherzo in F]; pp. 616-17 [Musorgsky, Scherzo in B♭]). Although Stasov was ever at pains to attribute Serov's later strained relations with the *kuchka* to an innate hostility exacerbated by Wagner-mania (see his monograph, "Tsezar' Antonovich Kiui," in *Izbrannye sochineniia III* [Moscow, 1952], especially pp. 396-98), it is clear that the first stones, among which Balakirev's dismissal of *Judith* was a boulder, were cast from the *kuchkist* side.

63. Cf. his letter to Anastasieva of August 29, 1862, cited in Findeisen, p. 99.

64. D.I. Lobanov, *A.N. Serov i ego sovremenniki* (St. Petersburg, 1889), p. 23.

65. Ibid.

66. Even the finale, with which he began work, was improvised, according to Lobanov, almost immediately after Serov heard Ristori's performance, and long before he had contacted Giustiniani.

67. Gozenpud, *Russkii opernyi teatr II,* p. 79.

68. Serov, *Izbrannye stat'i I,* p. 387. Italics original.

69. Serov, *Izbrannye stat'i I,* p. 372. The Assyrian acts, originally planned together as Act II, first became Acts II and III in the process of enlargement. The opera reached its total of five acts by July, 1862, when Serov informed a correspondent, the pianist Varvara Yefimovna Zhukova, that he had decided to split the first act into two. The irony of the situation was not lost on him: "So you see, it has come to five acts—*grand opéra en forme en 5 actes, avec deux divertissements!!*—by *Robert-le-Diable's* recipe, or *La Juive's* or the *Huguenots'!!* Precisely: whatever you mock the most you end up doing yourself!" (A.N. Serov, "Pis'ma k V. Zhukove," *Sovetskaia muzyka* 18 [1954], no. 7, p. 70.)

70. Cf. his review, *"A Life for the Tsar"* and *"Ruslan and Liudmila"* (1858) in Serov, *Kriticheskie stat'i II* (St. Petersburg, 1892), pp. 1019-21. See Chapter 1, above.

71. "Serov heard himself in the orchestra and gained a certain self-confidence, necessary if he was to see through to completion such an enormous and risky undertaking as a composer's debut with a grand opera in a severe style and on a serious Biblical subject" (Serov, *Izbrannye stat'i I,* p. 73). But the excerpts performed could have given but scant idea of that seriousness or severity.

72. Lobanov, p. 24.

73. May 19, 1862. *Russkaia starina* 31 (1888), p. 653.

74. *Preface* to the published libretto of *Judith* (St. Petersburg, [1863], n.p.)

75. Serov, *Izbrannye stat'i I*, p. 255.

76. Ibid., p. 258. These are the requirements of serious opera. Serov makes it clear that comic opera almost precisely reverses this weighting of elements.

77. Ibid., p. 259.

78. Ibid., p. 257.

79. *Preface*, n.p.

80. *Preface*, n.p.

81. Cf. Serov to Feofil Tolstoi (June 7, 1863), *Russkaia starina* 21 (1874), p. 361.

82. That he should have turned to this source shows Serov still receptive, Zvantzev's reproaches notwithstanding, to German idealist influences. *Judith* (1839-40) was Hebbel's first play; his second was *Genoveva,* which became the basis for Schumann's single operatic attempt.

83. Hebbel, too, gave Judith a lover (Ephraim), who even makes an abortive attempt on Holofernes' life. The German dramatist also enriched the action with a good many anecdotal and genre interludes—i.e., Samuel's narrative about Jonah and the whale (Act III, sc. ii)—but Serov probably did not object to such digressions, as genre set pieces of this kind can be found in any opera, and play a perhaps excessively prominent role in his *Judith.*

84. Edna Purdie, *Friedrich Hebbel* (London, 1932), p. 66.

85. Friedrich Hebbel, *Werke I* (Munich, 1963), p. 75.

86. Indeed, *Judith*'s scenario gives in a number of ways the impression of a de-Russified *Life for the Tsar:* are not Serov's Hebrews and Assyrians Glinka's Russians and Poles all over again? The static, oratorio-like action, the monumental, choral-dominated outer acts, and, of course, the embodiment of high "ethical" content all suggest kinship with Glinka's opera, as does the rather naive use of musical "genre" for characterization (the Hebrews by patently inapposite and anachronistic "church music," the Assyrians by an idealized "orientalism"). Serov's spoken and written utterances offer nothing but denials on this score (as indeed we could only expect). The parallels between *Judith* and *A Life for the Tsar* are so conspicuous and run so deep that the composer was understandably rendered hypersensitive. When Feofil Tolstoy asked Serov—rather fatuously—why the composer had chosen a legend of Biblical times for his opera, instead of "a subject from Russian life," as a Russian composer was expected to do, Serov made the brazen reply that he "did not wish to follow Glinka's footsteps" (*Russkaia starina 21* [1874], p. 361). But even Serov's initial conception of his drama belied this premise. As Lobanov recalled, at their first meeting

[Serov] played several sketches..., presumably to give me an idea of the flavor of the proposed musical work.... The music was in a sacred style. "What's that, some kind of Mass?" I asked. "No, that's the opera!" —"How can that be?" —"Because the third and fourth acts will have a different kind of music. Can you understand what a contrast this will make?" And he began to improvise his Assyrian themes (Lobanov, p. 23).

One will readily recall that Glinka's first glimmer of *A Life for the Tsar* took the same form: at root lay the musical contrast. Not at all coincidentally, moreover, the period of work on *Judith* also saw the flare-up of the notorious *Ruslan* controversy, in which Serov came down so heavily on the side of Glinka's first opera against his second. It seems evident that Serov strove to make the virtues of Glinka's work, as he extolled them in print, his own.

87.   A useful synopsis of Serov's libretto, together with a summary of the musical numbers and even a copious selection of musical citations, can be found in the English translation of Musorgsky's well-known letter on *Judith* to Balakirev (who was in the Caucasus at the time of the premiere) in Jay Leyda and Serge Bertensson, *The Musorgsky Reader* (New York, 1947; reprint ed. 1973), pp. 48-54.

88.   The name derives from Giacometti's Abra. Its source, it would appear, was Metastasio's oft-set oratorio libretto.

89.   To Anastasieva, July 25, 1862 (*Russkaia starina*, 21 [1878], p. 168).

90.   Musorgskii, *Literaturnoe nasledie I* (Moscow, 1971) p. 66.

91.   Cf. Mary Garland, *Hebbel's Prose Tragedies* (Cambridge, 1973), p. 24.

92.   Indeed it seems that his enthusiastic analysis of the Miller's Act III mad scene may, ironically enough, have been one of the strongest nudges Dargomyzhsky received in the direction of *The Stone Guest*, which represents a type of operatic style and dramaturgy as far from the Serovian as could be imagined. More on this in Chapter 5.

93.   *Russkaia starina* 17 (1874), pp. 363-64.

94.   The theme of this chorus is cited incorrectly in Musorgsky's letter to Balakirev. From this, Gerald Abraham infers that Musorgsky's citation shows "changes made by Serov before his opera was printed," for "there can be no question of a lapse of memory on Musorgsky's part" (*Essays Presented to Egon Wellesz*, p. 171). Why so? Musorgsky's memory shows itself in this letter to be impressive but by no means infallible. Elsewhere he cites just as inaccurately (e.g. the immediately preceding dance of the odalisques, where the rhythm is caught better than the melody—which is, by the way, the case with the present chorus of Assyrians, too) and admits having forgotten altogether the theme of Vagao's Indian Song, the most successful number in the opera, and later the obvious model for Rimsky-Korsakov's greatest hit, the "Song of India" from *Sadko*. There is no reason to assume that the chorus as published was not the one performed in 1863.

95.   Moscow: A. Gutheil [1885], pp. 161-68.

96.   Rostislav, *Razbor opery A.N. Serova "Iudif'"* (St. Petersburg, 1863), n.p.

97.   Baskin, p. 60.

98.   *Russkaia starina* 17 (1874), p. 368.

99.   Serov's eclecticism is "realistic." That is, musical style itself can play a characterizing role with him. Thus the music of the Jews is of a saccharinely "Protestant," Mendelssohnian, and instantly recognizable "religiosity," while even "Italianism" finds a use to fulfil: Judith's Act III arioso (and the ensuing quintet—the only ensemble in the opera) is based on a "seductive" Bellinian tune, by which Serov evidently sought to portray Judith's erotic and insincere appeal to Holofernes (cf. vocal score, pp. 202 ff).

   For a description of some of the more idiosyncratic elements in Serov's musical idiom (especially as regards "empirical harmony") see Gerald Abraham's article in the Wellesz Festschrift, especially pp. 177-79. We might additionally emphasize a flair for fresh-sounding yet purely diatonic ("modal") harmony and a propensity to build diatonic seventh chords on any scale degree as Serovian quirks. Example 2.3 above will serve to give an idea of his extremely freewheeling use of pedals.

100.   *Essays Presented to Egon Wellesz*, p. 176.

101. Stasov put this thought as damagingly as he could in "Twenty-five Years of Russian Art:"

Wagner's system particularly suited Serov not only because in many respects it really met the demands of reason and conformed to the intellectual concept of what opera ought to be, but also because Serov was totally incapable of developing themes, of treating form so as to build entire musical structures on a single melody or motive.... For this reason, the Wagnerian system, which gave him a chance to keep stringing together new and different bits of music—motives and melodies—served his purposes perfectly. Of course, this system, applied on a broad scale, characterizes all the latest and most advanced music of our time— Wagner's operas, Liszt's symphonic poems, and many of the songs, operas and instrumental works of the new Russian school. It is a bad thing, however, when this kind of writing stems, not from a system, but from the lack of talent and skill (V.V. Stasov, *Selected Essays on Music,* trans. Florence Jonas [New York, 1968], pp. 85-86).

102. Serov's attitude toward "symphonization" of opera was ambivalent, and one suspects an unconscious double standard. He took Glinka to task for an excess of "symphonic" development and plasticity of form in *Ruslan,* and his widely circulated remark that "the theater is not a symphony" came long after his own operatic career was well established, and after he was intimately acquainted both with *Tristan* and with parts of *The Ring.* Nonetheless, he wrote of the "Prelude and Liebestod" in orchestral performance that "singing is dispensed with, but the *symphonic* character of the whole, the unheard of richness of orchestral beauty, does not allow the listener even to notice this lack." (*Izbrannye stat'i I,* p. 558.) And this was not merely a propagandist's pose, for to Zvantsev Serov remarked in private that the entire *Tristan* was "Bach + Beethoven + Chopin + Shakespeare" [!] (*Russkaia starina* 31 [1888], p. 652).

103. "The very serious title of a very serious book [*Das Kunstwerk der Zukunft*] turned out to be a diplomatic blunder on Wagner's part. But he was not born a diplomat, but an artist, and carried away with his artistic thoughts and plans, he lost sight of the *pettiness* and *banality* with which the world greets the lofty and the beautiful, always and everywhere" (*Izbrannye stat'i I,* p. 545).

104. *Izbrannye stat'i I,* p. 549.

105. Here, incidentally, Serov indulges the heroine with a few coloratura roulades—the only such in the opera—in which we may perhaps discern the traces of his early flirtation with the Italian opera and with La Grua.

106. See its citation by Musorgsky (*The Musorgsky Reader,* p. 49), or more accurately and completely, by Abraham (*Essays,* p. 177).

107. *Perepiska s Balakirevym I* (Moscow, 1970), p. 163.

108. This ending greatly impressed the young *kuchkists.* See Musorgsky's and Balakirev's admiring comments, quoted in *Essays Presented to Egon Wellesz,* p. 173. The device was a favorite mannerism with Serov, who boasted of it as a sign of his seriousness: "With me—on purpose!—there is not a single aria, the duets are wildly impetuous and frantic, and each act (except the last)—again, on purpose!—ends *morendo, pianissimo!!*" (Letter to Zhukova, October 18, 1962. *Sovetskaia muzyka* [1954], no. 7, p. 74).

109. The quotation here is taken from the reprise of the march in the "Assyrian" tonality of D major, rather than the march's first appearance as *entr'acte* in B♭.

110. Gutheil vocal score, p. 200.

111. See Serov's letter to Zhukova, July 3, 1862 (cited in footnote 69, above). There seem to be a number of additional parallels between *Judith* and *Lohengrin*. One is the orchestral "introduction," which Musorgsky aptly characterized as an "espèce de Vorspiel" (*The Musorgsky Reader*, p. 48). It is a prefatory summation of the "idea" of the opera, in a free, agglutinative form. Here as everywhere, though, Serov is far more literal than Wagner. What he actually foreshadows is the plot. We hear first the theme of the "Chorus of Starving Judeans" from Act I, followed by music associated with the murder of Holofernes (Judith's prayer, "God of My Fathers," and the sword blows), and after a transition comprised of harp arpeggios which rather disconcerted Musorgsky, the "Introduction" concludes with Judith's canticle of praise.

There seems to be another parallel with *Lohengrin* in the structure of the scene of Judith's arrival in the Assyrian Camp (Act III). An exchange of ariosi by the principles is offset by choral repliques based on the material of the preceding "symphonic" chorus, just as it is upon Lohengrin's first entrance in Wagner's opera.

Finally, the climactic Act IV scene between Judith and Holofernes, where Serov, for once sufficiently "inspired" to break away from the deadening singsong regularity of his other "dramatic" scenes, seems to take the Telramund-Ortrud duet scene (*Lohengrin*, Act II) as his model. There is, at least in intent, the same free and flexible pliancy of form which so impressed Serov in Wagner's operas—an ease of movement from recitative through "arioso" to full-blown lyric utterance and back again, which sadly evaded the composer of *Judith* in the rest of the work, most deplorably in the analogous duet scene in Act III. The Act IV scene, which culminates in Holofernes' delirium, was the one that appealed most strongly to connoisseurs and literati (see, inter alia, Turgenev's letter to Pauline Viardot [January 18, 1864], quoted in A.A. Gozenpud, *Russkii opernyi teatr II*, p. 82).

112. *Perepiska s Balakirevym I*, p. 63.

113. *The Musorgsky Reader*, p. 53. Serov did recognize the difference between his style and Wagner's to the extent that he could confide to Varvara Zhukova that, "My *Judith* both in its subject (simple and fundamentally a bit crude) and in the style I have created for it, is infinitely more accessible than Wagner's creations." (Letter of September 8, 1862. *Sovetskaia muzyka* no. 7 [1954], p. 71.) He felt this necessary, he maintained in the same letter, because of the relatively unsophisticated audience he was addressing.

114. Quoted from V.S. Serova, *Serovy, A.N. i V.A.* (Moscow, 1914), p. 59. Serov's widow may possibly have softened Wagner's words; the remark appears in ruder form in Baskin (pp. 81-82) and in Findeisen (p. 106). Characteristically, Serov turned Wagner's faint praise to his advantage in his "Autobiographical Sketch": "Wagner read through much of the score with great attentiveness and praised its orchestration" (*Izbrannye stat'i I*, p. 74).

115. See Gozenpud, *Russkii opernyi teatr II*, p. 72.

116. Letter to Zvantsev (*Russkaia starina* 31 [1888], p. 658).

117. Serov, *Izbrannye stat'i I*, p. 74.

118. Pravdin in *Russkaia stsena*, 1864. Quoted in Gozenpud, *Russkii opernyi teatr II*, p. 17.

119. Tsezar' Kiui, *Muzykal'no-kritcheskie stat'i*, p. 191.

120. Notices collected in Gozenpud, op. cit., p. 74-75.

121. Ibid.

122. Kiui, op. cit., p. 192.

123. According to a letter to Zhukova (September 8, 1862), Serov at first expected Petrov to sing Holofernes, but without enthusiasm in view of the singer's age (*Sovetskaia muzyka* [1954], no. 7, p. 72).

124. *Sanktpeterburgskie vedomosti* (1866) no. 14.

125. Interview in *Peterburgskaia zhizn'*, November 12, 1892.

126. The really far-reaching and striking parallels and relationships between Serov and Musorgsky deserve a study in themselves. A beginning is made in Abraham's article in *Essays Presented to Egon Wellesz*, especially pp. 177-80.

/

Fig. 3.1   Serov in the 1860s

3

Pochvennichestvo on the Russian Operatic Stage: Serov and His *Rogneda*

Though Serov's second opera is by now about as thoroughly forgotten as an opera can become, when it was given its premiere on October 27, 1865, one of St. Petersburg's leading critics confidently predicted that "just as for the last thirty years we have dated our musical history from *A Life for the Tsar*, . . . so, from now on, will we date it from *Rogneda.*"[1] The venerable Prince Odoevsky declared that "in *Rogneda,* Russian music has taken nothing more nor less than a new step, marking a new period,"[2] while Tsar Alexander II took as great an interest in Serov's work as his father had in Glinka's. *"Coming to the stage himself,"* Serov emphasized in retelling his moment of glory, "His Majesty the Emperor ordered the composer summoned and spoke with me very graciously for about ten minutes."[3] For *Rogneda,* Serov was awarded by the crown a lifetime pension of 1000 rubles per annum. He was the first musician ever to be so honored in Russia, and the first creative artist since Gogol.

In its first five years the opera played seventy times to full houses in St. Petersburg alone, and continued to be enormously popular right up to the Revolution.[4] Nor was the work without its share of influence on later Russian operas which still hold the stage, even if it did ultimately disappoint those who saw in it the dawn of an era. Perhaps the greatest interest *Rogneda* possesses for the modern reader, however, lies in the fact that at the time of its creation Serov was extremely close to some of Russia's leading thinkers and writers—no less a figure than Dostoevsky among them—who had an important hand in its shaping. The opera was a kind of Russian *Gesamtkunstwerk* and a document of one of the most curious intellectual currents in Russian society around the time of the Emancipation. It is, then, as an embodiment of *pochvennichestvo* that we shall approach *Rogneda,* and through it hope to illuminate what has remained a dark corner in Russian musico-cultural history.

Fig. 3.2   Apollon Grigoriev at the time of *Iakor'*.

It was Dostoevsky himself who coined the term *pochvennichestvo* from the Russian word *pochva*—"soil" or "foundation." The movement it stands for centered around the short-lived journals the novelist edited and published together with his brother Mikhail. The first of these, *Vremia (Time)*, appeared from 1861 until early 1863 when it was suppressed by the censorship over an article contributed by Nikolai Strakhov (1828-95), a philosopher and critic and one of Dostoevsky's closest intellectual kinsmen. After the misunderstanding with the censor was cleared up, the brothers Dostoevsky resumed their publishing activities with a new journal (or rather the old one under a new name), *Epokha (The Epoch)*, which came out from January 1864 until it folded in March, 1865. In between *Vremia* and *Epokha* the center of the movement shifted to a weekly called *Iakor' (The Anchor)*, which was published as a stopgap by the critic and poet Apollon Grigoriev (1822-64), another collaborator of the Dostoevskys and in every way *pochvennik* par excellence. It is Grigoriev's name that now symbolizes the movement, thanks perhaps to his having died at its height.

These journals and the handful of *littérateurs* who manned them (besides the ones mentioned these included Alexander Ostrovsky and the poets Apollon Maikov and Yakov Polonsky) represented a recognized trend in the Russian thought of their time. All born within a decade of one another, the *pochvenniki* shared a common background: Dostoevsky and Grigoriev especially, having come from Moscow, knew well the patriarchal merchant society of *Zamoskvarechye*, the old-town quarter depicted so unforgettably in fellow Muscovite Ostrovsky's plays. From this sense of a shared heritage came a strong faith in the continuity and resilience of Russian traditions. Basing their outlook on Schelling's idealism, they held that "the world is a *coherent whole;* nothing in it exists 'in itself.'"[5] A bit inconsistently, perhaps, the wholeness of life was seen by them in terms of an "organic connection" with nationhood; this was the *pochva* in *pochvennichestvo*.[6] Every nation, in their view, brought to the world its own unique "idea." With the Slavophiles of the 1840s the *pochvenniki* of the sixties shared the conviction that Russia needed to renew contact with her ancient heritage; salvation lay in union behind the monarchy and the Orthodox faith. But unlike the later Slavophiles, their contemporaries, the *pochvenniki* were not primarily political or social thinkers, and for all their concern with a society based on Christian charity, they were anything but theocratic. For them, philosophy and art were the highest outcropping of the "soil." The national spirit, the *"pochva,"* received its highest expression in art and literature, through which it was made available to consciousness in concrete form.

Since in turn art and literature derived their vitality and validity from an "organic" connection with life, they needed to have firmly and deeply embedded roots in the national experience. But the *pochvenniki* were far from being anti-Westerners or nationalists in any narrow sense. Although in keeping with their name they were strongly committed to the development of indigenous literature and drama, they also welcomed foreign artists and artworks that met their criteria of "wholeness." Nor was their definition of Russianness without a tinge of eclecticism. *Vremia*'s subscription blank announced the new journal's position in terms that neatly straddled the fence between Slavophile and "Westernizer":

> We have at last persuaded ourselves that we too are a separate nationality independent and original in the highest degree, and that our task is to create for ourselves an indigenous form native to *our own soil*. ... We foresee that the Russian idea may well be a synthesis of all the ideas that have developed in Europe.[7]

Grigoriev's principles of "organic criticism," emphasizing such things as transcendence, inclusiveness, richness of allusion, ties to the soil and to ancient heritages, placed him—and the *pochvenniki* generally—among the few in Russia hospitable to Wagner and "Wagnerianism." Grigoriev's famous description of "life" as embodied in art—"something mysterious and inexhaustible, an abyss that engulfs all finite reason, an unspannable ocean"[8]— clearly owed something to such Wagnerian concepts as *Gesamtkunstwerk* and *unendliche Melodie*. When Wagner came to St. Petersburg in 1863, he found his warmest reception in the pages of Grigoriev's *Iakor'*. And this, of course, was Serov's doing. The future composer of *Rogneda* had already been famous as Russia's leading music critic for a dozen years, infamous as her Perfect Wagnerite, and was about to make his own unexpectedly spectacular debut as composer with *Judith*. Besides a critical appreciation of "Richard Wagner and His Concerts in St. Petersburg" (*Iakor'*, no. 2), Serov contributed to Grigoriev's weekly a huge study (ten installments!) of the *Nibelungen* poem, viewed as the quintessence of what might be oxymoronically described as German *pochvennichestvo* (to put a finer point on things than did V.V. Stasov, who had the habit of referring to Wagner—opprobriously—as a "German Slavophile").[9]

Serov and Grigoriev had known each other since the 1850s, when the literary man solicited from the musician some articles on Glinka for the journal *Moskvitianin*.[10] In 1860, Grigoriev took over the editorship of the foundering *Teatral'nyi i muzykal'nyi vestnik (Theatrical and Musical Courier)*, to which Serov had been a regular contributor since the journal's inception in 1856. It was there that their relationship flowered, and it was under Grigoriev's editorship that Serov first engaged in journalistic polemics on behalf of Wagner.[11] When Serov belatedly embarked on his own creative career, Grigoriev became his most devoted supporter. He bruited *Judith* about among his literary friends as much as a year before the opera was finished,[12] and when it was finally performed, the critic greeted it with a review that positively embarrassed the composer with its hyperboles of praise.[13] But if Grigoriev lacked the qualifications to pass musical judgments, still the very fact that he devoted so much space in *Iakor'* to Serov's opera was already a tribute: not since Glinka had a Russian opera attracted the attention of the literary community.

Grigoriev approached *Judith* with great seriousness. His review is in fact a prime document of *pochvennichestvo*.[14] Talk of realism filled the air and Grigoriev took Serov's opera as his pretext for defining the *pochvennik* position on the issue. "True realism," he wrote, "is that kind wherein, along with the fullest life-likeness and naturalism of form, the Ideal insinuates itself like a lining, or soars over the work."[15] Besides *Judith,* examples of "true realism" included Ostrovsky's plays, Hugo's *Les Misérables* and above all, Wagner's music dramas. "Wagnerianism," in fact, is taken to be a veritable synonym for "true realism," and in this sense Serov's opera, which Grigoriev acknowledges to be in its style and facture "less like a Wagnerian creation than anything on earth," is nonetheless a "victory for Wagnerianism," proof that the Wagnerian tendency "is not 'music of the future' but a direct expression of the forces and demands of life itself."[16]

By "naturalism of form" Grigoriev meant congruence of form and content dictated by no preconceived formal model. His description of the Wagnerian/Serovian reform marked by *Judith* no doubt derived in significant measure from the composer himself:

> Without vivid typicality of language and sharpness of image, drama and fiction are unthinkable today: and after Wagner (among us, after Serov) the old, conventional forms of opera are just as unthinkable, with their obligatory duets and quartets against all common sense, with the inevitable *primo tenore* in the inevitable lover's role, etc.[17]

For clarification of what Grigoriev meant by "the Ideal" in relation to true realism, we must turn to an article in the next issue of *Iakor'*, "On Realism in Art and Literature." This more extended piece was most likely written for the purpose of elucidating ideas that were expressed in passing, and for that reason, vaguely, in the review of *Judith*.

> The work of any true artist is composed of two elements—the subjective, or the striving toward the Ideal, and the objective, or the ability to reproduce the phenomena of the outside world in typical images. These elements can give rise to creativity only together and in harmony. The degree of dominance of one or the other of these elements is conditioned by the nature of the given artist; the relationship between the two, i.e., between the Ideal and reality, is conditioned by the historical moment....
>
> The true artist of our time, who has established the greatest possible equilibrium between the Ideal and reality within himself, treats reality in the name of the eternal and rational demands of the Ideal, seeks perhaps by comic or even negative means the fulfillment of noble and exalted tasks. But on the other hand he must observe reality assiduously, he must give its inviolable laws their just due, he must know how to distinguish its unique and basic traits from the superficial or the accreted. This unique and basic foundation is the Ideal in the contemplated model....

> Realism of form, then, is by now nothing that should surprise us.... Our realism of
> content is in essence only the revival of a direct and immediate, i.e., truly idealistic
> relationship to reality—simple, unspoiled and fresh.[18]

This is basic *pochvennichestvo*. It lies at the heart of what Dostoevsky
called "realism in a higher sense,"[19] and in its emphasis on what is direct and
immediate *(neposredstvennyi)* of apprehension it reflects what some have
identified as the single unique and indispensable criterion of the movement.[20]
The Ideal is nothing other than the "unique and basic traits" of reality
correctly observed, culled and presented by the artist in the interests of the
"noble and exalted tasks" of art. Artworks which successfully capture and
transmit this abstraction from reality can be said to embody what Grigoriev
called *veianie,* literally "drift" or "what is wafted in the air," but as Grigoriev
used the term, rather close in meaning to the German *Zeitgeist*. It is an
important criterion of artistic validity, which Serov's opera satisfied—despite
its non-"national" subject—by virtue of its high ethical content, its imagery
derived from reality with an emphasis on typicality, and an immediacy of
impression resulting from a spontaneous congruence of form and content.[21]

Grigoriev's *Judith*-inspired articles had a profound and immediate
reciprocal influence on the opera's composer. *Iakor',* no. 28 contains an article
by Serov which has largely escaped the attention of students of his work
thanks to its title, "A Musician's Remark on Non-musical Affairs" *(Zametka
muzykanta o delakh nemuzykal'nykh)*. This piece echoes Grigoriev's preachments on "true realism," which Serov defines by exposing its negative
counterpart, "naked realism." A new play, *The Whirlpool (Omut)* by the
minor dramatist Mikhail Nikolaevich Vladykin (1830-87), had aroused
Serov's indignation by virtue of its naturalism unguided by considerations of
moral uplift. Following Grigoriev, Serov saw this as a betrayal of art's
purpose. Comparing this new manifestation with an earlier artistic blind alley
at the opposite extreme, Serov finds even the latter preferable.

> Thought distorted in the service of the false principle of "didacticism" [he has in mind such
> Russian playwrights as Fonvizin and Sumarokov] nonetheless had at its foundation a noble
> aspiration to the "Ideal," and consequently was a thousand times worthier than the latest
> nakedly realistic tendency, which seeks to have nothing whatever to do with the "Ideal."
> Quite the contrary: it mocks and derides the latter in a blanket "trampling down" of
> everyone and everything on earth. The naked realists have forgotten that the absence of the
> Ideal is death to art! Without ideals one can and even should take pen in hand to write a
> memo between provincial offices. But to be a writer, an artist or a dramatist "without
> ideals" is positively impossible. [Even] satire is merely the *negative* of the ideal side of life,
> never a vile positive photograph of life's vilenesses.[22]

Serov's reference to "non-musical affairs" in his title is born of his
conviction that music is necessarily immune from the pestilence of "naked

realism." By its very nature concerned with the beautiful, hence with the Ideal, music is perforce a positive moral influence and cannot be otherwise, while literature is at its creator's mercy in the matter of ethical quality.

> In music, in the enjoyment of sounds, even from the standpoint of the most sensual ear-gratification, there is always an *ideal* quality. The sensation of musical sound and its effect upon man cannot be other than *"ideal,"* even if only to an insignificant degree. Such is in fact the basic characteristic of the language: it is chiefly ideal. Music does not even possess the means for expressing meanness or moral ugliness.[23]

It would seem, then, that a musician would be better suited than anyone else to give ultimate expression to the aims of *pochvennichestvo,* and Grigoriev lost no time in urging the newly-converted Serov to undertake the task. Shortly after *Judith*'s premiere, critic wrote to composer:

> Write an opera about your own people [*narodnaia opera*], Sashka! You have the talent for it. What is of one's own people, what is one's own, is more alive than anything foreign. After all, that's what the ancient Greeks wrote about, and the more their art was their own, specifically Greek, the more we value it. And as for there being no beauty among our people, that's nonsense! It all depends on the artist.[24]

This was a step Serov had long hesitated to take. He had tried and failed to write a "national opera" (*May Night,* after Gogol) in the 1850s. Later, he had nurtured dreams of more than the parochial success a Russian opera seemed likely to bring him.[25] Most of all, he was afraid of comparisons with Glinka. Having developed the reputation of being Glinka's (or at least *Ruslan*'s) major detractor in the Russian musical press, as composer he would have to offer concrete, not merely theoretical answers to the questions he had raised as critic. Any Serov opera on a Russian subject would be taken as an "answer" to *Ruslan,* and the composer felt this responsibility acutely. To Feofil Tolstoy Serov confided that indeed he wished to write a "Russian" opera but had to wait until he found "a way to give a specific twist to my musical speech, so as not to turn into one of Glinka's satellites."[26] He had also to avoid the dramaturgical pitfalls that had marred *Ruslan,* foremost among which had been the predominance of musical interest over action. "Give us the stage," he had promised, "and judge our dramatic and musical intentions by their effect in the theater."[27] *Judith* had passed this test with flying colors. Everyone, even the otherwise hostile *"kuchkists,"* acknowledged Serov's aspirations to "dramatic truth."[28] The time seemed ripe for him to take Grigoriev's advice.

Indeed, the long-feared step may well have seemed necessary to Serov at this point in his career, for *Judith* had failed to establish his reputation abroad. Serov had hoped to arrange performances of his opera in Paris through Liszt, and in Berlin and Vienna through Wagner.[29] These were not to be, for the Western musicians were unimpressed with Serov's work. Wagner's reaction to the score was confined, as we have seen, to some polite remarks about the orchestration, and things fared even less well with Liszt. The Weimar master played through the first two acts with the composer at Karlsruhe in 1864, and then declined to continue, with the words, "I do not recognize this opera; it is lacking in interest." He treated his "provincial" colleague with the greatest condescension. Pointing to a harp accompaniment in Judith's Act II monologue, Liszt insisted that it would be inaudible, to which Serov hotly retorted that he himself had heard the passage in the theater a good 32 times![30] These rejections by the Western musicians he most admired certainly played their part in turning Serov back upon his own heritage. He virtually ceased his propagandistic activity on Wagner's behalf, and welcomed in *pochvennichestvo* a native, not explicitly Wagnerian peg on which to hang his artistic theories. And so it is not surprising that the idea for Serov's second opera originated with his *pochvennik* friends, was worked out by the composer under their guidance, and that in the end the finished work mirrored the movement's ambivalences and inner contradictions.

It was Polonsky who first suggested to Serov the quasi-historical tale of Rogneda when the composer announced his intention to seek out for his next opera a "national, native" subject.[31] The story, which appears twice in the chronicles of Kievan Rus',[32] has obvious and striking parallels with the story of *Judith:* the murder (or attempted murder) by a woman of a sleeping ruler.

Around 970 the Varangian Rogvolod [Ragnvaldr in Norse chronicles] left his homeland and settled in Polotsk. He had a beautiful daughter, Rogneda [Ragnheidr], who had been promised in marriage to the Great Prince Iaropolk Sviatoslavich of Kiev. The latter's brother Vladimir, having declared war on Iaropolk and assembled an army of Varangians, Slovenians, Chudians and Krivichians, asked for Rogneda's hand. Rogvolod inquired of his daughter whether she wished to marry Vladimir. "I will not," she replied, "draw off the boots of a slave's son, but want Iaropolk instead." [NB: To draw off her husband's boots was one of the symbolic acts of the bride in the old Russian marriage ritual.] Enraged at Rogneda's refusal, Vladimir stormed Polotsk, killed Rogvolod and his two sons, and married Rogneda by force. She bore him a son, Iziaslav. Later, having defeated his brother Iaropolk and become Great Prince of Kiev, Vladimir grew tired of Rogneda and banished her and Iziaslav to the banks of the river Lybed, on the outskirts of Kiev. One day, happening that way, the Prince fell asleep. The vengeful Rogneda, approaching, was on the point of dealing him a fatal blow with her sword, when Vladimir awoke. He ordered her to don her wedding clothes and await death in her bedchamber. When Vladimir arrived for the execution, he was met by Iziaslav, who, on his mother's instructions, presented Vladimir with a sword, saying, "Father! You are not alone. Your son shall bear witness to your rage." The astonished Vladimir forgave Rogneda and sent her together with her son to a newly built city which he named Iziaslavl.[33]

From this kernel Serov developed his scenario in collaboration, as it were, with the whole editorial staff of the soon-to-be-launched *Epokha*. By this time, through Grigoriev and *Iakor'*, Serov had joined their inner circle. He mentions Maikov and Dostoevsky, among others, as his advisers in the shaping of the new opera,[34] while the task of writing the text had fallen to a younger-generation *pochvennik,* Dmitri Vasilievich Averkiev (1836-1905), Grigoriev's disciple and successor as theatrical reviewer for the Dostoevsky journals. (He later became a popular playwright on his own, specializing in romanticized and genre-dominated historical dramas.)[35]

The Rogneda story had been embodied more than once in nineteenth-century Russian literature before Serov turned his attention to it. One of these appearances took the form of a brief narrative digression toward the end of the famous historical novel *Askold's Grave* by Mikhail Nikolaevich Zagoskin (1789-1852), which in the author's own libretto had furnished the subject for the immensely popular opera of the same name (1835) by Alexei Verstovsky (1799-1862), the most famous and successful work of its kind before Glinka. Zagoskin's view of Russian history, conservatively patriotic and tinged with Slavophilism, had led to his giving the Rogneda episode a novel twist. The captive queen is spurred to her act of vengeance by the songs of her countryman Fenkal, a Varangian bard who, like Rogneda herself, has been taken prisoner by Vladimir. Fenkal sings to her of the exploits of Edwina, daughter of Rikmor, a Norse heroine who avenges the death of her father and her two brothers at the hands of a foreign invader.[36] Rogneda steals into Vladimir's chamber, where she finds him mumbling in his sleep about a Christian he had encountered that day. In the next chapter of Zagoskin's novel, the witch Vakhrameevna is seen recounting with some amazement how the Prince had foiled Rogneda's attempt upon his life but then showed her mercy. The implication is clear that Vladimir had acted under the impression of Christian teachings. Thus Zagoskin tied the Rogneda story to Vladimir's great historical role as Christianizer of Russia.

Serov seized upon this connection as the key to providing the Rogneda legend with the "lining of the Ideal" which would enable the opera to fulfill the "noble and exalted tasks" of "true realism" as Grigoriev championed them. And so the episode wherein Vladimir encounters the Christian was also appropriated from *Askold's Grave:* A pilgrim named Duleb (Ruald in the opera), whose bride Liubasha (rechristened Olava by Serov) had been abducted like Rogneda by Prince Vladimir, saves the Prince from a savage bear at the cost of his own life.[37] In the opera, the Prince is reminded once more of this object lesson in Christian charity at the very moment of Rogneda's intended execution, by the offstage approach of the pilgrim band to which Ruald had belonged. *Rogneda's* scenario thus became a kind of *pochvennik* manifesto, for all that it drew upon rather outmoded literary prototypes and harked back to the "kvass-patriotism" of the 1830s. In its opposition of bloodthirsty paganism and humane Christianity, the personification of their warring tendencies within the figure of the sainted Prince

Vladimir Sviatoslavich, founder of the Russian state, and the remotivation of the action in such a way that the Rogneda episode becomes something like the efficient cause of Russia's Christianization, Serov's scenario aspired infinitely higher than the one Zagoskin himself had derived for Verstovsky from the main line of his novel's action.[38] Moreover, by filling out the plan of his opera with a wealth of genre scenes depicting idol-worshipping, visits to witches' caves, royal hunts and feasts, *terems* full of captive maidens, wandering pilgrims and the like—some drawn from Zagoskin, others from different sources[39] or else freshly invented[40]—Serov would be able to supply it with plenty of "typical images of the external world," the other ingredient necessary for the attainment of "true realism."[41]

As a basic idea, then, as an operatic embodiment of all that *pochvennichestvo* stood for philosophically and aesthetically, the *Rogneda* scenario seemed ideal. Serov's preface to the opera's libretto, which he published in advance of the libretto itself in N.V. Mikhno's influential theatrical journal, *Russkaia stsena (The Russian Stage)* in October, 1865, shows to what an extent he thought of his work as just such an embodiment. Obviously modelled on the caustic prefaces of Gluck, the preface to *Rogneda* set forth the composer's credo in the most forthright, indeed belligerent, terms, as well as his conviction that in the new opera that credo—compounded of Wagner, Grigoriev's "true realism" and progressive operatic *"veianie"* generally—had found its ultimate, "organic" realization. One of the most curious documents in the history of Russian opera, this manifesto is a unique merger of Serov's creative and critical callings. As such, it demands quotation practically in full.

Preface to the Libretto of the Opera *Rogneda*

The relationship between the text and the music of an opera which is to be taken seriously as a musical drama, constitutes an essential, indeed vital question of contemporary art. A thinking artist is obliged to attempt its clarification in word and deed. That is why I consider it not superfluous to indicate here, in a few lines, what is in my opinion the only true viewpoint on the text and music of my second opera.

In the Preface to *Judith* I gave voice to my firm conviction that the truest solution to the problem occurs when both the canvas and the music of an opera take shape in one and the same mind. From this position I have not retreated a single step in my new work. Most important of all in this connection is the question, to whom belongs the initial idea of the drama and the invention of the scenario, both of the music-drama in its entirety and of each individual scene. Only afterwards comes the question of fashioning the speeches of the various characters, their *language,* the words of the opera per se.

Working on a subject taken in its general features from our national heritage (the legend of Rogneda can be found in any schoolbook), I had need of a collaborator who was at the same time an able and artistic versifier and could approximate the language of the chroniclers, so as to convey the flavor of tenth-century pagan Russia. D.V. Averkiev, as far as I am concerned, has accomplished this task with extraordinary success—a task which is in no case simple, but which was made particularly difficult by the fact that many scenes (almost all, it would be fairer to say) ripened in my musical sketches long before the fashioning of the words, so that my collaborator, in most cases, had to fit verses to altogether finished music according to a given detailed program.

In thus declining any responsibility for the literary merits or faults in the actual language of *Rogneda*'s text, I do not place the responsibility for the drama itself upon my collaborator. With only the smallest exceptions, it all, in the whole and in its details, belongs to me alone. Therefore I could not call my collaborator my "librettist" in the former sense, but have sought to avoid the usual heading: "An opera in five acts/ words by so-and-so/ music by so-and-so," where the composer would stand as one among a number of equal contributors to the success of an operatic production, hardly any higher than the ballet master, the costume designer, or the builder of the sets. Only when the composer is at the same time the author of the drama, when he works to his own plan, can the relationship between the text and the music gradually approach the desired rationality.

Voltaire, poking fun at the opera of his time, noted that "ce qui est trop bête pour être dit, on le chant." A whole century has passed since that time; such men as Gluck, Mozart, Cherubini, Méhul, Beethoven, Weber, and Glinka have walked the earth and accomplished their great deeds; Wagner lives and creates today. But have we in fact gotten so far away from Voltaire's sarcasm? Almost every day we find in all the European papers, and in ours as well, little phrases like this: "The dramatic situation in this scene is absurd, but the music is excellent." (?!) Or even better: "What a pity that this celebrated maestro was saddled (?!) with such a pitiful libretto!" Is an operatic libretto, then, nothing more than a lottery ticket, which falls to our lot at the caprice of blind Fortune? Where were this egregious maestro's eyes? Where was his taste, where were his long years of experience when it came to choosing the pitiful canvas for his music?

In judgments on the actual music of an opera, on the merits and faults of its style and workmanship, we find the same muddle-headedness and confusion. To clarify all this as it should be would mean writing not a short preface but whole volumes. Let us say in general that the public has not yet learned to demand of "opera" something decent in the way of sense. It still looks upon the canvas of an opera, that is, upon its libretto, as upon something "unimportant" in the general makeup of the work. This is just as if, in speaking of the human bodily organism, we were to ignore the structure of its skeleton. Such a fundamental blunder is much abetted by the general senselessness and the constant incongruity between music and text in famous Italian operas (zealously presented in translation upon all European stages), and also by the absence of true acting skill on the part of Italian songsters and songstresses. "Russian opera" must stand upon entirely different ground. It must give the first place, the place of honor, to "sense." But the public does not part with its old habits so easily. It will be a matter of time, of gradual, good-natured, but continual effort.

In direct connection with the nonrequirement of common poetical sense from the text of an opera, stands the nonrequirement of sense from the music itself. For many, music is still on the level of "a pleasant amusement, an easy gratification of the ear." The power of the language of music to transmit forcefully and faithfully the movements of the soul, portraying together with them the epic foundations of drama, and local as well as temporal color, and the congruence of music with all the profoundest requirements of true dramaturgy—all this is something of which many have as yet no inkling. The majority continues above all to seek pleasant, melodious singing in opera, that is, easily remembered motives and tunes, virtuosically rendered by sugary voices on the stage—as if this constituted the whole interest of opera!?—whence the majority goes no further in its demands than melodies of waltzlike or polkalike cast, with which all the favorite Italian operas are so copiously endowed. But the thinking musician of our day, without chasing after melodic appeal (which would be the height of absurdity), must nevertheless nurture the firm conviction that in a truly dramatic musical language full-fledged melody, with every right to be so called, can manifest itself a thousand times over without in the slightest resembling the work of those composers who "have a reputation for melody" with the musically uneducated crowd. Naturally, in such cases the melody will not be so easily and instantly memorable; but then why satisfy the demands of a taste corrupted by "organ-grinders'" tunes?

After all, there was a time when in literature there was demanded of "tragedy" above all, and without fail, the kind of exalted, sonorous and easily remembered tirades and individual lines— "des vers à retenir"—of which Corneille, Racine and Voltaire made a specialty. The "pseudo-classical" era has passed, and no one in our time will reproach a drama like [Lev Alexandrovich] Mey's *Pskovitianka* [*The Maid of Pskov,* 1860], let us say, for not containing magnificent apostrophes in the manner of Sumarokov's tragedies. . . . [Here Serov gives a number of examples of stilted "pseudoclassical" language.]

In those days such rhetorical rhyme-spinning was considered the summit of art. Now it is merely funny. Today one demands of a historical drama first of all historical truth, fidelity of atmosphere and character; in this, and not in sonorous verses, does one seek poetry.

Why, then, is the level of musico-dramatic understanding still so debased? It would seem to be high time to look upon music, too, more seriously. My ideal is dramatic truth in tone, although for this truth, for the sake of musical characterization, I have had to sacrifice "conventional" beauty, the "jewelled" elegance of musical form. Judge me from this standpoint.

Ask yourself two essential questions:

1) Is the subject chosen by the author for his musical drama (the whole conception of the play, together with its epic foundations) organically developed within itself, and is it or is it not suitable for embodiment in musical tones?

2) To what extent has this embodiment succeeded or failed; that is, does the music transmit the whole story, all the vicissitudes of the musico-dramatic canvas, or does it transmit only some of them but not all, or does it find itself altogether at odds with the drama, either throughout or in one or another scene?

"Why are there no formal 'arias'? Why so much recitative? Why so few easily remembered melodies? Why does the style recall Wagner and not Glinka, or Glinka and not Bellini?" and so on in this vein—all such questions, since they have no bearing upon my work, will expose, in my eyes, only the immaturity of those who pose them.

(St. Petersburg, September 1865)[42]

The ease with which *Rogneda*'s detractors were able to hoist the unfortunate composer on his own petard makes the history of the opera's reception by "progressive" critics a famous tragicomedy. For indeed, it cannot be said that Serov and his "collaborators" found satisfactory solutions to all the problems they had to face in transforming the "idea" of *Rogneda* into the finished libretto, to say nothing as yet of the music. First among these problems was that of focus and coherence. The opera's main plot line was compounded of two passing episodes in a novel whose well-plotted central intrigue had already, as it were, been "taken." Serov had to construct his opera's action out of a collection of "leavings" which had somehow to be woven into a persuasive whole. Some attempt was made to fuse the various elements of the scenario by having Rogneda, for instance, secretly visit the witch in the first scene of Act I to arrange an alliance with Ruald against Vladimir, or by having Ruald interrupt the idol-worshippers in the next scene. But the line of action initiated by Rogneda's visit comes to nought for she and Ruald never meet, while the action of the interrupted sacrifice revolves around Olava (Ruald's bride), a character over whom a great to-do is made through three whole acts, about whom no less than three musical numbers are sung—but who never appears on stage.

Serov's proud and principled description of his working methods in the Preface is apt to strike the modern reader as bizarre.[43] And no doubt these methods, familiar to those who know *Judith,* seriously exacerbated the difficulties inherent in the nature of the plot material. This time around Serov did not bother to write a single word of the libretto (whereas some of *Judith*'s text had in fact been his work), but once again this did not prevent him from regarding himself as poet-musician à la Wagner, for he was *Rogneda*'s scenarist (with some barely acknowledged assistance from Maikov, Polonsky, Dostoevsky et al.), and for an opera, that was the only dramaturgical role of consequence. We may compare the account of Serov and Averkiev's working relationship given by the composer himself with one given many years later by his widow. As Serov tells it, work went smoothly, the composer firmly at the helm, guided at all times by a well-defined and "organic" plan:

> Averkiev very aptly caught the intentions of the composer-dramatist in their, so to speak, embryonic form. Never departing from the composer's plan for each scene, Averkiev wrote the entire libretto in verse which well suited the matter at hand. This work went along almost imperceptibly, in the course of discussions with many other literary figures, and parallel to the composition of the music itself.[44]

Valentina Serova's account is rather less flattering:

> Averkiev wrote the libretto for Serov, and their working procedure in this collaborative effort was carried on rather strangely. First Serov would write the music for a given scene, then Averkiev would have to find words for it; in this way they wrote scene after scene, act after act, never knowing for sure if the whole operatic carcass would hang together.[45]

While *Rogneda*'s creative chronology cannot be reconstructed in detail, owing to the loss of the composer's manuscripts,[46] the structure of the libretto confirms Mme. Serova's account. While the opera seems to have been written straight through from first scene to last, rather little thought was given, especially at the early stages, to the proportions of the whole. As had happened with *Judith,* Serov allowed himself to be carried away with the decorative possibilities of the subject. The original Rogneda story was so crowded by all the accretions that in the end it shrank to a single act (the fourth) out of a luxuriant five in the finished scenario.[47] In this compressed form, the action rather closely follows the *duma* (narrative ballad) on Rogneda by Kondraty Fyodorovich Ryleev (1795-1826):[48] the scene opens on Rogneda grieving with Iziaslav over her captivity; to distract her, Iziaslav asks his mother to recall her childhood and ancestry (this provided Ryleev with the opportunity for "exposition"; Serov uses Iziaslav's invitation as pretext for the opera's most popular set piece, Rogneda's "Varangian Ballad"[49]); a messenger announces the imminent arrival of Prince Vladimir; the latter retires for the night and is awakened by a thunderclap just in time to save himself from Rogneda's sword. The only departure from Ryleev's version comes at the end: Iziaslav's intercession does not at first meet with success in the opera; Vladimir's decision to forgive his wife is made, as we have seen, on the arrival of the Christians in the next act. As for the other main event of the plot, the episode of Ruald and the bear from Zagoskin, it is cramped into the finale of Act III (and takes place, except for Ruald's death, offstage). All the really essential action in *Rogneda,* then, takes place in a clump of one-and-a-half acts starting at the opera's midpoint. The rest is given over to accretion, spectacle and genre—a world record?

The fact that two-and-a-half acts pass before the action fairly commences, and that the earlier scenes of the opera are not logically related to what follows, is all the evidence we need of the kind of outwardly smooth but actually planless work Mme. Serova described. There is a certain amount of corroborative evidence on *Rogneda*'s gestation to be gleaned from records of preview performances of various numbers and from Serov's correspondence. The first public hearing of any music from *Rogneda* took place in March, 1864, when the chorus, *"Slava solnyshku na nebe,"* and the 'Dance of the Skomorokhi" (both from Act II) were given at a concert sponsored by the Imperial Theaters Directorate.[50] The next month the pilgrims' chorus and the duet of Ruald and the Pilgrim Elder (both from Act III) were performed at a concert of Balakirev's Free Music School.[51] All of these numbers precede the essenial action. Three of them are purely decorative, while the quite extended duet only develops the dramatically futile Ruald-Olava subplot. During the late spring and summer of 1864, Serov went abroad with his wife (and had the unhappy experience with Liszt recounted above). It seems likely that it was during this trip that Serov found Ryleev's *duma,* which guided him in the dramatic structure of the fourth act. (As a Decembrist mutineer executed in 1826, Ryleev was under ban in Russia, and editions of his works began to appear in Russian only in Germany in the late 1850s.) Upon his return, Serov seems to have resumed work with the second half of the third act, where the action finally comes into focus. The text Averkiev fit to the Act III hunters' chorus was published in the "October" issue of *Epokha* (1864, no. 10), which had been delayed at the printers and only appeared in December. On the twenty-eighth of that month Serov addressed a letter to Dostoevsky in which he apologized for causing another delay: he had not submitted a promised article on time because he had been putting the finishing touches on the fourth act—the "most important"—of his opera.[52] The composition of the fifth act and last-minute alterations—we may assume that these included the invention of transitions and connections betwen the various numbers—kept Serov busy through the summer of 1865.

What we have observed of the scenario's structure at the overall level is confirmed by a closer examination of the individual scenes. The opera's plan having been gradually refined in the course of work, the earlier a scene comes in the action the more aimless and chaotically constructed it is likely to be. A glance at the second scene of Act I—the sacrifice to Perun—will suffice to illustrate. The scene is built around Ruald's interruption of a wild pagan rite. Christian and pagan elements are early brought into sharp and dramatic confrontation. But this "effect" (reminiscent of Glinka's Russians and Poles) seems to have been the scene's whole raison d'être. The attempted human sacrifice is pure genre and touches the plot in no way. Ruald's essential role is not played until two acts later, when his self-sacrifice provides Vladimir with an example and a motive for embracing Christianity. In Act I Ruald merely "contrasts" with the dramaturgically superfluous sacrifice, which makes him therefore doubly superfluous. His two sugary arias are not only devoid of dramatic necessity but create wholly avoidable and needless problems of coherence and plausibility. The first concerns the ever-elusive Olava, while the second is the "Prayer," which Ruald ostensibly utters in panic when the enormous crowd of pagans turns upon him with intent to kill. The Prayer causes them to stand still and listen to 37 bars of *andante, dolcissimo sempre* before resuming their murderous advance. This moment was so ridiculed by the critics after the first performance that the notoriously stiff-necked composer was actually brought round and made adjustments.[53] In the revised version of the scene the High Priest and the chorus of pagans accompany the Prayer with shouts of "Death to him!" set to snatches of their preceding chorus, worked in contrapuntally. To Serov this must have seemed the perfect solution, since the passage now included the kind of vivid "polyphonic" contrast he had handled well in *Judith*. But as Cui drily remarked, it is after all "better to stand still in silence than to threaten murder and stand still all the same."[54]

It might appear, then, that as a *dramma per musica, Rogneda* could only be improved by cutting the scene out. And yet—cruel paradox!—it was precisely this scene that made the strongest musical impression on the opera's viewers, even those otherwise ill-disposed to the opera. Cui, Rimsky-Korsakov and Tchaikovsky though they all to varying degrees denigrated *Rogneda* as a whole, singled out the Sacrifice to Perun as, to use Tchaikovsky's words, one of the "rare oases in the desert, an excellent number from the musical point of view."[55] But to justify this scene, or the opera, on grounds like these was comparable to the kind of defense of *Ruslan* that Serov had devoted a river of ink to opposing. Indeed, in the Preface Serov had gone out of his way to rule out such a defense of his own work. The irony of the situation was not lost on his critics. Cui, confronted with so easy a target as the Preface offered him, produced one of his most corrosive polemics.

It is with trepidation that I embark upon an examination of *Rogneda*. Trepidation, because Mr. Serov, in his Preface to the opera's libretto, intimidates public and reviewer alike. He himself has indicated "the only true viewpoint on the text and music of his second opera," and any judgment or question that does not conform to this point of view "in his eyes exposes only the immaturity of those who pose them."... Our esteemed critics, though, have dodged him well: they have praised *Rogneda* to the skies, and this clearly proves their maturity, plain as day.... Here we have the *only* two questions which Mr. Serov will permit one to apply to his work. I am in agreement with these questions, but besides them I will permit myself to touch also upon the *quality* of the music. For me, it is not enough simply that a Friday dish be made of fish; I am also interested in what kind of fish it is and the degree of its freshness.

[Here Cui summarizs the plot of *Rogneda,* not without sarcasm.]

All this is perfectly suitable for musical treatment, but where do you find here "an organically constructed musical drama?" The whole subject is contained in the fourth act alone, and *Rogneda* thus might as well have been a one-act opera or an eight-act opera, instead of the five-act opera it is in its present form.... What purpose is served by the scene at the witch's cave [Act I] or the sacrifice scene, whose characters never return in the course of the entire opera? Once again I say that this is a sequence of scenes, of tableaux, eminently suited to musical treatment, but without the slightest organic connection between them. And in this regard, the "text" of *Rogneda* is no better than the "libretto" of *Ruslan,* at whose expense Mr. Serov has so often amused himself.... Drama consists not in settings and accoutrements, but in the gradual unfolding of character and emotion. And of this development there is not a hint in *Rogneda.* Not a single act goes by without all manner of artifice: witches, high priests, hunters, dogs, horses, death scenes, processions, dances, dreams, moonlight—what isn't there in this opera! These effects can be wonderful if they proceed from the subject itself. But if the subject be fashioned to seek out these effects as if by compulsion, then this is hardly art.[56]

Cui's concluding sentences read like a paraphrase of Serov's own strictures against the grand opéra, particularly as expressed in "Spontini and His Music," the article that had made his critical reputation in 1852.[57] Indeed, it was *Rogneda* above all that earned Serov his sobriquet, "The Russian Meyerbeer." *Russkaia stsena,* the journal in whose pages Serov's Preface first appeared, carried in its letters column a lively exchange of views on *Rogneda*'s libretto. The most interesting of these letters is one signed pseudonymously "Ivanushka Durachok" (Little Ivan the Fool), which recent research has succeeded in attributing to Vladimir Vasilievich Nikolsky, Professor of History at Serov's alma mater, the Imperial School of Jurisprudence, and immortal in the annals of Russian opera as the one who later turned Musorgsky's attention to the subject of *Boris Godunov.*[58] His indignant critique of *Rogneda*'s libretto perhaps marks the beginning of Nikolsky's interest in the problems of "historical" opera. He chides Serov for having left so many dramatic possibilities inherent in the Rogneda legend unrealized: her love for Iaropolk, their engagement, Vladimir's rivalry for her hand, his war to the death against his brother, his conquest of Polotsk, the murder of Rogvolod and his sons, Rogneda's forcible abduction. All of this would have provided ample scope for the "unfolding of character and emotion" Cui had demanded. But Serov, on the contrary,

took for his drama only one moment out of the entire story of Rogneda: her attempted revenge—that is, only what would have been the denouement of the real drama. After that, one can hardly expect that Mr. Serov's play would have any organic structure. For Serov has thrown out the figure of Iaropolk, Rogneda's relation to him, her entire story up to the concluding moment, the whole development of her character, in a word, the whole drama.

As for Serov's handling of the one dramatic moment he did see fit to include:

Now comes the central moment of this organic drama—Rogneda gets ready to kill the Prince. But—o miracle!—her whole monologue at this moment consists of two (Shake-spearean) phrases: "The hour has come! I have sharpened my knife!" [Nikolsky misquotes here: Rogneda sings only the second of these phrases—but she sings it twice.] And the long interval between these utterances is taken up by a ballet sequence by moonlight [Vladimir's prophetic dream], during which Rogneda runs from the window to the bed and back again. In other words, the drama has let us down even here. And that's not all. Not only was it incapable of expressing this strong moment, Serov's scenario actually replaces it with the most paltry of all theatrical devices—a tableau vivant! ... Indeed, after this there is nothing to be said anymore about organic development, let alone artistic truth.[59]

Serov came to his opera's defense in a letter printed over the signature "A Constant Visitor of the Russian Opera." Its diction and tone, over and above its content, make attribution to the composer a virtual certainty, and the letter was so taken at the time. It expresses, at any rate, a viewpoint which accords so completely with the tenets of *pochvennichestvo* that it can only be regarded as an explication of *Rogneda*'s dramaturgy by one who was present at the creation. The "Constant Visitor" reminds us that "organic" drama has an Ideal as well as a surface subject, and that it is here that one must seek *Rogneda*'s "organic development." "The opera," he suggests, "might really be called 'The Dawn of Christianity in Russia,' which dawn is hinted at from the very first words of the sorceress [that is, the very first words in the opera]."[60] When viewed from this standpoint the work was not only coherent, but presented a continuous and "artistically true" unfolding of a single theme, proceeding from the opening scene straight through to the magnificent choral peroration (based on a reprise of a melody first sung in Act III by the Pilgrim Elder).[61] All the intervening vagaries of plot and stagecaft were meant to be seen as tributaries to this overriding current, however weak the connections between them may individually appear. As to the remaining question— whether in fact such a work, in which characters and their interaction count for so little, and whose complicated surface is so weighted down with static and poorly motivated spectacle, can be truly called a drama—the "Constant Visitor's" reply is one of the most characteristically Serovian pronunciamentos:

How is one to instill in you, stern critics and judges, the truth that a "musical drama," precisely because it is not simply a drama, but a drama created for music, can never conform to those standards and criteria which you apply to a nonmusical drama, nor should it.

Music and scenic dramaturgy are closely allied, but perhaps they can never be completely fused. In his Preface to *Rogneda* Mr. Serov nowhere speaks of a purely dramatic criterion for his opera, but on the contrary, he relies heavily upon the epic element as upon a broad background for the musical scenes with which the canvas of a Russian opera of a contemporary cast is to be filled. One easily notes that such epic pictures as the sacrifice to Perun, the prince's banquet, the hunt, the funeral singing of the Pilgrims, occupied the imagination of the author of *Rogneda* fully as much, if not more than the strictly dramatic moments of the play. But is one to reproach him for this? He was creating no drama in the narrow sense of the word, but a broad epic-dramatic canvas for his music, and, of course, no dramatist who is not a musician as well could have thought up a canvas more grateful for music than, for example, the whole third act of *Rogneda*.[62]

One is tempted to quote here from Serov's many articles on *Ruslan* in refutation of the arguments advanced here in defense of *Rogneda*. One refrains, however, because *Ruslan* made no pretense to a "lining of the Ideal," which was, according to the "Constant Visitor" as it might have been for Grigoriev himself, the redeeming virtue of *Rogneda*. As for Act III, that was the act which Cui, among others, had singled out for special mockery. It contains, as we have seen, only one piece of "action" (the fight with the bear), and even that one takes place off stage. To "Ivanushka Durachok," this only confirmed the essential futility of *Rogneda*'s dramaturgy: "[With Ruald's death] he vanishes from the stage; his role is finished . . . but why did he appear in the first place?"[63] For the rest, Act III contains three male choruses (smartly contrasting with the female choruses—the captive maidens—of Act IV), a full-fledged operatic duet replete with a high $B\flat$ for the tenor, a rousing orchestral showpiece (the hunt) to rival Wagner's Valkyries, and a comic patter-song "à la russe." Every one of these numbers may be dispensable from the "purely dramatic" point of view, but for the "Constant Visitor" their presence is justified, even demanded, by the special requirements of *dramma per musica,* and because the nature of *Rogneda* is such that scene-setting and genre are the true bearers of its "idea."

Few were satisfied with this special pleading, however, and all wanted to know how Serov, self-proclaimed seeker of "dramatic truth in tones" and "organic dramatic structure" that he was, could have fathered a work which, although it arrogantly purported to embody these ideals, patently perverted and distorted them. Serov's contemporaries could only suspect opportunism. The young Herman Laroche expressed the opinion of many when he observed that in *Rogneda* "one can't help but see a 'sign of the times' (Meyerbeer)."[64] Tchaikovsky, a great admirer of *Judith,* went further in his reproaches:

[Serov] wrote not out of the inner compulsion of a born creative artist, but because, having critically studied the whole realm of musical art over a period of many years, he was a past master of the technical side of things and saw the opportunity to embark quickly and easily upon a composer's career. . . . The public the world over is undemanding in matters of aesthetics; they love external effects and vivid contrasts, and they are altogether indifferent to profound and original creative manifestations if they are not fitted out colorfully, vividly and brilliantly in the highest degree. And one must give Serov his due: he certainly knew how to please the crowd.[65]

Even so partisan a chronicler as Mme. Serova asserts that "Alexander Nikolaevich could not have pandered more to the public and the theater of his time than he did with *Rogneda*."[66] And it is *Rogneda* above all that is responsible for the unfortunate view of Serov that prevails today among those who know his work only by reputation. Thus Rosa Newmarch, whose *The Russian Opera* reigned for half a century as the standard English-language source of information on its subject: "We shall look in vain in *Rogneda* for the higher purpose, the effort at psychological delineation, the comparative solidity of workmanship which we find in *Judith*. Nevertheless the work amply fulfilled its avowed intention to take public taste by storm."[67]

But such a view is facile, and it is false. We have no evidence of cynical intentions on Serov's part. We have, on the contrary, presented plenty of evidence to show that the composer's intentions were guided by the highest, most idealistic literary and philosophical thinking current in the Russia of his time. And as for Serov's courting public success, the only evidence of that is the success itself.[68] With regard to intentions and ideals, the unprejudiced investigator is bound to take the Preface at face value and then attempt to discover what went wrong.

At least since the Spontini essay of 1852, Serov had cast himself as the implacable enemy of unmotivated stage spectacle in opera. Yet the "Constant Visitor of the Russian Opera" could find no better motivation for *Rogneda*'s sacrifices, banquets and all the rest than that they provided a "canvas grateful for music." A seemingly irresolvable dilemma, this; and yet that very Spontini essay holds the key to the riddle of *Rogneda*. There Serov had sought to explain the genesis of the French "monster spectacle," as he called it. He began by defining the "goal of opera" as:

> that delight of the soul which dramatic music in conjunction with scenic action affords. Only beauty can afford spiritual delight, beauty in this case being either beauty of expression—truth of character, of dramatic situations transmitted by music, of declamation—or beauty of purely musical idea—of the musical phrases themselves, freely flowing from one another, though perhaps without any direct relation to the text.[69]

The operatic composer disregards either of these elements at his peril. But as neither is dispensable, so must neither be exaggerated. The results of exaggerating the second element, the purely musical, are familiar enough—the typical "Italian" concert-in-costume, the perennial whipping boy of all "progressive" operatic theory. But what is crucial to our understanding *Rogneda* is Serov's equally emphatic warning against exaggeration of "truth":

Strict truth of character, situation, declamation, truth of *expression* in general . . . may to a large extent be captured by deliberation, care and calculation, and can often replace real musical talent in dramatic music. All the rest—that is, real musical interest—will be decidedly lacking in the works of such a composer, extremely intelligent and experienced though he may be; his works, despite truth of character and situation, will possess hardly any real attraction, but will remain dry and dull. And since the composer's intuition causes him to see that there is much still lacking for effectiveness upon the stage, he does not fail to set in motion all manner of legitimate and illegitimate means to astonish, startle and stun the public. There you have the origin of those works, wherein *pretensions* to profound dramaturgy are everywhere apparent, these pretensions utterly replacing the *music.*[70]

Serov had been describing *La Vestale,* but it might as well have been *Rogneda.* For when it came to writing his own quasi-historical, "national" opera, he unwittingly recapitulated the phylogeny of the grand opéra just as he had so understandingly, even compassionately described it. Guided as before by the ideal of "true realism," Serov erred fatally in choosing a subject whose overriding "Ideal" was embodied not in his protagonists or their deeds, but in the mise-en-scène. Where Serov's initial stimulus for *Judith* had been the story itself, the "Ideal" emerging metaphorically from it, the underlying idea of *Rogneda* was simply—and vaguely—"the Christianization of Russia." Thus, the composer was seduced into contriving static "portraits" of pagan Russia on the one hand—sorceresses, high priests, idol-worshipping, sybaritic feasting and hunting—and of the Christians on the other—hymns, prayers, funeral services—and deluded himself into thinking that all of this was *eo ipso* "organic" to his plan. Thus the flaws of decorativeness and redundancy which had marred the Assyrian acts of *Judith* spread like a plague over the whole of *Rogneda,* without the compensating virtue of a direct, simple and coherent surface plot to govern the whole, which had saved the earlier opera.

As in the French grand opera, the spectacular element so dominated *Rogneda* that it inevitably took on the appearance of an end rather than a means. "Dramatic" moments pass almost unnoticed. The story line, such as it is, unfolds in tiny spurts, either carried by musically insignificant recitatives (which are nowhere nearly as prominent as Serov implies in the Preface) or else by declamatory passages cast against a spectacular background that dwarfs them utterly. There is nothing in all of *Rogneda* to compare with the much-admired confrontations of the two leading characters in the fourth act of *Judith.* But there is a moment in the scenario of the later opera which seems to be almost exactly analogous: the single confrontation between Vladimir and Rogneda (also Act IV), right before Rogneda/Judith attempts the murder of the sleeping Vladimir/Holofernes. Why, then, did Serov so blithely throw this scene away, as "Ivanushka Durachok" had noted with exasperation? The answer, seen from a properly *"pochvennik"* point of view, is neither difficult nor perplexing: in *Judith,* the two main characters were at the same time the bearers of the opera's "idea," while in the opera named for her,

Rogneda is neither fish nor fowl. As major representative neither of pagan nor of Christian world, she is part only of the surface drama. Her attempted murder of her husband, though it appears to be the culminating moment of the opera's action, is actually peripheral to the opera's real—that is, "Ideal"— line of development, and Serov quite logically wasted no time over it. The fatal contradiction in *Rogneda,* then, is the incongruity of its surface and "Ideal" subjects. The congruence of the same in *Judith* is what made the first opera a dramatically successful one. Cui sensed this when he wrote:

> *Rogneda* has proven that if many, including myself, saw in *Judith* a real dramatic flair and the desire to advance contemporary operatic standards, then this was an illusion accidentally created by the nature of *Judith*'s subject.[71]

Over and above the problematical libretto, *Rogneda* presents another, and perhaps even more disconcerting incongruity between theory, as stated in the Preface, and actuality, and that is the plethora of "numbers," vocal set pieces of every description, ranging from full-blown arias of the very kind Serov had boastfully and explicitly excluded in the Preface, through "easily remembered tunes, virtuosically rendered by sugary voices," all the way down to the most trivial little songs and dances. For anyone who knows the opera, quite the oddest part of the Preface is the conclusion—the series of baffled questions the composer smugly anticipated from the uncomprehending public. In fact the recitatives in *Rogneda* are in no way conspicuous by virtue of their quantity, and certainly not by their quality. Nor could anyone who ever heard *Rogneda* possibly have asked, "Why are there no formal arias?" Puzzling is not only the profusion of set pieces in Serov's opera, but the flimsiness of their pretexts. Ruald, in particular, seems to have accidentally wandered into *Rogneda* from the Italian opera house across town. And were it not for the Preface, with its strictures not only against Italian music but against "Italian songsters and songstresses," there would have been little cause for surprise, since the role was conceived for Fyodor Nikolsky (1828-98), a remarkable lyric tenor and a great favorite with the public, but a singer whose reputation was based amost exclusively on a non-Russian repertoire of a kind Serov despised: Rossini, Meyerbeer, Halévy. Serov himself gave a just evaluation of Nikolsky's talent in an article of 1870:

> His is a voice beyond all compare! But...we must leave it at that, [for] acting is not his province; he is only a singer, and, consequently not a finished artist.... He lacks, above all, artistic maturity.[72]

Not a singer, in other words, meant for a musical drama such as *Rogneda* purported to be. And neither was the role, unless in its honeyed, cloying phrases Serov had naively sought to express what his wife termed "pacific Christianity, all-forgiving in its holy simplicity."[73]

As for "jewelled musical forms," they are often smuggled into *Rogneda* in a way that would become a time-honored method among Russian composers who preached "dramatic truth": by "excusing" them. Situations are contrived in which one character entertains another, where one character is actually invited or ordered by another to sing. Often, too, Serov attempts to cover up the traces of his "jewelled" forms by failing to complete them. Both of the Jester's songs (Acts II and III) are interrupted by the sudden entrance of messengers bearing evil tidings. Abrupt diminished-seventh chords in both instances cut the songs off in midphrase. But such a transparent dodge can hardly disguise an "interpolated" set piece. Even Grigoriev (who was acquainted with two-and-a-half acts of *Rogneda* before his sudden death in September, 1864) was a little embarrassed, and felt constrained to justify the more conventional musical physiognomy of *Rogneda* vis-à-vis *Judith* before any music from the second opera had been heard in public.

> By now it is clear to all that *Judith* is grounded in rich and varied melody, although its melodies are developed only to the extent and degree necessary for a musical drama. The melodic element will be even more clearly marked in *Rogneda*—it will even predominate in some ways, for the drama takes place on Slavic soil. Its predominance is to be explained only by this fact, however, not by any compromise or concession.[74]

The static impression created by Serov's "musical frescoes"[75] in *Rogneda* is exacerbated by the composer's musical style. All musical structures and forms, "jewelled" or otherwise (and even the recitatives), are hamstrung in *Rogneda* even more than in *Judith* by an overwhelming compulsion toward symmetry and periodicity. In Cui's words, "monotony of rhythmic design . . . and overprecise *carrure des phrases* both characterize Serov's music and constitute its greatest deficiency."[76] Nor is this merely a "musical" deficiency, for it fundamentally affects the progress of the drama. Since the music came before the text, and since Serov was inclined to follow almost everywhere the line of least resistance in the construction of phrases, Averkiev was often forced to extend the text to fit the repetitive music by artificially repeating whole sentences. This not only slowed the pace of the action, but occasionally made for unintended comedy. In Act I, scene ii (the sacrifice), a tiny snatch of dramatic recitative is the slender thread by which the scene is bound to the main line of the plot (though the line, as we know, shortly comes to nought): Rogneda's slavegirl Malfrida informs Ruald of her mistress's intention to help him against Vladimir. The prefabricated music of the recitative forced the librettist into an unparalleled bit of dialogue that spreads the least possible verbal content over the most music, meanwhile endeavoring to maintain a semblance of "truth" in declamation (Ex. 3.1).

Ex. 3.1.   *Rogneda,* Act I, sc. ii
(Vocal score, Moscow: A. Gutheil, ca. 1885)
[Malfrida: Get ready for your exploit, knight! Help is
           coming your way.
Ruald: What did you say, messenger?
Malfrida: Help is coming your way!
Ruald: Help is coming! From where?]

In more formal musical numbers Serov pushes his disdain for the words of the text, as the saying goes, to the point of dogma. For him words count only on their first appearance. Having given a referential context to the music, from then on they act only as a pretext for that music, the only true bearer (in Serov's view) of musico-dramatic "meaning." This aspect of Serov's style particularly annoyed the "New Russian School" and its spokesman, Cui. For them, the words of an opera's text had an importance, at least theoretically, on an absolute par with the music. In writing about *Rogneda,* then, Cui reserved the full measure of his venom for the recitatives and the handling of prosody in general. Serov's modus operandi was for Cui already enough to disqualify him from consideration as a serious composer of dramatic music.

> Dramatic music must express all the nuances of meaning in the text. But Mr. Serov *adjusts* the words to music created *without text*: if a word doesn't fit because of its accent or the

number of its syllables, he simply replaces it with another, and all the while talks of "seriously conceived musical drama."

Small wonder, then, that Cui found Serov's recitatives "the worst possible." But his description of them, later to be echoed by Stasov, is not distinguished for its accuracy, and betrays moreover a prejudiced and surprisingly conservative ear.

> [These recitatives] consist of a fortuitous series of notes, interrupted by chords chosen equally at random, guided only by the proviso that they must constantly belong to different and mutually dissonant tonalities; this constitutes the only difference between [Serov's] recitatives and those of the Italians, which latter are accompanied by chords which *never* leave the tonic or dominant. But recitative, after all, is the very touchstone of a gift for dramatic music.

The last sentence, though an axiom for Cui, was of course one with which Serov could scarcely have agreed less. And the offhand quality of his recitatives shows it. The vocal line, far from a "fortuitous series of notes," generally arpeggiates the chord that "accompanies" it. The chord progression, likewise far from fortuitous, is usually a functional (if frequently enharmonic) transition from the key of one number to that of the next, interrupted, if at all, only by a few climactically placed and harmonically static diminished-seventh chords on appropriate words or exclamation. One recitative that is almost entirely "built" on a linking diminished-seventh chord is the one immediately preceding Ruald's death. One imagines a single chord variously resolved in the composer's sketches, awaiting Averkiev's text (Ex. 3.2).

Equally problematic questions of an altogether different kind were raised by Serov's understanding of "national character." While, in keeping with the nature of his subject and the aims of *pochvennichestvo,* he had sought to contrive music of a deliberately and recognizably "Russian" style in many of the opera's numbers, the sources of that style gave rise to controversy. In his wish to sidestep Glinka's influence, it was natural that Serov turned to *Askold's Grave*—that is to say not only Zagoskin's novel, but Verstovsky's opera as well. For by placing himself in a line of descent that proceeded from Verstovsky, Serov would be able to "circumvent" Glinka altogether. Not only in his activities as composer, but also in his public lectures and his critical articles Serov now attempted to downgrade Glinka's status as founding father. Stasov wrote of this to Balakirev in incredulous indignation:

> One of Serov's friends has related to me a few of his recent pronouncements, which I simply cannot credit. For instance, Serov (supposedly) has declared in his lectures, and innumerable times in conversation, that Glinka's music is not really Russian at all, but only Russian in its themes, which are elaborated in a non-Russian fashion (e.g., *Kamarinskaia*

Fig. 3.3   Alexei Verstovsky

Ex. 3.2.   *Rogneda,* Act III

[Prince: Thank the Lord! I am safe! I thought I was
done for. He almost had me, the cursed thing!
But where is the Varangian?

Dobrynya: They're bringing him in yonder! The bear
got him.

Prince: Unfortunate wretch!

Elder: My son, my son!]

and most of *Ruslan*). Also that if Verstovsky could have been given Glinka's talent and musical education he would have been a far more Russian musician and would have shown what our national music ought to be. But since this still has not been accomplished by anyone, it remains for *Rogneda* to show the way, to show what real Russian music ought to be, not only in its themes, but in its spirit as well, in its moods, its musical elaboration and its smallest details. In keeping with this, needless to say, "The Dance of the Skomorokhi" [*Rogneda*, Act II] is both *Kamarinskaia*'s indictment and its corrective. I would guess that all this is the result of Serov's lascivious cohabitation with the *pochvenniki* on *Epokha*.[77]

Stasov guessed right, of course, although he exaggerated the extent of Serov's anti-Glinka propaganda. Serov never belittled Glinka's achievement so much as he deplored the "Italianism" of Glinka's taste and technique. Such influence was entirely lacking in Verstovsky, whose style amalgamated Weberian harmony and orchestration with the vocal manner of the French vaudeville and opéra comique. Serov's most explicit comment on the relationship between Glinka and Verstovsky was made in an article entitled "Verstovsky and His Significance for Russian Art," which he published as early as 1862. Here he accused Glinka not so much of eclecticism as of having portrayed the many-sided Russian spirit in too limited a way. Considering that the article predates even *Judith*, one can hardly agree with Stasov that Serov's revisionism was simply a matter of self-glorification or the advancement of *Rogneda*'s cause. On the other hand, it is hard to deny that when Serov set about composing his Russian opera, he had it in mind to show what *Askold's Grave* could and should have been, that his purpose in his creative work, as in his journalistic activity, was partly polemical, and that he deliberately sought to provide a corrective not only to *Ruslan*, but to certain aspects of *A Life for the Tsar* as well. Serov wrote:

Askold's Grave, for all its beauties, is merely a dilettantish miscarriage when set beside the foremost operas of Europe or those of Glinka. But one cannot help agreeing with the admirers of Verstovsky's inspirations, that from the point of view of pure melodic invention he is *richer* than Glinka, that melody flows more freely in him and strikes chords within the Russian soul that Glinka never touched. In Glinka, for example, there is almost no element of *merriment*; his was chiefly an elegiac talent. Even in *Kamarinskaia* (which is a model of craftsmanship and orchestration), or even in the Trepak from *A Life for the Tsar* (at Sobinin's arrival), there is not that merriment and that bold exuberance which informs so many melodies in *Askold's Grave* (as for example Toropka's drinking song). In the expression of graceful femininity Glinka is a marvelous artist, but the chorus of the captive maidens in the third act of *Askold's Grave* (despite its rather modest polonaise format) expresses the spirit of Russian womankind no less, if not more, than the melodies of Antonida, Liudmila or Gorislava. Finally, in the role of Toropka the *gudok* player, Verstovsky captured the *humorous* strain of Russian song. This side of Russian life, and so important a one at that, remained alien to Glinka's nature because of the seriousness and melancholy of his temperament.[78]

Serov maintained that despite its technical immaturity, the derivativeness of its "dramatic" music, and its retention of the trivial style and couplet-dominated forms of the vaudeville, *Askold's Grave* nevertheless "exhibited the full measure of the gifts of a composer whose calling it was to lay before Russian opera a direct path to the truly national."[79] It is hardly a coincidence, then, that every one of the numbers from Verstovsky's opera enumerated in the foregoing citation has an exact counterpart in *Rogneda,* though that opera had not yet been envisioned at the time Serov had made his list. The merry drinking song *"Zakhodili charochki po stoliku" (The cups are passed around the table)* is mirrored in *Rogneda* by the Act III chorus, *"Pësh' charu, tak druguiu pit'" (Drink a cup then drink another)*; Verstovsky's chorus of captive maidens, *"Akh, podruzhen'ki, kak grustno" (Ah, maids, how sad it is)* is the obvious model for the entirely decorative chorus of captive maidens, *"Prizamokhli, prizatikhli" (Waving and lulling),* which opens the fourth act of Serov's opera, replete with a sentimental orchestral introduction to match Verstovsky's. And it scarcely needs pointing out that Serov's Jester, whose role is both anachronistic and disconcertingly "decorative" even in an opera so heavily reliant on genre and spectacle, is derived in every way from the figure of Verstovsky's Toropka. Nor do the borrowings stop there: the opening chorus of Act II in both operas shows a princely feast; and the scenes at the witch Skulda's cave in *Rogneda* are musically indebted to the witch scene in *Askold's Grave.*

Compared with the Verstovskian model, though, *Rogneda* seems ever to make trapping out of what had been substance, compounding yet further the already serious structural difficulties of the libretto. Toropka the *gudok* player was one of the major characters in *Askold's Grave*; the parallel character in *Rogneda,* the Jester, is there solely for the sake of the two amusing songs he sings. The chorus of captive maidens in *Askold's Grave* has a convincing internal motivation, since the plot of the opera revolved around the rescue of one of them. The parallel chorus in *Rogneda* serves no dramatic purpose at all: Serov's captive maidens have no further business in the opera than to sing it. It would seem, then, that Serov was willing to pay a high price in coherence to establish the links he sought between his opera and Verstovsky's.

And in so doing, moreover, he further alienated the "New Russian School," for whom Verstovsky's Russianness was quite spurious in its failure to distinguish between the "national" and the merely "popular" as the source of an indigenous Russian high art style. Serov shared Verstovsky's attitude on this point; indeed, he attempted to prove the genuineness of Verstovsky's musical nationalism by citing his enthusiastic public reception: "Admirers of Verstovsky's music (and there are incomparably more of them than of Glinka's)...are not wrong when they say that in *popularity* Verstovsky surpasses Glinka, that the Russian *people* (who visit the theaters) know and love *Askold's Grave* far more than *A Life for the Tsar.*"[80] An unwontedly vulgarian argument, this, and quite transparently pragmatic. In any case the "Russian people" Serov invokes here were merely the educated, theater-going population of St. Petersburg, an assemblage of aristocrats and parvenus whose aspirations and self-image were either patently cosmopolitan or else self-consciously and affectedly "Slavophile." "Folk music" for this segment of the population meant sentimental stylization of the Russian melos with a heavy infusion of gypsy elements (the so-called *russkie pesni*), most often the work of professional composers.[81]

This then, was Serov's ideal of Russian nationality in music at the time of *Rogneda,* and in this he was of one mind with, and perhaps guided by his friends among the *pochvenniki*. Grigoriev in particular was a fanatical admirer of gypsy songs, of which he became a great connoisseur and even an accomplished amateur performer to his own guitar accompaniment.[82] And it was to Grigoriev, appropriately enough, that Serov had dedicated his article on Verstovsky. The city-born and bred composer had at this time little knowledge of rural and peasant folk music, even tended to despise it, and fastened upon precisely those numbers in *Askold's Grave* that reflected the influence of "urban folk song," meanwhile ignoring those of its numbers (e.g., the unaccompanied chorus *Goi ty, Dnepr* [*Hey there, Dnieper*] in Act I) where even Verstovsky had exhibited considerable knowledge of and sensitivity to "peasant" musical culture. The *"kuchka,"* of course, was scandalized by Serov's sources and his treatment of national material in *Rogneda,* and vented its collective spleen particularly on the music of Act II, where in a drama that purported to take place in tenth-century pagan Kiev, one heard music of a kind one encountered every day on the streets of mid-nineteenth-century St. Petersburg, "in all its monstrous nakedness."[83] Of the Jester's part, Cui wrote:

> You hear it and can't believe your ears, that melodies of such banality could have been conceived by a human brain, while the Jester might have been given a completely new and original comic shading, the kind at which Dargomyzhsky is so adept. . . . The entire second act is the very apotheosis of banality and insipidity.[84]

Musorgsky, too, could not get over the fact that "at Vladimir's feast [Serov] admitted a contemporary tavern song."[85] As for the "Dance of the Skomorokhi," here, according to Cui, Serov "mixed up [even this style] with French quadrilles (the first strain) and phrases of pure Meyerbeer (the G minor strain)."[86] Recognizing that Serov drew inspiration from *Askold's Grave,* Cui insinuated that *Rogneda* was not only a retreat from Glinka's example, but even marked a retreat from Verstovsky's. Addressing the "Constant Visitor of the Russian Opera" who had come to *Rogneda*'s defense in the pages of the *Russkaia stsena,* Cui asked:

> Where do the innovations lie—in the plot? in the musical forms? or in the musical ideas? Everyone is astounded at the colossal idea of opposing paganism and Christianity.

But...*Askold's Grave* presents the same thing; consequently, Verstovsky is the real colossus, and Mr. Serov is only an imitation colossus. And in general, the plot of *Askold's Grave* represents an immense analogy to *Rogneda*. The same abduction, the same Jester striking up his song, the same witch—only better motivated in *Askold's Grave*. I do not propose to compare the music of *Askold's Grave* with that of *Rogneda*: in its forms *Askold's Grave* stands hardly higher than a vaudeville. But I would point out in passing, however, that the song *"V starinu zhivali dedy"* [*In days of yore our forefathers lived, Askold's Grave*, Act I] is no worse than the Prince's hunting song, and Toropka is far more musical than the Prince's Jester.[87]

Only two actual folk tunes can be certified in *Rogneda*: the "Dance of the Skomorokhi" (Act II) contains a passing snatch of the famous *khorovod* tune, *Kak u nashikh u vorot,* first noted down in the classic collection of Lvov and Pratsch (1790), while the Jester's song in Act III, *"Ty mne zhënka, ne perech,"* is based on a dance song *(Iz-pod duba, iz-pod viaza)* which is found in the same collection and which had been previously employed as early as 1787 by the Russian singspiel composer, Fomin, in his *Post Drivers.*[88] Serov's treatment of both recalls Glinka, not Verstovsky; the founding father's influence could not be altogether evaded after all. If we compare the Jester's song with Verstovsky's single utilization of a genuine folk song in *Askold's Grave* (Toropka's song with chorus, *"Zakhodili charochki po stoliku,"* one of the numbers cited with approval by Serov in 1862),[89] the shade of Glinka's *Kamarinskaia* is immediately evoked. For where Verstovsky was content with a simple strophic setting, Serov puts his song through a series of virtuosic variations in the orchestral accompaniment (some imitating folk instruments), for which Glinka had set the precedent.[90]

Representation of other musical "types" in *Rogneda*—the Christian hymn, the music of the pagan sacrifice, etc.—could not be drawn "from life," as it were, but had to be thought up by the composer in such a way as to evoke their subjects nonetheless. In his "Christian" music Serov sought to avoid the stereotyped "oratorio style," whose Protestant overtones had marred the characterization of the Hebrews in *Judith*. He hit instead upon what he fancied to be a "realistic" and brilliantly appropriate formula. He described it to Feofil Tolstoy in this way:

> What do you think the songs of the earliest heralds of Christianity in Russia were like? Yes indeed! That's hard to decide! So here is what I have thought up: create a mixture between the Palestrina style and our own church modes *(glasy).*[91]

Needless to say, the music of *Rogneda*'s Christians is hardly that. But it is the most original music in the opera. Absolutely diatonic and homorhythmic, it displays the oft-noted Russian knack for writing fresh-sounding music without recourse to chromaticism. A suggestion of modality plays about it, thanks to occasional cadences on the second and third degress. Also noteworthy are the pedals in the highest voice (Ex. 3.3).

The hymn quoted here on its first (orchestral) appearance in Act III is later developed into the grandiose concluding chorus in Act V. It is probably the 6/4 meter that has prompted comparison between Serov's Christians and the music of the ancient Russian *byliny* (epic songs).[92] Authentic *byliny* are not, however, characterized by such meters (nor, needless to say, by harmony-derived melody). The parallel seems better drawn with the mock-*byliny* of Rimsky-Korsakov's *Sadko,* in which a trace of Serov's influence may perhaps be detected.[93]

Ex. 3.3.   *Rogneda,* opening of Act III, melody in tenor

The Sacrifice to Perun, so often singled out for approval by otherwise hostile critics, is an effective number which sets the tone for a half-century of Russian genre music in its employment of ostinati.[94] While the "Dance Around the Altar" might have been lifted from *Robert-le-Diable,* and the diminished-seventh chord comes in for more than its usual share of abuse, there are also some rather unusual harmonic "barbarities"—a rather early instance of the deliberate cultivation of "ugliness" for the sake of realism— which found echo in later Russian operas, particularly Musorgsky's (Ex. 3.4).

Ex. 3.4.   *Rogneda,* Act I, sc. ii
[Chorus: Perun will drink (blood) and become more
benign; he is the lord, he will show mercy.]

For the supernatural element, Serov relied on *Der Freischütz,* filtered through *Askold's Grave.* Both as composer and as critic Serov lacked affinity for the "magical," and the scenes at Skulda's cave are perhaps *Rogneda's* least characteristic component. Perhaps recognizing as much himself, Serov cut the first scene of Act V from the premiere production ("He himself has no faith in the organic connections of parts in his opera," fumed Cui[95]). At any rate, the music associated in Verstovsky's opera with the witch Vakhrameevna (who conjures up Rogneda!) was Serov's starting point in his conception of Skulda, as the following pair of examples will show. The underlying model for both, of course, was Weber's "Wolf Glen" (Ex. 3.5).

The best scenes in *Rogneda* are those in which Vladimir comes into direct contact with the Christians—that is, where the surface and "Ideal" levels of the drama coincide. The finales of Acts III and V give a tantalizing hint of what *Rogneda* might have been. In them, genre music works impressively and "organically" as a backdrop to the dramatic interaction of characters. In Act III, the funeral service of the Christian pilgrims proceeds concurrently with Vladimir's troubled interrogation of the Elder in a fashion that strikingly adumbrates the monastery and death scenes in *Boris Godunov,* except that in Serov's scene background and foreground alternate rather than overlap (Ex. 3.6).

The finale of Act V pits a highly "naturalistic," fragmented treatment of the chorus (the gathering *veche,* or council[96]) against reminiscences of Vladimir's triumphal march from Act I. This episode sounded a really fresh note in Russian opera, one that had many reverberations in operas to come (Ex. 3.7, pp. 114-16).

Ex. 3.5.   a. *Rogneda,* Act I, sc. i

b. *Askold's Grave* (Moscow: A. Gutheil, n.d.), p. 78.

Ex. 3.6.   *Rogneda*, Act III, parts of Dobrynya and hunters'
chorus omitted
[Chor.: He suffered to the end.
Prince: Who are they singing about? To whom are they
singing? I am tormented by anguish and fear!
Chor.: Lord, terrible judge! By your fearful judgment . . .]

Later, the scene of Rogneda's pardon (symbolizing Vladimir's conversion) takes place against the hymn of the approaching Christians, who enter at the moment of forgiveness, their hymn growing into a general chorus that caps the opera with a monumental and satisfyingly theatrical climax signifying the triumph of the new faith. This scene has a striking analogue in Rimsky-Korsakov's *Pskovitianka* (1871), whose *veche* scene (Act I, sc. ii) begins with choral declamation and concludes with a mutineers' song that grows and finally sweeps all before it as one man after another joins up, in a manner recalling the general outlines of *Rogneda*'s closing scene no less than Rimsky's self-confessed unconscious plagiarism (in *Antar*) of the orchestral figuration at the end of *Rogneda*'s concluding hymn.[97]

Indeed, though no one derided *Rogneda* more loudly than the young composers of the Balakirev circle, they were nonetheless intrigued by many of the opera's imaginative details. Serov's score is strewn liberally with piquant, at times eccentric, harmonic and melodic turns, and these predictably attracted the *kuchkists*. For one of the outstanding attributes of *"kuchkism,"* as it was later to be defined by the group's critics, was a morbid fascination with "originality" on the smallest scale and at the most local musical levels. In his memoirs, Rimsky-Korsakov left a revealing record of his likings in *Rogneda*:

> *Rogneda* strongly interested me and a great deal in it pleased me, e.g., the witch, the idol-worshipping chorus, the chorus at the feast, the dance of the skomorokhi, the hunt prelude, the 7/4 chorus [of the hunt], and much else—in snatches. I was also pleased by the coarse

Ex. 3.7.   *Rogneda,* Act V, abridged
[Stop! Listen, they are coming!
What's in store for the people?
Look! Look! The armed guard is coming too!
And here is the Prince himself!
Greetings, Prince! Glad tidings to the bright sun!]

Ex. 3.7 (cont'd)

but colorful and effective orchestration.... I did not dare confess all this in the Balakirev circle and even, as one sincerely devoted to their ideas, abused this opera among my acquaintances. [But] I remembered a great deal, having heard the opera two or three times, and enjoyed playing excerpts from it by memory.[98]

Just how well Rimsky remembered *Rogneda* can be learned from *Sadko*, the "musical picture" that he began shortly after *Rogneda's* premiere. It was Musorgsky who spotted and "would not allow" the resemblance of one passage to *Rogneda*, asking Rimsky to "change this phrase—for God's sake as far as possible from Serov's witch"[99] (Ex. 3.8).

Musorgsky presumably had in mind the passage cited above as Example 3.5a. What is odd, however, is that Musorgsky missed the altogether obvious

Ex. 3.8.   Rimsky-Korsakov, *Polnoe sobranie sochinenii* V
(Moscow, 1963), p. 296.

Ex. 3.9.   a. Rimsky-Korsakov, *Polnoe sobranie sochinenii* V, p. 292.

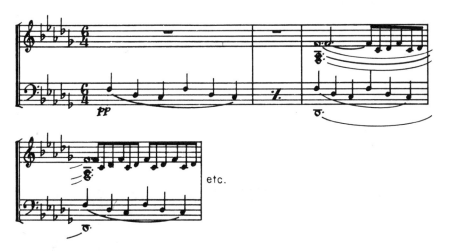

b. *Rogneda,* Act I, sc. i

resemblance between the very opening of *Sadko* and the opening of Skulda's
scene (Ex. 3.9).

Snegurochka also contains echoes of *Rogneda.* The popular "Dance of
the Skomorokhi" in Rimsky's opera owes a heavy debt to the similarly titled
number—not one of *Rogneda*'s finer pages!—that had come in, ironically, for
so much *kuchkist* abuse (Ex. 3.10).

Finally, the many oddly-metered numbers in Rimsky-Korsakov's operas,
beginning with *Snegurochka,* must owe something to the hunters' chorus in
Act III, whose 7/4 (4/4 plus 3/4) meter, by Rimsky's own testimony,
fascinated him. Here Serov had deliberately taken a step further than Glinka,
who had assayed nothing more adventurous than quintuple meter (one chorus
in each of his operas) (Ex. 3.11).

Ex. 3.10.   a. *Rogneda,* Act II

b. Rimsky-Korsakov, *Snegurochka* (Moscow, 1967), p. 275.

Ex. 3.11.   *Rogneda,* Act III, chorus parts only
[We'll hurl our spears at the bear, our faithful arrows at
the aurochs,
And for all, through all a damask sword.]

What Musorgsky picked up from *Rogneda* was even more striking, his blanket pro forma condemnation of Serov's work notwithstanding. For in the hunt prelude (Act III) we are startled to find a striking, original, and well-remembered chord progression (the oscillation of two dominant-seventh chords with roots a tritone apart), the very one on which Musorgsky was to base the "bell-ringing" ostinato in the coronation scene from *Boris,* perhaps the most famous page in all of Russian opera (Ex. 3.12).

Ex. 3.12.   *Rogneda,* Act III

With Musorgsky, similarities to Serov extend to a profounder level of musical thought than unconscious plagiarism of details, however striking. Not for nothing did Laroche note a "spiritual affinity" between the two composers (although he intended no flattery to either of them by the comparison). Serov's declamation, ridiculed and decried as it was by Cui, at times foreshadowed Musorgsky's. The Elder's recitatives in Act III are in places hardly distinguishable from Pimen's [100] (Ex. 3.13).

Ex. 3.13.   *Rogneda,* Act III
[Who is crying and moaning here? The voice is somehow known to me.
Who is this lying on the grass? O God! Ruald! What is the matter?]

The oddly placed rests and "mute endings" in some of *Rogneda's* recitatives are often naturalistic reflections of Russian speech (Ex. 3.14).

Ex. 3.14.   *Rogneda,* Act III
[Send them to Vyshgorod, to the poultry yard, for mattress-stuffing.]

And the brief passage in Act I where the chorus jeers at the prisoners from Pecheneg is an arresting anticipation of the crowd scenes in *Boris* (Ex.3.15).

Ex. 3.15.   *Rogneda,* Act I, sc. ii
[Look! There are our prisoners. Ha ha ha! What monsters!]

There was another side, however, to the *kuchka's* Serovian borrowings. As Stravinsky once remarked, the truest musical criticism is musical composition itself, and so we find, alongside the genuine (often unwitting) appropriations from *Rogneda,* a great deal of deliberate parody. The best known instance of this was Musorgsky's "Musical Pamphlet" of 1870, *Raëk (The Sideshow),* dedicated to Stasov. Here Serov takes his place alongside Zaremba,[101] Famintsyn,[102] Rostislav (Feofil Tolstoy) and the Grand Duchess Elena Pavlovna[103] in Musorgsky's series of biting vignettes. Serov is the "Titan" who bursts in upon the scene on his "emaciated Teutonic Bucephalus, under his arm a sheaf of lightning bolts ready for the press." The music that accompanies the Titan's rantings and blusterings is a cleverly wrought pastiche which shows, if nothing else, that Musorgsky knew *Rogneda* very well indeed. The Titan is heralded by the offstage trumpets that announce the triumphal entrance of Vladimir at the close of Act I; this gives way to the trumpet fanfares of the hunt prelude (Act III). The main body of the Titan's song is a ludicrously ponderous version of the Jester's trivially "vaudevillian" *Ty mne zhënka* couplets in Act III, followed by a variant of equally ludicrous frenzy. A passage from Holofernes' orgy in *Judith* is thrown in as transition to the climax where, with a prosodic clumsiness to match the original, Musorgsky cacophonously parodies the "Death to him!" chorus from the Sacrifice scene. Following this, the muse Euterpe (Elena Pavlovna) descends, and the entire company of the sideshow pays her homage in a hymn based on a reprise of the Jester's couplets.[104]

If Musorgsky's caricature of Serov and *Rogneda* seems directed more ad hominem than ad rem, the little-known operetta entitled *Bogatyri (The Heroic Warriors,* 1867) and subtitled "a musico-dramatic chronicle in five genre scenes" by Alexander Borodin in collaboration with the poet and *kuchkist* sympathizer Victor Alexandrovich Krylov, was a none-too-subtle lampoon of the whole trend *Rogneda* represented.[105] A resume of its plot will show how Krylov's libretto attempted to do for Russian legends and chronicles what Offenbach's operettas were doing for the Greek myths and their operatic offshoots.

The action takes place "in days of yore," in a certain princedom of Kurukhansk. The warrior Solovei Budimirovich, from a far-off kingdom, has fallen in love with the daughter of Prince Gustomysl, Zabava by name, and has boasted that he will abduct the princess in broad daylight "right under the noses of the good people." When the prince, the army and the people gather for a sacrifice to Perun, Solovei lulls them all to sleep with a song and steals off with Zabava. The warriors of Kurukhansk set out after the abductor. At that very moment a "numberless horde" approaches the capital—an Amazon brigade led by the warrioress Amelfa. Foma Berennikov, the head warrior of Kurukhansk who had stayed at home out of cowardice, is forced to come to the defense of the princedom. He defeats the women's army by outsmarting Amelfa. After this victory matchmakers appear at Gustomysl's court, sent by Solovei. The prince gives his blessing to Solovei and Zabava. The action concludes with a wedding feast and a general dissipated revelry.[106]

From this synopsis it is evident that the librettist's goal was not to mock the Russian epics themselves, but to spoof the stereotyped Russian genre scenes customarily portrayed on the contemporary dramatic and operatic stages. Of course *Askold's Grave* and *Rogneda* were the chief targets, but not even *Ruslan* was spared.[107] The theme of abduction is common to all three operas, but only in *Ruslan* does it take place "in broad daylight." Of the three, only *Ruslan* ends with a wedding feast. The cowardly warrior in *Bogatyri* is an obvious take-off on Pushkin-Glinka's Farlaf. On the other hand, the name of the abducted princess, Zabava—which means "fun" in Russian—is obviously derived from that of the invisible ingenue Olava in *Rogneda*. The sacrifice to Perun is another direct appropriation from Serov's opera, as is perhaps the "dissipated revelry."

Allusion to *Rogneda* is crystallized in Borodin's caricaturing use of its music. The score of *Bogatyri* is a farcical pastiche, in which only about a quarter is original music. The rest consists of parodies and straight citations from a wide variety of operas and operettas, the majority from Offenbach *(Barbe-bleu, Les Bavards, La Belle Hélène)* and the rest from Meyerbeer *(Robert-le-Diable, Le Prophète)*, Rossini *(Il Barbiere, Semiramide)*, Verdi *(Ernani)*, Hérold *(Zampa)* and other authors the *kuchka* held in low esteem.[108] The Russian school is represented by Verstovsky and Serov. The quotations are either presented exactly as in the original—in which case they are applied to action and situations with which they are wildly incongruous (e.g., the use of *Robert's* most melodramatic music to accompany a scene of domestic squabbling)—or they are distorted absurdly. It is to the latter type that most of the Serovian and Verstovskian quotations belong. (Most of these are given complete in Appendix B.) At the sacrifice to Perun, Serov's dance around the altar is turned into a ridiculous dance by Perun himself, while the populace gapes in amazement. Marked *"Tempo di polca,"* Serov's "barbaric" unison melody is given a banal harmonization and furnished with silly *"kazachok"* endings which underscore the commonplaceness of Serov's Russianisms as the *kuchka* saw them. The scoring for flute and piccolo soli accompanied by pizzicato strings and tubular bells broadly mocks Serov's "uncivilized" tutti. Serov's orgiastic hymn to Perun is parodied with a quotation of the same trivial "town song" that Serov had used in the "Dance of the Skomorokhi" (Ex. 3.16).

Ex. 3.16.   a. *Rogneda*, Act II

b. *Bogatyri,* Hymn to Perun (Sokhor, *A. P. Borodin,* p. 586)
[Ah, Perun, our Perun, we glorify thee! Ay, lyuli, lyuli,
lyuli, lyuli . . .]

The abduction scene is an even more pointed jab at *Rogneda.* The Tsaritsa Militrisa, Gustomysl's wife, bids Solovei sing, and in her order the librettist parodies the *Rogneda* Preface: "See particularly that [your song] answer to all the requirements of contemporary music, that in it you strictly observe the laws of musical truth: if you are going to sing about a wolf, then growl like a wolf; if about a frog, then croak like a frog." What Solovei then sings, though, is none other than the notorious Jester's song from Act II of *Rogneda,* Serov's *Allegro giocoso* turned into a lagging *Andante,* and the original *gusli*-like scoring replaced by soporific muted strings and sustained woodwinds. The dynamics begin at piano and make from there a steady decrescendo, while Solovei repeats hypnotically the first phrase of the Jester's song, to these words:

Za morem, za sinem	Beyond the blue sea
Opery daiutsia;	Operas are given;
V operakh premilo	In these operas most prettily
Pesen'ki poiutsia.	Little songs are sung.
Pesni eti chudno	These songs miraculously
Negu razlivaiut,	Exude the sweetest bliss,
I ot nikh nevol'no	And hearing them, involuntarily,
liudi zasypaiut . . .	People fall asleep.

Act III of *Bogatyri* is pure plotless parody. We are transported inexplicably to Gustomysl's *terem*, where, sure enough, we see the chorus of captive maidens familiar from *Rogneda* and *Askold's Grave*. This time they are lamenting neither their captivity nor their loneliness, but sheer boredom. The act begins with a verbatim quotation of Serov's chorus of captive maidens (the opening number of *Rogneda*, Act IV), followed by Militrisa's exasperated interjection, "God, how boring!" which is immediately taken up by the chorus to the tune of Verstovsky's captive maidens—"*Akh, podruzhen'ki, kak skuchno!*" Militrisa's young son Zadira tries to divert his mother with a parody of Iziaslav's song of consolation to Rogneda. Serov's cloying *Andante cantabile* melody is turned into another polka, this time marked "*Allegretto, scherzando*" and fitted out with Offenbachian chromatic roulades. Militrisa will have none of it: she breaks in after each line with an irritated "*Otstan'!*" (Get lost!). A return to the chorus of captive maidens is followed by the forced gaiety of a magnificently brainless pseudo-*Kamarinskaia*, whose text is a list of nine varieties of Russian berry. This last is finally too much for Militrisa. She flies into a rage and shouts, "Be quiet already! What is this?!... I've had it up to here!" And then she turns critic:

> You are driving me out of my mind! When, oh when will our authors stop dragging out this idiotic Russian *terem*, with its mamushkas and babushkas and captive maidens, its cherries and berries, its currants and raisins, its stupid fairy-tales and songs that drive you to distraction?!

The young *kuchkists* were not alone in their parodies of *Rogneda*. Its stereotyped Russian genre combined with the arrogant Preface made it a favorite caricaturist's butt. The humor magazine *Iskra (The Spark)* ran a series of drawings by A.I. Lebedev purporting to depict "*Rogneda, An Illustrated Musico-Dramatic Truth in Five Acts (Rhymes by D.V. Averkiev, tunes by A.N. Serov)." Budil'nik (The Alarm Clock)* parodied the libretto, having Ruald address Serov, "Tell me quick, where's Olava? Help me in my distress!" To which Serov replies, "Go ask Rostislav. I'm damned if I know!"[109]

But all such parodies and mockeries must be seen in the context of *Rogneda*'s resounding public and official success. Most critics, too, joined in the chorus of praise, at least at first. Rostislav gratified the composer by making the hoped-for comparison with *Ruslan:*

> Serov has embarked on the same path and has embarked equipped with the apparatus of German musical erudition, but has already freed himself from the influence of the *fantastic* or *fairy tale* element, embracing, if one may put it so, a *realistic-dramatic* tendency.[110]

Indicative of the inherent ambiguities of *pochvennichestvo* was the warm reception given *Rogneda* by the representatives of political reaction. The drift of these reviews, which touched little upon Serov's music, is well conveyed in the following appreciation by the minor littérateur and nobleman, Count Vladimir Alexandrovich Sollogub (1813-82):

> Serov's new opera, besides being a remarkable musical work, is a civic deed deserving of everyone's gratitude. We live in an era of doubts and hesitation [and so] one cannot help thanking Serov . . . for the underlying theme of his musical drama. A more felicitous theme we have never seen for opera. First we see before us pagan Rus', then the everyday life of ancient Rus', and all at once there blazes up in the distance the dawn of Orthodox Russia. The young Varangian [Ruald], who has sworn to kill the Kievan prince . . . saves his enemy from certain death and dies for him. Who brought about such a miracle? God! What God? The Christian God! The God of love and forgiveness. The God of the future Orthodoxy. . . . This scene will always remain an ornament of the Russian theater. In it there is so much religious faith, submission and withal, so much compelling force. . . . This scene, we repeat, is a civic deed. . . . Nowadays it is a great service to have stirred in the spectators such feelings of love, reconciliation and self-sacrifice.[111]

The "nowadays" of which Sollogub speaks was the troubled time that immediately followed upon the abolition of serfdom. In such a period it is easy to see why the aristocracy (and the Tsar himself) should have seized upon a dramatic representation with a theme like *Rogneda*'s. Great Prince Vladimir Sviatoslavich was not only the Christianizer of Russia, he was also the unifier and consolidator of the Kievan state. The existence of the Russian *samoderzhavie* (autocracy) as a political force in the world dates from his reign. The words Averkiev fit to Serov's concluding chorus seem to justify Sollogub's interpretation of the opera's "underlying theme":

Pokoris' krestu, prosviati narod,	Submit to the cross, consecrate thy people,
Veru pravuiu utverdiv zemle.	Affirming the true faith to all the land.
I vragam grozna, i na vek slavna	And awesome to her enemies, and in eternal glory,
Sviatorusskaia budet zhit' zemlia	The holy Russian land will ever live.

Once again it is easy to see evidence here of Serov's alleged pandering. But who was exploiting whom? The conservative press had attempted the same assertion of proprietary rights over *A Life for the Tsar,*[112] and would do so again when it came to Rubinstein's "Biblical operas."

Rogneda's production was one of its greatest assets and called forth the praise even of one as reluctant as V.V. Stasov. Historical verisimilitude was sought as far as possible, and counting with good reason on a smashing success, the Imperial Theaters Directorate was for once relatively generous in allotting funds.[113] This lavishness (the lighting and scenery changes alone were given forty rehearsals) provoked much jealous comment, including the oft-quoted remark by Dargomyzhsky to Serov that "your operas cannot fail: in one you have camels, in the other you have dogs."[114] The quest for "realism" was not without obstacles: it was only after the most strenuous effort that Serov was able to persuade the Directorate to allow the dancing girls in Act II to wear sarafans instead of the tutus that were mandatory for the dancers even in *Askold's Grave*. But in the end the costumes of *Rogneda*'s first production were able to withstand the scrutiny of even the most exacting Russian antiquarians. Stasov, who possessed eminent credentials both as antiquarian and as realist, wrote a long and largely approving review of certain aspects of the production in which, to one's disappointment, he carefully refrained from comment on Serov's music save the sardonic complaint that such laudable treatment had been wasted on so undeserving an object. Having divided the costumes into three groups—the historically accurate (the main characters); the wholly inacccurate (the chorus in its various roles); and the "invented"(the priests and acolytes, the Jester and the skomorokhi)—Stasov proceeded to analyze the last group in a manner that cleverly praised the production at the expense of the opera itself:

> In tenth-century Rus' there were no high priests for performing sacrifices, nor was the Tsar entertained by jesters. The authors of *Rogneda* apparently did not know this but, on the basis of universally accepted operatic principles, they considered it necessary to decorate the opera with idol-worshipping dances and a ballet (that eternal operatic commonplace), and therefore they needed priests and skomorokhi. What can a person do, even if he *knows* that this is all a fabrication, and that nothing of the sort had been in reality? Naturally there is only one thing to do—invent. That is what the costumeur did: his priests came out entirely conventional, but what of it? That is how it should be. If the librettists of the opera had no thought in their heads beyond the stock figures of Italian opera, then he could boldly content himself with costumes of the same order. Nothing better is needed.... The costumeur simply gathered up anything that came to hand: he brought in the ubiquitous fool's cap, rattle and jingles, our festival masks...and out of all this he fashioned the motliest, most unprecedented mishmash, which has nothing at all to do with historical fact and which offends the eye of anyone with the slightest sophistication. But what else do you need? In *Rogneda* the jester sings the most trivial, absolutely tasteless songs on motives of the very *latest,* not to say contemporary times, the skomorokhi dance to the strains of similar tunes—why should the costumes be any better, any more sensible?[115]

In Stasov's view, then, the designer (V.A. Prokhorov) was Serov's most trenchant critic. This rather restrained article was not Stasov's only public pronouncement on the subject of *Rogneda*. But it was the only one that was printed over his signature. Stasov's hatred of *Rogneda* was not founded merely on the opera's shortcomings. His rage took on a special virulence because he perceived the opera—correctly—as Serov's ultimate polemic against *Ruslan*. No article of Serov's had made critics write of the "end of the Glinka era," and yet his opera had done just that. Shortly after *Rogneda*'s premiere, in 1866, *Ruslan* finally achieved its long-awaited revival after the disastrous fire of 1859, and so the two operas could be viewed side by side. This circumstance brought about a reopening of the dormant feud between

Fig. 3.4   Stasov in the 1860s

Serov and the "Ruslanists." A.A. Gozenpud has rightly observed that "the bitterness of the dispute was the result of its being, for Serov, primarily a quarrel about *Rogneda,* while for the *kuchkists* it involved the resurrection of Glinka's position in history."[116]

It was Stasov who fired the most hostile salvo in the little war, since it was he who wrote the only article to compare *Rogneda* and *Ruslan* directly. "Would You Believe It?" *(Verit' li?),* which took the form of a letter to "***" (Cui's siglum in the *Sanktpeterburgskie vedomosti*), was published in Cui's paper on March 16, 1866. It was so insulting to Serov that Stasov hid behind a pseudonym—"M.S."—although there was never any doubt as to the author's identity. Stasov addressed himself to a question Cui had raised in an article of his own: why had *Rogneda* so smashingly succeeded where the newly-revived *Ruslan* had failed? Stasov's predictable answer was couched in terms so malicious as to border on libel. The *Ruslan* controversy had been going against him, after all, and Stasov dropped all pretense of a reasoned defense of Glinka's opera, lashing out wildly instead, first at the public, then at "its representatives the feuilletonists," and finally at the Antichrist himself in his incarnations both as critic and as composer. Although Stasov's arguments are scarcely distinguished for their logic (indeed, for the sake of exposing *Rogneda*'s repetition of all *Ruslan*'s alleged faults, Stasov quite effectively, if unwittingly, demolishes Glinka's opera), it is a major document, not only because of its focal position in the "War of the Russian Operatic Succession," but for the vivid and candid glimpse it affords of Stasov the strident polemicist and fearsome verbal brawler, which none of his better known essays can match. The concluding pages of "Would You Believe It?," in short, are simply too good to miss:

> To those individuals who have complained about the arias and suchlike in Glinka's opera, I would say: "And why have you never complained not only at the arias in Rossini, Bellini, or Verdi, but even in Meyerbeer, and, finally, in Mr. Serov's latest work? None of them is short on such goods." They go on: "What about Finn's ballad, what about the Head-chorus and such, which unmercifully force Ruslan or whoever is present to languish interminably; what should he do at such times, where can he hide himself, what business can he devise?" Yes, I say, that's true, and I am sorry indeed that Glinka's opera has such flaws and faults; but I would turn the question back upon them: "And why do you see twigs in Glinka, but not the logs in all the rest of those operas that everyone praises and raves about?" Thus, without even mentioning examples from bygone times, but focusing instead only on what is happening now before our eyes, I would ask: "And what are the other characters on stage supposed to be doing while Holofernes sings his aria, Vagao and Avra their songs, Iziaslav his ditty, Rogneda her ballad, her ladies-in-waiting their choruses, or while the maidens dance their khorovod and the skomorokhi do their dance?"
>
> No, this is poor reasoning, logic without coherence—it's hard to credit it. No, it is not for the libretto that *Ruslan* is unloved, not for the content, for the formal conventions, for the insufficiency of action that the opera is damned: the public and the feuilletonists have never even seen the opposite qualities, or at the very least, have seen them but not noticed. In

short, they have never needed them before. No, one must seek elsewhere for the reason for this antipathy on the part of the masses toward this great Glinka opera. All of the above is a mere dodge, a pretext, an excuse. The real reasons, in my opinion, are altogether different.

In the first place, in all the highest and best that Glinka has created (and this includes practically all of *Ruslan*), Italianism is no more, nor is there any other kind of stale, easily accessible banality: everything breathes poetry and profound original creativity. This the crowd will not soon forgive. In order to feel satisfaction, delight, enthusiasm, it needs pitiful, miserable things like the "Dance of the Skomorokhi," like Ruald's duet with the Elder, like the pilgrim choruses.

To go on: the expression of all emotions and feelings is too truthful in Glinka, too full of inspiration and genuine beauty. This, too, is useless to the majority of the public; they can't tolerate the astounding truth and beauty of Bayan's, Finn's, Ruslan's and Ratmir's recitatives: there is nothing colorless, habitual or customary about them. The public is happy only when the characters drawl, howl and mumble like Vladimir, Rogneda and the hermit do in the new opera.

Further, Glinka has such creative penetration and is so suffused with ancient national coloring, that he is far too rich for the stomachs of our "melomanes" (as our joker Rostislav calls them). Have they ever felt the full force of the depiction of the old-Slavic, pagan world in *Ruslan,* probably the most inspired, most brilliant creation in all Russian art? Have they been shaken by the beauty and tender atmosphere of the oriental pictures that Glinka has drawn? They need something cruder, something more ordinary. They will find their true nationalism in "Troikas" and "Sarafans". [The invidious reference is to the popular romances of Varlamov and Gurilev.] They have never needed such truth, such beauty, such an ambience [Stasov deliberately uses Grigoriev's word, *veianie*] of history. Not only do they not perceive insipidity, they positively rejoice in it. They imagine that a man who plays at composing need only to wish it, and he can create real Assyrian, Hebrew, Indian, Russian, or whatever style music he wants. That is why all of them together, these "melomanes," do not suspect that in these horribly trivial and tasteless "skomorokhi dances," jester's songs, etc.—in a word, in all of *Rogneda*—there is as much genuine Russian character, as much of ancient pagan Rus', as there is true Italian character in [Auber's] *Fenella* [*La muette de Portici*], Swiss in [Rossini's] *Guillaume Tell,* modern Russian in [Meyerbeer's] *L'Etoile du Nord,* or old German in Gounod's *Faust.*

Finally, Glinka's characters are presented too truly, too completely; they are drawn accurately down to their last hair. There is too much that is profoundly and genuinely dramatic in them. Just look: Farlaf, Ruslan, Ratmir, Susanin—what artfully fashioned, sharply profiled personalities and characters these are! Each of them is a complete, whole picture. Each of them embodies his era and his nationality. Most of the public have no need of such truth, fidelity or profundity; they recognize as wholly satisfactory and artfully realized the dramas and personalities of Mr. Serov, whose men are all women and whose women men. The former do nothing but drink and lurch about, the latter are always running around with swords and cutting off heads.

After all this I ask: in what, then, did the "Glinka period" consist? In the fact that it never existed? In the fact that, despite the work of a new and original composer of genius, the public as a whole has retained all its old tastes and ideas, changed not one iota and continued to love nonsense both old and new, to take delight in old and new trivialities? No, eras that carry the imprint of a given personality are not made that way. For example, the Rossinian, Verdian and Meyerbeerian periods—now these really did exist, without doubt. The work of these men, whatever its quality, did please *everyone,* attract *everyone,* suited *everyone*'s taste. They were the grounds for the intoxication and joy of *all* their contemporaries; they found dozens of imitators. Was there anything like this in the case of Glinka (except for his bad music)? Who was happy with it? Whose thoughts and feelings did his music modify, exalt or broaden? For whom among the public did it open a new path? Did anyone dare compare Glinka with even the most absurd and insignificant of the Italians, let alone the recognized "classical" authorities—Meyerbeer, Spontini, Cherubini, Spohr, Auber. No, at best Glinka was considered a *tolerable* composer, and only in private, and even then half out of simple patriotism. This means that he founded a "period"?

No, this is not the end of the Glinka period, nor is it the "beginning of Russian art" (as one paper would have it), but simply the appearance in the theater once again of that which again pleases everyone, fills everyone's needs and suits everyone's taste.

The Russian operatic public of today can be divided into two groups, like all European publics. One consists of people at the very lowest level of development, devoid of taste and understanding in equal measure and therefore up to their ears in the most pitiful, routine and cynical music: Italian. These people have no discrimination and, save the emptiest tunes and the most meaningless titillation, music is for them an impenetrable forest. The opposite group consists of people who are able to understand and love real art in all its exaltation and greatness, and can be satisfied only with such works as show real talent, truth and beauty. Between these two extremes we find the great majority, which consists of those who have nothing against the good but who also delight in the bad, who applaud works of genius but are moved to tears also by the uninspired. These are the people who are always ready to call Shakespeare great, but who lose sleep over Dumas as well, who give the palm to Rachel [Elisa Rachel Félix (1820-1858), French dramatic actress], but also to the most raucous bellower worthy only of Verdi's music, who will agree that Beethoven was a genius, but that so was Flotow.

This is the crowd, "neither fish nor fowl," who took Meyerbeer to its bosom. This musician unites a great quantity of the most diverse qualities; in him alone is combined the whole range of what any immature taste demands: decorativeness, effects every minute, the most ordinary Italian and French melodies and roulades, declamation without inner truth but full of rhetoric and affectation, occasional seriousness of intention and form, but more often vulgarity and banality; finally, accessibility and ease of comprehension, and all of it flooded with external, absolutely superficial, brassy brilliance and dandyism. How all this is bound to please the majority! This crowd, this majority, delighted with Meyerbeer's operas, is at the same time delighted with itself. They proudly proclaim: "Oh, we are not like those other poor souls who have no understanding of music! We are much higher indeed; we comprehend drama, we understand truth. Give us a 'page of history' in music; we nourish ourselves on the profoundest emotion." And preening themselves in their self-satisfaction, these people go and hear Meyerbeerian operas, fancying that they contain all that they boast of. But what must have been the joy of our public when in their midst appeared their very own Meyerbeer! Because without doubt Mr. Serov is of the purest Meyerbeerian strain, the most Meyerbeerian spiritual makeup, and if he once was given to attacking that musician, it was nothing more than a pure misunderstanding. Just like Meyerbeer, he thinks only of effects calculated to please the crudest taste. Just like Meyerbeer, he is inclined toward creating music of the most vacuous and trivial nature. Just like Meyerbeer, he has no gift for expression of the soul, its transports, sensations, joys and tears. He has no gift for portraying the merest jot of our inner spiritual world, no gift for creating even a single character. In his indifferent eclecticism he is equally ready to undertake the portrayal of any nation, epoch or scene. The whole difference between the two composers is only that Meyerbeer has nonetheless several times Serov's command of musical technique and form, as well as more imagination and, finally, that Meyerbeer's Italianate roulades are replaced in Serov's work by "dramatics" à la Verdi, and the old-fashioned French forms are replaced with the newfangled mannerisms and rhetoric of Liszt and Wagner, along with all the beauties of our Russian romance-makers. But it is obvious that precisely this is what our public demands and we see those same people who found a treasure trove of poesy in

Alicia's "Grâce" [*Robert-le-Diable*], the love duet of Valentina and Raoul and the profound historicity of the blessing of the swords in *Les Huguenots,* now melting with delight and happiness when they listen to similar but homegrown miracles. We now have our own "pages of history" marvelously expressed in music. We have our own conspiracies, our own brilliant "juxtapositions," feasts, marches, hunts, hymns! Naturally, we will soon likewise have our own simulated fires on stage, skeleton dances, resurrections from the grave and ice skating, and then we really will have no further cause to envy Europe its music. How much inspiration, invention, creative force there is in everything our Russian Meyerbeer has done! What blissful momements the multitude experiences, absorbing these precious sounds! And how could it be otherwise, when the composer has taken care to please everyone? See for yourself—there is nothing missing from Mr. Serov's new opera: requiems, hymns and the conversion of Russian for pious souls; hunts and carousals for merry bons vivants; popular councils and verdicts for Slavophiles and *pochvenniki;* Verdiisms for the "melomanes"; counterpoint and combinations of themes for scholars and pedagogues. To each his own pleasure, and everyone is happy, and grateful, and moved, and see how they applaud!

How can one even think of real music here, the kind where there are no crude effects, where there is no more nonsense and banality, where the author has not even given a thought to the question of becoming the public's pet?[117]

"So I'm a second Meyerbeer, it seems," Serov's friend Konstantin Zvantsev recalled his exclaiming on reading these lines. "Je ne demande pas mieux! Thank God there is at least a Meyerbeer in Russia!"[118] But of course he *had* wanted more: he had wanted to play Gluck to Glinka's Piccini, and he wanted to create a native Russian equivalent to Wagner's total art work. These goals he had fallen far short of achieving, and Serov had to own as much. A letter written at the very height of *Rogneda's* triumph unexpectedly reveals that:

From my inner viewpoint as an artist, I am still dissatisfied both with *Judith* and with *Rogneda,* notwithstanding the incredible success of the latter opera. ... With regard to my ideals they have been mere "experiments"—tests of style, means and artistic skills.[119]

There is more here than the usual conceited humility of the "successful" artist. For in fact Serov did not follow up on *Rogneda* with more Meyerbeerian spectacle out of Russian history, as he might have been reasonably expected to do. *Rogneda* was for its creator, no less than for Russian opera generally, a cul-de-sac.

In this the opera shared the fate of the movement that had spawned it. As an identifiable faction *pochvennichestvo* did not survive the mid-sixties. Grigoriev died, the Dostoevsky journals folded, and it was as if the movement had never been. Its demise was determined not so much by these outward events, though, as by its own internal contradictions and ambivalences, of which it was as full as *Rogneda.* Toward the end of his life a disillusioned Grigoriev wrote a series of essays in which he identified himself with Turgenev's ineffectual "superfluous man"—one of the literary archetypes of the period. It was a fitting epitaph for *pochvennichestvo* and for *Rogneda* as well. Serov had scored a colossal public succcess with his work perhaps, but it was a success only with those who did not count for him. Particularly bitter was the total rejection of Serov and his work by Stasov, his former bosom-friend. The very last preserved letter in the famously voluminous Stasov-Serov correspondence is separated from its nearest neighbor by some years. Dated October 13, 1865, it is an agonized refusal to send Stasov and Balakirev passes to *Rogneda*'s dress rehearsals, and—most poignant of all—it retains the familiar form of the second person (as great a rarity in Serov's mature correspondence as it was in Stasov's), testifying to the relationship they once had shared.

> At rehearsals of my opera I generally meet either people connected with the theater, or those sympathetic to me and my work. The two of you fall under neither category. If there were in you but a drop left of the sympathy that brought us together—*a quarter of a century ago*. ... But if you and Balakirev are running to the rehearsals of *Rogneda* just to be able to jeer at it in the presence of the composer, then that is first of all inhumane—I have enough worries without you—and in the second place, there will be time enough for that at the performance.[120]

In all the leading musical circles of St. Petersburg, from Rubinstein and the Conservatory to the young *"Balakirevtsy," Rogneda* cost Serov ground he had won with *Judith*. Having wished to assert musical leadership, Serov found himself more than ever before an outsider. Having wished to embody in tones the most idealistic of contemporary aesthetic attitudes, he found himself branded a panderer and a debaser of art. He became in effect Russia's "superfluous man" of music, and has remained so in history. But his fate, and that of his work, should not blind us to his prominence in the Russian musical world of the 1860s, when he alone among Russian musicians played a noteworthy role in the broader intellectual realm, and played it most effectively. Even if in some ways only by negative example, *Rogneda* exercised a considerable spur on the emergence of the "classic" Russian opera of the final third of the nineteenth century.

Notes

1. Rostislav (Feofil Tolstoi) in *Golos* (1865), no. 311.

2. V.F. Odoevskii, *Muzykal'no-literaturnoe nasledie* (Moscow, 1956), p. 342.

3. Serov to M.P. Anastasieva, January 11, 1866. V.S. Baskin, *A.N. Serov* (Moscow, 1890), p. 84.

4. Its last production was in Ekaterinburg during the season 1917-18. For obvious reasons having to do with its libretto, *Rogneda* has been dropped from the Soviet repertory.

5. Strakhov, *The World as a Whole,* quoted in V.V. Zenkovsky, *A History of Russian Philosophy,* trans. George L. Kline, vol. I (New York, 1953), p. 409.

6. Their insistence on the primacy of "shared roots in a common soil" over "artificial" divisions like social classes earned the *pochvenniki* a reputation for conservatism and the enmity of "progressive" thinkers of their own time and since. See U. Guralnik, *"Sovremennik* v bor'be s zhurnalami Dostoevskogo," *Izvestiia Akademii Nauk SSSR, otdelenie literatury i iazyka* 9 (1950), pp. 265-85.

7. Quoted in Zenkovsky, p. 414.

8. Grigoriev, "Paradoxes of Organic Criticism," quoted in D.S. Mirsky, *A History of Russian Literature* (New York, 1958), p. 219.

9. Cf. Stasov, *Sobrannye sochineniia III* (St. Petersburg, 1894), p. 275. Stasov used the term perfectly knowingly to portray Wagner as a sinister political force.

10. See Vera Nechaeva, *Zhurnal M.M. i F.M. Dostoevskikh "Epokha"* (Moscow, 1975), p. 171. The *Moskvitianin,* founded by the Slavophile historian Mikhail Pogodin and edited by Grigoriev from 1850 to 1856, might be looked upon as the prototype for the Dostoevskys' *pochvennik* journals. For more on the *Moskvitianin,* see Chapter 4.

11. "Parizhskii Feofilych," *Teatral'nyi i muzykal'nyi vestnik* (1860), no. 9. A long extract from this article is given above in Chapter 2.

12. See Serov to M.P. Anastasieva, July 25, 1862 *(Russkaia starina* 21 [1878], p. 165), where Grigoriev is credited with the following remark to the Dostoevsky brothers: "Herzen [Alexander Herzen (1812-70), the writer and political exile] is wrong to say that art has died in our time. Death is a good thing for art if it means writing such things as Ostrovsky's plays or *Judith."*

13. Serov to D.I. Lobanov, one of his librettists: "If you listen to Grigoriev's ravings (even if you attribute as much as half of his praises to the influence of alcohol), it would appear that in tragic power, in holiness and in beauty of sound I have surpassed Weber and Wagner and Glinka and everybody. But I cannot help seeing that Grigoriev has gotten carried away and, in particular, is not strong enough in purely musical matters" (D.I. Lobanov, *A.N. Serov i ego sovremenniki* [St. Petersburg, 1889], p. 31).

14. Indeed, it is treated as such in B.F. Egorov's article on Grigoriev in A. Ya. Al'tshuler, ed., *Ocherki istorii russkoi teatral'noi kritiki* (Leningrad, 1976), esp. pp. 44-45. This is a literary, not a musicological, essay.

15. *Iakor'* (1863), no. 12, p. 223.

16. Ibid., p. 222.

17. Ibid., p. 223. Compare this with Serov's summary of the Wagnerian reform given in "Parizhskii Feofilych." That these remarks were beyond the musically naive Grigoriev's independent judgment is amply suggested by such incompetent and tautological observations of his as this: "Since Serov's music drama contains nothing conventional, one cannot call the... scene between Judith and Avra [Act II] a duet, although it sometimes becomes something resembling one."

18. *Iakor'* (1863), no. 13, pp. 243-44, condensed. It is noteworthy that as early as 1842 Serov had sketched an "Outline for a Dissertation on the Subjective and Objective in Music" (published in *Muzykal'noe nasledstvo I* [Moscow, 1962], pp. 190-91).

19. Cf. Donald Fanger, *Dostoevsky and Romantic Realism* (Chicago, 1965), p. vii.

20. V.V. Zenkovsky actually renders the word *pochvennichestvo* as "the cult of primitive immediacy" (*History of Russian Philosophy I*, Chapter 14).

21. Grigoriev returned to these themes and amplified them in an article entitled "The Russian Theater," which he contributed to the maiden issue of *Epokha*. Despite its title, this was a review primarily of opera. Attempting to bring his ideas into line with the more "progressive" thinking of the day, Grigoriev declared himself, as his "profession de foi," to be a "democrat" in matters theatrical and operatic, and went on to aver that "as a democrat I am, it goes without saying, a Wagnerian, for the principle that opera is drama—of which Wagner is the highest and at the same time the purest representative in our time—is a wholly democratic principle which alienates the enjoyment of dilettantes and gives enjoyment to the masses." This will be worth remembering when dealing with the charges made against *Rogneda* that it pandered opportunistically to public taste. Grigoriev's rather long-winded article is reprinted in Tamara Livanova, *Opernaia kritika v Rossii II*, part 4 (Moscow, 1973), pp. 314-29.

22. *Iakor'* (1863), no. 28. Reprinted in A.N. Serov, *Kriticheskie stat'i III* (St. Petersburg, 1892), p. 1542.

23. Ibid., pp. 1541-42.

24. Quoted in Valentina Serova, *Serovy, A.N. i V.A.: Vospominaniia* (St. Petersburg, 1914), pp. 86-87.

25. Serov's correspondence with Varvara Zhukova on *Judith* is revealing in this connection. Even before his first opera was staged in St. Petersburg, Serov was looking ahead to its productions in Western Europe. Because of the quality of its singers and orchestra, he felt the Vienna opera to be "my ideal for the performance of *Judith*" (July 3, 1862). Still thoroughly cosmopolitan in his aspirations, Serov went so far as to assert that "*Judith* will surely find a *more* sympathetic reception in Germany than in St. Petersburg. There they have had time to accustom themselves to the strictest dramatic ideals and to the enormous demands on the *attention span* imposed by a through-composed A-to-Z musical drama, that is, a vocal-orchestral symphony" (September 8, 1862). And therefore, "As soon as the opera is produced on the Russian operatic stage, I shall immediately arrange to have its text translated into German (for Vienna, mainly) and into French—for Brussels. It is my good fortune that a Biblical subject is at home everywhere and is nowhere an impediment." There is even a kind of negative echo of Grigoriev in Serov's observation that "with *Ivan Susanin* and *Ruslan* it's another story; they are too strongly bound to *the soil*" (see *Sovetskaia muzyka* (1954), no. 7, pp. 69, 71).

26. *Russkaia starina* 21 (1874), p. 370.

27. Ibid., p. 369.

28. Musorgsky, for example, admitted *Judith* to have been "the first seriously conceived Russian opera since [Dargomyzhsky's] *Rusalka*" (M.P. Musorgsky, *Literaturnoe nasledie I* [Moscow, 1971], p. 64).

29. See Stasov to Balakirev, May 17, 1863 (*M.A. Balakirev i V.V. Stasov: Perepiska I* [Moscow, 1970], p. 202). Stasov names Serov's confidante, Maria Pavlovna Mavromikhaili (Anastasieva), as his source of information.

30. V.S. Serova, *Serovy*, p. 65.

31. "Podlinnaia avtobiograficheskaia zapiska A.N. Serova" (An Authentic Autobiographical Note by A.N. Serov), in Serov, *Izbrannye stat'i I* (Moscow, 1950), p. 75. Serov's choice of words is symptomatic. Instead of the usual words for "national" and "native" (*natsional'nyi,*

narodnyi), he uses the word *pochvennyi,*—in normal usage an agronomist's word—which is derived, like the name of the movement to which the composer allied himself, from "soil." Similarly, in an article on musical education in Russia ("Muzyka, muzykal'naia nauka, muzykal'naia pedagogika"), which was based on a series of lectures he delivered in 1864 and adapted for publication serially in Dostoevsky's *Epokha,* Serov consistently refers to "folk music" not by the normal and universally accepted term, *narodnaia muzyka,* but by a special coinage, *"pochvennaia muzyka"* (Cf. Serov, *Izbrannye stat'i II* (Leningrad, 1957), pp. 187-89.

32. For details, including the relevant passages in the original old Russian, see Ad. Stender-Petersen, *Anthology of Old Russian Literature* (New York, 1954), pp. 20-22.

33. Summary conflated from abstracts of various Kievan texts by A.V. Arkhipova and A.E. Khodorova in K.F. Ryleev, *Polnoe sobranie stikhotvorenii* (Leningrad, 1971), p. 117; and in George Vernadsky, *Kievan Russia* (New Haven, 1948), p. 57.

34. Serov, *Izbrannye stat'i I,* p. 75. Maikov had previously helped Serov polish the text of *Judith.*

35. Averkiev later collaborated with Anton Rubinstein on *Goryusha* (1889). His *Frol Skobeev* much later furnished the literary source for the comic opera of the same name by Tikhon Khrennikov.

36. *Sochineniia M.N. Zagoskina VI* (St. Petersburg and Moscow: M.O. Vol'f, 1901), pp. 302-6. This Norse ballad, with its references to Odin, Valhalla, Valkyries, etc., may well have been one of the main attractions of the Rogneda story in Zagoskin's version for the sometime Wagnerian Serov, though it did not find its way into the opera.

37. This episode takes place in Book III, chapter 4 of Zagoskin's novel (Vol'f edition, pp. 256-66). Up to this point Duleb had been wandering rather aimlessly in and out of the action in search of Lyubasha, much as Ruald does in the opera.

38. This concerns the rescue from Prince Vladimir's clutches of the captive maiden Nadezhda by the noble youth Vseslav, aided by the minstrel Toropka.

39. It seems evident, for example, that the direct juxtaposition of a pilgrims' chorus and a royal hunt in Act III was a possibly unconscious emulation of *Tannhäuser* (Act I, sc. ii).

40. The Pilgrim Elder and the pagan High Priest do not seem to be drawn from any literary source, but were standard operatic types (in the case of the High Priest, quite ahistorical).

41. It was this external element that Serov was inclined to emphasize in discussions of his work in progress, for it was chiefly this that set his work apart from Glinka's. "I've found a Russian subject for my lyric drama," he announced to Feofil Tolstoy (Rostislav). "It won't be anything like *Ruslan!* . . . I am choosing ancient, uncivilized, pagan Russia. And there can't be any sentimentalizing here; even the melodies of the Perun worshippers will have to be coarse and uncouth" *(Russkaia starina* 21 [1874], p. 369). When the time came, Rostislav echoed this line faithfully in his reviews of *Rogneda,* where he contrasted the idyllic, fairy-tale world of Glinka with Serov's "realistic-dramatic art" (see Tamara Livanova, *Opernaia kritika v Rossii II,* part 3, p. 382).

42. Serov, *Izbrannye stat'i II,* pp. 63-65.

43. We might note, though, that this method had a prestigious precedent in Russia: Glinka had collaborated in precisely this way with Baron Rozen, his librettist in *A Life for the Tsar.*

44. Serov, *Izbrannye stat'i I,* p. 75.

45. V.S. Serova, *Serovy*, pp. 45-46.

46. All manuscripts in the possession of Serov's widow were destroyed by fire in the summer of 1886. If Serov and Stasov had not become such bitter enemies by the end of Serov's lifetime, this probably would not have happened, since Stasov would then have collected the manuscripts in due course for preservation in the archives he supervised in the Imperial (now Saltykov-Shchedrin) Public Library. Cf. Findeisen, *A.N. Serov*, p. 61.

47. A full synopsis of the libretto and a list of the musical numbers is given in Appendix A.

48. See K.F. Ryleev, *Polnoe sobranie stikhotvorenii* (Leningrad, 1971), pp. 117-23.

49. Serov worked his "exposition" of Rogneda's history into Rogneda's monologue in Act I, sc. i. This was an afterthought, interpolated after the first performance.

50. Cf. Findeisen, p. 113.

51. Cf. the review by Tsezar' Kiui *(Sanktpeterburgskie vedomosti* [1864], no. 87), reprinted in Kiui, *Muzykal'no-kriticheskie stat'i I* (Petrograd, 1918), pp. 54-55. Cui did not hesitate, even on this much acquaintance with the music of *Rogneda,* to assert that it failed to come up to the level of *Judith.*

52. Nechaeva, *Zhurnal Dostoevskikh,* p. 173.

53. Other alterations made after the premiere in the interests of tightening the plot included Rogneda's "expository" aria to the witch in Act I, sc. i, which uses the same music as her monologue in Act IV (Cui: "The witch must know all this, since she *is* a witch; as for the public, this is, to say the least, neither the time nor the place for this narrative." [*Sanktpeterburgskie vedomosti* (1866), no. 327]), and the transferral of Vladimir's lines forgiving Rogneda from before to after the entrance of the Pilgrim Elder in Act V, thus rather neatly tying all of the opera's "themes" together.

54. *Sanktpeterburgskie vedomosti* (1866), no. 327.

55. P.I. Chaikovskii, *Muzykal'no-kriticheskie stat'i* (Moscow, 1953), p. 48.

56. *Sanktpeterburgskie vedomosti* (1865), no. 292.

57. Reprinted in Serov, *Izbrannye stat'i I,* pp. 357-87.

58. See Livanova, *Opernaia kritika v Rossii II,* part 3 (Moscow, 1969), p. 381.

59. *Russkaia stsena* (1865), no. 12. For the tableau vivant, at least, Serov was not to blame. Objections had been raised by the censor against showing a dagger raised onstage against even a tenth-century Tsar. The tableau vivant, showing Vladimir's prophetic dream, was introduced to divert the audience's attention from Rogneda (see Findeisen, p. 117).

60. *Russkaia stsena* (1865), no. 14.

61. Serov had been much impressed by a similar device in *A Life for the Tsar,* and had devoted a whole article to tracing prefigurements of the choral epilogue ("Slavsia") throughout the opera ("Opyty tekhnicheskogo kritiki nad muzykoiu M.I. Glinki: Rol' odnogo motiva v tseloi opere 'Ivan Susanin,' " *Izbrannye stat'i II* pp. 35-43).

62. *Russkaia stsena* (1865), no. 14.

63. *Russkaia stsena* (1865), no. 12.

64. *Russkaia stsena* (1865), no. 13.

65. Chaikovskii, *Muzykal'no-kriticheskie stat'i,* pp. 47-48. Rogneda's main faults, as Tchaikov-

sky enumerated them, were "the poverty of melodic inspiration, the crude decorativeness of the harmony and instrumentation, the absence of organic connection between separate numbers, [and] the utter feebleness of the recitatives with regard to the demands of true declamation."

66. V.S. Serova, *Serovy*, p. 73.

67. Newmarch, *The Russian Opera* (New York, 1914), p. 155.

68. Thus Richard Anthony Leonard in his widely-consulted *History of Russian Music* (New York, 1957): "The popularity of Serov's operas can be explained only by the way the composer had his eye firmly fixed on the 'grand' operas of Meyerbeer. His procedure is reminiscent of Wagner's in *Rienzi*, the imitation of Meyerbeer which had once captivated Germany like an operatic circus" (p. 71).

69. Serov, *Izbrannye stat'i I*, p. 374.

70. Ibid., pp. 374-75.

71. *Sanktpeterburgskie vedomosti* (1865), no. 292.

72. Quoted in A.A. Gozenpud, *Russkii opernyi teatr XIX veka II* (Leningrad, 1971), p. 36.

73. V.S. Serova, *Serovy*, p. 74.

74. "Russkii teatr," *Epokha* (1864), no. 2 (dated March 4, 1864), in Livanova, *Opernaia kritika v Rossii, II*, part 4, p. 326.

75. The term is Gozenpud's (see *Russkii opernyi teatr II*, p. 66).

76. This and the next two citations from *Sanktpeterburgskie vedomosti*, (1865), no. 292.

77. March 30, 1865. *M.A. Balakirev i V.V. Stasov, Perepiska I*, p. 241. Serov's lectures were frequently reported in the *pochvennik* journals. See, for instance, Averkiev's review of several in *Iakor'* (1863), no. 33.

78. Serov, *Izbrannye stat'i II*, p. 47.

79. Ibid.

80. Ibid., p. 46.

81. A good example is Varlamov's *Krasnyi sarafan (The Red Sarafan)*, which educated Russian city-dwellers are apt to take for a genuine folk song to this day.

82. Regardless of their origin, folk songs were regarded by Grigoriev as having roots, like their singers, in a common soil that transcended all distinctions of "class" or geographical provenance. His blanket assertion that "few or no folk songs are foreign to me"(*My Literary and Moral Wanderings*, trans. Ralph Matlaw [New York, 1962], p. 23) might have been seconded by Serov at this point in his career, but not by the more "purist" Balakirev circle. A good whiff of the atmosphere of "urban" folk music is given by Grigoriev's enthusiastic description of gypsy singing: "In Moscow, if you seek expression for those undefined, incomprehensible, sorrowful blues *(khandra)*, you make off to the gypsies, immerse yourself in the hurricane of these wild, passionate, oppressively passionate songs. And even if total disillusion has you in its grip, I am willing to stake my head that you'll be pulled out of it ... when Masha starts to afflict your soul with a passionate song, or when a mad furious chorus takes up the last pure, clear, silvery sound of Steshina's 'Oh, do you hear, or do you ken?'" ("Moskva i Peterburg," *Moskovskii gorodskoi listok* [1847], no. 43).

83. Kiui, "Zhurnal'nye tolki o 'Rognede'," *Sanktpeterburgskie vedomosti* (1866), no. 14.

84. *Sanktpeterburgskie vedomosti* (1865), no. 292.

85. To Rimsky-Korsakov, July 15, 1867. Rimskii-Korsakov, *Polnoe sobranie sochinenii V* (Moscow, 1963), p. 297.

86. *Sanktpeterburgskie vedomosti* (1866), no. 12. According to Viacheslav Karatygin, who saw Serov's sketches (*Ezhegodnik Imperatorskikh Teatrov,* 1901), Serov quite deliberately parodied the styles of older Russian composers in some of the genre numbers in Act II. The Dance of the Young Girls is labelled "imitation of Dargomyzhsky," while the opening chorus is designated "imitation of Villebois." See Gerald Abraham, "The Operas of Serov," in Jack Westrup, ed., *Essays Presented to Egon Wellesz* (Oxford, 1966), p. 181n.

87. *Sanktpeterburgskie vedomosti* (1866), no. 12.

88. See N.M. Bachinskaia, *Narodnye pesni v tvorchestve russkikh kompozitorov* (Moscow, 1962), p. 176. Gerald Abraham suggests (Wellesz Festschrift, p. 180) that the "women's chorus" (presumably he means *Leites' slëzy* ["Flow My Tears"] in Act V) is "probably also based on a real folk song," but it seems just as likely, especially in view of the information given in footnote 86, above, to have been an imitation of a Verstovsky or Villebois imitation.

89. The song is based on the folk tune *Charochki po stoliku pokhazhivaiut,* which had been published in the collection of Gerstenberg and Ditmar in the late 1790s.

90. The pizzicato evocation of balalaikas both in this song and in the "dance of the Skomorokhi" copies the procedure Glinka first used in the oarsmen's chorus from *A Life for the Tsar.* In the Jester's song (Act II), seemingly blind reliance on Glinka's example results in an absurdity, when the Jester demands a merry tune from a player of the *gudok* (a bowed string instrument) and from the pit we hear the combination of harp and piano that had been Glinka's inspired representation of Bayan's *gusli* (a kind of psaltery) in *Ruslan.*

91. *Russkaia starina* 21 (1874), p. 370.

92. E.g., Gerald Abraham (Wellesz Festschrift, p. 180).

93. Serov might possibly have had in mind a certain historical song, *Pro tatarskii polon,* when he wrote *"Pokoris' krestu,"* the concluding chorus of *Rogneda.* There are unmistakable melodic similarities between the two. But Serov could have known the song only from the collection of Stakhovich (Moscow, 1854), where it is notated in 3/8 meter:

Ex. 3.17.

The song reappears (in a transcription attributed to Balakirev) in Rimsky-Korsakov's folk song collection of 1876, this time cast in Serov's 6/4 meter.

Ex. 3. 18.

I would suggest that the new meter was prompted by memories of *Rogneda*, and that Serov's example lies behind its extensive employment in Rimsky-Korsakov's *Tale of the Invisible City of Kitezh* (1906).

94.   One recent writer has even gone so far as to imply a line of descent from this scene to *Le Sacre du Printemps* (Gozenpud, "Opernoe tvorchestvo Serova," *Sovetskaia muzyka* [1971], no. 7, p. 97). It is undeniable, of course, that Stravinsky knew the Serov operas well. His father sang leading roles in all of them. See also footnote 108 in Chapter 4.

95.   *Sanktpeterburgskie vedomosti* (1865), no. 292.

96.   It was from Karamzin's *History of the Russian State* (an important source of historical detail for many Russian plays and operas, including both Pushkin's and Musorgsky's *Boris Godunov*s) that Serov took the idea of Vladimir's convening the *veche* to help him decide Rogneda's fate.

97.   Rimsky-Korsakov, *My Musical Life,* trans. Judah A. Joffe (New York, 1923), p. 96.

98.   Ibid., p. 92.

99.   June 15, 1867. Rimskii-Korsakov, *Polnoe sobranie sochinenii* V, p. 296.

100. Perhaps this resemblance may help explain Cui's extremely negative reaction to the cell scene in *Boris*. He called Musorgsky's recitative "choppy" and unmusical, possibly because he sensed its kinship to Serov's *(Sanktpeterburgskie vedomosti* [1874], no. 37).

101. Nikolai Ivanovich Zaremba (1821-79), Professor of Harmony at the St Petersburg Conservatory under Rubinstein, who, at the time of Musorgsky's satire, was enjoying a brief tenure as Director.

102. Alexander Sergeevich Famintsyn (1841-96), a minor composer and conservative feuilletonist, Stasov's antagonist in a famous libel suit.

103. Rubinstein's patroness and founder of the Russian Musical Society.

104. In connection with Musorgsky's "pamphlet," the word *durak* might better be translated not as "jester" but in its more usual meaning, "idiot."

105. *Bogatyri* was performed once in Moscow and never published. The score is preserved in the library of the Kirov State Opera and Ballet Theater (formerly the Mariinsky), Leningrad, inv. 3766. Krylov was a longstanding collaborator of César Cui's (see Chapter 6).

106. Synopsis adapted from Arnold Sokhor, *A.P. Borodin* (Leningrad, 1965), p. 580.

107. On this point Asafiev ("Iz zabytykh stranits russkoi muzyki," *Muzykal'naia letopis'* I [Petrograd, 1922]), Sokhor, Gozenpud, and in fact all who have written about *Bogatyri* have understandably kept silent.

108. The attribution of these sources (and others) is clearly indicated in Borodin's manuscript by footnotes. These notes also contain instructions to the copyist for the transfer of music from other numbers of *Bogatyri* itself, and indicate, by means of measure numbers, exactly how much music from each source is to be used.

109. Cf. Livanova, *Opernaia kritika v Rossii II*, part 3, pp. 385-86. The Ruald-Serov exchange rhymes in the original.

110. Rostislav, *Muzykal'nyi razbor 'Rognedy'* (St. Petersburg, 1870). This pamphlet, an expansion of Rostislav's newspaper reviews of the opera, is a gold mine of comically inept musical misjudgments, and goes a long way toward explaining Serov's dissatisfaction with

his opera's success. For Rostislav the epitome of artistic realism and dramatic truth was the Act IV chorus of captive maidens, and the critic goes on to document the "archeological accuracy" of the Sacrifice to Perun in an irresistibly inane "musicological" disquisition: "It is remarkable that in this place the women's voices are written in parallel fourths, so that if by some chance the men's voices were to fall silent, there would result exactly the same progression as Guido d'Arezzo wrote in 1023 A.D. Of course, in the present instance this quartal cacophony is inaudible, since the women's voices are complemented by the harmony of the men's. But is this not written nonetheless with archeological intent? After all, 1023 is not far from the time when people did bow down before Perun!" (*Razbor*, p. 18) Rostislav saw in Rogneda an advance in melodiousness over *Judith*, which prompted Cui to observe acidly that "after *Judith*, Mr. Serov wrote *Rogneda*—that's fine. But when after *Rogneda* he writes *La Traviata*, only then will his genius achieve its full wingspread" (*Sanktpeterburgskie vedomosti* [1866] no. 14).

111.   *Vest'*, (1865), no. 19.

112.   Cf. Gozenpud, *Russkii opernyi teatr XIX veka I*, pp. 70ff.

113.   The one area in which the theatrical directorate saw fit to economize was sets. Only some of the scenery was created expressly for *Rogneda*. The rest was borrowed from other productions of the Mariinsky (operatic) or Alexandrinsky (dramatic) theaters. Vladimir's audience room (Act II) was the same as that used in the 1865 revival of *Rusalka*. Ostrovsky's play *The Voevoda* provided *Rogneda* with a forest (Act III). The set for the concluding scene—the "square of the settlement of Predslavino"—came, most fittingly of all, from *Askold's Grave* (further details in Gozenpud, *Russkii opernyi teatr II*, p. 91).

114.   Quoted from *Serovy*, p. 83. Mme. Serova claimed that the remark was made to Serov's face. It appears in many variants in the literature on Serov, and its original circumstances are obscure.

115.   V.V. Stasov, "Arkheologicheskaia zametka o postanovke 'Rognedy,'" *Sobranie sochinenii, III*, p. 187.

116.   Gozenpud, *Russkii opernyi teatr II*, p. 106.

117.   V.V. Stasov, *Izbrannye sochineniia I* (Moscow, 1952), pp. 147-51.

118.   *Russkaia starina* 31 (1888), p. 667.

119.   To M.P. Anastasieva, January 11, 1866. *Russkaia starina* 21 (1878), p. 172.

120.   *Muzykal'noe nasledstvo III* (Moscow, 1970), p. 189.

4

Drama Revealed Through Song: An Opera After Ostrovsky

It would be difficult to imagine a greater contrast than between *Rogneda* and *The Power of the Fiend,*[1] the Serovian opera that followed it. Both were based on subjects appropriated from Russian literature, and both were principled attempts at applying the tenets of *pochvennichestvo* to the ideal of musical drama. There, however, the resemblance ends. Where the earlier work had been a "grand," romantic interpretation of Russian history, its successor was realism itself: a "musico-dramatic picture of Russian life,"[2] a domestic melodrama executed on a decidedly petty, not to say "economical"[3] scale. Where the use of Russian national material was mainly decorative in *Rogneda* and vulnerable to criticism on grounds of naivete and inappositeness, *The Power of the Fiend* was a milestone in the incorporation of folk idioms into high art music, and occupies from this point of view a unique place in the annals of Russian opera. It embodies a new attitude toward the use of folk song, seeing it as the "organic" vehicle of musical drama on all levels from the lowliest recitative to the grandest ensemble, and represents the most thoroughgoing essay in this particular brand of musical nationalism ever attempted by a Russian composer. Moreover, where *Rogneda* (not to mention *Judith*) had aspired to the "formlessness" of contemporary operatic ideals as propounded first and foremost by Wagner, *The Power of the Fiend* is equally far from the worlds of Wagner and Meyerbeer. A numbers opera constructed on a libretto in rhymed couplets, its lineage is traceable to the opéra comique and the vaudeville, through such Russian practitioners of these genres as Verstovsky, Dütsch, Villebois and Artemovsky. Finally, and perhaps somewhat paradoxically in light of the foregoing, where Serov's previous operas had emphasized a "lining of the ideal" (as Grigoriev put it) in plot and musical realization, *The Power of the Fiend* came as close as Russian opera was ever to come to the "naked realism" Serov had loudly decried in his critical capacity. It seemed in places calculated to give the lie to his professed belief that music was incapable of ugliness or immorality.[4] From the standpoints both of subject and of treatment, and from that of its actual

Fig. 4.1   Alexander Ostrovsky at the end of the *Moskvitianin* period

musical materials, no other word will do to describe Serov's third opera than the untranslatable Russian *bytovoi,* from *byt,* the conditions of everyday life and environment. We will refer to all that is covered by this term as "genre realism," in which area, no less than in that of "national style," *The Power of the Fiend* represents a high-water mark in the Russian opera of its time and has remained unsurpassed—a realization that, given the importance of genre and of realism in Russian aesthetics and criticism then and since, comes with something of a start.

Since *The Power of the Fiend* was Serov's final work, it has retrospectively colored his career, and has looked to historians like another Serovian volte-face. Had the composer lived, as he expected, to write "another three or four operas,"[5] the work would probably seem more a detour than a reversal. At all events, probably the best way of approaching the opera would be as a *reprise de contact* with elements inherent in *pochvennichestvo* that had been neglected in *Rogneda,* elements that go even further back in the history of the movement, and which lie even closer to its heart.

The sources of *The Power of the Fiend* reach back to the early 1850s, to the journal *Moskvitianin*[6] and its "young editorial staff" with Grigoriev at the helm. This periodical had been founded in 1841 by Mikhail Petrovich Pogodin (1800-1875), an eminent historian and professor at Moscow University, and in its first decade it had faithfully reflected the founder's Slavophile predilections. By 1851, however, subscriptions had declined and the *Moskvitianin* faced serious difficulties. To forestall the imminent danger of folding, Pogodin agreed to turn the day-to-day editorial function over to Grigoriev, who promised to revive interest in the journal through an infusion of fresh blood. Grigoriev, then not quite thirty, surrounded himself with like-minded littérateurs of his own age. This so-called *molodaia redaktsiia* (young editorial staff) included, alongside the editor-in-chief, the poets and playwrights Boris Nikolaevich Almazov, Evgeny Nikolaevich Edelson, Lev Alexandrovich Mey, Tertii Ivanovich Filippov, and most important by far, Alexander Nikolaevich Ostrovsky. These young men, far more deeply committed to literature than to ideology, changed the *Moskvitianin* far more than Pogodin had bargained for, and relations between founder and "young editors" quickly became strained. In place of the "official nationalism" of the founder—a matter of rather formal adherence to autocracy, orthodoxy and the maintenance of the existing social order (which, in the 1840s and 50s, meant first of all the defense of serfdom)— the young editors emphasized the development of national character in literature, and the celebration of a rather loosely conceived national spirit. The journal became the rallying point of those romantically and idealistically national tendencies that crystallized a decade later into the *pochvennik* movement. In particular, his tenure at the *Moskvitianin* gave Grigoriev the opportunity to develop the approach to life and literature he called "organic criticism." Here is how he defined this immortal and notoriously slippery term some time later, in response to a request for clarification by Dostoevsky:

> The organic view acknowledges its point of departure to lie in creative, spontaneous, natural, vital forces. In other words, not only the mind, with its demands for logic and the theories which proceed inevitably from these demands, but rather the mind with its logical demands—*plus* life in all its organic manifestations.[7]

For Grigoriev, the most significant manifestations in the literature of the day were Ostrovsky's early plays, which he published regularly in the *Moskvitianin.* "Ostrovsky appeared," the critic later recalled, "and around him, as around its center, formed the circle of all my up-to-then inchoate beliefs."[8] Within the pages of the *Moskvitianin* itself, Grigoriev hailed his friend's achievement: "Ostrovsky's new word is the oldest word of all: nationality."[9] He attempted to formulate a rigorous definition of "national character" in literature in an article published by the Dostoevskys in *Vremia* in 1863 (but of course, rigorous definitions were never Grigoriev's strong point):

> Literature is national in the broad sense when ... in its types it reflects varied yet generally recognized types or aspects of the popular character, common to everyone's experience, embodied wholly and fully; and when in its forms it reflects beauty as understood by the people, elaborated to the point of becoming an artistic production, no matter whether that beauty be Greek, Italian, Flemish; and when in its language it reflects the whole of the people's common tongue, developed on the basis of its fundamental etymological and syntactical laws.[10]

What makes this rather vague theorizing important to us is the fact that the "forms" and to an extent the "language" of which Grigoriev speaks are strongly bound up with folk song. Folk songs, which lived among the people in nineteenth-century Russia to an extent unparalleled in other European countries, were among the greatest mediators between the individual art work and the national consciousness. One of Grigoriev's most seminal writings was an enormous review for the *Moskvitianin* of a sizeable collection of Russian folk songs compiled and harmonized by the lyric poet Mikhail Stakhovich who, like Grigoriev himself, was an enthusiastic amateur folk singer and guitarist. This "critical essay," which filled a good fifty pages of the issue of August, 1854, was dedicated to Ostrovsky, Filippov and the great actor Prov Sadovsky. Although for the most part concerned with the problems and methodology of establishing authentic verbal texts for the songs, the review gave Grigoriev the pretext for some memorably lyrical effusion on the place of folk songs in his scheme of things artistic.

> A song comes to birth we know not when and where, is created by we know not whom, thrives as a plant thrives, yes, precisely like a plant, which vegetates luxuriantly in congenial

soil. Have our readers ever taken note of a certain very ordinary, yet nonetheless striking fact? Have they ever tried to determine how many songs—of the most varied kind both in words and in music—are, as it were, preserved in the memory of any unlettered peasant singer? It will hardly seem likely if we were to suggest that they number in the thousands, and yet it is in fact so: one song leads to the next, a word in the song will recall a third, and so on. The most apparently diverse motives and phrases flow forth, perfectly distinct from one another, and yet linked together by their shared vegetative existence. The soil in this case is altogether virginal, unfurrowed, unsowed with anything that might impede the growth and proliferation of an organic produce. And now we ask, how much effort does it cost us so-called *educated* folk to memorize even the smallest number of folk texts and tunes, and at that, to memorize them so that the texts and tunes are not confused or interchanged, but come forth clearly with all their subtlest peculiarities (for to remove these subtle peculiarities from a song is just the same as trimming organic vegetation into a hedge, ironing it all out into a single, insipid shape).[11]

This striking image of folk song sending its roots down into the soil of racial memory is trumped (and—characteristically—slightly contradicted) in a passage a bit further on, where Grigoriev says of song (now from the point of view of the ethnographer practicing the comparative method) that it is "not merely a plant: song is the soil itself, on which layer after layer has settled: stripping away the layers by the collation of variants, one can sometimes easily arrive at the primal layer."[12]

Grigoriev's language is charged with all the key words and concepts that were later to crystallize around *pochvennichestvo,* and the critic fully recognized the centrality to his thinking of these pronouncements on folk song. In 1860 he reworked them into what was to prove one of his most widely noticed articles, "Russian Folk Songs in Their Poetical and Musical Aspects," in which he proceeded to suggest even more explicitly that, because its visible flower is the natural product of tangled roots in the national soil, folk song can become the medium or vehicle for relating art "organically" to life. Grigoriev made the prediction that with the rising tide of realism, folk song would become more and more important an element in art.

No one rejects any more the significance of nationality as an organic fact of life; what is rejected, and one must say justly, is the stagnation of the forms of life [in art], and what is opposed, again with perfect justice, is the barefaced denial of reasonable aspects of life, which if pursued to its logical conclusion ends up in bankrupt Utopias. Thought has recognized life as an organic network of manifestations, . . . and has recognized the need to learn from life, turning away from the vainglorious goal of teaching life or raising it to the level of the thinker or his ideals.[13]

A further testimony to the centrality of his remarks on folk song to his artistic creed is Grigoriev's reference to them—including the citation of the passages from the 1854 review we have quoted above—as part of his explanation of one of the most crucial yet elusive terms he habitually employed in the practice of "organic criticism": *rastitel'naia poeziia,* which may be translated literally as "vegetative poetry," and which Grigoriev defines as "a national, impersonal, artless kind of creation, as opposed to art in the usual sense, that is, personalized creativity."[14]

Grigoriev's views were fully shared by his fellow "young editor" Ostrovsky, who moreover was prepared to put them into artistic practice in a way that, as we have seen, made him for Grigoriev the most vital creative force on the Russian scene. Like Grigoriev, Stakhovich, and Filippov an enthusiastic amateur collector of folk songs, Ostrovsky made conspicuous use of them in his plays of the period, particularly in the group of plays he produced during the time of his active involvement with the journal—often referred to collectively as the *"Moskvitianin* plays"—which formed the brilliant culmination of the early phase of the dramatist's career.[15] They inaugurated an epoch in Russian drama, in which the dramatic action "tended to become a selected arrangement of slices of life, with the minimum of adaptation to scenic demands."[16] In short, they inaugurated the epoch of realism. The incorporation of folk songs was a hugely important instrument both for "detheatricalizing the theater" and for securing the connection with the soil that gave "true-realistic" art its validity. Ostrovsky succeeded to the point where, as Mirsky puts it, "the saturation of the atmosphere with the very essence of Russian *byt* and Russian poetical feeling makes it hardly understandable to a foreigner; for every detail...is intensified by the background of a whole emotional tradition (expressed perhaps best of all in the lyrical songs of the Russian people), and without this background it loses most of its appeal."[17] One might compare Ostrovsky's innovative use of folk song in his plays with Glinka's path-breaking achievement in *A Life for the Tsar*—what had been before a decorative trapping if present at all was made the "organic" bearer of dramatic meaning. Folk song became a prime vehicle of characterization; it provided the atmospheric foil against which the dramatic events stood in relief and from which they acquired resonance, and on occasion it could even be made to bear the weight of a dramatic turning point.

Integration of folk song reached its apogee with Ostrovsky in *Poverty Is No Crime* and in *Live Not the Way You'd Like,* two plays written consecutively at the end of his *Moskvitianin* period. While the former cites more than twice as many songs as the latter (no less than twenty, as compared with nine), it is generally agreed that *Live Not the Way You'd Like* represents the most "organic" wedding of song and drama. It was specifically with reference to this play that Grigoriev dubbed Ostrovsky a *narodnyi poet,* a "poet of popular life." A seamy "moral comedy" of life among the Moscow merchant class, the "dark kingdom" (as Dobrolyubov called it) inhabited by so many of Ostrovsky's best plays (and which, having been raised in it, the playwright drew from life), *Live Not the Way You'd Like* is woven around a rather commonplace situation: a young merchant from a stern patriarchal family feels constrained by his domestic circumstances, philanders, is found out, and ultimately returns chastened to his forgiving wife. The real dramatic meaning of the play lies in its evocation of the conditions of Pyotr Ilich's world as revealed in his relationships with the other characters: his father, his wife, his mistress, her mother (an innkeeper), and a squalid blacksmith who for a time seems to promise him a way out. And over and above these, the drama is revealed in the way in which the surface events are played against the rich background of the Russian Shrovetide festivities, the *maslenitsa.*

The manner in which Ostrovsky employed folk songs both as a means of defining the individual characters and their mutual relations, and as a way of ironically contrasting the unhappy action with the general rejoicing of the *maslenitsa* shows the playwright in pursuit of a kind of Slavonic *Gesamt-kunstwerk,* in which the penetration of Russian Geist (or to use a more Grigorievesque expression, *veianie*)—which in conventional spoken drama could only be accomplished as it were peripherally (in "idiom," in sets and props, in costumes)—could be made thoroughly "organic" through the agency of music.

Grigoriev seized upon this idea in an astonishingly prophetic article published by the Dostoevskys in 1864, in which the now mature *pochvennik* called for a union between his two greatest artistic enthusiasms, Ostrovsky's drama and Serov's music, with *Live Not the Way You'd Like* furnishing the ideal meeting ground. The critic quite rightly saw the essence of the play in its subtle but profound interrelation of foreground and background, which, he argued, could only achieve full fruition along lines implicit in Ostrovsky's methods if the play were turned into an opera:

> In this drama, alongside the palpable and visible characters, there reigns over all an invisible character, richly carnal—the altogether inebriated *maslenitsa*... This *"maslenitsa"* is one of the best-preserved remains of our ancient and even now residual pagan heritage... Maskers roam the streets, by night unclean forces go at will. ...Song and dance and minstrelsy are in full swing. With the first stroke of the Lenten matins bell the unclean powers disappear. But up to that minute the dark divinity with its sinister revelries and wild orgies is all-powerful.[18]

In the play, Pyotr Ilyich's philandering and debauchery reach their peak and crisis at the height of the Shrovetide, when he falls under the sway of the sinister beggar-blacksmith Eryomka, the embodiment of the "dark divinity" of which Grigoriev speaks. It is that first matins bell, however, that returns him to his senses and to his family (he hears it, symbolically, just as he is about to rush in a blind rage into an ice-hole in the river). But for Grigoriev, Ostrovsky's drama could not do justice to its own implications; the Shrovetide had not sufficient presence:

> Now here is where poesy might be dazzlingly assisted by another art—music—yes, and I am firmly convinced that Serov will write the musical poem to *Live Not the Way You'd Like.*

The drama is too subtly drawn but might yet be realized on the stage in all its glory with the help of music and a brilliant production. ... Let it be staged at the Mariinsky Theater, sparing not those various accessories which we so bounteously lavish on all kinds of "Fausts" or on the balletic fruits of M. Petipa's nonsensical imagination.... An ideal staging of the drama *Live Not the Way You'd Like* would be a spectacle worthy of a great people.[19]

It is more than reasonable to assume that this public pronouncement was accompanied by many private exhortations. Among the arguments Grigoriev might have marshalled is one that has a special significance in light of the controversies aroused by Serov's treatment of "national" material in *Rogneda.* The urban setting of Ostrovsky's play virtually assured a greater stylistic unity than the composer achieved in his more "historical" opera, for here his taste for "town song" could be indulged with impunity. Genre music and dramatic music might thus achieve the symbiosis that had eluded the composer of *Rogneda.* The musical atmosphere the young staff of the *Moskvitianin* had breathed was one heavily imbued with "impurities"—gypsy songs, "Russian romances", and the like. Grigoriev himself had been personally close both to Alexander Varlamov (1801-48), author of the "Red Sarafan," the very archetype of the "composed folk song,"[20] and to Konstantin Villebois (1817-82), a composer of light music who was also an intimate of Ostrovsky. Villebois and Ostrovsky, in fact, had participated together in a folk song-collecting expedition along the Volga in 1856, the result of which was a pair of published collections that might be looked upon as the central musical document of the *Moskvitianin/pochvennik* milieu.[22] (From what will be said below, it is certain that Serov so regarded them.) In short, Grigoriev's view of folk song, like Ostrovsky's, was broad enough to encompass the productions of the Varlamovs and Villeboises without embarrassment, and so, as we have seen, was Serov's. Then, too, Grigoriev must have called Serov's attention to the remarkable scene in Act III of *Live Not the Way You'd Like,* which as originally written is already virtually operatic in conception. Eryomka, sidling up to Pyotr Ilyich with a cure for his troubles, piques his interest by singing an old dance tune of the *Kamarinskaia* type *(Kumanechek, pobyvai u menia),* which was in very widespread current use as a street song. When Pyotr Ilyich succumbs to his wiles, Eryomka rushes him offstage singing a line from the song that is virtually a line of dialogue at that point in the drama:

Uzh i ia li tvomu goriu pomogu!	For I can help you in your woes!
Pomogu-mogu-mogu-mogu-mogu!	Yes I can-I can-I can-I can-I can!

The song Ostrovsky selected as the vehicle of such a strategic moment in his play was, significantly enough, one that was included in the Stakhovich collection Grigoriev reviewed in the *Moskvitianin* in 1854, that is, exactly as Ostrovsky was getting to work on *Live Not the Way You'd Like,* which appeared the following year. This scene is a very paradigm of the "organic" wedding of genre to drama along *pochvennik* lines, and just as Grigoriev's influence may have played a part in its conception, so was it obviously a factor in sparking Serov's interest in the play. When he came to propose collaboration with Ostrovsky, Serov singled out the third act—"all music!—songs, now solo, now choral, now in duet"—[23] as having exerted the decisive attraction on him.

But Grigoriev exerted this influence on Serov only posthumously. At the time he wrote of *Live Not the Way You'd Like,* and for a couple of years following the huge success of *Rogneda* (by which time Gregoriev was dead), Serov was cool to such suggestions, for all his intimacy with Grigoriev and despite the fact that he had expressed enthusiasm for Ostrovsky—even interest in musicalizing his plays—in the past.[24] But then came Wagner, the *Ruslan* controversy, his operatic career, and by the time *Rogneda* was finished, the "Meyerbeerization" of Serov's creative imagination appeared complete. Defensively, perhaps, but no less sincerely, the composer flaunted the mantle his critics had thrust upon him. He claimed that the "whole Meyerbeerian baggage" was necessary to his dramatic intentions,[25] and the prospective subjects he considered immediately after *Rogneda* certainly presaged a heady continuation along its lines. He once again sought out his unreconstructed Wagnerian friend, Zvantsev, and advised him that he was in the market for "something fast and bloody—slaughter, cannon fire (where appropriate)—though if we can't have all that (this time) it's no great pity. Drama and Chopinism will suffice."[26] Together, Zvantsev and Serov considered operas on Mazepa, on the haydamaks, and even on Gogol's *Taras Bulba,* which latter Serov finally rejected because Gogol had "changed everything and didn't know history."[27] To Zvantsev, though, such an objection only proved the truth of all the criticisms of *Rogneda,* and he argued valiantly but in vain for a return to their old romantic idealism and a stop to Serov's fatuous search for "Cossack Huguenots," that is, his misguided infatuation with "realism," which to Zvantsev meant only "brutalism, approached from the most trivial point of view, not organically but purely à la Meyerbeer."[28] For the second time collaboration between Serov and Zvantsev foundered on fundamental aesthetic differences. Here is how Zvantsev later described them:

> As an outrageous Wagnerian adept (a nickname given me by Apollon Grigoriev, who was himself an outrageous adept of Ostrovsky), I submit that on pure historical data one cannot base a musical drama. ... I argued with Alexander Nikolaevich to the point of tears. I tried to persuade him that the point is not a matter of history, this or that epoch or any given country, but rather the human heart in its eternal and unchanging nature and aspects. I tried to show him that Adam and Eve thought and felt exactly the same as we today, that in order

to depict feelings, thoughts, passions, characters and situations there is no need at all to resort to historical paraphernalia, to the outward trappings of different epochs and peoples. ... But no! Serov, that Russian Meyerbeer, attached the greatest importance to the incidental and superficial side of things. Why? Simply because he himself recognized and even admitted his inadequacy in the face of such a subject, for example, as *Hamlet!* There, street songs taken on loan, marches, hymns, trepaks and skomorokhi will get you nowhere.[29]

Serov had, it seemed, been captured utterly by the pomp and pageantry of the Meyerbeerian theater, and when Zvantsev offhandedly suggested a grand trilogy to be based on the history of the Hussite wars (*Vaclav IV, Jan Hus, Jan Zižka*), Serov had found his "Huguenots." Indeed, Serov offered this trilogy in his dreams not to the Mariinsky, but to the Paris Opéra itself.[30] The Hussite trilogy was a plan Serov cherished to the end of his life. In his *Autobiographical Sketch,* written only months before his death, he still announced his intention to write it, and his intention to "of course... collect preparatory materials in Prague."[31] But Serov never realized the plan, for he was sidetracked, with drastic consequences for his art, by his rediscovery of Ostrovsky, the very match Grigoriev had tried so hard to make for him. Zvantsev, of course, wanted to see in this change of course yet another instance of Serovian inconstancy and opportunism.

Seeing the public success writers of the realist tendency were enjoying, he read widely in the novels, dramas and stories of the day, loved to read them aloud (and read them very well indeed). In his readings I became acquainted with ... many of the fruits of such literature. Serov was also taken with Ostrovsky's dramas. I recall that on 22 May 1867 [*sic,* but 1866 was more likely the year] he read me his verse chronicle, *Tushino,* and considered turning it into an opera.[32]

That Ostrovsky's historical verse plays (of somewhat later vintage than those of the *Moskvitianin* period) were what first attracted Serov's attention at this point might have been expected. Besides *Tushino,* Serov considered *Dmitri the Pretender,* another "chronicle" of the Time of Troubles in the early 17th century, ever a fertile field for Russian historical dramatists. But Serov turned away from them in the end, finding in the case of *Dmitri the Pretender* that "it is a brilliant subject to be sure, but *in essence* not very musical. Politics plays the chief role in it and music, by virtue of its open, candid nature, is but a poor elucidator of political and diplomatic intrigue. Give us rather something *simpler, more heartfelt.*"[33]

Serov's return to the *Moskvitianin* plays seems to have been influenced to a significant degree by his growing friendships in progressive theatrical circles, notably with Alexei Antipovich Potekhin (1829-1908), whose plays of peasant life appealed strongly to the composer's imagination. Potekhin's great specialty was the crowd scene, and this undoubtedly stimulated Serov's conception of the *maslenitsa* as the embodied in Act IV of *The Power of the Fiend*. The possibility of such a scene had been at the heart of Grigoriev's call for a Serov-Ostrovsky collaboration, and Potekhin's plays evidently provided the necessary model. As Mme. Serova recalled:

> Serov never missed a new theatrical production, so that we spent every evening either in the theater or at Potekhin's home, and on Thursdays we entertained the same company ourselves. Almost imperceptibly we found ourselves taking part in debates and discussions on art, on drama and opera. ... Thus, the question of "muzhik" drama was raised for the first time in our "educated" circle. Potekhin held the initiative here: he knew the people in their actual, unadorned state, loved them, and was able to depict them in his plays and stories so vividly and artfully, that we were all completely won over and enchanted. From this proceeded the first embryonic thoughts of a national opera..."[34]

Having come round to it in this way, Serov vigorously pursued Grigoriev's line of argument for an Ostrovskian national opera in his own writings. He devoted an important article to the question in his own short-lived "specialized gazette," *Muzyka i teatr*.[35] Somewhat unlike Grigoriev, however, Serov places the main emphasis not on music's evocative power, but on its psychological force. Interest in Ostrovsky on the part of musicians, he maintains:

> is explained by two factors:... Music has gotten so strong that her desire to enter as an ingredient into drama has ripened. On the other hand, in those of his dramatic works in which this author delves deeper and deeper into the psychological realm, he himself is no longer satisfied with the word alone, but frequently introduces music into his plays, correctly perceiving that only by fusing it with drama can he realize his intentions. The stronger the emotion in a subject, the more appropriate a musical means of expression. The word is impoverished, colorless before the tone; we take for granted that the music correspond strictly to the general mood of the whole play. The works of Ostrovsky belong to this "new form": he has so many moments of purely musical impulse that at the present time musicians are, as it were, involuntarily choosing operatic subjects for themselves from among them. This will have a healthy effect on musicians in Russia. The absurd doctrine that music can only embody exalted feelings that do not recall the attributes of our daily lives will collapse. Ostrovsky's dramas prove the contrary: his characters are drawn from simple, everyday life; their feelings are as ordinary as they themselves are. How music will react—we cannot tell! Will she be able to complement the impression of Ostrovsky's drama with the means at her disposal? With all our heart, we wish her victory over the entrenched routinière opinion that would remove from life that art which flows from the innermost recesses of the soul.

But before he could write his own Ostrovskian opera one further step was necessary: Serov would have to revise some cherished attitudes toward the relationship between folk and art music. As early as his correspondence with Stasov in the 1840s Serov had been firm in his conviction that serious music was by its very nature cosmopolitan and that the Russian folk idiom was hopelessly limited in its expressive range. On the very eve of his collaboration with Ostrovsky, in "Ruslan and the Ruslanists," Serov had stated explicitly and categorically his belief (with reference to what he took to be the naive aspects of *A Life for the Tsar*) that "drama is not revealed through 'songs.'"[36] And his widow reports the following dialogue (presumably at an evening spent in the company of Potekhin), as having taken place after the premiere of *Rogneda:*

—"I don't understand why one has to portray *muzhiks?!*" Serov would exclaim after endless debates. "I can't stand what is far-fetched! Whatever comes to hand that is interesting, that awakens the musician's appetite to reproduce it in sounds, then thank the Lord, a subject is found! I don't know what it is, gentleman, that frightens me in this rage for so-called popular drama; [perhaps it is that] I don't know "the people" at all... —"What don't you know?!" interjected one fanatical admirer of Serov's. "You, after all, have never set eyes upon the Assyrians, but you have written such a march for them that there are no words to do it justice! I dare say you have never been a pagan, either, but you have given them such a chorus [in *Rogneda,* scene ii] that I, an honest Christian, was all but turned into a pagan when I heard it. All that you are saying now, old man, is nonsense!"[37]

But it is easy, after all, to see what frightened Serov, for "muzhiks," or Ostrovsky's merchants for that matter, unlike Assyrians or pagans, would have to be drawn from life, not from imagination. Once committed to Ostrovskian realism, however, Serov underwent a characteristically whole-hearted conversion. He became an ultrapurist in matters of folk song and its proper artistic treatment, and began to undertake learned disquisitions on the subject, both in print and in the lecture hall. From this final period in Serov's career, while *The Power of the Fiend* was in progress, date his "ethnological" articles, notably "On Great-Russian Song and the Peculiarities of Its Musical Style" (*O velikorusskoi pesne i osobennostiakh eë muzykal'nogo sklada,* 1868), which was reworked into the mammoth monograph, "Russian Folk Song as a Scientific Object" (*Russkaia narodnaia pesnia kak predmet nauki),* published in the journal *Muzykal'nyi sezon* over the years 1869 to 1871 in three large installments: "Russian Song in Contradistinction to Western European Music," "The Technical Structure of Russian Song" and "Collectors and Harmonizers of Russian Song." A huge debt to Grigoriev is announced in the very first sentence: "Folk song is a plantlike product purely of the soil."[38] This characterization, widely circulated since Serov's time (and particulary in Soviet polemical journalism), displays a pair of patented code words of "organic criticism." Serov's emphasis, of course, differs from Grigoriev's; he is concerned with possibilities for the artistic development of folk song, not its aesthetic experience per se. And so he immediately follows the sentence quoted above with a corollary that jars somewhat in the context of *pochvennik* doctrine: "Creativity is manifested here in its most primitive form, in musical *embryos,* a larval stage of art, capable of a magnificent further development, but as yet devoid of such."[39]

With such an attitude, the prospect of composing an opera on *Live Not the Way You'd Like* became doubly inviting, for it would be an opportunity for Serov to work out this magnificent development according to his own lights. Once again we shall have the chance to compare Serov's preachment with his practice. But before doing so, there remains a story to tell, and it is not a happy one. The creative history of *The Power of the Fiend,* far more amply documented than those of the other two Serovian operas, is the chronicle of an unfortunate mismatch of major talents, ending in perhaps the messiest "divorce" in the history of opera. Whatever the deleterious effects of stormy relations with Ostrovsky may have been on the work itself, though, the heaviest toll was evidently taken on the composer's health, for he died unexpectedly of a heart attack on the eve of the opera's completion.

It was, of course, inevitable that Serov turned to Ostrovsky himself for collaboration on the projected opera, even though this already meant an about-face of sorts for a composer who had always cherished a quasi-Wagnerian view of himself as poet-musician, and who had insisted not only upon the unique and highly specific demands of *dramma per musica,* but also on the notion that a literary mind was unequipped to satisfy them. Also unprecedented in Serov's career was the conception of an opera based in its entirety on a single preexistent work, and on a prepared libretto. For once he would have to go about composing this theatrical music in the conventional manner—that is, to specific *words,* not merely broadly imagined situations. And it would have to be composed in systematic order, scene by scene, as composer received them from librettist. Undaunted by these novel prospects, Serov wrote to his "dear namesake" (composer and dramatist had the same Christian name and patronymic) on April 23, 1867, with an earnest proposal that they pool their talents. He recapitulated Grigoriev's arguments with reference to *Live Not the Way You'd Like,* and assured Ostrovsky that with but a few minor exceptions (largely involved with augmenting the role of Ilya, the patriarch and embodiment of the moral order in the play), "there is nothing that need be changed."[80] Ostrovsky's answer must have come as a shock:

> The subject you have suggested seems to me, after much thought, to be unsuitable, and this is why: it is a petty one, the whole interest focuses upon dissipation, although the latter is not too serious. But all the same, that's not enough for opera: there are no deep passions, no strong situations. In my view such a subject will do for a little two-act operetta without recitatives, but not for an opera. And there is no reason for you—a man from whom we have a right to expect important and impressive noises—to reduce yourself to this level. Furthermore, there is little of the picturesque and scenic in this subject—that is also important. The first act takes place in a little room, the second—in a hut, the third—back to the little room. The costumes, too, are poor and lack variety. Let us rather look for another subject. We will hardly find one in my works; they are all drawn from everyday life and are visually unimpressive. One must look into other writers.[41]

In other words, Ostrovsky raised precisely the objections Serov himself might have voiced a couple of years earlier. Here indeed was a switch: Ostrovsky, the uncompromising "detheatricalizer" of the theater, advancing a "Meyerbeerian" argument with the Russian Meyerbeer himself! Although he goes on to assure Serov of his readiness to help if a suitable subject could be found, part of Ostrovsky's resistance can perhaps be attributed to the fact that he was already involved in collaborations with not one but two other Russian musicians at the time. For Vladimir Nikitich Kashperov (1827-94), a composer and vocal pedagogue recently returned from an eight-year sojourn in Italy, Ostrovsky had turned his most famous play, *The Storm,* into a conventional numbers libretto. And concurrently he was collaborating with the young Tchaikovsky on the latter's first opera, based on Ostrovsky's historical drama, *The Voevoda.* A brief look at Ostrovsky's contribution to these two works will show why, paradoxical though it may appear, Ostrovsky was in fact a less than ideal prospect for Serov in his project of realizing an "organic" Russian music drama along *pochvennik* lines.

If Serov was the Russian Meyerbeer, Kashperov was surely the Russian Donizetti. And this was precisely why Kashperov's collaboration with Ostrovsky was the most mutually satisfactory of all such projects the playwright entered into, and why the collaboration with the "reformed" Serov proved, as we shall see, to be the least. Ostrovsky, in the recollection of Ippolitov-Ivanov "a great lover of Italian singing,"[42] was only too happy to turn his most characteristic work into a vehicle for such singing, even if it meant doing violence to the content and meaning of the original. The dramatist, evidently, had not his admirer Grigoriev's aspirations to "organic" drama, at least where music was concerned, for in adapting his play into a libretto he blithely discarded the all-important background, the stifling "dark kingdom" that had made his heroine Katerina credible and moving, had given the work a significance that transcended its rather hackneyed plot, and had made it such a focal point of "progressive" Russian criticism. In the opera all that is left is that plot, or more precisely the love intrigue, which, stripped of its social and atmospheric milieu, is reduced to a banal tale of a fickle woman, a spineless paramour and a ridiculous cuckold. The roles of Kabanova and Dikoy are practically eliminated; that of Kuligin, the "conscience" of the play, entirely (his indispensible lines are taken variously by the chorus [!] and by Boris and Kudrash in duet). While music might, as Grigoriev and Serov envisioned, have sketched in some of the play's background, Kashperov's score is pure "Italianshchina" with a thin veneer of romancelike local color à la Varlamov-cum-Villebois, reserved almost exclusively for the roles of Varvara and Kudrash (the latter sings a song to his own balalaika accompaniment), plus a few genre choruses (village maidens and the inevitable Volga boatmen).

"Deep passions" and "strong situations," however, there are in plenty, and the librettist bent every effort toward ending each of the four acts with an

Fig. 4.2   Vladimir Kashperov, Ostrovsky's collaborator on *The Storm*

impressive ensemble finale. Thus, the play's first act, so crucial to an understanding of Katerina's situation, was largely cut since it apparently offered little in the way of "operatic" possibilities. The first act of the opera ends with Tikhon's departure (Act II in the play). Ostrovsky the librettist dwells interminably upon the farewell scene, constructing from it an enormous quintet (Tikhon, Katerina, Varvara, Dikoy, Boris) that centers around Tikhon's parting words to each in turn—a series of little duets that in Kashperov's unimaginative setting exemplify what Glinka had once sarcastically termed "typical Italian" behavior.[43] This trivial set piece altogether overshadows the really important events of Tikhon's departure: Katerina's forced vows and then the one she forces upon Tikhon herself.

In fashioning his libretto, Ostrovsky sought to gather into big arias the individual, scattered speeches and admissions of Boris and Katerina, which in their cumulative effect give such force, in the play, to their inevitable rendezvous. Thus, the opera begins right off (except for the conventional genre chorus) with an aria by Boris in which he sets forth at length his hopeless love for Katerina, instead of it being revealed gradually in dialogues and soliloquies spread over the first two acts. And Katerina's two scenes with Varvara, one before and one after Tikhon's departure in the play, are combined in the opera into one enormous scene that begins the second act (balancing Boris's opening number). But because of this, we know nothing of Katerina's passion for Boris throughout the first act, and so her hysterical insistence on swearing fidelity to her husband is as mysterious to the spectator as it is to Tikhon.

Of course, the opera *The Storm* was written for an audience presumed to be familiar with the play. But this only demonstrates to what extent Ostrovsky failed to regard the genre of opera as a fully independent and intrinsically viable form of drama. When music is involved, passions need only be "deep"; they need not be motivated. Situations need only be "strong"; they need not be plausible.[44]

Much the same can be said of Ostrovsky's adaptation of *The Voevoda* for Tchaikovsky. The original play is a rich tapestry woven out of history and fantasy in equal measure, in which the love intrigue plays a decidedly subordinate role. Tchaikovsky, however, was even at this stage a composer interested, by his own avowal, in "love, love and love,"[45] and so, with Ostrovsky's assent, the opera turned into a silly story of how, in Laroche's words, "a certain Shalygin stole Maria from Bastriukov, and Bastriukov stole her back from Shalygin."[46] Critics have since observed wistfully that the play contained the unrealized makings of another *Boris Godunov,*[47] and indeed there are parallels between certain aspects of Ostrovsky's drama that were omitted in the opera—the crowd scenes (complaints of the people against the *voevoda*), the *voevoda*'s dream-hallucination, etc.—and Musorgsky's treatment of Pushkin's play. But neither Tchaikovsky nor his distinguished librettist were interested in such things, and though it has become more or less accepted in the critical literature to blame the composer for the faults of *The Voevoda's* libretto,[48] it is impossible to doubt that Ostrovsky was responsible for the scenario.

The Storm, produced at the Mariinsky late in 1867, might have served Serov as a warning not to expect smooth sailing in his joint endeavor with Ostrovsky. Certainly, it placed Ostrovsky's early refusal in a new light. The Ostrovsky/Kashperov work was greeted with two important and eminently hostile reviews. One, by Cui, sought to dismiss the whole affair with some rather ham-fisted persiflage at the expense of "Il signor maestro Kasperoff."[49] But Serov, writing at length in his own journal, reserved the brunt of his thrust for the libretto.

> Whether it was the result of the hoary prejudice that an operatic canvas must remain *far removed* from dramaturgical criteria and automatically debase any subject it touches, or whether it was the desire to match the text to the capabilities of the composer, or yet whether it was because of his own Italianate predilections and inspiration, the fact remains that A.N. Ostrovsky has weakened his play extremely in adapting his text for the opera, and has hardly helped the cause of *serious* operatic standards in so doing. Even in its present form, of course, [this libretto] is nevertheless an excellent canvas for music, even, if you like, "the best Russian libretto up to now." But it recalls the play called *The Storm* only faintly. For anyone who knows and values the original (and what Russian theater-lover does not know or value it?) it is a patent "distortion" of a matchless and wonderful play. Why must this be? It is an insult to all musico-dramatic ideals. . . . That A.N. Ostrovsky placed one of his best creations at the service of *such* a conception of opera is his personal affair. That from an opera with such aims and means nothing can emerge but a profanation of the subject, is no less clear.[50]

These are amazingly strong, even tactless words, especially when one considers that at the time Serov and Ostrovsky had already embarked upon their own collaboration. The critic did attempt to soften his blows by calling attention to some of the difficulties attendant upon a musical adaptation of a play like *The Storm.* His discussion of the role of Kabanova is particularly revealing of the viewpoint from which Serov himself approached Ostrovsky as composer.

> In Kabanova's role there is absolutely *nothing* to connect her with the realm of tones. She must even speak in a hollow, toneless voice, which is *never* raised to a shout or any kind of forceful or impetuous exclamation. She nags her victims, but does it quietly, calmly, dispassionately, unemotionally. All this is antipathetic to music; music is a warm, heartfelt art. Dispassionateness, unemotionalism, heartlessness, hypocrisy—these are not music's domain (which is why Shakespeare's Richard III or Iago [!!] are hardly possible in music).[51]

Serov had been more tactful when he had addressed Ostrovsky directly a few months earlier, in a long letter (May 26, 1867) that had proved persuasive in getting the playwright to collaborate with him on *Live Not the Way You'd*

Like. His words are conciliatory, almost modest, as he outlines a new approach to opera—a musical drama that would conform to the standards and criteria of the realistic spoken drama to an extent unheard of, along lines he himself had vigorously opposed as recently as *Rogneda.* Serov's remarks on the success of the latter opera in this letter can hardly be taken as ingenuous.

> You approach operatic matters mainly from the external standpoint, from the point of view of pomp and lavish spectacle.
>
> Most operas which have existed up to now (including our Russian ones generally, as well as both of my own) might actually support such a view, that opera demands brilliance and magnificence of costumery and sets, bold dramatic situations, and crowds of people on stage as necessary conditions.
>
> The history of opera in all countries has shown that opera developed from festive court spectacles, combined with and inseparable from ballet. Traces of this element are still very strong in opera even in our time.
>
> But, on the other hand, the same history of opera in more recent times shows clearly that contemporary operatic goals are drawing closer and closer to the simplest, most profound dramaturgy, rich by virtue of its own inner strength, without need for luxuriant paraphernalia.
>
> If the occasion should arise for picturesqueness, for lavish dress and spectacle—well and good; all this must be attended to in the best possible way. But if there is no occasion for all this, then who needs it? One can certainly do without brilliance and magnificence.
>
> I have had occasion to note something of this in practice. The third and fourth acts of *Rogneda,* for example, please the audience not because of their luxuriance and picturesqueness, but because of something else. The first and second acts are more luxuriant by far, and yet they always pass completely without emotion on the part of the spectators. This means that for the Russian public, luxuriance of staging is no longer the strongest point.
>
> I would say further that I myself have nothing against picturesqueness in opera. I am even rather partial to broad historical backdrops for musical drama. This started with *Guillaume Tell* and *Les Huguenots* (here, with *A Life for the Tsar*), and of course it is a good thing and must remain true to itself. But whoever said that an everyday *(bytovaia)* drama is not operatically feasible?
>
> Right now I am strongly drawn to precisely that kind of drama (without any external adornment), as exemplified by your *Live Not the Way You'd Like.* I am convinced that its inner dramatic strength will call forth truly Russian, heartfelt tones, altogether in character with the matchless songs of the Russian people.
>
> You yourself are a connoisseur of these songs. You know what is in them! Remember that in this drama as you yourself have written it, all the characters—Dasha, Grunya, Pyotr, Vasya, even Eryomka, one and all—sing. At every opportunity they lapse into song.
>
> This shows that they are all full of Russian musicality. What could be better for opera? The background is Shrovetide revelry and carousal. Again what could be better? For goodness' sake! Apollon Grigoriev himself always saw in this drama a future Russian national opera. And you have to agree that Grigoriev had a nose for such things.
>
> It is precisely with this simple setting that you and I will perform a great deed! We will defeat many prejudices. For the time is ripe for a purely Russian music, without admixture of Western influences.[52]

Serov thereupon gets down to specific points. First of all, he rejects Ostrovsky's contention that the subject demands treatment as a little "operetta without recitatives." Such a work, writes Serov, "is unthinkable in our time; it has outlived its age and has been irrevocably banished from the operatic stage." Prose dialogue is out of the question, not only because it "cruelly destroys the unity of the musical impression," but also because "our singers have utterly lost the knack of 'talking' on stage."[53] One gets the impression that Serov, out of force of habit, was busily imagining the musical setting of the opera, not only in general terms but specific whole scenes, in advance of receiving Ostrovsky's text, or even his assent. Thoroughly warm now to the subject, Serov outlines the whole scenario as he conceived it:

First act—just as it is in the play, with only the most insignificant alterations (e.g., to begin it with Dasha's monologue). The role of Ilya is extraordinarily suitable for music in a strict, ecclesiastical Russian style (a venerable, God-fearing, patriarchal elder).

In the course of the whole first act it will be necessary to have the sounds of merrymaking, choral singing, troikas, etc., intrude from the street, just as Ilya speaks of it: "the people are all as if boiling in Hell; this noise, this uproar, these devilish songs."

The scene of Dasha and the inebriated, dozing Vasya—in music it will come off perfectly.

Dasha's wailing and her decision to run off to her parents—the most "musical" ending for the act you could possibly want!

The second act will have to begin on a *somewhat merrier* note. Drivers, merchants, riff-raff of all kinds carousing at Spiridonovna's. (She can be made more colorful than in the play. I see a very good role emerging, e.g. for Leonova). First Spiridonovna entertains the company, then Grusha (your play already hints at this). Grusha's entrance can be just as it is, only in the presence of the others. At the guests' departure, an animated duet for mother and daughter (Spiridonovna's and Grusha's "principles").

Grusha alone—sings of her merry maiden's way of life. Grusha and Pyotr—a big *love scene* (duet). A small reflective monologue for Grusha, then to the end of the act all the scenes can be combined into a big "ensemble" (the meter *continually* changing in accordance with the vicissitudes of the situation. Well, of course, you know all about that . . .)

Third act: scene one (the same set—the inn). To begin with a song for the girls, who have come to have fun with Grusha. She is pensive (an excellent contrast for music).

The scene with Eryomka—all music! Songs, now solo, now choral, now in duet.

The scene with Pyotr—coldness, mockery—the same at Vasya's entrance—in animated "ensemble."

Toast to Vasya and Grusha by the girls. They leave. Behind the scenes: sounds of songs and coach bells, further and further off.

Pyotr's bitter reflections and then—Eryomka. (The latter to be shaded in greater relief, in all his devilishness—sorcery—the magic stone.) A wonderful basis for a duet of altogether unique character.—They go off on a spree.

In the second scene, I propose, we can show *from the side,* that is, *from a point outside,* the last day of the Shrovetide fair on the Novinsky Boulevard (or wherever it was held in the eighteenth century, if we are to keep somewhat less than completely to a contemporary setting).

At dusk—scenes of popular life: crowds, songs, pipes, tambourines and the like (a merry fair for *Russian* opera—it will be a novelty).

Eryomka, so as to egg Pyotr on the more, points out Grusha and Vasya in the crowd. (In this way we can make a good ending for Act III.)

In Act IV—first scene, in Pyotr's house, just as in the play.

At Pyotr's exit with the knife (accompanied by Eryomka) *everyone* rushes onstage and

Vasya decides to send for Ilya, to look for Pyotr all over Moscow *(ensemble)*.
Second scene. Moonlit night over the River Moskva (a beautiful set).
Eryomka leads Pyotr to the edge of the ice hole.
The matins bell for Holy Week.
Eryomka disappears.
Pyotr's repentance. All (including Ilya) rush onstage.
Pyotr throws himself at his father's feet and embraces his wife.
General singing to Ilya's motive, "Live not the way you'd like" *(Ne tak zhivi kak khochetsia)*.

As you wished, here you have an excellent subject for a popular-Russian opera. It is not a large thing—but deep! The one is the price of the other. Think it over—other details will arise that will suit the opera. But even as I have sketched it here, the opera is *ready* and by no means without import.

I would be in despair to have to give this project up! Don't let me down; get right to work.

A great "historical" music drama will not come from our collaboration. What you have suggested to me, probably, is precisely right. But, for now, even if as an experiment, I will not let go of your *Live Not the Way You'd Like.*

And who will help me in it if not you? It is ridiculous even to contemplate it.[54]

On June 4, Serov wrote again, ostensibly to make sure that Ostrovsky had received the letter of May 26, but mainly to assure the dramatist that the detailed scenario was no more than a suggestion. He was concerned lest his zeal result in an overkill. He needn't have been. Ostrovsky's diary informs us that on that very day, June 4, 1867, he "began the libretto of *Live Not the Way You'd Like.*" Serov's letter had proved persuasive. More than that, his scenario proved helpful indeed. As far as we are able to judge, which is as far as the first scene of the projected Act III, Ostrovsky followed Serov's plan in virtually every detail. And so the lengthy citation from Serov's letter may be treated by the reader as a reliable synopsis of the opera through the third act, and Serov in the end could fairly claim, even in the opera on which he and Ostrovsky collaborated, to have been his own scenarist! In the past, of course, this much had entitled him to claim the title of "poet" outright.

Ostrovsky worked intensively and quickly, although he was then in the midst of the *Voevoda* libretto for Tchaikovsky. According to his diary entries, he worked on both concurrently, often devoting parts of a single working day to each. Only two days after beginning work, Ostrovsky was able to make a fair copy of "one-and-a-half scenes for Serov." Serov received the first scene on June 11, and went ecstatically to work. It was almost all sketched out in music by the following day, as he informed Ostrovsky by mail, adding that "if you continue at this pace, our work will go with unheard of speed." He broaches the subject of terms,[56] offering his coworker 100 rubles an act for a total of 400. He also takes up the matter of the opera's proper designation, rejecting the category "comic opera" as suggested evidently by Ostrovsky, preferring an adaptation from the original subtitle of *Live Not the Way You'd Like*: "a national Russian *(narodno-russkaia)* musical drama."

The librettist finished the first act on June 20.[57] Serov wrote to thank him on June 29. His next letter is dated August 20, and from its contents one may deduce that Ostrovsky had finished Act II except for the very complicated final ensemble. As for Serov's work, he boasts that

> I am practically caught up with you in the music. The first act I could begin orchestrating now, and in the second, except for a couple of recitatives I haven't touched yet, I have sketched almost all the scenes you have sent.[58]

The pace, however, did not keep up. Ostrovsky became engrossed in the composition and production of a major work, *Vasilisa Melentieva,* and kept Serov waiting (though he did supply the final ensemble of Act II by late fall, since Serov's letter of December 6 contains some requests for small changes). It took some rather importunate prodding from the composer, but by the beginning of 1868 the libretto was complete, and a grateful Serov could write to his collaborator that it was "a model of its kind."[59]

At this point comes a six-month hiatus in the Serov-Ostrovsky correspondence, during which the librettist probably forgot all about the project and the composer was presumably happily at work. We will take the opportunity here to interrupt our chronicle of *The Power of the Fiend*'s creative history for a comparison of the libretto with the original play.

First of all, the play was condensed as far as possible. Ostrovsky, already an experienced hand in matters of operatic adaptation, did not have to be instructed on this score. On receipt of the completed first act, Serov remarked approvingly, "Knowing, of course, that music has the capability of *diluting* its text, you have *compressed* it vis-à-vis the text of the play—and very sensibly."[60] He even complained that the playwright had gone too far in this direction, by cutting out important elements of Ilya's characterization (the playwright willingly restored them). There was a similar tacit agreement from the outset that Ostrovsky was to transform his prose play into verse for musical treatment, as he had done in the case of *The Storm* for Kashperov. When Zvantsev, playing devil's advocate, needled Serov about this ostensible compromise with "realist" principles, the composer replied that to set Ostrovsky's prose unaltered would have been a needless burden.[61] He might have added that the verse text was indeed necessary in order to achieve the particular *"pochvennik"* variety of spiritual (i.e., "true") realism through the medium of folk poetry and song at which he and Ostrovsky were aiming. To put matters this way would have defined his "realist" position vis-à-vis the more material realism of a Musorgsky, who at the time was turning out some remarkable songs on prose texts and who was about to make his now famous "experiment in dramatic music in prose" on the text of Gogol's *Marriage.*[62]

What Ostrovsky was after was an unprecedented recasting of his play into a kind of infinitely extended folk poem in anticipation of the song-saturated music Serov promised to write. A beautiful and wholly characteristic example is the very opening of the first scene. In the play, Dasha (Pyotr's wife) and Afimya (Pyotr's aunt) together lament the misfortune brought upon the household by Pyotr's errant ways. The main expository function is performed by Afimya's rather garrulous opening speech:

Chuet, chuet moë serdtse!...Ne dobro ono chuet!...Da chemu i byt-to khoroshemu? Ni miru, ni ladu v sem'e! Znat', uzh bog vovse ot-stupilsia ot nas, gliaduchi na nashe neputnoe zhit'ë. Za grekh za kakoi-nibud' nakazan'e ekoe Petru Il'ichu, da za nashe neumolenie. I na chuzhogo-to na besputnogo serdtse mrët, a to legkoe li delo, svoe detishche!...da eshchë zhenatyi!...Khorosho, chto mat'-to bog pribral, a to kakogo by ei na eto gliadet'-to!...Ottsu soprotivnik, zhenu zamochil!...U kogo takoi uro-dilsia? Teper' dni proshchen'e, i chuzhie miriatsia, a u nikh i vstava-iuchi, i lozhaiuchis' bran' da perekor. Nu, gde on teper' shliaetsia? Zhdali, zhdali obedat', a ego i slykhom ne slykhat'!...Vsiu maslianitsu guliaet, skruzhilsia, kak ugorelyi. Otets-to prishël poliubovat'sia na vashe zhit'ë: est'na chto radovatsia! Chem by po-gostit', a on domoi sobralsia.

There is an evil foreboding in my heart! And how could it be a good one? There is neither peace nor harmony in this household! You see how God has forsaken us altogether, seeing the disgraceful way we live! This is our punishment for Pyotr Ilich's sins and for our impiety. It's heartbreaking enough to see a total stranger go astray, but one's own flesh and blood!...And he's married, besides! It's a good thing his mother never lived to see this!...He's become his father's enemy and his wife's tormentor! Who could have given him birth?! Now are the days of forgiveness, and total strangers are reconciled, while with them it's bicker and strife, morning, noon and night! And where's he galli-vanting now? They've been waiting and waiting with dinner, and no word of him! The whole Shrovetide he's been gadding about like a house on fire. His father has come to admire the way you live—not much to rejoice about, is there? Some reception he's had, and now he's going home.

In the opera the focus is placed on Dasha and her feelings. Most of Afimya's lines, radically abbreviated, are transferred to her opening speech, and recast into rhymed quatrains. Afimya's role is confined to a single replique, uttered more in sorrow than in reproach. (Serov, in his setting, combined Afimya's lines contrapuntally with a reprise of Dasha's opening quatrain, which kept the focus on the young wife even here.) With great taste and skill, Ostrovsky poeticized his language, replacing the everyday vocabulary of the original with a more colorful, yet authentic, diction derived from the imagery of folk lyrics (e.g., *retivoe* for *serdtse,* etc.):

Dasha: Chuet, chuet retivoe,
        ne k dobru ego shchemit:
        pered gorem il' bedoiu,
        govoriat, ono bolit!

Dasha: There is a foreboding in my heart,
        its aching bodes no good:
        before sorrow or misery,
        they say, it always hurts!

Da chemu i byt' inomu,	And how could it be otherwise,
kol' ves' dom u nas vverkh dnom,	when our whole house is upside down,
koli muzhu, kak chuzhomu,	when my husband, like a total stranger,
opostyl rodimyi dom!	has grown sick of his own home!
Chto za zhizn'! chto den'-to slëzy,	What kind of life is it, when tears, day-long,
vmesto laski i liubvi,	replace caresses and love,
bran' poprëki da ugrozy,	when bickering, strife and threats
Khot' na svete ne zhivi!	make life impossible!
Dni proshchen'e miritsia	The days of forgiveness bring
i proshchaetsia rodnia,	reconciliation to families,
a on boga ne boitsia!	but he has no fear of God!
Propadët po tri dnia!	He disappears for three days at a time!
V gosti batiushku pozvali—	We invited Father for a visit—
syn i dumat' pozabyl!	And his son forgot all about it!
My ego k obedu zhdali,	We waited dinner for him,
i a sled ego prostyl!	But look, he's flown the coop!

Afimya: Vidno, ty neschastna, Dasha,   Afimya: It's plain you're unhappy, Dasha,
znat' talanu net ni v chëm,   you've had no luck at all,
vot i k nam, na gore nashe   and now, to our sorrow,
zaneslo neschast'e v dom!   misfortune has come to our door!

The next scene in the libretto embodies the contrast between Ilya's stern reprimands and the sounds of merrymaking on the street, as Serov had requested. For the rest of the first act the sequence of scenes follows the play faithfully.[63] The one given most expansive treatment is precisely the one singled out by Serov as the most "musical"—the seventh, between Dasha and Vasya.

In Act II, following Serov's suggestion, Ostrovsky provided a number of interpolated set pieces in folk style. These included Spiridonovna's song, "*Okh, kuptsy, molodtsy,*" and Grunya's (for so Grusha is called in the opera) "*Akh, nikto menia ne liubit,*" both sung ostensibly to entertain the guests at the inn. Between them Ostrovsky inserted Eryomka's Shrovetide song, "*Shirokaia maslenitsa,*" destined to become the opera's most popular number. This was a small masterstroke, for not only does it introduce Eryomka to the audience a full act earlier than in the play, and not only does it strengthen "the presence of the Shrovetide" in precisely the manner Grigoriev had envisioned, but it cements early the decisive bond between the quasi-pagan holiday and (through Eryomka) the "dark forces" of which Grigoriev had written so presciently. After Grunya's entrance song, there follows the "comic duet" for mother and daughter Serov had called for, after which (as in the play) Grunya sings her monologue (indistinguishable in style from her "song") and greets Pyotr. From here to the end of the act, Ostrovsky followed Serov's requests punctiliously: an extended "love scene" (in merry vaudeville style, rather than ardent), and the concluding ensemble which embodies the plot's turning point. This is handled in the traditional way, culminating in a quartet wherein the reactions of Dasha, her parents, and the horrified, eavesdropping Grunya are all superimposed.

At the beginning of Act III, Ostrovsky took over another happy idea from Serov: the opposition of the jolly maidens' song with Grunya's lamenting one. Serov's description of the ensuing scene with Eryomka—"all music! Songs, now solo, now choral, now duet"—fits the libretto as well, but Ostrovsky (or conceivably Serov himself, when it came to the setting) evidently felt the songs were getting to be too many, for the longest "interpolated song" in the original play, the girls' *Iskhodila mladen'ka vse luga i bolota* (a great favorite of Ostrovsky's),[64] is otherwise unaccountably omitted from the opera. Again, to the end of the act Ostrovsky was entirely faithful to the original action, and also to Serov's suggestions for musicalization, including the "toast" by the chorus of maidens, and the remarkable expansion of the *Kumanechek* dance song (by means of original verses in the same meter and rhyme) to carry the action of the concluding scene (Pyotr and Eryomka). It would appear, in sum, that not only was the libretto indeed, as Serov remarked, "a model of its kind," but so was the collaboration of the two artists a model of smooth interaction and mutual support between dramatist and musician.

But now the trouble began. Serov had called for a scene to follow the end of Act III,[65] which had no analogue at all in *Live Not the Way You'd Like.* This was to be a tableau of the Shrovetide fair, for which Serov's conceptual model was no doubt the crowd scenes he knew from Potekhin's genre plays. Ostrovsky fell in with gusto, but the act as he wrote it was rather different from the one Serov had imagined. He evidently had Grigoriev's description of the *maslenitsa* in mind, but interpreted the critic's remarks rather literally. The act, as Ostrovsky wrote it, is now lost, so we shall have to rely on the description given by Mme. Serova in her memoirs, written almost a half-century later:

> Ostrovsky was especially taken with the fourth act, and recommended to Serov that he apply himself with particular diligence to it, assuring him that the popular poetic and legendary element was captured in it. What this came down to was that Ostrovsky had introduced devils—real ones, with tails, horns and all the rest of the devilish paraphernalia—into the scene of the Shrovetide revels, as if to terrify the carousers. And Eryomka he put forth as some kind of Caspar out of *Freischütz,* a sort of homespun demi-devil.[66]

For Serov, this touch so literalized Grigoriev's idea as to trivialize it, and with it, the whole drama. To spell out the metaphor of "dark divinity" so graphically ill accorded with "true realism": Eryomka was already enough the representative of "unclean forces" without the horns and tails. These only served to remove the play from the real world and thereby lessen the sinister force of its message. Serov, who had always been skeptical of the place of the "fantastic" in serious drama (he had resolutely excluded it from his previous operas), suspected that Ostrovsky's devils were mainly intended "to soften the crudeness of the drunken crowd."[67] But that crudeness was the very last thing Serov was prepared to compromise. The composer was particularly insistent that Eryomka be drawn true to life, in all his squalor and unseemliness. Just as insistently he resisted the notion that Eryomka was—or represented—the devil in any literal sense. "Devils act disinterestedly," he said, "they scourge the soul of man simply for art's sake, while Eryomka demands pay for his dirty work, and, if possible, in advance."[68] Eryomka stood for the dark forces at large within the real world of man, and any attempt to make of him a preternatural force would turn the play into a Romantic caprice.

Accordingly, Serov returned the manuscript of the fourth act to Ostrovsky with the request that the sugar-coating be removed. "The slightest admixture of the unreal," he warned, "will spoil, nay, destroy the entire impression."[69] The only thing Serov wished to retain in the entire act was the phrase "*vrazh'ia sila,*" which became the opera's title.

One can imagine the playwright's indignation, not so much at Serov's disagreement as at his lack of tact, coming right on the heels of his withering review of the Ostrovsky-Kashperov *The Storm.* But one can also imagine him giving in to Serov's persuasion on this point, as he had given in so frequently in the past. But Serov sprang another, far more fundamental demand on his coworker, and this one meant the collapse of the whole project.

In the scenario Serov proposed in his letter of May 26, 1867, certain alterations are already apparent in the ending of the opera vis-à-vis the play. These, however, mainly involved matters of musical form and stage effect, not substance. In the play, the final act has only one scene and one set—Pyotr's house. Serov introduced a scene change not only for the sake of the "good set" he mentioned, but also in order to turn into action what in the play is narrative: Pyotr's epiphany at the ice-hole. Neither Eryomka nor Ilya appear in Ostrovsky's last act, though Pyotr, in his drunken raving, sees an apparition of the blacksmith. Ilya is brought onstage in Serov's version for the obvious purpose of rounding out the drama with an effective musical peroration of the opera's "title theme"—"Live not as you'd like, but as God commands."

But in the course of a year's work on the opera, Serov had a fundamental change of heart. As he put it to the actor A.N. Vitmer, "to end so, that is, Ostrovsky's way, would mean ending with nothing: the drama has come to the point of no return and must be brought to a tragic denouement, else why even set it in motion to begin with?"[70] If we may believe him (a problematical matter, since his hostile account of Serov's last opera is so full of wisdom after the fact), it was Zvantsev who first put the idea into Serov's head that an operatic treatment of the subject demanded a tragic conclusion. At the time, so Zvantsev recalled, Serov derided the idea.

> With all due respect to Ostrovsky's talent and his theatrical experience, I nonetheless tried
> to talk Serov into changing the end of the play and heatedly exhorted him: "Let your Pyotr

Ilyich come home and kill his wife like a chicken behind a screen—and just then over the villain's head let the first deep stroke of the Lenten bell resound!"—"Ah, my dear fellow," Serov objected with a grin, "my Muscovite hero is no Othello! Pyotr Ilyich still has a few years' carousing in store. All such tragic conclusions are out of keeping with our [Russian] disposition.[71]

But the Meyerbeerian bloodlust claimed its due and Serov came round to the paradoxical viewpoint that only a tragic ending befitted a serious, realistic music drama. According to Mme. Serova he fretted and procrastinated at great length before he could bring himself to take the matter up with Ostrovsky. Once he did, however, he expounded his newfound conviction to the dramatist at great and characteristically insulting length:

> It seems that from the very beginning [!] you and I have been somewhat at odds in our view of the subject. You have turned the text into a good-natured, half-amusing thing, going so far even as to call it "comic" (?) in the very title. Because of this the saccharine, feeble ending has not seemed inappropriate to you. For me, however, this subject is serious and tragic, with episodes of rough humor.
>
> By now I have come to certain conclusions and from the scenario that I herewith impart to you I will not retreat under any circumstances. In the play *Live Not the Way You'd Like,* there are in essence two plots: (1) a domestic drama; (2) the story of how "unclean forces" brought a drunken reveller to the edge of an ice-hole, and how that reveller came to his senses at the sound of a churchbell.
>
> It is now my firm belief that this second story about the ice-hole has to be thrown out altogether; this falling in with the unclean would demand for its scenic realization some kind of god-forsaken wilderness, an out-of-the-way forest clearing, a Russian "Wolf's Glen"—and not an ice-hole right in front of the Kremlin in the middle of Moscow. Hewing as close as possible to the implications of the domestic drama, I have taken your own characters and have brought their elements to their logical conclusion. There comes about a collision that inevitably calls for a bloody denouement.
>
> Your Pyotr gets the idea of killing his wife; for this he comes home in a fury, and let him kill her, if you please, right there at home. Such a young gallant you won't bring to reason with churchbells, with crosses, with clubs, with anything. *After* his fit of blind rage—repentance. And at this point comes the old father with his words of doom and distant churchbells (from the same church as in the first act). There you have a natural, simple and, it seems, a strong conclusion.
>
> I am not one to trifle with a subject. I am no "melodist" and find the transformation of your so very Russian dramas into canvasses for treacly Italianism a monstrous matter and a disgrace to art.
>
> Please forgive my tactlessness. Honorable devotion to ideas is more important than the observance of decorum and courtesy.[72]

How Serov could have expected any answer from Ostrovsky save the one he got—total silence—is unfathomable. Although Ostrovsky did actually accede to a few other minor revisions in the earlier acts which Serov requested in the same letter, the playwright quite understandably pocket-vetoed the conclusion. Mme. Serova indicates in her memoirs the extent to which relations between composer and librettist were strained while the opera languished:

> Not without reason had Serov feared a deplorable outcome from the change he contemplated: Ostrovsky stubbornly kept silent while Serov pined pending an answer. One time Serov caught sight of Ostrovsky in a theatre lobby; he called to him, ran after him, but the latter disappeared, ignoring Serov's shouts. From that time on they did not see one another.[73]

Finally, on December 24, 1868, an exasperated Serov sent Ostrovsky his "ultimatum": either he furnish the complete libretto according to Serov's specifications within two weeks "and not a day longer," or Serov would turn to another librettist. Again, Serov apologized for his brusqueness, but "everyone holds his work dear, and you are forcing me to sit with folded hands."[74] It goes without saying that Ostrovsky did not dignify Serov's ultimatum with a response, and that the composer was forced to carry out his threat.

The libretto of Acts IV and V of *The Power of the Fiend* was mainly the work of Pyotr Ivanovich Kalashnikov (1826-97), a versifier with considerable operatic experience, having made singing translations for the Mariinsky of *Les Huguenots, Le Prophète, La Traviata* and *Faust,* and having just collaborated with the Mariinsky's recently hired chief conductor Eduard Napravnik on the opera *Nizhegorodtsy.* Serov hired him (for 300 rubles) early in 1870, which means that for something over a year he had again been without a librettist—a familiar predicament!

He treated his new collaborator much as he had handled his pre-Ostrovskian librettists—as an underling to whom he would send detailed prose scenarios and expect their faithful transformation into verse. In this fashion the fourth act was completed to Serov's initial satisfaction (according to Kalashnikov's recollection) by the beginning of March, 1870. And then came the fifth act, with Serov's new resolution of the drama—and yet another falling out with the librettist, only this time with the roles curiously reversed (perhaps the tyrannical Serov unconsciously sought to avenge the wrong done him by his first librettist on his second). Here is how Kalashnikov recalled their parting of the ways:

> Having delivered the fifth act [in May or June, 1870], I considered my work done; when all of a sudden, at the end of July, I received from Serov an entire additional scene for the last act, which he himself had written in prose, along with a letter in which he requested that I translate his prose into verse. Against my better judgment I set to work, but at the same time I wrote him a letter in which I expressed my opinion that the scene was a weak one and made indications in the margins. This served as the grounds for severing our relationship. Serov took offense at my frankness. This scene was later destroyed as unsuitable by Serov himself.[75]

Serov vented his spleen at Kalashnikov in a letter written October 24, 1870, to an unnamed party,[76] in which he complained that Kalashnikov's text was "good for nothing and is undergoing revision." For this task, Serov engaged yet another littérateur, Alexander Fyodorovich Zhokhov (1840-72), a lawyer by profession, who put the finishing touches on the fifth act. Thus another typically Serovian committee of librettists had been assembled.

Freed of Ostrovsky's grip, Serov indulged his sensationalist inclinations more and more extravagantly. He surprised Zvantsev one day by telling him:

> You know what? It's turned out your way: I have decided to slit the wife's throat like a chicken, only not backstage, but in a wild ravine, in a tumbledown shack at the outskirts of town. From afar, beyond the snowdrifts, a church can be seen and the matins bell heard. This will be best of all. [The Mariinsky designer] Bocharov will make me a superb set.[77]

In other words, Serov came back to the Russian "Wolf's Glen" he had derided so early in his correspondence with Ostrovsky. For the sake of a "good set" he was even willing to work some tortured contrivances in the action so as to get all of the characters to the out-of-the-way murder scene.

Such was the tortuous and frustrating creative history of Serov's third and last opera, a work that seemed to have, in its composer's rueful words, "an evil star hanging over it."[78] Serov was more prophetic than he knew: the last unhappy episode in the opera's fate was his death from a sudden heart attack on January 20, 1871, when the opera was on the very brink of completion. The first four acts had gone to the theater's copyists, the artists were learning their roles for the premiere, and since "only a couple of days' work remains on the fifth act, I have a right to say that my opera is done," as Serov put it in the letter of October 24, 1870, quoted from, above.[79] That couple of days' work, however, was left to Mme. Serova to accomplish. It is usually said that the opera was finished by Serov's disciple Nikolai Feopemptovich Soloviov (1846-1916), best known as a critic, but a composer of some reputation in the late nineteenth century.[80] However, according to correspondence between Mme. Serova and Nikolai Findeisen following publication of the latter's life of the composer, it appears that the fifth act was more or less her work, composed "on the basis of sketches Serov had played on the piano but had never written down."[81] Soloviov's role was to tie up such loose ends as the orchestration of the Introduction to Act I and the second half of Pyotr's scene in the same act. In its posthumously completed form the opera was presented at the Mariinsky on April 19 (May 1), 1871.[82]

"I sit and pore over the 'songs' and feel in my bones the possibility of a completely new style for a Great-Russian national opera," Serov had written Ostrovsky in the palmy days of their collaboration.[83] At the heart of that style—"which has nothing in common either with ordinary operatic methods or with those of Serov himself in his two prior operas," in the composer's own words[84]—was the carefully planned and executed symbiosis of genre and dramatic content, two elements that so often impeded one another in "historical" or "national" musical dramas, including Serov's own *Rogneda,* as the composer surely came to be aware. The fundamental difference between the new opera and its predecessors was that the "organic" connection with "the soil" was to be sought in the music itself, all of which, from recitative to ensemble, was to be "permeated with that peculiar style of Russian genre *(bytovoi)* song, which reigned infectiously in the young Moscow circle that edited the *Moskvitianin* in the early 1850s, when the leading role was played by Apollon Grigoriev,"[85] and thus achieve the long-sought goal of a "purely Russian music, without admixture of Western influence."[86] In its tone, style and musical forms, then, Serov's opera was conceived in terms extraordinarily congruent with the aesthetic and cultural milieu that had surrounded Ostrovsky's *Moskvitianin* plays, of which *Live Not the Way You'd Like* was the last. In keeping with the character of the Stakhovich and Villebois folk song anthologies which provided their tunes with accompaniments in the style of the salon romance, Serov's was not a style of unimpeachable ethnological authenticity. It was not "pure." But it was highly distinctive, and it was carried through with remarkable consistency, imbuing *The Power of the Fiend* with a musical flavor wholly original and unique in Russian opera.

The logical starting point for an investigation of Serov's unique achievement is a comparison of Ostrovsky's own use of folksong quotations with Serov's. In the *Moskvitianin* plays, Ostrovsky often used folk songs as "arias," that is, as lyrical epitomes of emotion and mood in a fashion reminiscent of the way Nikolai Chernyshevsky described folk song in his "bible" of artistic realism, *The Esthetic Relations of Art to Reality (Esteticheskie otnosheniia iskusstva k deistvitel'nosti,* 1855). In that book, which appeared the same year as *Live Not the Way You'd Like,* the question of music's relation to the phenomenal world was resolved by looking upon spontaneous music, that is, upon folk song, as an artifact not of art but of nature: "Singing, being, in essence, an expression of joy or sorrow, does not by any means spring from our striving for beauty."[87] But:

> Natural singing as the expression of emotion, although a product of nature and not of art, which consciously concerns itself with beauty, nonetheless possesses great beauty; that is why a person is prompted by the desire to sing deliberately, to imitate natural singing. In what relation does this artificial singing stand to natural singing? It is more deliberate, calculated, embellished with everything with which human genius can embellish it. What comparison can there be between an aria of an Italian opera and the simple, pale, monotonous melody of a folk song! But all the training in harmony, all the artistry of development, all the wealth of embellishment of a brilliant aria, all the flexibility and incomparable richness of the voice of the one who sings it cannot make up for the absence of the sincere emotion that permeates the pale melody of a folk song and the ordinary,

untrained voice of the one who sings it not from a desire to pose and display his voice and art, but from the need to express his feelings.[88]

Table 1 gives a list of all the places in *Live Not the Way You'd Like* where Ostrovsky resorted to "natural singing," together with a breakdown of their appearance in the collections closest to the *Moskvitianin* circle, and an identification of the analogous place in Serov's opera. Ostrovsky's selection of songs is a tight-knit group. All of them, if their music was printed at all, were printed by Stakhovich or by Villebois, and one was later dictated by Tertii Filippov to Rimsky-Korsakov. Of those that were never published in musical notation, the text editors include Pavel Yakushkin (1822-72), the Slavophile ethnographer, and Grigoriev himself.

Serov limited himself just as stringently in his sources of folk songs for direct citation in *The Power of the Fiend*. With a single (highly significant) exception, all of the genuine tunes traceable in his opera came from Stakhovich or Villebois, thus maintaining their closeness to Ostrovsky and his world. Of the four songs cited by Ostrovsky that were available in published musical editions, Serov adopted three directly: nos. 2, 6 and 9 on Table 1. *Iskhodila mladen'ka* (no. 7), as we have seen, was dropped when either Serov or Ostrovsky decided to tighten the operatic version of the scene in which it appears by having Pyotr burst in just as the girls are preparing to sing it.

The dance song with which Eryomka teases the girls in the same scene (no. 6) is reproduced in the opera in a strikingly naturalistic way. Eryomka here sings (rather than "speaks") in the course of the action. His song is set forth unaccompanied, except for the laughter and patter of Grunya and the girls. Here folk song occurs in opera just as it does in life, and provides a means of rooting art in the "soil" (Ex. 4.1).

Another instance where unaccompanied "natural singing" is given real dramaturgical significance occurs near the end of Act I, where Ostrovsky has Vasya "sing his sorrow" at Grunya's fickleness. Serov used the song whose text Ostrovsky cited (our no. 2—he even wrote to the librettist to verify the "true motive" for this song[89]). This is the unique instance of an authentic *protiazhnaia*, that is, a melismatically lyrical "drawn out" peasant song, in all of Serov's works, and it is no wonder that Gerald Abraham, for one, was "incredulous" at the prospect that Serov had invented the tune himself.[90] As in the play, Ostrovsky's libretto builds an entire scene around the song: Dasha tries to question Vasya, who ignores her and goes on singing. Serov's problem was to differentiate the music that represents "speech" from the "natural singing." His solution was to use very quick notes, repeated pitches and chromatic touches that effectively removed the "spoken" music from the folk world. As in the preceding example, Dasha's musical "speech" is set in counterpoint against Vasya's otherwise unaccompanied song (Ex. 4.2).

Table 1. Use of Folk Songs in *Live Not the Way You'd Like*

Location and Title of Song in Play	Location in: Stakhovich	Villebois	Other Sources	Analogous Spot in *The Power of the Fiend*
1. Act I, sc. vi (Pyotr alone): "*Udalaia golova, ne khodi mimo sada*" (Hot-headed one, don't go by the garden)	Vol. I (St. P., 1851), no. 2		*Pesennik* (1808) —text only. *Pesni, sobrannye N. V. Gogolem* (1908) —text only. Rimsky-Korsakov (1877), no. 33.	Act I, no. 5 (Pyotr's monologue): "*Ekh! golovushka moia buinaia.*" Vocal score (Moscow, 1968), p. 46.
2. Act I, sc. xi (Dasha and Vasya): "*Vostoskuisia ty moia ty moia sudarushka*" (Lament, o my lady)		*Ruskie narodnie pesni*, no. 16	Balakirev, *Sbornik russkikh narodnykh pesen* (1866), no. 36: "*I chto na svete prezhe-stokom.*"	Act I, no. 7 (Dasha and Vasya): "*Ekh! vostoskuisia, vozgoriuisia.*"
3. Act II, sc. v (Pyotr and Grunya): "*Kak u molodtsa, u udalogo*" (As with a reckless youth)			Sobolevsky, *Velikorusskie narodnie pesni,* III (1897) —text only.	Act II, no. 13 (Pyotr and Grunya)
4. Same scene: "*Mne ne dorog tvoi podarok*" (It is not your gift I cherish) —an excerpt from the song, "*Po ulitse mostovoi*" (Along the bridge road)			*Pesennik* (1808) —text only. Sobolevsky, IV (1898) —text only.	Act II, no. 13: "*Mne ne dorog tvoi podarok*"
5. Act II, sc. x (finale): "*Polechu ia ptashechkoi, kukushechkoiu*" (I will fly away like a bird, like the cuckoo) —an excerpt from the song, "*Kalinu s malinoiu voda poniala*" (The water carried off the berries)			I. Sakharov, *Pesni russkogo naroda* (1838) —text only. A. Grigoriev, *Russkie narodnie pesni (sob. soch.,* vyp. 14, 1915) —text only.	Act II, no. 14 (finale)
6. Act III, sc. iii (Eryomka and the girls): "*Ia na kamushke sizhu*" (I sit here on a bench)		*Russkie narodnie pesni*, no. 21	Filippov-Rimsky-Korsakov (1882) no. 37. Yakushkin (1884) —text only. Sobolevsky, III and IV —text only.	Act III, no. 16 (Eryomka): "*Ia na kamushke sizhu*", p. 214
7. Same scene: "*Iskhodila mladen'ka vse luga i bolota*" (The girl wandered over meadow and field) [NB: Ostrovsky is said to have taken this song down from the gypsy singer Anton Sergeev.]		*Russkie narodnie pesni*, no. 7	Daniil Kashin, *Ruskie narodnie pesni,* II (1833-34) Yakushkin (1884) —text only.	(not used)
8. Act III, sc. iv (Eryomka and Grusha): "*Sirota l' ty moia, sirotinushka*" (My little orphan girl)			Sobolevsky, IV —text only. Dobrovol'ski, *Smolenkskii etnograficheskii sbornik,* Moscow, 1903.	Scene dropped from libretto, so apparently not used. But cf. Grunya's "Tale," p. 219ff.
9. Act III, sc. vi (Pyotr and Eryomka): "*Kumanechek pobyvai u menia*" (Come and see me, old pal)	Vol. II (1852), no. 8		Sobolevsky, IV ·text only. Ivan Vasiliev, "*Kumanēk, pobyvai u menia, russkaia narodnaia pesnia*" (separate publication) Moscow (Gutheil), n.d.	Act III, no. 17 (Pyotr and Eryomka): "*Ty, kupec, so mnoiu ne branis','* p. 242 ff.

*Information on text sources mainly derived from the critical commentary to the 1973 edition of Ostrovsky's works, ed. L.N. Smirnova (Moscow: "Iskusstvo"), vol. I.

Ex. 4.1.   *The Power of the Fiend* (Moscow: Izdatel'stvo "Muzyka," 1968), p. 215

The remaining instance where Ostrovsky's use of folk song was followed directly by the composer provided the spark for what is surely one of the most extraordinary numbers in *The Power of the Fiend,* or indeed in any Russian opera of the period—the song to the balalaika (cleverly imitated in the orchestra) that unites and dominates the Act III finale. Based as it is on the most conspicuously song-dominated scene in the original play, Serov's setting truly achieves the organic union of genre and dramatic action that had made Ostrovsky the great "people's poet" for Grigoriev, and for whose intensification through Serov's music the critic had so yearned. And fittingly so, one feels, since this scene was the last in which Ostrovsky and Serov were true collaborators. In the play, Ostrovsky had had Eryomka coyly hum and strum

Fig. 4.3   Konstantin Villebois, transcriber of folk songs from
Ostrovsky's rendition, whose published collections were
Serov's main source for *The Power of the Fiend*

Ex. 4.2.   *The Power of the Fiend*, pp. 61-63

the strains of the popular dance tune *Kumanechek, pobyvai u menia* between his sinister repliques, as he tightens his hold over Pyotr. In recasting the scene for the libretto, Ostrovsky expanded the role of the song by using its meter and rhyme for much of Eryomka's part. But Serov was able to effect a far more potent and thorough integration of the song into the action than was available to the author of the spoken drama, by actually setting Eryomka's repliques to its tune, and by having the strumming balalaika imitations in the orchestra accompany the whole scene. The music reaches a striking peroration on the words "Uzh ia li tvomu goriu pomogu! Pomogu-mogu-mogu-mogu-mogu!" which had been the blacksmith's exit line in the original play (Ex. 4.3).

Ex. 4.3.   *The Power of the Fiend*, pp. 242-44, voice part only

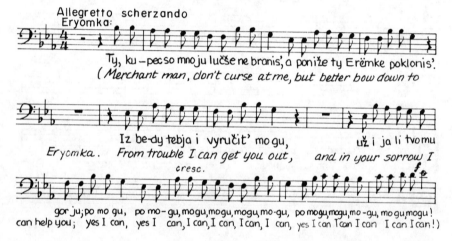

The whole scene proceeds as a series of ostinato variations on the *Kumanechek* motif—a kind of sinister *Kamarinskaia*. The effect of the ceaseless repetitions and the concluding refrain is insidious. The song, for all its surface gaiety, shudderingly casts Eryomka as the incarnation of the diabolical *maslenitsa*—the "power of the fiend"—and does so not through conventional Romantic supernaturalism, but through the employment of materials very much of the real world. This is *pochvennik* "true realism" at its most potent: surface and "ideal" plots are integrated by means of one of the most commonplace of Russian ditties. Drama has truly been "revealed through song," for the song is made a medium of dialogue.

Where Ostrovsky had resorted to folk verses in the play, but where there were no published tunes available, Serov adapted other songs from Stakhovich and Villebois. The duet scene in Act II (Grunya and Pyotr), which incorporates nos. 3 and 4 on Table 1, is mainly constructed on a series of free paraphrases of the fifth song in the Villebois collection, "Plyvët-vosplyvaet." One of them (Ex. 4.4c) is set to the folk verses ("Mne ne dorog tvoi podarok") cited by Ostrovsky in the original play (see Table 1).

Ex. 4.4.   a. K.I. Villebois, *100 russkikh pesen* (St. Petersburg, 1860), no. 5

b. *The Power of the Fiend*, p. 143

c. *The Power of the Fiend*, p. 144

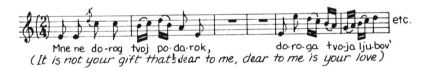

d. *The Power of the Fiend*, p. 147

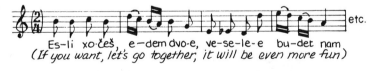

This lengthy duet, in its pervasive couplet structure, harks back to the Russian vaudeville style of the 1820s and 30s, as typified in the work of Verstovsky and Titov. Something of the color of a *bytovoi* romance à la Varlamov can be found in the passage in *The Power of the Fiend* corresponding to no. 5 on Table 1, the Act II finale where Dasha, unknowingly in the presence of her parents, pours out her heart in song. The folk verses are marked by Ostrovsky to be delivered "in a sing-song fashion, through her tears,"[91] a perfect application of Chernyshevskian "natural singing." At this point in the opera, Serov rather radically adapted another tune from the Villebois collection, as follows:

Ex. 4.5.   a. Villebois, no. 67

b. *The Power of the Fiend*, pp. 162-63

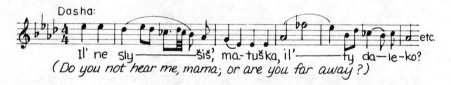

This mock-*protiazhnaia* has an interesting 5-measure phrase structure, but its plaintive rising minor sixth and its use of the leading tone (neither of them features of the original tune) reveal Serov's deliberate evocation of "urban" sentimentality as part of Dasha's characterization.

The remaining instances of adaptation of genuine folk song occur in spots that have no direct analogue in the original play. The beginning of Act II has three interpolated numbers (one each for Spiridonovna, Eryomka and Grunya). The last of these incorporates two songs from Villebois, as shown in Example 4.6. The second of them—the *khorovod* tune *U vorot batiush-kinykh*—is familiar to Westerners thanks to its citation in Tchaikovsky's "1812" Overture.

Ex. 4.6.   a. Villebois, no. 24

b. *The Power of the Fiend*, p. 116

Už ty ma-tuš—ka ro-di-ma, ty pečal' ni——ca mo-ja,
(Oh mother, dearest mother, do not send me off in

ne ot-daj men-ja ty za-muž za bo-ga————to-go!
marriage to a rich man!)

c. Villebois, no. 17

U vo-rot, vo-rot, vo-rot da vo-rot ba-tju-ški—nyx, aj, Dunaj,

moj Du-naj, aj ve-se-lyj Du-naj!

d. *The Power of the Fiend*, p. 116

Ax ni-kto men-ja ne ljub-it, ni-kto za-muž ne be-rët! Už ko mu li
(Ah, nobody loves me, no one will marry me.   And who-

ja pon-ra-vu, ja sa——ma nej-du!
ever does like me, I won't have!

The chorus of girls going skating at the beginning of Act III draws on yet
another *khorovod* from Villebois:

Ex. 4.7.   a. Villebois, no. 36

Ja po-e—du vo Ki-taj-go-rod gu-lja—ti;—— ja ku-plju li

mo-lo-doj že—ne po— kup——ku

b. *The Power of the Fiend*, p. 191, first soprano

This song, first heard in counterpoint to Grunya's lament, is consistently used by Serov for ironic juxtapositions. Heard offstage or in the orchestra alone, it forms an effective backdrop to sinister action in Acts IV and V. The last occurrence of it, though it comes from the "posthumous" act in which Serov's intentions cannot be judged with certainty, is particularly noteworthy not only for its irony but for its superimposition of two levels of "realism"— the background of genre music against the foreground of naturalistic declamation which is prevalent in the last two acts. The effect is one familiar in the works of Musorgsky (Ex. 4.8).

Ex. 4.8.   *The Power of the Fiend*, pp. 356-57

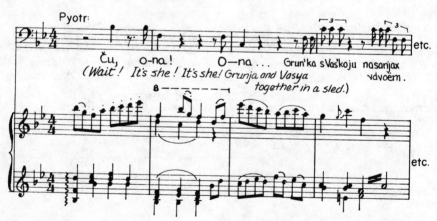

Finally, we may mention a kind of orchestral synthesis of the traditional *Kamarinskaia* and the dance tune, *Uzh ty, Van'ka, prignis',* from the Stakhovich anthology, which Serov introduced in the Act III scene between Eryomka and the girls, to support some recitative dialogue. The Stakhovich tune is familiar from its use by Rimsky-Korsakov in the famous "Dance of the Skomorokhi" from *Snegurochka* (Ex. 4.9).

Ex. 4.9.   a. *Kamarinskaya* (Field transcription printed in
Bachinskaya, *Narodnye pesni v tvorchestve russkikh
kompozitorov*, Moscow, 1962), p. 54

b. M. Stakhovich, *Sobranie russkikh narodnykh pesen,*
vol. II, p. 9

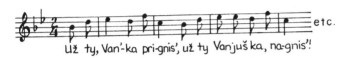

c. *The Power of the Fiend*, p. 210ff, orchestral theme

These citations have been documented at length not only because there are
more of them than in any previous Russian opera of importance,[92] and not
only because in some cases their working-in is unusually "organic,"[93] but
because of the notable freedom of approach evident in Serov's adaptations.
The only songs cited more-or-less unchanged were the ones taken over directly
from the play (Examples 4.1-4.3). All the rest have been willfully altered, some
to a degree that would seem to call their very status as citations into question.
Intervals are narrowed or widened at will, phrase structure is recast, even
modes are changed. The citations can, however, be accepted as genuine
because we fortunately possess some documentation of Serov's methods.
Ostrovsky had peppered the libretto's first act with a number of "Moscow
songs," as Serov called them. Upon receipt of the text, the composer wrote to
his collaborator rather urgently for their "genuine tunes." The librettist had
written, apparently out of dim recollection, the couplet *"Kak u nashego
dvora/priukatana gora,"* and Serov was "exasperated" to find that no

standard anthology seemed to contain what Ostrovsky assured him had been
a very popular song in his youth. "Won't you tell me where to find it? And also,
if possible any of the others: it is for me a matter of the utmost importance."[94]
Finally Serov located a variant of Ostrovsky's couplet buried within the text
of the song, *Kapitanskaia doch', ne khodi guliat' v polnoch',* as it appeared in
the old Lvov-Pratsch collection.[95] But having found the tune at last, Serov felt
he had to reject it, his chief reason being that its first phrase was too similar to
his own "Dance of the Maidens" in *Rogneda,* Act II (Ex. 4.10).

Ex. 4.10.   a. Lvov-Pratsch, *Sobranie narodnykh russkikh pesen*
(St. Petersburg, 1790), no. 61

b. *Rogneda* (Moscow: V. Bessel, ca. 1885), p. 79

As for the rest of the tune, Serov had this to say: "The second half of the
song (the "descent" as you call it, according to Apollon Grigoriev's notes)
begins animatedly enough, but ends up somewhat gloomy. Therefore I cannot
use this song in its entirety."[96] What he ended up doing, then, was to change
the pitch content of the melody to the point where only a few of the original
notes remained in place (while the mode was transformed in the process). The
rhythm, however, was maintained without alteration (cf. the comparable
approach to some of the tunes from Villebois, as given, e.g., in Example 4.4).
In its new guise the tune permeates the entire opera, beginning with the very
first notes the listener hears at the outset of the Introduction to Act I, from
which we quote it. On this first appearance it is immediately coupled with
balalaika imitations (Ex. 4.11).

We may now summarize the extent of Serov's appropriation of authentic
Russian folk songs in the first three acts of *The Power of the Fiend* in a table.[97]
(See Table 2.)

Table 2.   Folk Songs in *The Power of the Fiend*

Location in Opera	Title	Location in: Stakhovich	Villebois	Other Sources
1. Overture Act I, sc. ii: Chorus: "*Uzh ia skok na ledok*" (Well, I slipped on the ice) —and many other places—	*Kapitanskaia doch',* *ne khodi guliat' v polnoch'* (Captain's daughter, don't go out in the middle of the night)			Lvov-Pratsch (1790), no. 61
2. Act I, no. 7: Vasya: "*Ekh! vostoskuisia, vozgoriuisia!*" (Ah, moan and groan)	*Vostoskuisia moia, ty moia sudarushka* (Lament, o my lady)		no. 16	Balakirev, no. 36 Filippov/ Rimsky-Korsakov (1884)
3. Act II, no. 10b (Grunya's song): Introduction and second part	*Otdavala menia matushka* (My mother has given me in marriage)		no. 22	Rimsky- Korsakov (1877) no. 24.
4. The same, main theme: "*Akh, nikto menia ne liubit*" (Ah, no one loves me)	*U vorot batiushkinikh* (At father's gates)		no. 17	Balakirev, no. 38
5. Act II, no. 13 (duet): "*Ty khodi ko mne pochashche*" (Come and see me more often)	*Plyvët-vosplyvaet* (Swimming, oh a-swimming)		no. 5	
6. Act II, no. 14 (finale): Dasha: "*Il' ne slyshish* *matushka?*" (Do you not hear me, mother?)	*Za dvorom luzhok zelenëshenek* (A lovely green meadow)		no. 67	Rimsky- Korsakov, no. 65
7. Act III, no. 15 (girls' chorus): "*Ia ne znaiu kak mne s milym pomirit'sia*" (I don't know how to make up with my beloved)	*Ia poedu vo Kitai-gorod* (I'm going to Chinatown)		no. 36	
8. Act III, no. 16: Orchestral theme associated with Eryomka	*Kamarinskaya* *(Wedding Dance Tune)* *Uzh ty, Van'ka, prignis'* (Come here, Vanka)	 Bk. II, no. 3		Trad. (perhaps via Glinka)
9. Act III, no. 16 (Eryomka): "*Ia na kamushke sizhu*"	*Ia na kamushke sizhu* (I'm sitting on a bench)		no. 21	Filippov/ Rimsky-Korsakov, no. 37
10. Act III, no. 17 (Pyotr and Eryomka): "*Ty, kupets, so mnoiu ne branis'*" (Merchant man, don't curse at me)	*Kumanechek, pobyvai u menia* (Come see me, old pal)	Book II, no. 8		Ivan Vasiliev, *Kumanek*

Comparison of Tables 1 and 2 reveals one notable discrepancy: there is no song in Serov to correspond with *Udalaia golova* (Table 1: No. 1), the folk song around which Ostrovsky had originally built Pyotr's Act I soliloquy. And this is a very significant point regarding Pyotr and his musical characterization, which was the first stumbling block to interfere with Serov and Ostrovsky's working relationship. After a full year of work, Serov wrote to his librettist:

> In his monologue Pyotr must reveal himself *in full*. This scene I have *all this time* (NB!) left a blank (while otherwise three acts are all ready). I *have not been able* to write it! Now I understand *why*. There's a false note here; the words do not go with the character as I have understood him. You have given Pyotr too "light" a turn. I *don't want* a good-for-nothing tavern bum. For me he must be all energy and passion, a choleric from head to toe, the personification of ardor, impetuosity, and—rage.[98]

But behind these words lies the fundamental transformation of *The Power of the Fiend* into tragedy that ended the Serov-Ostrovsky partnership. The Pyotr of Serov's opera is an altogether different character from the Pyotr

Ex. 4.11.   *The Power of the Fiend*, p. 5

of *Live Not the Way You'd Like*: where the latter is an idle, unreflective simpleton, Serov's Pyotr is a dark, tortured soul capable of murder. Nevertheless (and even after the huge insult he was dealt by the composer with regard to the opera's ending), Ostrovsky complied with Serov's request for a new monologue for Pyotr; on October 1, 1868, the composer wrote to thank the playwright for the new version.[99] Whereas the older one (as we know from another passage in the letter quoted above) maintained the folk song "aria" from the original play, the revised scene did away with it. And so, except for the vaudevillesque duet with Grunya in Act II (which represents an early phase of the composer's work on the libretto and his attitude toward the characters), Pyotr is the character in *The Power of the Fiend* least given to "natural singing," or what later Russian critics would call "folk intonations." This peculiarity of his role very effectively underscores his dramatic isolation.

Otherwise, folk intonations are pervasive in *The Power of the Fiend*, and here we come to the most interesting aspect of Serov's music—independent creation in the folk style. This was Serov's response to Grigoriev's call for the idealized, spiritual portrayal of "life as it is," much as Ostrovsky had responded in turning the prose dialogue of his original play into simulated folk verses. Taking his cue from Grigoriev's view of folk song as a meeting ground between "life" and "art," since it occupied a position intermediate between the two and was "organically" related to each, Serov envisioned a musical style—and thence a dramatic style—in which elements of Russian folk music would penetrate the entire compositional fabric, in which, truly, drama *would* be "revealed through songs." "Western influences" would disappear not out of a conscious act of will, but by a natural process of replacement. Nor would mere incorporation of folk tunes or folklike melodic formulas do the trick. Alone, they led, even in *Ruslan* and *Rusalka* (to say nothing of *Rogneda*) to "decorativeness" and dramaturgical trivialization, most recently exemplified in the Kashperov-Ostrovsky *The Storm*. In reviewing this last opera, Serov attempted to point out the path along which an "organic" Russian style might develop.

> Russian folksong, without doubt, is *not* dramatic music; from songs—in their raw state— one cannot weave a musical drama. But the ideal of Russian music *after* Glinka and Dargomyzhsky demands unfailingly, nonetheless, that *every phrase* of a Russian opera on a Russian subject be molded in forms congeneric in their tonal resources and devices with Russian folk song. In the absence of that condition there will always be a gaping abyss between a Russian text and the "European" music written to it, an abyss which nothing can fill in or cover up.[100]

The first task, then, was one of definition: what were the "tonal resources and devices" that together made up an "organically" Russian style? Serov constructed a rather elaborate theory of Russian folk music that differed markedly from other "enlightened" views on the subject, as expressed notably by Laroche and by the Stasov/Balakirev party. They had maintained that Russian folk music was cast in the medieval "church modes" and that it had been given exemplary artistic treatment by Glinka. Serov rejected both these premises, holding rather that Russian folk songs are best analyzed according to the ancient Greek tetrachord system, from which position he proceeded to make rather extravagant genealogical claims. The sources of Russian music were to be found, he asserted, "among the ancient Hellenes, and perhaps even further back than that, all the way back to the very roots of music in the cradle of all culture, in India, in holy Aryan Bharat."[101] Though many of the specific points Serov prescribed to preserve the purity of the Russian style—strict diatonicism, avoidance of the raised leading tone and "dominant" harmony in the minor, etc.—were similar to the contemporary prescriptions of Laroche[102] and the practices of Balakirev,[103] Serov's insight (leaving aside the dubious "historical" underpinning) is a real one, not a quibble. For Serov recognized that Russian folk songs are often restricted to a very small range of pitches, that they are even more often pentatonic, and that there is apt to be a radical distinction between "structural" and "ornamental" tones within the pitch vocabulary of a given melody. The "church modes" theory accounted for none of these features, but Serov's reference to the tetrachord system shows at least that he perceived them accurately.

For an example of Serovian folk lyricism at its most characteristic, we may examine his sensitive setting of the libretto's opening lines, on whose derivation from those of the original play we have already commented in some detail (Ex. 4.12).

The first and second lines are set respectively to three and four bars of music, yielding a characteristically Russian seven-bar phrase. Characteristic, too, is the fleeting excursion to the relative major (ethnomusicologists call this *peremennost'*) at the beginning of the second line. Most remarkable is the spare accompaniment, particularly for its avoidance of dominant harmony and its reliance on plagal cadences. In the second measure the dominant is replaced by the subdominant under the second scale degree in the melody. The resulting harmony (which could be described either as a half-diminished-seventh or as an added-sixth chord) is a dominant-surrogate that colors much of *The Power of the Fiend,* and is one of the means by which Serov sought and achieved a consistent, distinctive and "organic" Russian flavor. At the end of the second line, the expected dominant chord is replaced by the premature arrival of the tonic, producing another plagal cadence and throwing the harmonic rhythm interestingly off balance. The one appearance of the dominant root (meas. 15) is conspicuously devoid of leading tone.

In the opera's best known number, Eryomka's Shrovetide song, *Shirokaia maslenitsa* (Act II)—a favorite vehicle of Chaliapin's—dominant chords are in a like manner consistently shorn of their thirds, except in the minor-

Ex. 4.12.   *The Power of the Fiend*, p. 13

mode section near the end, where Serov employs the natural minor dominant, without borrowed leading tone. (Curiously enough, when the song modulates from F major to C, Serov fastidiously marks a B natural to cancel the signature flat, but as that note is the new leading tone it never once appears in the music.) The melodic writing tends toward the pentatonic, as is especially clear in the unaccompanied invocation that precedes each section. The entire song is constructed in a fashion typical of Russian *pliasovie* (dance tunes)— endless rhythmic-melodic ostinato variations (Ex. 4.13).

If elements of genre and setting are at times strikingly invested with dramatic import (e.g., the Act III duet on *Kumanechek*), the interpenetration works the other way as well: dramatic scenes are suffused with elements appropriated from genre music. The recitatives of *The Power of the Fiend* contain many minuscule rounded structures of folklike cast, comparable on their smaller scale with the larger, more "concerted" numbers we have thus far examined. That it is often difficult to draw a stylistic line between "recitative" and lyric utterance in Serov's opera is, of course, very much a sign of the times. But the way in which Serov broke down the distinction was as radically different from the "Wagnerian reform," on the one hand, as it was from, say,

Ex. 4.13.   *"Shirokaia maslenitsa"*

a. The invocation

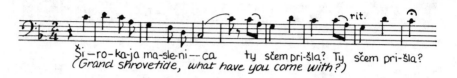

b. The main theme

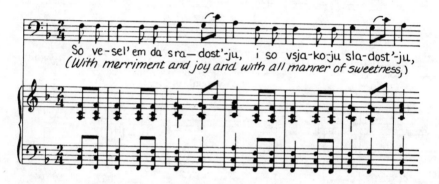

c. The dominant section

d. The minor section

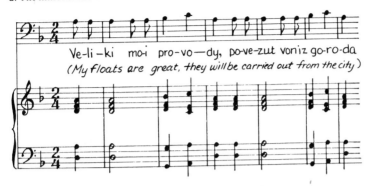

Dargomyzhsky's practice on the other. If the German and Russian reformers tended toward continuous declamation, Serov tended in the opposite direction—toward continuous lyricism, a constant penetration of the folk melos on all levels and "scales." Consider, for example, the little recitative that begins the last scene of Act III, the one that culminates in the *Kumanechek* variations. Eryomka's repliques form a perfect little "bar" in four rhythmically symmetrical lines, with a tonal excursion and return (Ex. 4.14).

Ex. 4.14.   *The Power of the Fiend*, p. 239, voice only

Extended scenes in dialogue are often treated in this manner. The opening of Act I, sc. iii offers a striking example of "drama revealed through song" according to Serov's first conception, when his ideas wholly harmonized with Ostrovsky's. In Dasha's arioso-like repliques, where the tempo is halved and the orchestra launches into figuration, the avoidance of the dominant leading tone is again conspicuous.[104] Pyotr's intervening outburst is set to the "dominant-surrogate" chord noted in connection with the opera's opening number[105] (Ex. 4.15).

Ex. 4.15.   *The Power of the Fiend*, pp. 25-27

Ex. 4.15 (cont'd)

One must, of course, acknowledge the possibility that Serov's continuous sing-song was not entirely deliberate. We have noted his weakness of rhythmic invention as far back as our discussion of *Judith*, and Ostrovsky's (and later Kalashnikov's) rhymed couplets placed further constraints on rhythmic plasticity. But if there are instances in *The Power of the Fiend* where sequences of rhythmically monotonous lines set off by dutiful caesurae effectively frustrate dramatic urgency, there are others where dramatic urgency is heightened equally effectively by means of rhythmic sequences derived, it would seem, from the ostinati of dance tunes. A striking example (the more so as such things are so rare in his part) is Pyotr's Act IV monologue, wherein he recalls the prophecy of the wizard whom Eryomka had taken him to visit (Ex. 4.16).

Perhaps the outstanding instance in *The Power of the Fiend* of recitative in the style of folk song is the entrance of Dasha's parents, Stepanida and Agafon, in the Act II finale. Both Stepanida's and Grunya's parts are marked by the composer *"govorkom"* (the equivalent of the Italian *parlando*), but the music is in no essential way distinguishable from that of the concerted numbers in style. The only difference is in the accompaniment, in the purest secco manner. The endless rhythmic repetitions do not entirely avoid monotony (perhaps Serov was counting upon the paralando delivery to take care of that), owing to the caesurae which are in most cases—but not always!—forced by Ostrovsky's obvious and unrelenting meter. The melodic writing is in the purest natural minor, with nary a "Western" leading tone. Within the pervading sing-song, Serov manages a neat characterization of the old, slow-moving Stepanida, who sings in eighths and quarters, vis-à-vis the young, frisky Grunya, who sings practically identical material in sixteenths and eighths (Ex. 4.17).

But Serov was not always content with such verse-imposed regularity of rhythm, however central to his conception of *bytovaia* opera it may have been. At times we see him straining to break the hold of Ostrovsky's couplets. Successive lines of identical metrical content are occasionally set a bit self-consciously to different musical rhythms. Sometimes the effect of this is natural and felicitous. In the Act II finale, the hamstrung rhythms of the scene between Dasha and her parents (not even the moment of recognition can jolt these "positive" characters out of their folklike cadences!) are to a certain extent "justified" and redeemed by their sudden and effective abandonment when Agafon angrily refuses to take his daughter back (Ex. 4.18, p. 198).

No less frequently, though, the effect is a bit contrived, and shows Serov's rhythmic ingenuity to have been a bit overtaxed by Ostrovsky's libretto. In the following passage from Act II, the triplets in Grunya's part refreshingly break the stranglehold of the preceding quarter-eighth dactyls. But the rhythmic flexibility thus achieved is immediately vitiated by the replique of the merchant, who chimes in with a parallel rhythmic period for no evident purpose save the satisfaction of the composer's compulsion for symmetry (Ex. 4.19, p. 199).

Ex. 4.16.   *The Power of the Fiend,* pp. 286-88

[I can't drink away my anguish with wine, I can't chase away my black thoughts with carousal; I'm drunk without wine, I wander like a madman; fear has clouded my fevered brain. . . That grey wizard is haunting me, and what he divined about my fate. Night and day he stands before me, and I hear his accursed speech all the time: "At midnight, in the dark forest, sharp beaks gnaw, furious owls and birds have spoken of you, that you will be married, youth, it must be, and the whispering wind at midnight will tell you what to do!" If that wizard is not lying, then there will be a wedding! But then how do I get rid of my wife? . . .]

A curious byproduct of the pervasive folk lyricism in the "dramatic" scenes of *The Power of the Fiend* was that it led Serov back to the extensive use of ensembles, which by the 1860s had become something of a bugaboo for progressive non-Italian composers. In Russian opera, in fact, the greatest breakaway from ensemble as dramatic resource had been Serov's own *Judith*, which contained only one (*Rogneda* contained no ensembles at all). But in *The Power of the Fiend*, Serov saw fit to reinstate the ensemble as a way of maintaining the all-important lyric impulse in this "drama revealed through song."

Two such scenes demand description. The Dasha/Vasya duet in Act I is remarkable for its freely unfolding, dramaturgically apposite structure. It starts off as a song for Vasya (quoted above as Example 4.2), in which he expresses his misery at the loss of Grunya's love. At this point Dasha's part is confined to short repliques—questions and interjections—as she urges Vasya to drink and tell all. As her suspicions mount, however, her lines become longer until, having guessed the truth (that Grunya's new lover is her husband), she bursts into a full-fledged song of woe to match Vasya's. (Here Serov is careful to mark over Dasha's part, "in her despair no longer listening to Vasya," so as to "justify" the simultaneous soliloquies that have been set in motion.) Once Dasha begins to participate with Vasya on an equal footing, Vasya begins to grow sleepy from drink, and Dasha gradually dominates the number which culminates in an *agitatissimo* that is hers alone, Vasya having fallen asleep. This is a superbly built and crafted scene, displaying a real dynamic (hence dramatic) structure, unified by means of an orchestral accompaniment based on the theme of Dasha's song (quoted above in Example 4.12). Its progressively unfolding shape is intensified by Serov's fluid modulatory scheme. The key shifts with each stage of Vasya's progressive revelation, as marked by Dasha's response. Beginning in f# minor, the duet passes successively through b♭ minor and c♯ minor, finally returning to the original key-signature (this time hovering freely between A major and its parallel and relative minors) at the moment when Dasha guesses that "My husband!" is the man who stole Grunya from Vasya. Both the Russian folk-influenced modal instability within a given key-signature and the Lisztian tendency toward cyclic modulation by thirds (except that rather uniquely, Serov does it with minor rather than major keys) are highly characteristic of the poignant harmonic texture of *The Power of the Fiend*; from this point of view the opera is remarkably consistent. (The whole number is given in Appendix C.) The opera's "grandest" ensemble, however, is considerably less successful. The moment near the end of Act II when Grunya overhears Dasha's complaint to her parents is made to order for ensemble treatment, and Serov did not evade the mandate of his text. But the result is curious. That Serov saw this number as one of the central musical moments of the opera is apparent from its inclusion almost in toto in the orchestral Introduction to

Ex. 4.17.   *The Power of the Fiend*, pp. 156-57

Что ж у вас о - на, видно, за москов-ско_го за_муж от_да_на?
Čto ž u vas o-na, vidno, za moskovskogo zamuž otdana?
[What kind of girl is she? You gave her in marriage to a Muscovite, it's plain to see.]

Лю_ди мы по -
Lju-di my po-
[We are peasant

-сад ски_е и жи_вем дом _ ком в го_ро_де Вла _ ди _ ми _ ре, на пу_ти боль.шом.
-sadskie i živëm domkom v go-ro-de Vla-di-mi-re, na pu-ti bol'šom.
[folk and live in a little house in Vladimir town, on a big road.]

p

День день_ской я стря _ па_ю, _ в хло _ по_тах о _ тец. К Да _ ше и под _ ла_стил_ся
Den' den'skoj ja strjapaju,-v xlopotax o - tec. K Da-še i pod-lastilsja
[I cook the livelong day, the father keeps busy. With Dasha there fell in love

мо _ ло_дой ку _ пец. (Ведь за дев _ кой- до_че_рью ну_жен глаз да глаз!)
mo-lo-doj ku-pec. (Ved' za dev-koj -dočer-ju nu-žen glaz da glaz!)
a young merchant. (You know, you have to keep your eye on a maiden daughter!)

pp

Ex. 4.18.   *The Power of the Fiend*, pp. 167-68, voice parts only

Act I (or rather—to call a spade a spade—the opera's overture). But, having made his decision to write a concerted quartet in disregard of what the *kuchkists* were fond of calling "contemporary operatic criteria," Serov evidently felt himself absolved of all dramaturgical responsibility. The piece begins promisingly enough, with Dasha singing one of her characteristic sentimental "romances" against horrified interjections from Grunya, in a fashion reminiscent of the Judith/Avra duet in Act II of *Judith*. But when all four members of the ensemble have joined in, the composer drops all effort at differentiating the characters—which, after all, is any ensemble's potential strength—and indulges himself in an unabashedly "decorative" confection.[106]

Ex. 4.19.   *The Power of the Fiend*, pp. 115-16, voice parts only
[Eryomka: Well, entertain our dear guests; sing them a
                  merry song.
Spiridonovna: Sing, don't be bashful.
Grunya: I would, but I don't know if they would like
              my song.
Merchant: Go ahead and entertain us the best you
                can; we love to listen and we'll gladly pay!]

At the climax, Dasha and Grunya—whose relationships to the events at hand are dissimilar, and who are supposed to be unaware of one another—sing *fioriture* in harmony that comes too close for comfort to the "thirds and sixths" that even old Glinka had ridiculed years before in conversation with Serov himself.

Pride of place in any consideration of Serovian handling of genre material must go, of course, to Act IV, which depicts the Shrovetide celebration—the *maslenichnoe gulianie*—in full swing. It remains one of the supreme evocations of urban folklore on the Russian stage. One can hardly better Asafiev's enthusiastic description:

The archaic quartal harmony (plus minor seventh) of Russian folk songs, the E♭ clarinet tunes, the witty tracery of the piccolos over the heavy tread of the trainer and his bear, the motley mixture of rhythms, the vividly characteristic and colorful phrases of the tavern drunks, the lurching muzhiks, the cries of the street vendors hawking their wares—spiced mead, hot rolls, honey cakes, *bliny*—the women's shrieks and the boisterous song of strolling couples against the background of shrill commotion, alcoholic fumes, intoxication, high spirits, alongside the exuberant, joyous, buzzing stream of lively, healthy revelry. It all hums, jangles, wails and culminates dazzlingly in the wild Shrovetide procession![107]

We have already noted the links between Serov's *maslenitsa* and the theatrical spectacles of Potekhin. The musical line to which it belongs extends back into the Russian opera's singspiel days (e.g. Matinsky and Pashkevich's *Sanktpeterburgskii gostinyi dvor* [1782] and Alexei Titov's *Maslenitsa* [1813]) and on, of course, to *Petrushka.* [108] The composer took extraordinary pains to achieve verisimilitude and authenticity in matters of genre, even to the extent of consulting the leading folklorists and historians of the day. To Pyotr Alekseevich Bessonov (1828-98), the librarian of Moscow University and editor of Kireevsky's and Rybnikov's collections of folk song texts, Serov addressed a request for, among other things, "a list of the various classes, etc., that might have comprised a crowd celebrating the Shrovetide somewhere on the outskirts of Moscow in the seventeenth century." [109] We may surmise that Bessonov's reply was the source for the assortment of "sellers of various goods and all manner of entertainers" that people Serov's stage. The music reflects this motley crowd with a patchwork of urban ditties and street cries. Serov's musical sublimation of the holiday din on the Moscow square includes some quodlibet passages that display remarkably Petrushkaesque "polytonal" combinations and superimpositions over pedals (Exs. 4.20 and 4.21).

As always, it is impossible without external evidence to tell exactly which tunes are authentic and which invented. The song Pyotr sings with Eryomka and a pair of drunks has as its text the authentic folk song *Kak u nas-to kozël.* The song had figured in Ostrovsky's *Poverty Is No Crime,* and we may suspect therefore that it figured in Serov's opera as a survivor from the playwright's rejected libretto for Act IV. It also appears, as we would have good reason to expect, in Villebois's folk song anthology. But Serov's tune is altogether different from the one recorded by Villebois (Ex. 4.22).

Later in the same scene, one of the drunks launches into a song about "the clink of copper coins." This time the text seems to be unknown in any recorded folk song, yet Serov's melody bears a conclusive resemblance to a Shrovetide tune known to all the world from *Petrushka* (Ex. 4.23).

These drunken ditties and the unappetizing characters who sing them show how, in his Ostrovsky opera, Serov finally redeemed the pledge he made in the Preface to *Rogneda* that "conventional beauty" would be renounced. This, of course, was an issue whose heated debate was raging precisely then, largely provoked by the work of another collateral *pochvennik,* Dostoevsky. [110] The high premium Serov placed on genre realism at whatever cost to beauty has led to his often being described as a proto-*kuchkist.* But actually, except for Musorgsky, the members of the Balakirev circle entertained rather more conventional ideas of beauty than is usually supposed. Cui, for example, writing in response to the *Rogneda* preface, had voiced the opinion that "any work of art, even one that represents the most monstrous phenomena, must necessarily impart to its subject a certain beauty, without which it would be no work of art." And he went on to assert (ironically enough, in the context of

Ex. 4.20.   *The Power of the Fiend*, p. 262

"Scene of Carousal"

Ex. 4.21.   *The Power of the Fiend*, p. 268

Ex. 4.22.   a. Villebois, no. 60

Kak u nas-to ko-zël čto za um-nyj byl, sam i po vo-du xo-
(What a smart goat we had: it went for its own wa-

-dil, sam i ka-šu va-ril.
ter and boiled its own kasha.)

b. *The Power of the Fiend*, pp. 274-75

Kak u nas-to kozël čto za um-nyj byl, sam i povodu xo-dil sam i

ka —šu va-ril.

Ex. 4.23.   a. *The Power of the Fiend*, pp. 280-81

Med-ny de—než-ki zven-jat, vka-ba-ček id -ti vel' jat! Ce-lo-
(Copper coins they jingle and turn us toward the tavern.

-val' ni-ček An-drej, ot-vo-rjaj ka-bak sko-rej!
Hurry up, Andrej, open up the bar.!)

b. *"Akh vy seni, moi seni,"* cited from F.W. Sternfeld,
"Some Russian Folk Songs in Stravinsky's *Petrouchka*
(rpt. in Charles Hamm, ed. *Petrushka:* Norton Critical
Scores, New York, 1967), text restored from Bachinskaya,
p. 35

Ax vy se-ni mo-i se-ni, se-ni no-vy-e mo-i, kak mne po vas po se—

ni-čkam ne xa — ži-va-ti.

The Power of the Fiend) that "foul language off the street, printed with complete literalness and fidelity, is no work of literature."[111] And this, of course, is a view to which Serov himself had subscribed, especially with respect to music, as in his critique of Vladykin's *Whirlpool,* as we have cited it in the last chapter. Now, however, he would not countenance protecting his own opera from the inevitable charge of vulgarity. When early private listeners to the first three acts of the work (without the *maslenitsa!*) already saw fit to raise the issue, Serov complained to his wife in no uncertain terms:

> What the devil do they want?! What's the use of delicacy here? If the subject is vulgar, then it has to be expressed in vulgar terms. Am I to sugar-coat it, or what?! No, let them swallow Eryomka.[112]

After the break with Ostrovsky, when the opera took its bloody turn, Serov's music began to owe somewhat less to folk song and rather more to a more literalistically naturalistic dramaturgy that took as its musical medium a recitative that was modelled not on song but on speech, supported by an empirically conceived, "ugly" harmony. It is as if Serov came to view folk song as too "soft" for his purposes, and too much of a generalizing agent, unsuitable for the kind of grim psychological drama his opera had all at once become. Thus, after its blazing apotheosis in the scene of the *maslenitsa,* the role of genre is much curtailed. Although folk song intonations are not abandoned, they now function largely as an element of contrast. In the next-to-last scene of Act IV (Pyotr and Eryomka, overheard by Vasya), Serov strives for once to make the libretto's relentless couplets disintegrate. The whole scene is marked "v polgolosa, chasto shëpotom" (mezza voce, often whispered), and the composer liberates the rhythm of his recitative declamation by peppering the vocal lines with a barrage of irregular, asymmetrically placed, "naturalistic" rests and pauses. The melodic line is chromatic and tortuous, with big leaps to accented syllables. One also finds the quick repeated notes of conventional parlando. All of this continues until Pyotr, wholly convinced that the plan will succeed, breaks into rapture at the thought of possessing Grunya—a rapture expressed musically in a great rush of "natural singing," a broad folklike melody (the only one of its kind in Pyotr's part), which dominates the conclusion of the scene and accompanies the conspirators' exit (Exs. 4.24 and 4.25).

The fifth act of *The Power of the Fiend* (the scene of the murder) contains, as befits its content, the least folk-derived material and the most naturalistic recitative. One hesitates to cite the music of this act, since the exact extent of Serov's contribution to it is indeterminable.[113] But one is even more reluctant to attribute the most novel aspects of the declamation to Mme. Serova or to Nikolai Soloviov. Here the naturalistic prosody forcefully reminds us that *The Power of the Fiend* was the only mature Serovian opera in which text preceded music, and reminds us what a crucial factor this is. In several ways Serov's declamation anticipates what was to be Musorgsky's practice (or rather, already was Musorgsky's practice, though unbeknownst to Serov or anyone else outside the narrow confines of the Balakirev circle). The stress pattern and tempo of Russian speech is faithfully transmitted by having successive tonic accents fall on successive metrical beats, while intervening unaccented syllables subdivide the beat evenly, making for an abundance of *gruppetti*. Rests placed in accented metrical positions following a string of unaccented syllables—"mute endings" *(glukhie okonchaniia)*, as Russian writers call them—become far more frequent here than anywhere else in Serov's works. Pitch inflection, too, tends to follow a speech model. The words "pomekha li?" in Example 4.26, for instance, faithfully adhere in their rising sixth to the Russian interrogatory intonation pattern in a naturalistic fashion Serov had eschewed in prior acts, where he was more concerned with song than with speech as a model for operatic dialogue (Ex. 4.26, p. 210).

As for "empirical" harmony—another point of kinship with Musorgsky—Serov carries forward what was shaping up as a Russian "tradition" of sorts, the exploitation of the coloristic properties of the whole-tone scale as pioneered by Glinka in his portrayal of Chernomor in *Ruslan*. But where Glinka had used the scale only as a descending bass progression, the composer of *The Power of the Fiend* built chords out of whole-tone clusters, most notably (predictably enough) at the moment of the murder, where they accompany Dasha's bloodcurdling scream (Ex. 4.27, p. 210).

Dasha's last lines are also typical of Act V's unique characteristics. When she realizes that she is about to be killed, she takes the psychological initiative from her husband for a brief moment, cursing him in an uncharacteristically naturalistic explosion of rage, deftly set by Serov to a phrase of extreme angularity and harmonic tension. But when this moment has passed, Dasha reverts to submissive character, and her last words are sung to one of her typical romancelike intonations (Ex. 4.28, p. 210).

But *pochvennichestvo* à la Grigoriev goes deeper yet into the substance and fabric of *The Power of the Fiend*. Two of Serov's most important critical articles in the period that immediately preceded the launching of his own career as operatic composer were attempts to apply principles of "organic criticism" to the operatic masterpieces of the past. In an "étude on Beethoven" entitled "The Thematic Structure of the 'Leonore' Overture," which was published serially for German consumption in the pages of none other than the *Neue Zeitschrift für Musik*,[114] Serov sought to lay to rest the "sophistries of Herr Hanslick" and demonstrate the means by which music is "the *life of the soul* expressed in tones," and, moreover, the carrier of "ideas."[115] This it was able to accomplish, as any Lisztian or Wagnerian knew, through the symbolic use of themes and their transformations (in one Russian word,

Ex. 4.24.   *The Power of the Fiend*, pp. 328-29

Duet, Pyotr and Eryomka

Ex. 4.25.   *The Power of the Fiend*, pp. 338-39

Ex. 4.26.   *The Power of the Fiend,* pp. 362-63

Vot i my   kak raz priexali.   Nam me-te-li-ca   po-me-xa li?
(Well, here we are right on time . A snowstorm doesn't bother us.)

Ex. 4.27.   *The Power of the Fiend,* p. 367

Ex. 4.28.   *The Power of the Fiend,* p. 366

Net   zlo dej!   Dol-go ja te—be molča-la!   Nu!   U-bej menja sko-
(No monster!   I have kept my silence with you long enough! Well,

rej,   sko-rej!   Sil mo-ix terpet,ter—pet'   ne sta lo...
kill me quick!   I cannot take anymore!)

tematizm, which we have translated above as "thematic structure"), creating
an "organism" which possesses "dramatic meaning."[116] Serov mounts an
elaborate argument, proceeding from the notes alone: "It will not do to depart
from the notes by so much as a single step: nothing must be sought beyond this
material," if the demonstration is to be "mathematically logical" and
convincing. [117]

Serov's main contention is that the themes of the third "Leonore"
Overture represent the main characters of *Fidelio,* and his major discovery is
the *"for the first time proven identity of the motives* of the Introduction and

the Allegro," as he himself triumphantly underscores it.[118] Another noteworthy touch is Serov's justification of third-related key centers within the sonata form, in a way that strikingly anticipates some twentieth-century analytical methods. The key of the second theme (E major) is related symmetrically to that of the first theme (C major) and that of the Introduction, whose melody it dramatically transforms (A♭ major). It also saves the dominant for the closing theme of the exposition, so that all the characters represented by themes (Leonore, Florestan and Pizarro in that order) will be tonally differentiated, without losing the maximum forward momentum in the tonal structure.

Two years earlier, in 1859, Serov had published the first of a projected series of "Essays in Technical Criticism Concerning the Music of M.I. Glinka" (and the only one completed), entitled "The Role of a Single Motif Through the Whole of the Opera 'Ivan Susanin.'"[119] The thesis presented there is that the concluding *Slavsia!* chorus is subtly foreshadowed throughout the opera, wherever the theme of kingship and legitimacy arises. Some of Serov's examples are more convincing than others, and Serov's purposes may have been to a certain degree ulterior in that the essay places Glinka in a proto-Wagnerian light,[120] but the essential insight is convincingly supported.

The prospect of analyzing Serov's own last and most progressive opera according to these lights is tempting. And the results are such that it will not be stretching a point to assert that criteria of "organic wholeness" through thematic and tonal interrelationships were very much on the composer's mind in the course of the opera's creation, and further, that through the derivation of the motifs so interrelated from the stylistic heritage—in some cases, the authentic repertoire—of Russian folk music, the method became a prime agency in the realization of *pochvennik* ideals through music.

Thematic recurrences and associations as such were nothing new in Serov's work: recall the Holofernian "headmotive" in *Judith,* or the dramatic reprises of the pilgrim's hymn in *Rogneda.* Their use in *The Power of the Fiend,* however, goes much deeper into the ideological and psychological fabric of the drama, and in one or two cases qualifies for full-fledged designation as leitmotiv.

Taking our cue from Serov's treatment of *Fidelio* in relation to the third "Leonore" Overture, we shall take the opera's modest overture (*vstuplenie,* or "introduction," as Serov fastidiously termed it) as our point of departure, and limit our detailed examination of *The Power of the Fiend's "tematizm"* to the themes encountered therein, regarding this as preferable to an exhaustive catalogue of all thematic recurrences in the course of the opera, in which significance would necessarily be sacrificed to statistics. Thus, we will pass over such conspicuous but comparatively superficial matters as Pyotr's signature tune, which serves chiefly as entrance music, without dramatically enlightening effect. And we will trust the musical examples already given to demonstrate the stylistic uniformity of Eryomka's part, derived as most of it is from the repertoire of ostinato dance songs.

The overture, given complete in piano reduction as Example 4.29, breaks down into two unequal halves (the first three pages of the example versus the last two).

Each half begins with arresting announcements of the tune Serov had adapted from the "Moscow song," *Kapitanskaia doch',* accompanied by balalaika imitations. These are pitched a third apart, in A♭ and E respectively (coincidentally or not, the keys of the two occurrences of the "Florestan theme" Serov had identified in the "Leonore" Overture). Thus the opera begins with an adumbration of the *maslenitsa* in Act IV. Following the *maslenitsa* theme, both halves of the overture provide transitions (meas. 24-39; 128-44) derived from the melody that closes Pyotr's solo *scena* in Act I, where he voices his determination to possess Grunya at all costs. This tune, too, is derived from *Kapitanskaia doch'* (cf. Example 4.10 above). Next, in both halves, follows a quotation (meas. 59-65; 145-56) of the theme that accompanies Ilya's exit in Act I, sc. iii after withholding his blessing from his son. The first half of the overture then continues into a long central passage drawn from Dasha's Act II lament at her broken home. At the analogous point in the second half of the overture, a transition is made directly into the opera's first number, which is also Dasha's.

Thus, "the content of the overture is the content of the opera," to quote Serov on Beethoven.[121] The major characters are all introduced (if we allow Eryomka to be represented by his balalaika), and all are placed in relation to Pyotr Ilich: Grunya desired by him, Ilya threatening him, Dasha injured by him, Eryomka tempting him. But most conspicuous in the overture is Grigoriev's "invisible character" that "reigns over all," that is, the *maslenitsa* itself. The opening motif, then, has as capital and programmatic a significance in *The Power of the Fiend* as the *Slavsia* motif had in *A Life for the Tsar,* and from the very outset, it would appear, the composer planned to treat it precisely as—according to his own famous analysis—Glinka had treated his theme. "If I come across a folk theme suitable to my needs at this point, I will construct *a great deal* in the opera on the basis of it," Serov had written to Ostrovsky,[122] and in the event he was as good as his word. Its symbolic status in the opera is made clear in the second scene of Act I, where the song, heard through an open window, contrasts impudently with the stern pronouncements of Ilya. At first song and sermon are heard alternately, but later Serov manages an artful contrapuntal juxtaposition, in which Ilya's plodding triple meter, played off against the swift duple meter of the street song, underscores their mutual antagonism (Ex. 4.30).

Elsewhere the balalaika sounds peep between the phrases of the old man's homily, or—dissonantly!—accompany them (Ex. 4.31).

Ex. 4.29.   *The Power of the Fiend*, pp. 5-9

Ex. 4.29 (cont'd)

Ex. 4.29 (cont'd)

(Attacca Nº1)

Ex. 4.30.   *The Power of the Fiend*, pp. 22-23, orchestra omitted

Thus, the lines are drawn upon which the "ideal" plot of *The Power of the Fiend* will turn. After this, the *maslenitsa* motif cannot return without bringing associations with Ilya, for whom it had served as such a conspicuous foil. For all its mirth and "rakishness,"[123] the tune casts a pall of doom. And thus, for all its picturesque and tuneful allure, Serov's *maslenitsa,* where the *Kapitanskaia doch'* motif really comes into its own, is no divertissement. It is fraught with portent that goes to the very heart of the drama, and the ostensibly merry genre music is what accomplishes this, just as Grigoriev had prophesied.

Stripped down to a three-note headmotive, the *maslenitsa* theme bears another set of associations. We first hear it in this form in the orchestra when, defying Ilya, Pyotr vows to continue his Shrovetide carousing (Ex. 4.32).

Ex. 4.31.   *The Power of the Fiend*, p. 22

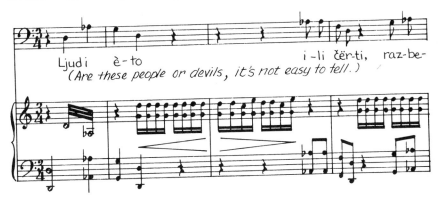

And we next hear it at the first mention of Grunya's name, near the end of Pyotr's Act I *scena* (and shortly before the closing *maslenitsa*-derived theme already noted in the overture, Ex. 4.33).

Thus Grunya, for all her merry innocence, is tied to the complex of sinister Shrovetide resonances. This association is reinforced at the very beginning of Act II, in the Prelude which sets the scene at the inn. This melody recurs four scenes later, as the basic tune of Grunya's monologue (Ex. 4.34).

We also find echoes of the *maslenitsa* motif when Spiridonovna urges Grunya to marry—that is, urges her designs on Pyotr (Ex. 4.35).

Finally, the third act is brought under the purview of the *maslenitsa* motif by basing the opening of its prelude (Ex. 4.36) on an expansion of the headmotive from Serov's habitual fourth to the sixth of the original tune in Lvov-Pratsch (again cf. Example 4.10).

And, transformed to the major, this motif forms a part of the girls' offstage chorus that provides an ironic backdrop to Grunya's lamenting

Ex. 4.32.   *The Power of the Fiend*, p. 31

Ex. 4.33.   *The Power of the Fiend*, p. 50

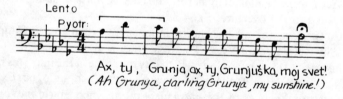

Pyotr's deception, just as formerly an offstage chorus on the *maslenitsa* theme had accompanied Ilya (Ex. 4.37).

The Ilya-Dasha complex adumbrated in the overture, which represents the forces of order and family obligation opposed to the "power of the fiend," receives a comparable development in the opera. Dasha's music, in particular, comprises a rich family of related themes, whose initial appearances are tabulated in Example 4.38.

Ex. 4.34.   a. *The Power of the Fiend*, Prelude to Act II

b. Grunya's monologue Act II, voice part only

Čto za ra-dost' žim'devič-ju na ne-vol-ju pro-me-njat'
What kind of joy is it to exchange a maiden's life for married bondage?

Ex. 4.35.   *The Power of the Fiend*, p. 127, voice only

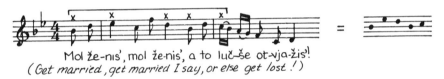

Mol že-nis', mol že-nis', a to luč-še ot-vja-žis'!
(Get married, get married I say, or else get lost !)

Ex. 4.36.   *The Power of the Fiend*, Prelude to Act III

These themes are all in minor, all are similarly harmonized, and all recur frequently both in Dasha's part and in the orchestra.[124] In addition, and most importantly, they are all variations on the scalewise descent from the fifth degree to the tonic (what Glinka once termed the "soul of Russian music"), as shown by the brackets.[125] This intervallic idea might then be termed the true "Dasha leitmotiv," with the various actual themes as given viewed as local surface embellishments. The falling fifth, along with a harmonization that prominently displays the half-diminished ii₇, characterizes Dasha in her sorrowful state and dominates all the scenes in which she appears, lending

Ex. 4.37.   *The Power of the Fiend*, pp. 194-95, choral parts only (reduced)

Ču——ži ljudi raz-go-vo-rom nas smu–šča-jut raz-go – vor— om nas   etc.
(*Strangers embarrass us with gossip.*)

Ex. 4.38.   Dasha themes:

a. Act I, sc. i

Ču – et ču-et re-ti –vo- e   ne kdo-bru e –go   šče—mit.
(*My heart aches and bodes ill.*)

b. Act II finale

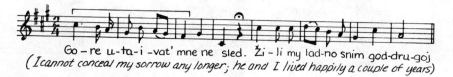

Go — re u-ta-i -vat' mne ne sled. Ži – li my lad-no snim god-dru-goj
(*I cannot conceal my sorrow any longer; he and I lived happily a couple of years*)

c. Act I, sc. iv

Sly — šal ba ——tjuš-ki-no slo-vo? Sly-šal ba —— tjuš-kin pri-kaz?
(*Did you hear your father's word? Did you hear his command?*)

d. Act I, sc. vi

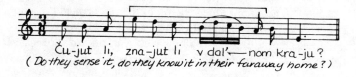

Ču-jut li, zna-jut li   v dal'——nom kra-ju?
(*Do they sense it, do they know it in their faraway home?*)

e. Act I, sc. vi

f. Act I, sc. vii, sung first by Vasya, then by Dasha

g. Act II finale

h. Act II finale, cf. Overture, mm. 66ff

i. Act II finale

them a distinctive color that is unique in Russian opera yet thoroughly "typical" and national.

Confirmation of our identification of the Dasha leitmotiv, as well as a striking testimony to the subtlety of Serov's *"tematizm,"* can be found in the music of Grunya's role, which undergoes a significant change between Acts II and III. In Act II, where she is identified primarily as one of Pyotr's temptations, her music, as we have seen, is strongly colored by the *maslenitsa* leitmotiv. In Acts III and IV, however, after she has been wounded by Pyotr and is no longer available to him, her music identifies her with Dasha (Ex. 4.39).

To the list of Dasha-Ilya devices can be added the characteristic modulatory rotation of minor keys by thirds. Table 3 summarizes the key relations in all the numbers of Act I. Except for scene vi, they all contain third-related juxtapositions, often enharmonically expressed.

Table 3	
Scene	**Key Scheme**
i. Dasha and Afimya	f-a♭-f
ii. Ilya and chorus	a-c (but ends in major)
iii. Ilya and Pyotr	E♭ (e♭)-B-e♭
iv. Dasha and Pyotr	g#-b-E♭-g#
v. Pyotr alone	b♭-c#-e♭-B♭-D♭
vi. Dasha alone	d-a
vii. Dasha and Vasya	A-f#-F#- f#-b♭-c#-A -f#-a

The last and most extended of these scenes, already described above, is the most striking example of minor-mode third rotations. Its central section (boxed in the table), where Dasha and Vasya both lament their respective unrequited loves, is built around such a rotation, in which the active modulatory agent is the Dasha theme we have identified above as No. 5 in Example 4.38. Its first downbeat is harmonized with a half-diminished seventh, which is immediately identified by the ear as a supertonic preceding the dominant of the new key—a very effective tonal wrench, uniting "leit-harmony" with "leit-modulation," and so giving almost unbearably poignant expression to the singers' anguish.

As Table 3 reveals, Ilya's role is also full of minor-mode third relations. It goes, in fact, much further than Dasha's into novel harmonic regions. If Dasha's leitmotiv is the falling fifth, Ilya's "leit-interval" is the minor third and its extensions, the tritone and the diminished-seventh. To characterize Ilya's melodic/harmonic language, we may cite one of his more extended utterances, the arioso he addresses to his errant son in the third scene of Act I, shortly before departing the stage (not to return until Act V). Here we find at short range many of the harmonic and tonal features we have already noted with respect to whole scenes: third-related rotations of minor triads (involving here the extravagant tonality of c♭ minor), the free substitution of minor thirds for diatonically occurring major ones, the pervasive tincture of tritones (Ex. 4.40).

Ex. 4.39.   Grunya in Acts III and IV

a.

Ax,   čtož————————ty, moj si-zyj go—lub————————čik
Ah, what has become of you, my grey dove ?

b.

Teš——te de-vuš-ki men—ja.
(Console me, girls.)

c.

V ne——————ko-to-rom car-stve de————vuš-ka ži-la.
(Once upon a time there lived a maiden...)

d.

Zdravst—vuj, mo-lo—dec u—da-lyj! Čto tak sko——(ro)
(Greetings, my brave young fellow, why so soon?)

Ex. 4.40.   *The Power of the Fiend*, pp. 32–33, voice only

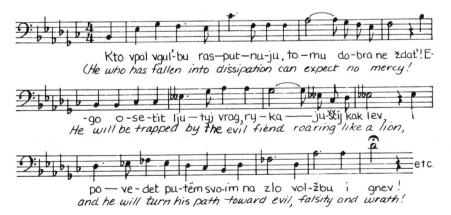

Kto vpal vgul'-bu ras—put—nu-ju, to—mu do-bra ne ždat'! E-
(He who has fallen into dissipation can expect no mercy!

-go o-se-tit lju—tyj vrag, ry—ka————ju-štij kak lev, i
He will be trapped by the evil fiend roaring like a lion,

po——ve-det pu-tém svo-im na zlo vol-žbu i gnev!
and he will turn his path toward evil, falsity and wrath!

So prone is this character to tritones (usually in the diatonic position of the minor scale locally in force—i.e., between second degree and sixth—but also frequently between fifth degree and a "Neapolitan" second), that the Vespers bell which gives him his exit cue is musically rendered as a diminished triad! Thus does Serov paint Ostrovsky's famous "dark kingdom" of the Moscow merchant class (Ex. 4.41).

Ex. 4.41.   *The Power of the Fiend*, p. 33

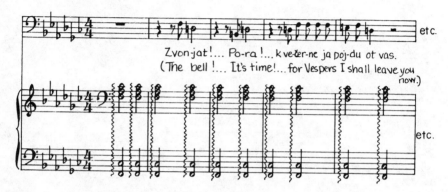

Ilya's harmonic language dominates much of the more dramatic recitative in *The Power of the Fiend,* especially the dialogues of Pyotr and Eryomka in Acts III and IV. The composer thus harnessed his musical resources to give Ilya a much greater "presence" in the opera than he had had in the play, and in fact much more than his relatively short time on stage in the opera would normally vouchsafe. "Immerse yourself in Ilya's speech," Serov had advised Ostrovsky. "This old man *frames* the whole piece, he is its alpha and omega, like the Commendatore in *Don Giovanni*. A fine opportunity for music."[126] Serov was not only defending his idea to have Ilya return to the stage at the end of the opera; he was hinting that by means of his music he wished to make of Ilya an "unseen character" throughout the body of the drama, almost on a par with the *maslenitsa* itself. The "ideal plot" of *The Power of the Fiend* is thus so vividly and so distinctively embodied in conflicting musical idioms—the one comprised of merry diatonic town song "intonations," the other of tortured diminished intervals and minor-third relations—that Serov may at last be credited with what had eluded him in his other operas, the creation not of an eclectic mélange, but of a cohesive musico-dramatic "reality." To an extent unapproached in the earlier operas, *The Power of the Fiend* invites and repays "organic criticism."

This was not the critical approach taken by Serov's contemporaries, however. For them, the great issue was realism and the place of "ugliness" in art. The reception of *The Power of the Fiend* thus became an interesting and significant little chapter in nineteenth-century Russian aesthetics. To say that reception was mixed would be an understatement: the work aroused one of the most heated responses accorded any theatrical presentation of the day.

The most favorable comment came from the aging Prince Odoevsky, who saw in Serov the legitimate heir to Glinka's mantle, a view that must have gratified the composer no end after the vicissitudes of the *Ruslan* controversy. In language strikingly reminiscent of his eulogy of *A Life for the Tsar* a quarter-century before, Odoevsky wrote, after a private audition in December 1868 of Act III, that "here Russian song is truly brought to the level of tragedy," and this while the unfinished opera was as yet designated a "comedy"![127] Odoevsky died in 1869, so he never heard the fourth or fifth acts of *The Power of the Fiend.* Thus, he could praise Serov's maintenance of "pure diatonicism" at a time when "in the West, ... a character can't even ask for a glass of water without a half dozen sharps and flats."[128]

The most contrary view, perhaps, was that of Eduard Napravnik, the conductor of the premiere production. Arguing from a conservative, avowedly Romanticist viewpoint, Napravnik held that Serov's last opera failed to come up to the mark set not only by *Judith,* but even by *Rogneda.* Though he is surely less than fair in charging that Serov's new-found realism was born solely of opportunism, his remarks well illustrate the suspicion with which Serov was widely regarded after *Rogneda*'s meretricious success. Now it was thought that the composer was trying to cash in on the vogue for Ostrovsky.

> Seeking ever greater popularity, [Serov] went to extremes and chose a subject which, though stageworthy, was trivial and, for some, positively repellent.... There are scenes deftly drawn right off the streets and taverns of Moscow, but ought such things to be transplanted to the stage?[129]

Napravnik was forced to admit that the music "successfully expresses the dramatic situations." His position, that such situations ought not be expressed at all, found wide agreement among critics who were unwilling to see music's scope broadened to encompass such aspects of daily life as had long since been accepted in literature. Music, as Serov himself had averred some years earlier, was for them the art of the Ideal par excellence. Even Cui was scandalized by the rampant drunkenness in Act IV, as if "drunkenness and reckless carousal were the highest manifestation of the vitality and the aspirations of the people."[130]

The pseudo-moral question raised by Cui was one to which Serov had had a ready answer at the time of *Judith,* when he was Grigoriev's apostle of "true realism." Then, he had written that

> The chief and fundamental power of art is the influence of *beauty,* either physical or spiritual, on man.... Horror, monstrousness, evil, the kingdom of darkness—all this has a

right to exist in art only as the negation of beauty, in juxtaposition with the kingdom of light. The soul of man demands light, demands beauty whether consciously or unconsciously; it lives by "ideals." That is the secret of the power all true artists wield over the crowd. Therein lies the basis of the law of *contrasts,* of oppositions and antitheses, without which art is unthinkable.[131]

But there is no "kingdom of light" in *The Power of the Fiend;* Ilya is hardly more attractive than Eryomka.[132] Pyotr, no less than Dasha, is a victim, and hence *The Power of the Fiend* (far more than the play from which it originally derived) can be assigned—uniquely among nineteenth-century Russian operas—to the category of "critical realism." From this standpoint the drunkenness and carousing upon whose representation Serov lavished such care, as well as the unflinching brutality of the opera's conclusion, may be viewed as integral and "organic" to the opera's conception. It would certainly be perverse to suggest with Napravnik that the opera's "ugliness" was merely "decorative," or that Serov sought "popularity" by providing the "repellent." It matters not whether Serov arrived at this new dramaturgical outlook "theoretically," or merely ad hoc, in the course of work. The moment he decided that *The Power of the Fiend* must end with Dasha's murder, "the kingdom of light"—"true realism" à la Grigoriev—was left behind.

Cui, for all the Romanticism that his own operas exhibit, was able to sympathize with Serov's artistic intentions to a considerable extent. In fact, he went so far as to aver that *"I know no better operatic subject"* than *The Power of the Fiend's* libretto:[133]

> The rational, natural union of drama, national character and the particulars of genre
> *(bytovye osobennosti)* in one subject constitutes the ideal for a contemporary operatic
> subject, and the subject of *The Power of the Fiend* satisfies this ideal completely.... The
> choice of this subject proves the correctness of Serov's view as regards operatic criteria and
> his intelligent and critical treatment of them.

In particular, Cui singled out Act IV—"in its subject, in its aims, it presents the most vital crowd scene in any opera imaginable"—and Act V as well, fully approving of Serov's emendation of Ostrovsky's ending, calling it "far more natural, consistent and effective" than the original had been. The only reservation Cui had about the libretto applied to Ilya, the foil by means of which the diabolical *maslenitsa* took on its full sinister significance. Cui had no interest in the moral overtones that fascinated the "true realist" in Serov, though without them the story of *The Power of the Fiend* would have descended to mere "naturalism," and in particular, the crowd scenes in Act IV that so impressed Cui himself would have descended to the level of unmotivated sensational spectacle. Cui's failure to grasp this was probably the reason for his squeamish objection to the scenes of drunkenness in Act IV. As for Ilya himself, Cui saw him as a "mannequin," who "appears in the opera without any organic necessity," and the critic actually objected to the old merchant's return in Act V, on which Serov had pinned the opera's whole message.

Cui was far less happy with the words of the libretto than with the scenario. His own experience as operatic composer enabled him to perceive the obstacles Ostrovsky had placed in the composer's way.[134]

> The libretto contains some good, strong verses, as well as some apt folk expressions taken mainly from Ostrovsky. But all too often the libretto transgresses by virtue of its short, extremely prosaic verses in dancing meters and tricky rhymes, perhaps worthy of contemporary satirical verse, but here serving for the most dramatic places.... Of course, imaginative musical declamation can to a considerable extent mask banal verses and the banality of overly clever rhyming. But one ought to take it as a rule that all dramatic moments in a libretto should be cast in blank verse, preserving meter, of course, since the latter in no small way assists the free flow of musical thought.

Rostislav, who ever since *Judith* had cast himself in the role of Serov's public defender, saw *The Power of the Fiend* from a point of view diametrically opposed to Cui's. His brochure on Serov's last opera starts out defending it against the enemies of realism, but as he goes along, Rostislav finds it hard to maintain his premise. It is fascinating to observe him gradually going over to the other side, seeing the ultimate failure of *The Power of the Fiend* precisely in those scenes upon which Cui had lavished the most praise— the scene of the *maslenitsa* (Act IV) and the whole of Act V. Rostislav encounters his first difficulties with the character of Eryomka, of whom he offers in passing an excellent description.

> Eryomka is by trade a blacksmith, by nature a bitter drunkard, for profit plays a fool in God *(iurodivyi)* and at times even a wizard. His reddish hair is tousled, his thin beard pointed, he lacks some teeth, his eyes are discolored. His bony shoulders (one of them humped) are covered with a threadbare patched rag of a shirt, his lumbering feet are shod in bast sandals. The whole figure of Eryomka smacks of poverty, of impenetrable ignorance, coarse aggressiveness and cunning. "Realism" can go no further, and the question arises unbidden, is such a personage suitable for opera, that is, for a lyric work of art?[135]

Rostislav manages to "swallow Eryomka," as Serov had put it, finding words of praise both for his song *Shirokaia maslenitsa* and for the scene in Act III where the employment of so lowly a tavern song as *Kumanechek* had aroused Cui's righteous indignation. Rostislav seems to enter into their spirit far more easily than the *kuchkist,* who maintained even in his attitude toward *The Power of the Fiend* his group's prejudice against urban folk songs as artistic material. Rostislav defends *Shirokaia maslenitsa* in words practically Stasovian in their sweeping and dogmatic generalization of the "rights" of

Fig. 4.4   The original set for the Shrovetide scene in Act IV of *The Power of the Fiend* (*Vsemirnaia illustratsiia*, 1871)

realism. "The lyric drama is not a concert, where banal or inelegant music would be inadmissible," he writes. "In drama life can and must be reflected in all its manifestations.[136] Later on, dealing with the *Kumanechek* song, Rostislav makes some penetrating and sympathetic comments, but qualifies the broad justification of realism he had issued earlier.

> *Trepaks and balalaikas* take on here an artistic significance comparable in force to the broad but coarse strokes by which the great painters of the Realist school have distinguished themselves. Here the limits, beyond which aesthetic taste does not permit one to venture, have not yet been violated. This is a bold juxtaposition of banality and musical pathos, but no degradation of art.[137]

Serov did exceed the limits, however, and with a vengeance, when it came to the *maslenitsa*. Significantly, it was the music rather than the dramaturgical conception that alienated Rostislav's sympathy. The critic was able to look upon Eryomka with equanimity, and was able to accept the intentions of the scene with enthusiasm, perhaps even unfeigned. But he could not condone the musical liberties Serov took in their name.

> [The scene of the *maslenitsa*] is boldly conceived, but conscience forces us to confess our firm conviction that it exceeds the limits of art. As a genre scene it is true to reality, but no longer music—rather it is discordant noise and uproar.[138]

The critic singles out for censure such "polytonal" effects as the E♭ clarinet playing in c minor over the double pedal G-F, or the superimposition of the *maslenitsa* leitmotiv in F major over an orchestral C major chord. Such effects were inadmissible for Rostislav, since art must never descend to a mere unmediated reproduction of reality.

> In a word, the chaotic mixture of sounds and keys vividly recalls, or rather depicts, the roar and hubbub of the Shrovetide fair. But this certainly does not correspond to the criteria of a lyric work of art.... We are amazed that the players can perform such chaos without "gnashing of the teeth."[139]

Ugliness itself is beyond the legitimate reach of music, Rostislav implies, when he writes of the drunken brawling that occupies so much of the action in Act IV:

> To elevate to a "pearl of creation," as Gogol used to say, such things as drunken carousal, fighting and street noises by means of music is flatly impossible. This inebriated ragamuffin of a muzhik who wriggles to the sound of Serov's pseudo-bagpipe is simply repulsive; the revellers crowding into the tavern likewise.[140]

Rostislav holds up *Judith* as his model of what opera should be, and what *The Power of the Fiend* was not. In *Judith*, too, the crowd shouts and participates in the action; in *Judith,* too, there is murder. But "the late Serov heeded the voice of reason and softened such places."[141]

The offstage murders in *Judith* and *The Power of the Fiend* do in fact pose an interesting comparison. In the earlier opera the thrust of the knife is transmitted conventionally, but effectively enough, by means of a *sforzando,* staccato orchestral diminished-seventh chord. In *The Power of the Fiend,* Serov no longer sought to conventionalize or "idealize" such a moment. We actually hear Dasha's scream, and the harmonies are original, empirical, and "realistically" horrible enough to drive Rostislav, if we are to believe him, to the very threshold of pain (and what else could have been Serov's intention?): "My God! What kind of wild, unheard of sounds are these?!"[142]

Nor does Rostislav approve of Serov's changes in the plot; he misses the "kingdom of light." The murder is but a "tawdry effect" (the old charge of opportunism); Ostrovsky's ending (*pace* Cui) had been far more "natural," and, "in any case, more comforting." Rostislav naively offers a compromise to satisfy the demands both of melodrama and of "ethics":

> The action of the fifth act might have been brought right up to the point where Pyotr seizes his knife. Then comes the sound of the churchbells. Pyotr, little by little, comes to his senses, becomes contrite, and when the other characters, led by Vasya, come down into the ravine, and as the pious old Ilya joins his voice to the uplifting sound of the bells, Pyotr is much affected and in heartfelt contrition falls at the feet of his father and the comforted Dasha.[143]

Cui's essential ploy in reviewing *The Power of the Fiend* was to deny Serov's express and, to a considerable extent, realized intention of creating an inseparable fusion of genre and drama. He radically divides the music of the opera into two unequal parts: "dramatic music (by far the larger portion) and another, by far the lesser, of genre music." It is not easy to guess what will fall into which portion with Cui—especially as in our own discussion we have found the genre portion to predominate—but since Cui's treatment of the "genre music" deals only with actual quotations of folk songs and with such major concerted numbers as the *maslenitsa,* we may assume that the "dramatic music" includes everything else. Cui's critique of the "dramatic music" is venomous; it is clear that his lavish praise of Serov's intentions was but a foil for his abusive, contemptuous dismissal of their attempted realization.

> Serov's dramatic music in *The Power of the Fiend* is *beneath all criticism.* It is even worse than Kashperov's or Afanasiev's. Not only is it paltry and lacking in ideas, it is sheer musical rubbish almost throughout.... Take any recitative in *A Life for the Tsar* [or] *Rusalka:* in all of them you will find natural, true declamation and an inspired musical idea, which, in its utter fusion with the word, strengthens the impression of the latter a hundredfold. Let us assert that Serov lacks this second quality of good recitative, which demands the greater talent and creativity. But even if there only be observed natural and correct declamation, a good text will stand on its own two feet and make a fitting impression.... But what do we

find in *The Power of the Fiend?* Complete distortion and perversion of the text to such an astounding and improbable degree that the whole dramatic side of this peerless subject is killed and produces on the listener *not the slightest impression.* [144]

Noting Serov's distinctively dark orchestration, in which low registers are tellingly exploited (*divisi* for the contrabasses, etc.), particularly in the scenes between Pyotr and Eryomka, Cui acidly satirizes Serov's compositional methods and proposes an absurd "recipe" for instant Serovian recitative:

> In the most dramatic places Serov arranges things thus: he divides the double basses, adds bassoons, clarinet, perhaps trombone, has them take their very lowest notes, notes which are practically not on the instrument, in some absurd chord which *you can't even make out* since the notes are too low, and over this chord the voice takes *any interval at all,* generally the most unnatural and senseless ones available.... I would suggest to Serov's followers, if such should yet arise (there are none at present), the following recipe for writing recitative à la *The Power of the Fiend:* arrange some music paper on your desk, catch a fly or a spider, dip its legs in ink and let it wander on the music paper. Then add stems and tails to the inkspots thus obtained, divide it all up into measures, copy in the text, and your dramatic recitative is ready.

Similar intolerance marks Cui's treatment of the genre music in *The Power of the Fiend,* especially evident in his preposterous objection to Serov's having based the Russian national element in his score precisely upon the type of music that was most appropriate to the time, place and social milieu of the action. Cui's criticism of the "genre element" is in actuality a tribute to Serov's success in realizing his intentions. Though he writes in condemnation, he describes the music in terms the composer himself might well have employed.

> There is none of the breadth and sweep we find in the introduction to *Ruslan,* or in many of the choruses from *A Life for the Tsar:* [the genre element] consists with Serov of a long series of little songs and choruses, paltry in form, in couplet style.... This genre side is fairly true to life [but] many of Eryomka's balalaika tunes positively astound one with their filthy and *inartistic* truthfulness.

Cui makes an exception for the Shrovetide procession, which he liked but nonetheless failed to understand, either because he was unfamiliar with the folk sources of Serov's ostinato construction, or because he was not willing to go as far as Serov in the employment of folk resources to generate structure in art music. In short, Serov's employment of folk music was too "organic" for Cui, who complained that although "highly successful as music" and "well harmonized," the Shrovetide procession was "rather poor in development and monotonous." [145]

Alongside the naturalism of Serov's music and that of the characters it portrayed, a strong if not entirely favorable impression was created by the style of performance on which the composer insisted, a development of the style evolved by Serov and Sariotti for the latter's portrayal of Holofernes in *Judith*. The barrier between song and speech was breached by an extensive use of parlando. When Serov employed the term (or rather its Russian equivalent, *govorkom*), he apparently meant it quite literally. He had the prospective cast of the opera[146] to his home and sang them the opera the way he wished it to go. The impression he made, according to the eyewitness E. Korsh, "was enormous; the artists warmly thanked the composer for this remarkable lesson in expression, which had given them a living conception of all the characters in the opera, not only in their inner, but even their external characteristics."[147] According to Serov, Sariotti, Leonova and Lavrovskaya captured his intentions to perfection in their performances.[148] Platonova, however, expressed a dissenting opinion. She felt that the constant reliance upon the style of the *bytovoi* romance in Dasha's part gave the role a monotonous, "whining" quality, and despite Serov's assurances and his example, she complained that she saw no way of "enriching" the character.[149] A. Abarinova, who replaced Leonova as Spiridonovna in 1872, left an account of her tribulations with the role that gives a vivid idea of the enormous difference between the performance style Serov demanded in his "realistic" opera and the more "normal" operatic style in which the singers had been trained. She also gives a revealing glimpse of Napravnik at work, much admired by composers and critics alike for his conscientious preparation of scores for which he personally had little sympathy. Both the conscientiousness and the lack of sympathy are evident in Abarinova's memoir.

> After the *bel canto italiano*, in which I had been brought up musically, the role of Spiridonovna seemed to me at first somehow outrageous. It was all I could do to learn the notes accurately by the time of the first rehearsal. But you can imagine my feelings when Napravnik, after my attempt to sing, closed the score and said, "That's all wrong; you are singing an Italian recitative. Here you don't need a voice; do it as if speaking, trivially." I burst into tears and did not know what to do. After the rehearsal Kondratiev came up to me, cheered me up and assured me that with the help of our mutual friend P.V. Vasiliev, everything would work out. But the next day, though they labored mightily with me, we got nowhere.... For a young woman, as I then was, it was hard to portray an old drunken crone in an inn. Suddenly Vasiliev had a brilliant idea: "Make her up, put a peasant blouse on her, get her some cheap boots, tie her in a headdress—then she'll know what to do." Jacoby, the makeup man, was called. He did me up as requested, and no sooner had I seen myself in the mirror, than all the right gestures and phrasing came to me. Later, Napravnik was to praise me for the role.[150]

This curious impromptu anticipation of the "Stanislavsky method" was done in the interests of a performance style that the critics, with one voice, pronounced false and pernicious. Not surprisingly, it was precisely those performers whom Serov himself had praised most highly that the critics cut down with particular vengeance, always in full awareness that their style of performance had the late composer's sanction. Cui, for example, saw in Serov's performance-ideal the ultimate confession of musical impotence.

> Acknowledging his complete inability to write any music at all to a given text, he has his singers not sing, but speak or shout. You can't imagine how inartistically this alternation of song and speech to musical accompaniment comes off, how completely it destroys any illusion, how melodramatic and farcical it is. . . . That the performers have not come to such a pass at their own initiative is obvious. Serov showed them the way. If you renounce the power of music, then why write music?

Rostislav, with reference to Grunya's exchange with Stepanida in Act II, saw in the pervasive parlando an exaggeration of what might have been in Serov's original conception a good idea. Rostislav's account indicates some purely practical problems inherent in the "alternation of song and speech" that may have made for some difficult moments at the premiere.

> In the score there is [probably] written in the late A.N. Serov's hand something like "in an altogether speaking style, not at all lyrically." *Not lyrical,* perhaps, but completely without pitch can't be the way, because, in the first place, this confuses the other singer, who must find the note of her entrance, and, in the second place, such a technique of toneless conversation is out of character for a lyric drama. We are conviced that the late Serov himself would have changed his markings if he had heard the beginning of the second-act finale on the stage.[151]

Indeed, the particular case to which Rostislav makes reference is a puzzling one, since Grunya's repliques show particular care in their modelling upon folk song. Lavrovskaya was one of the singers Serov singled out as "the best possible" in their roles, so the contradiction between the mutually exclusive elements of folk melody and "toneless" delivery must have been unresolved in Serov's own mind. It seems likely that his ideas on performance-style evolved along with his conception of the drama itself, and the practice applied to the whole opera at the posthumous premiere was one that had occurred to the composer in connection mainly with the "naturalistic" fourth and fifth acts.

The one character who seems to have been able to carry off Serov's experiments with complete success was Sariotti in the role of Eryomka. This remarkable singing actor had come in for criticism for exaggeration in his characterization of Holofernes. Now it would seem that he had a character beyond exaggerating. Even Cui grudgingly paid him tribute: "This artist's fate has been a strange one—to be excellent in monstrous roles and mediocre in excellent ones." And elsewhere, "Truly, he is great and touched by genius in his astonishing ugliness."[152] Somewhat more seriously, Rostislav, though he entertained some reservations about the character, was swept off his feet by Sariotti's performance:

Fig. 4.6   Caricature by Fyodor Stravinsky of himself in role of Eryomka

Fig. 4.5   Sariotti as Eryomka and Leonova as Spiridonovna in the première production

Sariotti communicated the role of Eryomka with amazing truth. From his first appearance on stage, from his very first words, he arrests the audience's attention, and one's eyes involuntarily follow his every move, now with dread, now with revulsion.... In his voice there is something inexpressibly coarse, hollow, almost sinister.... With a slightly shaky head (a sure sign of the inveterate drunkard), he raises a cup to his lips, downs it at a gulp, wipes his beard and whiskers with a rough hand, and moving to one side, he follows with hawklike glance everything and everyone in the shack.[153]

A like aspiration to realism-at-all-costs—to the representation of Russian *byt* in its coarsest, most brutal aspects, so as to suggest the diabolical forces that underlie the half-pagan *maslenitsa*—governed the staging of the opera, the work of the baritone Gennady Petrovich Kondratiev (1834-1905), who also sang Pyotr. His zeal to avoid varnishing the naked truth at times appeared gratuitous, particularly at the very end of Act IV, and managed to offend everyone. Apparently for the sake of comic relief between the planning and the execution of the murder, Serov and Kondratiev had the two drunks who had been accompanying Pyotr in his Shrovetide songs lurch suddenly out of the tavern and reel about, "quietly and incoherently crooning fragments of familiar themes," in the words of a scandalized reviewer.[154] This episode was found by Rostislav, and not only by him, to be not only inartistic but positively anti-artistic. Realism, for him, was not its own reward.

The appearance of these dead drunks... is true to life, all right, and not a bad contrast, perhaps. But in a lyric work of art such a thing is positively unthinkable, because it is so monstrous and ugly.[155]

The sets and costumes followed the principles of Kondratiev's staging. Although Serov had set *The Power of the Fiend* in the seventeenth century, there was little attempt, except in a few of the costumes (partly the work of Musorgsky's friend Victor Hartman, he of the "Pictures at an Exhibition") to achieve historical verisimilitude. Thus, ironically, the composer was denied his "aerial perspective" by the theater. On the other hand, enormous emphasis was placed upon what Gozenpud calls "the truth of everyday life" *(bytovaia pravda)*.[156] This truth often amounted to plain ugliness, to judge from surviving photographs. Indeed, the whole production seems to have been ruled by a zealous horror of idealization, and carried out with real experimental fervor. The integrity of Serov's conception was preserved and, if anything, intensified by its scenic realization.

This studied "ugliness" was what, ultimately, made it impossible to charge Serov with opportunism. However reluctant his detractors may have been to part with their comforting view of the composer as meretricious darling of the public, the intentions of his final work were so obviously noble and progressive, and so notably did they impede the work's popular success, that the "New Russian School" was forced to respect them, and even, after a suitable interval had passed, to claim *The Power of the Fiend* as one of their own. By 1874 Cui could write:

> *The Power of the Fiend* is yet a step further than . . . *Judith.* In it we see an early attempt to present a people rather than a chorus; we see the desire to set forth drama simply and truthfully, and we see an enormous, even excessive aspiration to realism. In these ways the opera may be counted as one of the New Russian School. [157]

Perhaps the greatest encomium came from the least likely source. Vladimir Stasov, in his published writings, maintained an abusive tone with regard to Serov's operas right up to the end. But in one of his letters to Musorgsky, while they were planning *Khovanshchina,* Stasov let out the following remark:

> How happy you make me with this serious consideration and hard work on the content of the opera, even before the musical work begins. I don't know any other example of this in music. (Not even Serov . . .) [158]

Serov, then, had set the standard, backhanded though Stasov's acknowledgment may be. The conventional wisdom, expressed as early as Laroche and Tchaikovsky, and as late as Asafiev, has always been that *Judith* was Serov's finest opera, a peak he was never to scale again. But this opinion needs revision. *The Power of the Fiend* was unquestionably Serov's most original, most unified, and most authentic achievement. There had been many Biblical operas before *Judith,* but there had never before been anything comparable to Serov's thoroughgoing attempt to integrate Russian *byt* with musical drama in *The Power of the Fiend.* The only prior opera to have displayed a comparably serious treatment of genre had been *A Life for the Tsar.* But Glinka's opera was a historical opera with a patriotic theme, reaching a full-blown Romantic apotheosis in the epilogue. Nor, it goes without saying, does Glinka ever transgress the canons of "beauty" for the sake of "truth." The national material in *The Power of the Fiend,* on the other hand, is not conditioned by patriotic concerns; it serves a disinterested and uncompromising realism, unprecedented in the Russian musical theater.

But if *The Power of the Fiend* was without precedent, it likewise failed to set one. No later Russian opera contains a character comparable to Eryomka or a scene comparable to the *maslenitsa,* though the impact of both upon the artistic imagination of Musorgsky is evident. [159] Musorgsky, like the rest of the *kuchkists* was strongly drawn to the historical costume play, and, following Dargomyzhsky, to a kind of psychological drama whose "truth" was independent of time and place. After *The Power of the Fiend,* Russian national elements in music were once again largely segregated from the dramatic elements of musical style; Serov's attempt at organic fusion of the two was never again taken up. The kind of permeation of the dramatic dialogue with "intonations" of folk music that Serov achieved remained a unique phenomenon and was still striking enough, long after the era of *kuchkism* had passed, for Asafiev to write, with reference precisely to this aspect of *The Power of the Fiend,* of the opera's "exceptional stylistic consistency."[160]

It is to Dargomyzhsky, then, that we must now turn our attention, to discover that other realism which took hold simultaneously with and parallel to *The Power of the Fiend,* and which, unlike Serov's brand, soon swarmed with avowed followers and imitators. Never were two equally innovative composers so close in aim and yet so opposed in means as were Serov and Dargomyzhsky. But since this aim was something so vague and unopposable as "truth," it is not so surprising that radically divergent paths were taken in quest of it.

Notes

1. The title is often translated (following Gerald Abraham) as "Hostile Power." The original Russian, however, makes quite specific reference to the devil, hence, "The Power of the Fiend" seems to be a more appropriate, as well as a more literal, translation.

2. *Muzykal'no-dramaticheskaia kartina russkogo byta,* as Serov termed it in a letter to Ostrovsky (June 12, 1867). See E.M. Kolosova and V. Filippov, eds., *Ostrovskii i russkie kompozitory* (Moscow, 1937)—henceforth to be abbreviated: *Ost RK*—p. 112. Elsewhere in the same letter he called it a "Russian musical folk drama" *(narodno-russkaia muzykal'naia drama,* p. 113).

3. The word has a special irony for Serov, for it was one that made him see red when used by followers of Anton Rubinstein to condemn Serovian excess. Serov alludes to this in a letter to O. Novikova (August, 1866), written before the plan of *The Power of the Fiend* had taken shape:

   As to the *profanation of the pure goals of art,* I have views of my own. There is profanation *only* when an artist, pandering to the public, acts *contrary* to his own convictions. If my whole nature and talent draw me to *vivid effects* and the *liveliest possible* coloration, then it would be a profanation of art if I were not to follow my inner urgings, but were instead to write for an *economical* orchestra on modest little subjects in a retrogressive, timid style. I find that "economical candles" can be good enough, likewise "economical soap," but economical orchestration, economical opera—that's nonsense. All I know is that with the backward view of art preached by the Director of the Petersburg Conservatory and Co., one can do nothing on the contemporary stage (quoted in Gozenpud, *Russkii opernyi XIX veka II* [Leningrad, 1971], p. 248-49).

4. Cf. his article for *Iakor'* on Vladykin's *Whirlpool,* quoted in the last chapter.

5. "Autobiographical sketch," in Serov, *Izbrannye stat'i I* (Moscow, 1950), p. 78.

6. In English the name would be *The Muscovite,* but the English word does not reliably convey the archaic overtones of the Russian.

7. "Paradoksy organicheskoi kritiki" (Paradoxes of Organic Criticism, an open letter to F.M. Dostoevsky), *Epokha* (1864), nos. 5-6. Reprinted in Vasily Spiridonov, ed., *Polnoe sobranie sochinenii i pisem Apollona Grigor'eva I* (Petrograd, 1918), p. 143.

8. Quoted in V. Friche, "Ap. A. Grigoriev," in A. Lunacharskii and V. Polianskii, eds., *Ocherki po istorii russkoi kritiki I* (Moscow, 1929), pp. 306-7.

9. "O komediiakh Ostrovskogo i ikh znachenii v literature i na stsene," in *Polnoe sobranie I*, p. 215. Grigoriev's word is *narodnost'*, literally, "the quality of being of the people."

10. "Russkii teatr i sovremennoe sostoianie dramaturgii i stseny," *Vremia* (February, 1863), no. 2, p. 160. This article is in large part a reworking of an open letter to Ivan Turgenev, first published three years earlier in *Russkii mir*.

11. *Moskvitianin* (August, 1854), no. 15, pp. 104-5.

12. Ibid., p. 106.

13. *Otechestvennye zapiski*, (April 1860), no. 4, p. 446.

14. "Neskol'ko slov o zakonakh i terminakh organicheskoi kritiki" (1859), in V.F. Sadovnikov, ed., *Sobranie sochinenii Apollona Grigor'eva II* (Moscow, 1915), p. 119.

15. These were *Svoi liudi—sochtëmsia!* ("Among Friends One Always Comes to Terms," or "The Bankrupt," 1850), the one-act *Utro molodogo cheloveka* ("A Young Man's Morning," 1850), *Neozhidannyi sluchai* ("An Unforeseen Occurrence," 1851), *Bednaia nevesta* ("The Poor Bride," 1852), *Ne v svoi sani ne sadis'* ("Sit Only in Your Own Sleigh," better known as "Stick to Your Own Station," 1853), *Bednost' ne porok* ("Poverty Is No Crime," 1854), and finally, *Ne tak zhivi, kak khochetsia, a kak bog velit* ("Live Not the Way You'd Like, but as God Commands," 1855). Except for "An Unforeseen Occurrence" and "Poverty Is No Crime," all these plays were first published in the *Moskvitianin*.

16. D.S. Mirsky, *A History of Russian Literature* (New York, 1958), p. 245.

17. Ibid., p. 250.

18. *Epokha* (1864), no. 3, pp. 230-31, condensed.

19. Ibid., pp. 231-33 passim.

20. Grigoriev knew him in 1845. In a letter to his fellow *Moskvitianin* editor Evgeny Edelson (December 1, 1857), Grigoriev names Varlamov, along with Lermontov and Gogol, as one of "the dear departed who have left their mark upon us." See Vladimir Kniazhnin, ed., *Apollon Grigor'ev: Materialy dlia biografii* (Petrograd, 1917), p. 194.

21. This was the second leg of an expedition organized in 1855 by the journal *Morskoi sbornik*. Other participants included Pisemsky, Potekhin and Afanasiev. (See Izalii Zemtsovskii, *Iskateli pesen'* [Leningrad, 1967], p. 60). Some idea of the extent of Ostrovsky's personal contribution to Villebois' anthologies is suggested by Ippolitov-Ivanov in his memoirs, where he purports to transmit an anecdote he heard from Ostrovsky himself: "Being a man of carefree temperament and a lover of good company, Villebois preferred to spend his time carousing with the merchants on the Volga barges, leaving the tedious work to Ostrovsky. 'And I,' Alexander Nikolaevich laughingly recounted, 'so as not to forget the melodies, used to sing them all day till I was hoarse, and only then, together with Villebois, noted them down.' " (Mikhail Mikhailovich Ippolitov-Ivanov, *50 let russkoi muzyki v moikh vospominaniiakh* [Moscow: Gosudarstvennoe muzykal'noe izdatel'stvo, 1934], p. 66.) One can imagine the unconscious distortion that must have occurred thanks to this "method."

22. These were *Sto russkikh pesen'* (St. Petersburg, 1860; 2nd ed., 1894) and *Russkie narodnye*

pesni, a supplement to the yearbook, *Dramaticheskii sbornik* (St. Petersburg, 1860).

23. *OstRK,* p. 108.

24. He had attended the first production of "Poverty Is No Crime" in 1854 and had written to Dmitri Stasov that he "would not even hesitate to call Ostrovsky a genius." (Letter of February 4, 1854. *Muzykal'noe nasledstvo III*[Moscow, 1970], p. 178.) In the same article in which he predicted that Serov would set "Live Not the Way You'd Like," Grigoriev took note of Serov's already expressed intention to "write an overture, entr'actes, and orchestrate all the songs in 'Poverty Is No Crime'." This is our only evidence of this unrealized project. Grigoriev's assertion rings true because Serov had at various other times expressed interest in furnishing incidental music in national style for Russian plays, and in one case actually wrote some. As early as 1851 he wrote from St. Petersburg to Aleksei Bakunin in the Crimea of his plan to compose "an endless array of songs, solo and choral—and all of it music of Russian character" for a play by P.P. Sukhonin entitled *A Russian Wedding at the End of the Sixteenth Century.* (In the end the job went to Otto Dütsch.) In 1867 Serov planned incidental music to Aleksei Tolstoi's *The Death of Ivan the Terrible.* A single number ("Dance of the Skomorokhi") from this projected score was discovered and published in 1952 (see Aleksander Nikolaevich Glumov, *Muzyka v russkom dramaticheskom teatre* [Moscow, 1955], pp. 200-203).

25. To Novikova. See footnote 3 above.

26. January 28, 1867. *Russkaia starina* 9 (1888), p. 669. The curious last term indicates Serov's fancy that Polish/Ukrainian history or literature would contain what he was looking for.

27. Ibid., p. 667.

28. Ibid., p. 669.

29. Ibid., pp. 669-70. Zvantsev chose his example slyly. Serov had indeed specifically rejected *Hamlet* as an operatic subject, but his reason was that "everyone knows Shakespeare's text practically by heart, and one could hardly set the whole thing to music." (Ibid., p. 661).

30. Ibid., p. 679. Zvantsev suggests that it was Wagner who put this idea in Serov's mind, in paying his Russian colleague what seems a rather dubious compliment. Speaking with reference to *Rogneda,* Wagner is supposed to have told Serov that, "if Meyerbeer, Halévy, Félicien David, Hérold, could all make brilliant careers for themselves in Paris, then so can you. That's the place for you, but not for me: I am steeped too deeply in my native German milieu." Zvantsev claimed to have heard this story from Serov himself. Interestingly enough, Liszt had the very opposite reaction to *Rogneda:* "Restez chez vous en Russie avec votre *Rognéda.* C'est une oeuvre toute *russe"* (V.S. Serova, *Serovy,* p. 66).

31. Serov, *Izbrannye stat'i I,* p. 78. The subject of the Hussites was briefly considered also by Tchaikovsky, who in his operatic works was not immune to Meyerbeerian predilections. He rejected the idea, however, writing that "I asked [Berg, the prospective librettist] whether he had any plan in mind. It turns out he had none; he just likes the fact that they sang hymns" (October 29, 1874. Quoted in Boris Iarustovskii, *Dramaturgia russkoi opernoi klassiki*[2nd ed., Moscow, 1953], p. 98).

32. *Russkaia starina* 9 (1888), p. 671.

33. Letter to Novikova (cf. note 3). Gozenpud, *Russkii opernyi teatr II,* p. 248.

34. V.S. Serova, *Serovy,* p. 82.

35. The article was unsigned and was therefore not included in Serov's collected critical works.

The very fact of its lack of attribution, however, in itself constitutes attribution in a periodical of which Serov was sole editor. Attention was first called to the piece by A.A. Gozenpud in "Opernoe tvorchestvo A.N. Serova," *Sovetskaia muzyka* (1971) no. 7, from which source we quote it.

36. Serov, *Izbrannye stat'i I*, p. 206.

37. V.S. Serova, *Serovy*, p. 85.

38. *Narodnaia pesnia—proizvedenie chisto-pochvennoe, rastitel'noe.* Serov, *Izbrannye stat'i I*, p. 97.

39. Serov, *Izbrannye stat'i I*, p. 97. Of course, Serov was bound to look upon the musical ideas of his *pochvennik* mentors with a certain condescension: they were dilettantes, he was by now Russia's foremost theatrical composer. Indicative are his comments on Stakhovich's collection, the publication that had given Grigoriev his initial pretext for formulating his theory of folk art: "Stakhovich, a dilettante who had certain pretensions to a scientific approach to his subject, invested a great deal of labor in his 'Collection of Russian Folk Songs' (Moscow, 1854). Unfortunately, he lacked the taste required for a successful selection and transcription, and lacked the training for a scientific treatment of the question or for successful harmonization" (p. 103). Serov has kinder words for Villebois's collection, which was prepared with the active participation of Ostrovsky, Grigoriev and Filippov, for here the dilettante folklorists had enlisted the aid of a professional musician as "secretary" (p. 104).

40. *OstRK*, pp. 102-103.

41. *Vestnik Evropy 10* (1916). Cited from *OstRK*, p. 93.

42. Statement made in conversation with S.S. Popov. *OstRK*, p. 79.

43. Instead of A, then B, then A-plus-B, "one character sings A, the other also A, and then together the same A in thirds and sixths." Quoted by Serov in a letter to Stasov, February 14, 1843. See Giorgii Khubov, *Zhizn' A.N. Serova* (Moscow-Leningrad, 1950), p. 16.

44. The description of the Kashperov-Ostrovsky *The Storm* is based on the separately published libretto (Moscow, 1867) and the piano score of Kashperov's music (without voice), arr. A. Diubiuk (Moscow: P. Jurgenson, n. d.).

45. To Modest Tchaikovsky, September 13, 1868. Chaikovskii, *Polnoe sobranie sochinenii V* (Moscow, 1959), p. 141.

46. Larosh, *Sobranie muzykal'no-kriticheskikh statei II*, part 1, p. 103.

47. Cf. N.V. Tumanina, *Chaikovskii, put' k masterstvu* (Moscow, 1962), p. 138.

48. Modest Tchaikovsky, in his biography of his brother, categorically asserts that "the fault seems to lie not with A.N. Ostrovsky, but with Pyotr Ilyich himself." (*Zhizn' P.I. Chaikovskogo I* [Moscow, 1900], p. 296.) This is because, through a series of rather improbable circumstances Tchaikovsky was forced to do some of the libretto-writing himself, having lost Ostrovsky's manuscript. With characteristic self-deprecation he later referred to his literary contribution as being "sickeningly banal and stupidly written" (*P.I. Chaikovskii i S.I. Taneev, Pis'ma* [Moscow, 1951], p. 89).

49. *Sanktpeterburgskie vedomosti* (1867), no. 304.

50. Serov, *Izbrannye stat'i II* (Leningrad, 1957), pp. 73-77 passim.

51. Ibid., p. 73.

52. *OstRK*, pp. 105-7.

53. Ibid., p. 107.

54. Ibid., pp. 107-9.

55. A.N. Ostrovskii, *Dnevniki i pis'ma* (Moscow, 1937), p. 64.

56. "With Averkiev [the librettist of *Rogneda*] I neglected to make stipulations, and in the end it was an unpleasant story for me . . . so I have taken it as a rule *always* to spell out these details as carefully as possible and *without ceremony*" (*OstRK*, p. 112).

57. Ostrovskii, *Dnevniki,* p. 66.

58. *OstRK*, p. 117.

59. Ibid., p. 123.

60. Ibid., p. 114.

61. *Russkaia starina* 9 (1888), p. 673.

62. Another conventionally operatic "compromise" by Ostrovsky initially took Serov by surprise: the setting was moved back in time a hundred years, to the seventeenth century. "You have done this," Serov wrote (June 12, 1867), "probably for the sake of the costumes, for the sake of externals. Well, that won't hurt, really. But this change will require, of course, some new shadings in the characters you have drawn" (*OstRK*, p. 112). When it came to explaining this un-"realistic" touch to Zvantsev, Serov adopted a rather pompously didactic tone: "In works of art one needs what painters call aerial perspective, that is, progressive remoteness in space. Remoteness in time is the same thing: that is, what is needed is some historical epoch, with its costumes, customs, mores, habits, etc" (*Russkaia starina* 9 [1888], p. 674).

63. The single exception is Pyotr's monologue, about which see below.

64. It is well known from Musorgsky's later use of it in Act III of *Khovanshchina.* Tchaikovsky also used it, in his very early overture to Ostrovsky's *The Storm.* His source for the tune may well have been the dramatist himself.

65. In early discussions (e.g., the letter of May 26 cited above) it is referred to as the second scene of Act III, but in the finished libretto it had become an independent act, for which, to judge by later correspondence, Serov seems to have agreed to pay his collaborator an extra 100 rubles.

66. V.S. Serova, *Serovy,* p. 111.

67. Ibid.

68. V.S. Serova, *Serovy,* p. 112.

69. See V.S. Serova's recollection, published in Findeisen, *A.N. Serov,* p. 127.

70. *Istoricheskii vestnik* (1915), no. 5. Quoted by L.N. Smirnova in the critical notes to A.N. Ostrovskii, *Polnoe sobranie sochinenii I* (Moscow, 1973), p. 570.

71. *Russkaia starina* 9 (1888), p. 672.

72. *OstRK*, pp. 124-26, somewhat condensed. On the matter of the "two plots," cf. the surface and ideal plots in Serov's conception of *Rogneda:* it was a *pochvennik* cliché. As a matter of fact, Ostrovsky's ending had raised previous objections among his intimates. Tertii Filippov had written (*Russkaia beseda* [1856], no. 1): "Here Mr. Ostrovsky has shown his usual

weakness: he never seems to be able to bring his action to a round conclusion, such as would satisfy the feelings of his reader." Cf. Ostrovskii, *Polnoe sobranie sochinenii, I*, p. 564. Serov reminded Ostrovsky of this critique in his letter.

73.   V.S. Serova, *Serovy,* p. 112.

74.   The letter appears in *OstRK*, pp. 138-39. Serov's threats included financial reprisals, too. Ostrovsky's fee would be lowered from 500 rubles to 300, so that his replacement could be paid. When the letter arrived, Ostrovsky was out of town. It was received by Mikhail Ostrovsky, who forwarded it to his brother with the note, "I don't know how I should answer lines like these, but I cannot refrain from observing that it would be better to have nothing further to do with the likes of Serov" (A.I. Reviakin, *Moskva v zhizni i tvorchestve A.N. Ostrovskogo* [Moscow, 1962], p. 390).

75.   *Peterburgskii listok* (1871), no. 6. Quoted in Findeisen, p. 129.

76.   It was published in 1881 in the *Sanktpeterburgskie vedomosti.* See Findeisen, p. 129.

77.   *Russkaia starina* 9 (1888), pp. 672-73.

78.   Letter to S.A. Yuryev (1868), quoted in V.S. Baskin, *A.N. Serov* (Moscow, 1890), p. 98.

79.   Findeisen, p. 130.

80.   His best known opera was a setting of the *Vakula the Smith* libretto by Yakov Polonsky which the Grand Duchess Elena Pavlovna had commissioned for Serov, and which after the latter's death was set by several composers in a famous competition sponsored by the Russian Musical Society and won by Tchaikovsky, whose setting has entered the repertory in a revision of 1885 entitled *Cherevichki.*

81.   See Gozenpud, "Opernoe tvorchestvo A.N. Serova," p. 100.

82.   For a synopsis of the scenario and a list of musical numbers, see Appendix A.

83.   *OstRK*, p. 111.

84.   Serov, *Izbrannye stat'i I,* p. 77.

85.   Boris Asafiev, *Kriticheskie stat'i i retsenzii* (Leningrad, 1967), p. 100.

86.   *OstRK,* p. 107.

87.   Nikolai Chernyshevsky, *Selected Philosophical Essays* (Moscow: Foreign Languages Publishing House, 1953), p. 346.

88.   Ibid., p. 347.

89.   *OstRK,* p. 116.

90.   In Westrup, ed., *Essays Presented to Egon Wellesz* (Oxford, 1966), p. 181.

91.   Ostrovskii, *Polnoe sobranie sochinenii I,* p. 399.

92.   Here is a breakdown: *Askold's Grave* (1835) cites only one actual Russian folk song; *A Life for the Tsar* (1836) cites two; *Ruslan* (1842) cites none at all; *Rusalka* (1856) cites five. The record-holder before *The Power of the Fiend* was actually an eighteenth-century singspiel, Pashkevich's (or Matinsky's) *Sanktpeterburgskii gostinnyi dvor* (1782), which includes at least eight songs found in the collections of Lvov and Pratsch (1790) and Trutovsky (1776). These appear for the most part as a medley in the Act II bridal scene *(devichnik).* The number of folksong citations in *The Power of the Fiend* was to be exceeded only by Rimsky-Korsakov, in *May Night* (1878), *Snegurochka* (1881), and *Christmas Eve* (1895). Most of

the foregoing information is taken from Vera Bachinskaia, *Narodnye pesni v tvorchestve russkikh kompozitorov* (Moscow, 1962).

93. For this there was precedent in Glinka: the dramatic turning point of *A Life for the Tsar* is supported by a running-bass ostinato derived from the folk song *Vniz po matushke po Volge.* See M.I. Glinka, *Literaturnye proizvedeniia i perepiska I* (Moscow, 1973), p. 271; or, in English, M. Glinka, *Memoirs,* trans. Richard B. Mudge (Norman, Oklahoma, 1963), p. 101.

94. *OstRK,* p. 111.

95. Serov had drawn upon this source for both of the folk tunes he cited in *Rogneda. Kapitanskaia doch'* had a long pedigree in the Russian theater, beginning with Fomin's *Post Drivers* (1788) and Davydov's *Rusalka.* See Bachinskaia, p. 43, and Gerald Seaman, *History of Russian Music, I* (New York, 1967), p. 145, including musical example 7.

96. *OstRK,* p. 116.

97. This list, of course, cannot pretend to be exhaustive. Given Serov's freewheeling methods of adaptation, on the one hand, and his probable access to unpublished or oral sources on the other, we may confidently assume that many more actual folk models lurk behind what from here on we shall have to treat as Serov's original music. Serov, for example, is thought to have had direct access to a number of folk tunes privately transcribed by Prince Odoevsky (see comments by E.V. Gippius in Bachinskaia, pp. 176-77). The identifications that have successfully been made have been made on the basis of two a priori clues: Ostrovsky's own use of folk material and Serov's known recourse to Villebois. It would take other such external hints to expand the list of identifications.

98. *OstRK,* p. 127.

99. Ibid., p. 137.

100. Serov, *Izbrannye stat'i II,* p. 76.

101. *O velikorusskoi pesne i osobennostiakh eë muzykal'nogo sklada,* transcript of a lecture delivered April 11, 1868 (Moscow, 1868), p. 23. Serov's remarks seem an echo of the "Benfeyism" that was just then spreading like wildfire through the field of folkloristic studies. In the preface to his edition (1859) of the *Panchatantra,* a third-century collection of Hindu tales, the German philologist Theodor Benfey (1809-81) traced the history of the work's transmission and migrations, and demonstrated the concordances between the Indian tales and those of Europe. The theory of cultural borrowing thus propounded was a direct assault upon the mystically Romantic attitudes toward folklore as embodiment of a unique national spirit, previously entertained, e.g., by Schelling, Herder and the brothers Grimm in Germany, or by the Slavophile folklorists (Kireevsky, Afanasiev) in Russia. The most spectacular application of Benfeyism in Russia was Vladimir Stasov's notorious essay on the origin of the *byliny* ("Proiskhozhdenie russkikh bylin," *Vestnik Evropy* [1868], six installments), which, transparently following Benfey's lead (and that of his Russian disciple, the orientalist F.M. Schiffner), Stasov located in India. The early installments of Stasov's work had just hit the stands at the time of Serov's lecture, and it is hard not to see Serov's rather half-baked theory as an attempt to keep up with his rival. For more on the Benfeyist controversies in Russia, see Iurii Sokolov, *Russkii fol'klor* (Moscow, 1938), Chapter 2 ("Istoriografiia fol'kloristiki").

102. In *Glinka i ego znachenie dlia russkoi muzyki* (1867); cf. chapter 1.

103. In his *Sbornik russkikh narodnykh pesen'* (1866) and such works as his "Overtures on Russian Themes" (1857, 1862).

104. In fact, in the whole example that follows, there is only one dominant chord (on Pyotr's "Ne ia vinoi!") and its resolution is suppressed.

105. Very obvious here is Serov's technique of deriving melody from harmony, especially by arpeggiating the half-diminished chords that are so conspicuous a component of *The Power of the Fiend*'s harmonic language.

106. Here, as in the early nineteenth-century "bytovoy" romance, the minor leading tone is very much in evidence, particularly under the natural third scale degree, producing a characteristically "Russian" diminished-fourth.

107. *Kriticheskie stat'i i retsenzii*, p. 100.

108. To trace the connections between Serov's opera and Stravinsky's ballet would exceed our present scope. Suffice it to point out for now that Stravinsky's father was one of the great Eryomkas; that Serov's operas were among Stravinsky's earliest musical impressions (cf. Stravinsky, *An Autobiography* [New York, 1936], p. 6); and that Serov's son Valentin, the famous painter, was extremely close both to Stravinsky and to Benois at the time *Petrushka* was created (cf. Alexandre Benois, *Reminiscences of the Russian Ballet* [London, 1941], Chapter 8, esp. p. 331).

109. March 1, 1869. *OstRK*, p. 187.

110. For a treatment of the aesthetic implications of the naturalistic treatment of drunkenness and crime in that part of Dostoevsky's work contemporaneous with Serov's (particularly *Crime and Punishment*, originally to have been entitled *The Drunkards*), see Donald Fanger, *Dostoevsky and Romantic Realism* (Chicago, 1967), Chapter 7, esp. pp. 184-91.

111. *Sanktpeterburgskie vedomosti* (1865), no. 292.

112. V.S. Serova, *Serovy*, p. 114.

113. Problems of this kind, as well perhaps as revulsion at the distortion of Ostrovsky, probably accounted for the widespread practice of omitting the fifth act in late nineteenth-century revivals of Serov's opera.

114. Vol. 54 (1861), nos. 10, 11, 12, 13. Reprinted in Russian translation in Serov, *Kriticheskie stat'i III* (St. Petersburg, 1895), pp. 1406-26, and in *Izbrannye stat'i I* (Leningrad, 1950), pp. 409-24.

115. Serov, *Izbrannye stat'i I*, pp. 409, 410.

116. Ibid., p. 412.

117. Ibid., p. 423.

118. Ibid, p. 423. He means the kinship of the opening woodwind melody of the Introduction and the second theme of the Allegro, related by tracing them both to a common origin in Florestan's Act II aria, "In des Lebens Frühlingstagen."

119. *Teatral'nyi i muzykal'nyi vestnik* (1859), no. 49. Reprinted in *Izbrannye stat'i II* (Moscow, 1957), pp. 35-43.

120. A point Serov made on numerous occasions, some of them cited in Chapter 1.

121. Serov, *Izbrannye stat'i I*, p. 412.

122. *OstRK*, p. 115.

123. Ibid., p. 116.

124. For example: accompaniment figures both for Act I, sc. iv and for the Act II finale are derived from theme no. 1; Act I, sc. vi (Dasha's solo scena) is preceded by a prelude played to an empty stage, constructed out of themes 1 and 2; the main theme of Act I, sc. iv (no. 2) is heard not only as given in the example, but as an accompanying figure throughout the scene.

125. Theme no. 2 falls not a full fifth, but a third (a fourth if the apoggiatura is counted). It is nonetheless clearly a member of the family, as it partially exhibits the significant shared trait.

126. *OstRK*, p. 134.

127. Odoevskii, *Muzykal'no-literaturnoe nasledie* (Moscow, 1956), p. 634.

128. Ibid., p. 343.

129. E.F. Napravnik, *Avtobiograficheskie, tvorcheskie materialy, dokumenty, pis'ma* (Leningrad, 1959), p. 48.

130. *Sanktpeterburgskie vedomosti* (1871), no. 111.

131. Serov, *Kriticheskie stat'i III* (St. Petersburg, 1892), p. 1543.

132. Ostrovsky had provided a way out "into the light" in *Live Not the Way You'd Like*, however. Ilya disappears after the first act and Pyotr makes his repentance in the end not at his own father's feet but at Agafon's, Dasha's gentle, all-forgiving parent. "Meekness, reconciliation and spiritual purity have defeated willfulness and pride," as Gozenpud puts it ("Opernoe tvorchestvo Serova," *Sovetskaia muzyka* [1971], no. 7). But having decided that Ilya is the "alpha and omega" of the drama, Serov plunged the story into unremitting night and it could be argued from this alone that the murder became inevitable. Pyotr's impossible situation was Serov's invention, not Ostrovsky's.

133. *Sanktpeterburgskie vedomosti* (1871), no. 111 (italics original). All further citations from Cui, unless otherwise noted, will be from this source.

134. Cui may actually have been unaware that Ostrovsky himself had written the text of the first three acts, since after the rift between composer and librettist, the latter's name was not mentioned in programs or advertisements, nor in the published score (a situation that has not been rectified even in the 1968 edition), where acknowledgement is made only that the opera "is derived from *Ne tak zhivi, kak khochetsia.*"

135. Rostislav (F.M. Tolstoi), *Novaia opera A.N. Serova Vrazh'ia sila* (St. Petersburg, 1871), p. 23.

136. Ibid., p. 27.

137. Ibid., pp. 49-50.

138. Ibid., p. 53.

139. Ibid.

140. Ibid., p. 54.

141. Ibid., p. 57.

142. Ibid., p. 65.

143. Ibid., p. 67.

144. The Afanasiev referred to by Cui was Nikolai Yakovlevich Afanasiev (1820-98), violinist and minor operatic composer, whose *Ammalat-Bek*, after Marlinsky's popular novel, had

been produced at the Mariinsky the year before.

145. An ironic footnote to Cui's relationship to *The Power of the Fiend* and his general development as musical thinker is his much later reminiscence of the work, entitled "A.N. Serov and his Posthumous Opera" *(A.N. Serov i ego posmertnaia opera).* His criticism of the work is much softened, but now, curiously, he attacks the subject: "The pity is that this subject is too realistic throughout, that it touches upon the less seemly, dirty side of our national life, and that there is not a drop of poetry in it, whereas the highest calling of music is to bring to our day-to-day existence some semblance of beauty, poetry and idealization" *(Novosti i birzhevaia gazeta* [1896], no. 38). This is hardly *"kuchkist"* thinking, but by then Cui had become a bit of a renegade. In the same article Cui quite rightly compares Serov with Musorgsky, not exactly meaning to flatter the latter.

146. It was an all-star assemblage: Kondratiev (Pyotr), Lavrovskaya (Grunya), Platonova (Dasha), as well as those faithful Serovians, Sariotti (who was to create another sensation as Eryomka) and Leonova (Spiridonovna).

147. *Istoricheskii vestnik* 125 (1911). Quoted in Gozenpud, *Russkii opernyi teatr XIX veka II,* p. 263.

148. Ibid.

149. Gozenpud, *Russkii opernyi teatr II,* p. 265. Platonova, one might add, was known particularly for her dramatic talent, and later became one of the *kuchka's* staunchest supporters. Thus, her objections hardly proceeded from prejudice or lack of artistic imagination.

150. *Istoricheskii vestnik 83* (1901). Quoted in Gozenpud, p. 266.

151. Rostislav, *Novaia opera,* p. 27.

152. *Sanktpeterburgskie vedomosti* (1872), no. 297.

153. Quoted in Gozenpud, p. 269.

154. Quoted in Gozenpud, p. 273.

155. Rostislav, *Novaia opera,* p. 62. Interestingly enough, this episode was cut when *The Power of the Fiend* was revived by the Bolshoi Theatre in 1947.

156. Gozenpud, p. 263.

157. *Sanktpeterburgskie vedomosti* (1874), no. 312.

158. A.N. Rimskii-Korsakov, ed., *M.P. Musorgskii: Pis'ma i dokumenty* (Moscow-Leningrad, 1932), p. 481.

159. But Musorgsky was so prejudiced against Serov by then that he was able to write to Stasov the day before *The Power of the Fiend's* premiere, that "suspecting the sincerity of his nationalism, I expect a caricature" (Musorgskii, *Literaturnoe nasledie I* [Moscow, 1971], p. 121). What Musorgsky thought after hearing the work is unrecorded, but it may be safe to assume that, like all prejudiced expectations, this one did not fail to come true.

160. Asafiev, *Kriticheskie stat'i i retsenzii,* p. 106.

5

The Stone Guest and Its Progeny

The realist ferment that took such a strong hold on Russian art of the 1860s received a rather extreme operatic expression, as we have seen, in *The Power of the Fiend*. And yet there was an even more extreme and, on the face of it, aberrant manifestation of the tendency in the domain of music—Dargomyzhsky's last opera, *The Stone Guest (Kamennyi gost')*, after Pushkin's Don Juan play. Serov's work and Dargomyzhsky's could hardly seem more different in the externals of method and aim: *The Power of the Fiend*'s realism was a matter of unflinching naturalism of genre and reliance upon the "natural" model of Russian folk song, neither of which play any significant role in *The Stone Guest*. The Spanish setting, needless to say, precluded Russian atmosphere, but even Spanish local color was an entirely peripheral matter with Dargomyzhsky, as it had been with Pushkin, whose play was not realist in inspiration at all, but purebloodedly romantic. Dargomyzhsky's musical realism, then, was concerned not with the content of the art work, but with means of expression. It was a realism of dramaturgical technique and psychological penetration, and as such issued a far more fundamental challenge to conventional operatic practice than Serov had ever envisioned.

The Stone Guest is in fact the very model of "reformist" opera. No other music drama had ever so self-consciously and resolutely refused to be "operatic," not even Wagner's. No other music drama was ever so literally experimental in conception. As is well known, Dargomyzhsky's opera is, quite simply, a setting of Pushkin's play to music with none but the most insubstantial and insignificant alterations in the text. The very idea that such a procedure was possible flew in the face of the entire history of opera, for it denied the fundamental premise upon which operatic dramaturgy had always rested, and by which opera differed radically from the spoken drama, that action and "passion" were separable. It was thanks to this premise that musical forms had been given the opportunity to achieve independent development within the dynamic processes of the drama. Although by the mid-nineteenth century operatic dramaturgy had become far more supple than the rigid alternation of action and soliloquy of the opera seria, no one, not excepting Wagner, had ever questioned the demand that the operatic

Fig. 5.1   Alexander Dargomyzhsky, engraving after a photograph of the late 1850s

libretto make suitable provision for the unfolding of purely musical structure, whatever the particular structure or the means of its unfolding. In short, no one ever questioned, as did Dargomyzhsky, the special and specific conception of the *dramma per musica*. Dargomyzhsky's example implied in terms more literal than ever before imagined, that the criteria of good opera and spoken drama were ideally identical, and *The Stone Guest* unleashed a storm of controversy over the most basic questions of the relationship of music to drama and to words themselves, a controversy that, in Russia at least, has still not completely died down.[1]

What brought Dargomyzhsky's creative path to such a pass? For most of his career he was the unlikeliest of candidates for such an exploit. His first opera, *Esmeralda* (1835-37, produced 1838) was based on his own translation of a libretto Victor Hugo himself had drawn from his *Notre Dame de Paris* for Louise Bertin (produced 1836), thoroughly "operaticizing" the work in the process, much as Ostrovsky would do with *The Storm*. If the music of *Esmeralda* was, as Dargomyzhsky himself later avowed, "nothing special, often banal,"[2] after the fashion of the grand *opéra*, his second stage work, *The Triumph of Bacchus* (*Torzhestvo Vakkha*, 1848), seems positively retrograde, especially when we consider that it achieved its first production as late as 1868. This "lyric opera-ballet," actually a sort of staged cantata, is a setting of a mock ode by the young Pushkin (1818), an unabashedly epigonous resurrection of ancien régime frivolity. Neither work succeeded in gaining much public recognition for Dargomyzhsky, and he might well have settled into a comfortable niche as dilettante composer and fashionable vocal pedagogue, on the order of an Artemovsky, a Varlamov or a Kashperov.

But friendship with Glinka spared Dargomyzhsky this fate, for the great man inspired in his younger colleague an enthusiastic wish to join in the quest for a national Russian style. In forsaking his fashionable Gallicism for the uncharted terrain of an indigenous musical language, however, Dargomyzhsky was faced with the same dilemma that was to confront Serov when he came to write *Rogneda:* how to join forces with Glinka without being overwhelmed by his example. If he was not merely to exchange one kind of derivativeness for another, he would have to find a new corner of the Russian vineyard to cultivate. He saw his opportunity in the controversies that surrounded *Ruslan.* These were reflected in an oft-quoted letter to Odoevsky (July 3, 1853):

> The more I study the elements of our national music, the more varied are the aspects I discern in them. Glinka, who alone up to now has given Russian music any breadth in my opinion, has touched upon only one of its sides—the lyric. His dramaturgy is too plaintive, the comic loses its national character. ... As far as possible, I am striving to develop the dramatic side of our national character.[3]

The opera on which Dargomyzhsky was working at the time of this letter, the one in which he sought to realize this goal, was *Rusalka,* after Pushkin's unfinished verse tragedy. This work was indeed taken to be a new departure in operatic dramaturgy at the time of its premiere in 1856, although those of its features that linked it with the past are apt to seem more conspicuous today than those which were viewed by contemporaries as portents of the future.[4] It was *Rusalka* that Stravinsky, for example, had in mind when he spoke of Dargomyzhsky's happy ability "to mingle the Russian popular *melos* and the prevailing Italianism with the most carefree and charming ease."[5] The opera contains arias derived from bel canto by way of Glinka, plaintive romances in the conventional *style russe* of the St. Petersburg salons, plenty of coloratura virtuosity for the heroine, along with a typical confinement of Russian local color to elements of divertissement (choruses, dances, strophic songs) that critics of the next decade would already characterize as naive. Its skimpiness of orchestration and episodic construction show the hand of the autodidact all too clearly. And yet a new note definitely was sounded in *Rusalka,* one which raised Dargomyzhsky to an incomparably higher plane in the eyes of his contemporaries—and of history—than had any of his previous work.

Unlike either of Glinka's operas, *Rusalka* was based on a literary souce that was itself dramatic in form. Despite the intermingling of the fantastic, Pushkin's *Rusalka* is fundamentally concerned with its characters and their interaction. The main protagonists are three: a Kievan prince, a miller's daughter (unnamed in Pushkin, Natasha in the opera) whom the prince seduces and abandons, and her father the miller. Natasha throws herself into the Dnepr when the prince forsakes her, and is transformed into the queen of the river mermaids, who wreaks cold supernatural vengeance upon her wayward lover. The old miller, meanwhile, is driven insane by the loss of his daughter. The music Dargomyzhsky composed for the confrontations between these main characters (leaving aside their extended solos, and considering Natasha only in her human guise) constitutes the "new" in *Rusalka:* a freewheeling declamatory style in which the composer's efforts were bent toward capturing the fugitive moods and meanings underlying the individual words of the text, rather than generalizing them into a closed structure governed by more purely musical exigencies. And the words were in many cases Pushkin's own. Dargomyzhsky, in fashioning his own libretto, had sought to preserve the original verses as far as possible, and advertised the fact in the opera's subtitle.

Though *Rusalka* enjoyed hardly more than a *succes d'estime* at the time of its premiere, it attracted to the composer the attention and enthusiasm of the best musical minds in Russia. First and foremost among them was Serov, who in 1856 was reaching the pinnacle of his critical career. He became Dargomyzhsky's ardent propagandist—much as Odoevsky had been Glinka's some twenty years before—and wrote an enormous essay on *Rusalka,* which was serialized in ten issues of the *Muzykal'nyi i teatral'nyi vestnik*. The critic, by that time deeply embroiled in controversy over the dramatic merits of Glinka's works, saw in *Rusalka* an advance "even over Glinka's first opera," to say nothing of *Ruslan*,[6] and used his essay on *Rusalka* as a pretext for the elaborate exposition of musico-dramatic theory we have already had occasion to sample for the light it shed on *Judith*. Almost alone among the early writers on Dargomyzhsky's opera, Serov recognized its innovatory side and valued it highly, if a bit tendentiously. Where most critics paid greatest attention to the elements of genre and the fantastic that linked *Rusalka* with its immediate tradition, Serov was at pains to point out that these were the opera's weakest, most derivative aspects. Instead, Serov called attention to the dramatic scenes, particularly the confrontation between the prince and the raving miller in Act III.

> Dramatic words by themselves, though they be declaimed to the highest degree of perfection by the foremost artist, cannot create so gripping an impression as the same words set to music and performed *as they should be* by a singer, as long as (NB) the scenic situation calls for "musical poetry" and as long as the author of the music is in full command of dramatic truth. In the present case both conditions are fully met. The meeting of the prince with the crazy old man contains strong drama of the truest musical character. And one of the most precious sides of [Dargomyzhsky's] talent is precisely this *truth* of musical expression. He serves this truth honorably at every turn, and oftentimes to the detriment of external effect, which latter might have easily been achieved by other, more conventional means. But in those places where all requirements of "effectiveness" *coincide* with "musical truth," there the triumph of *Rusalka*'s author is complete. His music profoundly and irresistibly affects even those who, for a variety of reasons, cannot appreciate the beauties of his style.[7]

From the entrance of the mad miller until his story of how he became a raven, all the words are Pushkin's. That is, these thirteen lines (eight of Pushkin's original verses are omitted) are composed in exactly the fashion that would characterize the whole of *The Stone Guest*. The music is given in Example 5.1. Here is Serov's *explication de texte:*

> The old man approaches the prince: "Greetings, greetings, son-in-law!" And from the first words one hears the speech of a man whose mind is deranged. "Who are you?" quickly asks the prince (unpleasantly struck by the appearance of this strange poor fellow). "I am the local raven!" The prince has not heard these quietly spoken words, which vividly characterize the madman; but staring at the old man he recognizes him: "Can it be? It's the miller! . . . " (High notes in the voice, in the orchestra *forte* on an extremely energetic figure). The old man has heard the loud outcry of the prince and is angered: "What do you mean miller?—" (In the orchestra, after the abrupt chords between this phrase and its repetition, a definite rhythm is established—the strings begin pumping with a sort of self-satisfaction). "I sold the mill to the demons behind the stove, and the money I gave for safekeeping to the mermaid, my prophetic daughter." The word "demons" is colored by a wild leap of the voice (in unison with the clarinet and bassoon). The words "and the money" take on a special coloration from the high notes of the bass voice, sung *piano*, by which the old miser (just as

Ex. 5.1.   *Rusalka* (Moscow: Izdatel'stvo "Muzyka," 1966), pp. 228-30

Ex. 5.1 (cont'd)

in Pushkin's text) is excellently drawn. At the words "to the mermaid," a mysterious solemnity appears both in the voice and in the orchestra. The interval between the lines of the miller is occupied by an original chord progression, culminating extraordinarily aptly in hollow, barely audible beats of the kettledrum. Here the music seems to dictate the proper gestures to the madman. "It is buried in the sands of the Dnepr; a one-eyed fish guards it," repeats the old man, fondly lingering in his thoughts over his treasure.... This last phrase of his, enunciated the second time no longer so loudly, but mysteriously, prompts the prince's replique, over a tremolo: "Unhappy man, he's lost his mind! Poor miller!" Once more this word angers the mad one: "What do you mean miller?" he cries, as distinctly as possible, "I'm telling you, I'm a raven. A raven, and not a miller." Every word is colored magnificently. The strange chords between the words "a raven...a raven" wonderfully depict the madman, deeply believing himself in his transformation into a bird.[8]

The most striking thing about Serov's extraordinarily sympathetic description of Dargomyzhsky's scene is his focus on the individual words of text, and the way in which the composer is seen as "performing" Pushkin's lines like an actor. Besides inflections and vocal colorations, the music supplies even the gestures. The irony, as one may recall, is that in the lengthy theoretical preface that had taken up the first part of Serov's essay, the critic had dismissed this level of detail as unsuitable for operatic music. Categorically and dogmatically he had asserted that in opera the actual words of the libretto "are absolutely subordinate to the music" and that the composer's real concern should not be with them but with "situations" and the broader aspects of the scenario, the "canvas" for the music. It was on this belief that Serov was to act in forming *Judith* and *Rogneda,* and yet his own creative predilections did not prevent him from empathizing as critic with Dargomyzhsky's tinycraft, even though this was precisely the point on which their two "realisms" so radically diverged. Serov recognized that what was new, daring and difficult in Dargomyzhsky's style was its demand for sustained spontaneous invention on the part of the composer and a continuously flexible response to the subtlest vicissitudes of the text. The sole yardstick by which the success or failure of such music could be measured was the degree to which the composer had been able to "perform" the text as the author had intended it. The composer is then judged as an actor is judged—an actor, to be sure, with hitherto undreamed-of resources. Truth of expression in such music utterly replaces all other criteria and functions of the art: music need no longer be "beautiful," but it must at all costs be accurate.

It seems clear in retrospect that Serov's essay on *Rusalka* exerted a powerful influence on the opera's composer. From Dargomyzhsky's own pen we have evidence that he never attached as much importance to the dialogue scenes in *Rusalka* as he did to other, more dated, ones. More than anyone else, it was Serov who opened Dargomyzhsky's eyes to the implications of his own achievement.

> Late last night I read your analysis of the duet between the miller and the prince. I thank you with all my heart not so much for your praise as for the uncommonly deep penetration of my innermost and even unconscious thoughts. In truth I had never thought that my duet was so successful, but I have already said that you possess the fortunate gift of being able to illuminate all sides of whatever you examine.[9]

After *Rusalka,* and especially after Serov's critique of it, there comes a definite change in Dargomyzhsky's artistic self-image, as reflected in his letters. Whereas during the period of work upon the opera his primary focus had been on national style and vague aspirations to the "dramatic," he now began to write the slogan-filled manifestos that characterize him today in Russian musical historiography. The aggressive tone that now asserts itself is to a degree attributable to the difficulties Dargomyzhsky was experiencing with the musical establishment of St. Petersburg. *Rusalka* was taken off the boards after eleven performances and was reinstated only after a public protest in which the composer had reluctantly played a part. The combination of Serov's encouragement and official discouragement led Dargomyzhsky to entertain radical musical ideals and to give them pungent and pugnacious expression in such letters as the following, to his admirer and pupil, the singer Lyubov Karmalina:

> I do not deceive myself: my artistic position in Petersburg is not an enviable one. The majority of our music-lovers and journalistic hacks do not recognize any inspiration in me. Their routine outlook seeks melodies that flatter the ear, which I do not chase after. I do not propose to lower music to the level of a pastime for their sake. I want sound directly to express the word. I want truth.[10]

The operative word here, of course, is "word" itself; Serov's influence is obvious. Ironic, this, that Serov guided the older composer into a position so contrary to his own, and one that was to make him the darling of the burgeoning "New Russian School."

Dargomyzhsky was hardly alone in his "radical" postures. The period between *Rusalka* and *The Stone Guest* was the heyday of the "radical democrats" and their clamorous utilitarian aesthetics, compared to which Dargomyzhsky's realism seems mild indeed. The most formal expression of the radical tendency was Chernyshevsky's *Esthetic Relations of Art to Reality,* which we have already cited in connection with Ostrovsky and "natural singing." A connection may similarly be drawn between Chernyshevsky's preachments on the relations between "real life" and art and Dargomyzhsky's views on the immediacy of musical expression as he now wished to practice it, along with the concomitant revolt against established canons of beauty and particularly of "form."[11] In the course of justifying his formulation of the concept of "natural singing," Chernyshevsky asked whether "it is to be

Fig. 5.2   Serov and Dargomyzhsky
(anonymous caricature from
around the time of *Rusalka*)

Fig. 5.3   Nikolai Chernyshevsky around 1860

expected that a person under the overwhelming influence of emotion will think about attaining charm and grace, will concern himself with form?"— and answered the question with one of his most notorious slogans: "Emotion and form are opposites."[12] This assertion certainly accorded with Dargomyzhsky's practice at moments of highest dramatic pressure in *Rusalka,* and flew in the face of conventional operatic dramaturgy, where it was precisely the expression of "pure" emotion that had called for, or excused, the generalizing, unifying sublimation of the music into rounded forms. Chernyshevsky even went so far as to claim that "in essence, . . . the music of a composer who wrote under the overwhelming influence of involuntary emotion will be a work of nature (of life) in general, and not of art."[13] We may allow for the pragmatic aspect of this conception in the face of the difficulties music presents to a positivist aesthetician, and still conclude that the ideal of vocal music Chernyshevsky describes is Dargomyzhsky's own. What counts in the final analysis is not the folk song (*pace* Ostrovsky and Serov) but what lies behind and motivates the folk song, the "sincere emotion" that "permeates" it.[14] And this is to be approached by the composer of art music by striving not for "art," but directly for emotion itself and the "truth" that transcends artistry. Vocal music written to such a prescription will be formally spontaneous and flexible, achieving coherence only in union with its text, and developing "organically" by a process of immediate, empathic reaction by the composer to words and situations.[15]

Such an aesthetic rests, of course, on the old assumption that music directly "represents" the emotions. To the mid-nineteenth century positivist, moreover, emotions were not inchoate, subjective feelings, but objective phenomena that could be observed and rendered "scientifically." What distinguished realism of this kind from romanticism was precisely this insistence on accuracy down to the most niggling distinctions and nuances, and success or failure in this regard was considered fair grounds for criticism.[16] But if this sounds like an incipient *Affektenlehre,* there was enough residual romanticism in the outlook of the "New Russian School" to prevent its being so. Horror of convention and routine precluded the establishment of any real musical symbology. Composers were, perhaps unreasonably, expected to be at one and the same time "accurate" in the representation of emotions and "original" in the means of that representation. In Chernyshevskian terms, the artwork had to contain the essence of the thing reproduced, but that essence had to be expressed in "individual" rather than "general" images.

Dargomyzhsky did not embark upon the realization of such a music immediately after *Rusalka,* however. For a full decade he maintained an embittered creative silence where opera was concerned, turning his attention to songs and to his series of curious short orchestral pieces of "national" character. He wrote to Karmalina, by way of acerbic explanation of his inactivity:

> You ask about my future opera? Actually, I did think of writing some opera or other back when music was still an art. But today it has become a craft. One must play the charlatan, accept subjects from the Tsar, seek a brilliant production, write about oneself in the papers. I felt I could never reconcile myself to all this—so I gave it up.[17]

But the composer was given a tremendous spur by the unexpectedly triumphant revival of *Rusalka* in 1865. While the original production had not exactly been a failure, this time the public as a whole valued those aspects of the work whose recognition in 1856 had practically been Serov's alone. Reviews of the new production were unanimous in pointing out, in the perhaps slightly self-satisfied words of the critic Rappaport, who wrote in the respected monthly *Syn otechestva,* that:

> In the course of a decade we have made positive progress in all things, not excepting musical development. The enormous success of *Rusalka* at its revival serves as the best proof of this. . . . Many of the opera's beauties, which formerly had passed unnoticed, have now been appreciated at their true worth; the majority has finally comprehended the nobility of the composer's aspirations. . . . Some, in an excess of musical purism, have even gone to extremes, as usually happens in the case of reforms, and have begun protesting those places in the opera which seem not to come up to the general level of serious operatic style. . . . Now they protest, for example, against the dances in the style of gypsy tunes, and against Olga's narrative.[18]

Perhaps there is irony in that Dargomyzhsky's original intention—to continue the national tradition established by Glinka—was now undervalued in favor of his real discovery, as first pointed out by Serov: the empathic *recitativo stromentato* of the dramatic scenes. To quote once more from Rappaport:

> If with respect to national character he seems but a follower, it is undeniable that he has created, in his own right, a genre that belongs exclusively to him and which gives him an important place in the history of music as an original figure. He has created Russian recitative, a model of musical declamation, meaningful and vital musical speech, which proves brilliantly how sounds may unite organically with words.[19]

The revival of *Rusalka* followed by a mere two months the sensational premiere of *Rogneda,* and many reviewers inevitably compared the two operas. The surprising result of the juxtaposition was that the modest and fairly unpretentious *Rusalka* cast the first cloud over the splendor of *Rogneda*'s reception. Little could Serov have dreamed in 1856 that the opera on which he was lavishing such praise would one day be entered as evidence against him, and precisely on grounds of "dramatic truth!" Some critics tried to maintain that Serov and Dargomyzhsky travelled the same creative path, that both were "inspired by the same ideal, they strive for truth in art and its cleansing from the coarse materialism that, alas, so firmly reigns in our time."[20] But for the majority, Dargomyzhsky's opera "revealed the advantage of a work that affirms the principles of dramatic truth over an opera in which these principles are merely declared."

Most eager of all to "expose" *Rogneda* by comparison with *Rusalka* was Cui. It is from the time of *Rusalka's* revival, and of Cui's ardent espousal of the opera's cause (very much on the order of Serov's championship a decade before) that we may date Dargomyzhsky's intimacy with the Balakirev circle, leading to his adoption by the "New Russian School" as their patron saint and elder statesman. Cui painted the sharpest possible contrast between Serov's opera and Dargomyzhsky's: "In *Rogneda* we encounter a tasteless overload of mere external effect under the emblem of so-called 'organic drama,' [while] in *Rusalka,* there is simple, truthful, stupendous drama without any emblems."[21] Cui's review was no less influential on Dargomyzhsky than Serov's had been, and was probably an important impetus specifically in the direction of *The Stone Guest.* Not only did Cui confirm approval of the dramatic tendency *Rusalka* represented in part, he suggested that recitative indeed was Dargomyzhsky's only strong suit, and that the composer's endeavors in more conventional aspects of opera were neither successful nor worthy of further cultivation.

> Uncommonly strong in dramatic music, in recitatives and declamation, Dargomyzhsky is much weaker in the choruses and other pure-musical numbers, which demand the development of musical thought and mastery of form which, generally speaking, have not been given to Dargomyzhsky.[22]

And:

> When a character, tarrying on a single emotion, begins a so-called full-fledged melody, or when several voices unite in a duet, a trio or other ensemble, the music is mostly weak, limp, devoid of originality, and weakens the profound impression created by the preceding recitatives.[23]

These comments betray that "shade of derision" which Rimsky-Korsakov remembered in the *kuchka's* early attitude toward the older composer.[24] Cui strongly, indeed somewhat patronizingly, suggested that what was needed from Dargomyzhsky was a work of major proportions written in his "dramatic" style exclusively. That *The Stone Guest* was conceived in response to this implication of Cui's critique, or at the general prompting of the Balakirev circle, seems clear from the fact that Dargomyzhsky began writing the long-contemplated work not with any thought to public performance, but rather for the private edification of his newfound friends. We begin finding casual references to the new opera in Dargomyzhsky's correspondence around this time, beginning with a letter to Karmalina of July 17, 1866:

> By the way, I have not entirely parted with the muse. I am amusing myself with Pushkin's "Don Juan." I am trying something unprecedented: I am writing music to the scenes of *The Stone Guest*—just as they are, without changing a single word. Of course, no one will ever listen to it. But how am I any worse than anyone else? For me it's not turning out badly.[25]

Dargomyzhsky now became a fairly regular participant, his failing health permitting, in the frequent get-togethers of the Balakirev circle, meeting with them at the home of Glinka's sister Liudmila Shestakova, at Balakirev's apartment, and occasionally at his own. A memoir by Cui strongly implies that these meetings (and perhaps his own *Ratcliff*, then in progress) were what got the old and embittered composer started on his magnum opus:

> We valued in him, especially in his romances and in the recitatives of *Rusalka*, a magnificently gifted prosodist, especially valuable and dear to us, who were agitating for the freedom of operatic forms, the equal rights of text and music, the complete merger of text and music. Dargomyzhsky acknowledged the truth of these theories, was stimulated by them and decided to apply them in his own *Stone Guest*.[26]

For years *The Stone Guest* remained more a contemplated idea than a work genuinely in progress. But in 1868, the last year of Dargomyzhsky's life, a serious aggravation of what was to prove his terminal heart disease, keeping him confined to his quarters, was oddly coupled with the greatest access of creative inspiration the composer had ever experienced. He confided this to Karmalina on April 9, 1868:

> Despite my grave condition, I have started up my swansong; I am writing *The Stone Guest*. It's a strange thing. My nervous state calls forth one idea after another. There is hardly any effort on my part. In two months I have written as much as would formerly have taken me a whole year. Perhaps you might be thinking that in my old age I am writing something trifling, limp (like what our dear friend Glinka wrote in your album at the end of his life). But the fact is, I'm not. It is not I that writes but some force I cannot fathom. *The Stone Guest* attracted my attention as much as five years ago, when I was in the best of health, and I shrank from so colossal a task. But now, sick, I have written almost three quarters of the opera in the space of two and a half months. . . . Of course, this work will not be for the many, but my own musical circle is pleased with my labors.[27]

The choice of Pushkin's *Stone Guest* for an operatic text seems eminently logical in some ways, audacious in others. One obvious asset of the play was its concision: one couldn't, after all, set just any play to continuous music, since it takes so much longer to sing than to speak. Pushkin's "Little Tragedies" *(Malen'kie tragedii)* of 1830, masterpieces of compression in their own right, had already stripped the drama of nonessentials, a task traditionally performed by the librettist, if only to make room for the musical "nonessentials" of conventional opera. *The Stone Guest,* the longest of the "Little Tragedies," contains a mere 550 lines. And these are of a quality that makes the play, in D.S. Mirsky's estimation, "one of the serious candidates" for the title of Pushkin's masterpiece.[28] For a composer bent on establishing the equality of words and music in opera, such quality was no small recommendation in itself.

Then, too, *The Stone Guest* embodied themes that had attracted Dargomyzhsky in the past. Like *Rusalka,* it is a drama of expiation and of supernatural nemesis. The parallels go further: the tragic heros of both plays are villain seducers (Belinsky had even called the prince in *Rusalka* a "Russian Don Juan"), and both meet their fate by returning to the scene of their past triumphs. (Was not Dargomyzhsky himself, in setting *The Stone Guest,* doing the same?) And so one can readily agree with Gozenpud's emphasis, in accounting for Dargomyzhsky's choice of subject, on the play's "uncommon poetic and philosophical qualities and its original resolution of a plot which had excited so many other writers and artists."[29]

Yet precisely here we encounter the chief audacity, for among the artists excited by that plot were the creators of one of the enduring masterworks of the operatic stage. For Pushkin, writing his play had meant polemicizing with Da Ponte. For Dargomyzhsky, it meant polemicizing with Mozart as well.

That Pushkin was familiar with a number of literary antecedents to his treatment of the famous story is evident. From the earliest written tradition, that of Tirso de Molina, he revived the original title.[30] An obvious borrowing from Da Ponte was Leporello's name. But Pushkin's treatment of the legend was completely alien, even opposed, to tradition. Where all previous Don Juan plays had been essentially farcical up to the last scene (whose serious treatment by Da Ponte and Mozart created such an abrupt and still problematical reversal of tone), Pushkin's is high romantic tragedy, diluted only by the "buffo" role of Leporello. His plot is simplicity itself:

Act I, scene i: Before the fence of a monastery, at the gates of Madrid. Evening.
Don Juan has secretly returned from exile, where he had been sent in punishment for having killed the Commander, Don Alvaro. While in the north he had "all but died of boredom." Nothing pleased him—neither the people, nor the place itself, nor particularly the women. With the help of his faithful servant Leporello he has decided to steal into Madrid, where a rendezvous with the actress Laura awaits him. From a chance conversation with a monk, Don Juan learns that every evening, Donna Anna, the widow of the slain Commander, comes to the monastery to visit her husband's grave, and that she is beautiful. Don Juan is enflamed with desire to meet her. Catching sight of the woman upon her arrival, her face mysteriously hidden behind a black widow's veil, Don Juan is drawn to her even more strongly. Night falls, and while the moon is as yet unrisen, Don Juan, together with Leporello, sets out under cover of night into the city.

Scene ii: Laura's room.

Laura is dining, surrounded by her admirers. At their request she sings two songs. One of the guests has appealed to her—the volatile, bold Don Carlos, the Commander's brother. He reminds Laura of her old love, Don Juan, whom she has not been able to forget. A knock at the door is heard; it is Don Juan. Don Carlos, who has long hated Don Juan for killing his brother, immediately challenges him to a duel. They fight, and Don Carlos is killed. Now no one can interfere with the Don's rendezvous with his inamorata.

Act II: In the cemetery, before the Commander's statue.

Calling himself "Don Diego de Calvado," Don Juan, disguised as a monk, has gained entry into the monastery. With impassioned avowals of love and artful speeches he has succeeded in enticing Donna Anna. Tomorrow evening she has agreed to receive him at her home. Don Juan is elated. Drunk with success he gives Leporello an impudent order: to invite the statue of the Commander to stand sentry at Donna Anna's door while he is there. To their horror, Don Juan and Leporello see the statue nod in assent.

Act III: Donna Anna's room.

Don Juan has revealed his secret to Donna Anna; the widow realizes that before her stands her husband's murderer. And yet she has not the strength to resist him. They agree to meet again the next day and as a sign of forgiveness Donna Anna bestows a kiss upon the Don. Suddenly there is a loud knocking at the door; the statue has come as invited. The stone guest seizes Don Juan's hand and drags him down to the underworld.[31]

The wealth of genre and low humor that still filled Da Ponte's "drama giocoso" could not have been less suitable to Pushkin's plan. Where the ending of Mozart's opera has always posed a problem of tone, in *The Stone Guest* every line points inexorably and severely to the denouement prefigured in the title. Don Juan is elevated to the status of tragic hero from the very beginning. Whatever he may have been or done before the curtain rises, we never see him in the role of wanton rake, nor do we ever see him in the act of amoral seduction. Pushkin's Don Juan is a poet and dreamer, a quintessential romantic hero (in keeping with this, Dargomyzhsky cast him as a lyric tenor). In the very first scene, he falls into a reverie while Leporello leeringly anticipates the nightly adventures that await them, recalling the "poor Inez" whom he had loved, and whom he had led to her downfall and death. Don Juan's return to, and recognition of, the scene of Inez's unhappy fate seals his own. It is the first link Pushkin forges between the twin forces of love and death that stalk the Don implacably throughout the play. Every dramatic stiuation strengthens this bond in Don Juan's person: he loved Inez for "her voice so soft and weak, like an invalid's"; he confesses his love to Donna Anna in a cemetery; both his tryst with Laura and his tryst with Donna Anna end in death: the first with Don Carlos's, the second with his own. Throughout, and in marked contrast to his literary prototypes, Pushkin's Don Juan behaves with a curious passivity. His only willful act is the invitation to the statue, and here, obviously, he does not expect results. For the rest, he is more the instrument of the forces he embodies than their exploiter. He does not seek the duel with Don Carlos, and when it is over he expresses not triumph but resignation. His meeting with Donna Anna is fortuitous, and he woos her without bravado. Once he sees her he is in the hands of forces beyond his control. One can only explain his revealing his identity to Donna Anna by the fact that, for perhaps the first time, Don Juan is truly in love. And no sooner is he touched by true love than he, like all his victims, must perish. He is killed as it were by his own sword, wielded by Donna Anna, her husband's unwitting avenger.

Of course, there is another, less "poetical" and "philosophical" side to Pushkin's handling of the Don Juan legend. His Don Juan is not only more profound and romantic than Da Ponte's, he is also far more morally repulsive. Pushkin's rearrangement of the relationships between the characters common to both versions of the story is indicative of his quest for a strong ethical motivation for the tragic ending. Above all, by making Donna Anna the Commander's widow and not his daughter, and by making the proposal to the statue not a mock-friendly invitation to share the Don's repast but a horrendous moral insult—a request that he actually assist his murderer in his widow's seduction—Pushkin involves not only Donna Anna's honor, but the Commander's as well. Yet this only strengthens the essential romanticism of Pushkin's conception: the audacious, intolerable challenge to the foundation of all social mores is issued by a poet.

The Stone Guest, then, is so thoroughly a play of poetry and ideas, so parsimonious in theatrical effect and action, that one is forced to wonder whether Pushkin actually intended it for the stage. If it seems to answer little to the demands of the expansive Romantic theater, though, how much less would setting it straightaway to music seem to answer, on the face of it, to the demands of opera.[32] Except for its directness of exposition and clarity of structure (qualities honored in conventional libretti perhaps as much in the breach as in the observance, anyway), *The Stone Guest*'s merits are precisely those qualities shunned by librettists as inimical to music. Its beauties are beauties of nuance and detail, and these are normally the first to go when plays are "stretched over a musician's canvas," as Serov would say. On the other hand, Pushkin resolutely excludes what operatic composers normally seek out and expand—local color and spectacle.[33] In short, where Ostrovsky's *Live Not the Way You'd Like* had seemed to Grigoriev to be incomplete without music, *The Stone Guest* seems to leave no room for it.

But there is an endless wealth of lyric poetry in the play: Laura's description of the Spanish night, Don Juan's amorous confessions to Donna Anna, and much more. This is truly the stuff of song, and Dargomyzhsky's music does it full justice. And here we must at once offer a corrective to the usual characterization of Dargomyzhsky's work, for there is scarcely another opera whose historical notoriety is at once so widespread and so misconceived. We quote the conventional assessment from a widely consulted popular history of music:

Dargomyzhsky offers the extreme example of the sterilizing effect of the uncritical espousal of foreign tenets, in this case the one form of vocal music that invariably baffled all non-Italian composers, the recitative. In his later works, notably in his operas *Russalka* and *The Stone Guest* (Don Juan), the purely musical element is totally submerged in abstract dramaturgical doctrines and the lyric drama emerges as a forbidding new *stile recitativo* of arid monotony.[34]

In fact, however, it would not even be correct to say that:

Dargomyzhsky developed from the spirit of the Russian language a new type of speech song.[35]

For Dargomyzhsky's music in *The Stone Guest,* far from an ascetic and uncompromising experiment in speech-derived musical declamation, or a continuous accompanied recitative, is almost unabatedly lyric in its fundamental impulse—far more so, in fact, than were the recitative scenes of *Rusalka,* which were its ostensible forerunners, and of which the new opera purported to be a continuation and development. The true sources of *The Stone Guest's* style are to be found in the through-composed romances of Dargomyzhsky's late years. One need only compare a song like *Mne vsë ravno* or *Eshchë molitva*[36] with one of the more extended speeches in *The Stone Guest*—say, Don Juan's reminiscence of Inez—to note the altogether striking similarity not only in the rhythmically supple vocal line (there are even whole measures in common between the pages given for comparison in Example 5.2!), but particularly in the regular harmonic rhythm of the accompaniment, expressed through a continuous figuration that is alien to recitative, but very much in the manner of the romance.

If the word "recitative" is to be used at all in connection with *The Stone Guest,* then, it must be specifically defined and understood. Cui coined the term "melodic recitative" to describe the music of Dargomyzhsky's last opera, and we may conveniently adopt it for our purposes. Its properties, which can be fully discovered only from a close examination of the score, involve chiefly the elegant "rounding" of melodic design and the construction of balanced, proportioned, memorably lyric phrases which differ from more conventional lyric forms only in that balance and rounding are applied locally to single phrases, not to their grouping. The absence of symmetry and repetition satisfies the realist demand of "formlessness," while the powerful characterization of each separate line of text satisfies the demand of "individuality." But in no sense can Dargomyzhsky's declamation be termed "naturalistic," save in a few isolated instances. Far more naturalistic was Serov's declamation in the final acts of *The Power of the Fiend,* for Serov was interested and involved in naturalistic dramatic tendencies, while Dargomyzhsky never gave any indication of such interest. Dargomyzhsky's realism was a realism of method,

Ex. 5.2.   a. *Mne vsë ravno (It's All the Same to Me)*, mm. 25-49
(words by F. Miller). A.S. Dargomyzhsky, *Romansy
i pesni*, vol. II (Moscow: Izdatel'stvo "Muzyka," 1971)

b. *The Stone Guest* (Moscow: Gosudarstvennoe
muzykal'noe izdatel'stvo, 1932), p. 16

which could easily accommodate the highly charged lyricism of Pushkin's
poetry and, indeed, the romanticism of his subject. The extended embodiment
of Pushkin's play in Dargomyzhsky's music, then, could perhaps best be
described as a gargantuan, kaleidoscopically varied, through-composed
"romance."

Early critics of *The Stone Guest* were mostly too preoccupied with
Dargomyzhsky's theory—or, indeed, like the *kuchkists,* actively propagandi-
zing it—to evaluate properly the composer's practice in this regard. The rather
exceptional accurate appraisals were to be found in the hostile camp. Thus,
Serov's disciple Soloviov wrote that "the musical form [of the opera] is not

recitative, but that of Dargomyzhsky's best songs—the supple, indefinite form of the arioso." And Laroche: "*The Stone Guest* is an excellent study in recitative, but that particular recitative-in-song, which is much closer to cantilena that to the Italian recitative, and constitutes a peculiarity of the Russian school (its first examples appeared in *A Life for the Tsar*)."[37]

Of course, the parity of words and music at which Dargomyzhsky aimed, as well as the general aesthetic approach of the opera, did demand that certain concessions be made to speech in forming the opera's melodic and prosodic style (but not only there—they can be found in the excerpt given from *Mne vsë ravno* as well). The first and most obvious of these is the absolute avoidance of melisma from one end of the score to the other. The one exception, truly "proving the rule," is Don Juan's little outburst on the word "sing" itself.[38]

Ex. 5.3.   *The Stone Guest*, p. 115

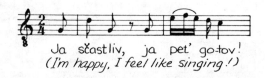

Ja sčastliv, ja pet' gotov!
(*I'm happy, I feel like singing!*)

Second, the note values in the vocal lines are very restricted. Essentially, the parts move in quarters, eighths, and eighth-note triplets, in a generally moderate tempo approximating a uniformly slowed down but still fairly natural speech tempo. Exceptions include the sixteenth-notes that are generally employed for asides and for parenthetical phrases, and the occasional longer values that are reserved for impassioned exclamations and ejaculations. Beyond that, Dargomyzhsky took great pains with prosody and hardly ever allowed a musically conceived rhythm to supervene over the rhythms of the language. Syncopation, foreign to Russian speech with its strong and regular tonic stress, is virtually absent.[39] On the other hand, upbeats of infinitely variable length are extremely common. The free and frequent use of triplets is an attempt to capture an important aspect of the rhythm of spoken Russian, which spaces accents regularly, like beats, filling in the unaccented syllables at whatever rate is necessary to maintain the regularity of the stress pulse.

Melodic contour is heavily influenced by the spoken language as well. Declarative statements, questions, exclamations and the like are generally transmitted by an accurate imitation of their spoken rise and fall. Also speech-derived are the fairly common passages of quick repeated tones, which reflect the strong orientation of the spoken language toward a single "intonational center" for every phrase.

Yet these influences of the spoken language never challenge the essentially lyric basis of Dargomyzhsky's vocal melody. They stem more from an avoidance of the unnatural than from active quest of the naturalistic. Dargomyzhsky's prosody is thus still a far cry from Musorgskian, or even Serovian realism. On the contrary, the composer seeks out what Mikhail Druskin has called "rounded intonational periods,"[40] even where this means departing noticeably from the rhythm of spoken Russian. Individual phrases are set off from one another and "characterized" by framing a series of (mostly) eight-notes with quarters at the beginning and the end. Where these beginning and ending syllables are unaccented, and especially when, as so often happens in *The Stone Guest,* the first word is a conjunction, the spoken language would have them short to the point of slurring, all intonational energy being directed toward that accented syllable which constitutes the "intonational center" of the phrase. But Dargomyzhsky is interested in melodic, "musical," no less than prosodic, naturalness and often decides in favor of the former, so long as the latter is not offensively distorted. A few examples will suffice to show the kind of completely formed and "rounded" periods in which Dargomyzhsky often embodies even the shortest repliques.[41]

Ex. 5.4.   "Intonational periods"

a. Donna Anna

I kak mo-gli me-nja vy o -skor-bit' ?
(*And how could you offend me?*)

b. Leporello

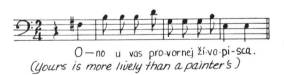

O—no u vas pro-vor-nej ži-vo-pi-sca.
(*Yours is more lively than a painter's*)

c. Laura

Ot — ku-da-ty? Davno li zdes' ?
(*Where have you come from? Have you been here long?*)

d. Donna Anna

O pjat' on zdes!
(*Again he's here!*)

In the example from Laura's part, two parallel phrases, identical in accent pattern and number of syllables, are given differing rhythmic settings so as to round off her replique. In other words, Dargomyzhsky molds a single phrase from her pair. If the composer's aim had been perfect naturalism, both questions would have been set to the rhythm of the second, which conforms far better than the first to the rhythm of the spoken language.

Not only lengths, but accent patterns too are regularly compromised in the interests of musical, lyrical shape. Polysyllabic words are often stretched over whole measures, so as not unduly to hurry the musical tempo. Thus they often take on secondary stresses which do not conform to their spoken pronunciation (in Russian, a word of no matter how many syllables carries a single stress). At such places, Dargomyzhsky generally contrives to give the real accent predominance either by lengthening it, by making it the highest note in the phrase, or, in the case of "gosudárstvennyi" in Example 5.5 by constructing a pair of sequential contours such that the accented syllable corresponds in placement to the last preceding accent (in this case, *"ia"*).

Any unnaturalness of prosody may be mitigated, of course, by a knowing performer. In those few places where Dargomyzhsky actually allows unaccented syllables to fall on the strongest beats, he makes doubly sure to place the accented ones on the highest notes (e.g., "polechù" in Example 5.6). The singer can make the passage come off naturally enough by not "observing the bar." Such phrases, however, demonstrate that at least occasionally Dargomyzhsky conceived melodic patterns independently of the speech values of the text.

Such musically dictated departures from the norms of spoken Russian should be distinguished from the many "expressive distortions" that show the composer-as-actor at his best, and which are among The Stone Guest's most positive accomplishments. In such places one can encounter the most egregious violations of the rules of normal prosody. But they are not only explicable, they are even "realistic" in context. One outstanding example is Don Juan's threatening admonition to Leporello, when the latter, in his cowardice, asks the Don to make the invitation to the statue himself. "Menacing with his finger," according to Dargomyzhsky's (not Pushkin's) stage direction, Don Juan tells Leporello to "watch out, good-for-nothing" *(Nu smotrí-zh, bezdél'nik)."* The first, unaccented syllable of *smotri* is drawn out to inordinate length, while Don Juan waves his finger in the air, and then the vocal line comes crashing down a minor seventh to the short accented second syllable (Ex. 5.7). In angry Russian speech, accented syllables are clipped in just this way. Contour is also exaggerated, as in Dargomyzhsky's setting. (In such contexts the composer resorts to sevenths throughout the opera.)

Dargomyzhsky's use of rests is also original and expressive. Melodic statements are often broken up by them in ways calculated to transmit subtle

Ex. 5.5.   Secondary musical stresses

a. Don Juan

ot – šél – ni - kom smi - rén - nym
(*a peaceful hermit*)

b. Don Juan

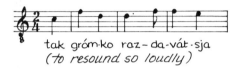

tak gróm·ko raz - da - vát·sja
(*to resound so loudly*)

c. Leporello

bla - go - slo – vi —li
(*blessed her*)

d. Don Juan

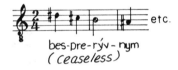

bes - pre - rýv - nym
(*ceaseless*)

e. Don Juan

ved' ja ne go —su–dár-stven-nyj pre-stup-nik
(*I'm no political offender, after all*)

Ex. 5.6.   *The Stone Guest*, p. 5

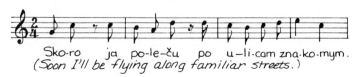

Sko·ro   ja po-le-ču   po   u –li·cam zna·ko·mym.
(*Soon I'll be flying along familiar streets.*)

shades of emotion and meaning. Leporello's terrified invitation to the statue is positively pulverized in this way. Here, of course, the rests literally imitate his gasping and panting (Ex. 5.8).

Elsewhere rests play a less naturalistic and more subtle role. When Laura fantasizes about the northern climate, we follow her train of thought by means of the pauses in her vocal line. Each new thought adds a refinement to her idea, and each is set off by rests that do not all conform to Pushkin's punctuation. Finally, when Laura's idea has taken definite shape, she continues surely and rapidly (Ex. 5.9).

One final example: when the disguised Don Juan declares his love for Donna Anna, Dargomyzhsky very effectively transmits the urgency of his speech not by an access of lyricism, but by means of breathless pauses that come more and more rapidly as the Don gets more and more carried away. In this case the music is made to conform not to a normal, but to an abnormal (though no less "real" and recognizable) pattern of speech (Ex. 5.10).

But even in this connection it would be unwise to overemphasize the speech derivation of Dargomyzhsky's musical language. The evocative potential of the musical medium and the emotive power of broad melody are given their due. Many of the most impassioned utterances of all are carried by frankly lyrical phrases which have nothing whatever to do with "speech song." The moment when Don Juan reveals his identity is an arresting example (Ex. 5.11).

Naturally enough, the love scenes (Don Carlos/Laura, Don Juan/Donna Anna) are the most consistently lyrical and least "declamatory" in inspiration and style. Even the breathless, rest-strewn example above from the graveyard scene is taken out of a context in which many of the phrases, taken individually, are of a practically Tchaikovskian lyric sweep and elegance of contour.

And they have to be taken individually. The special "realist" quality of Dargomyzhsky's vocal writing even at its most lyrical stems from the fact that there is practically no repetition, hence practically no "form," that Chernyshevskian "opposite" of emotion. Cui's observation, that the real difficulty in composing *The Stone Guest* lay in devising new melodic ideas for each individual phrase (whereas the usual method consisted in working up only a few themes), is a penetrating one. The high lyric moments, such as would have been worth an aria in a numbers opera, are here expressed in single phrases such as the one last quoted. These individual ideas are thus freighted with a very heavy musico-dramaturgical responsibility; Dargomyzhsky's lyric drama is thus in its own way as much a study in compression as Pushkin's original play. The long love-speeches of Don Juan in Acts II and III, the most extended lyrical moments in the opera, are best described as mosaics—nonsymmetrical arrangements and accumulations of individual aria- or romance-like gestures.

Ex. 5.7.   *The Stone Guest*, p. 127

Nu, smo—tri, bezdel'nik!
(*Watch out, good for nothing!*)

Ex. 5.8.   *The Stone Guest*, p. 124

Moj barin Don Žuan vas prosit   zavtra pritti po-poz-že, v dom su-
(*My master, DonJuan, requests that you come late tomorrow to*

-pru-gi va-šej   i stat' u...   u...   dveri...
your wife's house   and stand by...   by...   thedoor...)

Ex. 5.9.   *The Stone Guest*, p. 63

A da-le—ko   na se-ve-re v Pa-ri-že   byt'možet
But far away   up north in Paris, the sky is

ne-bo tu-ča-mi pokryto,
perhaps covered with clouds)

Ex. 5.10.   *The Stone Guest*, p. 100

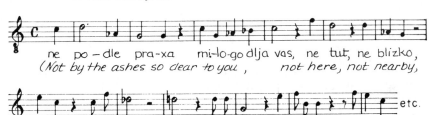

ne po—dle pra-xa   mi-lo-go dlja vas, ne tut, ne blizko,
(*Not by the ashes so dear to you ,   not here, not nearby,*

da-le gde ni-bud', tam, u dve-rej, u sa-mo-go poroga
further off somewhere , there, by the gate, by the very threshold...

Ex. 5.11.   *The Stone Guest*, pp. 151-52

Ja Don Žu-an   i   ja tebja lju-blju!
(*I am Don Juan,   and I   love   you!*)

Repetitions in the music are invariably the result of repetitions in the text, and they are deftly handled. The Second Guest at Laura's for example, has the same vacuous comment to make after each of her songs—"What sounds! What soul!"—and his music is likewise identical, except that the second time Laura impatiently cuts him off.[42] When in the graveyard scene Don Juan repeatedly importunes Donna Anna to give him "one minute" to speak to her, he repeats the words to the same insistent phrase. Between the repetitions, Donna Anna makes the frightened (and rest-ful) objection, "What if someone should come?" Don Juan having silenced her with his forceful entreaties, the musical phrase of Donna Anna's objection is relegated to the orchestra: she is silenced, but unconvinced (Ex. 5.12).

The most striking example of repetition as generator of "form" comes from the same scene. Don Juan protests against Donna Anna's suggestion that he must be mad. "Is it a sign of madness, then, to desire one's end, Donna Anna," he protests, and follows with these lines:

> If I were a madman, I would wish to remain among the living,
> I would nurture hope of touching your heart with tender love.
> If I were a madman, I would spend my nights at your balcony,
>   troubling your sleep with serenades; I would not hide myself,
>   but would try to be noticed by you everywhere.
> If I were a madman, I would not suffer in silence.
>
> [To which Donna Anna retorts, "You call this silence?"]

Dargomyzhsky sets the words "If I were a madman" as a threefold refrain, conveying the Don's mounting urgency by setting each repetition a step higher than the last. Between these "structural" refrains, however, the writing, while still songful rather than declamational, is altogether nonrepetitive and spontaneous: the meter changes, phrase-lengths are irregular, the harmonic scheme modulates constantly and meanderingly. With the possible exception of Don Carlos's little "aria" in Act I, scene ii (see below) this is as close to a "number" as Dargomyzhsky comes in *The Stone Guest*. In its relative self-sufficiency it might well serve as a paradigm of the curious musical ambience—hovering unstably between parlando and full-blown song—that characterizes Dargomyzhsky's "melodic recitative" (Ex. 5.13).

Ex. 5.13.   *The Stone Guest*, pp. 102-104

But although the intention behind Dargomyzhsky's procedures is one of economy and compression, his empirical, moment-by-moment method carries with it the obvious hazard of diffusion or, worse, incoherence. Dargomyzhsky seems to have been aware of this pitfall, for he often employs the accompaniment as a unifying, almost formalizing device. Don Carlos's admonition to Laura (Act I, sc. ii) is so thoroughly shaped by its accompaniment figures (and to a lesser degree by parallelism in its phrase construction) that it perhaps ought frankly to be described as an arioso or even a cavatina, its assymetry and tonal open-endedness notwithstanding. Its resemblance to Onegin's aria from Tchaikovsky's opera has often been pointed out (Ex. 5.14).

A unified orchestral accompaniment is also used to bind together passages of high-pressure dialogue and direct them to a climax in a fashion that calls to mind the *parlante* that was becoming widespread in Italian opera by the 1860s (Ex. 5.15, pp. 284-5).

Occasionally, Dargomyzhsky manages to make the formalizing accompaniment serve dramaturgical ends as well. The orchestral figure that accompanies Don Juan's reminiscence of Inez in the opening scene serves, in the ensuing colloquy between the impatient Leporello and the still-pensive Don, to differentiate the latter's inner world from his surroundings and so to characterize the state of mind that underlies his passive, noncommital repliques. The Inez episode also contains the first occurrence in the opera of the whole-tone harmony that will characterize the Statue, and thus forges the first musical link between love and doom[43] (Ex. 5.16, p. 286).

This use of the whole tone scale demands some comment. Dargomyzhsky had been drawn throughout his career to harmonic *piquanteries;* as early as *The Triumph of Bacchus* we can find mild *Ruslan*-influenced whole tone experiments (Ex. 5.17, p. 287).

In *The Stone Guest,* however, we find the most thoroughgoing and radical use of "Glinka's discovery" in all of Russian music. Like Serov, Dargomyzhsky seized upon the whole tone scale for the opportunity it afforded "realistically" to depict the horrible.[44] Dargomyzhsky epitomized the statue with a melodic phrase consisting of the whole tone scale ascending and descending through five degrees, achieving on its initial appearance the same augmented fifth (C-G♯) that had formed the harmony for the reminiscence of Inez (Ex. 5.18, p. 288).

This melodic idea is harmonized in a variety of ways, often (but not exclusively) with the augmented triads the melody itself suggests. At the statue's appearance at the end of the opera, however, Dargomyzhsky drops all restraint and harmonizes the whole-tone motif with the traditional chord of terror, the diminished seventh, not shrinking from the extreme harmonic clashes—false relations and double inflections—that result (Ex. 5.19, p. 288).

Similarly bold is the single piece of "action music" in the opera, the duel between Don Juan and Don Carlos. Here the active ingredient is a sharply clashing minor second, perhaps meant to represent the crossing of swords. Dargomyzhsky never bothers to resolve it, though Rimsky-Korsakov, in his second edition of the opera, was careful to turn these dissonances into well-behaved suspensions, just as he eliminated the wild whole-tone/diminished-seventh conflicts from the climactic scene[45] (Ex. 5.20, p. 289).

Crude, "empirical" harmonies like these are a crucial style ingredient of the opera, and are strongly bound up with the realist aesthetic. And it was that aesthetic that made *The Stone Guest* far and away the best-composed of Dargomyzhsky's large-scale works, paradoxical as that may sound in view of the realist aversion to "pièces bien faites." Until *The Stone Guest,* the two most "original" features of Dargomyzhsky's style—strong declamation and piquant harmony—had been more or less mutually exclusive. The latter effect was usually reserved for comic purposes, e.g. in the orchestra pieces, and had played no significant dramaturgical role. *Rusalka,* for example, contains few harmonic peculiarities to speak of, even in the music associated with the fantastic mermaid world. It was the "realistic" use of dissonance as the musical expression of the ugly and the frightening that finally enabled all the various components of Dargomyzhsky's style to cohere, and this gave *The Stone Guest,* for all its varied elements and all its empathic, empirical compositional method, a stylistic consistency that his other works lacked.[46]

Many have been misled, in their perception of *The Stone Guest,* by the use of recurrent themes as formalizing elements. Except for the Statue's whole-tone melody, these themes are static, unsymphonic, and inconsistent in their associations. It would be unwise, therefore, to call them leitmotivs. The most frequently employed "signature tune" is Donna Anna's: it announces every one of her entrances. The quotation is taken from its first appearance (Ex. 5.21, p. 290).

The only other identifiable musical calling card belongs to the monk, of all people. But actually, the theme in question seems to represent not "the monk," but monks in general, since in the second act it accompanies the appearance of the disguised Don Juan (Ex. 5.22, p. 290).

And yet even this much "leitmotiv," given Dargomyzhsky's reformist reputation, has led to his being linked with Wagner. In Riemann's *Musik-Lexicon,* the first edition of which appeared in 1882, we may read, for example, that "D. näherte sich mehr und mehr den Prinzipien Wagners und hat ihn schliesslich (nicht zu seinem Vorteil) überboten."[47] And R.A. Leonard confidently reminds us that:

> The similarity between Dargomyzhsky's theories in *The Stone Guest* and those by which Wagner revolutionized modern opera must be instantly apparent. Both composers were seeking release from the prison of Italian opera form; both hit upon the same general escape device.[48]

Ex. 5.14.   *The Stone Guest*, pp. 58–59: Don Carlos's "Aria"

Ex. 5.15.   *The Stone Guest*, pp. 149-50: "parlante"

Ex. 5.16.   *The Stone Guest*, p. 17: whole tone harmony

Ex. 5.17.   *Torzhestvo Vakkha* (Moscow: Izdatel'stvo "Muzyka," 1969), p. 25

Ex. 5.18.   Statue leitmotiv

Ex. 5.19.   *The Stone Guest*, p. 169, orchestra only

But these similarities were fortuitous and superficial. Far more revealing are the differences. As a matter of fact, Dargomyzhsky's acquaintance with Wagner was very limited, and his reaction decidedly unfavorable. When Serov, hoping to make a convert of his older colleague after detecting in *Rusalka* a kindred spirit, lent Dargomyzhsky the score of *Tannhäuser* in 1856, he was disappointed to read this epistolary response:

> He indicates a new and sensible path; but in his unnatural vocal writing and his overspiced (though occasionally very diverting) harmonies, a certain strain peeps through: *will und kann nicht!* Truth is truth, but taste, after all, is also necessary.[49]

When *Lohengrin* was first performed in St. Petersburg a dozen years later, Dargomyzhsky's attitude had not changed. Rimsky-Korsakov recalled the "inexhaustible torrent of humor, ridicule, and venomous cavilling" that came from Dargomyzhsky's corner of the box they shared.[50] By the time of Dargomyzhsky's death, only months later, Wagner's most advanced music dramas were still unperformed in Russia (and the composer's trips abroad had never taken him to Wagnerian centers). While even to Serov Wagner remained essentially the Wagner of *Lohengrin* and *Tannhäuser,* the Wagner whose unsuccessful imitator Dargomyzhsky is adjudged to be was certainly the Wagner of *The Ring.*

If looked upon as a Wagnerian, of course, Dargomyzhsky will inevitably appear unsuccessful. For *The Stone Guest* entirely lacks the "symphonism" that was the main prop of the Wagnerian solution to the problem of the number-less opera. Dargomyzhsky might thus be seen with greater justice as Wagner's complement, his opposite number, or even his antagonist. Rather than attempting to unify and articulate the music drama as a series of huge

Ex. 5.20. *The Stone Guest*, p. 176, Dargomyzhsky's original

Ex. 5.21.   *The Stone Guest*, p. 26, simplified

Ex. 5.22.   *The Stone Guest*, p. 19

symphonic spans embodying a gigantic, musically "organic" unity, Dargomy-zhsky preferred to leave—some might say abdicate—questions of structure to the writer of the words (who is never the composer). Dargomyzhsky's attitude toward the problem of form is wholly literary; Wagner's is thoroughly musical.[51]

Equally important, opera remained for Dargomyzhsky and the *kuchka* always preeminently a singer's medium. The essential focus was always on the sung lines; the orchestra was at all times essentially functional. For them, the Wagnerian system of Leitmotiv meant the reshackling of music in a rational straitjacket, rather than its liberation through an untrammelled, empathic response to words. Any attempt to impose abstract logic on vocal music ran counter to its nature, that is, to its "natural model." Cui put this explicitly and emphatically in his second major essay devoted to *The Stone Guest*.

> Without the text each musical phrase possesses its own beauty and meaning, but in the overall view and in their ordering there are no absolute musical connections, no abstract musico-logical development. For this is not pure, symphonic music; this is applied music, vocal music. Its development and coherence depend upon the text; it must be listened to only with the text, and then its potency is enormous.[52]

Dargomyzhsky's complaint that Wagner's vocal line was "unnatural" was a characteristic realist objection, manifestly akin to Chernyshevskian doctrine. Wagner's was, moreover, an unnaturalness born of reason. When Stasov, in his famous review, "Twenty-five Years of Russian Art" *(Dvadtsat' piat' let russkogo iskusstva,* 1881-82), came directly to grips with the Wagnerian view of Dargomyzhsky, he sought to lay it to rest precisely on this point. Wagner, to Stasov, was less an artist than "an inventor, a thinker, an imaginer." Dargomyzhsky, on the other hand, was "an artist from head to toe, ... creating with his inspiration and his nerves."[53] These ideas are echoed in articles and letters by all the *kuchkists,* and Rimsky-Korsakov was still fighting Dargomyzhsky's battle as late as 1892, when he sketched a long, unpublished article to be entitled, "Wagner: The Joint Work of Two Arts, or Music Drama." The original plan called for a companion piece on Dargomyzhsky, but this was never completed. While allowing that the two composers shared certain aims—"the development of musical drama and its removal from the conception of opera," whose peak of "formal perfection" had been reached with Meyerbeer and Glinka[54]—Rimsky-Korsakov nonetheless scathingly indicted Wagner for his artificiality and unnaturalness, and for indicating not a path to the future but a cul-de-sac. The ideal of "endless melody" was a monstrosity against nature because "in real life many phenomena have definite beginnings and clear endings: for example, a procession stops, a dance commences, a speech ends, etc."[55] In a similar vein of dogged literalism Rimsky-Korsakov ridiculed the "colossal abuse of symbolism" entailed by Wagner's "polyphonic fabric" of Leitmotivs:

> The listener cannot derive any immediate impression from all these Leitmotivs as they steal in and out of the contrapuntal web. And in point of fact, if character A, finding himself in a certain mood, were to speak with character B about character C, and if in the accompanying music we hear the contrapuntally interwoven motives A, B and C, perhaps with the addition of a fourth denoting their mood, then can one clearly distinguish such a situation from the reverse: i.e., where C speaks to A about B, or B and C discuss A?[56]

To attempt, like Wagner, to create a symbolic language of tones, was to force music into a job it was inherently incapable of performing. Cui, expounding upon the failure of musical expression in *Tristan,* put this view rather extremely and dogmatically:

> Its philosophical "lining" is the same old absurdity we find everywhere in the Wagnerian system. Music is powerless to tackle intellectual or philosophical problems; it can express only moods, feelings. It can express the joy or sadness brought about by the renunciation of earthly desire, but never the renunciation itself. Having admitted such inappropriate tasks for music, it is only a matter of time until some follower of Wagner will write a musical drama based on the Simplified Method for the derivation of logarithms.[57]

Even *Tristan,* however, was not as bad as *The Ring,* because, for one thing, "the singers are given little thematic phrases occasionally, and this at times even creates the illusion that they are singing."[58] Once again, "unnatural singing" is the issue. Dargomyzhsky had sought to fulfill the expressive tasks of his operatic setting by means of expressive vocal melody; thematic interest, with him, was always focused squarely upon the stage. This lyric element, on the other hand, was what seemed to matter least of all to Wagner, and it is this that prevented his "union of the arts," in the eyes of the *kuchkists*, from taking place. Rimsky-Korsakov is particularly harsh on this point:

> [Wagner's] solo singing is not singing at all in the true sense of the word. This is no idealized musico-dramatic declamation [NB: This is Rimsky's term for what Cui more simply called "melodic recitative."]; we can't call it recitative; it is merely declamation, distinguished from ordinary speech only by the presence of musical tones and intervals. It can reach— particularly in *Parsifal*—the point of arbitrary selection of pitches, which suggests nothing so much as repellent and monstrous musical meaninglessness.[59]

It is in this context that we may understand Stasov's strange pronouncement, on the face of it fashioned out of whole cloth, that Wagner was "little gifted, extremely artificial, and completely devoid of aptitude for recitative and declamation," while Dargomyzhsky "possesses the most flaming and burning gift, immediate, enchanted and enchanting; [he is] an artist full of dramatic power and pathos, but also of humor and comedy, always full of truth and naturalness, and, along with that, gifted more than anyone else specifically for recitative and declamation."[60] The ideal is not mere imitation of speech, but speech sublimated into real vocal melody, which preserves its "purely musical" beauty even as it exhibits all the flexibility and range of speech.

Positivist ridicule of Wagner reached its height with Stasov's imposing survey, *Art in the Nineteenth Century* (*Iskusstvo deviatnadtsatogo veka*, 1901). His choice of subject makes the German composer repellent to the Russian critic. His preoccupation with gods and heroes is seen as the nineteenth century's most retrograde tendency inflated to the point of decadence.

> To anyone who has not lost touch with simple, healthy ideas, who is unspoiled by pseudo-patriotism and metaphysics, the Wagnerian aversion to nature, to living reality, to simplicity and truth of thought, his mindless servitude to all manner of high-flown idealism, unreality and improbability, his boundless devotion to all manner of delirium, hallucination, any and all affectation and monstrous exaggeration, can inspire nothing but astonishment and antipathy. What sort of feelings or thoughts can arise from Wagner's endless absurdities—his fish-women, whom fauns drag from the water in nets, his Lohengrins, renouncing their beloved women forever because they dare ask, "What is your lineage, O Hero, and what are they like?"; his Tannhäusers, making pilgrimages to the Pope in Rome to ask forgiveness for overly long visits with Venus in the mountains; his Wotans, putting their daughters into sleep enchanted for all eternity under an oak tree, amid enclosures of fire; his regiments of gods, crossing bridges in midair from one castle to

another; the senseless secrets of the medieval Grail and a hundred more such stupidities—
what, I say, can all this inspire, if not indignation and scorn? And for installing such
nonsense, such monstrosities of thought upon the stage, are we to take Wagner for the great
reformer of opera, the creator of unprecedented, unheard of truth and profundity?[61]

Stasov was willing to grant Wagner a high place as German symphonist,
but of course that had nothing to do with opera.

Wagner's nature did not contain even one of the elements which comprise the operatic
composer. He hadn't the slightest feeling for life and reality, he did not possess any
understanding of character, of human nature, of types of human personalities or features;
he hadn't any comprehension of the human soul, its vicissitudes, movements and
impulses.[62]

And that is what made it possible for Stasov to accept as his paradigm of
operatic realism a work in which statues walk and talk! For Dargomyzhsky's
real concern, unlike Wagner's, was always the transmission of human feelings
as embodied in human speech. The characters in *The Stone Guest* (with the
aforementioned exception) are human beings in all their psychological
complexity, a complexity unprecedented in opera. And this is what precondi-
tioned the breakdown of "musical form" in the first place, since the musical
mood had to change to follow the peregrinations of the text with an
unprecedented rapidity, with no time to settle into a stable projection of a
"unitary affection." While there may have been no arias in Wagner, either,
Stasov argued that neither were there moods or characters. Wagner dealt not
with individuals but with what Stasov called "algebraic symbols." The one
Wagnerian opera which Stasov was willing to recognize as one of "the greatest
operas on earth" was, of course, *Die Meistersinger,* a bourgeois comedy, in
which for once Wagner dealt with human beings and human situations. It was
also the one mature Wagner opera in which the music was allowed frequently
to settle into set pieces; Wagner needed these far more urgently than
Dargomyzhsky, who had found the true key to dispensing with them. The
other Wagnerian operas, particularly *The Ring,* were compared acidly by
Rimsky-Korsakov to an enormous edifice "consisting entirely of a staircase
leading from the entrance to the exit."[63]

Though Dargomyzhsky's astonishing burst of creative energy in 1868 brought
him within a hairsbreadth of completing *The Stone Guest* (in vocal score),
death intervened at the last moment. Stasov has left a moving account of the
last stages of Dargomyzhsky's work on his swansong, which he accomplished
no longer seated at the piano, but literally on his deathbed.

In the autograph score of *The Stone Guest* there are a few pages upon which, amid all the
great things the opera contains, one cannot look without a special reverence. These are the

four pages, written in pencil, which comprise the end of the scene between Don Juan, the monk and Leporello [i.e., the end of Act I, sc. i]: this music was written by Dargomyzhsky sick in bed, when he already felt the nearness of the end. He was aware that he would never get up again; in the last days he often endured unspeakable suffering from the illness that finally carried him off. And nevertheless, despite everything, he continued to create, with enfeebled hands he tried to finish this opera, the best, most perfect of his creations, clearly comprehending its significance and hurrying lest death prevent him. This victory of the spirit over the flesh, this triumph of the creative spirit over the most unendurable suffering, this limitless devotion to work, with which alone his whole soul was filled—is this not greatness? And truly, such colossal creations as *The Stone Guest* may proceed from the heads of those only for whom the products of their creative spirit is all—all of life, all of love, all of their existence.[64]

Dargomyzhsky had a premonition that death was on its way and repeatedly reminded the members of the Balakirev circle of his wish that, in the event of his demise, Cui should finish the vocal score and Rimsky-Korsakov should orchestrate the whole, since "in our circle Cui was considered the vocal and operatic composer par excellence, since *William Ratcliff* was already his third opera, [while Rimsky-Korsakov] had the reputation of a talented orchestrator."[65] Cui had rather little to do; Dargomyzhsky had left only ten-and-one-half lines in Act I unset, which Cui covered in an economical 63 measures, including twenty bars of postlude derived from the opening of the act. Thus Cui managed both to round off the scene and to keep his own contribution down to a respectful minimum of newly invented music. He captured Dargomyzhsky's style well; one would be hard put to guess just where his hand took over.[66] Originally, Cui provided a brief orchestral prelude, too. But when in 1906 Rimsky-Korsakov completed a second orchestration of the opera (begun 1898), he replaced Cui's prelude with one of his own, drawn totally from Dargomyzhsky's music: a kind of mini-potpourri of themes associated with Don Juan, the Statue, and Donna Anna.

The Stone Guest's posthumous premiere was many times delayed. The expected production of 1870 failed to materialize because of a financial dispute. The executor of Dargomyzhsky's estate, the composer's brother-in-law, P. Koshkarev, had stipulated, according to the wishes of the deceased, that the estate receive 3000 rubles for the performance rights, while a law of 1827 allowed the theatrical directorate to pay a Russian artist no more than 1143 rubles (there was no limit to what a foreigner might receive). The theater offered three annual installments of 1000 rubles, but Koshkarev insisted upon 12 percent interest compounded after the first year, and this the theater would not allow.[67] Stasov and Cui began a loud publicity campaign, both to raise the money to satisfy Dargomyzhsky's executor, and to get the archaic law, so humiliating to Russian artists, repealed. In both of these goals they were successful. Thanks to a public subscription undertaken by the St. Petersburg

Fig. 5.4   Montage of scenes from the première production of *The Stone Guest*
(*Vsemirnaia illiustratsiia*, 1872)

artistic community and a number of benefit concerts, the required sum was raised and the opera was finally produced on February 16, 1872.

It was an event. The leading roles were all sung by artists of the first rank, including the veteran Osip Petrov as Leporello, Platonova as Donna Anna, and Fyodor Komissarzhevsky as Don Juan. *The Stone Guest*'s partisans were delirious in their praise of the performance, and small wonder: the singers had attended gatherings of the Balakirev circle, where *The Stone Guest* was read in private (Platonova and Petrov had been coming since as far back as Dargomyzhsky's time, when they had pleased and encouraged the ailing composer with their "furiously enthusiastic" reception of his experiment[68]), and they were well acquainted with the work's "performance tradition." This was a rather special thing, in keeping with the opera's very special nature, and demands some comment. The cast of characters at the private readings during the composer's lifetime, according to Rimsky-Korsakov's recollections, was as follows: Dargomyzhsky himself sang Don Juan, Musorgsky sang Leporello and Don Carlos, Lieutenant-General Konstantin Nikolaevich Velyaminov ("a music-lover and devoted amateur singer") took the smaller roles of the monk and the statue, while Alexandra Purgold sang both Laura and Donna Anna. Her sister Nadezhda (later to become Mme. Rimskaya-Korsakova) accompanied.[69] Nadezhda left a vivid glimpse of Dargomyzhsky as performer of his own music:

> He had no voice at all (he even spoke in a hoarse whisper), but—mirable dictu!—despite that, his singing in declamatory pieces made a very strong impression. His performances of [the romances] "Paladin" and "The Old Corporal"... and especially of the role of Don Juan in *The Stone Guest* were unforgettable. In the latter, the varied expression, the subtle understanding of all spiritual movements, the humor, the joie-de-vivre, the passion, and, ultimately, the tragic impulse of the final scene all combined in the author's performance with his strong music to affect the listener in a shattering way.[70]

For all that she speaks of "declamatory pieces," Purgold's examples indicate that the standards of performance applicable to *The Stone Guest* are closest to those of "Lieder singing." The experience of listening to Dargomyzhsky was a revelation to Platonova, who wrote generously of Alexandra Purgold's renditions of the feminine roles that they were "distinguished by particularly clear enunciation and astonishing diction, humor where needed, and sincerity as well."[71] Many of the writings left by the *kuchkists* testify to their high regard for Alexandra Purgold-Molas's performances. Her singing was the ideal medium for the new psychological realism they envisioned for Russian opera. Stasov repeatedly called attention to her "volatility"—a prime feature of Dargomyzhsky's music as well. The same was noted in Musorgsky's performances. It was at these readings of *The Stone Guest* that his talent as singing actor was first revealed. Nadezhda Purgold recalled that "his singing enraptured us. His small though pleasant baritone, his expressiveness, his subtle comprehension of all shades of emotion and his simplicity and sincerity withal, devoid of the slightest exaggeration or affectaton—all these worked their charms on us."[72] No description of these chamber renditions of *The Stone Guest* contains anything suggestive of Serovian stridency or of parlando; the pervasive lyric impulse of the music was matched in the performance style.

It is of great significance that the two composers most deeply involved in what we may call the New Realism, Dargomyzhsky and Musorgsky, were also gifted interpreters of their own works (and each other's). The idea of the composer as "performer" of the text, at the very heart of the new operatic aesthetic, is thus conformed at another level. The new style implied a reform not only in operatic theory but in practice, not only in composition but in execution as well. What is remarkable is that the singers of the Mariinsky Theatre were not only amenable to their new task but downright enthusiastic. The only discordant note was sounded by the contralto Lavrovskaya, famous for her portrayals of Vanya and Ratmir in Glinka's operas, who flatly refused the part of Laura as not offering sufficient reward to the singer (and Laura's is by far the most "singerly" role in the score!). As for Komissarzhevsky, he regarded Don Juan as the finest role of his career and made a number of acute observations on the role in his pedagogical handbook, *Advice to Young Singers*.

> The highest model of arioso style [*rechitativno-melodicheskoe penie*] for a Russian who understands the beauty of the Russian word, is provided by Dargomyzhsky's opera *The Stone Guest*. It is all written in the middle register, which actually constitutes, alongside its other attributes, the chief merit of this remarkable work. If this opera had been written with greater reliance upon vocal effect it would have pleased the masses more, but would hardly make such a profound impression upon the sophisticated listener. It is no wonder that the masses do not comprehend the musical significance of this opera, since the composer departed boldly from the time-honored operatic forms out of love and respect for the remarkable work of the great poet, wishing to clothe his wonderful verses with music in the most faithful and appropriate manner possible, which to the masses seems a strange and incomprehensible idea. The recitative in *The Stone Guest* is at one and the same time both a melodious, natural conversation and the highest eloquence, uncovering to all the richness of the Russian word, as it had been brought by the immortal poet to the highest level of art. All the characters in this opera are portrayed so vividly and truly that it is sufficient merely to perform what is written with accuracy and without alteration. And if the singer's voice be beautiful and true, he cannot fail to make a profound impression on the listener. Dargomyzhsky understood the singing voice in all its development, and therefore even at those moments where Don Juan's passion reaches the boiling point, he never gives the tenor a higher note than A, knowing that this note is the limit of voice production that is free and bright.[73]

Komissarzhevsky's insistence on vocal beauty defines the distance between Dargomyzhskian realism and Serovian. That his style of performance in this work was, however, not simply a modified bel canto (as might have been expected since Komissarzhevsky had received his vocal training in Italy under Repetto), may be determined from the reviews of the premiere production, which describe the performance of all the participants more in terms of acting than of singing. In fact, it would be hard to guess from many of the remarks on the performance that an opera is under discussion at all. Had such an approach been limited to the opera's partisans, it might fairly be written off as tendentious. But even critics less than ecstatic about the opera itself echoed the *kuchkist* encomia where the performance was concerned. Laroche, for example, wrote that

> Among the performers the palm must go to Platonova (Donna Anna). With inimitable artistry, or better yet, unfeigned inspiration, she recreated before us the image of a subdued, gentle woman, in whom the sense of duty and a profound piety repress, but cannot entirely extinguish, a passionate lust for life and happiness.[74]

About Petrov in the role of Leporello, the critic of the *Vsemirnaia illiustratsiia* wrote:

> We consider Petrov to be one of the greatest artists of our time. In the role of Leporello he displayed such mockery, so much cowardice (in the scene with the Statue), so much mirthful insolence in his relations with his master, he phrased his lines with such understanding and strength, that one is simply in awe of his artistry.[75]

Unanimity abruptly ceases, however, when we leave the area of performance. The opera called forth the most contradictory and strident polemics. Actually, Dargomyzhsky's "performance," like that of the singers, found universal favor; everyone agreed that he had succeeded in achieving his goal. The goal itself, however, became a matter of sharp controversy. This controversy actually preceded the premiere by a matter of some years. Cui's articles were its foundation. The first of them appeared as early as March 28, 1868, at a time when talk about the opera—then a half-finished pencil sketch—could be conducted only at the level of theory and rumor. Nonetheless, this early squib set the tone for all the ensuing debate, and is an important document in the annals of Russian operatic realism. We give it here in full.

Pushkin's "Stone Guest" and Dargomyzhsky's

What should we demand of operatic music? Here is a question as yet far from settled, though much indeed has been written about it. It seems to me that the answer to this question consists of two words: from operatic music we should demand *truth* and *beauty*. Truth, in that throughout the entire opera the music should express faithfully that which takes place on the stage, with all possible observance of local color, the spirit of the time of the action, and the development of the musical character of the various personages. Besides that, it is necessary that the phrasing be natural, that every phrase be enunciated correctly, the voice rising and falling as it should, and that every note strengthen the expression of the text by its effect upon the listener. But truth alone is not enough; such truth we encounter often enough in Auber, while his operas are completely unmusical. Musical *beauty* must be united with truth. Phrases must not be commonplace or hackneyed; musical ideas must be developed hand in hand with musical character, so that every note possesses as much musical significance as possible and thus interests the listener. There you have the ideal of opera, satisfied in part by certain sections of *Der Freischütz, Ruslan* and *Rusalka,* but never completely realized in any one opera. In some numbers there is likely to be a dominance of elegant musical beauty, as in the epic picture of the Russian pagan world in the prologue to *Ruslan;* in others, true dramatic declamation, as in the last moments of Natasha's farewell scene with the prince in *Rusalka.* But in any case such an opera, inspired in conception and in execution, would create an impression on a prepared audience such as our melomanes have never dreamed of. Before the emergence of these criteria (they trace their origins back to Gluck), or when they were deliberately neglected, the selection of a subject for an opera was never any problem; any subject would do. Any old music was written in response to the public taste and to the demands of singers, it was grafted onto the text, and thus laurels were easily earned. In such a fashion were written most of Rossini's operas, satisfying neither the condition of beauty, nor that of truth.

In light of today's demands upon opera the choice of subject has taken on great significance. The subject can be divided into three categories. The first—the plot—must have general interest and be potent enough to cut everyone to the quick. In the second place, the plan or scenario must present a full exposition and development of the subject and all its most important moments without padding. Third, the embodiment of the subject, that is to say the speeches of the characters, may be written in verse or in prose (the latter I consider to be entirely possible for realistic comic operas).

One rarely finds a person so luxuriantly endowed by nature as to unite within himself both a strong musical and a strong literary talent; consequently, if such a composer should succeed in writing a completely successful libretto for his own opera, that would be an exception which can in no way be elevated into a general rule. Still, the composer himself can pick his subject and plan it for musical purposes. With most remarkable literary works this is not especially hard. But to write the text for an opera—that's a difficult task.

Ordained librettists, to whom one usually turns, are in most cases unremarkable people, without gifts, devoid of any poetic feeling not even always equipped with decent verbal skills. It is true that even without a good text, so long as the plan is good, a series of good scenes can be accomplished, but beyond the good general impression they will turn out crudely, will be gaudy and decorative *(les Huguenots),* without that poetic beauty of detail which captivates us in so many songs written to good texts. Beyond the general picture, the text can contain no end of nuances of feeling and emotion, no end of subtle strokes, without which no picture can come alive, but will remain just that—a picture. For such a text one needs a strong poetic talent, one which will not always submit willingly to the musician, but will be far more inclined to create with complete independence.

It is quite possible that when the contemporary operatic ideal comes to be realized more frequently, when it finally declares war on those monstrosities that are nowadays called operas— so masterfully and dispassionately described by Count Tolstoy in the third part of *War and Peace*—then, perhaps, talented writers will begin to create dramas intended for union with music, and one of the most enormous difficulties in creating an opera will have been resolved. But in the meantime, one must seize upn those works of great artists that even in a limited way approach the criteria we have outlined. One work that comes near to the ideal operatic text is Pushkin's "Don Juan" *(The Stone Guest).* If Pushkin had added choruses (though there is no reason why operas must have choruses, for musical purposes the absence of such a powerful element is regrettable), if he had increased the number of purely lyric moments and cut down on the more prosaic exchanges in a few places, the text of *The Stone Guest* would have been perfect. But even in its present form, as Pushkin left it, this is a wonderful text, and it has attracted our most remarkable musical artist, who has had an enormous preparation for the deliberate creation of a contemporary music drama.

And at the present time, in fact, Dargomyzhsky, despite his illness, is writing music to the text of Pushkin's "Don Juan" with uncommon heat and perseverance, and without changing a single word. More than half of this great work is completed. Dargomyzhsky's "Don Juan" will be a marvelous, unheard-of phenomenon; it will be all the best things in *Rusalka* without the weaker things. It is the first conscious experiment in creating contemporary opera-drama without the slightest concession; it will be a codex in which Russian vocal composers will be able to check the truth of their declamation and the fidelity of their transmission of the inflections of the text; it is dramatic truth brought to its highest expression, combined with intelligence, experience and mastery of craft, along with a musical beauty that bears in many places the inimitable stamp of Dargomyzhsky's originality. Dargomyzhsky's "Don Juan" will occupy a place of honor, a *foremost* place, not only in the history of Russian opera, but in the history of world opera, as the first serious, honorable and uncommonly gifted attempt to attain so closely to the operatic ideal.[76]

Cui has obviously begged the focal question: is it right to base operas on texts written without premonition of, or provision for, the addition of music? He evidently wished it to appear that *The Stone Guest* differed in conception from conventional opera only in degree (of "truth" and "beauty"), not in kind, that it represented nothing more (or less) than the closest approximation to date of the Gluckian ideal. When he writes in praise of Pushkin merely that his poem is superior to the ordinary libretto, he states a platitude that is both self-evident and misleading. For unlike the conventional libretto, *The Stone Guest*, was intended to be a self-sufficient literary composition. And when Cui complains that Pushkin failed to supply choruses and "purely lyric moments," he effectively undercuts his own case. For if Pushkin had provided more in the way of musical opportunities for the composer, he would in effect have been writing a conventional operatic libretto.

Two names conspicuous by their absence from Cui's discussion are the two most closely identified with operatic reform in Russia before 1868: Wagner and Serov. But although he pretends to ignore their existence on the surface, Cui nonetheless polemicizes with them indirectly. This is most obvious where Cui dismisses the "requirement" that composer and librettist be one and the same. It is the reason for his rejection of the precept, however, that is the real bone of contention. Cui's somewhat artificial classification of the components of the "operatic subject"—plot, scenario, libretto (text)— is obviously borrowed from Serov's *Rusalka* essay of 1856. But what a difference in the ordering of priorities! Now it is the last category that is given preeminent importance: literary, rather than scenic considerations are held up as the primary criteria. Serov, we remember, had positively despised the "words" (the derisive quotation marks are his), and had given greatest weight to the scenario. When Cui cites *Les Huguenots* as his example of the "gaudy, decorative" result of the dominance of scenario over text, we may be sure that he wished his readers to substitute *"Rogneda."*

It is where Cui describes the ideal libretto that he, with misleading matter-of-factness, introduces the radical departure: the best thing to have in a libretto, says he, is "no end of nuances of feeling and emotion, no end of subtle strokes." Now this, of course, is what all previous operatic theory had specifically excluded from the libretto, for its presence inhibits musical expansion. Music had always been a generalizing, idealizing force in its relationship to the emotional content of the text. No operatic "reform" had ever challenged that. The "continuous opera" that began with Mozart's finales, for example, had sought to allow fully articulated musical structures to carry the action that had formerly been the province of dry recitative. The operatic ideal Cui described, on the other hand, is one that contained no larger structures, no broad musical strokes and, most emphatically, no "symphonization" of opera à la Wagner. In short, he called for a music which by no previously existing standard—save perhaps that of the Camerata, decidedly *hors de concours*—could be described as "operatic." The most revealing moment, the one that shows Cui to have been "present at the creation," is where he calls for an operatic music that would embody "that poetic beauty of detail which captivates us in so many songs written to good texts." For this was a precise description of Dargomyzhsky's aim and even implied his method. In short, the ideal Cui proposed amounted to nothing less than the destruction of opera as an independent art form with its own criteria, obedient to its own laws. The libretto was now to conform to the principles of the spoken drama, and the musical setting was to model its resources on those of the through-composed art song.

Stasov, for his part, stoked up his propaganda machine with a special vengeance after the premiere. In his wonted way, he tried to silence all criticism in advance by flinging it back at the critics.

> One mustn't go to hear *The Stone Guest* with prior operatic criteria, previous routine operatic ideas, in mind: one mustn't address oneself with these to such a work, which...opens up a new era in music—an era of realistic opera, approaching life and literature, rid of conventions of expression to an extent that approaches any contemporary drama or comedy.[77]

To voice any criticism at all, then, was merely to confess one's bondage to "routine operatic ideas." It was the old dodge Serov had tried in the Preface to *Rogneda,* and it didn't work any better for Stasov. For his main point, that *The Stone Guest* "approached any drama or comedy," was the main point of the opposition as well. Here was an opera whose text was already a fully viable contemporary drama. Where was the music's indispensable contribution? If an ascetic denial of music's full and independent powers and resources was considered an advance in the art, then would not eliminating music altogether be an even greater advance? As Laroche put it: "Who said you have to pursue the ideal of spoken drama? In that case the greatest realism would be not to write music at all but to leave Pushkin in peace."[78] The most hostile of *The Stone Guest*'s critics really saw it as the attempted abolition of music itself—"musicoclasis," as Rostislav termed it.

The fundamental error committed by critic and partisan alike in considering *The Stone Guest* was the exaggeration of its "declamatory" aspects. To read some of the early reviews (and later writings by some who obviously never heard the work), one might indeed think it to be an unremitting, unrelieved *recitativo secco*. Tchaikovsky's description, for example, is far from resembling:

> It is well known that Dargomyzhsky's strength resides in his astonishingly realistic and, at the same time, gratefully singable recitatives, which lend his magnificent opera *Rusalka* an enchantment of inimitable originality. The late composer recognized, apparently, the dominant strength of this gift, and this recognition, unfortunately not supported by firm critical foundations, moved him to the strange notion of writing an opera that would consist exclusively of recitatives. For this purpose Dargomyzhsky chose the text of Pushkin's *The Stone Guest* and, without changing a single letter, without adapting it to the requirements of operatic procedure as is usually done when a literary work is taken as the canvas for broad musico-dramatic forms, he strung his recitatives onto every line of the original text. As is well known, recitative, being without definite rhythm and clearly delineated melodic quality, is not yet a musical form—it is merely the connective cement between the separate parts of the musical structure, indispensable on the one hand because of the simple conditions of scenic movement, and on the other as a contrast to the lyric moments of the opera. What a pitiable delusion on the part of a bold talent unguided by a mature artist's sober understanding of aesthetics! To write an opera without music—is that not the same as writing a drama without words or action?[79]

One sympathizes with Tchaikovsky, the fully trained composer, who obviously felt that Dargomyzhsky's example challenged him to give up far too much. Realism, with its rejection of "form," was supremely the doctrine of the autodidact. What was liberation to the latter was tyranny to the professional. A revealing insight is gained from the entry in Tchaikovsky's diary for July 23, 1888. Once again fulminating against *The Stone Guest*, he set down the private thought that "if anything is more hateful and false than this unsuccessful attempt to introduce *truth* into a branch of art where everything is based on *pseudo* and where *truth* in the everyday sense of the word is altogether useless—I do not know it."[80]

The motives Tchaikovsky ascribed to Dargomyzhsky were purely pragmatic and practical—above all, simply to capitalize on what he recognized to be his strongest compositional suit. The work's history in fact reveals a grain of truth in this view. But more typical of Dargomyzhsky's critics was to regard *The Stone Guest* quite wrongly as a woeful subjugation of artistic instinct to cold, calculating theory. This attitude, too, was understandable. Stasov and Cui had so thoroughly identified the work with a specific "camp" and doctrine, that polemics on *The Stone Guest* were more likely to be directed at that camp than at the work itself.

It is in this light that one must evaluate Herman Laroche's articles on *The Stone Guest*. He was much drawn to the work; as a true connoisseur both of music and of literature, he was not deaf to the felicities of their union. But he objected strenuously to the way *The Stone Guest* was touted as a model: the work was in his eyes completely off the operatic mainstream—a "studio piece" *(kabinetnaia rabota)* of undeniable interest, even beauty, but essentially sterile. Quite perceptively catching the work's *romance* derivation, Laroche noted that "*The Stone Guest*'s true domain is the salon; its true orchestra, the pianoforte," for which reason "there is no pretense [in it] to musical drama."[81] For drama demanded breadth of conception, and, without fail, the employment of music's unique resources in their full bloom (epitomized for Laroche by the ensemble), and these Dargomyzhsky had deliberately nipped in the bud.

> To the extent that the realm of music is removed from the sphere of reason, to the extent that it is more fantastic than the realm of literature, compromise with the spoken drama, which is no more than a grim necessity, can be made more easily and willingly in musical drama. Instead of polemicizing against the vocal ensemble, sensible criticism ought to recognize in it the very nerve center of dramatic music: it constitutes a means unavailable to any other art of depicting the collision of characters and their interests. . . . If good recitative is the foundation of good opera, then ensemble is its crown.[82]

Laroche had a field day lampooning the realist-positivist operatic aesthetic, which admitted no situation into opera that was not faithful to the conditions of real life. Obviously, the ensemble was the furthest beyond the pale, along with the other "rounded forms," the conventional monolithic use of the chorus, and so forth. While it is not at all clear that Dargomyzhsky intended *The Stone Guest* as a protest against such things—he seems to have been more interested in the positive implications of the new aesthetic than the negative ones—his work was undeniably so used by the *kuchkist* party. As Laroche put it,

> Judge and jury have convicted contemporary opera of having too much music, of being *too musical*. With a self-sacrifice worthy of a martyr's halo, they lay their hands upon their own art and execute it for the excessive scope it had enjoyed. Opera must be drama and nothing else; drama must be a reproduction of real life and nothing else. And neither Italian, German nor French opera bears the slightest resemblance to real life. Examining existing models from this point of view, our hypochondriacs see contradiction and incongruity at every turn. Here their eye is offended by a beautiful aria, because it holds up the action; there they are offended by a sonorous *morceau d'ensemble* because it presents people singing completely different words simultaneously to the same accompaniment; further on, a chorus gives them no peace because in its text the same words are repeated a dozen times, while in real life it just isn't done that way. In a word, exceptional dramaturgy in operatic

music and exceptional truth to life in drama have not yet found practical application; . . . all composers up to now have concerned themselves, in opera as everywhere else, with the beauty of their music, the elegance of sound and of aesthetic impression, and hence the long faces with which our contemporary musical critics stroll through the gardens of musical composition.[83]

This laughable aesthetic asceticism has finally found a standard bearer in *The Stone Guest*—"far from music for the masses, this is music for the few, or rather, nonmusic for the not-many."[84] Dargomyzhsky's motives in writing it are held up to ridicule:

The moral fortitude with which the composer renounced everything capable of giving enjoyment to his audience must not be confused with talent or inspiration: we sense only that the composer has resolved not to allow the listener any pleasure.[85]

Once again the music of *The Stone Guest* is oversimply equated with recitative, so that, in keeping with recitative's usual function, the opera is said to give the impression of "an endless introduction, after which the main body is missing; a foyer without a building; a gate leading to an open field; a mountain laboring to bring forth a mouse."[86]

Laroche, of course, applied to *The Stone Guest* precisely the kind of "prior operatic criteria" that Stasov had ruled out. But with Laroche this was no simple matter of conservatism, rather a coherent aesthetic outlook that determined his reaction to Dargomyzhsky's opera. A disciple of Hanslick, as we have seen, Laroche insisted upon the futility of the very idea of musical realism, except in the very narrow sense Hanslick himself had admitted.

Music affords incomparably less food for realism, for the imitation of nature, for logical analysis, than the arts of word or of color. But since it exists in time and is expressed in the form of motion, it presents a certain analogy to many processes which are accomplished in the course of time, and with many kinds of motion.[87]

But there was as little "action music" in *The Stone Guest* as there had been action in the original play. Pushkin's work was chosen for its beautiful language and the subtlety of its emotional expression. And this was Dargomyzhsky's greatest mistake: Pushkin's exquisite poetry had throttled his music. For Dargomyzhsky actually to have desired this was merely symptomatic of the essential "pathology" of his aesthetic.

Criticism, as is well known, has complained exceedingly often that the operas with the most beautiful music are written to the most colorless, insipid texts. This is a pity, of course, but it does not follow that the creators of such operas would have profited had they set only the highest works of poetry. . . . In the words of a great poet, alongside the attractive exterior, there is a particularity of thought and an individual shading, and if these features are pursued by the composer, his music will lose its freedom and its breadth, which are attainable only where music soars in an atmosphere of vague and generalized mood. For the purposes of opera, then, one is better served by verses of negative merits: not stupid, not banal, not clumsy, not ungrammatical, but at all costs not profound or touched with genius.[88]

Half seriously, half sarcastically, Laroche suggests that the reason for the rise of realism as a leading artistic tendency among musicians was the decline in the level of operatic performance, which made maintenance of previous operatic standards untenable. Singers now "act" because they can no longer sing. A work like *The Stone Guest* merely attempts to exploit this sad situation, and, in catering to it, further dims the prospects for real opera.

Turning to the opera in its details—and "besides details there is *nothing* in *The Stone Guest*"—Laroche is compelled to admit that they include some "exquisite beauties."[89] But in opera, the chief interest must lie not in details, but in the broad strokes that depict "general moods." Anything else is a misunderstanding of music's inherent potential, and a deflection from its purpose. Laroche had dealt with this problem at some length in his defense of Glinka against the "Zukunftists" some years before:

Opera, as a form of lyric drama, must act upon the listener with the simplest and most accessible means and motives: there is no room in it for those psychological subtleties and fine points, which the contemporary novel, for example, seeks out with such avidity.[90]

The point was at the time directed against Wagner. But Dargomyzhsky was, if anything, even worse an offender, for Laroche now writes that:

Dargomyzhsky has addressed himself to his task more responsibly and conscientiously than Wagner; he is far purer as an artist and has not the Wagnerian sensuality which masquerades as lofty romanticism; he is far freer in his music from the commonplace, and in his declamation more careful and more successful. But for all that, *The Stone Guest* is infinitely less *musical* than any opera of Wagner's.[91]

Accordingly, when Laroche sets about to survey Dargomyzhsky's opera, he dwells little upon its "exquisite beauties" of detail, but is ever on the watch for lyric moments and expansions of "general mood," eager to "catch" the composer in an aria wherever he can, and thereby expose his aesthetic pretensions as a willful denial of his own natural artistic inclinations, thus proving that the numbers opera is the "natural" and inevitable procedure, and that no amount of theorizing can cause it to disappear. Naturally enough, Laroche fastens upon Don Carlos's monologue in the second scene.

There is...a place where the musician's inspiration came into open collision with his aesthetic catechism, his *passion* for beautiful sounds with the *duty* of the contemporary musical dramatist: one can observe this tragic accident in Don Carlos's scene with Laura, where the former, seemingly forgetting utterly about the theory of musical drama, undertakes to sing nothing more nor less than a cavatina.... But when he gets to the word "kill," he remembers that such singing is not part of the platform of musico-dramatic innovation, and, ashamed of his momentary weakness, he continues in good recitative style, which is all the catechism allows.[92]

Even more caustic are Laroche's comments on Laura's songs. If normal, rounded musical forms can be justified in realist opera so long as the character is actually supposed to be singing rather than speaking, then there is a way out for the poor realist who nonetheless wants to write real music:

One need take but one more step and take an operatic performance itself as the subject for an opera. Then not even the strictest realism could find anything objectionable in all manner of arias, duets, choruses and so on, or even in virtuosic cadenzas and fioritura! But what will libretti become when one of their chief tasks will be creating situations and inventing characters to ask one another to sing, whereupon the one asked takes up his guitar and charms the world with his art. As long as this cunning idea is new it will be bearable, but when it becomes a stock situation it will become funny and then begin to pall. The listener, suffering through half an hour or forty-five minutes of uninterrupted recitative, unimpeachable from the realistic point of view, will await this *invitation to sing* like manna from heaven: without such an invitation, singing will be unthinkable, and without singing, going to the opera is likewise unthinkable.[93]

The radically differing positions espoused by the professional critics was mirrored in the reaction of the public. Cheers and hisses mingled after each act, but the former began to predominate with the third scene (the cemetery). Laroche chose to explain the unaccountably large degree of enthusiasm by assuming that the public had been intimidated by Cui and Stasov's advance publicity, just as the professional critics had been cowed by Serov at the premiere of that equally doubtful work, *Rogneda*. How could the public really like a work that was patently not written for them at all? "To see *The Stone Guest* on the actual stage," he wrote, "is as strange as coming across a comprehensive treatise on differential calculus in a popular magazine."[94] This was no opera for music-lovers; it could appeal only to a literary mind.

But at least one eminently literary mind thoroughly despised *The Stone Guest*. This was Turgenev, Chernyshevsky's great antagonist, who (despite his notorious liaison with Pauline Viardot) might have been presumed receptive to a music so respectful of poetry. He was, however, apparently unable to accept the loss of scale, of "tone," that resulted from the application of realist methods to a tragic subject, and expressed himself to Stasov in no uncertain terms at the time of the premiere:

It will always remain one of the great mystifications of my life, how such intelligent individuals as yourself and Cui, for example, could find in these limp, colorless, feeble recitatives, drearily sprinkled here and there with excruciating little *frissons* for the sake of fantastic coloration—how can you, I say, find in this pitiful chirping—what?—not just music, but inspired, original "epoch-making music!!?!!"—Isn't this unconscious chauvinism?[95]

Stasov made a typical objection to the effect that Turgenev was voicing not his own true feelings, but those conditioned in him by unnamed "authorities." Turgenev replied angrily:

> I am thrilled by Gluck's recitatives and arias not because authorities praise them, but because at the first sound of them my tears begin to flow. And it is not authorities that compel me to regard *The Stone Guest* with utter contempt.[96]

But though *The Stone Guest* struck so many as the furthest imaginable extremity of antimusicality and radicalism, the *kuchkists* knew that it was not, that it was possible to go further. It was experience, not mere hypothesis, that caused Cui unexpectedly to hold up a warning sign in the midst of one of his orgies of praise:

> One must avoid texts, however perfect in literary style or thought content, if they are not written for music. One must avoid rational, prosaic conversations, one must seek lyric opportunities suited to broader melodic development, as much as possible; one must seek popular masses that live and take on an active part in the drama. Continuous dialogue and only dialogue becomes tiring in the end, and if *The Stone Guest* had been longer, then its qualities of genius notwithstanding, it would have been a chore to sit through it.... This type of opera—brief, intimate, small-scaled—is not the only one possible.[97]

This startling volte-face can be explained in part by Cui's wish not to allow his praise of *The Stone Guest* to be interpreted as a withdrawal of approval from *Ruslan,* for following the quoted passage is another in which Glinka's and Dargomyzhsky's works are held up as the "two complementary pillars" of Russian opera. Cui might also have wished to protect the rights of such grander operas as his own *Ratcliff* (or *Angelo,* then in progress). But, though he does not say so, it is clear that Cui's description of the realist blind alley was drawn, as it were, "from life," from his knowledge of the "experiment in dramatic music in prose" that had been directly inspired by *The Stone Guest*—Musorgsky's *Marriage.*

Musorgsky had been tending toward such a project in his songs of the mid-sixties, which reflected his preoccupation with naturalistic declamation as the key to truth of emotional expression. Two of these songs—"Yeremushka's Cradlesong" (*Kolybel'naia Eremushki,* 1867) and "With Nanny" (*S Nianei,* 1868), the first of the *Nursery* cycle—bear dedication to Dargomyzhsky, the "great teacher of musical truth." So when, at one of the *kuchkist* soirées devoted to *The Stone Guest,* Dargomyzhsky himself suggested that Musorgsky embark upon a "dialogue opera" of his own, the composer leapt at the chance. The work to which Dargomyzhsky directed the younger composer's attention—"(in jest), but seconded by Cui (not in jest)"[98]—was the most tendentious selection possible, one calculated, as it were, to put the tenets of the New Realism to the acid test.

Where Pushkin's *Stone Guest* had been a work of elegant lyric poetry and lofty romantic theme, Gogol's "altogether improbable occurrence in three acts," entitled *Marriage (Zhenit'ba,* 1833), must rank with the most "unmusical" prose ever penned. The play's literary idiom is naturalistic colloquialism exaggerated in its laconicism and bluntness to absurd hyperbole. Its themes are paltry, its humor the lowest sort of caricature. Not even that ardent Gogolian, Vladimir Nabokov, could summon up much admiration for the artistic qualities of this "rather slipshod comedy about the hesitations of a man who has made up his mind to marry, has a swallowtail suit made, is provided with a fiancée—but at the last moment makes a fenestral exit."[99] This roughness, this bluntness and, above all, this total lack of "poetry" may, however, have been just what made *Marriage* attractive to Musorgsky, the "thinking realist of the Russian operatic stage" (as Laroche was later to dub him). Such an ambience was absolutely uncharted terrain for music; here was a chance to widen the art's horizons, to free it from the shackles of the lyric and the "beautiful" and truly live up to the *kuchkist* slogan, "Toward new shores!"[100]

It was in his faith in prose texts and naturalistic declamation as the key to truth of emotional expression in music that Musorgsky went considerably beyond Dargomyzhsky's most advanced thinking and parted company with Chernyshevsky altogether. Chernyshevsky's model of "natural singing," we remember, was the Russian lyrical folk song *(protiazhnaia),* which the philosopher had viewed as a natural artifact in that it was a direct, untutored and spontaneous "expression of joy or sorrow."[101] Chernyshevsky's unwontedly nonempirical citation of these vaguely defined emotions as music's natural source and model could in any case be construed as leading back to the aesthetic of the Affektenlehre, and hence (paradoxically enough for a critic to whom "emotion and form are opposites") to the justification of rounded forms in dramatic music. Chernyshevsky in fact spoke of the aria, not the recitative, as the artful imitation of "natural singing." And the "melodic recitative" of *The Stone Guest,* though avowedly realist in its "formlessness," was, as we have seen, not particularly naturalistic as regards declamation, but essentially lyric in impulse.

Musorgsky, on the other hand, gave repeated expression to an aesthetic wholly found on imitation of speech as bona fide empirical model for his music. Here is a typical example, from a letter written during his period of work on *Marriage:*

> This is what I would like: for my characters to speak onstage as living people speak, but in such a way that their essential nature and force of intonation, supported by an orchestra that forms a musical canvas for their speech, shall hit the target squarely. That is, my music must be the artistic reproduction of human speech in all its subtlest twistings; that is, the sounds of human speech, as the exterior manifestation of thought and feeling, must, without exaggeration or strain, become music—truthful, accurate, *but* (read: which means) artistic, in the highest sense artistic.[102]

Striking and somewhat unexpected in this context is the neoclassical tint. In his call for the mimesis of speech, which in its turn is itself a mimesis—"the exterior manifestation of thought and feeling"—Musorgsky sounds like a regular Aristotelian, even a latter-day Galilei. Where could the Russian composer have encountered such ideas? Or is this merely an example of independent formulation of an obvious and endlessly recurring reformist slogan?

Though many have assumed the latter to be the case, Musorgsky left a strong clue to the true source of his aesthetic outlook and, in particular, his view of the relationship between music and speech. In the autobiographical sketch he prepared in 1880 at the request of Hugo Riemann for inclusion in the first edition of the *Musik-Lexicon,* Musorgsky followed the factual information with this self-styled *"profession de foi"*:

> Art is a means of communicating with people, not an end in itself.... Proceeding from the conviction that human speech is strictly regulated by musical laws (Virchow, Gervinus) he [Musorgsky] views the aim of musical art as the reproduction in musical sounds not only of modes of feeling [*nastroeniia chuvstva*], but mainly the reproduction of modes of human speech [*nastroeniia rechi chelovecheskoi*].[103]

Given the context, there was certainly something *pro forma* about the citation of the two German names. The composer seems to have wanted to show the German Musikwissenschaftler that he, too, was up on his Wissenschaft (and not only musical), as any self-respecting thinking man of the nineteenth century was supposed to be.[104] Rudolf Virchow (1821-1902), cellular pathologist, anthropologist and political activist, was a standard hero of positivists and progressives: a "scientific luminary" (as Chernyshevsky called him) who sought active participation in governmental and social reform and hence exerted an enormous appeal on the progressive intelligentsia in Russia, where more than anywhere else the arts and sciences were viewed as under an obligation to be *engagés.*

To the literary historian Georg Gottfried Gervinus (1805-71), on the other hand, the proposition with which Musorgsky associates his name may be directly attributed. Einstein calls him the "dry German pope of letters,"[105] and sees in Musorgsky's invocation of his name only a general reflection of the Russian composer's antiromanticism. But Gervinus was vitally interested in music and music aesthetics, and his writings on the subject provide the missing link between Musorgsky and the neoclassical thinking his letters reflect. Gervinus's great passion was Handel. In 1856 he was one of the founders— along with Chrysander, Hauptmann and Dehn—of the Deutsche Händelgesellschaft, and contributed many German translations of the oratorio texts (for which task he was eminently qualified as Germany's leading Shakespearean scholar), which remain in use to this day. His essays in the *Niederrheinische Musikzeitung* and later in the *Deutsche Musikzeitung* earned him a reputation as a leading practitioner of musical *Hermeneutik,* and during the 1860s that reputation spread to Russia. Some amusing oblique testimony to Gervinus's status as authority on the "meaning" of music is given by Cui, sarcastically reviewing the public final examinations for pianists graduating from Rubinstein's conservatory in 1866:

> These ladies are utterly finished pianists; each of them possesses all the attributes of a performing artist: calm self-assurance, excellent technique, stamina, scrupulousness and understanding. But the reader must not forget that one had to judge these qualities in performances of nothing but a repertory of study pieces—and what pieces? Concerti by Mozart, Beethoven, Chopin, Mendelssohn! These concerti have been performed for hundreds of years by hundreds of pianists; the expressive content of every little note in them has been explicated practically by Gervinus himself; nothing in their interpretation is up to the inspiration of the artist.[106]

Gervinus's major contribution to music aesthetics was his last book, *Händel und Shakespeare: Zur Aesthetik der Tonkunst* (Leipzig, 1868), dedicated to Chrysander. It came out, significantly enough, in the very year Musorgsky went to work on *Marriage.* As its title indicates, the book is devoted to establishing parallels between music and literature through a comparison of the two arts' greatest—to Gervinus, paradigmatic—exponents. Its thrust is against the newfangled formalism of Herbart, Dehn and an unnamed Hanslick, in favor of "the 3000-year-old, ever constant, never contested notion of the nature and essence of music," namely, that it is an art of "feeling and expression."[107] In defining musical expression further, Gervinus reaches back beyond the various aesthetic theories of the preceding hundred years and attempts, from his very first sentence, to reinstate the imitation theory à la Aristotle in all its glory.[108] The latest authority Gervinus cites with complete approval is Rousseau, and the earliest roots of his idea are sought among the pre-Socratics. The whole 3000-year history of musical expression is set out with Germanic thoroughness in a series of chapters tracing the development of music from the Greeks, through the Renaissance humanists and the early opera composers (with Peri at their head rather than Monteverdi, who is for Gervinus a madrigalist), up to the apogee of all *Tonkunst*—Handel. The story is told with all the traditional embellishments: the misguided deviance of "der polyphone Gesang des Mittlealters"; Palestrina's heroic rescue;[109] the salutary influence of folk song; the new deviance in the form of "die reine Instrumentalmusik."

But Gervinus's book is far more than an historical panoply. The author attempts to construct a coherent theory of musical expression in which the rationalistic Affektenlehre of Handel's time could be made consistent with more modern psychology[110] and with nineteenth-century scientific empiricism, so as to support the rather positivistic thesis that the composer objectifies through his work his own and his hearers' subjective, personal feelings. Like Wagner, whom he in most other respects opposes, Gervinus sees the greatest opportunities in the hybridization of the arts: "The range, strength, value and effect [of music] increase with the objectivity of the individual work and with the ever-expanding assemblage of means— instruments [combined] with voices, vocal expression with the sense of the words, words with dramatic action" (p. 244).

No matter how grand or complex, however, a work of musical art can ultimately derive its validity only from imitation, that is, by taking as its point of departure the reproduction of the sounds of animate and inanimate nature. But since real expression of emotion can be effected only by the human organs that make direct appeal to other human organs—that is, by facial muscles and the speaking voice as received by eyes and ears—music must take speech as its model, and in particular, the aspect of speech that effects expression in real life: stress or accent *(Betonung)*. "Accent is the mother of music" *(Betonung ist die Mutter der Musik)*, proclaims Gervinus at the outset of his study, and by way of emphasizing the point and its classical pedigree, he immediately restates the maxim in Latin: *accentus mater musices.* Three varieties of *Betonung* are distinguished: grammatical or syllabic stress, rhetorical empha- sis, and finally the third, "infinitely rich (by comparison with the other two), ruling a whole musical world, which alone will occupy us henceforth—the pathetic or affective accent [*der pathetische oder Empfindungsaccent*], which through the subtlest shading of the voice endows the speaker's feelings with a special language of their own" (p. 17). The first two kinds of accent are often indicated in writing, but "if one wanted to show *Empfindungsaccente* in written form, one could do it only by means of notes" (p. 18). It is precisely at this point that spoken language passes over into music.

Thus the special relationship between speech and music lies in the wide range of emotional communication that a speaker can convey over and above the lexical meaning of the uttered words, and it is precisely where expression and communication are concerned that speech appears to follow a system Gervinus describes as "ruling a whole musical world," or Musorgsky, paraphrasing him, describes as speech "governed by musical laws." If music itself were to act in harmony with these laws, objective and definite communication of meaning through the medium of musical sounds might become a real possibility. One can easily imagine the effect on Musorgsky's creative imagination of a passage in Gervinus such as this one:

> *Empfindungsaccent* introduces, behind the language of logic, a new language, by means of which ordinary speech is transformed by the raising and lowering of pitch, increase and decrease of volume, rushing and lingering, intensification and weakening, or by the muffling or amplification of the vowels of those words which are to be set apart by means of emotional accentuation. This makes possible not only the understanding of speech, but also empathy with that which is being said. It often happens that inner nervous stresses, which

arise in the soul under the influence of external vivid impressions, seek a keener outlet [than is provided by the verbal content of the utterance]. The resonator of emotion in such cases becomes not the given strictly delimited substance of the word, but the elastically pulsing and limitlessly flexible musical tone (p. 19).

Gervinus speaks here not of literal music, but of those paralexical attributes of speech—contour, pitch-level, volume, tempo—that often convey more emotion than words. When speech passes over into music according to the workings of Gervinus's *Betonung* theory, the first type encountered is recitative, and thus Gervinus saw the most potent manifestation of music in what for so many was its lowliest form. His description of Peri's achievement could also be a description of Musorgsky's, and provides a genuine point of contact between the seventeenth-century Florentine and the nineteenth-century Russian: "Through the observance of the natural accents of the emotions in joy and sorrow, and through attending to the delivery of such words in correctly enunciated speech, he was able to base his melody [*eine Harmonie*—after the Greek *harmonia,* a usage one finds in the writings and prefaces of the early Baroque monodists, including Peri] on their intonations" (p. 25).

In an especially characteristic passage, Gervinus observes that recitative as handled by Peri corresponds to the ideal of poetry as set forth by such latter-day classical writers as Martianus Capella: a genre lying midway between speech and music, which transcends their individual powers by uniting them (p. 26). We need not consider further Gervinus's application of his theory to actual music (chiefly Handelian recitative) in the second half of his book, for Musorgsky, "in the field," as it were, made his own application, which undoubtedly went much further than anything Gervinus might have imagined in his armchair (though he employed such prophetic terms as *Sprechgesang*[111]). It will suffice to compare the foregoing quotations with another from the numerous letters Musorgsky wrote during the time of his work on *Marriage,* to perceive the extent of the impression Gervinus's book made on him.

> In my opéra dialogué I am trying to underscore as vividly as possible those abrupt changes of intonation that crop up in the characters during their dialogue, seemingly for the most trivial of reasons, and on the most insignificant words, in which is concealed, it seems to me, the power of Gogol's humor.[112]

It is almost a paraphrase. And as a matter of fact Musorgsky cites Gervinus directly in the autobiographical sketch excerpted above, where he refers clumsily to "modes [or moods] of feeling" *(nastroeniia chuvstva).* This is a translation of Gervinus's term *Gefühlsstimmungen,*[113] one of the categories through which the German writer sought to rationalize the effects and "meaning" of instrumental music.

What Musorgsky got from Gervinus then, and patently not from Dargomyzhsky's example, was his overriding preoccupation with speech. Dargomyzhsky's professed preoccupation was with the expression of the *word*.[114] But Musorgsky, following Gervinus, recognized that words do not possess immutable meaning.[115] For emotional expression in music genuinely to qualify as "truthful" there must be an empirically real natural model, and such a model cannot be provided by words in themselves. Dargomyzhsky's aims and method had been empathic and subjective.[116] Musorgsky, in the spirit of nineteenth-century "scientism," wished to go beyond that. If speech is the exterior form given to the emotions, one must reproduce the former with the greatest objective accuracy if one is to capture the latter in tones. Musorgsky's letters of 1868 are full of such quasi-mechanistic thinking, which we may now confidently, with reference to Gervinus, call Aristotelian (at least in the sense that his nineteenth-century interpreters understood Aristotle). Some more examples:

> On nature's scale man is the highest organism (at least on earth), and this highest organism possesses the gift of word and voice without equal among terrestrial organisms. If one admits the reproduction by artistic means of human speech in all its subtlest and most capricious shades—to depict it naturally, as life and human nature demand,—would this not amount to the deification of the human gift of words? And if by this simplest of means, simply submitting strictly to artistic instinct in catching human vocal intonations, it becomes possible to capture the heart, then is it not a worthy enterprise? And if one could, along with that, catch the thinking faculties in a vise, then would it not be worthwhile to devote oneself to such an occupation?[117]

The musical mirroring of speech became a veritable obsession. To Rimsky-Korsakov, Musorgsky confided that "whatever speech I hear, whoever is speaking (or, the main thing, no matter what he is saying), my brain is already churning out the musical embodiment of such speech."[118] And, in language far more explicit and deliberate than any expression of Dargomyzhsky's, Musorgsky cast himself in the actor's, interpreter's role vis-à-vis his text:

> The success of Gogolian speech depends upon the actor and his correct intonation. Well, I want to fix Gogol's place and the actor's too; that is, to say it musically in such a way as it could never be said otherwise, and say it as Gogol's characters would wish to speak.[119]

It is doubtful whether Musorgsky ever intended *Marriage* seriously for public performance. He meant his "scientistic" subtitle literally, and constantly referred to *Marriage* in his letters as "an étude for chamber trial" and his "crossing of the Rubicon."[120] Speaking on behalf of the Balakirev circle, Rimsky-Korsakov wrote to Musorgsky that "your work is terribly interesting, and not only because it undoubtedly contains excellent things; besides that, it ought to clear up a great deal."[121]

Carried away in his experimental zeal, Musorgsky worked on *Marriage* with great urgency and unprecedented speed. He carefully entered the date of completion of each scene in his manuscript, and so we learn that, having begun the project on June 11, 1868, Musorgsky had the first scene (up to the matchmaker Fyokla's entrance) completed by the twentieth. The second scene (up to Kochkaryov's arrival) was done by July 2; the third and shortest (up to Fyokla's exit) was done in a mere four days (finished July 6), and the whole act was complete in vocal score by the eighth.[122] Then followed a long period of rest, reflection, and the voluminous epistolary activity we have been sampling. Musorgsky jocularly accounted for the speed of his work by reference to the inclement weather at his country estate (Shilovo), which kept him indoors. Another partial explanation is that the formal freedom of the *opéra dialogué* technique, in which the composer follows a ready-made text moment by moment, worked to the advantage of the autodidact. What is rather extraordinary, in view of the empirical method Musorgsky adopted, is that he worked (by force of circumstance) without a piano.

Musorgsky treated Gogol's text with greater freedom than Dargomyzhsky had treated Pushkin's. Lines were often shortened and changed slightly, but never in such a way as to affect meaning. The most conspicuous and significant alterations involved the interpolation of a plethora of hyper-Gogolian exclamations and expletives. The composer clearly desired to reduce the formal lexical content of the play to a bare minimum, leaving the greater room for paralexical play, that is, for the "musical" qualities of speech. Thanks to Gogol's prose medium, he was able to do this without much harm to the original. Further in keeping with Musorgsky's aims is the abundance of expression marks and directions, most of them his own invention, with which he attempted to "fix the actor's place" by imparting a special, individual character to almost every line.

The music with which Musorgsky clothed Gogol's prose, while it is usually lumped together with Dargomyzhsky's, is in fact utterly different and in some ways opposed to the latter in style and aim. It *is* recitative; there is no discernable lyric impulse, not the slightest kinship to the art song or romance. The rhythm and melodic contour of the vocal parts are so completely formed by the patterns of speech that they lose all significance, indeed all coherence, when divorced from the lines upon which they were modelled. There are no vocal melodies as such in *Marriage*. Rather, there are terse, laconic musical "statements," which certainly do justice to Musorgsky's description of his work as the "exercise of a musician, or rather a nonmusician, desirous of studying and mastering the flexes of human speech, and giving it the same immediate, truthful exposition as is transmitted by that greatest of geniuses, Gogol."[123] To observe Musorgsky's procedure at its most characteristic, we need only examine the very opening of the opera, the little monologue of the bachelor nonhero, Podkolyosin (Ex. 5.23).

Ex. 5.23.   Musorgsky, *Marriage* (Moscow: Gosudarstvennoe muzykal'noe izdatel'stvo, 1933), pp. 1-3, voice only

The primary essential attribute of Russian speech that informs the setting of these lines is the even distribution of accents, whose tempo varies according to affect. Podkolyosin is lying on a divan, smoking his pipe. Accented syllables fall regularly on the half note in "rather slow" tempo, as befits his lethargic state. Unaccented syllables are arranged in formations of short equal values between the accented ones. Two peculiarities in the treatment of accent in relation to rhythm and meter set Musorgsky's naturalistic declamation apart from all previous Russian recitative. First, an unaccented syllable is never allowed to occupy the beginning of a beat, lest it introduce an un-Russian secondary accent. Where the beat is the quarter note and the accents fall on the half note, as here, this means that the intervening quarter-note pulses will be occupied by rests, as is uniformly the case in the present example up to the words, *"nádo zhenít'sia."* The resulting strings of little notes evenly crowded into the duration of one beat and interrupted by a rest at the beginning of the next, are instantly recognizable as "Musorgskian," and remained a permanent feature of his style. Later in the scene, when Podkolyosin becomes more agitated, the accents fall on the quarter notes, and so the necessity for rests is obviated except at normal points of punctuation.

The other typically Musorgskian peculiarity is the utter fastidiousness with which note values are assigned. Musorgsky's ear for the tempo of Russian speech was superbly refined. The rhythm of *"na dosúge,"* for example, decelerates (triplets followed by eighths), while the next word, *"podúmyvat',"* reverses the order of note values and accelerates. These rhythms are not arbitrary or subjective; Musorgsky is drawing from life. Similarly, the lengths of upbeats vary according to the natural model. The first syllable of *"odín"* and the unaccented word *"chto"* are set as sixteenth notes, while the word *"tak,"* even when unaccented, is usually drawled in spoken Russian, and hence is entitled to an eighth note.

Naturalism notwithstanding, Musorgsky exercises a careful control ("in the highest sense artistic") over the shape of the line, directing all tension to release on the explosive *"nádo zhenít'sia."* This phrase is the first since the initial word, *"vót,"* in which the first syllable is an accented one, and hence unpreceded by an upbeat. It therefore gives the impression of being delayed, and this reinforces the sense of climax. It is precisely here that the accents begin falling on the quarter notes, suggesting the anxiety the thought of marriage has aroused in the confirmed old bachelor.[124]

Melodic contour is also handled naturalistically, but with artistic control. The climactic *"nádo zhenít'sia"* is exceeded, as melodic highpoint, only by *"takáia skvérnost'"* (what a horror). These affective climaxes stand out all the more because Musorgsky has surrounded them with neutral utterances that reproduce the characteristic Russian monotone quite accurately. Podkolyosin's initial turgid deliberations are deftly transmitted by sing-song oscillation between a "reciting tone" of sorts (E-E$\flat$), which takes the strings of unaccented syllables, and a higher pitch area (A-A$\flat$) that divides the accented syllables alternately with the lower pitch. Where irony is called for *("zhivesh', zhivesh'"),* the contour of this oscillation is widened to grotesque sevenths. The intonational model is always provided by the spoken language, and throughout *Marriage,* melodic contour is dictated by the type of utterance—declarative, interrogative, exclamatory, etc.—that the music is called upon to reflect.

One of the most fascinating "antimusicalisms" in *Marriage* is the harmonic ambience. In this musical prose, tonal motion is kept purposefully static and ambiguous for long stretches, Musorgsky being highly sensitive to the tendency of functional harmony to periodize phrase structure. As in *The Stone Guest*, but with far greater reason, there are no key signatures from beginning to end. In the vocal parts this tonal ambiguity is reflected in an unprecedented reliance on augmented and diminished intervals, with chords of corresponding intervallic content in the accompaniment. These, of course, are the "unsingable" intervals shunned by conventional vocal composers, and hence all the more desirable if lyric atmosphere is to be avoided and the illusion of speech maintained in the presence of fixed pitch. Occasionally Musorgsky even manages a witty conflict between the general tonal stasis and firm tonal resolution, as in Podkolyosin's first exchange with his manservant Stepan. Podkolyosin's queries end on suitably "interrogatory" tritones. Stepan's monosyllabic responses resolve the tritones abruptly by interpreting the last note of the question as a leading tone (Ex. 5.24).

As we have seen, Musorgsky attached special importance to his role as "actor," and to the quest for renderings of Gogol's lines that were original and characteristic even as they conformed to the normative patterns governing all Russian speech. His letters are full of enthusiastic references to "fortunate acquisitions" of this sort. The composer was particularly proud of the way he had managed the "sudden change from laziness to exasperation" in Stepan's responses to his master's idiotic questioning.[125] This change was not indicated by Gogol; Musorgsky invented a stage direction for Stepan—"at the threshold, looking back at Podkolyosin with irritation"—and has him say the perfectly innocuous line, "He didn't say anything," the music given in Ex. 5.25.

Here the affective communication is entirely on the paralexical level, completely at variance with the surface content of the words, and yet in context both appropriate and true to life. The rhythm (particularly the enormous elongation of the unaccented second syllable of *"nichego"* and the rapid explosion that follows) and the contour spanning an entire octave (and including the highest note in all of Stepan's small part), reproduce the Russian intonation pattern associated with the specified affect. Later in the act, Musorgsky gives special attention to the words "grey hair," and Podkolyosin's "bear-like agitation" at its mention.[126] Here the operative factors are the rather complex rhythm Musorgsky devised to reproduce the pronunciation of the words *"sedói vólos"* in a state of agitation, and the way he keeps returning to it (and to the progression A-E♭) upon Podkolyosin's obsessive repetitions. The composer must have been pleased with the "acquisition" of the dissonant secundal harmony as well (Ex. 5.26).

Musorgsky was generally leery of literal repetition of music even where there was repetition of text. Repetitions must have a reason, after all, and the reason is usually one of emphasis. So when lines are repeated in *Marriage*, the

Ex. 5.24.   *Marriage*, p. 3

Ex. 5.25.   *Marriage*, p. 14

Ni-če --—- go ne go-vo-ril!
(He didn't say anything!)

Ex. 5.26.   *Marriage*, p. 34

I s če—go vdrug u men-ja ...   se-doj volos!
(And since when do I have   grey hair?)

Gde? ...   Gdež sedoj volos?
(Where?... Where's the grey hair?)

music attempts to convey an intensification through changing "nuances of speech," as Gervinus would have said. An example is Stepan's repetition of the line, "He's already begun the buttonholes," when Podkolyosin fails to hear him the first time. There could scarcely be a less "affective" line than this, so any affective illustration must relate beyond the line to Stepan's attitude toward his master. This we hear (the beginnings of his irritation) in the drawling rhythm and the really weird intervallic structure of the repetition. One can appreciate that Musorgsky saw the affective neutrality and "unmusicalness" of lines such as these as a decided advantage. In setting them, all the affect has to come from the music. From this point of view the composer has an even larger and more vital responsibility in setting prose dialogue than in a more normal, lyric context (Ex. 5.27).

Ex. 5.27.   *Marriage*, p. 4, voice parts only

The only "purely musical" shaping in the score occurs in the orchestra (or piano: Musorgsky never got around to the instrumentation), and it is minimal. There are signature tunes for each character (Podkolyosin in fact has two), which crop up at entrances and at points where the characters mention or indicate one another. But these never provide a frame for musical elaboration or development even to the extent that, say, the Statue's music does in *The Stone Guest*. There is only one spot in all of *Marriage* where the accompaniment performs even a nominal unifying role, and that is the matchmaker Fyokla's description of the bride's dowry. Musorgsky set this longest speech in the act as a sort of *moto perpetuo*. The "orchestra" rips along in steady, rapid triplets, while Fyokla maintains a characteristic parlando declamation above it. Her part is cast wherever possible in triplets to match the orchestra's, but this is not always possible, lest fidelity to speech rhythm be disturbed. Thus, her part is actually in a rather complex rhythmic relationship to the accompaniment, with frequent 2:3 and 4:3 superimpositions. During this little number, the only "detachable" one in the opera, Musorgsky seems to have been at special pains not to let the regularity of the accompaniment impose itself upon the vocal part; Fyokla's phrase lengths are irregularity itself.

For the rest, the independent role of the accompaniment is limited to an occasional ironic commentary on the text. When the matchmaker describes the bride, the orchestra plays a sickly sweet little phrase (Fyokla never sings it, though; nor does she sing her signature tune, which is the only folk-style melody in the score). When Kochkaryov describes the joys of wedded life to Podkolyosin, we hear another tritely sentimental snatch. At mention of children, the orchestra breaks into what Nadezhda Purgold, who accompanied the early run-throughs, described as some "amusing curlicues."[127] When Kochkaryov mentions a washtub we hear a splash; when he mentions boots we hear them thump (even though the pair he refers to is lying on the floor); mention of snuff calls forth an orchestral sneeze, and so on.

Apart from such trivia, however, Musorgsky appeared determined to frustrate and stifle "purely musical" invention to an extent that disconcerted even his fellow *kuchkists*. What his experiment seemed to "clear up" most conclusively was that realism, after all, had its limits. When evening gatherings at Dargomyzhsky's resumed after the summer of 1868, *Marriage* received the "chamber trial" Musorgsky awaited. It was read concurrently with *The Stone Guest* and by the same "cast": Musorgsky himself as Podkolyosin, Alexandra Purgold as Fyokla, Velyaminov as Stepan, and Dargomyzhsky himself, who, "interested in the highest degree, . . . copied out the part of Kochkaryov in his own hand and performed it with enthusiasm."[128] But Dargomyzhsky was heard to mutter at times that "the composer had gone too far," and as for the "leaders" of the group, Balakirev and Cui, "*Marriage* [was] only a curiosity with some interesting moments of declamation."[129] Borodin, only recently involved in the Balakirev circle, wrote to his wife that Musorgsky's work was "an extraordinarily curious and paradoxical thing, full of innovation and at times of great humor, but as a whole—*une chose manquée*—impossible to perform."[130]

Borodin alone raised the question of practicability, but it is a fair point. Musorgsky at times allowed himself to get so carried away with his quest for accuracy in the transcription of speech patterns that at times his writing became quite unrealistically complex.[131] Notations like the following pair from Fyokla's part hardly admit of accuracy in rendition at the indicated fast tempi (Ex. 5.28):

Ex. 5.28.   a. *Marriage*, p. 29

Ta—ka-ja už na to   vol—ja bo-ži-ja!

(Such is God's will!)

b.   p. 33

Da ved', sam že pri stal: že-ni ba-buška da i tol'ko!
(You'd come to me yourself: Find me a wife, a good woman, that's all I ask!)

These passages are actually written at the speed of the spoken language (at least!) and this, of course, was a cardinal difference between Musorgsky's objective naturalism and the subjective lyricism of *The Stone Guest,* where the tempo "is all moderato, adagio, lento, occasionally andantino."[132] But finding the correct pitches (and the examples will show that these are not always easy to find!) inevitably slows the singer down. In both recordings of the score[133] the singers fail to maintain Musorgsky's tempi, nor do they even come close to the difficult rhythm of the second example. What they do is actually deliver the line "as it comes" in speech, which may, it could be argued, have been precisely Musorgsky's intention. But if so, then his finicky descriptive notation is merely obfuscating. And did he not declare, after all, that his aim was to "fix" and control?

In any case, the general consensus was that Musorgsky's excessive naturalism not only limited, but distorted musical values. When Rimsky-Korsakov issued his edition of *Marriage* in 1908, he made reference in his foreword not only to the "harmonic excesses" one is accustomed to hearing complaints about in Musorgsky's work, but also to "melodic and rhythmic monstrosities." But these were not the result of arbitrary novelty-seeking, nor even of unfinished technique (to cite the usual explanations where Musorgsky is concerned). They lie at the very heart of the composer's ruling aesthetic aim. One cannot agree with Rimsky when he protests that "the author obviously did much that went against his own excellent ear" in his "youthful and understandable impulse for progress."[134] No, it was in fact that excellent, indeed far *too* scrupulous ear that dictated them. But then Rimsky-Korsakov adds that "in general, the whole piece should be performed as if *a piacere,* which I, who heard the author's own interpretation many times, . . . can testify with authority."[135] Why then Musorgsky's fiendish exactitude of notation on the one hand, or Rimsky's complaints (and corrections!) on the other?

What *Marriage* "cleared up" for Cui was that prose was not a suitable musical medium. He had suggested that it was—for comedy—in his 1868 article on *The Stone Guest*. But later, he attempted to show the opposite, using *Marriage* as his prize exhibit.

> For us [Russians], with our tonic prosody, this question [of prose in musical setting] is one of the first importance, and a libretto written entirely in prose would have to be considered a liability for music. Of course, in vocal music the structure of the text determines and explains the given structure of the musical discourse. But even in vocal music one should not ignore the finish and symmetry of musico-architectonic forms. This finish is dependent to a large degree upon the definite and sustained meter of these musico-architectonic lines. Sustained meter in music written to prose is unthinkable; can one imagine, after all, that the music be an entity entire unto itself, and text likewise, or that the text be applied to music written without regard for it?
>
> Musorgsky attempted to write *Marriage* to Gogol's prose without adaptation. He wrote the first scene of the first act [sic] and saw that this was an ungrateful and inartistic task. So the opera has remained unfinished. And bear in mind that in this case the task was considerably lightened by the fact that Musorgsky was a man of remarkable talent and a skillful versifier. Our tonic verses not only allow, but demand sustained meter—that is their chief significance for music. But from this it does not necessarily follow that individual brief phrases of recitative must necessarily be turned into verse. On the contrary, they will sound truer in prose. Thus the use of prose in libretti is altogether possible and permissible, but only as an exception.[136]

Cui's assumptions about Musorgsky's own ultimate attitude toward his own work seem a tendentious extrapolation, for Musorgsky's letters are full of plans for the opera's completion. But the cool reception given *Marriage* by the rest of the *kuchka* undoubtedly played a part in his decision not to pursue his experiment beyond the one act he had written. It is true that he had chafed a bit in a letter to Shestakova about the limitations his task had set upon his musical imagination—"*Marriage* is a cage in which I am imprisoned until tamed, and then on to freedom."[137] And it was right at the time of the first act's trial readings that Vladimir Nikolsky suggested that the composer look into Pushkin's *Boris Godunov*. Musorgky needed no second hint.[138]

But, Cui and Rimsky-Korsakov notwithstanding, Musorgsky never renounced his early work. Quite the contrary, he remained not only convinced of his experiment's essential validity, he thought of it as the key to his dramatic style. On Stasov's forty-ninth birthday (January 2, 1873), Musorgsky presented his friend with the manuscript, adding in his inscription:

> How do you please one dear to you? The answer comes without the slightest hesitation, as it does to all reckless hotheads: Give him of yourself. And so I do. Take my youthful work on Gogol's *Marriage*, look at these essays in musical speech, compare them with *Boris*, juxtapose 1868 with 1871 and you will see that I am giving you myself irrevocably.... I

cannot abide obscurity and think that for one sympathetic *Marriage* will reveal much with regard to my musical audacities. You know how *dearly* I value it, this *Marriage*.[139]

Musorgsky chose his recipient well—the single noncomposer in the *kuchka*. Stasov alone "went into ecstasies" when *Marriage* was tried out chez Dargomyzhsky,[140] and no wonder. He had no reason to keep account of the price Musorgsky had to pay as composer for his achievements. For Stasov the opéra dialogué was an ideal whose time had come, the irresistible wave of the future. "*Zukunftsmusik* is not Wagner," he wrote to his brother Dmitri, "but Dargomyzhsky and Musorgsky."[141] And Stasov gave strident, even intolerant expression to this onesided view at every opportunity, most particularly, where *Marriage* was concerned, in his biography-necrologue of Musorgsky (1881):

> This "experiment in dramatic music in prose" is as yet insufficiently appreciated. It seems to me that it will not remain without consequence and followers. The time will come to throw off prejudices as to the inevitable necessity of a "text in verse" for libretti, and when opera, like all future art, will become more and more realistic in the hands of Musorgsky's heirs, *Marriage* will receive its due place and evaluation. . . . At every step one encounters that astounding truth of expression, that closeness to ordinary everyday human speech which can only be considered a great step forward in the affairs of art, even when compared with Musorgsky's own highly original songs of 1866-68. Musorgsky here has come upon a completely new terrain: he has thrown off to one side all conventions of form and artistic formalism. He has pursued only the expression of his text and in this he went even further than Dargomyzhsky, who even in his *Stone Guest* retained "conventional, rounded forms" in a few instances. Fidelity to the text cannot go further than this. There is no convolution of thought, feeling, transient mood, mimetic movement, spiritual or even purely physical expression that Musorgsky's music has not here reproduced.[142]

But what Stasov did not reveal is that if *Marriage* was "insufficiently appreciated," it was mainly because he was sitting jealously on the manuscript the composer had given him. In fact, once in possession of the score, Stasov went to great lengths to keep it under wraps. He would show it to no one, and when, in 1893, he presented his great collection of manuscripts and letters to the Imperial Public Library, he wrote upon the title page of Musorgsky's work, in his own hand, that "I earnestly request that it not be given or shown to anyone during my lifetime."[143] And he lived until 1906. Despite his published assurances that Musorgsky's opera was "endlessly talented, true and original," then, Stasov took every measure to suppress the work and leave the reputation he created for it unchallenged by actual performance, let alone publication. As late as 1901, when A.M. Kerzin, a Moscow impresario who was considering producing *Marriage* (doubtless after reading Stasov's exuberant encomia) wrote to the aging custodian of the work requesting the score, he received an astonishingly worded refusal:

It is an unsuccessful thing, an exaggeration, a monstrosity and a blunder on Musorgsky's part, and to facilitate a new public and popular "failure" for Mursorgsky when our poor Modest already has such a host of enemies—this is something we cannot do.[144]

One can hardly doubt that these were Stasov's true feelings, and his public encomia a propagandist's pose. After *Marriage,* disillusion with its whole tendency was complete within the *kuchka.* "Enough of *The Stone Guest!*" was Rimsky-Korsakov's exasperated exclamation in 1898, as recorded by his son, "Music, too, is needed!"[145] And Cui, when he set about packaging *kuchkism* for export in 1878, wrote of *The Stone Guest*—which he nonetheless continued to tout as "the capital work, the keystone of the New Russian Operatic School"—that

As a general rule, it is better to avoid such texts by great poets, seductive though their intrinsic beauty may render them in the eyes of musicians, because they are not made for music. Moreover, one must take care to avoid as much as possible both philosophical excursions and the familiar language of everyday speech. A truly *lyric* text, lending itself favorably to the development of vocal melody, is, in sum, that which should be sought above all in a libretto.[146]

The words were Cui's this time, but Laroche had said them first. Opéra dialogué had been a flash in the pan. Far from establishing the norms of Russian opera's future course, Dargomyzhsky's example had succeeded in providing precedent merely for a small corner of the repertoire, decidedly off the mainstream of operatic innovation. When, in later years, composers occasionally returned to the genre, it was without the sense of reform and adventure that had surrounded *The Stone Guest* and *Marriage.* It had become a mere curiosity.[147]

All the remaining Russian dialogue operas were drawn from the same source as Dargomyzhsky's: "The Little Tragedies" of Pushkin. When that source dried up, so did the genre. This was natural, since only Pushkin's "Little Tragedies" provided verse texts of sufficient compression for operatic purposes. But Dargomyzhsky had plucked the plum from that collection; only *The Stone Guest* contained the makings of a really viable operatic plot. *Mozart and Salieri,* set by Rimsky-Korsakov in 1898, seeks to lend motivation to Salieri's rumored murder of his more gifted colleague. His lengthy soliloquies focus sharply on the relationship between genius and morality. He rails at the injustice of a fortune that could favor Mozart with such transcendent genius without requiring of him the kind of diligence and sacrifice that Salieri had expended in order to attain his lesser standing. Mozart's genius, then, was itself an immoral thing. But it is Salieri, the learned craftsman, who is capable of murder, while Mozart, the naive genius, claims that crime and genius are mutually exclusive.

This play, for all that its protagonists are musicians, and although Pushkin sprinkles it with indications for quotations of Mozart's music, actually has little to recommend it for operatic treatment. There are only two characters, both male, and a near total dearth of action. There is much philosophical discourse, but little exposition of emotion, which, after all, had been the original raison d'être of dialogue opera as Dargomyzhsky envisioned it. Rimsky's reasons for setting the work, at that, were far from those that had motivated Dargomyzhsky. He was remarkable candid about them in a letter to his friend and sometime librettist V.I. Belsky:

> This type of music (or opera) is an exclusive sort, and in most ways not a desirable one; I have little sympathy with it. I wrote this thing out of a desire to learn (don't laugh, that's very necessary)—that is, on the one hand, to find out how difficult it is, and on the other, and more importantly, because some sort of egoism had been provoked in me.... Can it be that recitative-arioso à la *The Stone Guest* is more desirable than real, free music?[148]

Rimsky even suggests, in his admittedly often disingenuous memoirs, that his work, dedicated as was inevitable "To the memory of A.S. Dargomyzhsky," was in fact an implied musical critique of the older composer, a professional's polemic against the inherent dilettantism of Dargomyzhsky's resolutely empirical and empathic method: "[*Mozart and Salieri*] approached most closely the manner of Dargomyzhsky in his *Stone Guest,* however without the form and modulatory scheme . . . being quite as much an accident as in Dargomyzhsky's opera."[149]

But then was it a close approach at all? Dargomyzhsky's "accidentalism" was the alpha and omega of the New Realism. In attempting to remove it Rimsky cut the opéra dialogué adrift from its aesthetic moorings. He thought to solve the problems of style and method thus created by a rather meretriciously "realistic" touch: taking his cue from the period setting of the play, he cast much of the music in an academically tinctured distillate of eighteenth-century style. This can be seen most conspicuously in the scurrying orchestral music accompanying Mozart's first entrance, but it pervades the vocal writing as well (Ex. 5.29).

The result is a kind of superficially "neoclassical" resurrection of the Mozartean recitative, replete with all its attendant clichés: *appoggiature,* "secco" chordal punctuation, etc. Rimsky's contribution to a genre frankly futuristic in its origins thus became a paradoxical glance into the past. Cui sensed this and wrote surprisingly unfavorably about Rimsky-Korsakov's purported contribution to the Dargomyzhskian tradition. In place of Dargomyzhsky's exalted lyric declamation, Rimsky had substituted plain recitative, which impoverished the genre to the point of futility.

> All the recitative phrases are of the most ordinary sort (they are distinguished only by the exquisite accompaniment, harmonizations, modulations). There is not a single characteristic

Ex. 5.29.   Rimsky-Korsakov, *Motsart i Sal'ieri* (*Polnoe sobranie sochinenii*, vol. 35, Moscow: Gosudarstvennoe muzykal'noe izdatel'stvo, 1950), p. 15

phrase that merges inseparably with its text in our memory.... The absence of such typical, musically substantial vocal phrases in *Mozart and Salieri* lends these scenes a notable aridity.[150]

But Cui's own *Feast During the Plague* (*Pir vo vremia chumy,* 1900) was scarcely an improvement. Rather, it testified further to the decline of the genre, and to the decline of its putative adherents' faith in it. Cui's choice of this one from the two remaining "Little Tragedies" offered him a return to the medieval, romantic atmosphere of *William Ratcliff,* and could be thought thus an inevitable choice. But musically, the *Feast* is an opera not less but far more conventional than the earlier one. Cui got around the question of "characteristic recitative" by begging it altogether. Everywhere, his effort to "reoperaticize" this most antioperatic of musico-dramatic genres is apparent. The composer seized every opportunity to impose standard musical formats upon Pushkin's verse: long speeches are treated not as freely lyrical ariosi, but as far as possible as strophic (!) songs, with the words squeezed into the most banal rhythmic stereotypes, even where the prosody must suffer. The center of gravity in the opera, as in the play, resides in the two songs, Pushkin's only wholly original addition to what was otherwise a fairly close adaptation of a scene from John Wilson's *The City of the Plague* (1816). Laroche's prediction had come true: the entire work hinges upon the "invitations to sing." No less than Rimsky-Korsakov, then, but in practically the opposite way, Cui missed the essence of the Dargomyzhskian reform. The form of *The Feast During the Plague* is not truly dictated by the words; Cui's treatment of Pushkin's play is in no way distinguishable from the arrangement and deployment of materials in a conventional libretto, save perhaps for its brevity.

The work that exhausted the "Little Tragedies," and thus effectively finished off the opéra dialogué in Russia, was Rachmaninoff's *Covetous Knight* (*Skupoi rytsar'*, op. 24, 1903-5). This was an anomalous work, the only opéra dialogué that did not proceed from Dargomyzhsky's original circle. Its stylistic allegiance is to Moscow, to Taneev and the Conservatory. The musical language is unabashedly symphonic, owing much to Tchaikovsky (though not to his operas!). The sustainer of the fundamental musical line and continuity is always the orchestra; the "accompaniment" was written first in this opera just as obviously as the vocal parts were the starting point and unchallenged shaper of the whole in all the rest of the operas comprising the genre. *The Covetous Knight* is thus perhaps the most thoroughgoing representative of a trúly indigenous Russian Wagnerianism (Rimsky-Korsakov's extensive but essentially unsymphonic employment of Leitmotiv in *Snegurochka* notwithstanding). As such it possesses interest, but can hardly be considered a part of any tradition spawned by *The Stone Guest*.

But while this tradition failed to become the main current of Russian operatic practice, the opera's prestige hung on and its influence, though attenuated, may be distinctly felt in many a *kuchkist* opera. Opéra dialogué could not hold on as a genre, however; not only did it not provide sufficient musical breathing room, it came to be viewed as an essentially "chamber" medium. At the beginning of the 1870s the imagination of the leading Russian composers was captured and held by the then-popular historical costume drama, a genre whose musical embodiment obviously demanded a breadth of conception and of staging inimical to the intimacy implied by the kind of psychological lyric drama *The Stone Guest* typified. But to the extent that within a grand-opera framework Russian composers continued to strive for psychological depth and immediacy of emotional depiction, the spirit of *The Stone Guest* lived on, providing the next generation not only with an ideal, but with new technical resources for its realization.

Notes

1. The most recent flurry of this continuing controversy was the result of the 1948 Resolution on Music of the Communist Party of the USSR. In keeping with its call for the reinstatement of the "lyrical basis" in opera, Dargomyzhsky's stock fell precipitously, and severe criticism of his work appeared in several influential books, among them Iarustovskii's *Dramaturgiia russkoi opernoi klassiki* (1952; revised, 1953) and Druskin's *Voprosy muzykal'noi dramaturgii opery* (1952). Yuri Keldysh's 1948 *History of Russian Music* emphasizes, in its treatment of *The Stone Guest*, "the stamp [it bears] of a somewhat hermetic and raffiné intellectualism" (pp. 465-66), and underscores, to the point where it emerges as a kind of warning, that the work—and works like it—can never achieve popularity. The otherwise inexplicable revival of Dargomyzhsky's early and inept grand opera *Esmeralda* in Leningrad (1949; revived again with unpublished episodes restored in 1958) seems to be related to this "revision" of his historiographical assessment. "Rehabilitation" of Dargomyzhsky's late work began in the 1960s, with the work of Mikhail Pekelis and Avram Gozenpud, and culminated in the revival of *The Stone Guest* at the Bolshoi Theatre in 1976.

2. Letter to Liubov Karmalina, November 30, 1859. Nikolai Findeisen, ed., *A.S. Dargomyzhskii: Avtobiografiia, pis'ma, vospominaniia sovremmenikov* (Peterburg, 1921), p. 63. This collection will hereafter be referred to as Darg:*APV*.

3. Darg:*APV*, p. 41.

4. Dargomyzhsky's opera had a Russian pedigree that went back into pre-Glinka times. Its native forebears include no fewer than four singspiels on the subject of *Lesta, the Dnepr Mermaid*, which were based in turn on the famous Viennese singspiel by Ferdinand Kauer, *Das Donauweibchen* (1798). These works, which had a direct influence on Pushkin's *Rusalka* (which was intended in the first instance as a singspiel libretto), are discussed (and the interrelationships between them clarified) in Seaman, *History of Russian Music*, pp. 143-46.

5. *Poetics of Music* (New York, 1947), p. 97.

6. Serov, *Izbrannye stat'i I*, p. 337.

7. Ibid., p. 323.

8. Ibid., pp. 324-25.

9. Dargomyzhsky to Serov, Autumn, 1856. Darg:*APV*, pp. 43-44. In another letter, Dargomyzhsky tells Serov that his own favorite among *Rusalka*'s scenes had been the fourth-act finale, which Serov for his part had criticized rather severely. It is the most "symphonic" of all the numbers in the opera and one in which Dargomyzhsky must have taken special pride for the additional reason that it had fallen to him to provide the ending to Pushkin's unfinished plot. In short, this was the most "Serovian" scene in the opera!

10. December 9, 1857. Darg:*APV*, p. 55.

11. It is easy to overdraw this connection. The chapter on Dargomyzhsky in Gerald Seaman's *History of Russian Music* starts right off with a misleading paragraph in which Chernyshevsky's name is rather patly dropped (p. 210), and my own "Realism as Preached and Practiced: The Russian *Opéra Dialogué*" (*Musical Quarterly* 56 [1970], no. 3, pp. 431-54), is perhaps the worst offender of all. One can actually go a long way toward accounting for Dargomyzhsky's "conversion" to realism without taking Chernyshevsky (or any other Russian thinker) into consideration, given the composer's interest in the latest French literary and artistic fashions. On his first trip abroad (1844-45), Dargomyzhsky was impressed above all with the Parisian vaudevilles for their topicality—their "bite and wit" as

he put it in a letter home (Darg:*APV*, p. 20). It is from this period that the earliest of Dargomyzhsky's "realistic" romances date. These satirical treatments of petty or low life subjects (à la Daumier, one might say) gradually overtook the conventionally romantic sentimental or exotic romance and come to dominate Dargomyzhsky's output by the end of his career. Two of the most famous and characteristic of these songs—"A Worm" *(Cherviak)* and "The Old Corporal" *(Staryi kapral)*—were written to texts by Béranger, further testimony to the French sources of Dargomyzhsky's realism. The translations were made by Nikolai Kurochkin, one of the editors of the satirical journal *Iskra,* with whose staff Dargomyzhsky was on very friendly terms during his final decade. (Another *"Iskrovetz"* was P.I. Weinberg, who wrote the text for another of Dargomyzhsky's notably "realistic" romances, "The Titular Counselor" [*Tituliarnyi sovetnik*].) *Iskra* was hospitable to the thinking of the "radical democrats," and thus at last a circle encompassing Dargomyzhsky and Chernyshevsky may be closed, if need be. For more on Dargomyzhsky's late romances and their connection with realistic tendencies and with *The Stone Guest, vide infra,* and also see Jennifer Baker, "Dargomïzhsky, Realism and *The Stone Guest," The Music Review* 37 (1976), no. 3, pp. 193-208.

12.   Nikolai Chernyshevsky, *Selected Philosophical Essays* (Moscow: Foreign Languages Publishing House, 1953), p. 346.

13.   Ibid., p. 347. This assertion allows Chernyshevsky to sum up as follows: "Instrumental music is imitation of singing, its accompaniment or substitute; and singing as a work of art is only an imitation of and substitute for singing as a work of nature. After this, we have a right to say that in music, art is only a feeble reproduction of the phenomena of life, which are independent of our strivings for art."

14.   Loc. cit.

15.   In one of his articles devoted to *The Stone Guest,* Cui was quite specific on the relationship of music to words and the contribution of each to the musico-dramatic totality: "Many have come to recognize that music and word can complement one another, that music can give to the expression of passion a depth, strength and fascination, and express an inner psychic state inaccessible to words. And conversely, the word imparts to music that definite meaning which by itself it does not possess" (Kiui, *Izbrannye stat'i* [Leningrad, 1952], p. 194).

16.   Although it is in operatic criticism that we encounter insistence upon representational accuracy most often, instrumental music was by no means exempt from the requirement (hence the strong preference for program music). The thoroughly positivistic view of emotion entertained by the Balakirev circle is well demonstrated by the well-known letter from Balakirev to Tchaikovsky on the "love theme" from *Romeo and Juliet:* "I will say one thing against this theme: there is little inner spiritual love, but only physical, passionate torment with even a hint of the Italianate. Romeo and Juliet were certainly not Persian lovers, but European. I do not know whether you understand what I mean. I always feel I lack the gift of words when I enter into musical criticism and so I try to clarify to some degree by example. I cite the first theme I come across in which, in my opinion, love is more deeply felt: the second theme in Schumann's overture, *The Bride of Messina.* The theme has its defects—sickly toward the end and a bit sentimental—but the basic feeling of which it is full is true" (December 13, 1869. Quoted from Sam Morgenstern, ed., *Composers on Music* [New York, 1955], p. 236).

17.   Darg:*APV*, p. 119. The reference to "some opera or other" is to *Rogdana,* a fantastic opera which was abandoned in its early stages (a few choral numbers survive). Other opera subjects Dargomyzhsky entertained between *Rusalka* and *The Stone Guest* included Pushkin's *Poltava* ("Mazeppa"), which had also briefly interested Serov, and "Ilia

Murometz" (after old *byliny*). See Mikhail Pekelis, "Dramaturgicheskie iskaniia pozdnego perioda," *Sovetskaia muzyka* (1980), no. 5, pp. 100-108. This short article, based on material intended for the third and last volume of the late author's definitive biography, *Aleksandr Sergeevich Dargomyzhskii i ego okruzhenie*, is a poignant reminder of what the student of Russian opera has been deprived of by Pekelis's death.

18. Quoted in Gozenpud, *Russkii opernyi teatr II*, p. 116.

19. Ibid., p. 114.

20. *Peterburgskii listok* (1865), no. 191. Quoted by Gozenpud, loc. cit.

21. Kiui, *Muzykal'no-kriticheskie stat'i I* (Petrograd, 1918), p. 349.

22. *Sanktpeterburgskie vedomosti* (1865), no. 100.

23. *Muzykal'no-kriticheskie stat'i, I* p. 356.

24. Rimsky-Korsakov, *My Musical Life* (New York, 1923), p. 19. This attitude is reflected, too, in Balakirev's early reaction to the news that Dargomyzhsky had embarked upon *The Stone Guest*: "I have no doubt that in his 'Don Juan' there will be uncommon things, but I am just as sure that of the real essentials, what should be certainly will not be" (January 30, 1866, to Stasov. *Perepiska I*, p. 151).

25. Darg:*APV*, p. 119. The actual beginning of work probably dates from the beginning of the year (see the preceding footnote).

26. Tsezar' Kiui, "Iz moikh opernykh vospominanii," *Izbrannye stat'i*, p. 535.

27. Darg:*APV*, p. 124. From this letter we learn that Dargomyzhsky was attracted to the subject of *The Stone Guest* as much as two years before *Rusalka*'s revival. But there is no reason to asssume that had he written the opera then it would have taken the radical form it did.

28. D.S. Mirsky, *Pushkin* (New York, 1963), p. 164.

29. *Russkii opernyi teatr II*, P. 277.

30. Tirso de Molina called his play *El Burlador de Sevilla y Convidado de Piedra*. It is true that the name resurfaced in Righini's opera (*Il Convitato di Pietra ossia Il Dissoluto*, 1777) and in Gazzaniga's (*Don Giovanni Tenorio ossia Il Convitato di Pietra*, 1787), not to mention a slew of minor settings and pasticci (see Alfred Loewenberg, *Annals of Opera*, 3rd ed. [Totowa, N.J., 1978], col. 358-59), but these were probably unknown to Pushkin. Mozart's *Don Giovanni*, on the other hand, was performed regularly in St. Petersburg beginning in 1797, with an important revival in Russian translation in 1828, that is, two years before the completion of *The Stone Guest* (cf. Loewenberg, col. 451). Loewenberg also mentions a Polish opera by Albertini (1783, text by Boguslawski probably translated from an Italian libretto).

31. Adapted from B. Kremnev, ed., *Opernye libretto* (Moscow, 1954), p. 43.

32. The completeness of Dargomyzhsky's fidelity to Pushkin has occasionally been challenged on account of those few discrepancies with the original text that exist in the opera. The biggest of these is the apparent excision of twelve lines in the final scene, which would seem crucial, for it is precisely here that Don Juan confesses to Donna Anna that she is the only woman whom he has really loved. A rather accusing letter to the editor (from one V. Karpov) was published in the *Sanktpeterburgskie vedomosti* (no. 59 [Feb. 29] 1872), almost immediately after the opera's belated premiere. The explanation, as Cui pointed out in his reply to Karpov, is a simple one: these lines were not included in the edition of the play from

which Dargomyzhsky worked, the one published in 1841 by Glazunov, Zaikin and Co. as part of the first collected Pushkin. Not only do we have the word of one of Dargomyzhsky's close associates (easily verified by a glance at the 1841 text), the point has been repeatedly made in the secondary literature, beginning with Porfiry Alexeevich Trifonov's long-standard monograph, "Aleksandr Sergeevich Dargomyzhskii, po ego avtobiografii, pis'mam i proizvedeniam" (*Vestnik Evropy* [1886], nos. 11-12), and most recently by Mikhail Pekelis's posthumous article in *Sovetskaia muzyka* (1980), no. 5 (see note 17 above). It is therefore strange indeed to find A. Tsuker, in the *same issue* of *Sovetskaia muzyka*, taking this apparent omission as his point of departure for a discussion of "*The Stone Guest* as a Musical Conception" (*Kamennyi gost' kak muzykal'naia kontseptsiia*, pp. 108-13), in an article that begins with an affectation of wonder that "no one has as yet turned his attention to this... most significant alteration." It is in fact no alteration at all. Dargomyzhsky's *additions* to the Pushkin text, on the other hand, are occasionally telling. He repeats the exclamations of the guests after Laura's second song, both for the sake of adding to the extremely small but "characteristic" comic role of the second guest, and because the acclamations of the guests provide the only opportunity for even the most minuscule "choral relief." The most conspicuous interpolations, of course, are Laura's songs. In the original, Pushkin merely indicated that "she sings" upon her guests' invitation. Dargomyzhsky took this opportunity to inject a little Spanish color and supplied Laura with two pretty romances of Iberian cast. The first of them, *Odelas' tumanom Granada (Granada was covered in mists)*, apparently to the composer's own words, was a song long in his portfolio, published as early as 1856. Its ritournelle is the tune Glinka had made famous as the first theme of his *Jota Aragonesa*. Laura's second song, *Ia zdes' Inezil'ia (Inezilia, I am here)* is a stylized serenade to words by Pushkin (after Barry Cornwall). Its ritournelle is employed as the curtain music for the opening of the scene at Laura's.

33.   This is not, however, to minimize the attractions of the Spanish setting for the composer. Not only was Spain a long-standing creative stimulus to the Russian artistic imagination, and not only had Dargomyzhsky himself written a number of Spanish romances (one of which he plundered for *The Stone Guest*), but perhaps most important, the volatile play of passion that made Pushkin's drama suitable for such musical treatment as Dargomyzhsky envisioned was notably "Southern."

34.   Paul Henry Lang, *Music in Western Civilization* (New York, 1941), p. 947.

35.   Alfred Einstein, *Music in the Romantic Era* (New York, 1947), p. 307.

36.   Dargomyzhskii, *Romansy i pesni*, ed., M. Pekelis, vol. II (Moscow, 1971), pp. 94-5, 117-8.

37.   Both passages quoted in Gozenpud, *Russkii opernyi teatr II*, p. 290.

38.   There are two additional departures from this norm. In the scene at Laura's apartment, the first guest has one phrase that contains some melismatic writing. That, plus the banal "tunefulness" of his musical expression in the style of a salon waltz, coupled with the dandified "Gallic" misaccentuation of the word "music" (the composer as actor again, and a witty touch indeed!) are all elements of characterization, in this case of foppery. Dargomyzhsky was extraordinarily careful to give even the most minor characters a distinct musical profile (Ex. 5.30).

The only other instance of nonsyllabic prosody in the entire opera—an isolated pair of notes on one syllable in one of Laura's speeches (p. 61 of the Muzgiz vocal score)—does not seem to have any special significance.

39.   All exceptions to this "rule" are found in Leporello's part, which retains certain elements of buffo style. His occasional syncopations (the placement of an accented syllable on a weak beat, or, conversely, the placement of an unaccented syllable on a strong one) suggest his blustering, somewhat ungainly manner (Ex. 5.31).

Ex. 5.30.   *The Stone Guest*, p. 40

Ex. 5.31.   a. *The Stone Guest*, p. 22

b.   p. 123

40.   Druskin, *Voprosy muzykal'noi dramaturgii opery*, p. 83.

41.   Druskin (loc. cit.) gives a useful sampling of typical Dargomyzhskian "periods," in which the tension between the rhythm of the spoken and "lyricized" language is well demonstrated. We reproduce it here, with some minor adaptations (the addition of accents, the changing of page references from the Bessel edition to the Muzgiz score of 1932). *Italicized* syllables are set as quarter notes (or larger values), all other as eighths or eighth-note triplets.

    1.   *Ty* dúmaesh' on stánet revnovát? *Uzh* vérno *nét.* (Don Juan, p. 116)
       [You think he'll be jealous? Not at all.]

    2.   *Vy* múchite menia, *ia* strákh kak liubo*pý*tna. (Donna Anna, p. 144)
       [You are tormenting me; I'm dying of curiosity.]

    3.   *Kak* dúmaesh', uznát' meniá nel'*ziá*?
       [What do you think? Will they recognize me?]

    4.   *Ni*któ iz nás ne vídyval e*ë* (Don Juan, p. 24)
       [None of us has ever seen her.]

    5.   *I* króv' neidët iz treugól'noi ránki. (Laura, p. 73)
       [His little three-cornered wound is not bleeding.]

6. *Ia* prinialá vas, don Di*égo*. (Donna Anna, p. 131)
   [I have received you, Don Diego.]

7. *Slëzy* s ulýbkoiu mesháiu kak ap*rél'*. (Donna Anna, p. 132)
   [Like April, I mix tears with a smile.]

42. This character's only other replique, "How she developed [her role], with what force!" is also set to the same silly phrase, as if to put a fine point on the Second Guest's obtuseness.

43. In this connection let us also call attention to the curtain music at the close of Act I: Laura and Don Juan retire to her bed chamber, while the orchestra replays Don Carlos's death—a masterly juxtaposition. Resonant moments like this, where the music contributes so tellingly to the development of the dramatic "theme," are all the justification the idea of "opéra dialogué" needs.

44. It ought perhaps to be reemphasized here that Dargomyzhsky and Serov knew each other's last operas only by reputation.

45. In his vocal score, however, Rimsky-Korsakov did scrupulously provide Dargomyzhsky's originals whenever he saw fit to amend them, either as footnotes or as appendices.

46. This consistency has made problems for some, in fact. As Aleksei Kandinskii quite rightly points out, very often dialogue scenes are carried by a kind of composite melodic thread, to which both parts contribute in turn. This impression is strongest in the love scenes between Don Juan and Donna Anna—that is, the most lyrical scenes in the opera, where the stylistic influence of the romance is at its height. "Not uncommonly," writes Kandinskii, "a succeeding vocal phrase will begin with the last tone of its predecessor, or will be built on the 'accrual' of a kindred intonation. In many instances the inner kinship of phrases belonging to different characters is conditioned by the natural logic of the general melodic line.... At times it even appears that the dialogue recitatives have been conceived as a single melody" (O. Levashova, Iu. Keldysh and A. Kandinskii, *Istoriia russkoi muzyki* I [Moscow, 1972], p. 573). This specific observation would tend to confirm the general one that Dargomyzhsky's goal was to "portray" Pushkin's verses sooner than his characters, and gives rise to the oft-heard complaint (voiced especially by non-Russians) that the various personages in *The Stone Guest* are insufficiently distinguished from one another (see, inter alia, Gerald Abraham, " 'The Stone Guest'," *Studies in Russian Music* [London, 1935], esp. pp. 74-76; Jennifer Baker, "Dargomïzhsky, Realism, and *The Stone Guest*," pp. 207-8). Despite the fact that the complaint is ill-founded, based as it is on a misapprehension of the composer's aims and methods (and, perhaps, on an insufficiently immediate apprehension of the text on the part of foreign critics), a sizeable literature in recent years has been devoted to refuting it. Most extended is G. Belianova, "Osnovnye zakonomernosti formoobrazovaniia v opere Dargomyzhskogo 'Kamennyi gost,'" in *Stranitsy istorii russkoi muzyki* (Leningrad, 1973), pp. 18-36, and most recent is the article by Tsuker cited in note 32 above. The task these authors have set themselves is to show how Dargomyzhsky, "establishing a unified system" (Tsuker, p. 109), succeeded in "achieving a wholeness of development thanks to the unity of the rhythmic-intonational sphere which characterizes each of the main characters throughout the entire opera" (Belianova, p. 21). In both cases, the argument is constructed out of a rather banal description of each character's musical profile as it emerges from Dargomyzhsky's setting (Don Juan's "impulsiveness," Donna Anna's "reserve," etc.). But nothing is demonstrated that cannot also be seen in terms of the empathic spontaneous reaction to the individual lines of text (or, if one prefers, the "impersonation of the actor") which was Dargomyzhsky's avowed method. What these articles seem to betray is a twentieth-century squeamishness about what Belianova rightly calls Dargomyzhsky's "inductive" methods (p. 36), and a determination to prove that he sought to control "the construction of large

sections" according to what Tsuker calls the overriding "musical conception," imagined as having been outlined as it were in advance of composition. This seems to be little more than willful "revisionism," with the aim of gaining respectability for the composer and the work in accord and latter-day notions of "responsible" compositional behavior. To oppose this view is by no means to deny Dargomyzhsky's surprising and remarkable success in achieving what Asafiev, in an encomium widely quoted by Soviet scholars, called "a cohesive, coherent scenic production" (Boris Asafiev, *Russkaia muzyka XIX i nachalo XX veka* [Leningrad, 1968], p. 18). The cohesion, however, is best accounted for (and seems all the more remarkable) in terms of the local devices Kandinsky notes (along with such other local devices as "ritournelles" and accompaniment figuration) than by making generalized assertions of higher organizing principles. To observe the apparent influence of criteria derived from Western academic analysis—the very height, after all, of "formalism"—on Soviet discussions of what is beyond doubt the very apogee of one kind of "realist" opera, is not without its irony.

47. Cited from the third edition (Leipzig, 1887), p. 208. The sentence was allowed to stand until the tenth edition (1922), revised after Riemann's death by Alfred Einstein. The 1902 Shedlock translation of the Riemann work gives the sentence as follows: "D. adopted more and more the principles of Wagner, until at last (and not to his advantage) he went further than the master." (*Dictionary of Music* by Dr. Hugo Riemann [London: Augener & Co., 1902], p. 178.) It may be of interest to note that Riemann gives credit in the preface to the first edition (reprinted in the third) to "Wjätscheslaw Rossolowski" of St. Petersburg as correspondent.

48. *A History of Russian Music* (New York, 1956), p. 62.

49. Darg:*APV*, p. 43.

50. *My Musical Life*, p. 101.

51. This is the antithesis—"opera as sung play" versus "opera as symphonic poem," that Joseph Kerman calls the two complementary sides of the "famous operatic 'reform' of the nineteenth century" (*Opera as Drama* [New York, 1956], p. 194). Apparently ignorant of *The Stone Guest*, or perhaps discounting its significance, Kerman ascribes the "sung play" position to Debussy, who made an experiment comparable to Dargomyzhsky's in *Pelléas*.

52. Kiui, *Izbrannye stat'i*, p. 199. On Russian aversion to "symphonism," cf. Musorgskii to Rimskii-Korsakov (August 15, 1868): "*Symphonic development in the technical sense* is just like German philosophy—all worked out and systematized. But lately that philosophy has been overturned by the English psychologists. When a German thinks, he *reasons* his way to a *conclusion*. Our Russian brother, on the other hand, starts with the conclusion and then might amuse himself with reasoning" (M.P. Musorgskii, *Literaturnoe nasledie I* [Moscow, 1971], pp. 106-7).

53. Stasov, *Izbrannye sochineniia II* (Moscow, 1952), p. 534.

54. Rimskii-Korsakov, *Polnoe sobranie sochinenii II*, pp. 47-48.

55. Ibid., p. 51.

56. Ibid., p. 54.

57. Kiui, *Izbrannye stat'i*, p. 483.

58. Ibid., p. 484.

59. Rimskii-Korsakov, op. cit., p. 56.

60. Stasov, loc. cit.

61. Stasov, *Izbrannye sochineniia III* (Moscow, 1952), p. 699, somewhat abridged.

62. Ibid., p. 703.

63. Rimskii-Korsakov, op. cit., p. 57.

64. Stasov, *Izbrannye sochineniia I* (Moscow, 1952), pp. 217-18.

65. *My Musical Life,* p. 90.

66. Druskin (*Voprosy muzykal'noi dramaturgii opery,* p. 89) has pointed out that Cui's prosody is a trifle more "naturalistic" than Dargomyzhsky's in one particular: the quarter-note upbeats with which Dargomyzhsky had rounded off "intonational periods" are dispensed with, and the rhythm of Cui's lines are therefore somewhat closer to that of normal conversational Russian. But the change is too subtle, and the duration of Cui's contribution too brief, for any incongruity of style to be noticeable.

67. See Stasov to his brother Dmitri, July 29, 1870. V.V. Stasov, *Pis'ma k rodnym I,* part ii (Moscow, 1954), pp. 55-56.

68. To K.N. Velyaminov, February 14, 1868. Darg:*APV,* p. 123.

69. The Purgold sisters were young admirers of Dargomyzhsky who made the acquaintance of the Balakirev circle through him. They were among the *kuchka*'s foremost early champions. Alexandra (married name Molas) was a well-regarded song recitalist who premiered many of the group's art songs and romances, and Nadezhda was of even greater practical help: it was she who made the piano reductions for publication of all the early *kuchkist* operas and orchestral pieces.

70. Quoted in Gozenpud, *Russkii opernyi teatr II,* p. 295.

71. Ibid.

72. Ibid., p. 297.

73. F. Komissarzhevskii, *Sovet molodym pevtsam* (St. Petersburg, 1882), pp. 18-19. Komissarzhevsky used scenes from *The Stone Guest* very extensively in his teaching, and staged student performances in the 1880s and 90s, considering that "mastery of Dargomyzhsky's recitative style was the best schooling in musical truth" (Gozenpud, p. 303). In a way even more noteworthy is the testimony of the great actor and director of the Maly Theater in Moscow, Alexander Lensky (1847-1908), who recalled that "when I was working on the role of Don Juan in Pushkin's *Stone Guest,* the late [Grigory] Lishin [composer, 1854-88] sang me Dargomyzhsky's *Stone Guest,* accompanying himself at the piano, and thanks to this I was able to assimilate some very apt intonations and clear up a great deal for myself" (A.P. Lenskii, *Stat'i, pis'ma, zapiski* [Moscow, 1935], p. 424).

74. Quoted in Gozenpud, p. 309.

75. Ibid., p. 311.

76. Kiui, *Izbrannye stat'i,* pp. 144-47. Dargomyzhsky called this article "an echo . . . of the whole Balakirev party" (to Karmalina, April 9, 1868. Darg:*APV,* p. 124). It was taken as such by Serov, too, who wrote as follows of *The Stone Guest* (which he did not live to actually hear) in his obituary for Dargomyzhsky: "Dargomyzhsky's ecstatic followers (lately he has been surrounded by a group of rather clumsy flatterers) would have us believe—they have announced as much in print—that the as yet unfinished opera *The Stone Guest* is *perfection itself* in all respects, the *nec plus ultra* of dramatic truth, and finally—*the last word in*

musical drama. . . . If we are talking about a work which is as yet in the portfolio, if it is written on a theme already realized in the celebrated opera of Mozart, if this is a work in the nature of a curious experiment, for the purpose of solving a certain problem, and at that, to a text not intended for music at all, then perhaps it will be permitted for us to remark that such anterior and at the same time comically inflated advertisements sooner hurt the as yet unknown work than work to its advantage. They call forth caution on the part of the public" (*Izbrannye stat'i II,* p. 54).

77.   Stasov, *Izbrannye sochineniia I,* p. 218.

78.   *Russkii vestnik* 87 (1887), p. 390.

79.   P.I. Chaikovskii, *Muzykal'no-kriticheskie stat'i* (Moscow, 1953), p. 149.

80.   P.I. Chaikovskii, *Dnevniki 1873-1891* (Moscow-Petrograd, 1923), p. 215.

81.   *Russkii vestnik* 87 (1887), p. 385.

82.   Ibid., p. 389.

83.   *Vestnik Evropy* (1872), no. 4, pp. 883-84.

84.   Ibid., p. 885.

85.   Ibid.

86.   Ibid.

87.   Ibid., p. 886.

88.   Ibid., p. 888.

89.   Ibid., p. 893.

90.   Larosh, *Sobranie muzykal'no-kriticheskikh statei I* (Moscow, 1913), p. 112.

91.   Quoted by Stasov in "Tormozy novogo russkogo iskusstva" (1885). *Izbrannye sochineniia II,* p. 680.

92.   *Vestnik Evropy* (1872), no. 4, pp. 894-95.

93.   Ibid., p. 895. Laroche chooses to ignore the obvious fact that both of the "invitations to sing" in *The Stone Guest* were Pushkin's idea, not Dargomyzhsky's. They are motivated entirely aptly and naturally, and even possess an "excuse" beyond mere entertainment: the first song, whose words are putatively the work of Don Juan, is the pretext for mentioning his name and arousing Don Carlos's anger; the second is the means by which Laura attempts to assuage that anger.

94.   *Golos* (1872), no. 153.

95.   Letter of March 27/15, 1872. *Severnyi vestnik* (1888), no. 10, p. 166.

96.   May 26/14, 1872. Ibid., p. 167.

97.   Kiui, *Izbrannye stat'i,* p. 205.

98.   Musorgsky to Stasov, January 2, 1873. Musorgskii, *Literaturnoe nasledie I,* p. 144.

99.   *Nikolai Gogol* (New York, 1959), p. 158.

100. The phrase turns up in several letters from Musorgsky to Stasov. It was chosen by James Billington, fittingly enough, as the emblematic epigraph for his treatment of the 1860s and 70s in his "interpretive history of Russian culture," *The Icon and the Axe* (New York, 1966).

101.   Chernyshevsky, *Selected Philosophical Essays*, p. 346.

102.   To Liudmila Shestakova, July 30, 1868. *Literaturnoe nasledie I*, p. 100.

103.   *Literaturnoe nasledie I*, p. 270.

104.   Musorgsky may have also intended a nod in Chernyshevsky's direction. Both Virchow and Gervinus are mentioned in the latter's "nihilistic" novel of 1862, *What Is To Be Done?* (cf. the Vintage edition, trans. Benjamin Tucker [New York, 1961], pp. 176-77, 223). From 1865 to 1868 Musorgsky had lived in what was known as a "Chernyshevsky commune," a living arrangement modelled on those described in the novel.

105.   *Music in the Romantic Era*, p. 314. Einstein probably refers to Gervinus's magnum opus, the five-volume *Geschichte der poetischen National-Literatur der Deutschen* (1835-42).

106.   *Sanktpeterburgskie vedomosti*, January 31, 1867. Kiui, *Izbrannye stat'i*, p. 83.

107.   *Händel und Shakespeare* (Leipzig, 1868), pp. 201-2. Henceforth, simple page references to this work will be given in the text.

108.   "Der älteste Erforscher der Kunstgesetze hat den Satz aufgestellt, dass alle Künste, und so auch die Musik, dem Wesen nach auf Nachahmung beruhen" (*Händel und Shakespeare*, p. 3).

109.   This, too, may have found echo in Musorgsky's autobiographical sketch, where Palestrina is listed among the "artist-reformers" who alone have the right to "lay down laws for art" (*Literaturnoe nasledie*, p. 270).

110.   A major portion of Gervinus's book is given over to a consideration of "Die Forderungen an eine geistig begründete musikalische Kunstlehre," with subsidiary headings embodying an exhaustive classification of feelings and emotional states (pp. 203-44).

111.   "Der entscheidene Schritt, der zu dem Grössten und Tieffsten in der Gefühlswelt und der Tonkunst zugleich führte, geschah erst mit dem entschlossenen Übertritt auf die Bühne, wo Dichter und Tondichter ihre Chöre und Sprechgesänge und lyrischen-dramatischen Arien vor eine Zuhörschaft tragen, welche die Gegenstände jener gewaltsameren Seelenbewegung lebendig vor sich sieht... " (*Händel und Shakespeare*, p. 247).

112.   To Cui, July 3, 1868. *Literaturnoe nasledie I*, p. 98.

113.   Carefully distinguished, be it noted, from the more active *Stimmungsgefühle*. See *Händel und Shakespeare*, pp. 225-34.

114.   Cf. the letter cited above (note 10).

115.   Cf. Gervinus on interjections: "Das O, zur Interjection geworden, empfängt wie A und Ach von dem Empfindungsakzente jeden Ausdruck der Freude wie des Schmerzes" (*Händel und Shakespeare*, p. 19).

116.   Cf. Taruskin, "Realism as Preached and Practiced," pp. 445-46.

117.   To V.V. Nikolsky, August 15, 1868. *Literaturnoe nasledie I*, pp. 102-3.

118.   July 30, 1868. *Literaturnoe nasledie I*, p. 102.

119.   To Shestakova, July 3, 1868. *Literaturnoe nasledie I*, p. 100.

120.   Ibid.

121.   August 17, 1868. A.N. Rimskii-Korsakov, ed., *M.P. Musorgskii: Pis'ma i dokumenty* (Moscow, 1932), p. 464.

122. See the description of the MSS in the foreword to the vocal score, ed. Pavel Lamm (Moscow, 1933), p. xii.

123. To Arsenii Golenishchev-Kutuzov, August 15, 1877. *Literaturnoe nasledie I*, p. 232.

124. A comparison of Gogol's text and Musorgsky's here will show that the process of shaping was an altogether deliberate one, and that Musorgsky's changes in the text were anything but capricious:

Gogol	*Musorgsky*
Vot kak nachnësh' edak odín na dosúge,	Vot, kak nachnësh' etak odín na dosúge,
podúmyvat', tak vídish' chto nakonéts	podúmyvat', tak vídish', chto
tóchno núzhno zhenít'sia.	tóchno,—nádo zhenít'sia.

Musorgsky omits the word *nakonéts* (finally), apparently for the reason that if he had included it, the word *tóchno* would have had to be set as an accented syllable after a rest, unpreceded by an upbeat. This would have paralleled, and hence mitigated the effect of the climax (*nádo zhenít'sia*). The replacement of *núzhno* by its near-synonym *nádo* was apparently also in the interests of climax, since *nado* is the stronger word, and is invariably given a strong accent in Russian speech.

125. To Cui, July 3, 1868. *Literaturnoe nasledie I*, p. 98.

126. *Literaturnoe nasledie I*, p. 97.

127. She further recalled that when singing the part of Kochkaryov at a *kuchkist* soirée, at this place Dargomyzhsky "was always obliged to stop, he was so overcome with laughter, and he said to me, 'You're playing some sort of symphony there, you're getting in my way'" (Jay Leyda and Sergei Bertensson, *The Musorgsky Reader* [New York, 1947], p. 124).

128. *My Musical Life*, p. 89. Dargomyzhsky's copy survives in the Saltykov-Shchedrin Public Library in Leningrad, and was collated by Lamm in preparing his critical edition (cf. his preface, p. xii).

129. *My Musical Life*, pp. 90-91.

130. September 25, 1868. A.P. Borodin, *Pis'ma*, ed. S. Dianin, vol. I (Moscow, 1928), p. 109.

131. This had been a matter of concern, apparently, from the very beginning, for Musorgsky wrote to Cui from the country (July 3, 1868) that "guided by your comments and Dargomyzhsky's, I... have considerably simplified what I showed you" (*Literaturnoe nasledie I*, p. 97). Reference is to the first scene, which had been begun in St. Petersburg before Musorgsky's departure.

132. Larosh in *Muzykal'nyi svet*, quoted in Gozenpud, *Russkii opernyi teatr II*, p. 291.

133. Oceanic OCS 36 (orch. Duhamel, cond. Leibowitz; reissued on Olympic 9105) and Westminster OPW 1202 (cpl. and orch. Ippolitov-Ivanov, cond. Kovalëv).

134. Rimskii-Korsakov, *Polnoe sobranie sochinenii II* (Moscow, 1963), p. 72.

135. Reprinted in the 1934 edition of the Ippolitov-Ivanov version of the vocal score.

136. Kiui, *Izbrannye stat'i*, p. 427.

137. *Literaturnoe nasledie I*, p. 100.

138. After *Marriage*'s publication in 1908 (ed. Rimsky-Korsakov) and its first performance in that year under Arkady Kerzin's auspices (Moscow), there were a number of orchestrations made of Musorgsky's act, and at least one completion of the score. The latter was the work

of Ippolitov-Ivanov, commissioned in 1931 by the USSR radio. Musorgsky's act has been orchestrated by Alexander Gauk (1917), by Antoine Duhamel, and by M. Béclart d'Harcourt. Both Lamm (preface to the critical edition, p. xi) and Loewenberg (*Annals of Opera,* 3rd ed., col. 1292) refer to an orchestration by Ravel (ca. 1923), but this appears to be an error. In 1946, Alexander Grechaninov made his own setting of the entire three-act play, in a style very far from Musorgsky's. This was first performed under Boris Goldovsky at the Berkshire Music Festival (third act only) and premiered officially in Paris in 1950. For the record, operas on Gogol's play have been written by two Czech composers: Jaroslav Jiránek and Bohuslav Martinu (1953). Somewhat ironically, Cui became interested late in life in the prospect of completing *Marriage,* following his completion of *The Fair at Sorochintsy,* but decided that the task was "utterly unthinkable; I don't even want to try" (To M.S. Kerzina, December 12, 1916. Kiui, *Izbrannye pis'ma* [Leningrad, 1955], p. 471).

139.   *Literaturnoe nasledie I,* p. 144.

140.   *My Musical Life,* p. 90.

141.   July 29, 1870. Quoted from Vladimir Karenin (pseud. for Varvara Komarova-Stasova), *Vladimir Stasov* (Leningrad, 1927), p. 395.

142.   Stasov, *Izbrannye sochineniia II,* p. 194.

143.   Cf. the description of the MS in Lamm, foreword to the critical edition, p. xii.

144.   "17 pisem V.V. Stasova k A.M. Kerzinu," *Muzykal'nyi sovremennik* (1916), no. 2, p. 14.

145.   Andrei Rimskii-Korsakov, *N.A. Rimskii-Korsakov: Zhizn' i tvorchestvo,* part IV (Moscow, 1937), p. 127.

146.   César Cui, *La musique en Russie* (Paris, 1880), p. 108. The contents of this book had appeared two years earlier as a series of articles in the *Revue et Gazette Musicale.*

147.   Still, it should be remembered that the earlier version of *Boris Godunov* (1869) was virtually identical to *Marriage* in approach and method. And when Musorgsky's "chose manquée" was finally given a public hearing in St. Petersburg in February, 1909, at one of Karatygin and Kryzhanovsky's "Evenings of Contemporary Music," in the audience was the 17-year-old Serge Prokofiev, whose early operatic outlook was strongly shaped by the experience of hearing it. (See my "Tone, Style and Form in Prokofiev's Soviet Operas: Some Preliminary Observations," forthcoming in *Studies in the History of Music II* [New York: Broude Bros., 1982].) Stravinsky heard *Marriage* even earlier, at a private performance at Rimsky-Korsakov's home on January 4, 1906 (see V.V Iastrebtsev, *Vospominaniia o N.A. Rimskom-Korsakove II* [Leningrad, 1960], pp. 370-71). A trace of its influence may be found in *Le Rossignol:* he recalled (*Memories and Commentaries* [Garden City, 1960], p. 125) having written himself a note while at work on his opera, "Why should I be following Debussy so closely, when the real originator of this operatic style was Musorgsky?" The influence of the published score spread even beyond the borders of Russia. It prompted Ravel to set Franc-Nohain's farce *L'Heure espagnole* to music in a similar idiom of naturalistic recitative. Ravel referred to Musorgsky's work as his opera's "only direct ancestor" in a manifesto published in *Le Figaro* in 1911 (see Arbie Orenstein, *Ravel: Man and Musician* [New York, 1975], p. 55).

148.   Quoted in Andrei Rimskii-Korsakov, op. cit., p. 118.

149.   *My Musical Life,* p. 310.

150.   Kiui, *Izbrannye stat'i,* pp. 496-97.

6

"Kuchkism" in Practice: Two Operas by
César Cui

During the years that separated Dargomyzhsky's demise and *The Stone Guest*'s posthumous premiere, the "New Russian School," which had adopted the recently deceased as its patron saint and made his work a bible, had its own formal operatic debut with *William Ratcliff*. This was César Cui's third opera, but the first by him or any of the Five to achieve production. What historical significance the work possesses is partly due to its fortuitous chronological primacy. But over and above that, *Ratcliff* is a work of considerable, albeit not entirely intrinsic, interest. In Cui, who like Serov was a professional critic, we have another opportunity to compare operatic preachment with practice. Unlike Serov, Cui was no maverick but spoke for a then monolithic group. The music of *Ratcliff* was taken as a manifesto of *"kuchkism"* on a par with the pronouncements of "***" (Cui's journalistic siglum) in the *Sanktpeterburgskie vedomosti*, and was so regarded by Cui's confreres themselves. Musorgsky, speaking on behalf of the Balakirev circle, confided to Cui his conviction that *Ratcliff* was "as much ours as yours."[1]

César Cui, of course, presents a famous paradox when viewed from our present historical perspective. What was this man doing in the *kuchka*, one can't help wondering, this miniaturist among epic bards, this Francophile among "nationalists," this precious aesthete among iconoclasts? He shares so little, it seems, in the Mighty Five's historical image, having in common with the rest of them only their nonprofessional, autodidact status and concomitantly limited technique. But in the 1860s the perspective was quite the contrary. After Balakirev himself, Cui was the senior member of the group.[2] In all the discussion and debate that marked their private gatherings, the most important questions had to do with opera—in particular, with operatic "forms"—and here Cui's voice carried special weight, since he was the first of them, and for a long time the only one, to put theory into practice. The very first *kuchkist* "private spectacle" was a work of Cui's, a one-act opéra comique entitled *The Mandarin's Son* (*Syn mandarina*, 1859). Nor was even that Cui's first operatic attempt. As early as 1857-58 he had produced a two-act opera on

Fig. 6.1   César Cui around the time of *Ratcliff*'s première

Pushkin's *Prisoner of the Caucasus (Kavkazskii plennik)*, which he had submitted for performance to the Mariinsky, and which was at first accepted for inclusion in the 1859 season at the contralto Latysheva's bénéfice. But the performance was cancelled after the first orchestral rehearsal, so inadequate and amateurish was Cui's instrumentation.[3] Though a failure, this attempt brought Cui much prestige within his circle; it made him, in Rimsky-Korsakov's words, their "operatic composer par excellence."[4] And we have seen how Musorgsky, at work on *Marriage,* regarded Cui—and not Balakirev, who never wrote an opera despite many plans and projects—as his mentor alongside Dargomyzhsky.

After 1864, when Cui began his journalistic career, his prestige within the Balakirev circle was matched by his notoriety without. The identity of "***" was always an open secret to the musical cognoscenti, and for all that Balakirev was the leader and teacher of the *kuchka,* to the world at large the "New Russian School", was synonymous with the name of its tribune. Even Dargomyzhsky, in his single extant letter to Musorgsky, addressed the latter as a "Cui-composer."[5]

The articles with which Cui made not only his own reputation but that of his group were primarily concerned with opera, which he (along with the rest of the world at the time) regarded as the most important musical genre. They reveal a quasi-dialectical view of operatic history as a linear progress toward freedom of form, the cardinal condition of musico-dramatic truth. A characteristic example of this evolutionary view is a very early and surprisingly favorable essay on Meyerbeer (published May 5, 1864), whom Cui viewed in dialectical relationship with Rossini, the chief representative of the detested Italian taste according to which "music is not the expression of feeling, but...a pleasant tickling of the ear."[6] To this depraved hedonism Meyerbeer opposed "German weightiness, if not German profundity," and offered, in his French grand opéras to Scribe texts, a music that was

> crude and decorative, but at least strove for dramatic truth and was distinct from Rossinian vocalizing. Meyerbeer's operas are no longer concerts in costume—they are dramas; there is little humanity in them and little soul, but nonetheless we perceive that on the stage stand something other than puppets and buffoons. In the music itself...there is discernable a desire to impart a musical identity to the various characters and to strengthen with music the impression the drama itself makes upon the viewer....It would be silly to pay unconditional homage to Meyerbeer today; his music and the sensibility it expresses are too crude and devoid of poetry. But without him, perhaps, the public would be even more hostile to, and even more inclined to shun the operas of Schumann and Wagner, in which we see the extreme expression of the contemporary operatic trend.[7]

In another article written during his first year of critical activity, Cui elaborately compares four schools of operatic composition—Italian, French, German and Russian—as he perceived them at the time. Here he gives a more detailed description of the "contemporary operatic trend" (identified with the German school) toward which Meyerbeer had pointed the way.

> German music is profoundly suffused with feeling, often passing over into sentimentality, and with Wagner, into sensuality. It seeks through its magical sounds to tear the listener from the real world and transport him to the world of imagination. Every sound, every note is called forth by the situation of the characters. There are no boundaries and designated places for recitative or for lyricism; both the one and the other pour forth freely from the breasts of the protagonists according to the play of passions. If we add to this the fact that [German] musical ideas are frequently imbued with national character, it will be evident how beautiful, how ideal is the general tendency of German opera.[8]

But already the downgrading of Wagner begins:

> Wagner is almost everywhere unequal to his task.... His music suffers from contrivance and unnaturalness; in it one senses impotent desires aroused by an unbalanced imagination. One senses an essential feebleness, poorly concealed by swagger and outward brilliance. With his farfetched, morbid harmonies and overbright orchestration he endeavors to hide the poverty of his musical thought much as an old man might hide his wrinkles under a thick layer of powder and rouge![9]

This attack on Wagner, based mainly on concert performances (including Wagner's own the year before) rather than on staged productions (Cui first heard *Lohengrin* complete in 1868; *Tristan* not until 1898!), is mostly one more tendentious diatribe of a kind familiar by now. Its primary motivation is not difficult to locate in the hardening antipathy between the *kuchka* and Serov, which broke into open polemical warfare as soon as Cui began to intrude upon the terrain of serious criticism, which had been Serov's undisputed preserve. The systematic underrating of Wagner was one facet of the *kuchka*'s refusal to recognize Serov the composer. But there were other sides to it as well. By disposing of Wagner, Cui was able to point to the contemporary "decrepitude" of German opera (its other outstanding protagonists in the nineteenth century—Weber, Marschner, and Schumann— being safely dead) and clear the way for the assumption of leadership by the Russian school, more specifically, the "New Russian School," that is, the *kuchka,* and most particularly, himself. In Cui's discussion of the character of Russian opera, the protagonists named—Verstovsky, Glinka, Dargomyzhsky—were either dead or inactive at the time of writing, and yet Cui averred that "[In Europe] music has outlived its time, while with us it is only beginning to live," and went on to prophesy, "let there only appear among us talented men (and how can they not appear!) ... and music will receive from us its renewal and begin a new era."[10]

Cui's treatment of the Russian school is notable above all for its brazen exclusion of Serov from consideration or even mention, a full year and more after *Judith*'s impressive premiere. Nor is this the only instance of bizarre selectivity. His discussion is generally prescriptive rather than descriptive, sooner reflecting ideals and desiderata than facts. National character is conspicuous by its absence from the list of Russian operatic virtues, save perhaps by implication when Cui says of Russian opera that it is "closer to the German than to the others." Beyond that, Cui notes the Russian penchant for recitative, and its unique use: "With us, the strongest outbursts of passion and emotion are expressed in a recitative of utterly unique character, unlike any other. It is full-blooded, melodic, expressive."[11] The context makes it clear that it is to Glinka's work that Cui refers, presumably to the scene in the woods from *A Life for the Tsar*, or to Ruslan's apostrophe to the battlefield. These are scenes of undeniably "declamational" character, but it would be difficult to describe either of them as recitative in the normal sense. Similarly odd are Cui's remarks on the progressive Russian use of the chorus: "This is no longer a mindless crowd gathered for the mere purpose of singing; this is a collection of people who act consciously and on their own initiative; from this, music gains a new element of profundity and breadth."[12] Here again, Cui ostensibly has Glinka in mind. But it would be hard to maintain that Glinka's choruses were other than decorative. His Polish soldiers, a simplistic choral multiplication of a single character, could hardly be counted among Glinka's happier dramatic strokes, and his choral masterpiece, the Epilogue to *A Life for the Tsar*, was, for all its outstanding musical qualities, precisely the kind of "crowd gathered for the purpose of singing" that Cui claims Russian opera has outgrown. True dramaturgical integration of the chorus had been attempted in only one Russian musical drama as of 1864, and that one belonged to the unnameable name. There can be no doubt that Cui sought to claim the merits of *Judith* for the Russian school without giving credit where it was due.

Nor, in the end, was this simply a matter of pique or jealousy. The *kuchka* was reluctant to acknowledge Serov's accomplishments even when his results approached their ideals. For Serov proceeded to these results from an aesthetic stance the New Russian School found inadmissable because it denied their cardinal principle of equality of music and text. The ultimate expression of the *kuchka's* disapproval of Serovian denigration of text in favor of music—disingenuously (they thought) masked by his insistence upon the identity of composer and librettist—were Cui's scathing essays on *Rogneda*, which we have already examined at length.

To recapitulate briefly, Cui asserted categorically with reference to *Rogneda*—and continued to maintain throughout his career—that for a true marriage of text and music to take place, the libretto must precede the music. Vocal music had to be fashioned within an explicit dramatic, conceptual, and—not least—verbal context. Because "combinations of tones are far richer in possibilities than combinations of words, since tones do not possess the rigidly defined meaning of words," the creation of music to a given text offered the composer far greater freedom and inhibited his fantasy far less than the opposite situation would inhibit the librettist. Cui could not imagine good spontaneous verse written over ready music:

> Because of the vagueness of musical mood, the poet would have to solve an uncertain equation with many unknowns.... Instead of sonorous, handsome verses, one would end up in most cases with prose, and clumsy prose at that.[13]

Thus, while words could inspire the musician, music could only constrain the poet. The usual result, as evidenced by numerous passages in Serov's operas, was a skewed proportion between imposing musical dimensions and the paltry quantity of text on which the music "dangles like a robe on a hook." Cui cautions that "the text should not have to be artificially extended [to fit the music] by means of repetitions of stanzas, lines or individual words,... distorting the artistic elegance of the verses' form."[14] On the contrary, such form must be respected by the composer even to the extent of observing the text's punctuation, to say nothing of its meter.

But just as Cui could not accept Serov's shaping of musical drama according to overriding considerations of purely musical contrast, we have seen that he came to view the opposite extreme—the notion that the criteria of opera could be made to coincide with those of the spoken drama—as equally onesided, though *The Stone Guest* ever remained for him a summit of Russian operatic achievement. Dargomyzhsky's exemplary success was due to the happy and unrepeatable coincidence of one particular composer's creative strengths with the specific demands of his task. Musorgsky's *Marriage* had proved that dominance of text over music was just as real a danger as the more common dominance of music over text. Cui often complained that too many composers "seek in poetry not a friend, not a support, not their equal, but a subordinate and a servant."[15] But neither ought it be the unconditional master. In any case, Dargomyzhsky had advanced only one of the elements—"melodic recitative"—that the *kuchka* prized in the Russian operatic legacy. In his theoretical essays, Cui sought a doctrine of operatic procedure that would be more inclusive, particularly one that would allow for the development of Russian predilection for monumentality, expressed in "dramatic" choral scenes:

> An opera in which the movement of the people would unite directly with the action of the principle characters of the drama, where the people would be depicted in colors as vivid and true as those Dargomyzhsky employed to animate each of the individual figures of his opera, would make an even more profound impression than the beautiful creation of dramatic music we call *The Stone Guest*.[16]

This ideal is based on a kind of opera that in the 1870s became the *kuchkist* favorite: an intense personal drama unfolding against a rich historical or genre background. The description also fits such a work as *The*

Power of the Fiend—which opera Cui after all did at least recognize as congruent in aims with those of the New Russian school—and has its prototype in *A Life for the Tsar*. Cui thus seems to suggest that it was on Glinka, the more inclusive talent, rather than on Dargomyzhsky, that the *kuchka* ought most profitably to build. Dargomyzhsky's accomplishments were to be assimilated as an indispensable part of the *kuchkist* equipment, but if accepted as the alpha and omega of Russian operatic practice, they could only lead Russian opera into a cul-de-sac.

For the realization of his operatic ideal, Cui put forth a doctrine of operatic form that purported to be all-inclusive, encompassing everything from the simplest to the most complex structures, from the freest declamation to the strictest canon or fugue. The all-governing principle in this moderate and reasonable platform was the apparent platitude that *"vocal music must correspond strictly to the meaning of the text."*[17] As a statement to which objection is impossible, it seems an empty one. But there is one very significant element: the use of the word "text," rather than the narrower "word" preferred by Dargomyzhsky (let alone Musorgsky's "speech"). Situation is once again the prime formal determinant, as it had been with Serov. (Dargomyzhsky's emphasis upon the individual word had made only one "form" possible.) But for Cui, the words of the libretto are no mere veneer, a "medium for music" to be despised and violated as the composer sees fit, but an integral part of the "situation," to be treated with respect. "Our New School," he wrote, outlining his middle-of-the-road position, "is averse neither to ensembles nor to choruses, so long as the ensembles be reasonably motivated and do not hold up the course of the action, so long as the choruses depict not choristers, but the people in all their animation and passion."[18]

The next step was to prescribe which forms were suitable when. This Cui attempted to do in "A Few Words About Contemporary Operatic Forms," which is, its title notwithstanding, a fairly lengthy essay. His list is rather arbitrary and verges at times on simplemindedness, but the general bent of the argument is clear: operatic forms are to be arrived at not out of any preconceived routine or sense of musical propriety, but in spontaneous response to the exigencies of the individual text. In the following extracts Cui's examples from the literature are mostly omitted, except where they appear to have solely prompted the inclusion of the form they represent.

Operatic forms depend generally upon the subject, the cast of the libretto and the scenario, and in particular, upon the text and its lines. And since subjects and their planning can be endlessly varied, they are able to call forth in operatic music forms of comparable variety, ranging from the simplest to the most complex.

Thus, song can appear in its most pristine and primitive [i.e., strophic] form when in the course of the play one of the characters sings a song or romance. The form of variations is a slight adaptation of the song form and can be reasonably used in similar instances. The rondo form will be appropriate where a character is obsessed with an idée fixe, and constantly returns to it, e.g., Farlaf's rondo in *Ruslan*.

All of these are the simplest forms.

But in opera the most complex symphonic forms of the broadest thematic development can also be appropriate: in all orchestral numbers, like overtures, entr'actes, dances; in ritual choruses, and generally in scenes where there is no dramatic action; in operatic tableaux (festivals, ceremonies, processions, divine services and so forth), in which passions have not yet come into their own. Even fugue and canon can fit in suitably. Thus, in the first chorus of *A Life for the Tsar* there is a fugue, and *Ruslan* sports a four-voice canon *("Kakoe chudnoe mgnoven'e"),* where so cleverly and so truly each character, under the impression of the same physical phenomenon, is made to sing the same melody. [19]

Note here the lingering echo of Chernyshevsky, when Cui maintains that "symphonic forms" are appropriate only when "passions have not yet come into their own." For him, emotion and "form" are still opposites. But Cui does admit the appropriateness of a kind of modified leitmotiv technique. This, however, is apparently borrowed in conception from Liszt rather than Wagner: "Thematic development is ideally suited to the depiction of the varied sides of a character's personality. In such a way one and the same theme, altered in rhythm, tempo, meter, harmonically embellished in varied colors, can depict different manifestations of one and the same personality without detriment to its unity."

The use of "rounded" forms, up to and including the ensemble, "where there may be the simultaneous singing of characters motivated by identical, or even diametrically opposed moods," is altogether natural so long as the situation "does not demand movement or action," or where "a single feeling of any kind reigns." But as soon as there is interaction of characters, volatility of emotion, crucial configurations of events, in short, as soon as "drama" rears its head, Cui reveals himself the loyal musical child of Dargomyzhsky.

However, besides the above-mentioned kinds of scenes, opera contains dramatic ones as well, which frequently dominate. In them, feelings, often contradictory ones, swiftly succeed one another; the action is developed without delay; speech becomes impetuous, troubled, irregular. For such scenes all of the above-mentioned forms are unsuitable; here one must have recourse to another form—the most varied, freest form of all: *melodic recitative.* Here there can be no question of placidly rounded forms, regular melodies or symmetrical phrases. These would contradict truth, delay the action, dampen and ultimately destroy the impression of the dramatic situation. . . . The music [must] flow ever forward without a backward glance, just as the drama itself develops without pause.

The recitative style must be at the same time a melodic style; besides correct declamation, there must be music as well—and especially inspired music at that, in response to the power and pressure of passions in dramatic situations. This style demands of the composer a special talent, inexhaustible invention and melodic suppleness. Inexhaustible invention, because here one cannot dwell upon one theme and its development; here phrase must follow upon phrase, theme upon theme, and they must all be meaningful and inspired so as to answer to the power of emotion and passion called forth by dramatic collision. Melodic suppleness, because here it is necessary to unite music with the most capricious phrases of text, differing in length and in meter. The result will be not melody, strictly speaking, but phrases. They must, however, be *melodic* phrases, embodying musical ideas. Dramatic scenes, swiftly developing, written with warmth and talent, intensified by music of comparable warmth and talent, bringing to the emotions contained therein an even greater depth, and to the passions an even greater fire—such cannot fail to produce an irresistible impression on a spectator equally receptive to the charms of poetry and of music.

But if musical numbers and forms are governed and "motivated" by the text, what motivates the text itself? With this question Cui never adequately comes to grips, and by this omission places a fatal limitation upon the usefulness of his theories. Cui seems to assume that all operas have preexistent literary sources; a drama created expressly for opera is never envisioned in his critical works, nor did he ever write such an opera. While he accepted the necessity of adapting the literary source to operatic purposes and means—*The Stone Guest,* to repeat, was for him at once a masterwork and an aberration— Cui never promulgated a philosophy of the libretto, that is, of the structure of the musical drama as a totality. For this reason, Cui cannot ultimately be taken as seriously as a musico-dramatic theorist as Serov, who did some to grips with first principles of operatic aesthetics. Unless the purview of operatic criticism is enlarged to include the structure of the libretto, no valid argument can be marshalled against the Rossinis or the Donizettis, or even the Handels. For no one could fairly demonstrate any incongruity between the typical Italian libretto and the musical forms in which its composers clothed it. In other words, if it is the shape of the libretto that determines the shape of a "rational" nineteenth-century opera, a theory of operatic form must for this very reason begin (as did Wagner's and even Serov's) with the text.

Nor was this the only shortcoming of Cui's recipe for "rational" opera. The overriding criterion in the choice of musical forms was merely the opposition of "lyric" and "dramatic," and this crucial polarity was construed by Cui as theorist in the most primitive possible way: he equates "lyric" with tranquility and "dramatic" with impetuosity. Now no opera, not even Cui's own, makes such an arbitrarily rigorous distinction. The lyric high points of both of Cui's major operas were ardent love duets. Could one call them tranquil? One of the stormiest passages in *Ratcliff* was Douglas's narrative about a fierce and bloody ambush. Its form is entirely "rounded," even strophic. There is nothing impassioned at all in the first scene of *The Stone Guest,* and yet it, like all the rest of the opera, is cast in "melodic recitative" throughout.

In the end, Cui offered no guide to a more "rational" *dramma per musica* beyond the remark that "subjects and their planning can be endlessly varied." And with this disappointing observation comes the realization that Cui's vagueness was necessary. His prescription for rational opera had to cover all cases admired by the *kuchka* from *Ruslan*—in which (to quote Cui) "there is no drama"[20]—to *The Stone Guest,* which had attempted to break down all boundaries between the lyric and spoken stages. As spokesman for the *kuchka* he had to enunciate a theory that could be subscribed to by talents and personalities as diverse as, say, Musorgsky on the one hand and Cui himself on the other. Small wonder then that Cui's purely theoretical writings have the ring of platitude. His attempt to be all-inclusive and, particularly, to mediate between *Ruslan* and *The Stone Guest,* involved him in logical difficulties, especially when it came to justifying Dargomyzhsky's extremism. "Would it not have been better," Cui asked rhetorically, "had the work been revised from the musical point of view, . . . so as to fashion arias and duets and add choruses (of monks, of villagers, nobles, etc.)?"[21] The answer implied by his writings would seem to be affirmative, but *The Stone Guest* being an untouchable masterpiece and the source of the "melodic recitative" style, Cui was forced to prevaricate:

> Dargomyzhsky could not content himself with a run-of-the-mill libretto and run-of-the-mill verses: he was a vocal composer. And he was a thousand times right to compose his last opera on Pushkin's text without alterations, despite the . . . drawbacks of this text for music. These drawbacks he overcame by the force of his talent, . . . and in recompense he was inspired by a work that was artistic not only overall, but in all its details.

But, he hastens to add:

> It would be a gross error to consider *The Stone Guest* the prototype of contemporary opera. . . . This type will hardly repeat itself, for it will hardly fall to the lot of another composer to write music to the text of a work so marked with genius, but not intended for music. . . . And we have already said that another kind of text will call forth other musical forms, less profoundly intimate.[22]

It was for opinions like these that Stasov came to regard Cui as a backslider.[23] In so doing, however, Stasov revealed in part his growing aesthetic isolation from the increasingly professional composers of the New Russian School. But he had a point: only Musorgsky found realism appealing after the first flush of excitement; he alone was immediately moved to test the implications of recitative opera to their very limits, while Cui was preoccupied with synthesis. Cui's was, in the final analysis, a conventional musical mind, and his conception of musical "truth" did not carry with it any positive commitment to innovation or reform. He maintained the cardinal romantic distinction between empirical truth and "artistic" truth, and abhorred any attempt to make music the medium of naturalistic representation, though he was more vociferous in his condemnation of Serov's endeavors along such lines than he was of Musorgsky's, at least in print. "Of course, opera is a stylized presentation," he wrote. "There is nothing of real, photographic truth to be sought in it, but in order for it to produce an impression, it must contain artistic truth."[24] And Cui did criticize Musorgsky for his "inclination to exaggerate, to carry correctness of declamation to the point of reproducing the actual intonation of the voice, of carrying picturesqueness to the point of onomatopoeia, of carrying musical truth to the point of realism."[25]

So Cui was not out to change opera fundamentally, although he was charged with such an intention often enough by his journalistic antagonists. He only sought to regulate the genre according to some vaguely Ciceronian "right reason." His "reform" was little more than a crusade for the suppression of abuses,[26] and Cui was the first to "concede" that his outlook on opera contained nothing new. "Twice it has already been promulgated and realized: at the time of the first sproutings of opera and at the end of the last century with Gluck."[27]

It was perhaps precisely because of the vagueness of his aesthetic program that Cui became such a pedantic, intolerant critic. About the only aspect of his conception of "musical truth" to which he could give definite formulation was correctness of declamation, and so, although he cautioned time and again that mere correctness was no guarantee of "truth," he became a virtual fetishist when it came to assessing prosody in the operas of others. A misplaced accent, a repeated word, a melisma of suspect "virtuosity" was enough for him to damn a whole opera.[28] So regularly did Cui allow himself to be caught up in such minutiae as to exasperate even a colleague as sympathetic as Dargomy-zhsky, who wrote to Karmalina that though Cui was a good musician, and "a clever and amusing 'original,' as a critic he is unfortunately far from well-rounded. Melodic invention is Greek to him [*tarabara*]. But those aspects of music which he manages to understand, he understands in depth."[29]

In view of the impression of Cui's theoretical writings, then, and in the absence of positive criteria for the all-important structure of the libretto, one turns eagerly to his works themselves as exemplars of Cui-style *kuchkism* in practice. The only fair place to start is *Ratcliff*, since it was the first of Cui's operas to reflect a serious, conscious response to the operatic questions raised by Cui the critic. The opera took shape during Cui's early years of journalistic activity and, as we shall see, reflects profoundly the changes that its author's outlook underwent as a result not only of contact with Dargomyzhsky, but also of the conscious formulation of thought forced upon him by the exigencies of his critical work. Neither *The Mandarin's Son* nor *The Prisoner of the Caucasus* is worthy of serious consideration: neither gives any indication of deep evaluation of aesthetic problems, or of serious artistic ambition.

The first of them (actually the second in order of composition) was a silly vaudeville of mistaken identity, whose music—compounded from Auber, Schumann and *A Life for the Tsar* (in descending order)—was fitted to Victor Krylov's text in a shoddy, haphazard fashion, not only as regards prosody, but also with regard to the later Cui's cardinal desideratum of appropriateness of musical form to action. The Mandarin's air (No. 7), for example, does something no operatic number should—it merely recapitulates the content of the preceding dialogue, and sticks out as superfluous even in so egregiously trivial a work as this. The innkeeper and his employee Zai-Zang conspire to defraud the Mandarin to the strains of a pretty, strophic couplet romance. And Cui's treatment of ensembles is pitiful: they are scarcely more than choruses sung one-to-a-part. When the texture gets too complex for the dillettante-composer's technique in the concluding quintet, he blithely doubles vocal lines, unconcerned that the characters singing identical music may have different, even dramatically opposed, words. Rimsky-Korsakov, who did not assist at the private premiere of the work in 1859, described his impressions upon coming in contact with it more than three decades later. His judgment, while harsh, is fair, and of interest because it measures the work by characteristically *kuchkist* standards of a kind that Cui himself had made a career of promulgating: "a talented composition with music unsuited to the subject, which in itself needs no music at all and is so poor that it is nauseating to hear and see it."[30] There is no need to tarry over *The Mandarin's Son,* nor to reproach its author. It is typical of the productions of the Russian dilettanti of the period—the Famintsyns, the Lvovs, the Fitingofs. The music itself actually possesses a certain charm and elegance, and is fluently written. What is surprising, though, and then revealing, is that Cui authorized the Moscow performance of this jejune piece of juvenilia that Rimsky witnessed in 1893, and continued to give indulgent approval to the work even later. The reason for his affection for it, as revealed in a letter of 1911, was that it alone of all his operas achieved any success with the public.[31]

No reproach could be made against the subject of Cui's other fledgling opera. It came from the mother lode itself, from Pushkin, albeit minor, uncharacteristically Byronic (and therefore popular) Pushkin. Cui's composition of *The Prisoner of the Caucasus* (again to a text by his school chum Krylov), followed closely on the heels of *Rusalka*'s premiere. While Dargomyzhsky's opera may have prompted Cui's choice of a Pushkin subject (there are surface plot similarities between *Rusalka* and *The Prisoner*—the theme of unrequited love, the death by drowning), there is no evidence that Cui paid any heed at this stage to those features of Dargomyzhsky's work he was later to value so highly. Recitative plays an altogether negligible role in his opera's scheme. Dramatic dialogue of whatever nature is almost invariably formalized into duet, with intercourse between characters taking the form of alternating couplets and quatrains to begin with, later merging into musically decorative simultaneous singing, to a text recapitulating the previous exchange. Pushkin's narrative poem is very short on action and long on description, Krylov's libretto follows suit, making luxuriant provision for oriental genre and color. Cui's corresponding music is of the most hackneyed sort, copied not "from life" but from French romantic models (Félicien David et al.)—a matter of augmented seconds, chromatic basses and ostinato accompaniments. Nor is there any effort to integrate genre with action. The only verses of Pushkin that Krylov retained were two stanzas of the "Circassian Song." Cui's setting of this number attained a certain popularity as morceau de salon after the opera's belated premiere in the 1880s. It is fully characteristic of the opera's style and tone.

Ex. 6.1.   *Kavkazskii plennik* (St. Petersburg: Bessel & Co., 1882)

Composer and librettist, naturally, were at pains to extract theater out of Pushkin's undramatic, contemplative poem, and at times this had to be accomplished by main force. The ending of the opera is typical. In order to gain a "strong" conclusion, Fatima's suicide, so subtly and ambiguously handled by Pushkin (indeed, this is the poem's high point for admirers of the original), is turned into a blatant operatic denouement, with the Caucasian armies (chorus) returning prematurely from their campaigns just in time to shout "O horror!" as Fatima melodramatically hurls herself into the river.

Cui's overblown treatment of Pushkin's delicately romantic *Prisoner of the Caucasus* makes his attraction to the lurid romanticism of Heine's *William Ratcliff* understandable. It seems a natural for opera: "seven murders, one case of insanity, and one duel to the accompaniment of lightning, squalls and corpses—that's what takes place before the eyes of the frightened spectator," according to the reckoning of an early reviewer.[32] The suggestion came from Balakirev, and though from a standpoint of *kuchkist*-realist hindsight the choice may seem problematical, it was at the time entirely natural. The *Ratcliff* Balakirev and Cui knew was the translation by the famous poet Alexei Nikolaevich Pleshcheev (1825-93), which appeared in 1859. Pleshcheev was a member (along with Dostoevsky) of the Petrashevsky circle of Utopian socialists, and was undoubtedly attracted to Heine's play as an example of "liberalism in art" (to cite Victor Hugo's definition of romanticism). Heine had called the piece a "work of ideas" and an "intuitive cultural analysis," and it is possible (if one wishes) to see in its action not only the working out of Heine's parricidal fantasies and his infatuation with his cousin Amalie (the standard modern interpretation), but also an allegorical social tract (though to call the duel at the Black Stone a collision between "the representatives of different classes"[33] is surely to go several steps too far). Pleshcheev's translation was dedicated to Chernyshevsky himself, and this may have contributed to exciting the interest of Balakirev, who at the time was even considering an opera on the subject of *What Is To Be Done?* Thus, some see in the choice of *Ratcliff* as operatic material yet another manifestation of the "Aesopian language" with which Russian "revolutionary democrats" sought to mask radical discussion of social problems. N.V. Tumanina even goes so far as to assert that the subject "indicates the composer's attention to the immediate problems of contemporary life, in particular the problem of the family, of free choice in love, and so forth."[34]

But this is already far from the truth. There is no reason not to take Cui's word at face value when he states simply that what attracted him to *Ratcliff* was "its fantastic qualities, the indefinite though passionate character of the hero himself in his submission to the forces of Fate; I was much taken with Heine's talent and Pleshcheev's lovely translation (beautiful verses have always enticed me and have doubtless influenced my music)."[35] In other words, Cui approached the subject appropriately, in the spirit of Heine's own romanticism, attracted by its beauty and not put off by its lack of "truth," seeking in it neither veiled message nor indeed any definitive, "positive" meaning at all. If anything, he made of *Ratcliff* an even purer expression of romanticism than Heine had done by purging his libretto as if deliberately of all the quasi-political and satirical lines that had been the play's appeal to the Petrashevskians.

What was left was something many found hard to swallow. When Cui acknowledged the attractions of indefiniteness, he placed himself outside the Russian tradition altogether, after all. Even Stasov could not refrain, in an essay he wrote in 1893 to celebrate *Ratcliff*'s twenty-fifth anniversary, from pointing out what were for him the inherent deficiencies of the subject.

> This ballad [sic: Heine called his drama a *Tragödie*] was created by Heine in the days of his youth and contained rather many of the elements of the first youthful flush of French *Romanticism*, a certain exaggeratedness and monstrousness, a certain "dishevelment": it had endless killing, it had sweet picturesque highwaymen, and, as leader of the gang, it had the noble hero Ratcliff, all together with psychopathological Scottish "second sight."[36]

Stasov put it mildly; *Ratcliff* is an embarrassment to Heine critics, even the most sympathetic of them finding in it a hodgepodge of "thick melodrama and thin mysticism."[37] Cui's colleagues could think of no better praise for his opera than to tell him how much he had improved upon his source, which in fact represented a literary tendency that was obsolescent and even retrogressive by the 1860s, especially in Russia. A synopsis of the libretto will easily bear this out.

> *Act I. Scene 1:* In the rich, ancient castle of the Scottish lord MacGregor merriment reigns. The wedding of the lord's only daughter Mary to the valiant Count Douglas is being celebrated. The nuptial couple receive the congratulations of the guests. Suddenly the joyous chorus is interrupted by the voice of Margaret, Mary's demented nurse: she sings a song about Edward, who killed his beloved. ("O why is thy sword with blood so red, Edward, Edward?") Douglas is confounded: this sorrowful song can bode no good at the wedding. Mary soothes her groom: the song has reminded her of her childhood; Margaret had always used to sing it over her cradle. To distract her beloved from his dark thoughts, Mary bids him recount his journey. Why has he come to MacGregor's castle alone, unexpected, without his friends and servants? The count begins his story: he rode as far as the Scottish border with his friends, but the slow trip had bored him and he made his way alone through the mountains and woods. Not far from the castle he was suddenly beset by three robbers. It would have gone badly for him ... At this point Mary suddenly interrupts Douglas' story. "William, William! Again these persecutions!" she cries in despair, and falls senseless. The shaken count throws himself upon his bride. But Mary comes to herself. In a state of agitation she asks her groom to continue his account. And Douglass concludes: "It would have gone badly for me, had a stranger not suddenly appeared. Together we set the robbers fleeing." The guests find this incident strange and mysterious. But in any event Count Douglas is alive, unharmed and celebrating his wedding. The guests hurry into the dining hall for a joyous feast. MacGregor remains with Douglas. He must impart to him a secret. Mary's faint was no accident. Six years before, William Ratcliff, the son of an old

acquaintance of MacGregor's, had come to the castle. He fell passionately in love with Mary at first sight. But the maiden rejected him and Ratcliff had left the castle. Since that time fortune had deserted Mary. Twice she had stood at the altar, and twice her groom had mysteriously disappeared. Both were later found dead at the Black Stone. The murderer was sought zealously until Mary finally discovered his identity. It seems that William Ratcliff appeared to her and brought her the engagement rings of her slain bridegrooms. At the fearful Black Stone MacGregor had had a cross erected, on which he had inscribed the names of the unfortunate victims. Hearing this story, Douglas is seized with a terrible rage. So that is who deprives Mary of peace! No, Ratcliff will not take the ring from his finger! Douglas resolves to avenge the murders.

Scene 2: The wedding feast continues. The guests make merry and honor the young couple. Unnoticed, Ratcliff's comrade Lesley makes his way into the hall. He gives Douglas a letter from Ratcliff challenging him to a duel. They are to meet that very night at the Black Stone.

Act II. Scene 1: Noisy carousal in a tavern. Tramps, robbers and their friends sing a racy song. In a mirthful skirmish they chase away a drunken and importunate tramp named Robin. The noise dies down and all ask Lesley to sing one of his songs. In a merry ballad Lesley sings the praises of wine and free love. Ratcliff enters—the merrymaking comes to a sudden halt. He orders everyone to go to bed. Ratcliff impatiently asks Lesley what Douglas' answer had been. Lesley calms his friend; the count has agreed to the duel. But William must be more careful: everyone knows that he is the murderer of the two noble lords. Ratcliff rejects outright the insinuation: he has been twice victorious in honorable combat and is now preparing for the third victory. Lesley is intrigued; what wrong has Douglas done Ratcliff? None at all, answers the latter, "I don't even know him." A mysterious force possesses Ratcliff and forces his hand. In his earliest childhood he had beheld two apparitions: a beautiful woman and a gallant man who held out their arms to each other in anguish but could not be joined. Years passed and Ratcliff forgot about this vision, when all of a sudden, on a visit to MacGregor, he caught sight of Mary. In her he recognized the features of the mysterious woman who had appeared to him, and a passionate love was kindled in his heart. But Mary rejected his enflamed avowals. Since then he had known no peace and had bound himself to a terrible oath: all who wish to call Mary their own shall die by Ratcliff's hand. Spurred with thirst for revenge, Ratcliff hurries to the Black Stone.

Scene 2: A stormy night. The wind howls fearsomely, clouds streak swiftly across the sky. Ratcliff appears in a dark cloak. Impatiently he awaits his adversary. Douglas enters and recognizes in Ratcliff the stranger who had saved him from the robbers. Gladdened, he offers Ratcliff his friendship, but is rejected. The duel begins. Ratcliff is sure of victory. But his hand grows weak and he is wounded. The magnanimous Douglas leaves his foe alive and departs. The darkness thickens. Ratcliff regains consciousness. In the howling of the wind he fancies he hears human voices. But all at once he remembers the duel. Rage and impotent despair seize him. To the evil laughter of invisible witches, Ratcliff sends curses at heaven and hell. He rushes crazed to MacGregor's castle. Together with the whistling of the wind the witches' laughter accompanies him.

Act III: Sad and anxious, Mary comes into her bedroom. She is not gladdened by the noisy feast. She confides her sorrow to her nurse. Margaret reveals to the maiden a horrible secret. Long ago Mary's mother Betty had loved William Ratcliff's father, Edward. One day he frightened her in some way, and she, rejecting him, married Mary's father. Edward, too, married. Time passed and Betty found out about his marriage. She wept bitterly, and her former love kindled afresh within her with a new force. Edward had been similarly unable to forget Betty. Every night he wandered beneath her window. Unable to restrain herself, Betty would rush to the window and stretch her arms out toward Edward. One night this was witnessed by Mary's father MacGregor. The next morning Edward was found lifeless; in three days' time Betty, too, went to her grave. Pale and trembling, Mary listens to Margaret's story. Suddenly Ratcliff appears at the door. With a cry— "There he is! Edward!" — the nurse faints away. Mary is terrified. With horror, she thinks that Ratcliff is about to give her the ring from Douglas' hand. But this time Ratcliff is wounded. At the sight of his blood Mary suddenly feels her mother's soul take possession of her. She sees before her not William, but Edward Ratcliff. Passion rises in her breast. Tenderly she caresses Ratcliff. William and Mary forget the world in a passionate embrace. All at once Margaret's voice is heard. It proclaims the will of those forces of evil that hound Ratcliff. He must kill Mary; then indeed she can never belong to another. In despair the maiden shrinks from Ratcliff. It is too late; Ratcliff's sword overtakes her. MacGregor runs in and falls, struck down by a blow from Ratcliff. Edward's murder has been avenged. By Mary's body Ratcliff stabs himself. Guests, servants and Douglas all rush in and, horrified by the fearsome sight of carnage, are rooted to the spot. The apparition of Edward and Betty united appears to all. "By the hand of the son the father is avenged," cries Margaret. All bewail the tragic victims of cruel fate.[38]

Now this story could be told infinitely more simply, and perhaps ought to be here, in the interests of clarity:

Edward Ratcliff had loved Betty and was killed by Betty's jealous husband MacGregor, Betty herself dying shortly thereafter. Edward's son William is haunted from childhood by a vision of the ill-starred lovers. Catching sight of Betty's daughter Mary, he conceives a violent passion for her, recognizing the woman of his vision; but, rejected by her, he becomes a bandit and resolves that he will kill anyone who attempts to make Mary his own. But Douglas, Mary's third bridegroom, overcomes Ratcliff, who then rushes in a frenzy to MacGregor's castle and kills Mary, her father, and himself. At this point the vision of Edward and Betty reappears, only this time they embrace; the death of their children has united them at last.

It will immediately be seen that in this "clarified" version, the events up to the denouement are related in almost precisely the reverse order. Needless to say, the author's primary concern had not been optimum clarity or immediacy. Nor was concentration of action his purpose. *William Ratcliff* was a *Schicksalsdrama* after the fashion of Kleist and Grillparzer, and the genre carried with it a special set of methods and aims. The action is kept deliberately diffuse and mysterious as long as possible, with causes and motivations not stated at the outset but rather hinted at through signs and portents (Margaret's song), and only gradually revealed in the course of the action, decisive explanatory factors being witheld up to the last minute. In the case of *William Ratcliff*, the all-important first cause, the story of Edward and Betty, is revealed only in the last scene, directly before the baroque orgy of bloodshed that brings the drama to its foreordained conclusion. Thus the distant cause and the horrific effect are brought into bald and lurid juxtaposition. Before the climactic scene, the action, though inevitably tending toward it, had been kept under a veil of mystery—the perfect embodiment in terms of dramatic action of the romantic ("musical," as E.T.A. Hoffmann would say) ideal of an expression powerful and vivid, yet inchoate and ambiguous.

But the Schicksalsdrama, which by the time of *Ratcliff*'s creation (1822) was already past its prime, contained, implicit in its very nature, all but insoluble dramaturgical problems. In such a work the action that takes place within the play constitutes merely the result and culmination of a fatal necessity set in motion by events long preceding the raising of the curtain. Therefore much, if not most, of the actual text must be given over to narrative, so as to inform the spectator progressively of these events and persuade him of the inevitability of the action he is witnessing. Then, too, the "drama of fate" is essentially inimical to character portrayal. The protagonists act not out of an inner necessity, but one imposed from without. Notwithstanding Heine's subtitle, there can be no tragedy here, at least not in the classic, Aristotelian sense, and that is why *Ratcliff* is so often referred to as a "dramatic ballad." Such a form afforded little room for the "exploration of human nature" (Musorgsky) such as appealed to the musical realists, and which Cui himself valued highly in his criticism.

But needless to say, Cui followed Heine's sequence in the presentation of the plot, making no attempt at all to convert passive narration into dynamic action. For one thing, this would have been impracticable: it would have meant writing a whole other opera about Edward and Betty, and perhaps one about William Ratcliff's childhood and his meeting with Mary, resulting in a *Ring*-like trilogy brought about by the very same conditions that begot *The Ring* itself. And for another, it would have deprived Cui of his "beautiful verses"; the narratives are very much the heart of the play, viewed as a work of poetry. The most important principle of all, the "equality of music and text" was at stake.

Cui claimed that his libretto respected the Heine/Pleshcheev text as much as Dargomyzhsky's had respected Pushkin's. On this point, the opera might be neatly divided into two halves. The second half (beginning with Ratcliff's narrative in Act II, sc. i) boasts a level of fidelity to the original that actually can bear comparison to *The Stone Guest*. Virtually all the words are Heine's (through Pleschcheev), though the text is abridged, given the greater length of the original vis-à-vis Pushkin's "Little Tragedy." All other modifications are minor indeed.[39] The first half, however, at best approximates the practices of Dargomyzhsky in *Rusalka*: lines and speeches from the original are maintained intact to a greater extent than in more "normal" librettos, but the drama is thoroughly adapted to musical purposes, along lines that will appear surprisingly conventional when measured against *kuchkist* theorizing (or against the opera's second half). It is almost as if we were dealing with the first and second halves, respectively, of two different operas, an anomaly that disconcerted many of the early critics. The explanation is to be found in *Ratcliff*'s creative history.

Although *William Ratcliff* is the last opera we are treating in our survey of Russian opera in the 1860s, it was not the "latest." Although it was completed when the air surrounding the composer was full of *The Stone Guest, Marriage,* and rumors of *The Power of the Fiend,* it was begun around the same time as *Judith.* This extraordinarily protracted gestation can be explained by factors both external (in Cui's own words)—

> Since the salary I received [as instructor in military fortification] was insufficient for subsistence, my wife and I opened a preparatory boarding school for youths wishing to enter the Engineering Academy, and, with the exception of languages, I took it upon myself to give instruction in all subjects. Even the summer with its holidays was not free. On the contrary, this was the most feverish preexamination time. Besides, one had to bring the boarders up, not just instruct them. So we were together at all times, as if one big family, eating, living in the country, taking walks, boating, and so on, all together. It is understandable that in such conditions I could write only in snatches, and I wrote the opera not sequentially, in order, from first scene to last, but in separate scenes from various acts, whatever I was most interested in at a given moment.[40]

—and internal (in the less kind words of Tchaikovsky):

> By his own admission to me, he can only compose by trying over and picking out little melodies at the piano, and fitting them out with little chords. Having hit upon some nice little idea, he plays around with it, works it up, embellishes it, powders and rouges it every which way—and all this takes a long time, so long that, for example, he was ten years [*recte* seven] in writing his opera *Ratcliff.*[41]

If there were no stylistic inconsistencies in an opera that came into being under these conditions, *that* would have been a wonder. When one considers the technical abilities of the composer and the circumstances in which he was forced to work, the opera—whatever its faults—is an astounding achievement. And in fact it astounded Tchaikovsky on first acquaintance, during the days of his greatest cordiality with the St. Petersburg composers he later came to despise. He wrote Balakirev (October 28, 1869): "I go through Cui's opera every day and am delighted. I never expected that his opera would be so remarkably good."[42]

There is good reason to think that *William Ratcliff* was initially planned as a conventional numbers opera along the lines of *The Prisoner of the Caucasus,* and that the point at which Cui started to compose in 1861 was the beginning of Act II. This is a typical second-act divertissement, replete with a drinking chorus, a laughing chorus, some dancing and a brilliant concerted strophic song with choral refrains. The words are not Heine's but Krylov's, replacing a gentle genre scene wherein, in the original play, the innkeeper Tom teaches his little son the *Pater noster*. If the whole opera had been written in this vein it should have turned out a kind of Russian *Fra Diavolo*, in a musical style not far removed from that of the Auberian *Mandarin's Son*, and with a libretto by Krylov as tenuously related to Heine's text as that of *The Prisoner of the Caucasus* had been to Pushkin's.

The situation does not change materially if we look next at Act I. This act can be pretty securely dated 1862, on the basis of a number of scattered bits of evidence. One is a curious reminiscence of Rimsky-Korsakov, made during an intermission at a private performance of the opera (at the home of Alexandra Purgold-Molas) on April 11, 1893: "When I was listening to [the opening chorus] today, I noticed two harmonies that I borrowed for my First Symphony; and since that symphony was written by me during my ocean voyage and even before it, it means that the chorus must have already been in existence in 1862."[43] Some excerpts from Act I were performed under Anton Rubinstein's baton at a concert of the Russian Musical Society in January, 1863. MacGregor's narrative contains a sizeable section lifted bodily from a "Symphonic Allegro" in E♭ major, "at that time [i.e., the winter and spring of 1862] often played at Balakirev's."[44] (This, by the way, was a procedure Cui was later often to deplore in the works of others.) Finally, we have a letter of December 3, 1862, in which Cui asked his librarian friend Stasov (who had performed a similar service for Balakirev when the latter needed English folk tunes for his *King Lear* music) to furnish him with "Scottish melodies, which I need for *Ratcliff* (which, parenthetically, promises to be not a bad opera)."[45] In the event—and this is significant—he used only one: the second scene of Act I is introduced by a chorus of wedding guests, the first part of which (for the men) quotes the Scottish song, "Tibbie Fowler."[46] Example 6.2 gives Cui's chorus and his presumable source, as supplied by Stasov, James Johnson's *Scots Musical Museum*. The fact that more such songs were not included in the finished opera again testifies to a fundamental change in its conception over the long period of its coming into being.[47]

Act I owes more to Heine than the opening scene of Act II. Its core is the pair of narratives (Douglas and MacGregor), taken over from the original without much change save abridgement. But, surrounding them and even within them, there is an enormous infusion of operatic paraphernalia. Forty years later, Cui recalled asking Krylov to make some "insertions...for the sake of a greater development of the role of the chorus,"[48] and we recall that failure to provide for the chorus had been Cui's only substantial objection (in the early days, anyway) to Dargomyzhsky's handling of *The Stone Guest*. So extensively did he provide for it in the first act of *Ratcliff*, that an early reviewer was moved to complain about the "choruses, choruses, and more choruses," that impeded the dramatic action.[49] And the texts were not all by Krylov. We have Cui's direct testimony (in a letter to Musorgsky) that the "rather awful" words to the final chorus of Act I were his own creation.[50]

Throughout the opera, but especially in Act I, the handling of the chorus is conventionally "operatic," that is to say, monolithic and decorative. Cui and Krylov solved the "choral problem" in an obvious way, by providing a troupe of wedding guests (comparable to the robber band that sings in Act II), who are available to frame the opening act with huge choruses of lusty congratulation. The first of these is a tableau of little or no dramatic significance and hence (in Cui's words) could accomodate "the most complex symphonic forms" without offending his *kuchkist* conscience. But the second big concerted chorus (the one that contained "Tibbie Fowler") was problematical. It crushes with its musical weight an important bit of dramatic action: Lesley's transmission to Douglas of Ratcliff's challenge. In Heine, Lesley's exchange with Douglas occupies the last three lines of the scene that contains MacGregor's narrative, and follows immediately upon Douglas's vow to avenge Mary's slain bridegrooms. But Cui and Krylov did not allow the impression of thickening plot thus to take hold, for they extracted these three lines from their context in the play and built around them the whole scene of the wedding feast. The brief encounter between Lesley and Douglas is flanked and engulfed by lengthily "symphonic" choral acclamations. Their actual moment of contact comes off well against the background of the rejoicing guests, oblivious to the fateful encounter. But this effective musical contrast is bought at a high price: because of the similarity between the congratulatory choruses in both scenes of Act I, the predominating impression is one of stasis, even redundancy.[51]

Elsewhere in the act an attempt is made to integrate the chorus actively into the unfolding drama—a prime *kuchkist* desideratum. It is a failure, for there is really no "organic" place for a chorus in Heine's dramatic conception. Thus, the chorus's role is never truly an active one, but that of a passively commenting "Greek chorus" of onlookers. When Mary faints during Douglas's narrative, Cui interpolates a short chorus that sententiously proclaims the obvious:

Kak ispugalas' Maria.	How frightened Mary has become!
Kak pobledneli uzhasno shchëki Marii,	How terribly paled are Mary's cheeks.
Uzh eto verno ne k dobru.	Surely this bodes no good.
Predveshchaet gore Marii	This foretells grief for Mary,
Etot strakh vnezapnyi eë.	This sudden fright of hers.
V den' svad'by, v den' torzhestva,	On her wedding day, a day of triumph,
Veseliia i schast'ia,	Of merriment and joy,
Ne k dobru ona tak ispugalas',	It bodes no good that she took fright,
Tak poblednela.	Became so pale.

This interpolation drags out and deenergizes the single tiny moment of action in the first scene. In Heine, Mary remains unconscious for the length of seventeen lines; in Cui's version, her faint lasts for 62 measures in slow tempo.

Ex. 6.2.   a. *Vil'iam Ratklif* (St. Petersburg: Bessel & Co., n.d.), p. 81

b. James Johnson, *The Scots Musical Museum* (1853),
reprint ed. (Hatboro, Pa.: Folklore Associates, 1962), p.452

Tibbie Fowler.

440

Tibbie Fowler o' the glen, There's o'er mony woo-in at her, Tibbie Fowler o' the glen, there's o'er mony wooin at her.

Slow

Chorus.

Wooin at her, pu'in at her, courtin at her, can-na get her:

Filthy elf, its for her pelf, that a' the lads are wooin at her.

Ten cam east, and ten came west, ten came rowin o'er the water;
Twa came down the lang dyke side, there's twa and thirty wooin at her.
Wooin at her, &c.

There's seven but, and seven ben, seven in the pantry wi' her;
Twenty head about the door, There's ane and forty wooin at her.
Wooin at her, &c.

She's got pendles in her lugs, Cockle-shells wad set her better;
High-heel'd shoon and siller tags, And a' the lads are wooin at her.
Wooin at her, &c.

Be a lassie e'er sae black, An she hae the name o' siller,
Set her upo' Tintock-tap, The wind will blaw a man till her.
Wooin at her, &c.

Be a lassie e'er sae fair, An she want the pennie siller;
A flie may fell her in the air, Before a man be even till her.
Wooin at her, &c.

Cui seems resolved not to let things move, and the reason seems to be his determination that the chorus shall have a piece of the action, whatever the cost.[52]

The most curious and dramaturgically disconcerting interpolation in Act I, however, is not choral. It is Mary's song about Margaret's song—yet another narrative in an opera already suffering such a hypertrophy in that department. Apparently unsatisfied with MacGregor's explanation of the song in Heine—that Margaret sings simply out of lunacy—Cui and Krylov abridged MacGregor's speech and gave to Mary a newly invented one. Objecting to Douglas's characterization of Margaret's song as "sad and funereal," she sings:

> Oh no! not sad; to me it is a song both sweet and pleasant.
> It brings back my childhood, this quaint old tune.
> To it, I, as yet a child, often fell peacefully asleep in my cradle.
> Later I used to listen with delight to it, when in my breast
> Unbidden, there first arose sweet dreams of love.
> Yes, this song brings back much to me,
> Youthful fancies and sweet dreams.

Now this song serves a number of perfectly rational purposes. First, it focuses additional attention upon what will be the prime musical symbol in the opera; second, it gives a female character a chance to sing an extended solo, offsetting to some extent the preponderance of male characters; and third—probably most cogent from the *kuchkist* point of view because it is the least "operatic"—it constructs a parallel between Mary's childhood and Ratcliff's, which in Cui's version are thus both dominated by the specters of Edward and Betty. And yet, it *is* another narrative. Its insertion exhibits a remarkable indifference to the requirement of action in musical drama, and if nothing else, puts Cui's defense of *Ruslan* in a new light. The number (frankly labelled "Romance" in the opera's table of contents) sounds exactly like what it is—an "inserted" (and hence detachable) set piece. No "melodic recitative," this (remember, it was composed in 1862), but a shapely little barcarolle, unified and "rounded" in structure, with a deftly prepared climax on high A♭ (Ex. 6.3). Borodin remembered it well when he wrote the "Nocturne" movement of his second string quartet.

Mary's song is followed immediately by another narrative set piece (Douglas), which in turn gives way to a third (MacGregor), all within the opera's first half hour. Douglas's and MacGregor's narratives, though they are set to Heine's practically unchanged text (except for the excision of Douglas's prefatory account of the London socio-political scene), are treated, like Mary's, more as "song" than as musical "speech." Each has a leading musical motif upon which hangs a unified number. Cui's apparent lack of

Ex. 6.3.   *Vil'iam Ratklif*, p. 35 (Mary's song)

discomfort with such a procedure, despite the acute lack of dramatic action that is its inevitable result—indeed, his positive eagerness to seek out opportunities for such static, "musical" narrrative, else why insert Mary's song?—has made it difficult even for some of his most sympathetic critics to take him seriously as a musical dramatist. Those who have tried have had much to explain away. Besides the ever-faithful Stasov, their number included one of the early non-Russian propagandists of the New Russian School, the French critic Camille Bellaigue, who was sorely nonplussed by Cui's aggravation of the dramaturgical problems already inherent in the structure of Heine's play.

If these [narratives] can be admitted as a last resort in a tragedy, they weigh down the action of an opera in a singular fashion. Now we are not at all sure but that the composer saw an advantage precisely in this—a perfectly natural opportunity to give free rein to melodic recitative, that cornerstone of the lyric drama as he conceives it.[53]

But perhaps we, like Bellaigue, are asking too much, on the basis of our knowledge of the later Cui, the *kuchkist* polemicist. The music thus far discussed was all written before Cui even began his journalistic career. And what is more, we have a mysterious hiatus in *Ratcliff*'s creative history, precisely at the point when Cui took up his duties on the *Sanktpeterburgskie vedomosti*. On February 25, 1863, Cui wrote to Rimsky-Korsakov (then on his cruise) with news that he expected to finish the third act that year.[54] And on May 5, again to Rimsky-Korsakov, he announced the completion of Mary's Act III romance.[55] On July 26, 1864, in a letter to Balakirev, Cui wrote that "this morning I forced myself to finish my Scene at the Black Stone, and with it the whole of the second act."[56] He expected to finish *Ratcliff* in 1865, as he told Rimsky-Korsakov, adding, "In what I have written there are good places and also mediocre places, but all of it is in any case thought through and written seriously."[57] But then silence descends on *Ratcliff*, to lift only in the fall of 1867, when Rimsky-Korsakov informed Musorgsky in a letter that Cui had finished the third act (for the second time?).[58] From then until the summer of 1868, Cui's correspondence resumes with news of the opera, still in progress. The last scene he mentions working on (after Acts II and III had gone to the copyists, where they were held up pending the copying out of the first two acts of *The Power of the Fiend*) is the last scene in Act I.[59] What happened?

Well, many things: the height of the *Ruslan* controversy, the commencement of Cui's journalistic activity, the revival of *Rusalka,* friendship with Dargomyzhsky, the realist ferment surrounding *The Stone Guest* and *Marriage*. And with all this, we must believe, came a sudden and decisive maturing of Cui's outlook and a complete revision of the opera-in-progress. Is this not what Musorgsky alluded to when he wrote Cui in a letter otherwise full of news about *Marriage* (August 15, 1868), that *Ratcliff* "crawled out of your artistic womb before our eyes, grew, became strong, and now is about to go out into the world, still before our eyes"?[60] Laroche, reacting to the stylistic disparities in the second act of *Ratcliff,* noted perceptively:

The differences in execution are not premeditated but involuntary.... All the inconsistencies can be explained by a difference in maturity and a radical change of taste.[61]

Indeed, with Ratcliff's narrative in Act II we arrive suddenly upon a wholly new operatic and aesthetic terrain. Though the composer still strove in it to achieve the impression of a "rounded" musical form, it is significantly freer in construction than the narratives in Act I. The story is told in three parts, set off from one another by Lesley's repliques. Each of these three major sections is dominated by a leading melodic idea, which characteristically penetrates both the vocal line and the orchestra. The vocal writing remains essentially periodic in phrasing, full of melodic repetitions (though not textual, the words having been adapted faithfully from Heine).

The first section deals with Ratcliff's childhood visions and his meeting with Mary. Musically, it is the most extended and impressive of the three, containing as it does the melodic germ that is to reach its full development in the Act III love duet, when Edward and Betty's frustrated embrace (which Ratcliff here describes) finally achieves consummation.

Ex. 6.4.   *Vil'iam Ratklif*, p. 138, vocal line only

This is contrasted with a theme that characterizes Ratcliff's "wild dissipation."

Ex. 6.5.   *Vil'iam Ratklif*, p. 139

This theme is to be associated with Ratcliff throughout the rest of the opera.[62] The first section of Ratcliff's narrative closes with the return of the theme quoted in Example 6.4, lending the section an elegantly rounded da capo structure. It is, however, quite "rationally" motivated by the narrative content: Ratcliff has visions (A); he forgets them in later life (B); he sees Mary and recognizes the woman of his dreams (A').

The first indication that the theme quoted in Example 6.5 is going to be an important leitmotiv comes in Lesley's repliques, which are built on a transformation of it.

Ex. 6.6.   *Vil'iam Ratklif,* p. 145

From then on there is not a theme sounded in Ratcliff's narrative that does not make a significant return in some other scene. When Ratcliff recalls how Mary's "No" resounded in his ears like "hellish laughter," we hear it in the orchestra, and hear it again, sung this time by an offstage "chorus of witches" to accompany Ratcliff's ravings at the end of the Scene at the Black Stone. Again, the music of Ratcliff's fatal duel with Douglas is prefigured in the middle section of the narrative, where Ratcliff sings of his thirst for blood and revenge[63] (Ex. 6.7).

Many of these thematic returns can be considered no more than petty "cross references," as Abraham puts it[64]—very small-scale *Erinnerungen.* There is one theme, however, that must be described as a leitmotiv: the one given in Example 6.4. It lies at the root of the Scene at the Black Stone and in a way may be said to have made the scene possible. This, the most "dramatic" scene in the opera, is the first to present direct action without reliance on flashback or narrative. Its core is the duel between Ratcliff and Douglas, flanked on both sides by impassioned monologues for the title character. In these the Heine/Pleshcheev text is followed faithfully by Cui and set as broadly conceived *scene* to which the term "melodic recitative" may be fairly applied. Mood succeeds mood with great rapidity and the vocal line responds with unexampled freedom and plasticity. What binds the whole scene together

Ex. 6.7. a. *Vil'iam Ratklif*, pp. 149-50

is the "leitmotiv of Ratcliff himself, developing and changing in conjunction with the scenic situation and mood," as Cui put it later (after the word "leitmotiv" had in fact entered the universal musical vocabulary; in 1869 it did not yet exist).[65] Its many vicissitudes may be suggested by a tabulation of a few of its appearances in the Scene at the Black Stone (Ex. 6.8).

It surfaces once more in the final scene, once before Ratcliff kills Mary, and then again when he kills himself (Ex. 6.9, p. 374).

Whereas this leitmotiv may be said to provide the continuity in the Scene at the Black Stone, the climaxes are articulated by means of another recurrent musical idea: an interesting five-beat phrase characterized by a "modal" diatonicism (the major triad on the natural seventh degree as dominant surrogate), all of which makes it perhaps the most "Russian" phrase in the opera (Ex. 6.10, p. 375).

b. p. 169

Cui gives this motive very prominent play: it recurs no less than four times (the last time in augmentation, transposed up a whole step), and on each occurrence it is immediately repeated, for a total of eight iterations in all. As a melodic idea its impulse is essentially lyric, not declamational (unlike the leitmotiv, it occurs only in the voice part). It is never altered or developed; its function is that of a point of reference. Each time it is used the words are different, made to fit by greater or lesser adjustment (typically involving melisma, that most un-"realistic" of devices).[66]

Ex. 6.8.   The Ratcliff leitmotiv in the scene at the Black Stone

a.

b.

c.

d.

e.

Ex. 6.9.   The Ratcliff leitmotiv in Act III

a.

b.

Ex. 6.10.   *Vil'iam Ratklif*, p. 161, orchestra part simplified

By the use in conjunction of these two recurrent motives—one dynamic and flexible, the other climactic and lyrical—Cui was able to construct a lengthy scene in "free" style, which took its formal cues at all times from the text, but which was nonetheless musically coherent. A notable achievement, this: by all odds Cui's high-water mark as practicing *"kuchkist"* and the most valuable and influential scene in the opera. It was admired by Rimsky-Korsakov and Musorgsky to the point of emulation. Rimsky acknowledged having composed the main theme of *Antar* "under the indubitable influence of certain phrases from *William Ratcliff*."[67] A comparison of the theme cited in Example 6.10, plus the following phrase, quoted here from its initial appearance in the Scene at the Black Stone (later Cui abstracted it along with the Example 6.10 theme for very prominent use in the opera's overture, which he intended as a portrait of the hero),

Ex. 6.11.   *Vil'iam Ratklif*, p. 168

with the *Antar* theme:

Ex. 6.12.   *Antar*, theme from first movement

will be sufficient to prove the point.

Musorgsky's debt to *Ratcliff* went deeper. His treatment of the title character in *Boris Godunov* (and perhaps, too, Rimsky's treatment of Ivan the Terrible in *Pskovitianka*) owed a great deal to the figure of William Ratcliff.[68] The phrase quoted in Example 6.11, moreover, is clearly the model for this famous replique from Tsar Boris's farewell to his son:

Ex. 6.13.   *Boris Godunov* (ed. D. Lloyd-Jones, Oxford University
             Press, 1975) p. 778, vocal line only

Ne sprăši·vaj   ka-kim pu-tëm ja car-stvo pri·o·brël —
(Don't ask me how I obtained the throne.

te-be   ne nuž-no znat'!
You don't need to know!)

This phrase is the only remnant in the 1874 version of *Boris* of what had been a very important leitmotiv in the 1869 version of the second act, which owed the most, both in conception and in many details of execution, to the Scene at the Black Stone.

Some have objected to the use of the term "leitmotiv" for these *Ratcliff* themes, among them Gerald Abraham, who insists that *Erinnerungsmotiv* is the proper handle to apply, since nowhere does Cui go beyond the Weber of *Euryanthe* in their "plastic transformation."[69] Of course all these terms are necessarily applied ex post facto to Cui's opera, and distinctions therefore are bound to be subjective. (Perhaps the term Rimsky-Korsakov invented in his review—"thematic dramaturgy"—might be the best one to use, to avoid quibbling.) But distinctions are nonetheless worth drawing here. The Eglantine motif in *Euryanthe* (to which Abraham evidently refers) is hardly more than accompaniment figure. The *Ratcliff* themes are far more deserving of the label "theme." And besides, *Ratcliff* contains one classic "*Erinnerungsmotiv,*" whose progress through the opera may be instructively contrasted with that of the hero's themes.

This last, of course, is Margaret's song, "O why is thy sword with blood so red, Edward, Edward?" (Ex. 6.14).

Its place in Cui's scheme of things musical is practically dictated by Heine, since it already stalks the play as a prime cog in the mechanism of the Schicksalsdrama, as a musical symbol of the fatal love of Edward and Betty, which keeps on acquiring new meaning as characters and audience acquire new information.[70] As an actual musical phrase within the world of the play, it

Ex. 6.14.   *Vil'iam Ratklif*, p. 210 (Margaret's song)

plays the same direct dramatic role in Cui's opera as its celebrated prototype—
to which analogies are inevitably drawn—*"Un fièvre brûlante"* from Grétry's
Richard Coeur-de-lion (1784). Idées fixes like these ought to be distinguished
from leitmotivs. They are stable and static, quoted rather than organically
developed into the fabric of the music. Unlike leitmotivs, their use does not
contribute to the "freeing" of musical form, but is dictated solely by
dramaturgical considerations. They function as easily and meaningfully
within a numbers opera as within any other kind. Unless distinctions like these
are made, to quibble about terminology is futile. And if they are made, then
the *Ratcliff* themes must be counted as leitmotivs—the first of their kind in
Russia. Rimsky-Korsakov acknowledged *Ratcliff*'s primacy in this regard as
late as 1908, in conversation with Yastrebtsev. He expressed the opinion,
when asked about it, that the leitmotiv came to Russia by way of Berlioz
rather than Wagner, but advised Yastrebtsev to ask Cui, who, having used
them first, "should know better than I."[71]

As for Margaret's Erinnerungsmotiv, Cui's handling of it is effective, if a
bit crude. Except for one brief snatch of it which may or may not appear (the
connection is tenuous) in the accompaniment to Ratcliff's narrative,[72] its use
is confined to the outer acts, that is, to the acts in which Margaret appears. But
she is not the only one to sing it. Cui constructs two of his interpolated
choruses on the tune: the one in Act I at Mary's faint (Ex. 6.15), whose text has
been already cited on p. 361 above, and the one that concludes the opera, thus
putting the final seal of fate over the completed action. Another good
dramatic stroke was to transfer the tune to Ratcliff's part, once he has fulfilled
the song's "behest" by killing Mary (Ex. 6.16, p. 379).

Elsewhere, it must be owned, Cui tends to weaken the dramaturgical
potency of the motive by diffusing it. When Margaret attempts to rouse Mary
from her faint in Act I by singing the song to her, the effect is strong: not only
does Margaret alone realize its full significance, but singing it as she does right
after the faint symbolically links Mary's cry, "William!" with William's father
Edward (though the audience is not yet explicitly informed of this relationship—unless they have read their program synopses!). However, when not
only the chorus chimes in but even Douglas—who remains in Heine curiously

Ex. 6.15. *Vil'iam Ratklif*, p. 46

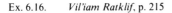

Ex. 6.16.   *Vil'iam Ratklif*, p. 215

(and significantly!) passive throughout the episode—the effect approaches that of a decorative morceau d'ensemble, and the musical symbol loses its focus.

An interesting insight into Cui's dramatic and musical predilections comes from a comparison of the dramatic centerpieces of the Scene at the Black Stone and of the final act. The central episode of the Scene at the Black Stone, the colloquy and duel between Ratcliff and Douglas, is given extremely short shrift. The text is cut down to the bare bones: a mere 24 lines remain from Heine's already terse 40. Almost all the dialogue that takes place during the actual fight is cut, its place being taken by a quintessentially "operatic" outcry from *Ratcliff:* "O Death!" Thus, the most important, potentially spectacular piece of action in the opera is rather spectacularly underplayed.

But if the Scene at the Black Stone is abridged, the culminating scene is conspicuously expanded. With Ratcliff's entrance, Heine had embarked upon a swift course of action involving two murders and a suicide in the space of six pages. In Cui's opera, however, the emphasis is placed not on the grim and bloody working out of Fate's decree, but on the ecstatic embrace of the lovers Edward/William and Betty/Mary. This passes in a moment with Heine, but Cui, evidently finding in love the raison d'être of opera itself, blows the moment into a gigantic love duet, the only full-scale ensemble in the opera.[73] Here Heine's text is treated by Krylov as the basis for a free paraphrase, which finally degenerates for the peroration into typical "ensemble verses," empty of literary value but full of affective iteration—the kind of thing Serov might have called, approvingly, a "canvas for music":

Mary: Calm, stand calm, my beloved,
        Let me look upon thee.
        My darling, my William!
        My darling, I love thee,
        I love thee, my William,
        I love thee, my precious.
        My darling, my darling William,
        I love thee, I love thee.

William: I see myself at my Mary's feet.
           But still I cannot believe my eyes.
           Am I dreaming, or is this real?
           I cannot tell, but I am happy,
           But I am happy with thee, my Mary.
           I am happy with thee, my Mary,
           My Mary.

This duet reaches a conventional but effective and assured musical climax replete with high B♭ for the soprano, a fermata at the cadence and an orchestral postlude to accompany their kiss. There is even a closed cadence at the end of the postlude (to accommodate applause?) (Ex. 6.17).

But now Cui faced a serious problem. In the play the sequence of murders is set in motion by Ratcliff's ecstatic line, "Mir ist die Nacht vom Auge fortgeküsst;/Die Sonne kann ich wieder sehn—Maria!" This mention of her name brings Mary out of her trance: she is not Betty but Mary; before her stands not Edward but William. She begins immediately to resist him, and this is what impels him to kill her. But in the opera this turn of events is made impossible by the love duet. Apparently for the sake of giving the number an emotional "reality" lacking in Heine, Cui had had the lovers call each other by their right names throughout. And so Cui skips directly to Margaret's sinister reprise of her fateful ballad. Hearing the grand Erinnerungsmotiv reminds Ratcliff of his fatal "duty," and he turns without any other motive upon the still enamored and unresisting Mary. The murders, toward which all the events of the preceding narratives had pointed inexorably, are at the last moment seemingly rendered superfluous. Far from the ineluctable climax they comprise in Heine, where Fate leaves Ratcliff no other recourse than murder, they now appear a mechanically contrived and trivially "romantic" denouement forced upon the composer by the ending of Heine's play. For with his love duet Cui had in fact created another alternative: Mary, in the opera, is made to love William, not Edward. The opera, unlike the play, could thus have plausibly ended with the lovers' union. In the context of the love duet, this might even have been (on the opera's terms) a more convincing resolution of the Fate motif, since the consummation of Edward and Betty's love obviously interested the composer far more than the avenging of Edward's murder, which, just as obviously, had mattered most to Heine.

This is not necessarily to imply that a happy ending would have been a sound or convincing culmination of the drama, only that such a conclusion would have been more consistent with Cui's distorted view of Heine's play. Throughout the opera one senses the underlying predicament: Cui wishes to make love his dominant theme, and wishes to make of his hero a rounded and complex character along the lines of psychological realism mapped out for music by Dargomyzhsky. He could not have picked less fertile soil for such fruit than *William Ratcliff,* for the Schicksalsdrama was by nature inhospitable to "real" motivations and characters. The opera's dramaturgical failure was thus foredoomed: the conclusion was no longer an organic outgrowth of the action. Margaret's concluding speech proclaiming the triumph of Fate could no longer arise spontaneously and naturally out of the situation, but had to be "prepared" by an incredibly stilted interpolated chorus of wedding guests, to a text by Krylov:

Ex. 6.17.   *Vil'iam Ratklif*, p. 209

Chorus: Vengeance! Bloody vengeance! We thirst for vengeance for MacGregor's death! (Etc., etc.)

[Stage Direction: Margaret, unnoticed up to now, slowly rises from her corner and slowly makes her way to the alcove through the crowd, which parts for her.]

Chorus: There goes mad Margaret. Her gaze is wandering; her gaze is frightening. She wishes to tell us something.

Margaret (drawing the screen aside and pointing to Ratcliff's corpse): Thus did Edward Ratcliff lie pale and bloody against the old tower. The evil MacGregor did kill the poor wretch! It was not my doing; I only knew. But that very one did William Ratcliff send on his way, and then fell peacefully asleep by Mary's side for all eternity.

Chorus: Unhappy victims of cruel Fate!

Despite, or even because of all this spelling-out, Margaret's interpretation of the bloody events lacks the chilling force it had possessed in Heine's play. For one cannot have it both ways. *Ratcliff* can be either a drama of fate or a tragedy. The two genres cannot be made to mix.

But the composer and his confreres failed to see that he was working at cross-purposes with the poet. His attempt to imbue the drama with the stuff of tragedy was in fact singled out for special praise. Musorgsky, naturally enough, approved heartily of his colleague's characterization of William Ratcliff not as mindless instrument of Fate, but as tragic hero goaded by unrequited love: "The amazing thing is that while Heine's Ratcliff is a stick figure, yours is a personality of frenzied passion, so alive through your music that one sees no sticks—one is dazzled."[74] And in his blindly eulogistic review of the opera, Rimsky-Korsakov paid particular homage to the love duet. While Cui unquestionably did succeed in breathing some real musical life into his hero—the monologues in the scene at the Black Stone are, after all, far and away the best things in the score—it was in the end a Pyrrhic victory: to strengthen the character was fatally to weaken the drama.

Given his historical position and the group with which he is identified, one looks hard for the realist in Cui. But one is looking for a chimera. His aesthetic allegiance was always to romanticism; whatever realistic touches one finds are mere quirks that rubbed off on him from his fellow *kuchkists* or from Dargomyzhsky, and sit rather incongruously on the surface of his work. Among these we might place first the obeisance to the whole tone scale in MacGregor's narrative:

Ex. 6.18.   *Vil'iam Ratklif*, pp. 68-69

If this passage sounds forced, compare the variant of one of the Ratcliff leitmotivs that was originally to have concluded the opera's overture, blared out by a solo trombone:

Ex. 6.19.   Rejected sketch for the Overture (Yastrebtsev,
Vospominaniia o Rimskom-Korsakove, vol. I, p. 71)

This was scrapped at the insistence of Balakirev himself, who went so far in his usual dictatorial way as actually to write for Cui the present conclusion of the overture.[75]

Similarly uncharacteristic and trivial is the one touch of "naturalism" in *Ratcliff*, which inevitably attracted attention far out of proportion to its significance in Cui's scheme of things: the yawning and snoring chorus with which the second act concludes following Ratcliff's narrative. The handling of the chorus here is really anything but realistic—it is a typical "monolithic" operatic chorus that replaces a pair of genre episodes in the original play. First (in Heine) the robbers, Robin, Dick and Bill, discuss their leader's strange behavior and go out to "work"; whereupon Tom the innkeeper steals the money from the pockets of the remaining members of the band, John and Taddie, who then wake up and go off. Krylov and Cui rejected this "realistic" individualization of the minor characters, preferring a scene in which the robber band, divided into impersonal groups of tenors and basses, goes back to sleep after having been awakened by Ratcliff's rantings. The "naturalistic" touches are offset by conventionally absurd choral announcements (e.g., "Our eyes are closing"). Curious as it may seem, this quaint passage was taken as the *ne plus ultra* of musical realism and ultramodernism, suggesting that early listeners to *William Ratcliff* responded more to the composer's reputation than to the actual sounds they heard[76] (Ex. 6.20).

On the other hand, when Cui gave himself up to his romanticist inclinations, he produced some of the best and most "authentic" pages in the score. The beginning and end of the Scene at the Black Stone stand out in this regard. The stage is set for Ratcliff's first monologue with a brief orchestral "storm" based on the leitmotiv first introduced in the middle section of the narrative in the preceding scene, where the hero had described his dissipations and his bandit's life. This is a fine embodiment of the romantic solipsism which reduces the phenomena of nature, the outer world, to a reflection of the protagonist's inner life. After the duel, Cui accompanies Ratcliff's onstage ravings with the "hellish laughter" of an offstage "chorus of witches." This is the hallucination (in dissonant major seconds) Ratcliff had described to Lesley in the preceding scene. The witches' laughter is at first a very effective component of the texture, particularly when it is brought into conjunction with Ratcliff's lyrical leitmotiv (Ex. 6.21).

Ex. 6.20.   *Vil'iam Ratklif*, p. 159

Ex. 6.21.   *Vil'iam Ratklif*, pp. 173-74

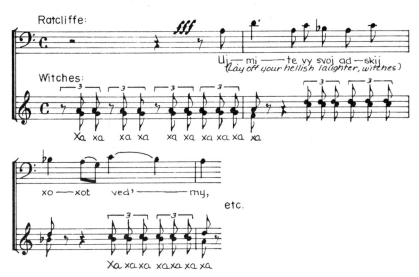

But when the witches laugh their last laugh after Ratcliff's exit, the effect is considerably vitiated. What Cui may have regarded as an innocuous touch of spooky coloration à la *Freischütz* gives the witches a "reality" independent of their demented observer and retroactively compromises their "artistic truth."

In his critical writings Cui gave matters of declamation and prosody such exaggerated weight that it becomes irresistible to look at his own work from this narrow perspective. If we proceed from this bias we perceive what seems perhaps the greatest gulf between preachment and practice to be found anywhere in the repertoire surveyed in this book. The opening chorus, for example, gets hardly a better mark than the choruses in *Judith*. Its text (by Krylov) runs as follows:

Drużia! Pust' zhizn' sulit vam
   vsegda liubov' i radost'.
	Friends! May life vouchsafe you
	   ever love and joy.

Pust' ni gore, ni nuzhda
   ne opechalit vas.
	Let neither want nor sorrow ever
	   make you sad.

Puskai pred vami zhizn' proidët
   tsvetushchei gladkoiu dorogoi.
	May your lives travel a smooth,
	   flourishing path.

Puskai i siryi i ubogii vsegda
   uchast'e v vas naidët.
	May the wretched and lonely ever
	   find a friend in you.

Pust' vasha zhizn' dast vam liubov'
   i veselie i radost'.
	May your lives grant you love,
	   merriment and joy.

Nam dana po srok ved' eta zhizn'   This life is granted us for but a time.
No pust' zhe do mogil'noi seni   But before the shroud comes,
Puskai rok vas ne lishit liubovnykh   Let not Fate deprive you of the ecstasy
   upoenii i char liubvi.   of love, nor of its charms.
Blaga vse vam sulia vashe zdorov'e   God grant you all good things, to your
   p'ëm.   health we drink.
Vivat! Vivat!   Vivat! Vivat!

This text, with its none too subtle memento mori, is serviceable enough for its conventional purposes, and upon it Cui constructs a huge and quite elaborately "symphonic" choral set piece. But from a doctrinaire *kuchkist* point of view—that is, from Cui's point of view—the chorus betrays an alarming willingness to sacrifice textual values to musical. The musical form is allowed to expand by means of endless fragmentary repetitions of text, and some egregious transgressions against prosody are committed in accommodating the words to what are obviously independently conceived musical ideas. The first line, for example, is set as two massive choral ejaculations that begin imitatively and come quickly to decisive cadences. There is no punctuation in the line, nor anything else to suggest dividing it in this way save a penchant for musical symmetry. The imitative entries, while musically effective, play havoc as always with textual intelligibility. Because of the quickly approaching cadence, Cui is forced to give successively entering voices progressively truncated versions of the text, with the result that each part sings a different set of words. (He even resorts to subterfuges like employing two different forms of the Russian word "may"—*pust'* and *puskai*—so as to gain or lose a syllable where needed.) And in the second phrase, the tenors and basses mindlessly repeat "love and joy, joy and love," so as to end on the word *liubóv'*, which has its accent in the right place. The altos and sopranos are not so lucky, they are forced to end on *rádost'* (joy), which by virtue of the musical meter comes out *radóst'* (Ex. 6.22).

Elsewhere, the words "smooth and flourishing path" are punched out a syllable at a time, in a fashion Cui the critic loved to deride (Ex. 6.23).

As an interesting documentation of the "radical change of taste" Laroche so rightly discerned in the opera, we may compare this opening chorus with the little choral *scena* that immediately precedes the most Auberian number of all, Lesley's song in Act II. Although this little "invitation to sing" is part of the earliest scene to have been composed, it was a very late addition, described in a letter to Musorgsky (July 27, 1868) in which Cui boasted that "to my own words I have written music which is, I submit, *unimpeachable in facture,*" and in a footnote to the letter admitted that by unimpeachable he really meant "exemplary."[77] Exemplary, that is, according to standards very recently set by *The Stone Guest* and *Marriage*. In this scene, for once, the chorus is not treated as a monolithic mass, but as a collection of "individuals." Sometimes

Ex. 6.22.   *Vil'iam Ratklif*, pp. 11-12

Ex. 6.23.   *Vil'iam Ratklif*, p. 13, choral parts only

this is accomplished by means of imitation, that is to say, "artificially." But at other times the chorus is fragmented more freely, one passage in particular bringing Musorgsky's rhythmic practices to mind:

Ex. 6.24.   *Vil'iam Ratklif*, p. 122, vocal parts only

But passages like this are very, very much the exception in *William Ratcliff*. Even Cui's "melodic recitative" sometimes violates correctness of declamation and clarity in the projection of text in a way that, if it does not cast doubt on the sincerity of the composer's critical preachments, it at least raises questions as to his ability to live up to them. Not even in *Rogneda* at its worst can one find a ʼpassage that transgresses Russian prosody more fundamentally than this line of "melodic recitative" for MacGregor:

Ex. 6.25.   *Vil'iam Ratklif*, pp. 24-25, vocal line only

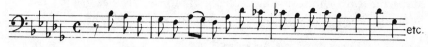

Da bu-det že nad va-mi dvoj-no-e   ix bla-go-slo-ve-n'e de-ti
(*May both their blessings be over you, children.*)

Here not only does the Russian word *vámi* recieve an unwarranted accent on the second syllable, but a similar stress falls upon the intensifying particle *zhe*, which is invariably slurred over in normal Russian speech. Cui has set the line, in short, like a foreigner, which stylistically speaking, perhaps he was.[78]

Because of his respect for musical meter over prosodic freedom, Cui's melodic recitative is rhythmically monotonous. Note values are generally limited to eighths, quarters and dotted quarters, with longer values at moments of extreme emphasis. Gruppetti (even triplets) are so rare as to be negligible. Phrases are welded into long periods, which by their similarity of rhythmic motion lose that "characteristicness"—that memorable alliance of verbal and musical phrase—which Cui prized so highly as a critic. Moreover, Cui's frequent lengthening of the last two notes of a phrase (quarters, say, in a context of eighths) and his reliance upon the characteristic device of appoggiatura at "feminine cadences" are both patently derivative of French prosodic habit, and suit the Russian stress-length pattern poorly. For illustration, refer to Example 6.9b above, and Example 6.26 as follows:

Ex. 6.26.   *Vil'iam Ratklif*, p. 163

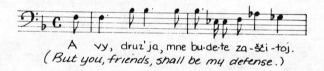

A   vy, druz'ja, mne bu-de-te za-šči -toj.
(*But you, friends, shall be my defense.*)

For any pretense at all to naturalistic declamation in the solo parts one must look to Ratcliff's hallucinatory ravings at the end of the Scene at the Black Stone, where his utterances lose their syntactical coherence under pressure of his fevered emotional state. Here Cui responds with a few lines of music that exhibit the gasping pauses and syncopations—violations of normal musical "syntax"—that we associate with so much of Musorgsky's prosody. Here, too, we find another rare occurrence in *Ratcliff* of characteristically *kuchkist* "empirical harmony"—this time employing a tritone ostinato à la *Boris*. The two styles—prosodic and harmonic—are really the two faces of one coin.

Ex. 6.27.   *Vil'iam Ratklif*, p. 177

Though Musorgskian harmonies like these are not common in *Ratcliff*, the general harmonic and textural style of the work may fairly be called *"kuchkist"* in its overelaboration. This was something Tchaikovsky was particularly sensitive to in his critiques of the work of his St. Petersburg rivals. He put it this way with reference to *Ratcliff:*

> In this opera there are delightful things—but unfortunately they suffer from a sickly sweetness and a certain sleekness in the voice leading. It is apparent that the author lingered over every bar and shaped them all lovingly, and that consequently his musical line is not sufficiently free, his strokes are too obviously artificed. Besides, he is undone by what you might call "originalizing." By the nature of his gift, Cui is inclined toward light, piquantly rhythmic music in the French manner. But the demands of the circle to which he belongs have forced him to overstrain his talent and get himself involved in such pseudo-original harmonic tricks as prevent him from being fertile.... *Ratcliff* took him ten [sic] years to write. Obviously the opera was composed in bits and pieces, each very conscientiously crafted,—but seeing it whole one feels a lack of unity and an unevenness of style.[79]

Vsevolod Cheshikhin has made some perceptive observations on this point as well:

> At a cursory glance (away from the piano), the music seems very simple.... But one has only to hear it in the theatre, or even play it over at the piano, to be convinced of the effort to

which Cui subjected his essentially simple compositional gift.... In every bar of *Ratcliff* there is some kind of harmonic vagary, in the guise of a chain of suspensions, anticipations, passing tones, auxiliaries or pivots, enharmonic modulations, altered chords and the like. In every bar there is an effort to conceal the harmonic structure, to hide the basic triadic progression from the listener!...This recherché harmonization of his cannot be the immediate product of his creative fantasy; it is obvious that the composer first thought up some simple tunes and afterwards embellished them with every conceivable harmonic affectation.[80]

One may recall that Tchaikovsky said some very similar things about his own opera *Vakula the Smith,* which he attributed directly to the influence of *"kuchkism,"* and which he attempted to exorcise in recreating that opera as *Cherevichki.* In the eyes of non-*kuchkists,* anyway, *kuchkism* always involved an overwrought harmonic texture, full of inner-voice activity, and excessively preoccupied with piquant "finds" at the local level, to the detriment of long-range design. For an example in *Ratcliff,* besides those given we may add this especially characteristic one from Ratcliff's Act II narrative:

Ex. 6.28.   *Vil'iam Ratklif,* pp. 138-39

The justice of Cheshikhin's observations is borne out in the use of pedals, of modal mixtures and of chromatic passing tones and neighbors (with particular emphasis on the raised fifth/lowered sixth so beloved of Balakirev). These are all rather obtrusively in evidence and spray a thick perfume over the rather simple melodic substance (almost all of it derived from Ratcliff's leitmotiv). But, as we shall see, where his critics saw in all this harmonic "tinycraft" only the paralysis of drama and a deviation from proper operatic style, Cui and his confreres saw in it a courageous embodiment of their shibboleth that "operatic music must be good music."[81]

William Ratcliff had its premiere on February 14, 1869, in a lavish production that marked the debut not only of the composer but of the conductor as well. Eduard Napravnik's long and distinguished career at the Mariinsky may be said to have begun with *Ratcliff,* since the only previous opera premiered by him had been his own *Nizhegorodtsy,* a month and a half before (December 27, 1868). *Ratcliff's* cast included such veterans as Leonova (Margaret), "Vasiliev the First" (MacGregor), and Nikolsky (Douglas). Platonova, then reaching the height of her career, sang Mary. Even the minor roles were assigned to first-string artists: Sariotti, Serov's favorite, sang Robin, and the part of Lesley was performed by the well-known vocal pedagogue and composer Pyotr Petrovich Bulakhov (1822-85), author of the still-popular "Troika." The title role went to Ivan Alexandrovich Melnikov, later the creator of *Boris Godunov,* who brought to three the number of auspicious debutants of the evening. Ratcliff was the first of many roles that were to make Melnikov the reigning baritone of the Russian lyric stage for many years.

In spite of the efforts of this excellent cast, *William Ratcliff* enjoyed not even a *succes d'estime*. Stasov recorded the opera's honorable failure with a self-righteousness that bordered on delectation:

> After the great operas of Glinka and Dargomyzhsky, this was at the time the best, the most significant opera written in Russia. Well then, what was the fate of this remarkable creation? The answer, it would seem, would be simple. Of course, anyone would say, this opera was received with open arms, was cherished, taken immediately for something precious and important, was greeted from its first appearance with enthusiasm and delight, and later was... lovingly preserved on the stage, constantly admired and surrounded with best wishes and infinite care. Not here. That would merely have been common sense, natural, innate. With us such logic is in many things utterly unknown, while what is known is another kind of logic peculiarly our own, utterly unique, unseen and unheard of. It consists in not rejoicing at the appearance of an opera of talent... but lamenting it instead, reacting not with delight but with indignation and rage, making it an object of hatred and persecution, and banishing it as soon as possible from the face of the earth.... And so it was that Cui's wondrous opera, the work of the highest talent, met the common fate and was immediately hated, ridiculed, run down and cast away from the stage like so much worthless rubbish.[82]

Cui himself, while naturally avoiding Stasov's shrillness, sought similarly to place the blame for his opera's failure on the public's backwardness and upon the enmity he had earned among the critics for his own activity in that field. While slanted and self-serving, his reminiscences are not without poignancy:

> Beginning in 1864 I had been engaged in musical criticism. My aim consisted in propagandizing our ideas and in supporting the composers of the New Russian School, whose music I valued and continue to value highly.... It was hard at the beginning. A bunch of officers out of nowhere plus a chemist had taken it into their heads to claim recognition as serious composers, and I, in the field of criticism, had presumed to rebel against the time-honored laws of routine, pass disrespectful judgment upon the authorities, and so on. All of this called forth the public's enmity toward us all, and particularly toward me as the mouthpiece, and from the critics it called forth a malice that was transferred from my "critical" shoulders to my composer's ones. With particular energy I carped in those days against the Italian opera in favor of the Russian, and among us there were then many Italomanes. Their desire for retribution went so far, that on the day of *Ratcliff*'s premiere they took a loge next to the directorate's, and when I came out to take my bows there (it was considered unseemly for a uniformed military man to appear on stage for such a purpose), they hissed right in my face, I answering them with bows (admittedly, I had been warned of this demonstration in advance, was prepared for it, and had amply fortified myself with sang-froid). Another reason for *Ratcliff*'s failure may have been the novelty of its forms. In it I had endeavored to realize our operatic ideals; it was the first opera to do combat for them.... In it, in place of the usual arias comprised of the obligatory andante and allegro, the listeners found narratives written in completely free form, they found choruses with modest symphonic developments, they found Ratcliff's leitmotiv, developing and changing in conjunction with the scenic situation and mood, while of Wagner's tendencies we had at that time practically no idea at all.[83]

Of course, Serov's operas, especially *Judith,* could be described in the same terms, but of course both Stasov and Cui, were, as ever, careful not to acknowledge their existence. Their composer was at the premiere, though, and Serov, who had so often tasted the bitter gall of *kuchkist* attack, seized his opportunity to even the score. Serov's review was the model which Cui and Stasov falsely represented as the general standard. Astonishingly, he began his offensive by questioning the credentials of critic as composer, which amounted to casting an enormous boulder at his own glass house.

A real artist is *always* a critic, but from this it does not follow that any old musical reporter can become a real artist by merely wishing it. The "Scottish" (!) opera entitled *William Ratcliff*... testifies to its author's complete unsuitedness to the career upon which he has set out.... The most insignificant "bravura" aria by Donizetti or Verdi is a veritable colossus of dramatic truth—in its own way—beside this absurd jumble of syncopations and disharmonies expressive of nothing because they strive to express too much.... With such exponents as Messrs. Stasov and Balakirev our musical maturation cannot get very far; we can already admire one operatic product of their camp. From there one could have expected nothing for the theater except monstrosities and lo!—the monster is before us! It is a totally failed attempt, exuding overwhelming ennui, and it is therefore no wonder that after its sixth [*recte* seventh] performance came the final death-throes. Nothing else could have been expected of one who despises Mozart, Rossini, Meyerbeer and Wagner, and who accepts as his ideal of *dramatic music* such unfortunate miscarriages as Schumann's *Genoveva* and Berlioz's *Troyens.* Art takes its revenge upon those who slander it.[84]

Serov's review of Cui's operatic "galimatias" mostly sustains this malicious, captious tone and empty posture: Serov the defender of the musical mainstream in valorous battle against rampant philistinism. But Serov could not write an entire piece, however strident and parti-pris, without some perceptive flashes. He cuts right to the heart of the trouble with *Ratcliff* in his comments on Cui's choice and treatment of his subject. A committed rationalist, Serov had not the slightest sympathy with Heine or with his play.[85] Unable to comprehend the romantic outlook embodied in the Schicksalsdrama as a genre, Serov preferred to view Heine's *Ratcliff* as a deliberate mockery, a "whole series of scenes taken straight out of Bedlam," in which the German "tooth gnasher" had "poured out his rage against the theatrical customs of his time."[86] This was far from the case, and yet Serov caught well the glaring incongruity between the essential nature of Heine's play and Cui's operatic treatment.

Imagine a gentleman who decides to take this parody seriously (!), who sees in it a foundation for profound psychological drama, a man who in all conscientiousness sets out to realize this drama (!!) and do it by means of rhythmic and harmonic miniatures in the manner of Berlioz and Schumann. —Is this not the manifestation of a sick brain?[87]

If one divests this passage of its ad hominems and hyperboles, it remains the single contemporary critique of *Ratcliff* to note the fatal flaw—Cui's attempt to introduce elements of tragedy and psychological realism into a completely inhospitable terrain. All other critics agreed that *William Ratcliff* was a poor subject—even Stasov, as we have seen, had his doubts—but none defined the reason as aptly as Serov, even though he understood and sympathized with Heine's drama less yet than Cui, perhaps less than anybody.

Others were more inclined to take the view expressed by Musorgsky, that Cui's departures from Heine were more or less successful improvements. Laroche was particularly intrigued with the apparent incongruity between the bloody subject and Cui's tender, Schumannesque music.

> In [MacGregor's] narrative there is an extremely pretty, warm phrase—"In that night, when the crime was accomplished," which exemplifies our author's manner at its best. Its harmony seemed to me at first glance to be too soft, too rich for this terrible moment which it illustrates; subsequently I became convinced that Cui deliberately gives this soft tone to those places where Ratcliff's bloodthirstiness manifests itself as the consequence of his love, and I came to the conclusion that the composer does this with the intention of characterizing Ratcliff as the victim of his hallucinations and his morbid sensitivity, as a man who acts under the spell of hallucinations and is cruel against his will. The tenderest, sweetest music in the whole opera is contained in the entr'acte that prepares us for the horrors of the third act: the same quality appears, for example, right before the very murder of Mary, when Ratcliff says, "O, be not afraid, death is so sweet."[88]

But even Laroche had to "leave open the question whether the mass of spectators and listeners will guess the composer's idea and will not see merely a contradiction where he has striven for the highest truth."[89] Ultimately, Cui was wrong, says Laroche, to have chosen such an "emptily violent" subject, "devoid of characters, poor in ideas and founded upon a plot as repellent as it is implausible." Such a story may be all right for Germany, where "there has never been and never will be a Gogol or an Ostrovsky," and where there is "a whole school of dramatists...who *consciously and deliberately* avoid depicting on the stage that which may be encountered in real life." But in Russia, a composer placing such an opera before the public "is doomed to wage a long, hard and essentially hopeless war" against progressive taste.[90]

Laroche complains that *Ratcliff*'s style is fundamentally unoperatic and ineffective on the stage. This is not simply a matter of "forms" but one of general style and facture. Cui's textures are overelaborated, his instrumentation (partly the work of Balakirev and Rimsky-Korsakov, though Laroche did not know this) overly subtle, his vocal line overly complex; he misses the grand manner necessary to support the weight of the opulent production, the enormous forces employed, and the sheer length of the work. This grand manner, Laroche asserts, is primarily a function of simplicity of style:

> It may be said that in opera the dominance of the top voice is stronger than in works of any other type; that operatic music is thus more inclined to homophony than chamber or church music; that in keeping with this the property of opera consists in the most vivid, distinct and

easily remembered melodies; that in operas musical form is not so organically developed, and thematic work is not so strict and logical as in music where polyphony reigns to a greater extent; that operatic music is generally more popular, more plastic and less inclined than other forms of music to go in for subtle details and technical intricacies accessible chiefly to specialists.[91]

Now one of the *kuchka*'s most idealistic and firmly shared positions was in strong reaction against precisely this (to them) vulgarian notion. For them, and for Cui especially, "operatic music must be good music,"[92] meaning that it need not differ in style and tone from any other kind. Laroche, however, refuses to grant this and actually challenges Cui upon his own *kuchkist* terms. Where is the formal freedom, where is the much-touted organic connection with the text that is supposed to be the *kuchkist* hallmark? Laroche cites endless examples from *Ratcliff* to prove, as we have already had occasion to note, that Cui's melodic conception was often independent of the text, and that Cui's musical imagination was hamstrung by the need for symmetrical repetition and formal rounding carried on at the very smallest, most local levels. And this is what made Cui's style essentially miniaturistic and "chamber" rather than theatrical.[93] Laroche hastens to make it clear, however, that he is not being "plus royaliste que le roi": "I would be the last," he assures us, "to take it into my head to raise against any composer the rusty sword of 'artistic truth'; all art is founded on compromises, and only little children and madmen can believe in the possibility of complete artistic truth."[94] His intention is rather to call Cui's bluff: the musical style of *Ratcliff* is not the fruit of operatic reform, but simply the result of Cui's blind adherence to the model of Schumann's opera and oratorios—and a very bad model it is. The whole apparatus of Cui's musical language—the endless suspensions, overdressed harmonies (sevenths, ninths), his ways and means of modulation, his tonic and dominant pedals—all comes straight out of Schumann, except that Cui uses these devices even more manneristically than the German master. And these devices above all are what impede dramatic flow and "effectiveness."

Laroche cannot accept "melodic recitative" as a desideratum. He regards it primarily as the admission of a lack of melodic inspiration, and its use as essentially fraudulent. Its effect is not so much to elevate the status of the recitative as to debase the quality of the lyric element. To blur the distinction between recitative and aria, moreover, is to ensure a general greyness and monotony of musical style, which, like so much else in *Ratcliff*, militates against theatrical effect. For the dramatic moments and lyric high points no longer stand out from the mass, but are swallowed up in an undifferentiated musical miasma.

If one is in fact to raise the melodic level of recitative, if recitative is to be everywhere turned into arioso, then one must *to the same degree* elevate the lyric numbers as well, which would mean to give us in the arias and [ensembles] such chefs d'oeuvre of melody and polished form as to cause all operatic music of former days to pale. . . . Here it might be appropriate to add that Mr. Cui's melodic gift is insignificant.[95]

Laroche's summation shows him not insensitive to the merits of Cui's work and the integrity of his ideals. But *Ratcliff* remained essentially a work for the connoisseur, not for the operatic public at large, and its failure with the audiences at the Mariinsky Theater was to be explained by its very nature as an opera. The critic, as we have seen, was to have similar things to say about *The Stone Guest,* except that Dargomyzhsky's opera was *not* a failure. Laroche ends his review with the rather kind remark that, "for one who values elegant detail, for one who knows how to enjoy lyric moments expressed with talent, *William Ratcliff* will always remain a musical work that inspires both respect and affection."[96]

This is hardly the kind of merciless attack we read about in Stasov and in Cui's reminiscences.[97] But while most critics were willing to grant *Ratcliff*'s individual felicities, no one outside the *kuchka* regarded the work as a viable "spectacle." Most critics did not bother to penetrate as deeply as Laroche into *Ratcliff*'s musical style; it was far easier to pin the opera's unsatisfactoriness on more obvious flaws in its dramaturgy, inherent in the subject itself. Cui's use of the chorus especially incensed Rostislav. The one that concludes the first act seemed particularly ill-conceived: an arbitrary and doctrinaire substitute for the traditional end-of-the-act ensemble, vouchsafing no gain in dramatic truth, but rather exacerbating painfully the impression of dramatic stasis, for all the protagonists are immobilized for its duration. Nor is there any musical gain, argues the critic, since the chorus as Cui deploys it is "nothing else than a morceau d'ensemble, save that it is rendered by mediocre voices rather than more-or-less artistic ones."[98] Rostislav protests predictably enough against the modernity of Cui's actually rather gentle music. What modernistic touches there were had long since become the common coin of progressive Russian composition: the use of the whole tone scale, for example, was by then practically de rigueur for moments of operatic terror. For his modest forays Cui hardly merited the epithet "harmonicide," but at least Rostislav caught the fact that Cui the composer shared at this time the preference of Cui the critic for harmony over melody as the main carrier of musical expression. Not surprisingly, Rostislav's favorite part of the opera was the tavern scene in Act II, whose derivative, Auberian style he rather bizarrely justified on grounds of "realism."

If drama is to be the reproduction of life, then a diversity of styles may be admitted in it, since life is a *kaleidoscope,* in which there mingle all manner of people, places and things. Of course, in a Scottish tavern it would make more sense to hear tunes from that country, but it is hard to see what difference there is between the carousal of inebriated Scotsmen and their French counterparts.[99]

But where Cui had deliberately attempted to incorporate attributes of psychological realism that we associate with Dargomyzhsky and the *kuchka,* Rostislav could not go along. For him, realism was solely a matter of genre and local color. The melodic recitative was an incomprehensible obfuscator rather than a clarifier of dramatic values, and Rostislav's criticism centered precisely on that aspect of Cui's style which was for the *kuchka* its greatest merit: the quick progression from one mood to another, faithfully mirroring the actual mechanics of human thought and feeling. Music could never achieve this end, claimed Rostislav, for there is an essential difference between our perception of music and our perception of words. The melodic recitative, even in a set piece like Ratcliff's narrative, must fail because of its

lack of unity and its indefinite musical character.... Hearing any musical phrase of strong profile, the ear expects its development. But here it is immediately replaced by another, perhaps no less interesting phrase, and the ear is baffled, as the eye is dazzled at the sight of diverse and multifarious objects.... If it is in fact useful to diversify musical phrases according to the meanings of the words, this should not prevent one's taking into account that musical thoughts do not penetrate human understanding as quickly as thoughts expressed in quick speech. Perhaps there will come a time when prepared listeners will be able to catch such thoughts on the fly and absorb the meaning of every fugitive musical idea, but in the meantime, we repeat, a system of kaleidoscopic musical declamation cannot satisfy the majority.[100]

To this Cui might have answered, with Schoenberg, "I can wait," and in fact the wait was not to be such a long one: the surprisingly warm reception accorded Dargomyzhsky's far more "systematic" declamation in *The Stone Guest* three years later belied Rostislav's comments. It was not on this issue that *William Ratcliff* fell, but on those summed up neatly by its conductor: "the absence of dramatic tension ... and ignorance of the stage"—the faults, in short, of Heine's play itself, which Cui was not equipped to overcome. Added to these, however, was "a musical style [that was] not operatic, but suited best for the recital stage, the concert hall, or even the salon."[101]

The only wholly favorable review of *Ratcliff* came, naturally enough, from within the bosom of the *kuchka.* "***" obviously could not publish a review of his own work in the *Sanktpeterburgskie vedomosti,* so he turned to the youngest member of his group, the twenty-three-year-old Rimsky-Korsakov, who obliged him with an ecstatic eulogy that reflected the sincere admiration he felt for one of the Balakirev circles's elders.[102] Not even the young *kuchkist* could find in Heine's play an ideal subject, nor in Cui's opera a model of dramatic structure, but all faults were excusable as necessary, for the sake of greater gain.

Belonging among the weakest of Heine's creations, *Ratcliff* cannot, of course, withstand strict criticism as a work of literature, but at the same time it offers the operatic composer much good material and the most tempting scenes, though far from easy in execution.[103]

This assertion will not stand strict scrutiny, either, for it suggests the kind of relaxed double standard for opera against which the New Russian School was ostensibly pitted. Moreover, it gives tacit sanction to Cui's method of composing his opera in pieces, scene by scene. And while this indeed was the method of Cui the composer, we remember with what glee Cui the critic had flailed at Serov for a similar transgression in *Rogneda*. But this is only the first inconsistency. Only a few weeks earlier Rimsky-Korsakov had sought to demolish Napravnik's *Nizhegorodtsy* on the grounds of eclecticism. Now, confronted with Cui's colossal stylistic debts to Auber and Schumann by turns, he sought to minimize the first by emphasizing (in the tavern scene) Cui's "original and rather piquant rhythmic accents," and, in the case of Schumann, by a bit of outright casuistry: "The style of most of Cui's opera is quite original, but the similarity of this style to that of Schumann is noticeable here and there, though this similarity is only a matter of kindred talents."[104]

No fan of Auber,[105] Rimsky considers the opening scene of Act II to be "one of the opera's weakest numbers," and makes a characteristically *kuchkist* demand for "something more national, more Scottish."[106] But there is something in the scene of which Rimsky heartily approves, and that is the little choral *scena* à la Musorgsky, preceding Lesley's song. This, according to Rimsky's rather hyperbolic description, was "one of the few places in any known opera where the chorus appears as a real character, and not simply a singing mass."[107]

If for no other reason than credibility's sake, Rimsky felt called upon to write negatively about one of *Ratcliff*'s numbers. For this purpose he selected Douglas's narrative in the first act, and subjected it to a very severe *kuchkist* critique, which of course it could not begin to withstand. Over and above the patently "inserted" and decorative character of the number as a whole, Rimsky objected to what happens during its interruption and reprise. Specifically, he cited the use of the chorus as a backdrop to Douglas's solo—a choir of "singers," not characters—and also, more importantly, to Douglas's singing his lines during Mary's faint to the tune of Margaret's song, for this compromises the song's symbolic quality. This scene, in Rimsky-Korsakov's words, "is a long way from satisfying contemporary operatic standards."[108]

Elsewhere Rimsky singles out Cui's use of symbolic themes for special praise, glorifying his colleague's use of reminiscence motifs with a new term, "thematic dramaturgy." Rimsky hails the overture as an absolutely unprecedented dramaturgical breakthrough, since, in place of the usual potpourri, Cui had drawn a vivid portrait of the hero, restricting himself only to themes associated with the title character in the course of the opera. (But it is only within the context of the opera itself that the various themes are given their dramaturgical associations; in the overture the listener cannot know their significance, and so he cannot possibly interpret the "meaning" of the overture in the way Rimsky suggests Cui intended.) The scene in which Rimsky saw "thematic dramaturgy" carried to its height was the last scene. About the duet, Rimsky is emboldened to declare that "we do not hesitate to say that there has never been such a love duet in any other opera,"[109] and the reason given is the obviously Wagnerian one that the whole scene is so tightly constructed on Margaret's song, Ratcliff's motifs and "several reminiscences of various preceding moments in the opera," while at the same time its form is "utterly free."[110] It seems odd that Rimsky should have made so much of the concluding scene, and for such a reason, while he has scarcely a word to say about the Scene at the Black Stone (save to note the correctness of its prosody). In fact, he only mentions the scene at all in order to demonstrate the length of time Cui spent in writing the opera; he contrasts the "inexperience" in declamation one encounters in many of the recitatives with the "complete mastery" of the Scene at the Black Stone, and cites this as the salient yardstick of Cui's artistic growth. But Rimsky leaves the larger aesthetic questions of melodic recitative untouched, suggesting that he himself was perhaps untouched by them.

Perhaps dissatisfied with the quality of Rimsky's praise, and particularly with the reviewer's emphasis upon the quasi-Wagnerian element of "thematic dramaturgy" rather than on Dargomyzhskian recitative, Cui eventually did write his own review of *Ratcliff*—pseudonymously, of course. This was a piece entitled "Three Russian Operas," published in the pages of the *Sanktpeterburgskie vedomosti* over the initial "M." (for Malvina, his wife's name?), on March 16, 1873. The article ostensibly dealt with all of the *kuchkist* operas performed up to that time, namely *Ratcliff, Pskovitianka* and *The Stone Guest.* As the first one to have achieved performance, *Ratcliff* was given pride of place, and Cui's claims for the opera were not distinguished by their modesty. He hails the work as the marker of an epoch, the "boundary dividing the new school from the old." The composer begins by dismissing the charge of Wagnerianism and emphasizing the direct link between *Ratcliff* and the works of Dargomyzhsky.

One cannot deny, of course, that Wagner, and to an extent his extreme adherent the late Serov, have had their measure of influence . . . on the tendency adopted by our young composers, but this influence, if it existed at all, was merely peripheral. . . . Developing and perfecting the orchestra, and at the same time enriching us with new harmonic combinations of tones. [Wagner and Serov] not only failed to ennoble melody, but gave it for the most part a crude, trivial character, and in their handling of voices reached such heights of unnaturalness and impossibility, that certain of their operas, from the vocal point of view, might serve best not as models of how to write, but rather as models of how not to. It is solely to the influence of Dargomyzhsky's romances and to the revival of his *Rusalka* that one can attribute the appearance in 1869 of Cui's opera *William Ratcliff*, which was so remarkable in many respects. . . . In it, for the first time after *Rusalka*, we witnessed that extremely rare combination of all means of operatic expression, which constitutes the real task of the contemporary operatic composer. . . . We heard melody that was noble and passionate in the highest degree, interesting harmonic combinations, a marvelous orchestra, and impeccable handling of voices.[111]

Why then did *Ratcliff* fail? Because of "a not completely successful choice of subject" and an occasional lack of restraint in the orchestration that caused the singers here and there to be drowned out. Not a word about opera-as-drama, nor about expressive declamation ("melodic recitative"). The author of the article, if in fact he wrote at all ingenuously, is an altogether different Cui from the critic of the sixties, who saw melody as a dried-up well, and all future musical progress as stemming from ever-expanding harmonic possibilities. Here he writes of *Ratcliff* as if of a bel canto opera, lumping the declamatory monologues together with the narrative set pieces as equally representative of his opera's extraordinary melodic distinction.

> Particular evidence of talent is the melodic side of the opera. Whoever among our musicians and cultivated amateurs was present at the performances of this opera will remember the enchanting and fresh impression created upon him at the time by the baritone (Ratcliff) and bass (MacGregor) parts, and in part by the feminine roles as well. Something completely new and gorgeous wafted from the passionate monologues and narratives of MacGregor, Douglas and Ratcliff, while the beautiful duet of Mary and Ratcliff in the third act and the whole Scene at the Black Stone will doubtless live forever, or at least for a long time, as model works of art.[112]

The Scene at the Black Stone received its due only from Stasov. His positively vertiginous praise of this scene, in an article intended primarily as a counterattack against *Ratcliff*'s detractors, seems like a practice run for the virtuoso polemics he would unleash in defense of *The Stone Guest*. Stasov alone made the point of Cui's aesthetic kinship with Dargomyzhsky at the time of the premiere. That other critics should not have noticed this is not surprising: *The Stone Guest* had not yet been perfomed. For Stasov, the Scene at the Black Stone

> belongs to the highest there is in music.... Never before in any opera had the expression of the most secret, deep-seated heartstrings been transmitted with such staggering force, passion and alluring beauty.[113]

Nor did Stasov stint where it came to the love scene—the "greatest love duet in the world." Stasov had not Rimsky's scruples; absolutely everything in the opera is praised in hyperbolic terms without any pretense to objectivity. Douglas's narrative for Stasov is "a miraculous model of picturesque description"; the rather sketchy women's parts (Mary and Margaret) "contain an inexhaustible treasure of drama and beauty"—and so it goes. In sum, *Ratcliff* "occupies in Russian music the next place after the great works of Glinka and Dargomyzhsky."[114] Stasov was not inclined to give reasons for his conclusions; his article was not, properly speaking, a work of criticism, but of musical forensics.

When he did come to make a more dispassionate critical assessment of Cui's work, in his synoptic *Twenty-Five Years of Russian Art,* Stasov had to recognize the problematical aspects of the opera and of its author, and had to admit that "two musical elements have always remained foreign to Cui—the national and the comic," and that all Cui's attempts to incorporate them into his work were failures. For *Ratcliff* this meant the role of Lesley and such Scottish local color as Cui had felt impelled to include. More significantly, from the point of view of dramatic quality and that prime *kuchkist* hobby horse, "operatic forms," Cui's opera could no longer be defended, only excused. And Stasov's efforts to excuse the work are not free of special pleading bordering on prevarication:

> In his first [sic] opera ... Cui still held to generally accepted forms; he still had arias, duets and choruses. When he embarked upon this opera, Dargomyzhsky had not as yet come to that musical turning point which he achieved in *The Stone Guest*, and Cui himself was not a reformer by nature. But nonetheless *Ratcliff* belongs to the company of the most important creations of our age, notwithstanding even the opera's unstageworthiness, the plethora of narrative that dampens its effect, and the deficiency of true characters. The force of passion, the dazzlingly poetical and fragrant manifestation of the emotion of love, the dark and menacing tragic overtones, expressed in the attractive forms of new, post-Schumannesque art make this opera a truly remarkable phenomenon.[115]

In short, *Ratcliff* was another *Ruslan,* whose objective failings were redeemed by subjective enjoyment, and whose static projection of mood was sufficiently vivid to compensate for the deficiency of dynamic drama. Stasov seized upon the "expressive" attributes of Cui's music to serve an additional purpose as well; by means of them, he could be shown to be, after all, a "belonging" member of the New Russian School. Though his talent may have been "exclusively lyrical," his emotional expression was profound, and what is more, "accurate," and this is enough for him to qualify as a realist!

> The main features of Cui's work are poetry and passion, combined with an uncommon sincerity and heartfeltness that go straight to the deepest recesses of the heart. It is true that Cui's talent was always directed exclusively to the depiction of amorous emotions in all their diverse manifestations (jealousy, despair, self-sacrifice, etc.), and therefore, it might seem, must appear one-sided. But the depiction of this emotion reaches with Cui such depth and focus as had never been reached before, not only by his comrades in the Russian school, but, perhaps, by anyone in the whole world of music.[116]

As in the case of his defense of *Ruslan,* one feels that Stasov is listing the virtues not of a composer of operas, but of a songwriter or "tone poet." One feels just as strongly, however, that Stasov knew his man. When it came to following *Ratcliff* with another operatic subject, it was Stasov who ended Cui's search with one that, as he put it, "completely satisfied him, and at the same time seemed to answer to many of the chief peculiarities and demands of [Cui's] creative nature."[117] This was Victor Hugo's drama, *Angelo, Tyran de Padoue,* which shared all the virtues of Heine's *William Ratcliff,* and perhaps even more pertinently, many of its vices. Once more we quote from Stasov:

Of course, here as everywhere in Hugo's dramas and novels, there was not a little exaggeration and needless violence typical of French Romanticism in the thirties, but together with that there were also such wonderful elements of passion, devotion, love, self-sacrifice—coupled with all manner of spiritual beauty and fascination—as could not help but act with intoxicating force upon Cui's exuberant fantasy.[118]

Hugo's play is a complicated drama of intrigue in which the "divers manifestations of love" provide virtually the sole motivating force. Angelo the *podesta* of Padua has a wife (Caterina) and a mistress (Thisbe), both of whom love not him but Ezzelino da Romana (alias Rodolfo), scion of the former ruling clan of Padua. Homodei, a spy for the Inquisition, is also enamored of Caterina, and out of jealousy arranges a tryst for her and Rodolfo so as then to denounce her to Angelo and achieve her ruin. Caterina is saved by Thisbe, whose abrupt switch from vengefulness against her rival to self-sacrifice is brought about by the revelation that Caterina had saved the life of Thisbe's mother in Venice, years before. Though the play, like much romantic theater, hinges crucially upon improbable coincidence, at least the characters are motivated by real passions and feelings, and are not mere puppets of Fate, as in *Ratcliff.* Moreover, the work abounds in strong theatrical situations and confrontations, striking peripeteia, and a wealth of lyrical love scenes that in their rhetoric and emotional stasis seem positively Metastasian, fairly crying out for musical setting.[119] There is even a rather contrived use of music within the play. Caterina, reminiscing about Rodolfo, picks up a guitar and begins to strum "their song." Rodolfo, waiting outside the window, sings along with her, and thus their love scene begins. A drama like this seems tailor made for Dargomyzhskian, opéra dialogué treatment, no adjustment being necessary save perhaps application of a blue pencil. Stasov had long had his eye on it: as early as 1846 he had recommended the subject to Serov.[120]

But now, a quarter century later, Cui, his librettist Victor Burenin,[121] and (one suspects) Stasov above all, could not leave *Angelo* alone. By the 1870s after the composition of *Pskovitianka* and *Boris Godunov,* a new operatic ideal had replaced the Dargomyzhskian psychological drama for the New Russian School. The tendency now dominant called for the placement of personal drama in relief against a broad social background whose protagonist was the chorus. Accordingly, Cui and Stasov planned a scenario that sought to adapt Hugo's quintessentially erotic play to these new criteria. Taking their cue presumably from an impromptu fabrication of Thisbe's in Hugo's play, where she explains her unlikely presence in Caterina's quarters to Angelo by saying that she had come to warn him of a plot against his life, the Russians invented a whole subplot of insurrection against Angelo's tyranny, at the head of which stood—Rodolfo! But the insurrection, immediately quashed, is futile both politically and dramaturgically. The love intrigue, the real plot of the play, is absolutely untouched by it; Rodolfo functions as lover completely independently of his role as revolutionary. Thus, the third act of the opera, given over as it is entirely to the insurrection, could be omitted entirely without any loss to the coherence of the drama. The only character directly affected by the new subplot is the inquisitorial spy, whose name is changed in the opera to Galeofa.[122] He now acts not as a rejected lover set upon Caterina's downfall, but as Angelo's own spy, a sort of agent provocateur with Rodolfo as his target. This of course necessitated the replacement of jealousy by some other motivating force behind Galeofa's actions. The best Cui-Stasov-Burenin could come up with were a few bombastic lines wherein Galeofa gives vent to a silly neo-Mephistophelian philosophy of universal negation, mere moustache-twirling. The libretto tries hard to make his death at "the people's" hand seem a blow for freedom against tyranny, but the same event, motivated in Hugo by a lover's rage, is far less unconvincing.

How little the insurrection motif mattered to the real drama is revealed by the fact that elsewhere in the opera the libretto hews very closely to Hugo's original, often reading like a paraphrase, even a translation. With the exception of Angelo's monologue (Act IV, scene i), an interpolation obviously if unsuccessfully modelled on analogous scenes in *Boris Godunov,* which seeks crudely to tie the abortive events of Act III to the rest of the drama, Cui's second and fourth acts are practically straight Hugo (allowing for a few minor interpolations and deletions). Indeed, the composer claimed for the opera as a whole that "I have kept as close as possible both to Hugo's scenario and even to his text,"[123] in keeping with Dargomyzhskian precepts. Act I follows Hugo's drama faithfully, too, except for the opening three scenes, in which the insurrection is planned. Hugo's opening scene between Thisbe and Angelo, in which she tells the story of how her mother's life had been saved by the young Venetian lady who later turns out to be Caterina, was transposed to a later position within the act (obviously Angelo could not be present at the plotting of the revolt).

Cui handled this narrative of Thisbe's in Act I—the only one of its kind in *Angelo*—precisely as he had done with the numerous narratives in *Ratcliff,* as a "free" lyric set piece. It is quite revealing that when a really professional operatic librettist—"Tobia Gorrio" (Arrigo Boito)—adapted Hugo's *Angelo* (far more freely than Cui, Stasov and Burenin) for Ponchielli's *La Gioconda* at the same time that Cui was at work on his version, even this much narration of essential action was too much for him. Boito gave over the greater portion of the first act of *La Gioconda* to a direct presentation of the events of Thisbe's narrative, in the form of a grand scena that freely intermingled the lyric with the declamatory, supported by a chorus that participates in the action far more directly than anywhere in Cui's opera save the "interpolated" insurrection scenes. Ironically, then, in this instance the Italian libretto approximated more closely the *kuchkist* ideal than the *kuchkist* libretto itself, which was content to present straight narration in "rounded" rather than declamatory form.[124]

Cui worked on *Angelo* over a five-year period. As always with him, it was written in bits and pieces; the last act was the first to be completed.[125] The next step was submitting the work to the Musical Committee of the Mariinsky Theater for its approval. This phase of *Angelo*'s career is amply and interestingly documented, thanks to a strategem which Cui (perhaps remembering Musorgsky's difficulties with *Boris Godunov*) adopted to expedite his work's acceptance. The committee had been recently restructured by direct order of the Imperial Court, in an unexpected move toward liberalization. Besides such musical functionaries of the theater itself as Napravnik (chief conductor), Pavel Fyodorov (director of repertoire), and the double bass player Fererro representing the orchestra (the same one who had so insulted Musorgsky), the panel was now enlarged to include the critics Laroche and Famintsyn, as well as Musorgsky and Rimsky-Korsakov, the two representatives of the New Russian School (besides Cui himself) to have by then had operas produced at the Mariinsky. Encouraged by the presence of friends on the committee, Cui thought somewhat to intimidate the opposition by requesting that in addition to his verdict, every member of the panel give his reasons for it. The result, as he expected, was unanimous approval. Besides the predictable encomia from his *kuchkist* colleagues,[126] Cui thus won the grudging praise of the "opposition" party, including Famintsyn, who wrote that the new work exhibited, among its other virtues, "lyricism in the vocal writing (taking into account the predominance of the recitative style in the work)"[127]—which only shows, really, how little of the "recitative style" remained in it. Napravnik's opinion was the most candid, and in its wickedly back-handed manner managed to convey both the conductor's intense distaste for Cui and his "mighty band," and his prideful resentment at having to justify his verdict.

> Not wishing, for good reasons, to enter into an evaluation of the opera *Angelo* by Mr. Cui, I propose that there is no reason to refuse the author a production of the submitted work.... After all, the operas *Naida* [Flotow], *The Storm* [Kashperov], *Ratcliff, Ammalat-Bek* [Afanasiev], *Pskovitianka, Boris Godunov, ...* none of which, with minor exceptions, were distinguished by any particular musical value and most of which (despite the unfavorable report of the Musical Committee) were produced on the Mariinsky stage, were valued by the public at their true worth and quickly and deservedly went out of the repertoire. The production of *Angelo* will doubtless refresh the repertoire of Russian opera for a time.[128]

Napravnik's words were prophetic. *Angelo* failed to hold the stage after its premiere on February 1, 1876, despite an excellent production (conducted with characteristic devotion to duty by Napravnik himself). The new work was compared invidiously even with Cui's own *Ratcliff,* the reason lying primarily in the failure of the music adequately to measure up to the grand romantic gestures of Hugo's play. As Nikolai Solovyov put it, "Cui, choleric in his articles, is, in his music, a phlegmatic."[129] He went on to state what was the critical consensus, that:

> Hugo's drama, in order to become an opera, needs music of a strong dramatic nature, with vivid contrasts and clear, well-marked delineation of characters and situations.... By the nature of his gifts Cui is a gentle, elegiac lyricist. He creates music that reveals above all a striving for the euphonious and the elegant.... Cui's opera gives the impression of a long, endless cantilena. The lyric mood that never abandons the author, unrelieved and undifferentiated in the melodic writing, imparts a great monotony to the opera; the work is further harmed by the predominance of moderately slow tempi and ceaseless repetitions of the motives without development. In Cui's opera there is no shading, no brushstrokes by which one mood is distinguished from another.... The melodic surface is smooth as glass, without highs and lows. There are many pretty spots, but the author has no knack for dramatic music.[130]

Even more clearly than in *Ratcliff*, Cui revealed his true composer's colors in *Angelo* and set the pattern for all his ensuing operatic output. He emerges here more clearly than before as a miniaturist, preoccupied with surface elegance and particularly with harmonic detail, as ill at ease with large-scale "theatrical frescoes" as with the kind of free-form musical speech he so eloquently championed as critic. The dramatic scenes in *Angelo* are devoid of any sense of climax, hamstrung by Cui's overweening need for a fundamentally static periodicity in phrase structure, coupled with an addiction to a manneristically "chromaticized" harmonic texture that vitiates the potentially tensile force of tonality. Cui was never able to harness the power of harmonic resolution to propel his musical utterances to a forceful conclusion. He remained insensitive throughout his career to this fundamental "secret" (so well understood by Dargomyzhsky and even Serov) of effective musical drama. His overdressed, decorative harmony often works against dramatic tension where he needs it most. A good example, noted by Laroche, is the opening of Act IV, scene vi, one of the tensest dramatic moments of the opera, where Caterina refuses on pain of death to reveal to Angelo the name of her lover. Cui could not refrain from setting Angelo's two questions as sequential phrases, imparting an untoward element of predictability to Angelo's lines, and hence undermining the menacing, threatening tone they are meant to convey. That these phrases were conceived "purely as music" is further indicated by the prosody: the stress and intonational structure of the first of them *"Obdúmali svoë reshén'e vy,"* is altogether at variance with the patterns of the language. But the main point is that the questions are set to rather definite plagal cadences, while the defiant answers are set to tonally remote, unresolved dominant seventh chords. The simple expedient of reversing the harmonies accompanying question and answer would go a long way toward restoring the dramatic tension this scene notably lacks, for, as Laroche put it, "because of the harmony, the questions come out as more affirmative than the answers"[131] (Ex. 6.29).

Ex. 6.29   *Andzhelo* (St. Petersburg: Bessel & Co., 1876), p. 293

As in *Ratcliff,* Cui sought out every opportunity to fashion fleeting set pieces on any even slightly extended speech. Not that there is any reason to assume that Cui himself thought that he was creating anything other than "melodic recitative." But his ingrained, automatic habits of periodic phrasing, of sequential repetition, of antecedent-consequent progression, are so ascendent in *Angelo* as to destroy any impression of freedom in the melodic writing. The recitatives and *scene* in *Angelo* are veritable chains of such "involuntary"

mini-arias (perhaps "songs" would be a better word) which succeed one another in a random, static fashion that seems not so much "formless" in Stasov's approving sense of the word, as merely undirected. The music is extremely formal at the lower levels of design, chaotic at the larger ones. Thus Cui was plagued by the disadvantages of both the older and the newer operatic styles, and could avail himself of the benefits of neither. As an example, we might examine Act I, scene vi, the scene of Rodolfo and Thisbe which Musorgsky pronounced a "chef d'oeuvre."[132] It takes the form of a love duet between one sincere and one dissembling lover, in which Thisbe's impassioned outbursts are contrasted in the text with Rodolfo's evasions and attempts to change the subject. Such a situation might have been handled effectively according to conventional operatic methods by assigning contrasting themes to each of the singers at first successively and then in combination. Or, alternatively, it might have been handled à la *The Stone Guest* in a series of varied and ever more animated repliques for Thisbe, answered by relatively flat responses from Rodolfo, with brightly diatonic, versus subtly chromatic, harmony underscoring the differences in their attitudes and characters. Cui's plan clearly inclines toward the latter method, but he could not resist the impulse to give Thisbe's love a more outwardly lyrical embodiment, with the result that the scene seems ever to aspire to a broad climax that is never achieved. Moreover, many of the formal gestures in the music have no counterpart in the text. After a preliminary exclamation, "O my Rodolfo!" the scene begins with an eighteen-bar song for Thisbe, in which her ardent excitement is rather well captured by the 12/8 accompaniment to her common-time tune. In structure, Thisbe's melody is conventionally rounded with a vengeance: the first two measures are repeated in the next two, bar five is reproduced in bar six, and the concluding two measures have a clear cadential role. Cui then gives Rodolfo two measures of "recitative" in which he tries to quiet Thisbe down. Undaunted, she launches into another song, this one in 9/8 with a phrase structure almost as square as the first. Its fifteen measures are grouped 4 + 4 + 3 + 4 (2 + 2). This is followed by a literal restatement of the first "song" to new words that demand a slight adjustment in the rhythms of Thisbe's part. The little ABA structure that results is arbitrarily imposed upon a fragment of Hugo's text that is by no means self-contained. After this, there follows an exchange between the two lovers that is apparently meant to contrast with Thisbe's lyrical effusions and approach more closely the ideal of "free" declamation. But even here, the composer is shackled by his fatal compulsion to periodize symmetrically. Rodolfo's replique is an even eight measures long and consists of four two-bar units of which the first three are all sequential repetitions, thinly disguised by elisions. These factors, plus the steady accompaniment figure in the orchestra, make Rodolfo's replique hardly less formal a little "song" than its more overt counterparts in Thisbe's music. Thisbe's answer to Rodolfo seems less formal on the surface: the orchestral part degenerates into tremolandi, and her replique is cast as a five-bar phrase. But the five are really four, extended by a sequential repetition. The *poco meno mosso* in 3/2 that follows is the heart of the duet: here the voices are finally combined, after an initial statement by Thisbe of predictable eight-bar length. This, potentially the strongest moment in the scene, becomes the weakest because Cui's characterization of the two lovers breaks down in the face of his greater desire for decorative lyricism. The text contrasts a passionate avowal by Thisbe with a classic evasion from Rodolfo:

Thisbe:	Akh zachem tebia ne uznala ia v dni rannei iunosti, kogda liubvi poryvy v dushe tak byli chisty, tak goriachi, tak zhivi! Togda ia byla dostoinei tebia milyi ty moi.	Ah, why did I not meet you in the days of my early youth, when the love transports in my soul were so pure, so warm, so vivid! Then I was more worthy of you, my darling.
Rodolfo:	O Tizba, ty mne pover'! chto ia liuboviu tvoei ochen', ochen' schastliv: ty mne darish' mnogo sladkikh mgnovenii, polnykh vostorgami strastnoi liubvi.	Thisbe, believe me, your love makes me very, very happy: you give me many sweet moments, full of the delights of passionate love.

But Cui's lovers sing in harmony, not in contrast. Given the fact that at moments of voice combination the words of the text are lost, there is no way for the audience to perceive their irony. Both characters sound equally ardent; the melodic and rhythmic motion of their parts is undifferentiated.

The rest of the duet consists of repetitions of the melodies heard previously, placed like tesserae one after another, with no apparent textual motivation, and no sense of dramatic progress. The scene does not build; as a whole it is no more than the sum of its parts. The one attempted touch of real musical irony comes at the very end, when Thisbe departs and Rodolfo's thoughts turn immediately to his real love, Caterina, and their impending rendezvous. Cui sets this passage to the music of the Rodolfo-Caterina love duet in Act II. But this is a miscalculation: not having yet heard the Act II duet, the listener cannot make the intended association to the theme Rodolfo quotes, and hence cannot grasp its significance or its intended ironic import.

The most successful numbers in *Angelo,* though dramaturgically they are of least importance, are the decorative choruses that grace each act. Here Cui did not try to evade a "concerted" effect, and was able therefore to paint effectively on a larger canvas. The chorus that opens the opera is a grandly "symphonic" affair in ternary form with an ingenious coda that combines both its themes. Cui was obviously pleased with the piece: he reprised it four times in the course of the first act. Besides this chorus, there are a number of choral genre pieces: a barcarolle (Act I), a nocturne and tarantella (Act III), and couple of pleasant folklike settings for three-part women's chorus with which Caterina's attendants seek to divert her from her troubles at the beginning of Act II. To this list one might add the closing "De profundis ad te clamavi" (on which the overture to the opera was also based), sung offstage by a chorus of luckily passing monks to accompany Thisbe's demise. Cui, who had habitually been exceedingly slapdash with genre and local color, for some reason strove like a real *kuchkist* for authenticity in this one detail. He wrote to Stasov (April 13, 1872) to inquire whether the psalm or the Requiem introit would be more appropriate for his passing monks. Characteristically, his letter also reveals that the music for this passage was already written at the time of his query.[133]

But Cui's unregenerate romanticism (and his incorrigible conventionality) notwithstanding, there is ample evidence that he was affected by the post-*Ratcliff* operas of his younger *kuchkist* colleagues. Temperamentally alien he may have been to the explorations of Musorgsky and Rimsky-Korsakov (as his reviews of *Boris Godunov* and *Pskovitianka* attest!), but he could not remain indifferent to them, and tried occasionally to incorporate some of their features into his own style. Although the lyric if anything predominates in *Angelo* even more than in *Ratcliff,* what declamatory writing remains is apt to exhibit a naturalism that was wholly lacking in the earlier opera. This new manner is found largely in the parts of Thisbe and Caterina and is reserved for "special effects." Thus, when Thisbe discovers the crucifix in Caterina's room and asks for an explanation, Cui recognized that another set piece recapitulating the content of Thisbe's Act I narrative would have been even for him de trop, and went instead to the other extreme, setting Caterina's answer in rapid quasi parlando.

Ex. 6.30.   *Andzhelo,* p. 182, voice part only

Here we encounter typically "Musorgskian" features of prosody: the spreading of unaccented syllables evenly through beats, the frequent use of triplets, the "mute endings," in which a string of short unaccented notes is cut off by a rest on the strong beat. But just as conspicuous even here is the tendency to periodize, along with a continuous "organizing" accompaniment of a type that Musorgsky rarely employed. Moreover, Cui makes up for this uncharacteristic foray into naturalism with the line, "I beg of you, have pity on me," which interrupts the narrative. Though this is the emotional high point of the passage, or perhaps because it is, it is set to longer values whose organization is "musical" rather than naturalistic. The reinstatement of "bel canto" for emotional projection is underscored by the composer by rather supererogatively marking the line "molto cantabile," while the ensuing resumption of the narrative is once again labelled "quasi parlando." For Cui, apparently, naturalistic declamation was a kind of musical discourse on a par with *recitativo secco*—a neutral medium for neutral text.

Ex. 6.31.   *Andzhelo,* p. 183, voice part only

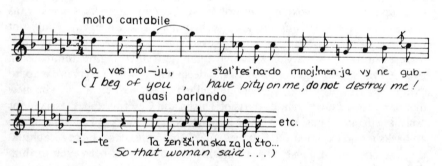

The other notable appearance of naturalism in *Angelo*'s melodic style occurs in Act IV, where Thisbe reads a letter from Rodolfo to Caterina that Angelo had intercepted. The use of parlando. or even of plain speech, for representing the tonelessness of letter reading was a device that had gained currency even in the Italian opera but the *kuchkists* habitually used it wherever a character recited words that were not his own. (The passage in *Angelo* owes much to Vlasevna's "Tale of the Tsarevna Lada" in *Pskoviti-anka.*) Here, too, Cui contrasts parlando with cantabile as soon as Thisbe speaks her own thoughts. Compare the neutral reading-tone with her anguished aside at finding herself referred to in the letter as "that woman." The "lection tone" is resumed as Thisbe resumes reading, despite the fact that the next words in the letter are "I love you" (Ex. 6.32).

The most overtly *"kuchkist"* part of *Angelo,* as noted above, was the third act, given over in its entirety to the ill-fated rebellion against the tyrant. It was modelled on the "veche" from *Pskovitianka* and the Kromy Forest scene in

Ex. 6.32.   *Andzhelo, p. 277, voice part only*

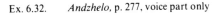

(Se) godnja ot muža tvœgo i ot ètoj zenšciny."
(We were saved) today from your husband and from that woman" – From that wo-

         Ot   e ——toj zenščiny

           "Ja ljublju tebja...
man! —" I love you . . .

Boris, both of which Cui had praised highly in his reviews. The chorus, which elsewhere in *Angelo* fulfills the prominent but mainly decorative role it had been assigned in *Ratcliff,* is here moved up to center stage and made to carry the burden of the action. This kind of choral drama required that Cui give the chorus not only "arias" but also "recitatives," that it be treated not only as a mass, but as an aggregation of individuals acting not always with unanimity. This free fragmentation of choral texture reaches its peak in the third act immediately following the genre set pieces—nocturne and tarantella—that open the scene, in which the chorus is treated altogether "monolithically" and conventionally. The choral dialogue that sets the scene for the rebellion commences with an ironic commentary on the tarantella itself, giving that decorative number as it were ex post facto, an "organic" connection to the main business. The basses are the insurrection's instigators:

Basses:	Ah, my friend, in our time there is not much to dance about. One might sooner howl.
Tenors:	What's to howl about?
Basses:	Well, for a start, how about the fact that we no longer have our former freedom!
Tutti:	Yes, what freedom have we got now that that beast of a Venetian who lives in that lair [pointing at Angelo's palace] has got us so firmly in his clutches?
Basses:	But have you heard the talk, comrades, that there are those who would smoke the beast out of his lair?
Others:	Who will smoke out the accursed beast?
Basses:	Men will be found! The Paduan nobles, you know, have not forgotten their old freedoms. Let them but sound the call..... Quiet!
Tutti:	Quiet! Quiet!
Basses:	The regent's guards! (They pass)
Tutti:	Venetian dogs! One day we'll be well rid of you. They've gone to the regent. He's taken to surrounding himself with bodyguards. He's afraid to go out among the people alone. The foreigner senses how we all hate him for his pride and his tyranny! But it's late, the evening passes and we must be up at dawn. Let's drink one more cup, comrades, and go to our homes, to safety.

The basses' lines are set to fragments of "melodic recitative" indistinguishable in facture from those of the protagonists in dramatic confrontation. But Cui found it difficult to sustain the free fragmentation of the choral texture: the tutti statements are organized around simple repetitive patterns, sometimes in ostinato fashion, more typically in imitation, to convey the impression of a crowd's hubbub.[134] Ironically, it was precisely this choral scene that contemporary critics cited as evidence not of any newfound realism, but, quite the contrary, of Cui's retreat from the free "formlessness" of the Dargomyzhskian style. The critic of the *Birzhevye vedomosti,* for example, wrote that

> Cui, one of the most ardent and most talented of Dargomyzhsky's adherents, departs very far in *Angelo* from the forms of *The Stone Guest.* Apparently he has realized their inadequacy. In *Angelo* there are embryonic arias, *even embryonic fugues.*[135]

Act III, scene iii, the height of the rebellion, could be called Cui's Kromy Forest scene. Dynamic treatment of the chorus is attempted on a grand scale. Two choruses—one of conspirators led by Ascanio, Rodolfo's second-in-command, the other representing "the people"—are played off one against the other. Ascanio whips them all to a frenzy, expressed in massive shouts of "Accursed Angelo!", "Let us all rise up against the foreigner," etc. The choral writing is partly realistic-imitative, partly monolithic-homorhythmic, culminating (exactly as in the Kromy scene) in a terrific shout on the word "Death!". But even in this scene, there are traces of the antidramatic and the decorative in the handling of the chorus. The most obvious, indeed comical, is the 33-measure choral diminuendo preceding Ascanio's incendiary harangue, taken up with endless repetitions of "Quiet!" and "Let us hear what Ascanio has to say." This sort of thing had long been the special object of Cui's journalistic vitriol,[136] and the stock-in-trade of parodists (cf. *Trial by Jury*). One would think that Cui, stern preacher of right reason that he was, could have viewed his own work with greater objectivity. But this is but one of many signs that while the immediate stimulus for *Angelo*'s third act may have been the operas of Musorgsky and Rimsky-Korsakov, the real model was Meyerbeer. In fact, the leading musical theme of the scene, initiated by Ascanio and taken up in force by the chorus, is a typically Meyerbeerian "alla marcia," replete with accented triplets and syncopated half notes (Ex. 6.33).

By all accounts Act III was the best received at the premiere performance. In a polemical move that only he could have brought off, Stasov noted this fact with tendentious approval of the public's maturity (as contrasted with the backwardness of the critics), while in the same essay even Stasov is forced to admit that "the national, the historical and . . . the comic elements in *Angelo* are weak, [since] they are all facets of musical composition alien to Cui's talent."[137] Any aspect of musical creation not directly concerned with the

Ex. 6.33.   Andzhelo, p. 224

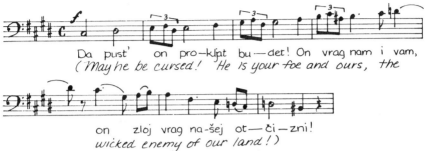

Da pust' on pro—kljat bu —det! On vrag nam i vam,
(*May he be cursed! He is your foe and ours, the*

on   zloj vrag na-šej   ot — či — zni!
wicked enemy of our land!)

theme of love was alien to Cui's gift in Stasov's view, and so Stasov holds up the characters of Thisbe and Caterina—contrasting and therefore complementary portraits of feminine character under the influence of amorous passion—as *Angelo*'s highest achievement. "The expression of the deepest, most gripping and touching movements of the feminine soul is realized in Cui's opera with such power," Stasov insists, "with such stunning truth, that one can only bow down before the divine gifts of the author of these miracles of true dramatic music."[138] Thus Stasov once again invokes the line of defense he had employed in the case of *Ruslan:* the equation of musical drama with mere "portrayal."

But in fact this was Cui's real retreat—a move back to generalized and monumentalized representation of static, unitary moods. The composer sought not so much the representation of Thisbe or Caterina's feelings as the expression of love itself; its human bearers are mere vessels. It is not surprising, therefore, that it was precisely in the area of characterization that Cui's opera received the lowest marks. Where Stasov pointed to the portrayal of two radically contrasting feminine types—"meek, tender, submissive and loving [Caterina], and . . . fiery, strong, intense, enflamed with uncontrollable passion [Thisbe]"[139]—other critics found little to choose between them. Laroche actually used the part of Thisbe, not Caterina, to make his point that Cui appeared in *Angelo* in the best light where he "permitted himself to write in that gentle, Schumannesque, melodious manner which suits him."[140] A.A. Gozenpud assumes that the failure of these two characters to impress themselves upon the listeners at the premiere production was the fault of the singers who gave the work its only performance. "And if so," he writes, "it means that the dramaturgical basis of the opera was not made clear."[141] But Laroche had made no mistake: the fault was Cui's. For both women's parts are submerged in the overriding love-ambience of Cui's music, an ambience created largely by means of a rather pettily voluptuous salon lyricism which the composer never thought to sacrifice to "higher" dramatic purposes.

In view of all that we have said about *Angelo*'s style, it is clear that whatever Cui's dramaturgical intentions or pretensions, *Angelo* turned out to be very much a singers' opera. This in fact might well have been predicted from a revealing passage in Cui's pseudonymous defense of *Ratcliff:*

> We hope with all our heart that in the new work that society has a right to expect of such a strong talent... there will be a greater concentration of effect in lyrical places on the singing voice, and not on the orchestra.[142]

So it is not surprising that the one recorded response to the opera comparable to Stasov's in warmth and enthusiasm should have come from a singer. The role of Caterina had been intended for Julia Platonova, who of all the leading singers of the Mariinsky had been the most favorably disposed toward the works of the New Russian School. But she never got to sing the part. Platonova's contract came up for renewal around the time of *Angelo*'s premiere, and as a result of an intrigue on the part of the Mariinsky's director of repertoire and the stage director, she was dropped from the roster on the pretext of a weakening voice.[143] Disappointed, she went to hear the opera anyway, and identified strongly with the role that was to have been hers.

> I cannot describe the impression that *Angelo* made on me! I grieved with Caterina, languished with Thisbe, suffered along with them, wept unashamed, sitting alone and unnoticed in my seat. I don't know, perhaps I was predisposed thus, seeing once more the Mariinsky, where I had spent my whole life; all I know is that upon my return home I lay awake all night, haunted by heartbreaking tones. I still saw the tortured figure of Caterina. Oh, how I wished to play that role even once in my life![144]

The failure of *Angelo* marked the end of Cui's career as a leading Russian dramatic composer, though he lived to write three more full-length operas as well as a number of smaller works for the stage. As a composer he finally gave himself entirely over to his Gallic leanings and forsook the Russian school in fact as well as spirit. The next stage work after *Angelo* was a French opera written to a French text and premiered not in St. Petersburg but at the Opéra Comique in Paris (1894). *Le Flibustier,* to a text by Jean Richepin, seems never to have been staged in Russia, though Gutheil brought out a vocal score in Russian translation (entitled *U moria*—"By the Sea"). *Le Flibustier* was followed by *Saratsin (The Saracen),* after Dumas Père, which although also based on a subject from French literature, was written to a Russian libretto and first performed in St. Petersburg in 1899. In musical style, the composer observed that the work "lay somewhere between *Angelo* and *Flibustier*."[145] By this time Cui was so committed to the numbers-opera format he had once derided that a return to the old ideals was impossible.[146] His attempt to do so—*Kapitanskaia dochka (The Captain's Daughter)* after Pushkin's novella

(1909, produced 1911), Cui's one full-length opera on a Russian subject—was perhaps the least successful of all his theatrical works.[147] Cui found it increasingly difficult to get his operas produced. His letters are full of forced-jocular allusions to himself as musical "pariah," "boycott victim," and the like. He turned to one-act forms and to children's theater, but still his subject matter and its treatment was almost exclusively French: Merimée *(Matteo Falcone),* Maupassant *(Mademoiselle Fifi)* and Perrault ("Puss in Boots," "Red Riding Hood," etc.). About the only exception was Pushkin's "Feast in Time of Plague," on which Cui based the nostalgic emulation of *The Stone Guest* we have already examined.

But *William Ratcliff* remained a treasured memory for all the *kuchkists.* For Liudmila Shestakova and for Balakirev it was always "the best opera after *Ruslan.*"[148] For the latterday Rimsky-Korsakov circle it was "a kind of Russian *Tristan und Isolde,*" exhibiting the best use of leitmotiv outside the *Ring* itself.[149] That it remained for all an enduring symbol of *"kuchkism"* at its freshest and best should serve as an eternal reminder that *"kuchkism"* should never be equated, in the fashion of facile historiography, with musical nationalism, even though the sobriquet arose in a nationalistic context.[150] What made the *kuchka* in the days of *Ratcliff* truly a *kuchka*—that is, a united "little band"—was their common devotion to operatic reform, to the "freedom of operatic forms, the equality of text and music, indeed the complete merger of text and music," as Cui himself summed it up.[151] The contribution made by the composer of *William Ratcliff* to the furtherance of these aims—aims achieved perhaps more successfully and certainly more enduringly by the composers of *Boris Godunov* and *Pskovitianka*—was in its day an indispensable, even crucial, one. Cui belonged in and to the *kuchka* after all.

Notes

1. August 15, 1868. M.P. Musorgskii, *Literaturnoe nasledie I* (Moscow, 1971), p. 104.

2. The very existence of the *kuchka* as such, in fact, can be traced to Cui's chance meeting with Balakirev in 1855 at a chamber music soirée. See his reminiscences, "Pervye kompozitorskie shagi Ts.A. Kiui," in Kiui, *Izbrannye stat'i,* p. 544.

3. In 1881 Cui revised the work, completely rescored it, and inserted an additional act between the original two, and in this form *The Prisoner of the Caucacus* was performed and published. See "Pervye kompozitorskie shagi," *Izbrannye stat'i,* p. 546.

4. *My Musical Life,* p. 100.

5. The letter is undated, but appears to have been written in 1867. See Darg:*APV,* p. 121.

6. Kiui, *Muzykal'no-kriticheskie stat'i I* (Petrograd, 1918), p. 70.

7. Ibid., pp. 71-2.

8. Kiui, *Izbrannye stat'i*, p. 36.

9. Ibid.

10. Ibid., p. 37. The downgrading of Wagner has perhaps another meaning when taken in conjunction with the conclusions of the Meyerbeer article as to the leaders of the "contemporary operatic tendency." Removing Wagner from contention meant the elevation of Schumann, and specifically of his single opera, *Genoveva,* to the pinnacle of world operatic achievement. In later life Cui was to retract this rather improbable evaluation. But he did continue to regard Schumann's work as exemplary until the arrival of *The Stone Guest.* Some additional insight may be gained from a curious and, be it said, rather inane passage in the course of Cui's predictably disparaging treatment of Italian opera, to the effect that "new melody cannot be created; salvation must be sought in harmony" (Ibid., p. 32). Thus, the usually cited faults of *Genoveva*—its overelaboration of texture and its neglect of lyric melody—were perhaps its very virtues for Cui. Sound or not, these were Cui's convictions and preferences while in the thick of work on *Ratcliff.*

11. Ibid., p. 37. Order of phrases rearranged.

12. Ibid.

13. Kiui, "Neskol'ko slov o sovremennykh opernykh formakh" ("A Few Words About Contemporary Operatic Forms," 1889), *Izbrannye stat'i*, pp. 405-6. Although this article comes somewhat later than the period under discussion, it contains no substantive reversals, and puts Cui's theoretical views more concisely than his individual reviews of the 1860s.

14. Ibid.

15. Ibid., p. 408.

16. Cui, *La musique en Russie* (Paris, 1880), p. 109.

17. Kiui, "M.P. Musorgskii (kriticheskii etiud)" (1881), *Izbrannye stat'i*, p. 289.

18. Ibid.

19. This and next four citations from Kiui, *Izbrannye stat'i*, pp. 408-11 passim.

20. *Sanktpeterburgskie vedomosti*, September 16, 1864. He adds that consequently *Ruslan* "has been subjected and is subjected to powerful attacks, . . . as if no other kind of opera may exist than the dramatic kind!"

21. *La musique en Russie*, p. 102.

22. *Izbrannye stat'i*, p. 414.

23. Stasov strongly recommended to Cui that he completely rewrite his French book *(La musique en Russie)* because, "loving his talent, . . . I would be mortified if he should leave behind him such a false and superficial book." He added that if there was no time for revision, then let Cui "destroy it so that not a trace remained" (Letter to Rimsky-Korsakov, August 9, 1889. Quoted by I.L. Gusin in the introduction to Kiui, *Izbrannye stat'i*, p. xlviii).

24. *Izbrannye stat'i*, p. 410.

25. Ibid., p. 287. A decisive factor in any artist's attitude toward realism will of course be his view of the relationship between "truth" and "beauty." Cui obviously held them to be seperate and equal; we need no further demonstration of this than his early review of *The Stone Guest* quoted in the last chapter, where he laid down the primitive "law" that *"truth and beauty"* were the two indispensable elements of operatic music, and went on to caution that neither one will suffice in the absence of the other. Such a warning was hollow for an

artist like Musorgsky. For him truth was all and beauty none. One need only compare Cui's truth-beauty precept with Musorgsky's oft-quoted letter to Stasov (October 18, 1872) to appreciate the ideological chasm that separated these two representatives of what was taken at the time, and too often is still taken, to have been a monolithic musical "camp": "The artistic representation of beauty alone, in the material sense of the word, is coarse childishness, the babyhood of art. The subtlest aspects of human nature, . . . the unremitting exploration of these uncharted regions and their conquest—there you have the true calling of the artist" (*Literaturnoe nasledie I*, p. 141). It is curious that A.A. Gozenpud, for example, cites precisely these two passages (from Cui and Musorgsky, respectively) as demonstrating *kuchkist* solidarity. He attempts to smooth over their almost diametrical difference with the laconic observation that "Musorgsky and Cui did not invest these words with identical meanings; but despite all discrepancies between individuals, the *kuchkists* were united in the sixties in their understanding that the first principle of art lies in its content" (*Russkii opernyi teatr XIX veka II*, p. 209). Gozenpud shows here, no less than Cui himself, that Cui and Musorgsky can be made to meet as thinkers only on the level of platitude.

26. One might add that the abuses Cui is apt to cite are so bald as to be trivial: "One recalls choristers ardently crying 'corriam, corriam,' and not budging from their places. One recalls catastrophes stilled by lengthy ensembles with the characters ranged neatly along the footlights, promptly to resume upon the ensemble's satisfactory conclusion. One recalls arias, duets and trios turned out by a cooky-cutter, consisting of the obligatory two tempi, preceded by the obligatory recitatives" (*Izbrannye stat'i*, p. 28).

27. *Izbrannye stat'i*, p. 415.

28. We have seen Cui at this game in the case of *Rogneda*. He played it no less avidly with other composers with whom he was not in sympathy—among the Russians, primarily Rubinstein and Tchaikovsky.

29. July 17, 1866. Darg:*APV*, p. 119.

30. *My Musical Life*, p. 329.

31. Kiui, *Izbrannye stat'i*, p. 418.

32. See Gozenpud, *Russkii opernyi teatr II*, p. 233.

33. Ibid., p. 217.

34. *Istoriia russkoi muzyki II* (Moscow, 1958), p. 287.

35. *Izbrannye stat'i*, p. 547.

36. Stasov, *Izbrannye sochineniia III* (Moscow, 1952), p. 395.

37. Louis Untermeyer, *Heinrich Heine, Paradox and Poet* (New York, 1931), p. 90.

38. Adapted from Boris Kremnev, ed., *Opernye libretto* (Moscow, 1954), pp. 51-53.

39. The exchange between Ratcliff and Lesley before Ratcliff's narrative is slightly rewritten to allow the elimination of a third character (Tom); a chorus replaces the concluding repliques of various minor characters in the same scene (Robin, Dick, Bill, Tom, John, Taddie); the cry "O Death!" is inserted at the moment when Douglas stabs Ratcliff, and an unseen chorus of cackling witches ("Ha-ha-ha-ha-ha") accompanies Ratcliff's second monologue at the Black Stone. These are the only additions to Heine's abridged text. In Act III the only significant deletion is the name of Edward's bride (Jenny Campbel [sic]) from Margaret's narrative. One line is transferred from Margaret to William and another from "a servant" to the chorus. Act III contains two sizeable interpolations, however: the text of the love duet and the concluding chorus.

40.   "Pervye kompozitorskie shagi" (*Izbrannye stat'i*, p. 546). Cui might have added to his list of distractions his work on the *Sanktpeterburgskie vedomosti* beginning with the issue of March 8, 1864. Cui's job was not that of a daily reviewer. He contributed occasional lengthy essays, which usually collected a number of events under the rubric *Muzykal'nye zametki* (Musical observations), or (in the case of opera) *Teatr i muzyka* (Theater and music). In 1865 (his first full year on the paper) he published 17 such articles; his most prolific year was 1876, with 55 (mostly shorter) pieces. The next year was his last on the *Vedomosti*. Later Cui published articles in *Novoe vremia, Golos* (where Laroche was the regular critic), *Iskusstvo* and *Nedelia*. From 1885 to 1888 he contributed more or less regularly to the journal *Muzykal'noe obozrenie*, and last, from 1896 to 1901, he was a staff writer for the stock market newspaper, *Novosti i birzhevaia gazeta*. For the two last named publications, he signed his articles with his own name, rather than "***." Only the *Vedomosti* articles, published at a time when the *kuchka* was a recognized faction on the vanguard of Russian musical life, have retained their interest and importance, and they are usually the only ones remembered. As for Cui's habit of working piecemeal on his operas, this cannot be explained solely in terms of "Sunday composing." It was a long-established habit. Victor Krylov described Cui's methods in composing *The Prisoner of the Caucacus* in terms almost word for word identical to Cui's description of himself at work on *Ratcliff:* "It was written number by number, whichever he felt most disposed to write at a given time" (Viktor Krylov, "Kompozitor Ts.A. Kiui," *Prozaicheskie sochineniia II* [St. Petersburg, 1908], p. 297).

41.   Letter to von Meck, Dec. 24, 1877. V.A. Zhdanov and N.T. Zhegin, eds., *P.I. Chaikovskii: Perepiska s N.F. fon-Mekk* I (Moscow, 1934), p. 136.

42.   M.A. Balakirev, *Vospominaniia i pis'ma* (Leningrad, 1962), p. 141.

43.   V.V. Iastrebtsev, *Vospominaniia o Nikolae Andreeviche Rimskom-Korsakove I* (Leningrad, 1959), p. 96.

44.   *My Musical Life*, p. 22.

45.   Tsezar' Kiui, *Izbrannye pis'ma* (Leningrad, 1955), p. 55.

46.   This chorus was given its first performance at the Free Music School under Balakirev on April 6, 1864. See A. Orlova, *Trudy i dni M.P. Musorgskogo* (Moscow, 1963), p. 114.

47.   It also testifies to Cui's general indifference to local color (which can be observed in his other operas, too), an indifference born of a romantic idealism shared by none of his fellow *kuchkists*. When Semyon Kruglikov was preparing his silver anniversary article on *Ratcliff* for the journal *Artiste*, he queried Cui on this point and received this answer: "One must not be too demanding where local color is concerned; it is desirable only in genre scenes. The language of passions is a universal language" (February 26, 1894. *Izbrannye pis'ma*, p. 164). He goes on to cite *The Stone Guest*, where local color plays perhaps an even smaller role than in *Ratcliff*, as "exemplary." Even in the genre scenes (e.g. the tavern in Act II), Cui gives local color amazingly short shrift. And so we are not surprised to find not the slightest Scottish "intonation" in any of the solo parts, or that even Margaret's Edward song, that prime musical symbol, is given a setting that emphasizes its Scottishness far less than its vague "antiquity" (the natural minor seventh, etc).

48.   "Pervye kompozitorskie shagi" (*Izbrannye stat'i*, p. 546).

49.   *Vest'* (1869), no. 47. Quoted in Gozenpud, *Russkii opernyi teatr II* p. 233.

50.   July 27, 1868. *Izbrannye pis'ma*, p. 75.

51.   The Act I finale is also highly reminiscent of the "Polish Act" of *A Life for the Tsar*, wherein a lengthy ballet divertissement is interrupted for a single tiny but decisive burst of action,

and then resumed. Could this act have served Cui and Krylov as model, or at least as justifying precedent?

52. Another motivation, or justification, of this chorus is the fact that it is built on a dramatically pregnant *Erinnerungsmotiv*, about which more below.

53. "Notice sur César Cui," appendix to Cui's *La musique en Russie*, p. 167.

54. *Izbrannye pis'ma*, p. 56.

55. Ibid., p. 58.

56. Ibid., p. 66.

57. Ibid., p. 61.

58. Jay Leyda and Serge Bertensson, *The Musorgsky Reader* (New York, 1947), p. 103.

59. To Musorgsky, July 27, 1868. *Izbrannye pis'ma*, p.75.

60. Musorgskii, *Literaturnoe nasledie I*, p. 104.

61. Quoted in Gozenpud, *Russkii opernyi teatr II*, p. 221.

62. It is prefigured rather inconspicuously eleven measures before 34, where Ratcliff describes Edward and Betty's unhappiness.

63. The continuation of the duel theme in Example 6.7a links it with the theme given in Example 6.4 (which Cui later referred to as the hero's leitmotiv). It is hard to see why Gerald Abraham writes this "motivic relationship" off as "probably unintentional" ("Heine, Queuille, and 'William Ratcliff'," *Musicae Scientiae Collectanea* [Festschrift K.G. Fellerer] [Köln, 1973], p. 18). On the contrary, it seems both deliberate and meaningful.

64. Loc. cit.

65. "Pervye kompozitorskie shagi' (*Izbrannye stat'i*, p. 548). On the origin of the term *leitmotiv*, see W. Apel, *The Harvard Dictionary of Music*, 2nd ed. (Cambridge, Mass., 1969), p. 465-66.

66. This theme, too, recurs in the final scene of the opera, where it is in fact treated to a modicum of "development."

67. *My Musical Life*, p. 89.

68. To go into this in detail would exceed our present scope. But the figure of the complicated protagonist who combines elements of hero and villian was obviously a favorite in Russian operas of this Dostoevskian period, and Ratcliff was the prototype. I hope to return to the matter elsewhere.

69. "Heine, Queuille, and 'William Ratcliff'," p. 18.

70. Heine's source, of course, was Herder's translation from Bishop Percy's *Reliques of Ancient English Poetry* (London, 1765). By Heine's time, the Herder translation had been set by at least three German composers, including Loewe (1818), whose famous Ballade was more likely the poet's immediate source than Herder's original publication (*Alte Volkslieder*, two vols., 1773-75. Cf. Otto E. Albrecht, "English Pre-Romantic Poetry in Settings by German Composers," in H.C. Robbins-Landon (ed.), *Studies in Eighteenth-Century Music: A Tribute to Karl Geiringer on his Seventieth Birthday* [New York: Oxford University Press, 1970]). But of course all of this has little to do with Cui, who took the Edward motif as he found it in Heine and composed his own pseudo-archaic melody. As Bertrand Bronson notes, "all the tunes that have been found for this ballad . . . come from the Appalachians,

and all have been recovered only in the present century; the ballad would seem to have died out of tradition in Scotland before Greig began his labors." (*The Traditional Tunes of the Child Ballads*, vol. I [Princeton, 1959], p. 237.) The reference is to John Greig, compiler of *Scots Minstrelsie: A National Monument of Scottish Song* (Edinburgh, 1892-95).

71.   Iastrebtsev, *Vospominaniia II* (Leningrad, 1960), p. 460.

72.   See figure $\boxed{33}$ in the Bessel vocal score, p. 135.

73.   Ensembles, of course, were something *kuchkists* handled with extreme caution. This one is presumably "justified" by the fact that the two entranced lovers, oblivious to the world, are hence insensible to one another's words.

74.   Letter to Cui, August 15, 1868. *Literaturnoe nasledie I*, p. 105.

75.   Iastrebtsev, *Vospominaniia I*, p. 71. In the same entry Iastrebtsev reveals that Mary's romance in Act III was orchestrated by Balakirev ("who also made some corrections in the duet"), and that the first chorus was orchestrated "very poorly" by the still inexperienced Rimsky-Korsakov (all of this is corroborated in *My Musical Life*, p. 96). This kind of thing is no doubt part of what Musorgsky meant when he wrote to Cui that "your *Ratcliff* is not only yours, but ours." Relevant, too, is an amusing anecdote recalled by Cui in his necrologue for Balakirev: "*Ratcliff* was written completely under [Balakirev's] influence, while I wrote *Angelo* independently. Balakirev tells me, 'But, you know, your *Ratcliff* was much better.' I ask, 'And have you seen *Angelo*?' He answers calmly, 'No, not yet.' There you have the whole Balakirev" (*Izbrannye stat'i*, p. 549).

76.   It was apparently this passage that Saltykov-Shchedrin recalled in his rather heavy-handed lampoon of "*kuchkism*" in *Nedokonchennye besedy* (St. Petersburg, 1885). Ivan Nikiforovich Neuvazhai-Koryto (Stasov) takes the author to hear some new compositions by the latest genius, "Vasili Ivanych." As the latter plays, he emits yawns and belches, which, Neuvazhai-Koryto explains, are ideas for future compositions. It is usually thought that Vasili Ivanych was meant to personify Musorgsky. This example, however, would indicate that the purview of Saltykov's satire was a bit broader, and took in the entire "New Russian School."

77.   *Izbrannye pis'ma*, p. 75.

78.   As he wrote to Felipe Pedrell in 1897: "Bien que russe, je suis d'origine mi-française mi-lithuanienne et je n'ai pas le sens de la musique russe dans mes veines" (Higinio Anglés, "Relations epistolaires entres César Cui et Philippe Pedrell," *Fontes Artis Musicae* (1966), no. 1, p. 18). He might have added "de la langue russe" as well.

79.   To von Meck, Nov. 26/Dec. 8, 1879. Quoted from Modest Chaikovskii, *Zhizn' Petra Il'icha Chaikovskogo II*, p. 337.

80.   Vsevolod Cheshikhin, *Istoriia russkoi opery* (Moscow, 1905), p. 233.

81.   A partial explanation for Cui's overly elaborated harmonic style can be found in his critical pronouncements of the time (already noted) to the effect that melody was a dried-up well, and only harmony still offered room for innovation, and also in his inordinate admiration for Schumann as operatic composer. It was as a Schumannist above all that Cui was known to his contemporaries, and this predilection has even been used to account for the otherwise puzzling choice of *Ratcliff* as a subject: "He places Schumann so high, and so willingly shares his musical tastes that one might perhaps suppose that their literary tastes should likewise coincide. And if so, then is this not the reason why our composer set out to find the subject for one of his operas in the dramatic works of Schumann's favorite?" (Semyon Kruglikov, quoted in Gozenpud, *Russkii opernyi teatr, II*, p. 216).

82. Stasov, *Izbrannye sochineniia III*, p. 387.

83. *Izbrannye stat'i*, pp. 547-48. Of course the reference to Wagner is gratuitous and tendentious. A more direct precedent was set by Berlioz, as the *kuchkists* even then acknowledged (see Rimsky-Korsakov via Yastrebtsev, footnote 70 above). Nevertheless, Cui was beaten with the Wagnerian stick by some of the critics, notably Rostislav, who discerned Wagnerianism in the modulatory vagaries Cui's "musical speech," especially in the Scene at the Black Stone. The true forerunner here, *The Stone Guest,* would not be heard, remember, for another three years.

84. Serov, *Kriticheskie stat'i IV* (St. Petersburg, 1894), pp. 2011-12.

85. This, like so many of Serov's aesthetic opinions, was one he shared with Apollon Grigoriev, who saw in Heine's work the expression of "the morbid disorder of an epoch" (see Gozenpud, *Russkii opernyi teatr II,* p. 215).

86. *Kriticheskie stat'i IV,* p. 2011. As early as his correspondence with Stasov, Serov had complained of Heine's "absurdly destructive spirit" (*Muzykal'noe nasledstvo I* [Moscow, 1961], p. 189).

87. *Kriticheskie stat'i IV,* p. 2011.

88. Larosh, *Muzykal'no-kriticheskie stat'i* (St. Petersburg, 1894), p. 93. The passage cited last is given in Example 6.9a.

89. Ibid.

90. Ibid., p. 75.

91. Ibid., p. 77.

92. For one formulation among many, see *La musique en Russie*, p. 77.

93. Laroche cites in particular a passage from the Scene at the Black Stone, where Ratcliff's line, "Yes, Count, William Ratcliff stands before you," and Douglas's response, "The very one by whom Duncan and MacDonald were slain," are set to repetitions of the same melodic phrase, in apparent contradiction not only of the precept of formal plasticity in recitative, but of dramaturgical sense as well, as if Cui cast his music symmetrically in spite of himself, compelled by habit.

94. Larosh, op. cit., p. 80.

95. Ibid., p. 82.

96. Ibid., p. 103.

97. The real, legendary hostility between Laroche and Cui came later, in the early seventies. One curious memento of their polemical warfare was an article in two parts published by Laroche in the newspaper *Golos* (1873, nos. 94 and 115), entitled, "The William Ratcliff of the Musical Press," which compared Cui himself with the hero of his opera, the point being that Cui's exacting and severe critical postures were the result merely of a frustrated and unsuccessful compositional career:

The popularity of an operatic composer who reaps laurels on the lyric stage took the form in his mind of a seductive but haughty woman, to possess whom he was ready for any sacrifice, for any exploit. Cruelly rejected by this beauty, our lover's sufferings were made complete by being forced to witness every day the success of his rivals, to see the caresses she lavished upon Mozart, upon Rossini, upon Verdi and Meyerbeer.... Cui swore that a beauty who had laughed in his face should be possessed by no one. He condemned to death a priori all new seekers after her favor; he thought to slay as well all those who enjoyed such favor at the time.... He pleased himself so in this new and unaccustomed role, he came so frequently to view himself as going knife in hand after his carefree rivals, that he got the idea of depicting himself in a grand musical drama.... For his war against all musicians who appeared to be obstacles in his path to musical glory, Mr. Cui drew up a plan in which one can see both high intelligence and an acquaintance with the fundamentals of military fortifications—not for nothing did he teach this science in one of our institutions of higher learning! In his hands the musical feuilleton of the *Sanktpeterburgskie vedomosti* was turned into a stormy fortress, from which he opened fire on all contemporary musical figures with the exception of Messrs. Balakirev and Berlioz (*Golos* [1873], no. 94).

98.   *Otechestvennye zapiski* (1869), p. 156.

99.   Ibid., p. 157.

100. Ibid.

101. E.F. Napravnik, *Avtobiograficheskie, tvorcheskie materialy, dokumenty, pis'ma* (Leningrad, 1959), p. 46. It was characteristic of Napravnik's professionalism that despite his disdain for Cui's opera, he turned out a performance marked, in the composer's words, by "rare skill, talent and conscientiousness" (*Izbrannye stat'i*, p. 547).

102. Rimsky had done Cui a similar favor a short while before in connection with Napravnik's *Nizhegorodtsy*, which Cui felt it impolitic to judge at a time when his own opera was in Napravnik's hands.

103. Rimskii-Korsakov, *Polnoe sobranie sochinenii II*, p. 20.

104. Ibid., p. 28.

105. Rimsky-Korsakov's correspondence with Cui contains an interesting letter (November 15, 1862) in which the latter tried, apparently without success, to convert him to Auber's cause (cf. Kiui, *Izbrannye pis'ma*, pp. 53-4). Much later, his pupil N.I. Shvanvich recalled Rimsky-Korsakov coming into class and saying, "Last night I was at the theater for *Fenella* [i.e., *La Muette de Portici*].... But what do you find there!?!..Tonic—dominant, tonic—dominant." (M.K. Mikhailov, "N.A. Rimskii-Korsakov—vospitatel' kompozitorov," in S.L. Ginzburg (ed.), *N.A. Rimskii-Korsakov i muzykal'noe obrazovanie: stat'i i materialy* [Leningrad: Gosudarstvennoe muzykal'noe isdatel'stvo, 1959].)

106. Rimskii-Korsakov, op. cit., p. 23.

107. Ibid, p. 24.

108. Ibid., p. 22.

109. Ibid., p. 27.

110. Ibid., p. 23.

111. *Sanktpeterburgskie vedomosti* (1873), no. 74.

112. Ibid.

113. Stasov, *Sobranie sochinenii III* (St. Petersburg, 1896), p. 267.

114. Ibid.

115. Stasov, *Izbrannye sochineniia II*, p. 551.

116. Ibid., pp. 550-51.

117.   *Izbrannye sochineniia III,* p. 403.

118.   Ibid.

119.   Hugo's drama offered such an *embarras de richesses* in the love department that Cui felt he could afford to drop one love scene altogether. Thus the wholly superfluous and redundant, though mightily impassioned, scene of Caterina and Rodolfo in the last act was wisely omitted from the scenario. Had Cui gained a belated appreciation of the value of swift timing as the denouement is approached?

120.   See Serov's letter of May 15, 1846. *Muzykal'noe nasledstvo II,* p. 94.

121.   Originally the libretto was to have been written by Pleshcheev, the translator of *William Ratcliff,* but he later backed out for reasons unknown. See Gozenpud, *Russkii opernyi teatr XIX veka III* (Leningrad, 1973), p. 134. *Angelo* was the journalist Burenin's first libretto. He went on to collaborate with Tchaikovsky *(Mazepa)* and others. See Cheshikhin, *Istoriia russkoi opery,* p. 397.

122.   The name had been used by Hugo for a minor character.

123.   *Izbrannye pis'ma,* p. 86.

124.   This observation, of course, extends only to Boito's contribution to *La Gioconda.* Ponchielli's music, for all its adumbrations of verismo, remains very much within traditions almost all Russian composers despised. Even Tchaikovsky, more receptive than most Russians to things Italianate, and certainly no fan of Cui, had to confess in comparing the two operas on the Angelo theme, that he could not help but "give preference to the Russian composer; in any case Cui has incomparably more talent and taste" (To von Meck, October 10, 1880. *P.I. Chaikovskii ob opere* [Moscow, 1956], p. 150). It is perhaps not without ironic significance that *Ratcliff* also became the subject of a famous Italian opera: *Guglielmo Ratcliff* (1895), music by Mascagni, libretto by A. Maffei. Loewenberg (*Annals of Opera,* 3rd ed.) also lists operas on the subject by Emilio Pizzi (1889), Cornelius Dopper (1909) and Volkmar Andreae (1914). To this list Abraham ("Heine, Queuille, and 'William Ratcliff,'" p. 12) adds an opera by Xavier Leroux (1906).

125.   Cf. *Izbrannye pis'ma,* p. 82.

126.   Rimsky-Korsakov: "Cui's opera is a remarkable work of the highest talent and only its production on the stage remains to be desired." Musorgsky: "The author has applied himself sincerely to the musical realization of character in the musical drama he has created on the canvas of Hugo's play. In my opinion, the personalities of the Venetian actress Thisbe, of Caterina Malipieri (the wife of the Paduan tyrant), and of Galeofa (spy in the service of the tyrant) are particularly successful. Thisbe's scene with Galeofa is very characteristic; Thisbe's duet with the young Rodolfo is a chef d'oeuvre; and the finales of the second act (Thisbe and Caterina) and of the opera (Thisbe's death) are bound to produce a stunning impression. The work's technical execution shows the author's best side. The opera is also rich in melodic beauty. Among the opera's weaknesses I would place certain *longueurs,* but these weaknesses, mainly in the first act and to some extent in the fourth, can be easily corrected in rehearsal, where the final polishing of any dramatic work, be it literary or musical, always takes place" (Kiui, *Izbrannye pis'ma,* p. 556). It is noteworthy that Musorgsky makes no reference to those parts of the opera (especially the third act) where Cui had been most indebted to his example.

127.   Gozenpud, *Russkii opernyi teatr III,* p. 138.

128.   Ibid., pp. 138-39.

129.   Quoted by Stasov in "Tsezar' Antonovich Kiui," *Izbrannye sochineniia III*, p. 404.

130.   Gozenpud, op. cit., p. 141.

131.   *Muzykal'no-kriticheskie stat'i*, p. 62.

132.   The entire scene will be found in Appendix D.

133.   *Izbrannye pis'ma*, p. 82.

134.   Glinka's treatment of the chorus in close imitation in the prologue to *Ruslan* had long been admired for its "realism" and presumably served Cui as a model.

135.   Cited after Gozenpud, op. cit., p. 136.

136.   Cf. footnote 26 above.

137.   *Izbrannye sochineniia III*, p. 404.

138.   Ibid.

139.   *Sobranie sochinenii I* (St. Petersburg, 1896), p. 679.

140.   Quoted in Gozenpud, op. cit., p. 141.

141.   Ibid., p. 140. The role of Caterina was sung by V. Raab, that of Thisbe by M. Kamenskaya.

142.   *Sanktpeterburgskie vedomosti* (1873), no. 74.

143.   See Gozenpud, *Russkii opernyi teatr II*, p. 19.

144.   Quoted in Gozenpud, *Russkii opernyi teatr III*, pp. 139-40.

145.   *Izbrannye pis'ma*, p. 192. He also went around boasting that "in *The Saracen* he finally achieved the 'ideal of the union of word and music,' and was thus the first Russian composer to have written a real opera" (Iastrebtsev, *Vospominaniia II*, p. 109). Iastrebtsev's report is made with irony. The Rimsky-Korsakov circle no longer took Cui seriously as an operatic composer by that time.

146.   Stasov wrote to his brother Dmitri as early as 1884 that "I have long noticed that in all our . . . musical company only [Cui] has backslided" (Stasov, *Pis'ma k rodnym II* [Moscow, 1958], p. 173).

147.   Tchaikovsky had toyed with this subject too and had finally rejected it as not containing sufficient dramatic possibilites, despite its attractive historical background of the Pugachov uprising.

148.   Iastrebtsev, *Vospominanija II*, p. 317.

149.   Ibid., vol. I, pp. 50-51.

150.   The phrase *moguchaia kuchka* was coined in the concluding sentence of Stasov's review, "Mr. Balakirev's Slavonic Concert," which appeared in the *Sanktpeterburgskie vedomosti* on May 13, 1867: "We conclude our remarks with a wish: may God grant that our Slavonic guests never forget today's concert, that they will forever preserve the memory of the poetry, feeling, talent and sophistication that is to be found in our small but already mighty band of Russian musicians" (*Izbrannye sochineniia I*, p. 173). Though the phrase was coined as it were within the *kuchka*, it was the group's enemies that took it up and popularized it. By the time of *Ratcliff*'s première, it was on everyone's lips.

151.   *Izbrannye stat'i*, p. 535.

Epilogue

"Between Glinka and his 'grandsons'," wrote Asafiev, "stood three: Dargom-yzhsky, Cui and Serov." But his characterization of this middle generation—the musical vanguard of the 1860s—is disconcertingly negative. Dargomyzh-sky is "helpless and, compared with Glinka, a veritable beggar." Cui is "an outsider and an alien, who created a world of lyrical moods, utterly isolated." And as for Serov, the most important of them, he "traveled a true path, but as if blind and deaf." The period they dominated is viewed as one of "pathlessness," of "indirection" (*bezdorozh'e*), during which Russian music, and Russian opera in particular, chased its own tail, until at last the generation of grandsons found its way back to Glinka's legacy and inaugurated the classical period of Russian opera.[1]

We would like to think that no one who has read this book will entertain such a judgment of the middle generation. If Glinka was the undisputed grandsire and Tchaikovsky, Rimsky-Korsakov, Musorgsky and Borodin (to cite Asafiev's list in his order) the undisputed generation of heirs, that still leaves open a number of interpretations of the admittedly ambiguous role of the men who came in between. Neither the inherent qualities of their work nor their relationship to the classical repertoire can justify viewing them with Asafiev merely as prodigal sons. They were fathers, too.

For not only—to recall the premise with which the present study opened—did they bring a conscious "high-mindedness" to Russian opera (think now of *Judith, The Stone Guest* and *William Ratcliff* above all), but their work is an enduring monument to the close involvement of music in the realist explorations of the sixties, when for a time it looked as though Russian opera and art song were going to be transformed as thoroughly and permanently as the novel and the short story. If this did not happen—if the generation of the sixties now looks like a generation of extremists, off the mainstream—it does not mean that paths were not broken or that all their experiments were sterile. The generation of grandsons is as unthinkable without the fathers as without the grandfather.

The realism of the 1860s found many different kinds and levels of embodiment in operatic music, some obvious, others contradictory, some fruitful, others barren. There was first the matter of subject. If "low" subject matter is a hallmark of realism, then Russian art has no better example than *The Power of the Fiend.* Nor is "lowness" a matter only or necessarily of social class: witness *Marriage,* whose pettiness of subject matter is matched by a prosaic style both in language and in music that no other operatic work has ever exceeded.

But any subject could be treated "realistically"—though here we enter a more nebulous realm of values and judgments. Contemporary opinion was unanimous that *Rogneda,* for example, set a new standard in operatic realism, even though its subject matter was virtually identical with *Askold's Grave,* or even *Ruslan,* both paradigmatic examples of historical and fantastic romance. For in Serov's work the witch is not shown creating "real" magic, the idol-worshippers are depicted as brutal and ugly, the Christians sing in a style of deliberate and recognizable archaism, and (perhaps paradoxically) the element of Russian genre is portrayed in terms of what was most contemporary and familiar to the opera's audience. In other words, the opera did not attempt to create its own "reality," but presented and judged its own action rationalistically and objectively from the standpoint of its own time and place: "artistic truth" was rejected in favor of empirical truth. Thus Asafiev is quite wrong to characterize *Rogneda* as simply one more "historical romance" in a line going back as far as *The Early Reign of Oleg.*[2]

The centrality of genre—both in terms of subject matter and in terms of musical style—is of course the most conspicuous component of Serovian realism as encountered in *The Power of the Fiend.* Here, too, Asafiev errs in drawing a line from Serov back to such paltry forebears as Fomin, Matinsky and Titov,[3] for all that Serov adhered in the early stages of his work to the "style vaudeville." The crucial difference was that eighteenth-century folklorism never regarded folklore as representative of "nationhood," but merely (at best) of "regions" or (more typically) of lower social classes.[4] Thus, folk music could occupy a position in a Russian singspiel no more central or "organic" than that of the character type who might sing such music. For forebears to *The Power of the Fiend* and its approach to folklore, one must look outside of music altogether. The only relevant antecedents can be found in literature and the dramatic theater, and these were no more than a couple of decades old when Serov began his work.

Finally, and no doubt most important, there is the level of "forms." If realism and romanticism can be contrasted as a matter of replacing breadth with depth, of sacrificing exaltation to poignant penetration, then we have a perfect musical analogue in the methods and procedures of *The Stone Guest* and the best pages of *William Ratcliff,* and a new motivation for the "petty" forms in *The Power of the Fiend.* And we have an effective means of accounting for the aloofness of the Russian school (even of the late Serov) toward the Wagnerian reform, which was after all aimed at ever greater breadth and at "Dionysian" exaltation, at the total sacrifice of the poignant, affecting moment, or of personal empathy.

Now every one of the matters raised here has endless resonance in the work of the "classical generation" of Russian composers, most obviously in Musorgsky and Rimsky-Korsakov, but in Tchaikovsky and Borodin, too. The result of the "age of exploration" of the sixties was an immeasurably enhanced range of possibilities, approaches and precedents, And yet it is impossible to deny that a retrenchment did take place, and that the generation of "heirs" was in fact in many important respects closer to Glinka than to the generation of the sixties. While a full accounting of this phenomenon will entail the writing of another book, its seed is not difficult to locate in the eternal and inevitable problem of artistic realism—the problem of tone.

"Tone," as a category of aesthetics and criticism, has largely to do with scale. Thus no characterization of Dargomyzhsky omits the obvious point that his was a "chamber" rather than a "theatrical" style, and for many this loss of scale disqualified him as a viable operatic creator. Among those for whom the loss was irremediable was, once again, Asafiev, who invidiously compared Dargomyzhsky's Miller with Ivan Susanin "in the dimensions of his musical language."[5] But Asafiev here echoed a sentiment expressed by Borodin, too, when it came to choosing a manner of discourse—of musical rhetoric, one might say—for *Prince Igor:*

> I must point out that in my view of matters operatic I have always parted company with many of my comrades. The pure recitative style has always gone against my grain and against my character. I am drawn to singing, to cantilena, not to recitative, even though, according to the reactions of those who know, I am not too bad at the latter. Besides, I am drawn to more finished, more rounded, more expansive forms. My whole manner of treating operatic material is different. In my opinion, in the opera itself no less than in the sets, small forms, details, niceties should have no place. Everything should be painted in bold strokes, clearly, vividly, and as practicably as possible both from the vocal and orchestral standpoints.... In *tendency,* then, my opera will be more like *Ruslan* than like *The Stone Guest.*[6]

But tone has not only to do with scale. It has to do with categories of style and their traditional associations with genres, with congruence of subject and manner of treatment. We have seen how Ostrovsky tried to dissuade Serov from basing a serious opera on *Live Not The Way You'd Like* on grounds having to do with a basic difficulty of realist art, viz., that every one of its essential characteristics—low subjects, sharp characterizations, small scale forms, predominance of genre—had its origins in comedy, and retained ineluctable associations with the comic. And in the minds of most, these bonds could be broken even less easily in the sung than in the spoken theater. In the end, of course, Serov seems to have agreed with Ostrovsky, to judge not only by what he did to the ending of his opera's plot, but what happened to the musical style of his work in the process.

Another who evidently came to agree was Musorgsky. One of the enigmas of his career has always been the stylistic retreat he seems to have made around the time of the revision of *Boris Godunov*. No one has ever quite been able to explain why he went so much further in reshaping his masterpiece than what was demanded of him by the much maligned Imperial Theaters Directorate. The new-old direction initiated by the second version of *Boris*, moreover, was confirmed and carried much further in the two unfinished operas that ensued. Without presuming to give in passing here a definitive answer to such a substantial and complex question, we may nonetheless draw attention to a seldom noticed document. In a letter to Rimsky-Korsakov written right after a private runthrough of some scenes from the first version of *Boris* at Stasov's summer estate, a rather bemused Musorgsky reports that some of his audience found his peasants "bouffe", as he put it, while "others saw tragedy."[7] This certainly suggests a stylistic crisis in the making: Musorgsky, perceiving that in the eyes—or rather, ears—of his audience the prose recitative of his choral scenes was inseparably bound up with comedy, its traditional vehicle, began to rethink his whole operatic technique with an eye toward elevating its tone—as Odoevsky had said of *Ivan Susanin* so many years before—"to the level of tragedy." Such a hypothesis seems to account for all the various kinds of changes he made in the second version of *Boris*—changes which involved the elimination of some of the crowd music and the unwonted introduction of a rather formal aria into the title role. A wish to elevate the tone of his work may also have prompted Musorgsky's otherwise fairly baffling decision to interpolate such a wealth of often trivial genre numbers—particularly into the second act, which also contains Boris's aria—that (ironically enough) at least one of them is almost invariably cut in performance. By making more decisive the contrast between what is *bouffe* and what is tragic, these conventional genre interpolations helped to define and focus the latter.[8]

The example of *Boris* is symptomatic of a general movement in Russian opera away from realism and *"kuchkism"* in the 1870s and '80s. We might also have cited Rimsky-Korsakov's two revisions of *Pskovitianka* or Tchaikovsky's transformation of *Vakula the Smith* into *Cherevichki*. But the new operatic works represented not an about-face or a reaction so much as a synthesis in which the contributions of the sixties generation were assimilated into a well balanced and truly "classical" Russian operatic style. In the 1870s two dominant operatic genres emerged: the grand historical costume drama (*Pskovitianka, Boris Godunov, Khovanshchina, The Oprichnik*), in which psychologically complex character portrayal à la Dargomyzhsky was successfully wedded to Serovian "frescoes," and the peasant comedy after Gogol (*Vakula the Smith, The Fair at Sorochintsy, May Night*), in which the cultivation of Russian folklore at the heart of the drama, along with a kind of specifically Russian patter declamation, were given a further development in a comic context that created no problems of tone. The folk-song recitatives in Musorgsky's *Fair,* for example, seem to be directly and heavily influenced by Serov's example (in *The Power of the Fiend*), though of course Musorgsky would have been the last to acknowledge this influence. And the connection of the remaining two Gogolian operas to the Serovian tradition is patent: Serov actually composed a *May Night* himself in the early 1850s, though he later destroyed it, and at the time of his death he was embarked on a setting of the very libretto that was to become the basis of Tchaikovsky's *Vakula.*

And if we may make one more plea for Serov's decisive influence on the younger generation, it will be this: he set the precedent for regarding opera as a "civic deed" (as one critic called *Rogneda*), and in so doing brought opera into the mainstream of nineteenth-century Russian social and intellectual life. Like *Rogneda,* the historical operas of the 1870s aspired higher than mere costumed entertainments, but were principled attempts to interpret Russian history, particularly that of the period of Ivan the Terrible and the "Time of Troubles" that followed his reign.[9] We have come full circle to the high ethical considerations and the notions of the exalted place of art in the national life with which we opened this study, and it seems as well a fitting place to close it. It is hoped, moreover, that our exposition of the principles and the protagonists of Russian opera in the 1860s—the first study to focus detailed attention upon this period so much richer perhaps in ideas than in accomplishments—will serve as a prelude to a more critically rounded and historically grounded understanding of the classical repertoire—that of the grandfather and the grandsons—than has heretofore been possible.

Notes

1. Citations in this paragraph from Boris Asafiev, *Simfonicheskie etiudy* (Leningrad, 1970), pp. 124-26 passim.

2. *Simfonicheskie etiudy,* p. 125.

3. Ibid., p. 126.

4. For an interesting exposition of this distinction, see Carl Dahlhaus, *Between Romanticism and Modernism* (Berkeley, 1980), pp. 87-90.

5. *Simfonicheskie etiudy,* p. 125.

6. To Lubov Karmalina, June 1, 1876. Sergei Dianin, ed., *Pis'ma A.P. Borodina II* (Moscow, 1936), p. 109.

7. Letter of July 23, 1870. M.P. Musorgskii, *Literaturnoe nasledie I* (Moscow, 1971), p. 117.

8. It seems worth pointing out, both for the light it sheds on the revised *Boris* and on a possible model, that the new second act seems heavily indebted in its dramatic shape to the second act

of the recently premiered *William Ratcliff:* a rather lengthy divertissement full of songs, dances and games is suddenly interrupted by the entrance of the stern protagonist, who, having banished the revellers, proceeds to sing a crucial and self-revealing monologue.

9. Thus, Tchaikovsky's *Oprichnik,* following Lazhechnikov's historical drama of the same name, propagates the "orthodox" historiographical view of Ivan, following Karamzin, as bloodthirsty tyrant. This view is "challenged" by *Pskovitianka,* whose literary model, the play by Lev Alexandrovich Mey, presented the "revisionist" view of the "Grozny Tsar" advanced by the historian Sergei Soloviov, who portrayed Ivan as a positive force in Russian history, since his policies promoted the formation of a unified Russian nation state. And Musorgsky, by adding the Kromy Forest scene to *Boris,* brought his opera into line with the most radical historical thinking of the day, that of the populist historian Nikolai Kostomarov. The latter is the one who made the oft-cited remark that *Boris* was "no opera, but a page of history."

Appendix A

Synopses of the Serov Operas

Scenarios are adapted from B. Kremnev, ed., Opernye libretto *(Moscow, 1954).*
Enumeration of the musical numbers follows the respective vocal scores.

Judith

Act I

The ancient Judean city of Bethulia has been besieged for many days by forces of the Assyrian commander Holofernes. Worn out by hunger and deprivation, the city has not the strength to resist any longer the hardships of the cruel seige. Women, children and old men, exhausted by thirst and scorching heat, have gathered at the city's walls.

With downcast heads the elders of the city Ozias and Charmi appear, together with the priest Eliachim. Scouts have reported that at dawn Holofernes had blocked off all roads from the city to the valley and mountains; the last source of water is in enemy hands.

Eliachim is steadfast in his faith that the city will be delivered from the foe. He believes that a miracle must come to pass.

But the inhabitants of the city do not hope for a miracle; they demand that the elders turn the city over to the enemy—better death by Holofernes's sword than to perish in agony from hunger and thirst.

The elders calm the crowd, promising that the miracle will occur within five days. If by then the city has not been saved, the gates will be opened to the Assyrians.

Cries and shouts resounding from beyond the walls seize the attention of the populace. Soldiers bring in Achior, the leader of the Ammonites, a people conquered by Holofernes. He is bound hand and foot. Achior relates how Holofernes had become enraged at him for his having dared to speak in defense of the inhabitants of the beseiged city. For this Holofernes had ordered him tortured and thrown unconscious upon the road, where he was discovered.

(Orchestral prelude)

Serov's stage direction: "Square in the beseiged city, beneath a scorching midday sun. Over the city wall, which has big, securely locked iron gates, tall stone mountains can be seen. When the curtain rises the people are seen ranged in various groups at the rear of the stage; they wear gloomy, despairing faces, cruelly wasted by thirst."

No. 1: *Scena and arioso of the Levite (sic).*

Recitative (Ozias and Charmi): *Kontsa ne budet bedstviiu . . . ostavil nas Gospod!* [There will be no end to our misery; God has forsaken us].

Arioso (Eliachim): *Umolkni ropot bogokhul'nyi* [Cease this abusive grumbling].

No. 2: *Chorus of the People*, in four parts:

Nashi muki, nashi skorbi [Our trials, our woes], 2/2;

Umiraiut pered nami docheri i zheny [Our daughters and wives are perishing before us], Lento e mesto;

Vas zaklinaem [We implore you]: Fugue, mosso ma non troppo—risoluto;

Molim tak dolgo [We have prayed so long], Più lento, lamentoso assai.

(Then reprise of fugue).

Recitative (Ozias) with chorus: *O brat'ia* [O brethren].

No. 3: *Scena with Achior:*

Chorus, Chto eto? [What's this?];

Recitative (Achior) with chorus, *Ia vozhd' Ammonitian* [I am the leader of the Ammonites];

Achior narrates the history of the Jews and tells of Holofernes's vow to destroy the city and slay all its inhabitants.

All fall to their knees and pray for salvation from the cruel enemy.

Act II

Enveloped in sorrow, Judith, the widow of a brave soldier killed in battle with the enemy, sits in mourning in her bedchamber. She knows that it has been decided to surrender the city in five days. Expecting salvation from no one, Judith decides to carry out a bold plan of her own devising. Donning her richest attire, she will set out for the enemy camp and will captivate Holofernes with her beauty, and then execute her deed. Judith knows how dangerous her idea is, but fears nothing.

Judith bids her servant Avra summon the elders, and to give her courage she asks Avra to sing to her a song of the exploits of the heroine Yail.

Judith informs the elders she has summoned of her intentions, and the elders bless her upon her heroic scheme.

Avra endeavors in vain to dissuade Judith from her contemplated mission, but Judith is unshakeable. Avra begins to suspect that Judith has forsaken her people and for the sake of her own salvation has turned traitor.

Act III

Holofernes lies upon a couch in his camp under a rich canopy. Odalisques entertain him with songs and dances.

Aria (Achior): *V sud'be svoei narod evreev* [In its fate, the Hebrew people . . .];
Choral interpolation: *Tak, ty pravdu rëk* [Yes, thou hast spoken the truth].

No. 4: *Finale, Chorus:*
Spasi rabov tvoikh Izrailia Gospod [Save thy servants, O Lord of Israel], Andante maestoso appassionato.
[Final *tableau vivant:* The people praying.]

(Orchestral prelude)
No. 5: *Judith's monologue:*
Recitative: *Cherez piat'dnei reshili gorod sdat'* [They have decided to surrender the city in five days' time];
Aria: *Ia odenus' v visson* [I will don my purple robe].

No. 6: *Scena* (Judith and Avra), culminating in the *Voinstvennaia pesnia evreev:Gory debri i doliny* ["War Song of the Jews": Mountains, thickets and valleys].

No. 7: *Scena with the Elders,* culminating in the Duet (Ozias and Charmi): *Da! nashei kliatvoi my greshny* [Yes, by our vow we have sinned].

No. 8: *Duet* (Judith and Avra), culminating in reprise of the aria, *Ia odenus' v visson* with interjections by Avra, followed by an arioso (Cantabile, molto espressivo) for Avra: *Ty u grudi moei vzrosla* [You grew up at my breast], with interjections by Judith.

No. 9: *Entr'acte:* Holofernes's March

No. 10: *Chorus of Odalisques*
a. Odalisques' song (with two coryphei): *Na reke na Evfrate* [On the banks of the Euphrates]

b. Dance (D major, 2/4, allegro vivace).
c. Reprise of (a.) in parallel minor.
d. Dance (D minor, 2/4, moderato).
e. Reprise of all the foregoing alternately and in combination.

No. 11: *Recitative and arioso* (with offstage trumpets): *Proch'vy s glaz moikh!* [Get you all out of my sight!].

No. 12: *Reprise of March* (with *orchestre d'harmonie* on stage). Directions call for procession on stage including "infantry and cavalry, chariots, mules and camels."

No. 13: *Chorus of Assyrians: Prishla k nam evreika* [A Jewess has come to us].

No. 14: *Scena* (Judith, Holofernes and others):
a. Recitative (Vagao) with offstage trumpets: *Vot k Olofernu vest' doshla* [The news has come to Holofernes];
b. Fragmentary reprise of no. 13;
c. Recitative (Holofernes): *Ne boisia nas, Evreika* [Have no fear of us, Jewess] and arioso (Judith): *Vnemli, o vozhd' velikii* [Give ear, great leader];
d. Another fragmentary reprise of no. 13;
e. *Arioso* (Judith), on material from Achior's Act I aria (no. 3): *Toboiu byl k nam prislan* [By you was sent to us . . .];
f. *Arioso* (Judith): *Vnemli raby tvoei recham* [Hear the words of thy servant];
g. *Arioso* (Judith): *Gory nashi bedny* [Our hills are poor];
h. Fragmentary reprise of no. 13;
i. *Quartet* (Judith, Avra, Holofernes, Asphanes) on material from "f" above: *On parazhën moei krasoi* [He is taken with my beauty];
j. *Final recitative* (Holofernes, Judith, later Asphanes): *Ostan'sia s nami zdes'* [Remain with us here].

No. 15: *Final chorus: Net v svete sily, ravnoi nam!* [There is no power on earth to equal ours!].

But Holofernes is preoccupied with a single thought: the sooner to destroy his enemies and wipe their very memory off the face of the earth. He decides to unleash all his forces upon the beseiged city the very next day. He orders his retainer Asphanes to communicate this plan to his men and begin preparations.

The eunuch Vagao reports that from the enemy side there has come a woman of dazzling beauty who wishes an audience with the Assyrian commander. Judith, accompanied by Avra, enters Holofernes's tent and falls to her knees before him. Struck by her beauty, Holofernes asks Judith tenderly the purpose of her coming. Quietly and submissively Judith tells him that she is prepared to help Holofernes take the Hebrew city and will show him a secret path. All she asks for herself is guarantee of safe conduct in and out of the Assyrian camp for the saying of her morning and evening prayers. The deceived Holofernes promises to raise Judith above all earthly queens. Affectionately taking leave of Holofernes, Judith goes with Avra into the inner sanctum of the tent.

Holofernes and his retinue exult over their impending victory and the inability of the Hebrew God to protect his people.

Act IV

Holofernes triumphantly feasts with his retinue.

Divertissement.

All praise Judith's beauty, but Asphanes calls her "inaccessible."

Judith enters with Avra. She sees slaves carrying off the body of Asphanes, whom Holofernes has slain in pique. Restraining her disgust and horror, she approaches Holofernes and promises her love as soon as the enemies of the Assyrians are destroyed.

In the last stages of drunkenness, Holofernes attempts to embrace Judith, throws himself at her but falls and loses consciousness. His bodyguards lift him to his bed. The tent empties. Vagao asks Judith to remain in the tent until Holofernes should awaken. At last the hour has come for the execution of Judith's deed. She sends Avra out of the tent, seizes Holofernes's own sword and disappears under the tent canopy. The blows of the sword and a muffled cry are heard, followed by a deathly silence. Judith reappears pale and trembling, with the bloodied

No. 16: *Prelude and Chorus of Revellers*
  a. Orchestral enr'acte: "Holofernes's Orgy";
  b. Chorus: *Polynye chashi vina* [The wine cups are full].

No. 17: *Dances*
  a. Bacchanalian dance of the odalisques.
  b. Dance of the two almahs.

No. 18: *Chorus and dances.* (Reprise of 16b and 17b in combination)
No. 19: *Indian song* (Vagao): *Liubliu tebia mesiats* [I love thee, moon].
No. 20: *Recitative and War Song of Holofernes: Znoinoi my step'iu idëm* [We cross the torrid steppes];
Scena (Vagao, Holofernes, Asphanes).

No. 21: *Scena with chorus*
  a. *Recitative* (Holofernes, Judith, Avra): *Iudif priblizh'sia* [Judith, come forward];
  b. *Arioso* (Holofernes): *Kogda vernëmsia v Vavilon* [When we return to Babylon];
  c. *Arioso* (Judith): *Satana, Satana!* [Satan, Satan!], based on 5a above, chromaticized.
  d. *Arioso* (Holofernes): *I ty so mnoi razdelish vsë* [You shall share it all with me];
  e. *Scena* (Judith, Avra, Holofernes, Vagao, chorus): *Gospod' Izrailia* [O Lord of Israel].

No. 22: *Finale*
  a. *Recitativo accompagnato* (Holofernes, Judith): *Gde zh ty, evreika?* [Where are you, Jewess?];
  b. *Arioso* (Holofernes), with offstage trumpets: *Chego zh ty medlish'?* [Why do you tarry?]; based on No. 11.
  c. *Duet* (Holofernes and Judith), based combinations of No. 22a in the orchestra, No. 17b in Holofernes's part, and interjections by Judith: *Ty ostaësh'sia* [You will remain];

d. Scena, "Holofernes's delirium". *Opiat' protivish'sia* [Again you resist me];

e. *Recitative* (Judith and Vagao): *On umiraet?* [Is he dying?]

f. *Recitative* (Judith and Avra): *Vot ona! Eta strashnaia noch'!* [Here it is, that fearful night!];

g. *Arioso* (Judith): *Gospod' otsov moikh* [God of my fathers];

h. *Orchestral Representation of the Murder of Holofernes;*

i. *Concluding repliques* (Judith and Avra): *Izbrannitsa Gospoda* [O chosen one of the Lord].

No. 23: *Chorus of the Starving Populace*

a. Prelude (Orchestra), largely a reprise of the Prelude to Act I.

b. *Chorus* (on same material): *Esli v neschastii, v tiazhkikh mucheniiakh* [If in our misfortunes, our dire sufferings];

c. *Recitative* (Achior): *K bogokhul'nomu narodu* [To the blasphemous people];

d. *Chorus* (fugue): *Otvoriaite vorota skoree* [Open up the gates at once].

No. 24: *Scena*

a. *Recitative* (Judith and Achior): *Vot golova Oloferna* [Behold the head of Holofernes];

b. *Chorus* (People, soldiers) on same material;

c. *Arioso* (Eliachim): *Kto protiv Boga* [He who opposes God];

d. *Chorus*, with Avra, Achior, Eliachim: *Iudif' ty slavnee Devvory* [Judith, you are more glorious than Deborah];

e. *Choral scena* (rout of the Assyrians heard from offstage): *Chu! brannye kliki razdalis'* [Hark! martial cries resound];

No. 25: *Final chorus*

a. *Chorus: My pobedili* [We have triumphed];

b. *Recitative* (Judith): *Boga vy tol'ko edinnogo chtite* [Honor but the one God], with choral repliques;

c. *Judith's canticle, with chorus: Trikraty sviat nash Iegova* [Thrice holy is our Jehova].

sword and Holofernes's severed head in her hands. She calls Avra in a weak voice, indicating the bed with her eyes, and bids her servant put the head in her sack. Avra at last understands her mistress's undertaking and falls down on her knees before Judith. Together they make a hasty exit from the tent.

Act V

In the dead of night the inhabitants of Bethulia have gathered upon the square. They have lost all hope of salvation. The fifth day is about to run out and the miracle has not occurred. The people are mutinous; they are about to stone the elders and open the gates to the enemy themselves.

All at once the sentry's trumpet resounds, and women's voices are heard from behind the walls. Torches are lit and all rush to meet Judith. She appears triumphantly with Holofernes's severed head in her hands and faces the crowd. The people, rejoicing, surround her, kiss the fringes of her garments, bless their deliverer. The Assyrian armies retreat in disarray from their encampments outside the city, deprived of their leader. Sounds of their rout are heard from offstage.

Joyfully, soldiers enter with news of the final victory of the Hebrews. The rising sun brightly lights the city square, as Judith leads the inhabitants of Bethulia in an ecstatic canticle of praise.

Rogneda

Act I

Scene i: In a dark cave on the banks of the Dnepr the sorceress Skulda receives the High Priest of Perun. He is alarmed; Christianity is spreading widely among the people and the Kievan Prince Vladimir the Bright Sun (*Krasnoe solnyshko*) is not taking measures to preserve the old pagan faith. He must be killed, and the priest has chosen Rogneda, one of the Prince's wives, as the instrument for realizing his plan. Skulda must incline the princess to murder. Rogneda enters wrapped in a cloak. She thirsts for revenge upon Vladimir. The latter, in the course of conquering the Polotsk lands, had killed Rogneda's father, the prince Rogvolod, and has forsaken his wife for the delights and diversions of war. The sorceress throws herbs upon the altar. A bright flame blazes up; in its reflection a knife gleams in Skulda's hands. With this knife Rogneda will wreak her vengeance.

Scene ii: A great crowd has gathered on the banks of the Dnepr before a hill dominated by an idol of Perun. The priests prepare to greet the Prince who is to return that day from his campaigns. In honor of his victory over the enemy they have decided to sacrifice two adolescents to Perun.

The knife is already poised over one of the victims when the Christian youth Ruald, looking for his bride Olava whom Vladimir has abducted, emerges from the crowd. Seeing the impending sacrifice he stays the priest's hand. Enraged by the Christian's bold deed, the priests fall upon him and are ready to tear him limb from limb. Suddenly the sound of hunting horns is heard from afar. Ships appear on the river. The High Priest lets Ruald go, thinking that the youth will yet prove useful to him, for Ruald, too, hates Vladimir. The Prince and his retinue disembark. A rejoicing people greets the victors.

(Orchestral introduction)
No. 1: *Scene in the sorceress' cave.*
   a.   Arioso (Skulda), *Beda i zla* [Troubles and woe]
   b.   Recitative (Skulda and High Priest)

No. 2: *Rogneda's divination*
   a.   *Scena* (Rogneda, Skulda and High Priest), including Rogneda's arioso, *On pogubil vsiu zhizn' moiu* [He has ruined my whole life].
   b.   The divination—arioso (Skulda)
   c.   Trio, *Nevol'nyi strakh, ostav' menia* [Unbidden fears, leave me now]

No. 3: *Sacrifice to Perun*
   a.   Chorus, *Zhaden Perun, popit' okhota* [Perun is thirsty, needs a drink]
   b.   Dance around the altar (vivace)
   c.   Arioso (High Priest), *Segodnia kniaz' s pobedoi vozvratitsia* [Today the Prince returns in victory]
   d.   Reprise of chorus
No. 4: Aria (Ruald), *Nigde ne otyshchu Olavy* [Olava is nowhere to be found]
No. 5: *Finale*
   a.   Continuation of no. 4, over reprise of chorus.
   b.   Recitative (Ruald and High Priest); Arioso (Ruald), *Edin Gospod'!* [The Lord is One]
   c.   Chorus, *Smert' emu!* [Death to him!]
   d.   *Ruald's Prayer* (Aria), *O Bozhe istinnyi* [O God of Truth], over continuing fragments of preceding chorus.

e. *Entrance of Vladimir* (March with Chorus), *Krasnoe solnyshko veselo v Kieve gorode svetish'sia* [Bright sun, thou merrily shinest over Kiev]

No. 6: Chorus, *Slava solnyshku na nebe* [Glory to our Sun on high]
No. 7: *Dances of the Maidens*
a. Moderato, Bb major, 4/4
b. Cantabile assai, Eb major/c minor, 4/4
c. Giocoso scherzando, G major, 4/4
d. Reprise of all three in combination, g minor/Bb major
No. 8: *Dance of the Skomorokhi (Minstrels).* Prestissimo, D major, 4/4
No. 9: Recitative and Jester's Tale, *Za morem, za sinem* [Beyond the blue sea]
No. 10: *Finale*
a. *Scena* (Hunter, Prince, Dobrynya, Jester and chorus)
b. Reprise of no. 6

No. 11: Prelude and Chorus of Pilgrims, *V Iordan-reke my ot grekhov otmylis'* [In Jordan's river we washed away our sins]; arioso of Pilgrim Elder, *S molitvoi, brat'ia, otoidëm na otdykh* [With a prayer, brethren, let us take our rest]

Act II

Vladimir celebrates his victories with his retinue and knights at a magnificent banquet. Girls and minstrels entertain the prince with songs and dances.

The prince's minstrel spins a tale.

The merrymaking is interrrupted by a huntsman who runs into the palace with the news that Ruald and his companions have attacked the tower and have attempted to steal Olava back. The sentry succeeded in beating back the attack, but Ruald has gotten away. The Prince orders Ruald caught and executed. The knight Dobrynya Nikitich speaks up on behalf of the courageous youth: Ruald is not to blame, he was only defending his bride. The knight asks that Ruald be forgiven and Olava returned to him. The enraged Vladimir pays no attention to Dobryna's just words. In a fury, he threatens to banish the knight. A merry joke by the jester calms the Prince's anger, and Vladimir orders the entertainment resumed.

Act III

In a thick forest near Kiev, Ruald meets with a group of Christian wanderers returning from worship.

No. 12: Recitative and duet (Ruald and the Elder), *Kak mne tosku zagubit'* [How can I assuage my grief]

No. 13: *The Hunt*
a. Orchestral interlude
b. Chorus, *Vo temnom lesu zver'e zhivët* [Beasts in the dark forest dwell]

No. 14: *Scene of the Hunters at Rest*
a. Recitative (Prince, Dobrynya, Jester, chorus)
b. Drinking song, *Pësh'charu, tak druguiu pit'* [Drain one cup and then another]
c. Jester's song with chorus, *Ty mne zhonka, ne perech'* [Don't cross me, woman]

No. 15: *Finale*
a. Scena (Hunters, Prince, chorus)
b. Reprise of Duet (no. 12)
c. Ruald's death (Arioso), *Gospod' nam povelel* [God has commanded us]
d. Funeral chorus of the Pilgrims (Repliques of Elder and Prince Vladimir superimposed), *Bozhe! Prosti ego* [God! Forgive him]

No. 16: Prelude and Chorus of Captive Maidens, *Prizamolkli, prizatikhli* [Waving and lulling]

No. 17: Recitative and song (Izyaslav), *Matushka kniaginia, rodnaia moia* [My dear mother, princess]

No. 18: *Scena* (Rogneda, Izyaslav) and *Varangian Ballad* (Rogneda), *Zastonalo sine more* [The blue sea moaned]

No. 19: Arioso (Izyaslav). *Akh, rodnaia, ty snova plachesh* [Ah, my dear one, thou art weeping again], with choral reprise of no. 17.

Ruald tells the Elder of his woe and announces his intention to take revenge upon Vladimir. The Elder bids Ruald repay the Prince not with evil but with good. The prince and his retinue happen by on a hunt and stop to rest.

The hunters amuse themselves.

Suddenly a bear attacks the Prince. In keeping with the Elder's command, Ruald coolly comes to the Prince's aid, saves his life, but is himself mortally wounded. The Prince is astounded at the magnanimity of his adversary. In deep meditation he gives ear to the words of the Christian Elder. The old man predicts that that very night Vladimir will be saved once again by a miracle, and calls upon the ruler to enlighten his people with the new faith. Then will Russia be truly holy and powerful among nations. It grows dark and it is too late to travel back to Kiev. Vladimir sets out instead to pass the night in Rogneda's tower, which is not far.

Act IV

Rogneda sits lost in gloomy thought, oblivious to the songs of her attendant maidens. Her son Izyaslav tries to console her, too. At Izyaslav's prompting, Rogneda recalls her youth and momentarily forgets her woe.

But only momentarily.

No. 20: *Rogneda's Monologue* (grand scena)
 a. Adagio sostenuto, *Snova s toskoiu ostalas'ia* [Again I am left in misery]
 b. Allegro (orchestral reprise of no. 13a), *Okhota!* [The hunt!]
 c. Allegro molto (reprise of no. 2c), *A! Nakonets!* [At last!]

No. 21: *Finale*
 a. Scena (Vladimir, Rogneda, chorus), *Kniaginia zdravstvui* [Greetings, Princess!]
 b. Orchestral interlude with violin solo [The Prince's vision and attempted murder]
 c. Final scena (Vladimir and Rogneda), *V tvoei ruke sverkaet nozh; Rogneda?* [Is that a knife there gleaming in your hand, Rogneda?]

No. 22: *Scene in the Witch's Cave*
 a. Orchestral introduction (Storm over the Dnepr)
 b. Scena (Skulda, High Priest), *Krepko ozlilasia buria* [The storm has gotten much much worse]

No. 23: *Scene in the Tower*
 a. Chorus of Captive Maidens, *Leites' slëzy* [Shed your tears]
 b. Scena (duet) (Rogneda, Izyaslav, later Vladimir), *Pusti menia k rodnoi, pusti!* [Let me see my mother]

No. 24: *Finale*
 a. Orchestral prelude (with *veche* bells)
 b. Scena (Chorus, Dobrynya Nikitich), *Zachem nas sozval kniaz'na veche?* [Why has the Prince called us to council?]
 c. Chorus (Entrance of Vladimir), *Chu! slyshite* [Hark! Listen!], based on material of no. 5e.
 d. Aria (Izyaslav with chorus), *Pozhalei rodimuiu, prosi* [Have pity on my mother, forgive her]
 e. Concluding chorus, *Miloserd Gospod'* [The Lord is merciful],

The princess cheers up only when she learns that her husband is approaching her quarters. At last she will get her revenge.

Vladimir, having sent his entourage away, retires to the bedchamber. Rogneda noiselessly steals up on the couch on which he sleeps, her sharp knife in hand. Suddenly Vladimir awakens, roused by a prophetic dream in which Ruald and the Elder had appeared to him warning of his danger. Jumping up, the prince disarms Rogneda. In the morning, he tells her, she will be executed.

Act V

Scene i: A storm rages on the Dnepr. During the tempestuous night the High Priest has once again come to Skulda. He is terrified: what lies in store for the pagan priests? Skulda works her magic. The walls of the cave part. Shrouded in heavy mist, the banks of the river are seen, covered with the populace. At a sign from Vladimir the crowd topples the idol of Perun and casts it into the river, where it sinks.

Scene ii: Rogneda's maidens bewail her fate. Izyaslav has decided to intercede with his father the Prince on behalf of his mother or else die with her. The boy interposes himself between Rogneda and the approaching Prince. Vladimir gives Rogneda over to be judged by the people.

Scene iii: The Prince's court is filled with people. The Kievan populace demands the death of Rogneda. Izyaslav falls down at the feet of Vladimir and begs for mercy. Touched by the child's prayer, the Prince forgives his wife. The Christian pilgrims arrive and lead the crowd in praise of the Prince's conversion.

The Power of the Fiend

Act I

Dasha, the young wife of the Moscow merchant Pyotr Ilyich, has become sad. Her husband is almost never at home of late; he has strayed altogether from his family. Pyotr's father, the rich Moscow merchant Ilya, also condemns his son. The devout, staid old man is getting ready to leave, so as never to have to set eyes upon the sinful, dissolute Pyotr. From the street, the merry sounds of balalaikas, songs of revelry, the footfalls of the dancing crowd are heard.

Pyotr enters. To his father's questions—where has he been hanging out?—the son makes evasive answer: in Moscow there are many places where one can roam to one's heart's content. Pyotr pays no heed to his father's admonitions; he is occupied with his own thoughts. Churchbells are heard and Ilya leaves for vespers.

Left alone with her husband, Dasha caresses him, entreats him to love her once again, but Pyotr pushes his unloved wife away with irritation. Pyotr's mood is dark; he considers his marriage a misfortune. His wife has grown hateful to him. He has become fond of Grunya, the young and pretty daughter of the innkeeper Spiridonovna. Once more he absents himself from the house. Dasha is left in misery.

The young merchant boy Vasya appears, a bit tipsy, wishing Dasha a merry Shrovetide. Dasha gives him some wine and easily draws from the inebriated Vasya that Pyotr is infatuated with Grunya. The latter had once loved Vasya, but has thrown him over for Pyotr. In despair, Dasha resolves to leave Moscow and set out for Vladimir, where her parents live.

Orchestral "Introduction," potpourri style. Based on nos. 2, 3 and 14f, below.

No. 1: Dasha sola, then with Afimya: *Chuet, chuet retivoe* [My heart aches].

No. 2: Ilya and offstage chorus: *Ia razvrata nenavizhu* [I hate depravity]. The chorus sings an adaptation of the folk song *Kak u nashikh u vorot*.

No. 3: *Scena* (Pyotr, Ilya, Dasha, Afimya): *Gde, byl, synok rodnoi* [Where have you been, my son?].

No. 4: *Scena* (Pyotr, Dasha): *Slyshal batiushkino slovo?* [Did you hear your father's word?].
No. 5: *Scena* (Pyotr solo): *Ekh, golovushka moia buinaia* [Hey, wild head of mine].

No. 6: a. Prelude (stage empty)
   b. Dasha sola, *Chuiut li, znaiut li v dal'nem kraiu?* [Do they sense it, do they know it off afar?].
No. 7: *Scena* (Dasha and Vasya): *S shirokoi maslenoi!* [Shrovetide greetings!].

No. 8: a. Orchestral prelude, based on No. 12, below.

    b. *Scena* (Spiridonovna with chorus): *Chto rano tak sobralis' v put' dorogu!* [Why are you setting off so soon?]

    c. Spiridonovna's song: *Okh, kuptsy-molodtsy* [Oh, good merchants]

No. 9: Eryomka's song (with Spiridonovna and chorus): *Shirokaia maslenitsa* [Grand shrovetide].

No. 10: a. *Scena* (Grunya, Spiridonovna, Eryomka): *Akh! esli khochesh', tak rabotai* [Ah, work if you like];

    b. Grunya's song: *Akh, nikto menia ne liubit* [Ah, no one loves me].

No. 11: *Recitative and duet* (Spiridonovna and Grunya): *Uekhali, i ladno!* [They're gone, and good riddance!].

No. 12: Grunya sola: *Chto za radost' zhizn' devich'iu nevol'no promenia!* [What's the good of giving up the maiden's life?].

No. 13: *Recitative and duet* (Grunya and Pyotr):

    a. Recit: *Chto serdi?* [What are you angry at?];

    b. Duet: *Ty khodi ko mne pochashche* [Come see me more often].

No. 14: *Finale*

    a. Grunya sola: *Prilaskai, tak ne otstanet* [Be nice and he'll never go away];

    b. *Recitative* (Stepanida and Grunya): *Gde mne, krasna devitsa, obogret'sia tut?* [Where can I warm myself here, pretty girl?];

    c. *Scena* (Dasha and Spiridonovna): *Ty, konei poka vpraiut, posidi u nas* [Sit with us while your horses are being harnessed];

    d. *Arioso* (Dasha, repliques from others): *Il' ne slyshish', matushka?* [Don't you hear me, mother?];

    e. *Scena* (Dasha, Agafon, Stepanida, later Grunya): *Batiushka! Matiushka!* [Father! Mother!];

    f. Quartet: *Smeisia, razluchnitsa* [Laugh, homewrecker];

    g. *Scena* (The same, plus Spiridonovna): *Chto zh delat', dochushka* [What can we do, daughter?].

Act II

There are many guests at Spiridonovna's inn, merchants and coachmen making a stopover. The hostess busies herself regaling her guests with wine and mead.

At Spiridonovna's request, Eryomka, the blacksmith attached to the inn, entertains the company with a swaggering Shrovetide song. Spiridonovna bids her daughter too to sing for the guests. The guests go wild over the comely girl and her song.

When all are departing, the wily and calculating innkeeper persuades her daughter to turn her charms upon the young Moscow merchant Pyotr Ilyich. Not for nothing has he lately been stopping by so often. Grunya must not let her opportunity slip by to marry this well-to-do young merchant. Grunya does not want even to think about the consequences of marriage; above all she values her freedom, but she has in fact grown fond of Pyotr in spite of herself. When Pyotr arrives, Grunya showers him with caresses and arranges with him that he will return that evening and that together they will go out sleighriding.

After seeing Pyotr to the door, Grunya remains alone, but not for long. Soon some new faces appear at the inn—Dasha's parents, Stepanida and Agafon. They do not suspect the misfortune that has befallen Dasha, but are simply on their way to Moscow to visit their daughter and her husband. Here at the inn, Dasha unexpectedly encounters her mother and father. The unhappy woman pours out her sorrow to her parents and tells them of her decison to leave Pyotr and seek refuge in her father's home. But Agafon will not hear of it: it is a sin to leave one's husband. Having overheard the entire conversation, Grunya realizes that Pyotr has deceived her, having passed himself off as a bachelor.

Act III

Grunya laments the turn her fate has taken.

When Pyotr comes for Grunya according to their arrangement, she receives him very coldly, as if totally transformed in his absence. He quickly guesses the reason for the change. Grunya chases Pyotr away with reproaches at his deception. Pyotr thinks tensely, who could have given away his secret? None other than Vasya, he concludes. His hostility to the young merchant boy grows greater yet when Vasya appears, and Grunya, having spurned Pyotr, goes out riding with Vasya. Pyotr gazes darkly after the couple. Eryomka sidles up to him. He is prepared to deliver the merchant from his troubles: if Pyotr turns to a certain witch Eryomka knows, his sorrow will be over. Pyotr, submitting to the smith's persuasions, agrees to go with him to see the witch.

Act IV

Shrovetide revelries are in full swing. At one of the Moscow gates the people are making merry. Sonorous songs of tipsy cavaliers and street vendors resound. A trainer and his bear appear, accompanied by a big crowd. Pyotr, Eryomka, and two drunken carousers appear onstage. Pyotr, intoxicated, sings a song to the balalaika, the two drunks humming along. Friends try to cheer him up, call him into the tavern, but nothing can dispel Pyotr's gloomy brooding. He cannot forget the divination of the witch, who had predicted a wedding in his future. How can he get rid of his repellent wife? Vasya enters with Grunya. Not noticing Pyotr, Vasya tells Grunya how Dasha found out about Grunya's relations with Pyotr. Hearing this, Pyotr hurls himself at Vasya and tries to kill him. Grunya and Vasya leave, Pyotr is humiliated.

No. 15: Grunya's song with chorus: *Akh, chto zh ty, moj sizyi golubchik,* against *Ja ne znaiu, kak mne s milym pomirit'sia* [Ah, what is the matter, my blue dove—I don't know how to make up with my sweetheart].
No. 16: *Scena* (Grunya, Pyotr, Spiridonovna, Vasya, Eryomka, chorus).

No. 17: *Duet scene* (Pyotr and Eryomka): *Pokatilisia devki udalye* [The lively girls have gone a-sleighing].
No. 18: Eryomka's song to the balalaika: *Ty, kupets, so mnoiu luchshe ne branis'* [Merchant man, you'd do better not to quarrel with me].

(Prelude-Intermezzo, based on no. 18 above)
No. 19: Scene of Shrovetide Revelries (*Scena gulianki*).

No. 20: *Scena* (Pyotr and the drunkards): *Kak u nas-to kozël chto za umnyi byl* [What a smart billy-goat we had].
No. 21: *Scena* (Pyotr and Eryomka), including Pyotr's monologue, *Ne zalit' vinom mne tosku moiu* [I cannot drink my sorrow away].

No. 22: *Scena* (Grunya, Vasya, chorus of girls; including Vasya's arioso, *Kak liubliu tebia, nenagliadnaia* [How I love you, sweetheart!]).
No. 23: Fight Scene (Vasya, Pyotr, Eryomka, chorus): *A! Tvoë, sobaka, delo!* [So it's your doing, dog!].
No. 24: *Scena* (Grunya with chorus): *Zdravstvui, molodets udalyi* [Greetings, brave fellow!].

The merrymaking continues. A sleigh passes with the shrovetide dummy and mummers. The crowd follows it off.

Left alone with Pyotr, Eryomka advises him to have done with his wife; then Grunya will return to him. They go into the tavern to discuss the matter further.

Vasya unexpectedly returns onstage, his sleigh having collided with another. He overhears Pyotr and Eryomka plotting from within the tavern.

Vasya hides as Pyotr and Eryomka hatch their plot. Pyotr is to set out at night into the forest and await his friend in a "wolf's gully" near a half-wrecked hovel. Eryomka is to go to Dasha and tell her that her husband has been taken dangerously ill and bring her into the forest. Vasya hurries to Dasha, to warn her of the imminent danger.

Act V

The dead of night. Through the clouds shine moonbeams now and then, illuminating with dim, unsteady light a deep, snow-bound ravine and a tumbledown shack. In its window a light is flickering faintly. A fierce snowstorm rages. In horror Pyotr listens to the howling of the blizzard. He seems to hear in it by turns the voice of Grunya, the laughter of the girls, the moans and entreaties of Dasha. In exhaustion he falls into a snowdrift and leaps to his feet—footsteps are approaching. It is Eryomka with Dasha. As soon as she had heard that woe had befallen her husband she had come hurrying to this "wolf glen," despite the late hour and evil weather. Eryomka urges his pal on—he must finish the "business" without delay. Pyotr falls upon Dasha with a knife. Attempting to save herself, Dasha rushes into the shack. Pyotr forces the door. The light in the window goes out. Dasha lets out a frightful scream.

No. 25: The Shrovetide Procession (*Poezd maslenitsy*), largely based on no. 9, above.

No. 26: *Scena* (Pyotr and Eryomka): *Chto, snegiriushko, nevesel?* [Still unhappy, old fellow?].

No. 27: *Scena* (Vasya, with voices of Eryomka and a drunkard from offstage): *Eko delo! Zatolkali!* [Some break! We collided!].

No. 28: *Duet* (Pyotr and Eryomka): *Nu skazhi mne, golova, chto nadumal?* [So tell me, smarty, what have you come up with?].

No. 29: Vasya solo, later followed by the two drunkards: *Akh, ty, Gospodi!* [Oh my God!].

No. 30: *Enr'acte*: "Storm in the Wolf's Gully."

No. 31: *Scena* (Pyotr solo): *Ne ubit' zmeiu, ne izzhit' bedu!* [If you don't kill the snake, your troubles will never end].

No. 32: *Murder scene* (Pyotr, Dasha, Eryomka): *Vot i my kak raz priekhali* [Looks like we arrived just in time].

Silence sets in, but is interrupted by the distant sound of sleighbells, coming nearer and nearer. Eryomka takes off in fright. Vasya, Ilya, Agafon, Stepanida, Afimya enter. Not finding Dasha at home, Vasya has come hurrying with her near ones to the "wolf's gulley" to avert the murder. But too late. With a hollow moan, Pyotr falls at the feet of his unforgiving father.

No. 33: *Final scene* (Eryomka solo, then Vasya, Stepanida, Ilya, Agafon, Afimya, Pyotr): *Vot-te na! Tam skachet kto-to!* [What's this! Someone's coming!]

Appendix B

Three numbers from the unpublished Borodin-Krylov operetta *Bogatyri* (Leningrad: Muzykal'naja biblioteka teatra opery i baleta im. S.M. Kirova, Ms. 3766), together with their models in *Rogneda* and *Askold's Grave*

The full title of this pastiche is "The Heroic Warriors: a musico-historical drama or chronicle in five scenes of everyday life by V. Alexandrov (i.e., Krylov). Music compiled [*sic*] by A.P. Borodin." There are twenty-two separate numbers. They are listed below, together with the indications of their "sources" as given in the margins of the manuscript. While there are many quotations beyond those acknowledged by the "compiler," no attempt has been made here to identify them. The credited citations are given merely to show the range of material drawn upon by Borodin. The Russian models account for only a fraction of the quotations. Asterisks denote the numbers given in full in this appendix.

Act I:

   1. Introduction *(Robert-le-Diable, Barber of Seville, Les Bavards)*
   2. Solovei Budimirovich's cavatina *(Barbe-bleu)*
   3. Solovei's couplets (*Barbe-bleu*, "Austrian March")

Act II:

   4. Procession of Prince Gustomysl with his retinue and troops (all original?)
   5. Aria, Gustomysl and chorus *(Robert-le-Diable, Barber of Seville)*
   6. Sacrifice to Perun (folk song, *Kak u našego dvora*)
   7. The March of the Bogatyri and chorus *(La Belle Hélène)*
  *8. Perun's Dance, chorus and scena (*Rogneda*, not credited)
  *9. a. Solovei's lullaby *(Rogneda)*
      b. Scena *(Barbe-bleu)*
  10. Finale *(Ernani)*—includes reprise of No. 8

Act III:

 *11. Chorus of maidens and scene in Militrisa's terem (*Rogneda*—plus *Askold's Grave*, not credited)
  12. Couplets of the High Priest Kostryuk Sidorovich (original?)
  13. Scene of the Bards' Arrival *(Le Prophète, Robert-le-Diable, Barbe-bleu)*
  14. Quartet, finale *(La Belle Hélène)*

Act IV:

  15. Alyosha-Popovich's love song (original?)
  16. Chorus of Bogatyri and scena *(Les Bavards)*
  17. Xenia's couplets *(Barbe-bleu)*
  18. Chorus of Bogatyri and Bogatyrshi, i.e., their wives *(Barbe-bleu)*
  19. Duel of Foma and Amelfa *(Robert-le-Diable, Zampa)*
  20. Finale *(Semiramide)*

Act V:

  21. Chorus of Congratulation *(Barbe-bleu, La Belle Hélène)*
  22. Finale (Song in honor of Foma and general dance)

#8: Perun's Dance (Pljaska Peruna)

Source: Rogneda, Act I (Dance around the idol)

Rogneda, Act I, sc. ii: Dance around the idol.

Dance around the idol (cont'd)

ЖРЕЦЪ.

Се_год-ня   князь съ по _ бѣ_дой возвра _ тит _ ся.   Мы въ честь по _   бѣ_ды

#9a. Solovei's Lullaby (Usypitel'naja pesenka Soloveja)

Source: Rogneda, Act II (Jester's Song)

jut-sja. Pes-ni è-ti čud-no   ne-gu raz-li-va-jut, i ot nix ne-vol'-no lju-di za-sy-pa-jut. Ge-nij mu-zy-

kal'-nyj daj mne vdox-no-ven-'e, čtob pro-iz-ve-sti zdes' sla-dost' u-sy-plen'-ja. Spi-te spi-te krep-ko, mir-no na-slaž-

daj-tes', i kak mož-no dol'-še vy ne pro-buž-daj-tes". [Spoken: Nu, kažetsja zasnuli.]

#10, – Full reprise of #8 [Militrisa's and Gostomysl's soli to new words]

Rogneda, Act II: The Jester's Story *(Skazka duraka)*

Си - не мо - ре   у - блажать!   Станемъ же-ре - бій ки-дать,   си - не мо - ре

у - бла - жать!   Гость въ от - вѣтъ про - мол - вилъ: Что - же,   брат - цы!..

#11: Chorus and scene in Militrisa's terem. [Xor i scena v tereme Militrisy]

NB: The text of the opening chorus (meas. 1 - 33) is missing in the ms. It has been supplied
from Rogneda, Act IV, in keeping with the author's evident intention. **Source:** Rogneda, Act IV
(Chorus of Captive Maidens)

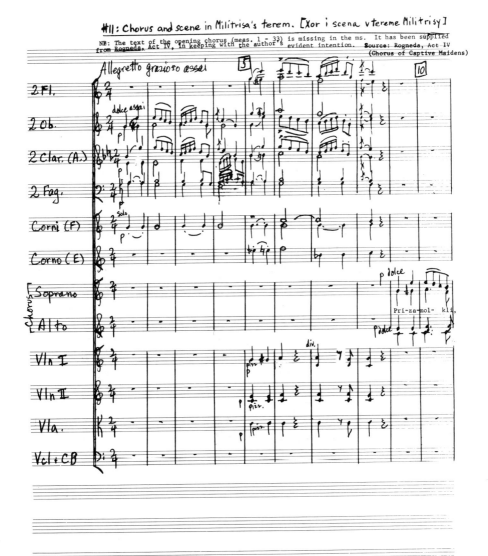

Aj, kak skučno oj,kak skučno Aj,kak skučno oj,kak skučno nam!

Source: <u>Rogneda</u>, Act IV (Izyaslav's song)

Rogneda, Act IV: Chorus of Captive Maidens

Askol'dova mogila (Verstovsky): Chorus of Captive Maidens *(Ax,
podruzhen'ki, kak grustno),* Act III. Vocal score, ed. B.V. Dobrokhotov
(Moscow: *Muzgiz,* 1963)

Rogneda, Act IV: Izyaslav's song *(Matushka kniaginia).*

Appendix C

The Power of the Fiend, Act I #7, Scene of Vasya and Dasha (later Afimya).

Vocal score (Moscow, 1968)

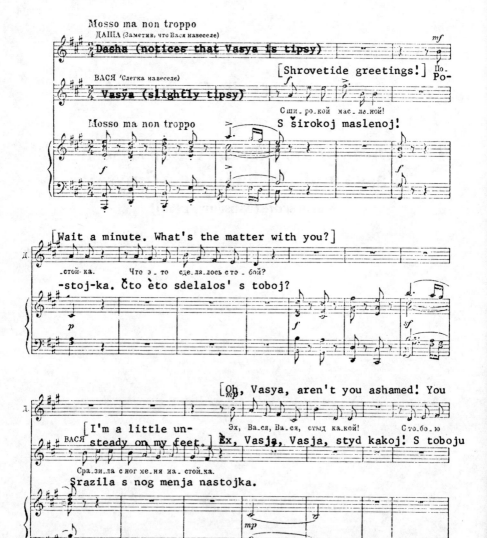

(In great despair and jealousy)

[Farewell, husband mine! The time has come for us to part!]

[I'm going to my family!...]

Appendix D

Love Duets from *Angelo*

The first of these scenes is closely described in the text. The other is given because it contains some of Cui's finest and most characteristic love music, giving a measure of credence to Stasov's hyperbolic praise of the composer as "realistic" portrayer of love ("the representation of which reaches with Cui a depth and a sharp force unequalled by any of his colleagues in the New Russian School and perhaps unequalled by anyone in the whole realm of music" [Izbrannye sočinenija, vol. II, p. 551]). Though they are formally unimaginative and static, and though their harmonic piquanteries will probably tend to justify Napravnik's dismissal of Cui as a salon composer, these duets reveal a composer of surprising individuality and polish.

a. Rodolfo and Thisbe (Act I, sc. vi). Bessel vocal score (St.
   Petersburg, 1876)

b. Rodolfo and Caterina (Act III, sc. ii), Bessel vocal score

из _ ме _ ни _ лась.   Ахъ,   э _ то другъ мой от _ то _ го, что каждый день   я
ich ge _ al _ tert!   Ach,   trautes Herz, wie hab' ich mich gehärmt um dich,

пла _ ка _ ла въ раз _ лу _ кѣ.   А ты,   что   дѣ _ далъ?
Tag   für Tag ge _ wei _ net!   Doch du,   wo   bliebst du?

poco ri _ te _ nu _ to.   *a tempo.*

О бомнѣ грус _ ти _ лъ ли ми _ лый мой?   Твой го _ лосъ хо _ чу   я
Hast du gleich _ falls dich nach mir ge _ sehnt?   Der Klang dei _ ner Red'   ist

poco ri _ te _ nu _ to.   *a tempo.*

mf

РОДОЛЬФЪ.
RODOLFO.

слы _ шеть;   го _ во _ ри _ же, го _ во _ ри   Ро _ дольфъ!   О Ка _ та _
Won _ na!   Re _ de, sprich doch, o Ro _ dol _ fo sprich!   O Ca _ tha _

КАТАРИНА.
CATHARINA.

a tempo.

бѣ.   И я,   я   то _ же о _ щу _ ща _ ла...
sagt!   Und   ich...?   ob   Glei_ches ich nicht fühl _ te?

Мнѣ
O

мно _ го нужно разска _ зать те _ бѣ...   Съ че _ го на чать?
vie _ les hab' ich mit zu_thei _ len   dir!   Wo fang' ich an?

Вотъ
Denn

ви _ дишь ли,   ме _ ня здѣсь за _ пер _ ли,   не мог _ ла я прид _ ти къ те _ бѣ,
weisst du's schon,   Ge_fan_gen   bin ich hier.   Konnte   nim_mer mehr hin   zu dir,

Ро _ дольфъ.   Ког _ да у _ слы _ ха _ ла   я   твой го _ лосъ
Ro _ dol_fo!   Und   plötz _ lich ver _ neh _ me   ich   be _ kann _ ten

О, по смот ри, какъ ночь ти ха, какъ звѣз ды бле щутъ
O schau, wie still und klar die Nacht! Die Ster ne flam mn

яс но въ ла зу ри не ба!
hell am Fir ma men te!

Все во кругъ насъ у
Und rings um schlum mert

сну ло! Са ма при ро да на ру шать не
Al les! Ja die Na tur selbst mag nicht uns' re

хо четъ бла жен ства на ше го...
see li gen Stun den stö ren!

Те бя я люб лю, ме
Mein Herz, es ist dein! und

Bibliography

Books and Articles

Abraham, Gerald. "Heine, Queuille, and 'William Ratcliff.'" *Musicae Scientiae Collecteanae: Festschrift Karl Gustav Fellerer zum 70. Geburtstag.* Cologne, 1973.
_____. *On Russian Music.* London, 1936.
_____. "The Operas of Serov." *Essays Presented to Egon Wellesz.* Ed. Jack Westrup. Oxford, 1966.
_____. *Slavonic and Romantic Music.* New York, 1967.
_____. *Studies in Russian Music.* London, 1936.
_____. "Tchaikovsky's First Opera." *Festschrift Karl Gustav Fellerer zum 60. Geburtstag.* Regensburg, 1962.
_____, ed. *The Music of Tchaikovsky.* Second edition. New York, 1973.
Abramovskii, Georgii Konstantinovich. "'Rogneda' A.N. Serova." *Sovetskaia muzyka,* 1976, no. 12.
_____. *Russkaia opera pervoi treti XIX veka.* Moscow, 1971.
Alshvang, Arnold. *Izbrannye stat'i.* Vol. I. Moscow, 1962.
Altshuler, A.Ia., ed. *Ocherki istorii russkoi teatral'noi kritiki.* Leningrad, 1976.
Anglés, Higinio. "Relations epistolaires entres César Cui et Philippe Pedrell." *Fontes Artis Musicae,* 1966, no. 1.
Artem'eva, E.N. and N.N. Grigorovich, eds. *Nauchnaia muzykal'naia biblioteka imeni S.I. Taneeva. Ocherk.* Moscow, 1966.
Asafiev, Boris. *Glinka.* Moscow, 1947.
_____. "Iz zabytykh stranits russkoi muzyki." *Muzykal'naia letopis'.* Ed. A.N. Rimskii-Korsakov. Vol. I. Petrograd, 1922 (signed Igor Glebov).
_____. *Izbrannye trudy.* Vols. III-V. Moscow, 1954-57.
_____. *Russkaia muzyka XIX i nachalo XX veka.* Leningrad, 1968.
_____. *Simfonicheskie etiudy.* Leningrad, 1970.
Bachinskaia, Nina. *Narodnye pesni v tvorchestve russkikh kompozitorov.* Moscow, 1962.
Baker, Jennifer. "Dargomizhsky, Realism and *The Stone Guest.*" *Music Review,* vol. 37, no. 3 (August, 1976).
Balakirev, Milii Alekseevich. *Milii Alekseevich Balakirev: Letopis' zhizni i tvorchestva.* Ed. A.S. Liapunova and E.B. Iazovitskaia. Leningrad, 1967.
_____. *Perepiska s Chaikovskom.* St. Petersburg, 1912.
_____. *Perepiska s notoizdatel'stvom P.I. Iurgensona.* Moscow, 1958.
_____. *Perepiska s N.G. Rubinshteinom i M.P. Beliaevym.* Moscow, 1956.
_____. *Perepiska s V.V. Stasovym.* 2 vols. Moscow, 1970-71.
_____. *Vospominaniia i pis'ma.* Leningrad, 1962.
Barenboim, Lev Aronovich. *Anton Grigor'evich Rubinshtein.* 2 vols. Leningrad, 1957-62.

Baskin, V.S. *A.N. Serov: Biograficheskii ocherk,* (Russkie kompozitory, III). Moscow, 1890.

Bazunov, S.A. *A.S. Dargomyzhskii. Ego zhizn'i muzykal'naia deiatel'nost'.* St. Petersburg, 1894.

Belianova, G. "Osnovnye zakonomernosti formoobrazovaniia v opere Dargomyzhskogo 'Kamennyi gost'.' " *Stranitsy istorii russkoi muzyki.* Ed. E.M. Orlova and A.E. Ruchevskaia. Leningrad, 1973.

Belinskii, Vissarion. *Sobranie sochinenii.* Vol. II. Moscow, 1948.

Benois, Alexandre. *Reminiscences of the Russian Ballet.* London, 1941.

Bernandt, Grigorii Borisovich. *Slovar' oper vpervye postanovlennykh ili izdannykh v dorevoliutsionnoi Rossii i v SSSR, 1736-1959.* Moscow, 1962.

——, and I.M. Iampolskii. *Kto pisal o muzyke: Bio-bibliograficheskii slovar' muzykal'nykh kritikov i lits, pisavshikh o muzyke v dorevoliutsionnoi Rossii i SSSR.* 3 vols. Moscow, 1971-79. In progress.

Berkov, V. *Ruslan i Liudmila M.I. Glinki.* Moscow, 1949.

Bogdanov-Berezovskii, V. *Teatr opery i baleta imeni S.M. Kirova.* Leningrad, 1959.

Bondarenko, F.P., ed. *Leningradskii gosudarstvennyi ordena Lenina akademicheskii teatr opery i baleta imeni S.M. Kirova.* Leningrad, 1960.

Borodin, Aleksandr Porfirievich. *Pis'ma.* Ed. S.A. Dianin. 4 vols. Moscow, 1928-50.

Braudo, Evgenii Maksimovich. *Istoriia muzyki.* Second edition. Moscow, 1935.

Brown, David. *Mikhail Glinka. A Biographical and Critical Study.* London, 1974.

——. *Tchaikovsky: The Early Years, 1840-1874.* New York, 1978.

Bykov, A., ed. *Iz arkhivov russkikh muzykantov.* Moscow, 1962.

Calvocoressi, M.D. *Musorgsky.* New York, 1962.

——, and Gerald Abraham. *Masters of Russian Music.* New York, 1936.

Chaikovskii, Modest Il'ich. *Zhizn' Petra Il'icha-Chaikovskogo.* 3 vols. Moscow, 1900-03.

Chaikovskii, Petr Il'ich. *Dnevniki 1873-1891.* Moscow, 1923.

——. *Muzykal'no-kriticheskie stat'i.* Moscow, 1953.

——. *P.I. Chaikovskii ob opere: Izbrannye otryvki iz pisem i statei.* Moscow, 1952.

——. *Perepiska s P.I. Iurgensonom.* Moscow, 1938.

——. *Perepiska s N.F. fon-Mekk.* 3 vols. Moscow, 1934-36.

——. *Perepiska s S.I. Taneevym.* Moscow, 1951.

——. *Pis'ma k blizkim.* Moscow, 1955.

——. *Pis'ma k rodnym.* Moscow, 1940.

——. *Polnoe sobranie sochinenii.* Vol. II (Literaturnye proizvedeniia). Moscow, 1953.

——. *Polnoe sobranie sochinenii.* Vols. V-IX (Perepiska 1848-80). Moscow, 1959-65.

Chaliapin, Fëdor Ivanovich. *Stranitsy iz moei zhizni.* Perm, 1961.

Chernyshevsky, Nikolai Gavrilovich. *Selected Philosophical Essays.* Moscow: Foreign Languages Publishing House, 1953.

——. *What Is To Be Done?.* Trans. B. Tucker. New York, 1961.

Cheshikhin, Vsevolod. *Istoriia russkoi opery (s 1674 po 1903 gg.).* Moscow, 1905.

Chudnovskii Mikhail Aleksandrovich. *Modest Petrovich Musorgskii.* Moscow, 1957.

Dahlhaus, Carl. *Between Romanticism and Modernism.* Berkeley, 1980.

Danilov, Sergei. *Ocherki po istorii russkogo dramaticheskogo teatra.* Moscow-Leningrad, 1948.

Dargomyzhskii, Aleksandr Sergeevich. *A.S. Dargomyzhskii. Avtobiografiia. Pis'ma. Vospominaniia sovremennikov.* Ed. N.F. Findeisen. Peterburg, 1921.

Druskin, Mikhail Semenovich. *Voprosy muzykal'noi dramaturgii opery, na materiale klassicheskogo naslediia.* Leningrad, 1952.

Fanger, Donald. *Dostoevsky and Romantic Realism.* Chicago, 1965.

Ferman, Valentin Eduardovich. "Nekotorye osobennosti muzykal'noi dramaturgii russkoi opernoi shkoly." *Sovetskaia muzyka,* 1946, no. 10.

Findeisen, Nikolai Fëdorovich. *Mikhail Ivanovich Glinka: Ocherk ego zhizni i muzykal'noi deiatel'nosti.* Moscow, 1903.

_____. *A.N. Serov, ego zhizn' i muzykal'naia deiatel'nost'*. Second edition. Moscow, 1904.

Frid, E.L., ed. *Russkaia muzykal'naia literatura*. Moscow, 1958.

Galperin, M.P. *"Iudif' " Libretto opery*. With an introductory article on Serov by L. Obolensky. Moscow, 1930.

Garland, Mary. *Hebbel's Prose Tragedies*. Cambridge, 1973.

Gervinus, Georg. *Händel und Shakespeare*. Leipzig, 1868.

Ginzburg, Semën Lvovich. *Istoriia russkoi muzyki v notnykh obraztsakh*. Second edition. 3 vols. Moscow, 1968-70.

Glinka, Mikhail Ivanovich. *Literaturnoe nasledie*. Vol. I: *Avtobiograficheskie i tvorcheskie materialy*. Leningrad, 1952. Vol. II: *Pis'ma i dokumenty*. Leningrad, 1953.

_____. *Zapiski*. Leningrad, 1953.

Glumov, Aleksandr Nikolaevich. *Muzyka v russkom dramaticheskom teatre*. Moscow, 1955.

Gordeeva, E.M., ed. *Kompozitory moguchei kuchki ob opere. Izbrannye otryvki iz pisem. vospominanii i kriticheskikh statei*. Moscow, 1955.

_____. *Kompozitory moguchei kuchki o programmnoi muzyke*. Moscow, 1956.

Gozenpud, Abram Akimovich. *Izbrannye stat'i*. Leningrad, 1971.

_____. *Muzykal'nyi teatr v Rossii*. Leningrad, 1959.

_____. *N.A. Rimskii-Korsakov. Temy i idei ego opernogo tvorchestva*. Moscow, 1957.

_____. "Opernoe tvorchestvo A.N. Serova." *Sovetskaia muzyka*, 1971, no. 7.

_____. *Opernyi slovar'*. Moscow, 1965.

_____. Russkii opernyi teatr XIX veka. Vol. I (1836-1856); vol. II (1857-1872); vol. III (1873-1889). Leningrad, 1969-73.

Grigor'ev, Apollon Aleksandrovich. "Moskva i Peterburg." *Moskovskii gorodskoi listok*, 1847, no. 43.

_____. *My Literary and Moral Wanderings*. Translated with an introduction by Ralph E. Matlaw. New York, 1962.

_____. "O realizme v iskusstve i literature." *Iakor'*, 1863, no. 13.

_____. *Polnoe sobranie sochinenii i pisem*. Ed. V. Spiridonov. Vol. I. Petrograd, 1918.

_____. Review of *Judith* by Serov. *Iakor'*, 1863, no. 12.

_____. Review of *Sobranie russkikh narodnykh pesen* ' by Stakhovich. *Moskvitianin*, 1854, no. 15.

_____. "Russkie narodnye pesni s ikh poeticheskoi i muzykal'noi storony." *Otechestvennye zapiski*, 1860, nos. 4-5.

_____. "Russkii teatr i sovremennoe sostoianie dramaturgii i stseny." *Vremia*, 1863, no. 2.

_____. Russkii teatr v Peterburge." *Epokha*, 1864, no. 3.

_____. *Sobranie sochinenii*. Ed. V.F. Sadovnikov. Vol. II. Moscow, 1915.

Gruber, R., ed. "Pis'ma A. Serova k ottsu." *Muzykal'noe nasledstvo*. Moscow, 1935.

Guralnik, U. "*Sovremennik* v bor'be s zhurnalami Dostoevskogo." *Izvestiia Akademii nauk SSSR, otdelenie literatury i iazyka*, vol. 9 (1950).

Gusin, I.L. "Ts. A. Kiui v bor'be za russkuiu muzyku," in Ts. Kiui, *Izbrannye stat'i*. Leningrad, 1952.

Hebbel, Friedrich. *Werke*. Vol. I. Munich, 1963.

Hofmann, R. *Un siècle d'opéra russe*. Paris, 1946.

Iakovlev, Vasilii. *Izbrannye trudy o muzyke*. Vol. I. Moscow, 1964.

Iarustovskii, Boris Mikhailovich. *Dramaturgiia russkoi opernoi klassiki*. Second edition. Moscow, 1953.

_____. *Opernaia dramaturgiia Chaikovskogo*. Moscow, 1947.

Iastrebtsev, Vasilii Vasilievich. *Vospominaniia o N.A. Rimskom-Korsakove*. 2 vols. Leningrad, 1959-60.

Il'inskii, A. *Biografii kompozitorov s IV-XX vek s portretami*. Moscow, 1904.

"Ip. M—v" [pseud.]. "Po povodu 'Rognedy.' " *Russkaia stsena*, 1865, no. 11.

Iuriev, S. Letter on *The Power of the Fiend.* Published as preface to A.N. Serov. *O velikorusskoi pesne i osobennostiakh eë muzykal'nogo sklada.* St. Petersburg, 1868.

Ivanov, Georgii Konstantinovich. *Russkaia poeziia v otechestvennoi muzyke.* 2 vols. Moscow, 1966-71.

"Ivanushka Durachok" [pseudonym for Vladimir Vasilievich Nikolskii]. "Libretto 'Rognedy.' " *Russkaia stsena,* 1865, no. 12.

Kandinskii, Aleksei Ivanovich, et al., eds. *Istoriia russkoi muzyki.* Vol. I. Moscow, 1972.

Kashkin, Nikolai Dmitrievich. *Stat'i o russkoi muzyke i muzykantakh.* Moscow, 1953.

Kerman, Joseph. *Opera As Drama.* New York, 1956.

Keldysh, Georgii Vsevolodovich. *Istoriia russkoi muzyki.* 2 vols. Moscow, 1948.

————. *Russkie kompozitory vtoroi poloviny XIX veka.* Moscow, 1960.

————. ed., with Vasilii Iakovlev. *M.P. Musorgskii. K piatidesiatiletiiu so dnia smerti. 1881-1931. Stat'i i materialy.* Moscow, 1932.

————, et al. *Muzykal'naia entsiklopediia.* 2 vols. Moscow, 1973-74. In progress.

Khrushchevich, Iraida Pavlovna. *Gosudarstvennyi ordena Lenina akademicheskii teatr opery i baleta imeni S.M. Kirova.* Leningrad, 1957.

Khubov, Georgii Nikitich. "Aleksandr Serov, voinstvuiuschii realist," in A.N. Serov, *Izbrannye stat'i.* Vol. I. Leningrad, 1951.

————. *A.P. Borodin.* Moscow, 1933.

————. *Musorgskii.* Moscow, 1969.

————. *Zhizn' A.N. Serova.* Moscow, 1950.

Kiui, Tsezar' [Cui, César]. *Izbrannye pis'ma,* Leningrad, 1955.

————. *Izbrannye stat'i.* Leningrad, 1952.

————. *La Musique en Russie.* Paris, 1880.

————. *Muzykal'no-kriticheskie stat'i.* vol. I. Petrograd, 1918.

————. Articles and reviews not included in anthologies:

Novosti i birzhevaia gazeta:

1896, no. 38: "A.N. Serov i ego posmertnaia opera." no. 106: Mariinskii teatr. 144-e predstavlenie 'Rognedy' Serova."

1899, no. 74: " 'Iudif' ' Serova s inozemnymi gostiami."

Sanktpeterburgskie vedomosti:

1865, no. 292: " 'Rogneda,' opera v piati deistviiakh A.N. Serova, stikhi D.V. Averkieva (po programme kompozitora)."

1866, no. 14: "Zhurnal'nye tolki o 'Rognede' g. Serova." no. 327: "Vtoroe izdanie 'Rognedy,' dopolnennoe i ispravlennoe."

1867, no. 304: "Repertuar russkoi opery. 'Groza,' opera g. Kashperova."

1868, no. 23: "Eshchë odna galliutsinatsiia g. Serova"; " 'Torzhestvo Vakkha' Dargomyzh-skogo."

1869, no. 132: "Korrektsiia g. Serovu."

1871, no. 6: "K istorii postanovki 'Kamennogo gostia' i k kharakteristike 'Golosa' (Polemika s Rostislavom po povodu op. Dargomyzhskogo)." no. 41: "A.N. Serov"; "Eshchë k kharakteristike 'Golosa.' " no. 111: " 'Vrazh'ia sila,' opera A.N. Serova." no. 303: "Pisk g. Famintsyna. Khvala Klassitsizmy. Katon starshii i ia." no. 311: " 'Askol'dova mogila' Verstovskogo"; " 'Demon' g. Rubinshteina."

1872, no. 297: " 'Vrazh'ia sila' Serova."

1873, no. 74: "Tri russkie opery" (signed "M"). no. 99: "Niderlandskoe chado g. Katkova ili g. Larosh. Ego zigzagi, naivnichan'e, istericheskie pripadki, rytsarskie svoistva" (Response to Laroche's "Vil'iam Ratklif muzykal'noi pechati").

1874, no. 37: " 'Boris Godunov,' opera g. Musorgskogo, dvazhdy zabrakovannaia vodevil'nym komitetom."

1876, no. 8: "Benefis g. Napravnika ('Rogneda')."

Kniazhnin, Vladimir, ed. *Apollon Grigor'ev: Materialy dlia biografii*. Petrograd, 1917.

Kolosova, E.M. and V. Filippov, eds. *A.N. Ostrovskii i russkie kompozitory: pis'ma*. Moscow, 1937.

Koltypina, Galina Borisovna. *Bibliografiia muzykal'noi bibliografii. Annotirovannyi perechen' ukazatelei literatury, izdannoi na russkom iazyke*. Moscow, 1963.

―――. *Spravochnaia literatura po muzyke*. Moscow, 1964.

Komarova-Stasova, Varvara [Vladimir Karenin]. *Vladimir Stasov: Ocherk zhizni i deiatel'nosti*. Leningrad, 1927.

Komissarzhevskii, Fëdor. *Sovet molodym pevtsam*. St. Petersburg, 1882.

Kremlev, Iulii Anatolievich. *Russkaia mysl' o muzyke*. Vol. II. Moscow, 1958.

Kremnev, Boris, ed. *Opernye libretto*. Moscow, 1954.

Krylov, Viktor, *Prozaicheskie sochineniia*. Vol. II. St. Petersburg, 1908.

Kunin, Iosif Filippovich. *Milii Alekseevich Balakirev: Zhizn' i tvorchestvo v pismakh i dokumentakh*. Moscow, 1967.

"L. N—va" [Pseud.]. "Otvet na stat'iu uchenika konservatorii o 'Rognede.'" *Russkaia stsena*, 1865, no. 11.

Lamm, O.P., compiler. *"A.N. Serov." Vystavka, Moskva 1945 (125-letie dnia rozhdeniia)*. Moscow, n. d.

Lamm, Pavel Aleksandrovich. "Ot redaktora." Introductory article to vocal score of *Marriage* by Musorgsky. Moscow, 1933.

Larosh, German Augustovich. *Izbrannye stat'i o Glinke*. Moscow, 1953.

―――. *Muzykal'no-kriticheskie stat'i*. St. Petersburg, 1894.

―――. *P.I. Chaikovskii kak dramaticheskii kompozitor*. St. Petersburg, 1895.

―――. *Sobranie muzykal'no-kriticheskikh statei*. Vol I. Moscow, 1913. Vol. II (O P.I. Chaikovskom). Moscow, 1922.

―――. Articles and reviews not included in anthologies:

Golos:
   1872, no. 153: Review of *The Stone Guest*. no. 184: Review of *The Power of the Fiend*.
   1873, no. 45: "Benefis g. Kondrat'eva v Mariinskom teatre." no. 94: "Vil'iam Ratklif muzykal'noi pechati." no. 115: (continuation of above) no. 308: "Russkaia muzykal'naia kompozitsiia nashikh dnei," part 1. no. 315: ibid., part 2. no. 329: ibid., part 3.
   1874, no. 9: ibid., part 4. no. 18: ibid., part 5. no. 29: "Novaia russkaia opera." no. 44: "Mysliashchii realist v russkoi opere." no. 308: "Russkaia opera."

Muzykal'nyi svet:
   1873, no. 5: Review of *The Stone Guest*.

Russkaia stsena:
   1865, no. 9: " 'Rogneda,' novaia russkaia opera" (signed "Uchenik konservatorii"). no. 13: "Eshchë o 'Rognede' (Pis'mo k redaktoru)."

Russkii vestnik:
   Vol. 187 (1887): "Po povodu 'Kamennogo gostia' v Moskve."

Severnaia pchëla:
   1864, no. 110: "Zametka po povodu lektsii o muzyke g. Serova" (signed "Uchenik konservatorii")

Vestnik Evropy:
   1872, no. 4: "Kamennyi gost' ' Dargomyzhskogo."

Lenskii, Aleksandr. *Stat'i, pis'ma, zapiski*. Moscow, 1935.

Lerner, N.O. "Pis'ma A.N. Serova k Iu. F. Abaze." *Biriuch petrogradskikh gosudarstvennykh akademicheskikh teatrov*. Petrograd, 1920.

Leyda, Jay, and Sergei Bertensson. *The Musorgsky Reader*. New York, 1947.

Livanova, Tamara Nikolaevna. *Muzykal'naia bibliografiia russkoi periodicheskoi pechati XIX veka*. 6 vols. Moscow, 1960-74. In progress.

_____. "Polemika V.V. Stasova i A.N. Serova ob operakh Glinki." *Pamiati Glinki 1857-1957.* *Issledovaniia i materialy.* Ed. V.A. Kiselev. Moscow, 1958.

_____. *Opernaia kritika v Rossii.* 4 vols. Moscow, 1966-73. In progress.

_____. *Stasov i russkaia klassicheskaia opera.* Moscow, 1956.

_____. and Vladimir Protopopov. *Glinka. Tvorcheskii put'.* Vol. II. Moscow, 1955.

Lobanov, D.I. *A.N. Serov i ego sovremenniki.* St. Petersburg, 1889.

Loewenberg, Alfred. *Annals of Opera.* Third edition. Totowa, N.J., 1978.

Lunacharskii, A. and V. Polianskii, eds. *Ocherki po istorii russkoi kritiki.* Vol. I. Moscow, 1929.

Mirsky, D.S. *History of Russian Literature.* New York, 1958.

_____. *Pushkin.* New York, 1963.

Molchanov, A.E. "A.N. Serov." *Russkaia starina,* vol. 39 (1883).

_____. *Bibliograficheskii ukazatel' literatury o A.N. Serove i ego proizvedeniiakh.* St. Petersburg, 1888.

Musorgskii, Modest Petrovich. *Izbrannye pis'ma.* Moscow, 1953.

_____. *Literaturnoe nasledie. Pis'ma, biograficheskie materialy i dokumenty.* Moscow, 1971.

_____. *Pis'ma i dokumenty.* ed. A.N. Rimskii-Korsakov. Moscow, 1932.

_____. *Pis'ma k A.A. Golenishchev-Kutuzov.* Moscow, 1939.

Muzykal'noe nasledstvo. Sborniki po istorii muzykal'noi kul'tury SSSR.
    Vol I. Moscow, 1962. Vol. II, part 1: Moscow, 1966; part 2: Moscow, 1968. Vol. III. Moscow, 1970.

Nabokov, Vladimir. *Nikolai Gogol.* New York, 1959.

Napravnik, Eduard Frantsevich. *Avtobiograficheskie, tvorcheskie materialy, dokumenty, pis'ma.*
    Leningrad, 1959.

Nechaeva, Vera. *Zhurnal M.M. i F.M. Dostoevskikh "Epokha."* Moscow, 1975.

Newmarch, Rosa. *The Russian Opera.* New York, 1914.

Odoevskii, Vladimir Fëdorovich. *Izbrannye muzykal'no-kriticheskie stat'i.* Moscow, 1951.

_____. *Muzykal'no-literaturnoe nasledie.* Moscow, 1956.

Ogolevetz, Aleksei Stepanovich. "A.N. Serov ob ispolnitel'skom iskusstve." *O muzykal'nom ispolnitel'stve.* Ed. L.S. Ginzburg and A.A. Solovtsov. Moscow, 1962.

_____. *Materialy i dokumenty po istorii russkoi realisticheskoi muzykal'noi estetiki.* 2 vols. Moscow, 1954-56.

_____. *Slovo i muzyka v vokal'no-damaticheskikh zhanrakh.* Moscow, 1960.

Orlova, A.A. *Trudy i dni M.P. Musorgskogo. Letopis' zhizni i tvorchestva.* Moscow, 1963.

_____. *Glinka v vospominaniiakh sovremennikov.* Moscow, 1955.

Orlova, E. *B.V. Asafiev.* Leningrad, 1964.

Ornstein, Arbie. *Ravel: Man and Musician.* New York, 1975.

Ossovskii, A.V., ed. *M.I. Glinka. Issledovaniia i materialy.* Leningrad, 1950.

Ostrovskii, Aleksandr Nikolaevich. *Dnevniki i pis'ma.* Moscow, 1937.

_____. *Polnoe sobranie sochinenii.* Vol. I. Moscow, 1973.

Pekelis, Mikhail Samoilovich. *A.S. Dargomyzhskii i ego okruzhenie.* 2 vols. Moscow, 1966-73.

_____. *Dargomyzhskii i narodnaia pesnia.* Moscow, 1951.

_____. "Dramaturgicheskie iskanie poslednego perioda." *Sovetskaia muzyka,* 1980, no. 5.

_____. *Istoriia russkoi muzyki.* Vol. II. Moscow, 1940.

_____. "Risunok A. Serova, podarennyi Glinke." *Sovetskaia muzyka,* 1957, no. 2.

Pogozhev, V.N. "Vospominaniia o P.I. Chaikovskom." *P.I. Chaikovskii: Vospominaniia i pis'ma.* Ed. Igor Glebov. Leningrad, 1924.

Popova, Tatiana Vasilievna. *Russkoe narodnoe muzykal'noe tvorchestvo.* 3 vols. Moscow, 1955-57.

Protopopov, Vladimir Vasilievich. *"Ivan Susanin Glinki. Muzykal'no-teoreticheskoe issledovanie.* Moscow, 1961.

Pougin, A. *Essai historique sur la musique en Russie.* Turin, 1897.

Purdie, Edna. *Friedrich Hebbel.* London, 1932.

Raeff, Marc, ed. *Russian Intellectual History: An Anthology.* Introduction by Isaiah Berlin. New York, 1966.

Reviakin, A.I. *Moskva v zhizni i tvorchestve A.N. Ostrovskogo.* Moscow, 1962.

Riesemann, Oskar von. *Moussorgsky.* Trans. Paul England. New York, 1971.

———. "Alexander Seroff and His Relations to Wagner and Liszt." *Musical Quarterly,* vol. 9 (1923).

Rimskii-Korsakov, Nikolai Andreevich [Rimsky-Korsakov]. *Letopis' moei muzykal'noi zhizni.* Moscow, 1955.

———. *Muzykal'nye stat'i i zametki.* St. Petersburg, 1911.

———. *My Musical Life [Letopis'].* Trans. Judah A. Joffe, New York, 1923.

———. *Polnoe sobranie sochinenii.* Vol. II: *Literaturnye proizvedeniia i perepiska.* Moscow, 1963.

———. *Polnoe sobranie sochinenii.* Vol. IV. Moscow, 1960. Vol. V. Moscow, 1963. Vol. VII. Moscow, 1970.

Rubinshtein, Anton. [Rubinstein]. *Autobiography.* Trans. A. Delano. Boston, 1892.

———. "Die geistliche Oper." *Vor den Coulissen,* Bd. II. Ed. Josef Lewinsky. Berlin, 1882.

———. *Izbrannye pis'ma.* Moscow, 1954.

Ryleev, Kondraty Fedorovich. *Polnoe sobranie stikhotvorenii.* Leningrad, 1971.

Ryzhkin, I. *Russkoe klassicheskoe muzykoznanie v bor'be protiv formalizma.* Moscow, 1951.

Saltykov-Shchedrin, Mikhail Evgrafovich. "Mezhdu delom. Zametki, ocherki, rasskazi i t. d." *Otechestvennye zapiski,* 1874, no. 11.

———. *Nedokonchennye besedy.* St. Petersburg, 1885.

Seaman, Gerald. *History of Russian Music.* Vol. I. New York, 1967.

Serov, Aleksandr Nikolaevich. *Izbrannye stat'i.* Vol. I. Moscow, 1950.

———. *Izbrannye stat'i,* Vol II. Leningrad, 1957.

———. *Kriticheskie stat'i.* 4 vols. St. Petersburg, 1892-95.

———. "Pis'ma V.K. i A.P. Anastas'evym." *Russkaia starina,* 1878.

———. "Pis'ma k V. Zhukove." *Sovetskaia muzyka,* 1954, no. 7.

———. "Po sluchaiu stat'i 'Libretto Rognedy.' " *Russkaia stsena,* 1865, no. 13. (Signed "Postoiannyi posetitel' russkoi opery.")

———. Preface to the libretto of *Judith.* St. Petersburg [1863].

Serova, Valentina Semënovna. *Serovy A.N. i V.A.: Vospominaniia.* St. Petersburg, 1914.

Sheffer, Tamara Vasilievna. *A.N. Serov.* Kiev, 1951.

———. "Ukrainskie temy v tvorchestve A. Serova." *Iz istorii russkogo-ukrainskikh muzykal'-nykh sviazei.* Ed. T.I. Karysheva. Moscow, 1956.

Shteinpress, Boris Solomonovich and Izrail Markovich Iampolskii. *Entsiklopedicheskii muzykal'nyi slovar'.* Moscow, 1966.

Smirnova, Irina. *Esteticheskie printsipy Serova-kritika. Avtoreferat dissertatsii.* Moscow: Institut istorii iskusstv akademii nauk SSSR, 1954.

Sokhor, Arnold. *A.P. Borodin.* Leningrad, 1965.

Solovtsov, Anatolii Aleksandrovich. *Kniga o russkoi opere.* Moscow, 1960.

Soubies, Albert. *Histoire de la musique en Russie.* Paris, 1898.

Starchevskii, I.G. "Kompozitor A.N. Serov." *Nabliudatel',* 1888, no. 3.

Stark, E. *Peterburgskaia opera i ee mastera.* Leningrad, 1940.

Stasov, Vladimir Vasilievich. *A.P. Borodin, Ego zhizn', perepiska i muzykal'nye stat'i.* St. Petersburg, 1889.

———. *Ts. A. Kiui. Biograficheskii ocherk.* Edited with an introduction by A.S. Ogolevetz. Moscow, 1954.

———. "Dvadtsat' pisem Turgeneva i moë znakomstvo s nim." *Severnyi vestnik,* 1888, no. 10.

————. *Izbrannye sochineniia.* 3 vols. Moscow, 1952.

————. *Izbrannye stati'i o M.I. Glinke.* Moscow, 1955.

————. *Nezabvennomu V.V. Stasovu* [Collection of articles and reminiscences]. St. Petersburg, 1910.

————. *Pis'ma k deiateliam russkoi kul'tury.* 2 vols. Moscow, 1962.

————. *Pis'ma k rodnym.* 3 vols. Moscow, 1953-62.

————. *Selected Essays on Music.* Trans. Florence Jonas. New York, 1968.

————. *Sobranie sochinenii.* 4 vols. St. Petersburg, 1894-1906.

Stasova, E.D., ed. *V.V. Stasov 1824-1906.* Moscow, 1949.

Stender-Petersen, Ad. *Anthology of Old Russian Literature.* New York. 1954.

Strakhov, Nikolai. *Zametki o Pushkine i drugikh poetakh.* Kiev, 1897.

Stravinsky, Igor. *An Autobiography.* New York, 1936.

————. *Memories and Commentaries.* Garden City, N.Y., 1960.

————. *Poetics of Music.* New York, 1947.

Strelnikov, N.A. *A.N. Serov. Opyt kharakteristiki.* Moscow, 1922.

Swan, Alfred J. *Russian Music and Its Sources in Chant and Folk-song.* New York, 1973.

Taruskin, Richard. "Realism As Preached and Practiced: The Russian Opéra Dialogué." *Musical Quarterly,* vol. 56 (1970).

Tolstoi, Feofil Matveevich [Rostislav]. "A.N. Serov, Vospominaniia." *Russkaia starina,* 1874.

————. *Muzykal'nyi razbor 'Rognedy'.* St. Petersburg, 1870.

————. *Novaia opera A.N. Serova "Vrazh'ia sila."* St. Petersburg, 1871.

————. "Peterburgskie teatry." *Otechestvennye zapiski,* 1869.

————. *Razbor opery "Iudif' " g. Serova.* St. Petersburg, 1871.

————. " 'Vil'iam Ratklif,' opera g. Kiui." *Otechestvennye zapiski,* 1869.

————. "Zapadnaia reklama, perenesennaia na russkuiu pochvu." *Severnaia pchela,* 1863, no. 126.

Trifonov. P.A. "Aleksandr Sergeevich Dargomyzhskii, po ego avtobiografii, pis'mam i proizvedeniiam." *Vestnik Evropy,* 1886, nos. 11-12.

Tsetlin, Mikhail. *Piatero i drugie.* New York, 1953.

Tsuker, A. " 'Kamennyi gost' ' kak muzykal'naia kontseptsiia." *Sovetskaia muzyka,* 1980, no. 5.

Tumanina, Nadezhda Vasilievna. *Chaikovskii. Put' k masterstvu.* Moscow, 1962.

————. *Istoriia russkoi muzyki.* Vol. II. Moscow, 1958.

Untermeyer, Louis, *Heinrich Heine, Paradox and Poet.* New York, 1931.

Uspenskaia, S.L. *Literatura o muzyke.* Vol. I (1948-53): Moscow, 1955. Vol. II (1954-56): Moscow, 1958.

Vanslov, Viktor Vladimirovich. *Opera i ee stsenicheskoe voploshchenie.* Moscow, 1963.

Vasina-Grossman, V.A. *Russkii klassicheskii romans XIX veka.* Moscow, 1956.

Vernadsky, George. *Kievan Russia.* New Haven, 1948.

Vodarsky-Shiraeff, Alexandra. *Russian Composers and Musicians. A Biographical Dictionary.* New York, 1940.

Zagoskin, Mikhail. *Sochineniia.* Vol. VI. St. Petersburg, 1901.

Zemtsovskii, Izalii. *Iskateli pesen.* Leningrad, 1967.

Zenkovsky, V.V. *A History of Russian Philosophy.* Trans. George L. Kline. 2 vols. New York, 1953.

Zvantsev. Konstantin Ivanovich. "Aleksandr Nikolaevich Serov v 1857-71 gg. Vospominaniia o nëm i ego pis'ma." *Russkaia starina,* 1888.

Zotov, R.D. "Vospominaniia o Serove." *Russkaia muzykal'naia gazeta,* 1896.

Musical Sources Consulted

[N.B.: Included here are only those works that figure with some importance in the text. For other citations, see within.]

Borodin, Aleksandr Porfirievich. *Bogatyri*. *Muzykal'no-istoricheskaia drama ili khronika v piati bytovykh kartinakh* (1867). Unpublished. Muzykal'naia biblioteka teatra opery i baleta im. S.M. Kirova, Leningrad: Ms. 3766.

Chaikovskii, Petr Il'ich. *Voevoda* (1868). Reconstructed and edited by Pavel Lamm. *Polnoe sobranie sochinenii. Vol. I (dopolnenie)*. Moscow: *Muzgiz*, 1953.

Dargomyzhskii, Aleksandr Sergeevich. *Kamennyi gost'. Opera v trëkh deistviiakh*. Moscow: *Muzgiz*, 1932.

――――. *Rusalka. Opera v chetyrëkh deistviiakh, shesti kartinakh*. Moscow: Izdatel'stvo "Muzyka," 1966.

――――. *Torzhestvo Vakkha. Liricheskaia opera-balet v odnom deistvii, dvukh kartinakh*. Moscow: Izdatel'stvo "Muzyka," 1969.

Glinka, Mikhail Ivanovich. *Ruslan i Liudmila. Volshebnaia opera v piati deistviiakh*. Moscow, Izdatel'stvo "Muzyka," 1968.

――――. *Zhizn' za Tsaria. Bol'shaia opera v chetyrëkh deistviiakh s èpilogom*. Moscow: A. Gutheil, 1885.

Kashperov, Vladimir Nikitich. *Groza. Opera v chetyëkh deistviiakh*. Arranged for piano (without voice) by A Diubiuk. Moscow: P. Jurgenson, n.d.

――――. Libretto of same (Ostrovskii). Moscow: P. Jurgenson, 1867.

Kiui, Tsezar' Antonovich. *Andzhelo. Opera v chetyrëkh deistviiakh*. St. Petersburg: Bessel & Co., 1876.

――――. *Kavkazskii plennik. Opera v trëkh deistviiakh*. St. Petersburg: Bessel & Co., 1882.

――――. *Pir vo vremia chumy. Dramaticheskie stseny A.S. Pushkina*. Leipzig: Edition M.P. Belaieff, 1901.

――――. *Vil'iam Ratklif. Opera v trëkh deistviiakh*. St. Petersburg: Bessel & Co., n.d.

――――. *Syn mandarina. Komicheskaia opera v odnom deistvii*. Leipzig: D. Rahter, n.d.

Musorgskii, Modest Petrovich. *Zhenit'ba. Sovershenno neveroiatnoe sobytie v trëkh deistviiakh (Opyt dramaticheskoi muzyki v proze)*. Ed. Pavel Lamm *(Polnoe sobranie sochinenii, tom IV, vypusk 2)*. Moscow: *Muzgiz*, 1933.

Rachmaninov, Sergei Vasilievich. *Skupoi rytsar'. Opera v odnom deistvii, trëkh kartinakh na tekst odnoimennoi tragedii A.S. Pushkina*. Moscow: Izdatel'stvo "Muzyka," 1968.

Rimskii-Korsakov, Nilolai Andreevich. *Motsart i Sal'eri. Dramaticheskie stseny A.S. Pushkina*. Ed. I.F. Belza *(Polnoe sobranie sochinenii,* vol. 35). Moscow-Leningrad: *Muzgiz*, 1950.

Serov, Aleksandr Nikolaevich. *Iudif'. Opera v piati deistviiakh*. Arranged for voice and piano by A. Evgeniev and G. Dütsch. Moscow: A. Gutheil, 1885.

――――. *Rogneda. Opera v piati deistviiakh*. Moscow: A. Gutheil, 1885.

――――. *Vrazh'ia sila. Opera v piati deistviiakh*. Arranged for voice and piano by G.O. Dütsch. Moscow: Izdatel'stvo "Muzyka," 1968.

Verstovskii, Aleksei Nikolaevich. *Askol'dova mogila. Romanticheskaia opera v shesti kartinakh*. Revised and edited by B.V. Dobrokhotov. Moscow: *Muzgiz*, 1963.

Villebois, Konstantin Ivanovich. *Sto russkikh narodnykh pesen*. St. Petersburg, 1860.

Index

Abarinova, Antonina Ivanovna (real name
    Reichelt), 234
Almazov, Boris Nikolaevich, 143
Ambros, August Wilhelm, 25
Anastasieva (née Mavromikhali), Maria
    Pavlovna, 42, 44, 46, 72 n.61
Artemovsky. *See* Gulak-Artemovsky,
    Semyon Stepanovich
Artôt, Désirée, 45
Auber, Daniel François, 45, 129, 351, 360,
    400, 424 n.105
    Works: *La Muette de Portici (Fenella)*,
        129, 424 n.105
Averkiev, Dmitrii Vasilievich, 87, 88, 91,
    125, 135 n.35, 137 n.77

Balakirev, Milii Alekseevich, 263, 354
    and folk song, 186, 245 n.103
    conducts Glinka's operas in Prague, 19
    on *Ruslan and Liudmila*, 27
    on *The Stone Guest*, 331 n.24
    on *William Ratcliff*, 417, 422 n.75
    positivistic aesthetics, 330 n.16
    reviews *Judith*, 46, 72 n.62
Beethoven, Ludwig van
    Works: *Fidelio*, 7, 60, 205, 210-11
Belinsky, Vissarion Grigorievich, xv n.3, 3
Benfey, Theodor, 245 n.101
Bertin, Louise, 251
Bessonov, Pyotr Alekseevich, 200
Bianchi, Valentina, 65-66
Boito, Arrigo ("Tobia Gorrio"), 405
Borodin, Alexander Porfirievich
    on *Marriage*, 321
    operatic aesthetics, 429
    Works:
        Bogatyri (operetta), 121-24, 139 n.105,
            139 n.108, Appendix B
        Prince Igor, 429
Bulakhov, Pyotr Petrovich, 393
Bulgarin (Bulharyn), Thaddei

on *A Life For the Tsar*, 29 n.9
Burenin, Victor Petrovich, 404-5, 425 n.121

Cavos, Catterino, 2
    Works: *Ivan Susanin*, 2
Chaliapin, Fyodor, 67, 186
Chernyshevsky, Nikolai Gavrilovich, 169-
    70, 177, 258-60 (incl. Fig. 5.3),
    329 n.11, 330 n.13, 338 n.104, 354
"Continuous finale," 60
Cui, César Antonovich
    and Auber, 351, 360, 400
    characterized as "William Ratcliff of the
        musical press," 423 n.97
    completes *The Fair at Sorochintsy*
        (Musorgsky), 139 n.138
    completes *The Stone Guest*, 294, 336 n.66
    defends *Ruslan and Liudmila*, 21-23, 299,
        418 n.20
    general characterization, 341-43 (incl. Fig.
        6.1)
    journalistic career, 343-45, 420 n.40,
        423 n.97
    La Musique en Russie, 418 n.23
    on *Judith*, 34-35, 66-67, 100
    on local color, 420 n.47, 422 n.78
    on *Marriage*, 323, 339-40 n.138, 346
    on Meyerbeer, 343
    on *Mozart and Salieri* (Rimsky-Korsakov),
        326-27
    on "operatic forms," 347-50
    on *The Power of the Fiend*, 227, 228-29,
        232-33, 235, 238, 248 n.145
    on realism, 200-204, 211, 227
    on *Rogneda*, 93-94, 96, 99, 100, 101-2,
        107-8, 139-40 n.110
    on *Rusalka*, 262, 299, 401
    on *The Stone Guest*, 263, 290, 298-301,
        307, 325, 330 n.15, 350
    on *The Storm* (Kashperov), 157
    on Wagner, 290-91, 344, 401

Cui, César Antonovich *(continued)*
  operatic aesthetics, 343-51, 419 n.26
  Works:
    Angelo, 307, 403-16, Appendix D
      adaptation of source, 403-5
      influence of Meyerbeer on, 414-15
      naturalistic declamation in, 411-13
      realistic use of chorus in, 412-14
    The Captain's Daughter, 416-17, 426
      n.147
    Feast During the Plague, 327-28, 417
    Le Flibustier, 416
    Mademoiselle Fifi, 417
    Mandarin's Son, 341, 351-52
    Matteo Falcone, 417
    Prisoner of the Caucasus, 341-43, 352-
      44, 417 n.3
    Puss in Boots, 417
    Red Riding Hood, 417
    The Saracen, 416, 426 n.145
    William Ratcliff, 307, 341, 417
      compared with *A Life For the Tsar,*
        420 n.51
      compared with *The Stone Guest,* 358-
        59, 401
      creative history, 359-60, 366
      declamation in, 385-91
      dramatic structure and flaws, 357-58,
        376-82
      interpolated songs in, 364-66
      leitmotivs in, 367-75, 376-77, 400-401
      musical style, 390-93
      narratives in, 358, 364-68
      production, 393-94
      realism in, 382-83, 428
      reception, 394-403
      relationship to literary source, 354-
        55, 358, 419 n.39
      scenario, 355-57
      use of chorus in, 361-64
      whole tone harmony in, 382-83

Da Ponte, Lorenzo, 264-65
Dargomyzhsky, Alexander Sergeevich
  and Cui, 343, 351
  and French realists, 329-30 n.11
  and Glinka, 251-52
  and Musorgsky, 296-97, 307-8, 313-14,
    321, 339 n.129
  and "truth," 54, 258
  and Wagner, 281, 288-92
  career, 251
  compared with Serov, 189, 238-39, 249
  on *Rogneda,* 125
  Works:
    Esmeralda, 251, 329 n.1

Rogdana, 330 n.17
Rusalka, 252-58, 260-62, 329 n.9
  compared with *Rogneda,* 261-62
  folk songs in, 244 n.92
  text-music relationship in, 253-57
The Stone Guest
  compared with Wagnerian opera, 249,
    288, 290-91
  creative history, 263-64, 293-94
  "empirical" harmony in, 280-81, 286-
    89
  fidelity to Pushkin text established,
    331 n.32
  leitmotivs in, 281, 290
  performance style, 296-98
  production, 294-96
  realism in, 249, 257, 274, 281, 301-2,
    303-6
  recent criticism of, 329 n.1, 334-35
    n.46
  reception, 298-307, 324-25
  scenario, 264-65
  text-music relationship in, 266-80
The Triumph of Bacchus, 251, 280
Debussy, Claude, 335 n.51
Dehn, Siegfried, 310
Dostoevsky, Fyodor Mikhailovich, 79, 81,
  87, 91, 92, 144, 200, 246 n.110,
  354, 421 n.68
Dütsch, Otton Ivanovich, 141

Edelson, Evgenii Nikolaevich, 143
Elena Pavlovna, Grand Duchess, 121
Epokha, 81, 86, 92, 105, 135 n.31

Famintsyn, Alexander Sergeevich, 121
Fillippov, Tertii Ivanovich, 143, 144, 170,
  243 n.72
Folk song
  and *pochvennichestvo,* 144-46
  in *A Life For the Tsar,* 2, 245 n.93
  in *Askold's Grave* (Verstovsky), 106, 107,
    138 n.39, 244 n.92
  in *The Power of the Fiend,* 141, 163,
    170, 171-85 (incl. Table 2)
  in *Rogneda,* 102-8, 129, 138 n.88
  in *Rusalka,* 244 n.92
  in *Ruslan and Liudmila,* 244 n.92
  Ostrovsky and, 146-47, 171 (Table 1)
  Serov's attitude toward, 13-14, 107-8,
    152-53, 168-69

Gervinus, Georg, 309-13
Giacometti, Paolo, 44, 51, 54
Giustiniani, Ivan Antonovich, 46, 48
Glinka, Mikhail Ivanovich, 1-32 passim

and Dargomyzhsky, 251-52
and later generations, 1, 427
and nationalism, 6-7, 29 n.9, 31 n.55
Beethoven's and Cherubini's influence on, 7
fusion of dramatic and national styles, 2-3
on *Ruslan and Liudmila,* 30 n.40
Works:
  A Life For the Tsar
    and "Wagnerian ideal," 18-19, 211
    folk song in, 245 n.93
    historical significance of, 1-3, 6
    leitmotiv in, 3, 29 n.9, 211
    national character in, 6-7, 13-14, 30 n.26, 138 n.90
    reception, 1-2
    Serov on, 16, 211
    Stasov on, 17-18, 31 n.55
    use of contrast in, 2
  Ruslan and Liudmila
    as an aesthetic problem, 3-4 et seq.
    attacked by Serov, 14-17, 19, 20-21, 23, 30 n.35, 42
    compared with *Rogneda,* 124, 128-31
    defended by Cui, 21, 23, 418 n.20
    defended by Stasov, 10-13, 17-18, 20, 26-27
    national character in, 138 n.90
    realistic use of chorus in, 426 n.134
    satirized, 122, 139 n.107
    whole tone harmony in, 4, 205, 280, 288 (Exx. 5.18-19)
Gluck, Christoph Willibald von, 18, 38, 59, 88, 351
Gogol, Nikolai Vasilievich
  Works: *Marriage,* 308
Gounod, Charles, 129
Grechaninov, Alexander Tikhonovich
  Works: *Marriage,* 339-40 n.138
Grétry, André Ernest Modeste
  Works: *Richard Coeur-de-lion,* 377
Grigoriev, Apollon Alexandrovich, 80-85, 87, 107, 131, 170
  as editor of *Moskvitianin,* 143-46, 169
  on drama through song, 147-48, 164
  on folk song, 137 n.82, 144-46
  on Heine, 423 n.85
  on *Judith,* 82-84, 133 n.12, 133 n.13, 133 n.17
  on national character, 144-46
  on "organic criticism," 144, 145-46, 185
  on Ostrovsky, 144, 172
  on *Rogneda,* 100
  on "true realism," 83-84
  on "vegetative poetry," 145-46
  on Wagner, 134 n.21

Grillparzer, Franz, 357
Gulak-Artemovsky, Semyon Stepanovich, 141, 251
Gurilyov, Alexander Lvovich, 129
Gypsies, 137 n.82

Hanslick, Eduard, 23, 205, 304, 310
Hartman (Gartman), Victor Alexandrovich, 237
Hebbel, Friedrich, 73 n.82
  Works: *Judith,* 51-54
Heine, Heinrich
  Works: *William Ratcliff,* 354-55, 357-58, 421 n.70, 423 n.85, 423 n.86
Herbart, Johann Friedrich, 310
Herder, Johann Gottfried von, 60, 245 n.101, 421 n.70
Hérold, Louis Joseph Ferdinand, 122, 450
Herzen (Gertsen), Alexander Ivanovich, 133 n.12
Hugo, Victor, 251, 354
  Works: *Angelo, Tyran de Padoue,* 403-4, 425 n.119

Iakor', 81-84, 137 n.77
Iskra, 41, 43 (Fig. 2.1), 71 n.43, 124, 329-30 n.11
Italian Opera (St. Petersburg), 30 n.39, 45

Kalashnikov, Pyotr Ivanovich, 167-68
Karamzin, Nikolai Mikhailovich, 139 n.96, 432 n.9
Kashperov, Vladimir Nikitich, 154-55 (incl. Fig. 4.2)
  Works: *The Storm* (opera after Ostrovsky), 154-57
Kauer, Ferdinand
  Works: *Das Donauweibchen* (singspiel), 329 n.4
Kerzin, Arkadii Mikhailovich, 324, 339 n.138
Khrennikov, Tikhon Nikolaevich, 135 n.35
Kleist, Heinrich von, 357
Komissarzhevsky, Fyodor Petrovich, 296-98
Kondratiev, Gennadii Petrovich, 237
Kostomarov, Nikolai Ivanovich, 432 n.9
Krylov, Victor Alexandrovich, 121-22, 351-54, 359-61, 364, 420 n.40, 450

La Grua, Emma, 44-46
Laroche, Herman Augustovich, 21-22 (incl. Fig. 1.4)
  and realism, 24-25
  and Hanslick, 23
  journalistic rivalry with Cui, 423 n.97
  on *Angelo,* 407-8, 415

Laroche, Herman Augustovich *(continued)*
on Glinka, 23-26
on Musorgsky and Serov, 119-20
on *Rogneda,* 96
on Russian folk music, 186
on *The Stone Guest,* 298, 301-2, 303-6
on *The Voevoda* (Tchaikovsky), 156
on *William Ratcliff,* 396-98, 423 n.93
Lavrovskaya, Elizaveta Andreevna, 234-35,
297
Leitmotivs
in *Judith,* 61-64
in *A Life For the Tsar,* 3, 29 n.9, 136
n.61, 211
in *Marriage,* 320
in *The Power of the Fiend,* 205, 210-26
in *The Stone Guest,* 281, 290
in *William Ratcliff,* 367-75, 376-77, 400-
401
kuchkist attitude toward, 291-92
Lensky, Alexander Pavlovich (real name
Verbitsiotti), 336 n.73
Lenz, Wilhelm von, 38
Leonova, Daria Mikhailovna, 45, 234, 236
(Fig. 4.5), 393
Lessing, Gotthold Ephraim, 60
Lesta, The Dnepr Mermaid (series of
singspiels), 329 n.4
Lobanov, Dmitrii Ivanovich, 46, 48, 55-56,
73 n.86
Loewe, Johann Karl Gottfried
Works: *Edward,* 421 n.70
Lvov, Nikolai Alexandrovich, and Ivan
Pratsch, anthology of Russian folk
songs *(Sobranie narodnykh russkikh
pesen s ikh golosami,* 1790), 182,
244 n.92, 245 n.95

Maikov, Apollon Nikolaevich, 48-49, 81,
87, 91
Martinu, Bohuslav, 339-40 n.138
Melgunov, Nikolai Alexandrovich
on *A Life For the Tsar,* 7
Melnikov, Ivan Alexandrovich, 393
"Melodic recitative," 54, 267-80, 345, 348-
49, 389-91
Mey, Lev Alexandrovich, 143
Works: *Pskovitianka,* 90, 432 n.9
Meyerbeer, Giacomo, 14, 60, 122, 129-31,
149-50, 154, 343, 450
Works: *L'Étoile du Nord,* 129
"Moguchaia kuchka," 417 n.2, 426 n.150
Moskvitianin, 143-44, 146, 169
Mozart, Wolfgang Amadeus, 10, 18, 36,
68 n.13
Works: *Don Giovanni,* 226, 264-65, 331
n.30, 336-37 n.76

"M.P.M." *See* Anastasieva
Musorgsky, Modest Petrovich
and Dargomyzhsky, 296-97, 307-8, 313-
14
and realism, 350-51, 418-19 n.25
and Serov, 77 n.126, 119-21, 180, 205,
238, 431
"Aristotelian" aesthetics of, 309-13
on *Angelo,* 409, 425 n.126
on *Judith,* 65, 74 n.87, 74 n.94, 75
n.108, 134 n.28
on musical form, 335 n.52
on *The Power of the Fiend,* 248 n.159
on *Rogneda,* 107, 116
on *William Ratcliff,* 341, 382
Works:
Boris Godunov, 110, 119-20, 139 n.100,
340 n.147, 376 (incl. Ex. 6.13),
417, 430, 431 n.8, 432 n.9
The Fair at Sorochintsy, 339 n.138,
430-31
Khovanshchina, 430
Marriage, 307-25
compared with *The Stone Guest,* 308,
314
creative history, 314
reception, 321-25
text-music relationship in, 314-22
use of prose in, 308
The Sideshow (Raëk), 121
songs, 307

Napravnik, Eduard Frantsevich, 400, 424
n.101
on *Angelo,* 406
on *The Power of the Fiend,* 227
Works: *Nizhegorodtsy,* 167, 400
Nikolsky, Fyodor Kalinovich, 99, 393
Nikolsky, Vladimir Vasilievich, 94-95

Odoevsky, Prince Vladimir Fyodorovich,
xviii (Fig. 1.1), 38, 245 n.97, 251
on *A Life For the Tsar,* 2
on *The Power of the Fiend,* 227
on *Rogneda,* 79
on *Ruslan and Liudmila,* 4-5, 11
Offenbach, Jacques, 121, 122, 450
"Official nationalism," 29 n.9, 31 n.55, 143
"Organic criticism," 82, 185
and folk song, 146, 152
applied to *The Power of the Fiend,* 205-
26
defined, 144
Ostrovsky, Alexander Nikolaevich, 81, 142-
44 (incl. Fig. 4.1)
as collector of folk songs, 148, 240 n.21
as librettist for Kashperov, 154-57, 161

as librettist for Serov, 153-54, 157-67,
  184-85, 243 n.62, 244 n.74
as librettist for Tchaikovsky, 156-57,
  160, 242 n.48
historical verse plays, 150, 161
"Moskvitianin plays," 144, 146-47, 169-
  70, 240 n.15
use of folk songs, 146-49, 163-64, 169-76
  (incl. Table 1), 181-82
Works:
  *Live Not The Way You'd Like But as
    God Commands,* 146-49, 153-54,
    157-60, 247 n.132, 266
    turned into libretto in verse, 160-67,
    193, 228, 243 n.62
    use of folk song in, 169-82 (incl.
    Table 1)
  Poverty is No Crime, 146, 200, 241
    n.42
  The Storm, 154
    turned into libretto in verse, 154-57,
    161

Pashkevich, Vasilii Alekseevich
  Works: *Sanktpeterburgskii gostinnyi dvor,*
    200, 244 n.92
Patti, Adelina, 45
Petipa, Marius, 148
Petrov, Osip Afanasievich, 45, 296, 298
Platonova, Julia Fyodorovna (real name
  Garder), 234, 296, 298, 393
  on *Angelo,* 416
Pleshcheev, Alexei Nikolaevich, 354, 425
  n.121
Pochvennichestvo, 81-86, 133 n.6, 141,
  143, 243 n.72
  and folk song, 145, 148
  and "true realism," 83-85, 176, 226-28
  and "the young editorial staff" of
    Moskvitianin, 143-44
  defined, 81-82, 134 n.20
Pogodin, Mikhail Petrovich, 143
Polonsky, Iakov Petrovich, 81, 86, 91,
  244 n.80
Ponchielli, Amilcare
  Works: *La Gioconda,* 405, 425 n.124
Potekhin, Alexei Antipovich, 150-51, 200,
  240 n.21
Pratsch (Prač), Ivan (Jan Bogumir). *See*
  Lvov
Prokofiev, Sergei Sergeevich, 340 n.147
Prose libretti, 308, 323
Purgold, Alexandra Nikolaevna (married
  name Molas), 296, 336 n.69
Purgold, Nadezhda Nikolaevna (married
  name Rimskaya-Korsakova), 296-
  97, 321, 336 n.69

Pushkin, Alexander Sergeevich
  Works:
    Boris Godunov, 50
    The Covetous Knight (Skupoi rytsar'),
      328
    *Feast During the Plague (Pir vo vremia
      chumy),* 328
    Mozart and Salieri, 325-26
    Ruslan and Liudmila, 3
    The Stone Guest (Kamennyi gost'),
      249, 263-66, 331 n.30, 331 n.32
    *Triumph of Bacchus (Torzhestvo
      Vakkha),* 151

Rachmaninov, Sergei Vasilievich
  Works: *The Covetous Knight,* 328
Ravel, Maurice
  and *Marriage,* 339 n.138, 340 n.147
  Works: *L'Heure espagnole,* 340 n.147
Realism, 24-25, 146-47, 169-70, 258-60,
  330 n.13, 350-51, 418-19 n.25,
  427-30
  Cui and, 350-51, 382-83, 411-14, 420
    n.47
  Dargomyzhsky and, 54, 249, 257, 274,
    281, 301-2, 303-6, 313, 329 n.11
  Musorgsky and, 307-24, 335 n.52, 350-51
  Serov and, 74 n.99, 84-85, 135 n.41, 141,
    143, 161, 164-65, 200, 204-5, 226-
    39, 246 n.110
Riemann, Hugo, 281, 309
Rimsky-Korsakov, Nikolai Andreevich, 170
  edits *The Stone Guest,* 294
  on *Angelo,* 425 n.126
  on Auber, 424 n.105
  on *The Mandarin's Son* (Cui), 352
  on *Marriage,* 322-23
  on *Rogneda,* 113-14
  on *The Stone Guest,* 325
  on Wagner, 291, 293
  on *William Ratcliff,* 377, 382, 399-401,
    417
  Works:
    Antar, 113, 375 (incl. Ex. 6.12)
    Christmas Eve, 244 n.92
    May Night, 244 n.92
    Mozart and Salieri, 325-27 (incl. Ex.
      5.29)
    Pskovitianka, 113, 376, 411, 412, 417,
      430, 432 n.9
    Sadko, 116-17 (incl. Exx. 3.8 and 3.9)
    Snegurochka, 117-18 (incl. Ex. 3.10),
      180, 244 n.92
    *Tale of the Invisible City of Kitezh and
      the Maiden Fevronia,* 138 n.93
Ristori, Adelaide, 44, 46
Rogneda, legend of, 86

Rossini, Gioacchino, 122, 129, 343, 450
Rostislav. *See* Tolstoy, F. M.
Rousseau, Jean-Jacques, 39, 49
Rubini, Giovanni Battista, 45
Rubinstein, Anton Grigorievich, 19, 55,
    125, 135 n.35, 239 n.3
Ryleev, Kondratii Fyodorovich, 91-92

Sadovsky, Prov Mikhailovich, 144
Saltykov-Shchedrin, Mikhail Evgrafovich
    lampoon of "kuchkism," 422 n.76
Sariotti, Mikhail Ivanovich, 66-67, 235-37
    (incl. Fig. 4.5), 393
Schelling, Friedrich Wilhelm Joseph von,
    81, 245 n.101
Schumann, Robert, 344, 397, 400
    Works: *Genoveva,* 24, 73 n.82, 418 n.10,
        422 n.81
Senkovsky, Osip Ivanovich, 5
Serov, Alexander Nikolaevich
    activity as critic, 38
    and Balakirev circle, 72 n.62
    and Cui, 300
    and Dargomyzhsky, 252-59 (incl. Fig.
      5.2)
    and Glinka, 6, 15
    and Liszt, 69 n.23
    and Meyerbeer, 69 n.24, 72 n.69, 130-31,
      149-50
    and Musorgsky, 77 n.126, 119-21, 180,
      205, 238, 431
    and the *pochvenniki,* 82-83, 86-87, 135
      n.31, 137 n.77
    and Wagner, 14, 19, 20-21, 37, 39-43
      (incl. Fig. 2.1), 49, 58-65, 75 n.102,
      75 n.103, 82
    attitude toward folk song, 13, 106-7, 148,
      151-52, 185-86, 245 n.101
    difficulties with collaborators, 37
    dramaturgical theories, 49-51, 70 n.37,
      88, 89-90, 97-98
    education, 35-36
    historical position of, 33-35
    hostility to supernatural, 39, 164-65
    on Beethoven, 205, 210-11
    on French grand opera, 97-98
    on *A Life For the Tsar,* 13-14, 16, 19,
      136 n.61, 211
    on Mozart, 36, 68 n.13, 59, 226
    on national opera, 30 n.35, 85, 149, 151,
      185
    on Ostrovsky, 151, 241 n.24
    on realism, 84-85, 204, 227
    on *Rusalka,* 15, 252-57
    on *Ruslan and Liudmila,* 14-17, 19, 20-
      21, 23, 30 n.35, 42

    on *The Stone Guest,* 336 n.76
    on Verstovsky vs. Glinka, 102, 105-7
    on *William Ratcliff,* 395-96, 423 n.86
    operatic ideals, 38, 97-98
    relationship with Stasov, 6, 13, 30, 68
      n.17, 132
    Works:
      Ave Maria d'una penitente, 71 n.54
      Basurman (unrealized operatic project),
        35, 70 n.37
      La Meunière de Marly (unfinished opera),
        36, 37
      Merry Wives of Windsor (unrealized
        project), 36
      Hussite Trilogy (unrealized operatic
        project), 150, 241 n.31
      Judith
        compared with *A Life For the Tsar,*
          73 n.86
        compared with *Lohengrin,* 76 n.111
        compared with *The Power of the
          Fiend,* 231-32
        cosmopolitanism of, 134 n.25
        creative history, 44-49
        general characterization, 33-35
        musical idiom, 65, 74 n.99
        performance style, 65-67
        Preface, 48, 51
        reception by Liszt and Wagner, 85-86
        scenario, 51-54, 434-38 (Appendix A)
        text-music relationship in, 54-58
        thematic relationships in, 61-64
      May Night, 36-37, 68 n.17, 85, 431
      The Power of the Fiend (Vrazh'ia sila),
        Appendix C
        compared with *Judith,* 231-32
        creative history, 153-54, 157-68, 184-
          85
        folk songs in, 141, 143, 168-85 (incl.
          Table 2), 245 n.97
        national style in, 168-69, 185-204
        performance style, 233-37
        "predicted" by Grigoriev, 147-48
        production, 237
        realism in, 200, 204-5, 226-39,
          428-30, 431
        reception, 226-39
        scenario, 159-60, 443-47 (Appendix
          A)
        thematic structure, 205-26
      Rogneda
        and *Ruslan* controversy, 128-31
        as "civic deed," 124-25, 431
        attacked by Stasov, 125-31
        compared with *Judith,* 98-99
        compared with *Rusalka,* 261-62

compared with *Ruslan and Liudmila*, 124, 128-31, 135 n.41
compared with Tannhäuser, 135 n.39
creative history, 85-92, 136 n.39
dramaturgical flaws, 92-99, 169
influence on younger composers, 113, 116-21
musical style, 108-10
musico-dramatic structure, 99-104, 110, 112-16
national character in, 102, 105-8, 138 n.86, 138 n.88, 138 n.90, 138 n.93, 182
Preface, 88-90, 93-94, 123
production, 125-26, 136 n.59, 140 n.113
realism in, 110, 428
reception, 79, 124-25
satirized, 119-24, Appendix B
scenario, 439-42 (Appendix A)
Serov's defense of, 95-96
Undine (unrealized project), 42, 44
Vakula the Smith (unfinished opera), 244 n.80, 431
Serov, Valentin Alexandrovich, 246 n.108
Serova, Valentina Semyonovna *(née* Bergman)
on *Rogneda*, 91, 97
finishes *The Power of the Fiend*, 168
Shestakova, Liudmila Ivanovna, 263, 417
Sollogub, Count Vladimir Alexandrovich
on *Rogneda*, 125
Soloviov, Nikolai Feopemptovich, 168, 244 n.80
on *Angelo*, 406-7
Soloviov, Sergei Mikhailovich, 432 n.9
Stakhovich, Mikhail Alexandrovich, 138 n.93, 144-45, 148-49, 169-70, 180, 242 n.39
Stasov, Vladimir Vasilievich
and Pan-Slavism, 19-20
hostility to Serov, 33
on *Angelo*, 403-4, 414-15
on Cui as backslider, 418 n.23, 426 n.146
on folk song, 186
on *Judith*, 65, 75 n.101
on *A Life For the Tsar*, 6-7, 10, 31 n.55
on *Marriage*, 324-25
on nationalism, 6-7, 245 n.101
on *The Power of the Fiend*, 238
on *Rogneda*, 103, 105, 125-31
on *Ruslan and Liudmila*, 11-13, 17-18, 20, 26-27
on *The Stone Guest*, 293-94, 301
on Wagner, 291, 292-93
on *William Ratcliff*, 355, 394, 402-3

on "Zukunftists," 18-19, 41, 70 n.39
opposes founding of Conservatory, 32 n.57
Strakhov, Nikolai Nikolaevich, 81
Stravinsky, Fyodor Ignatievich, 67, 236 (Fig. 4.6)
Stravinsky, Igor Fyodorovich, 121, 340 n.147
on Dargomyzhsky, 252
Works:
Petrushka, 200, 203 (Ex. 4.23), 246 n.108
Le Sacre du Printemps, 139 n.94
"Superfluous man," 131-32

Tchaikovsky, Pyotr Ilyich
on *Angelo*, 425 n.124
on Glinka's operas, 27
on *Judith*, 67
on realism, x
on *Rogneda*, 93, 96-97, 136 n.65
on *The Stone Guest*, 302
on *William Ratcliff*, 359, 391
Works:
Cherevichki (Vakula the Smith), 244 n.80, 431
Hussites (rejected subject), 241 n.31
The Oprichnik, 430, 432 n.9
Romeo and Juliet, 330 n.16
The Voevoda, 156-57, 242 n.48
Titov, Alexei Nikolaevich, 2, 177
Works: *Maslenitsa*, 200
Tolstoy, Feofil Matveevich (Rostislav), 55, 58, 121
on *The Power of the Fiend*, 229, 230-31, 235-36
on *Rogneda*, 124, 139 n.110
on *The Stone Guest*, 302
on *William Ratcliff*, 398-99, 423 n.83
Turgenev, Ivan Sergeevich, 131, 306-7

Ulybyshev, Alexander Dmitrievich, 38

Varlamov, Alexander Egorovich, 129, 132 n.81, 177, 240 n.20
Verstovsky, Alexei Nikolaevich, 103 (Fig. 3.3), 141, 177
Works: *Askold's Grave*, 2, 87-88, 102, 105-8, 110-11 (incl. Ex. 3.5), 126
satirized, 122, 124, Appendix B
Verdi, Giuseppe, 45, 122, 450
Viardot, Pauline, 45
Villebois (Vil'boa), Konstantin Petrovich, 141, 148, 169-71, 173 (Fig. 4.3), 176-79, 200, 203, 240 n.21, 240 n.22, 242 n.39

Vremia, 81-82

Wagner, Richard
and the *pochvenniki,* 82-83, 134 n.21
and Serov, 14, 34, 37, 39-43 (incl. Fig.
2.1), 49, 75 n.102, 75 n.103, 82
contrasted with Glinka, 25-26
aesthetics, compared with Dargomyzhsky's, 249, 281, 288, 290, 300
influence, ix
kuchkist attitude toward, 290-93, 344,
401
on *Judith,* 65
on *Rogneda,* 241 n.30
reforms, compared with *The Power of the
Fiend,* 187, 189
Works:
Lohengrin, 19, 21, 40, 60, 76 n.111,
288, 344
Die Meistersinger, 293
Tannhäuser, 19, 40, 48, 60, 135 n.39,
288

Tristan und Isolde, 75 n.102, 344
Der Ring des Nibelungen, 21, 288, 293
Weber, Carl Maria von
Works:
Euryanthe, 376
Der Freischütz, 70 n.37, 110, 164, 166,
168, 299, 385
Whole tone harmony, 4, 205, 210 (Ex.
4.27), 280, 286-89 (incl. Exx. 5.18
and 5.19), 382-83

Yakushkin, Pavel Ivanovich, 170

Zagoskin, Mikhail Nikolaevich
Works: *Askold's Grave,* 87-88, 92, 135
n.36, 135 n.37
Zaremba, Nikolai Ivanovich, 55, 121, 139
n.101
Zhokhov, Alexander Fyodorovich, 168
Zvantsev, Konstantin Ivanovich, 42, 44, 48,
149, 161, 165-66, 168